D1454727

TODAY IN HISTORY

BOB JOHNSTONE

Warwick Publishing Inc.
Toronto   Los Angeles

ISBN 1-895629-35-7

Published by Warwick Publishing Inc., 24 Mercer Street, Toronto, Ontario M5V 1H3

Cover Design: Dave Hader/Studio Conceptions
Project Editor: Jacqueline Lealess
Text Design: Jacqueline Lealess
Proofreader: Mary Englesakis

Distributed by:
Firefly Books Ltd.
250 Sparks Ave,
Willowdale, Ontario
M2H 2S4

Printed and bound in Canada.

A WORD OF THANKS

Deep in the works of the Canadian Broadcasting Corporation in Toronto is a department called Infotape. It's a collection of people who work with skill and patience and talent and, some days, a few cuss words. They put together the columns and features that are the backbone of CBC Radio, the best radio service in the world. Bar none, past or present.

Over the years, dozens of Infotapers have gently held my hand, firmly corrected my errors, bravely endured my abrasiveness. Some of them are still at it. Many have moved on.

If I tried to name them all, I'd miss a few. So I won't. But they know who they are. And how heavily *Today in History* and I have leaned on them over the years.

CONTENTS

INTRODUCTION

Today in History started almost by accident about a dozen years ago as a Monday-to-Friday feature on CBC Radio. It's usually carried on the 6-to-9 morning programs.

Summer is a quiet time for news, and the producer of a morning program asked for some old Canadian crime stories to fill in gaps in his program. I was assigned to the job because before I worked at the CBC I was a newspaper crime reporter. But Canada is a law-abiding country, and I was soon running low on crime stories. So, without any conscious effort, I found myself looking at other fields: battles and political crises and shipwrecks and feuds and lawsuits . . . all the stuff that makes history.

That's how *Today in History* became a regular feature on CBC Radio. I can't recall when it was decided to run a story on the anniversary of the day it happened.

Nor can I recall when the listeners took over. But the suggestions and criticisms and old yellowed clippings soon started to pour in.

Today, I don't pretend to know if *Today in History* belongs to me or to my listeners. Or, if it's just like the past: something that belongs to all of us, something to look back on with awe and tears and wonder and pride (or sometimes with shame). And, most important of all, the odd laugh.

Bob Johnstone
Toronto

A TAXING SITUATION

In 1791, the newest nation in the world, the United States of America, was almost broke. When the American Revolution ended in 1783, the Americans made their wartime general, George Washington, their first president.

Washington faced some terrible problems. The worst was money.

The new federal government had assumed the debts that the various states had run up fighting the Revolution. But virtually all the taxes were collected by the states so there was no income to satisfy those huge bills.

In 1791, Washington tried to solve the problem with a tax on whisky. It wasn't a big tax; 9 cents a gallon or 60 cents a year on each gallon a distiller had the capacity to produce. And in most of the country it caused no trouble.

But in western Pennsylvania, which was the frontier in those days, it was an awful hardship. The farmers couldn't get their grain to market. Roads to the east, where the population was concentrated, were almost non-existent.

The obvious market lay down the Ohio and Mississippi Rivers, through the port of New Orleans to Europe. But Spain owned New Orleans and wouldn't let in American ships.

So, farmers distilled their grain into whisky. A pack horse could carry two kegs of whisky. It would take six horses to carry the grain that made that much whisky.

And there was a money shortage in the remote western counties of Pennsylvania. So, pretty soon, whisky became currency in that barter economy.

It should have come as no surprise to Washington when his tax collectors were met first with surliness, later with violence. They were shot at, tarred and feathered, chased away.

In the summer of 1794, the violence escalated. A pro-tax faction led the a hero of the Revolution fought a battle with an anti-tax faction, also led by a hero of

There was a money shortage in the remote western counties of Pennsylvania. So, pretty soon, whisky became currency in that barter economy.

the Revolution. Four were wounded and two killed. One of them was the anti-tax hero.

The anti-taxers even had their own flag. The 13 red and white stripes on the American flag represent the 13 original states that started the revolution. The anti-taxers had a flag with six red and white stripes, representing the six westernmost counties of Pennsylvania where the protest was centred.

The anti-tax army, if you could call it an army, actually captured the city of Pittsburgh and did a bit of looting.

That did it. Washington assembled an army of 13,000 men, a bigger force than fought most of the battles of the American Revolution. He ordered it into western Pennsylvania to collect the whisky tax.

It grabbed about a million and a half dollars. Mind you, it wasn't all profit. The army used up a third of all it collected. And the soldiers drank huge amounts of the very whisky they were coming to tax.

No anti-tax leaders were caught. They all faded into the forest until the army left.

But all in all, the expedition was a success.

On the first of January in 1795, Washington announced the new nation had weathered its first internal crisis. The army was disbanded and sent home and a day of thanksgiving was declared.

Local governments realized they'd better do something about those isolated people in the west and they began a serious road-building program. The diplomats realized those western markets needed an outlet to Europe and they negotiated with the Spanish for passage through New Orleans.

But, most important of all, that army that George Washington sent into the west was well equipped with cash which it spent for supplies. Long after the army left, the cash stayed in circulation and whisky was no longer needed as the medium of exchange.

This entry was written expressly for this collection.

AN ADVOCATE OF DEMOCRACY

William Lyon Mackenzie was a terrible little man. Nevertheless, he has gone down in our history books as some sort of a saint. I guess that's because much good came of what he did. Even if he did it unpleasantly.

Mackenzie was very small, probably less than 5'5". When he became first mayor of Toronto, one of his political enemies wrote that when he sat in the mayor's chair, his feet didn't touch the floor. It's hard to tell what's true about him and what's gross exaggeration.

But if Mackenzie's image suffers from the irresponsible journalism of the day, it's his own fault. No one did more to set the tone than he did.

Mackenzie was a very poor Scotsman who came to Canada in 1820. He started off, within a day or two of landing, as a timekeeper on the Lachine Canal, which was under construction. He accused the workers of cheating the boss and the boss of being an incompetent who didn't know how to run the job.

A fitting start for Mackenzie. He would sooner argue than eat.

When that job ended — and it didn't last long — he went to Toronto, York as it was called then. He went into business as a merchant and made big money. He might have become one of the millionaire merchants that that era produced. But he couldn't. He had a fixation: a double fixation, really, politics and journalism.

In 1824, at Queenston, near Niagara Falls, he started a newspaper called the *Colonial Advocate*. Right from the first issue, he tore into the establishment. The establishment gave him lots to be critical about: high taxes, poor services, virtually no roads, all the good jobs going to people from England, and so on.

After four years he moved back to York. He was in constant hot water with the governor. He decided to not just write about politics; he wanted to play the game. So he was elected to the house of assembly.

Whenever Mackenzie was angry, he would tear off his wig and throw it on the floor and jump on it. The poor wig was good for about 10 trips to the floor on a fairly calm day.

The fact that Mackenzie was right didn't make him any more lovable. He suffered from a fever that kept him ill most of the time and short-tempered. It also made him bald. He wore a cheap red wool wig. Whenever he was angry, he would tear off the wig and throw it on the floor and jump on it. The poor wig was good for about 10 trips to the floor on a fairly calm day. Mackenzie was an even-tempered man, always furious.

Mackenzie had the contract to print the debates of the house. The government just didn't pay him. He could get resolutions passed, voting him his money, but the governor and his officials just ignored them.

That's exactly what Mackenzie was campaigning against, democratic government that didn't follow the will of the people, government that wasn't responsible.

Late in 1831, the government members in the house finally mustered up enough votes to have Mackenzie thrown out of the house and his seat declared vacant. Mackenzie ran for that vacant seat.

There were no secret ballots in those days. People went to the polling place and loudly declared their vote.

On the second of January in 1832, Mackenzie's supporters flocked into York from as far away as 50 miles. They went to the polling place and declared for their boy.

By three in the afternoon the vote stood at 119 for Mackenzie, one for the other guy. The other guy conceded.

Two years later, Mackenzie became mayor when York became Toronto. But he still couldn't get the sort of government he wanted. Three years later he led a revolution, very un-Canadian.

But perfectly logical for the sort of man who gets so angry he stomps on his own wig.

Originally broadcast January 2, 1987

HANGING IN

In late 1776, the British Army was very much in control of the American colonies.

After years of complaining about British rule, the Americans had broken into rebellion in 1775. The British had a fair-sized army there at the outset. In the next year they sent plenty more.

Not all those British troops were British. The king of England was descended from Germans and had many friends and relatives in German royal families.

So he recruited a lot of German soldiers. Many of them came from the duchy of Hesse in Germany, so the Americans called all German troops in the British Army Hessians.

By the end of summer and fall campaigning of 1776, the British had taken the whole colony of New Jersey and chased the American troops across the Delaware River into Pennsylvania. The Americans had been badly beaten and they knew it. Most of them were in favor of surrender.

George Washington, the American commander-in-chief, knew he couldn't beat the British army. But that doesn't mean he thought the British army couldn't be beaten.

Time and distance could do it. The British had to ship all their men and equipment 3000 miles across the ocean. If he could hang on a year or two he just might pull it off.

But there was no American army. Washington commanded what was called the Continental Army, a collection of militiamen from all the 13 colonies that were now calling themselves independent countries. Most of his command consisted of men who had signed on to the end of the year.

So, as Christmas approached in 1776, Washington knew he had to do something fast. The town of Trenton, New Jersey was garrisoned by a regiment of

Hessians under a big, happy drunk, Colonel Roll.

Roll's officers had suggested they fortify the town. But Roll said they didn't have to bother. Washington's pathetic army was across the river in the hills in Pennsylvania, half-starved and freezing to death.

He was right about that. But he was wrong about there being no danger.

Washington had decided to capture Trenton, not because it was any use to him, but because he had to do something spectacular before the end of the year.

He sneaked across the river on Christmas night, when the Hessian sentries were drunk. He attacked suddenly and chased Colonel Roll out of the town. Roll rallied his men and tried to recapture Trenton but he was killed.

Washington captured 918 men and a lot of supplies, especially boots. His men were so poorly dressed that they left a trail of blood on the snow from their frozen feet whenever they marched.

Quite a few of the American soldiers stayed on at the end of the year. But it was a terrible winter and Washington realized he had to do something else to keep his men's spirits up.

So on the third of January in 1777, as the British converged on Trenton with thousands of men to take it away again, Washington slipped out of the town and moved, not away from them, but toward them. He slipped off to one side and passed the British on their way to take Trenton back.

He hit them at their supply base at Princeton, a dozen miles away. In half an hour he'd won another spectacular victory. He had to fade away after that. But he'd shown he could win if his men would only hang in. And they did. For another six years until the British admitted they were beaten and sailed away.

> *George Washington, the American commander-in-chief, knew he couldn't beat the British army. But that doesn't mean he thought the British army couldn't be beaten.*

Originally broadcast January 3, 1989

WHERE THERE'S A WILL . . .

Cornelius Vanderbilt was the richest man in the United States when he died on the 4th of January in 1877.

He was 82 and was known as The Commodore, not because he'd ever been in the navy, but because he had started as a poor farm boy and had made his way in the world by owning a ferry boat.

Later, he had gone into the stock market. On his death he owned the New York Central Railroad and a whole bunch of other things.

The 4th of January, 1877, might have been the end of the Commodore's life. But it was the beginning of something much more fascinating: the fight over his will.

Cornelius Vanderbilt left his wife, Frankie, half a million and their mansion in New York plus horses and carriages and household items like that.

Five of his eight daughters got a quarter million in bonds. The other three daughters got a little more. Of the two sons, Cornelius Jr., a ne'er do well in his late 40s, was given the income from a $200,000 trust fund. Not outright. It was to be administered by a panel of trustees, including his older brother William. And William got the rest, way more than $100 million.

It was by far the biggest fortune any American had accumulated up to that time. More than twice as big as any other.

Needless to say, Cornelius Jr. and his sisters weren't amused. But the joy of William was shared by two professional groups: lawyers and reporters. Both could smell big business in the offing. They didn't have long to wait.

Cornelius Jr. and one sister soon filed papers to contest the will. They claimed the old Commodore had been of unsound mind and he'd been unduly influenced by William, the brother who got the bundle.

First, they brought witnesses to show that the Commodore was easily influenced by women, especially those whose activities in those Victorian times had to be described as unwholesome or unsavory or unmentionable.

It might have been the end of the Commodore's life. But it was the beginning of something much more fascinating: the fight over his will.

There was plenty of hinting and even a little bit of outright accusing along that line. Then young Cornelius himself took the stand and told how his father had demanded that he reform and abandon his wicked ways and he would be rewarded. Cornelius said he had indeed reformed before the will was signed, two years before the Commodore's death. Therefore, he should get a bundle.

Then William's lawyers produced affidavits from private detectives who had had occasion to watch Cornelius a few years earlier. They went into great detail about following him from one low dive to another, watching him drink, gamble and consort with loose women.

Then the other side's lawyers produced affidavits from the same private detectives saying they had been deceived and had just learned that the man they had been following wasn't young Cornelius and they would be willing to appear to testify to that.

Then a woman appeared to testify that her husband, a doctor of spiritualism, had treated the Commodore. And he had taken a bribe from William to convince the Commodore that his first wife had spoken to him from The Great Beyond and warned him to leave it all to William.

Then the other side countered with evidence that Frankie, the widow, who was 50 years younger than the Commodore, had a first husband rattling around out there somewhere so maybe they weren't legally married so that would mean the will . . .

"Hold it," said William's lawyers. "Maybe we can settle out of court." More than two years had gone by. William gave Cornelius and the one sister who fought the will a million each and paid their legal fees. They were enormous, maybe even more than the million apiece. At least two of the lawyers retired soon afterwards.

Cornelius killed himself within a couple of years. William died seven years after his father. But he learned a valuable lesson. He left plenty to everybody.

Originally broadcast January 4, 1988

A MONUMENTAL LOVE STORY

Prince Kurram was born in India on this day, the fifth of January, in 1592. You probably never heard of him. Or of Shah Jehan. That was the name he took after he became the emperor. He ran an empire half the size of Europe and infinitely richer.

Politics in India in those days was neither democratic nor gentle. Shah Jehan's first order, when he became emperor, was that the male children of all his uncles and cousins be killed. He didn't want to take any chances on someone claiming his throne. And stayed in power for the next 30 years by a series of similar stunts.

Shah Jehan had several wives and girlfriends and children by most of them. But the favorite, by far, was Mumtaz Mahal. They had been married for 16 years before he became the emperor.

Shah Jehan was so in love with Mumtaz Mahal that he couldn't bear to be away from her. He insisted that she travel with him wherever he went. That travel was hard on her, especially when she was expecting a baby, which was most of the time.

Shah Jehan had only been emperor for three years when she died on one of his trips, having their 14th child. Poor, grief-stricken Shah Jehan ordered the finest architects from all over his empire to assemble at his palace at Agra.

> *Shah Jehan had several wives and girlfriends and children by most of them. But the favorite, by far, was Mumtaz Mahal. He was so in love that he couldn't bear to be away from her.*

He ordered then to start work, around the clock, on a tomb for his beloved empress that would be the finest the world had ever seen.

Shah Jehan was head of an empire of Indians, the Moguls, and his people had fallen lock, stock, and elephant for the charms of the ancient Persian civilization. They adopted its language and literature, its art and music, with the enthusiasm of converts. And, above all, its delicate architecture.

Quarrying began on tons and tons of the most delicate white marble. When the construction began, it took 20,000 men 22 years to finish the job.

What emerged was the Taj Mahal, the most beautiful single piece of architecture ever produced on the face of the earth.

Shah Jehan intended, when it was finished, to get started on another one nearby of black marble. Mumtaz Mahal would lie in the white one, he in the black one.

But it wasn't to be. Even before the great tomb was finished, Shah Jehan's four sons began fighting over his empire. The winner was Mumtaz Mahal's son. He ordered his father shut up in a fort near the Taj Mahal. But he made sure the old man was kept in a room with a good view of the Taj Mahal.

And when he died, the son ordered that he be buried in it, alongside the woman he loved so much.

Originally broadcast January 5, 1993

GREAT EXPLORATIONS

Robert Cavalier was made a nobleman by the King of France for his exploration of North America and he took the noble name of Lasalle. So history knows him as Lasalle.

Lasalle was a mathematics teacher who intended to be a priest. But he had a fiery temper and the church turned him down. So he came to Canada and settled just west of Montreal.

He had a theory that if he went as far as the St. Lawrence River and Great Lakes would take him, he would get to China. His neighbours thought he was crazy and called his place China. In French, that's Lachine and there's still a town there with that name.

Over the next 15 years Lasalle became one of the greatest explorers in the history of the world. He went to the west end of the Great Lakes and down the Mississippi to the Gulf of Mexico. He was the first white man to reach the gulf that way.

Lasalle intended to make his fortune in the fur trade. But he was no businessman. As well, he got all tangled up in the complicated politics of Quebec. He was a pal of Frontenac, the governor, but Frontenac fought with everybody else and made enemies for them both.

In 1682, after Lasalle had been in Quebec 15 years, Frontenac sent him back to France to talk to the king. The king was impressed and that's when he made him a nobleman.

Lasalle had a plan to establish a colony at the mouth of the Mississippi, where New Orleans is today. But the king had other plans for that part of the world. He wanted to invade Mexico, which was owned by Spain, and grab the silver mines there.

Now, Lasalle, like most promoters, was a bit of a con man. He said: my new colony would be the perfect base for an invasion of Mexico.

The king said it sounded to him like a long way from Mexico. "No," said Lasalle, "they're right beside each other." Lasalle had been there and he was a mathematician and navigator, so the king was convinced.

The expedition to found the colony was a disaster. Lasalle fought with everybody else involved. The weather was against him. Enemy ships captured one of his loaded with vital supplies.

When Lasalle landed in the Gulf of Mexico, on the 6th of January in 1685, he was 400 miles off course, away to the west in Texas. The experts still argue over whether it was careless navigation or part of Lasalle's scheme to con the king.

No matter. It was the end of Lasalle. He had several hundred colonists with him and most either starved to death or were killed by Indians.

Lasalle's men had enough of him and shot him. And they left him where he fell. One of the great figures in Canadian history and he ended up making a meal for the buzzards down in Texas.

When Lasalle landed in the Gulf of Mexico, he was 400 miles off course. The experts still argue over whether it was careless navigation or part of Lasalle's scheme to con the king.

Originally broadcast January 6, 1993

THE CARPETBAGGERS

The Peltzer murder trial was the sensation of Europe a hundred years ago. It gave rise to books and plays and songs and verses. And rightly so. It's a fascinating tale. But even more fascinating is the story of the carpet the victim was standing on when he was killed.

The story starts in the 1870s. Leon and Armand Peltzer were Germans, brothers from a family of politicians and aristocrats. The family had fallen on hard times but the brothers worked their way back into prosperity. Leon was a merchant in Antwerp in Belgium. Armand was in Buenos Aires.

Leon got into trouble. He went broke and was facing fraud charges. Armand didn't hesitate for a moment. He sold everything he had and sailed for Antwerp right away. He searched out everyone Leon had swindled and paid him off in cash.

It seems Armand had done very well in Buenos Aires because, after everybody was paid off and brother Leon was shipped off to the United States, he had enough money left over to let him live a comfortable life.

Armand became a close friend of a wealthy young lawyer named Guillaume Bernays. And, more important, of Bernays' wife, Julie.

They quickly became a threesome. Armand was always at the Bernays house. In fact, he was almost like a brother-in-law. He just showed up at mealtimes and there was always a place set.

One reason he was welcome was that Guillaume and Julie didn't have a happy marriage. They fought all the time and only Armand seemed to be able to calm them down.

This kept on for four years. Then, in 1881, the Bernays decided to get a divorce.

To collect evidence, Guillaume started questioning the maids in the house and soon heard things about Armand he'd never suspected. He wrote Armand a letter accusing him of impropriety with Julie. Armand denied all.

Just about then, Guillaume got a series of letters

> *Guillaume showed up, stepped into the hallway, and was shot in the back of the head. He fell forward, spattering the carpet with blood.*

from an Englishman named Henry Vaughan, asking him to do some legal work. It looked like a job that would pay very well. Vaughan arranged by letter to meet Guillaume in Brussels, at a private house on Law Street, of all places. That was on the 7th of January in 1882.

Guillaume showed up, stepped into the hallway, and was shot in the back of the head. He fell forward, spattering the carpet with blood. The body wasn't found for almost two weeks.

By then, there was a lot of evidence that Henry Vaughan, the Englishman who set up the meeting, was around somewhere. A wedding ring with Henry and Lucy engraved inside it was found by the washbasin as if someone had washed his hands and forgotten the ring.

Printers were easily found who had been turning out Henry Vaughan business cards and Henry Vaughan letterhead. Just no Henry Vaughan.

The house had been rented by a dark-haired man who had also rented that carpet in the hall and just enough furniture to fill one room. But, in the stuff left behind was a comb with some light hairs in it. How could this be if Henry Vaughan was dark?

The cops quickly charged Armand and his brother Leon, the fair-haired one who was supposed to have been in the United States. It seems he had returned to Belgium just about then.

Both were convicted after a sensational trial. Armand died in jail within a couple of years. Leon did 30 years then was released. He killed himself by drowning at Ostend, a Belgian city on the sea, in 1922.

When the body was washed ashore, the police hired a farmer to cart the body to the morgue. The farmer covered it with an old bit of threadbare carpet. When the body arrived at the morgue they found an evidence tag on one corner of the carpet. It was the same carpet that Guillaume had been standing on when he was shot 40 years earlier.

Originally broadcast January 7, 1987

LADY KILLER

From Confederation in 1867 until Canada did away with capital punishment, about 50 women have been sentenced to be hanged in this country. In fact, only 11 were executed.

Most of them were involved in plots in which the actual killing was done by a husband or boyfriend.

But the last woman to be hanged in Canada, Marguerite Pitre, was a real killer. Her brother made a bomb and she took it to the airport and put it aboard a plane. The plane blew up in mid-air and 23 people were killed.

Marguerite Pitre's motive for those murders was secondary. She had no direct interest in seeing them dead.

Marguerite Pitre's maiden name was Ruest. She was married twice, once in 1934 and again in 1948. She came from a little place in Quebec called St. Octave-des-Metis. During the war, when there was good money to be made in war plants, she moved to Quebec City and worked in a munitions factory.

There she met a flashy young man named J. Albert Guay. Guay was one of those people who comes on as a loser but who can achieve a sort of leadership if he hangs around with other losers. During the war, Guay worked in the ammunition factory with Marguerite Pitre and, on the side, sold jewelry to his fellow workers.

Between his two incomes, Guay was able to live a flashy life. He drove a pretty good car and liked to show the girls a good time.

Marguerite Pitre was just about the opposite. Her friends called her the Raven. She always wore black and she was quite fascinated with cheap, shiny things like the tasteless jewelry that Guay peddled.

Short, dumpy Marguerite Pitre seemed healthy herself, but those around her weren't. Her brother, Genereux Ruest, lived in a wheelchair. His legs had been attacked by tuberculosis. Of her two boys, the younger was sickly.

After the munitions plant closed at the end of the war, Guay started his own jewelry shop and Marguerite Pitre went to work as a waitress.

A girl of 17 nameed Marie-Ange Robitaille worked with her. Her old friend, Guay, started having an affair with Marie-Ange, although he was married and a father.

Marguerite would often loan Guay the key to her apartment so he could spend the afternoons there with Marie-Ange. Guay was good to Marguerite. He loaned her money, never charged interest and never bugged her for repayment. He employed her crippled brother in his jewelry shop. The brother was a bit of a mechanical genius, very good at watchmaking and anything complicated.

Pretty soon, Guay was so deeply involved with Marie-Ange that he had to do something about his wife. She was due to fly from Quebec City to Baie Comeau in early September.

In mid-August, Marguerite Pitre went into a hardware store and bought 10 sticks of dynamite. She said it was for a friend who wanted to blow up some stumps. She took the dynamite to Guay's jewelry shop and there her brother made a bomb.

Then Marguerite took the bomb in a taxi, on the day of Mrs. Guay's flight, to the airport. She told the clerk to handle the parcel carefully because it was a delicate religious statue.

The plane blew up in mid-air. It should have been over the St. Lawrence River. But it was a little slow that day and the wreckage came down on land where the police recovered the pieces. They soon saw it was a bomb job.

Everybody in Quebec knew about Guay and Marie-Ange so the cops didn't have to look very hard. When Guay was arrested he ratted on Marguerite and her brother. Guay was hanged in 1951, Marguerite's brother in 1952 and Marguerite herself on the 8th of January in 1953. She insisted she'd done nothing wrong.

> *The last woman to be hanged in Canada, Marguerite Pitre, was a real killer, putting a bomb her brother had made aboard a plane.*

Originally broadcast January 8, 1988

THE GREAT SEA QUEENS

In the 1930s, the way to get from Europe to North America was by ship. A couple of dozen huge ocean liners carried passengers in luxury, more elaborate than in any hotel in the world. The British decided to build the two most fantastic ships the world had ever seen, the Queen Mary and the Queen Elizabeth.

One would leave England as the other left New York and between them, they would grab most of the North Atlantic passenger trade, taking five days to cross either way.

The Queen Mary was built first and was actually in service when the war came along in 1939. The Queen Mary was repainted a dull wartime grey, the luxury interior was torn out and it was converted to a big troopship.

The Queen Elizabeth was launched in 1938, but by the time it was fitted out luxuriously the war had started. As soon as the peacetime interior was built, it was torn out and the Queen Elizabeth, also, was turned into a troopship.

Both ships were so huge they could each carry an infantry division at a time, 15,000 men.

They were both so fast they travelled without any escort ships. They could outrun any submarine that might be hunting them. When the war was over, it was estimated that those two ships alone had carried so many soldiers all around the world that they had shortened the war by a year.

The Queen Elizabeth alone travelled half a million miles and carried more than 800,000 soldiers.

Once the war was over, they were refitted again, ready for the luxury trade they had been designed for. For a few years they made big money for their owners,

Suddenly in the mid-1950s, everything changed. Passengers started flying instead of sailing, and the two great Queens were terrible liabilities for the Cunard Line.

the Cunard Line.

Then suddenly in the mid-1950s, everything changed. Passengers started flying instead of sailing and the two great Queens were terrible liabilities for the Cunard Line.

The Queen Mary was sold to an American company that anchored it an Long Beach, near Los Angeles, and there it sits today, a money-making venture and a major tourist attraction.

The Queen Elizabeth, alas, had a sadder ending.

First, the Cunard people refitted it as a cruise ship for the West Indies and Mediterranean trade. That didn't work.

It was sold to an American company that intended to anchor it in the Delaware River near Philadelphia, as a hotel and convention centre. But the Delaware River was too shallow.

Then the same outfit went into partnership with Cunard to anchor the Queen Elizabeth at Port Everglades in Florida, as a hotel and tourist attraction like the Queen Mary. That venture fell apart amid an investigation about corruption and mafia connections by some of the Americans in the deal.

Finally, the great ship was sold to a Chinese multi-millionaire who intended to sail it out of Hong Kong, partly as a cruise ship, partly as a sea-going university.

It was being refitted for that new job when it caught fire on the 9th of January in 1972 and burned and sank. The investigation that followed said it couldn't prove that sabotage was involved. But the fire seemed to start in three places at once.

Originally broadcast January 9, 1992

INDEPENDENCE DAY

Going into the First World War, Canada was a very bush-league power on the international scene. In fact, even that might be overstating the case. Canada was no power at all. It was part of the British Empire, and Britain handled all our foreign affairs.

The situation was so ridiculous that if the Canadian government wanted to deal with the American government, the message went from our government in Ottawa to the governor-general. He sent it to his boss in London, the colonial secretary, who sent it to Britain's department of external affairs, the foreign office. And the foreign office sent it to the British ambassador in Washington. And the British ambassador handled it as if it were a British affair, not a Canadian one.

In 1919, the powers that won the First World War sat down together to come up with a peace treaty. The American president, Woodrow Wilson, wanted to take that process one step further. He wanted to create an organization called the League of Nations, that would prevent future wars by bringing countries to the conference table before the shooting started.

That seemed like a good idea and practically everybody went for it. Then came the next problem: who would join the League?

Most of the countries of the world agreed that Britain would be a member and would represent the entire British Empire. There was no need for Canada, Australia, South Africa and the others to be members in their own right.

But Robert Borden, the prime minister of Canada at the time, wouldn't hold still for that. The Americans didn't want the various British dominions to be in the League because it assumed they would all vote together with the mother country. That, in effect, would give the British a half-dozen votes to one each for America, France, Italy, Japan, and the other nations.

The British didn't want Canada to have its own membership because it was afraid that would be the first step in the breakup of its empire.

The British didn't want Canada to have its own membership because it was afraid that would be the first step in the breakup of its empire.

But Borden was in no mood to knuckle under. He pointed out to the British that they had only won the war because the Canadians, Australians, and others had stood by them. In fact, with more accuracy than good manners, he pointed out that the British Army had been on the verge of collapse when the Canadians stood firm and saved the day at Ypres.

It was the Canadians who had stormed up Vimy Ridge and taken the strongest fortress the Germans had. That had been the beginning of the end for the German Army. And it hadn't been easy. Fifty thousand Canadians died. Three times as many were wounded.

No one could deny that incredible effort by a nation of fewer than 10 million. So Canada got its own delegation to the peace conference. And when the League of Nations was formed, on the 10th of January in 1920, Canada was one of the founding nations.

In 1922, when Britain threatened to go to war with Turkey, it pointed out that that would mean Canada would be at war, too. Canada said, "No such thing. You get involved in some stupid war over there and you're on your own."

The next year, 1923, Canada signed a fishing treaty directly with the United States. It had been 56 years since Confederation and Canadians were finally cutting the apron strings.

It would be nice to end the story on a high note and report that, once in the League of Nations, Canada became a major power for good in the world. Alas! That's just not so.

Canada's record was as sad as any nation's. The League didn't work. Our place in it also entitled us to our own place in the International Labor Organization. But we didn't go along with all that organization's progressive plans, because we insisted on the right to discriminate against Japanese and Chinese workers in British Columbia.

We had joined the big guys. And we were as nasty as they were.

Originally broadcast January 10, 1984

A BORN LEADER

The Macdonalds lived in the north of Scotland, on land owned by the Countess of Sutherland. In the late 1700s and early 1800s, the Countess saw that there was more money to be made by raising sheep than people on her land, so she chased the people off and raised sheep whose wool would make the Industrial Revolution.

One of the Macdonalds who was dispossessed moved south and went into business as a merchant. His son did the same. And *his* son, John Alexander Macdonald, was born in Glasgow on the 11th of January in 1815.

Five years later the Macdonalds moved to Canada and settled in the town of Kingston. In those days that was away out west, though today it's just halfway between Toronto and Montreal.

Young John A. Macdonald got a pretty good education for those days. The Scots have always had a great reverence for learning. John's father was a shopkeeper and a miller and never did make much money.

But the family scrimped and saved to put John in a private school that was a bit better than the public schools of the day. They moved to Picton, a small town a little to the west, but they left John in Kingston because that's where the private school was.

He was not a bad student although certainly not brilliant. He liked to read a lot. When he was 16, he was apprenticed to a Kingston lawyer. There were no law schools in those days.

The theory was that he would serve as a clerk in the lawyer's office for six or seven years then be made a lawyer. In practice in those days, nothing went as planned and many lawyers were called to the bar with only a few years' apprenticeship.

Young John was good enough that, after only a year, he was sent to Picton to open a branch office for his boss. Then, after another couple of years, he was asked to take over the law practice of a sick cousin. So he did that.

The pictures and descriptions we have of Macdonald in those days are of a tall, gangly young man, rather ugly but with quite an engaging sense of humor.

All his life Macdonald would be a boozer and a joker. Somebody once put a dead horse in the pulpit of the local church and Macdonald, although denying it, had to make a rather abject apology.

In later years, when Macdonald was the first prime minister, the governor-general wrote back to London that he met a man who was a pal of his in those days of his youth. The man told him that he and Macdonald and another man loved to cross the border to the States.

There, they would make the rounds of the bars. Macdonald would play some sort of crude instrument, a mouth organ or a jew's harp, one of the three who was a big man would prance around like a dancing bear and the third man would lead him by a chain and pass the hat. They paid for their drinking and occasionally even came home with a dollar or two.

When Macdonald was only 20, the lawyer he was apprenticed to died suddenly. Macdonald was then called to the bar with only five years' apprenticeship.

He started to practice law in Kingston. He had two famous criminal cases, one of treason, one of rape. Both clients were hanged.

So Macdonald abandoned criminal law and went into commercial law. He was well on his way to being a rich man.

Then he was smitten by politics. Once he was elected an alderman in Kingston he could never turn back. He was on the path that would make him Canada's first prime minister.

All his life Macdonald would be a boozer and a joker. Somebody once put a dead horse in the pulpit of the local church and Macdonald, although denying it, had to make a rather abject apology.

Originally broadcast January 11, 1990

THE AGONY OF DEFEAT

The British arrived in India in the late 1500s. In the next 200-odd years they conquered it and made it the jewel of their empire. But they were always afraid of invasion from the northwest, especially by the Russians.

Only the mountainous land of Afghanistan lay between the Russians and India. The Russians sent ambassadors to make alliances with the Afghans. But the Afghans would have nothing to do with them.

Some British officers in India figured they had nothing to worry about because the Afghans would never let the Russians cross their territory to attack India.

But the British leaders in London weren't that confident. They figured the British had better conquer Afghanistan just to be sure.

The British figured the best way to do it would be to ally themselves with one of the many Afghan leaders. The Afghans were always fighting amongst themselves.

In the 1830s, one of the losers fled to India and the British treated him well. They gave him a pension and a palace to live in and let him recruit an army.

Then, in the summer of 1839, they encouraged him to return to Afghanistan and take it back from the faction that had chased him out. They even sent an army of their own along to help him.

It took a year, but the combined British and Afghan force took the country back.

A couple of times, the defending Afghans tried to stop the British force. But the British attacked vigorously with their small but highly professional force. And, every time, they succeeded, just as they had in the past couple of centuries. No force in the world could stand up to the British army.

The officers who had warned against the invasion

British officers in India figured the Afghans would never let the Russians cross their territory to attack India. But the British leaders in London weren't that confident.

in the first place pointed out that the Afghans weren't defeated. When they saw the British were too strong for them, they just retreated.

There was still a strong Afghan force out in the hills, they said, and it would attack at the appropriate moment. The British leaders said they were crazy.

The British captured the few major towns in Afghanistan, even the capital, Kabul.

They put an army of 4500 men in the city as a garrison but they didn't bother to build themselves a strong fort.

The officers even moved in their families and settled down.

Then, the Afghans started to wear them down. They began a series of small attacks, seldom anything big. They killed off the British one and two and three at a time.

It finally got so bad that, around Christmastime in 1841, the British commander asked the Afghans if they would hold off their attacks long enough for him to assemble his army and march home. The Afghan leaders said, sure, go ahead.

So just after New Year's in 1842, the British force started home. As soon as they were strung out in a line through the rocky hills and narrow passes of the mountains, the Afghans attacked.

On the 12th of January in 1842, the sole survivor of the British column arrived back in India. The Afghans had killed or captured the whole force and allowed one man, a medical officer, to return to tell the British in India what had happened. It was the single most humiliating defeat the British Army ever received. One hundred and forty years later, the Russians invaded Afghanistan. With the same success.

Originally broadcast January 12, 1990

SHOOTOUT AT THE OK CORRAL

On the 13th of January in 1929, the wild west gunfighter, Wyatt Earp, died peacefully in his home in Los Angeles. The old west that he and his buddies had created was already dead nearly a generation.

To me, the most amazing thing about the wild west has always been that it occurred so recently. Wyatt Earp, the most famous of the western lawmen, died quietly in his suburban bungalow amid his orange groves in Los Angeles, in a house with electric light and a phone and washing machine — this man who made his name with a horse and a gun and a badge and not much else.

Wyatt Earp was born in Illinois in 1848 and he went west as a teenager. He and his father and brothers worked all over the west, as far as California, as laborers, stagecoach drivers, miners, cops, gamblers, and saloonkeepers.

In Canada, frontier justice was imposed in an orderly manner by the Mounties. In most cases, they arrived in new territory before the settlers.

Just the opposite was happening in the States. The people flocked into the empty land. They settled and started making money raising cattle or mining or farming. When crime cropped up, they appointed a member of the community to control it.

There was no point in hiring a Sunday school teacher to go up against a gunfighter, so they usually hired another gunfighter. If they hired the best gunfighter, the town got law and order. If they hired the second best, the town got disorder and violence.

From the late 1860s on, Earp and his brothers were sheriffs and marshalls in various towns from Kansas south and west. They were also part-owners of saloons, gambling halls and houses where women were available to cowboys and miners.

It sounds like the recipe for corruption and, by today's standards, it was. But on the whole, the Earps were fairly honest lawmen.

Most of those positions Wyatt Earp held were elective, so his life was a mixture of business, law-enforcement and politics. His politicking brought him into conflict with a sheriff named Billy Behan. I'm not sure why screenwriters have picked up on Wyatt Earp's exploits and not on Billy Behan's. He was at least as colorful a character.

Since both were lawmen, you might think they would have been on the same side. But they weren't. That rivalry led to the most famous gunfight in the history of the west, the shootout at the OK Corral. The OK Corral was in Tombstone, Arizona, where Wyatt's brother Virgil was town marshal.

A gang of crooks called the Clanton Gang, friends of Billy Behan, went up against the Earp brothers and their pal, Doc Holliday. Holliday was a strange character, a southern gentleman, a dentist who quit his practice and moved west hoping the dry air would cure his tuberculosis. He was probably the best gunman the west ever produced.

The shootout itself probably lasted about 30 seconds. Seventeen shots were fired and three men were killed, all Clantons. Virgil and Morgan Earp were wounded. Five months later, two men shot Morgan in an ambush and killed him.

Wyatt went on the warpath and nailed one of them.

One of the best parts of the story escaped Hollywood as far as I know. While all this shooting was going on, Wyatt and Billy Behan had eyes for the same girl, a circus girl named Josey Marcus. Wyatt won her and they moved to California.

Wyatt made his living as a saloonkeeper in Alaska during the gold rush. Then he returned to California and became a fight promoter and racehorse owner.

None of his fighters were champs. But one, Jack Kearns, quit to become a fight manager. He took over the career of another youngster from those wild west days. That kid was called Jack Dempsey.

By the time Wyatt Earp closed his eyes and died quietly in bed, on the 13th of January in 1929, the wild west had become just memory — and legend.

> *If they hired the best gunfighter, the town got law and order. If they hired the second best, the town got disorder and violence.*

Originally broadcast January 13, 1984

THE ART OF DARKNESS

Josef Teodor Konrad Korzeniowski was born in Poland in 1857, the son of well-to-do landowners on both sides of his family. Poland in those days was part of the Russian empire.

Young Korzeniowski's father was involved in plotting against the czar, and when he was caught, the whole family was sent into exile in northern Russia. His mother got sick in the harsh climate and died.

The young boy lived with his father who was allowed to return to Poland after the death of his wife. Then the father died and the boy was raised for a couple of years by his mother's brother.

The boy announced when he was 17 that he wanted to be a sailor. So he left home and went to the great seaport of Marseilles.

In 1875, the records show, young Korzeniowski sailed to the French West Indies on the ship Mont Blanc as an apprentice. It was the beginning of a career as a seaman that lasted until 1894 and saw him a captain. And more importantly, it was the beginning of a career that was to be the foundation of another career, one that made him world-famous.

For three years Korzeniowski sailed as a seaman and studied to get his officer's papers.

In late 1877, he was involved in some sort of gun-running enterprise, taking munitions into Spain which was in the middle of one of its many revolutions.

If it had worked he would have made a bundle. It didn't, and he was left almost broke. He took his last 800 francs to the casino at Monte Carlo and took a chance with it.

He lost and tried to kill himself. But the bullet went in his chest and out his side without hitting his heart. He just might have been drinking at the time.

Joseph Conrad became the greatest writer of sea stories in the history of the greatest seafaring nation of all time.

Korzeniowski then went back to sea. A few months later he arrived in England. He figured if he was going to make his living as a seaman he would be better off in the British merchant service since Britain ruled the world and the waves.

In 1880 he passed his exams as a second mate. He kept studying while he was at sea and passing his officer's exams. He became a British subject.

He sailed all over the world, especially to the Far East and to Africa. He would fill in his spare hours at sea writing short stories, mostly for his own amusement.

While he was up a river in Borneo in 1887, he met a Dutchman named Ohlmeyer who had spent his life as a trader in the Far Eastern jungles. He started scribbling a story, based on Ohlmeyer's life. He called it *Aylmayer's Folly.* Sometime in late 1893 he sent it to a publisher in London.

Then he reported to the French port of Rouen where he was to sail an immigrant ship to Canada. But the shipowners had some sort of trouble and that voyage was cancelled so he went back to London.

When he arrived, there was a letter waiting for him from a publisher.

It wasn't a letter of acceptance. But it was encouraging. So Korzeniowski decided to leave the sea and to settle down as a writer.

The date was the 14th of January, 1894. And he changed his name to something an Englishman could pronounce: Joseph Conrad. And he became the greatest writer of sea stories in the history of the greatest seafaring nation of all time.

Originally broadcast January 14, 1986

THE WORD OF THE LORD

At the beginning of 1838, Lord Melbourne, the prime minster of Britain, had a big problem on his hands: Canada. There had been rebellions in both Ontario and Quebec. They were over but the causes remained, whatever they were.

Melbourne needed somebody with clout in Britain to go to Canada, assess the situation and come up with solutions.

He had asked Lord Durham, but Durham had said no thanks. Durham was fabulously rich, so he was trusted by the moneyed and titled people who ran Britain. On the other hand, he had been one of the movers of the great reform bill of 1832 that allowed the poor to vote. For that he was known ever afterwards as Radical Jack, usually not with much affection.

Melbourne was desperate so he asked Durham again, this time with a speech about duty and responsibility.

On the 15th of January in 1838, Durham said yes. He arrived in May, accompanied by crates of champagne, his own silverware and monogrammed dishes and two regimental bands. He rode through the streets of Quebec City on a white horse, wearing the uniform of a field marshall although his military career had ended before he was 19 and the highest rank he ever held was lieutenant.

There were 800 prisoners in the jails of Ontario and Quebec from the rebellion. Durham freed all but eight who were under death sentences. He exiled them to Bermuda then started travelling around, looking for the causes of the rebellion.

They weren't hard to find. The French-Canadians felt oppressed by the English-speaking minority in Quebec. The Ontarians were ruled by a bunch of retired British officers who ignored elected representatives.

Durham lived like a lord as he moved around, impressing everybody with his charm and generosity. He didn't spend much time in any one place.

Back home, the opposition jumped on his order to exile those rebels to Bermuda. He had no authority in Bermuda. The prime minister fired him rather than face any more grief in Parliament.

Durham left Canada after only five months. He wrote a report recommending that Ontario and Quebec be made one colony. He said the Quebec problem was caused by the people insisting on keeping their own language and culture.

Durham arrived in May, accompanied by crates of champagne, his own silverware and monogrammed dishes and two regimental bands.

The union would eventually put them in the minority and they would disappear under waves of British immigration.

Durham's anti-French-Canadian feelings led to much of this country's subsequent grief. And his union of Ontario and Quebec was so unworkable that parliament ground to a halt.

Mind you, it created a situation so bad that Canadians had to solve it themselves. We call that solution Confederation.

Originally broadcast January 15, 1993

THE FABULOUS BARKER BOYS

Donnie Arizona Clark was an awful name for a girl so, as she grew up, she insisted on being called Kate. Kate was born in the dirt-poor hills of Missouri in 1872. That was Jesse James country with a long history and culture of banditry. In fact, Jesse James wasn't killed until Kate was 10 so, for all we know, she might have met him at one time, although history doesn't say she did.

Anyhow, Kate grew up to be the leader of a gang of criminals much tougher and smarter and more successful than Jesse James or any of the famous bandits.

The records are obscure and a lot of pure nonsense has been written about Kate, some of it by the cops who spent years trying unsuccessfully to catch her. When Kate was fairly young, in her late teens, she married a man named Barker and had four boys by him.

The four all turned out to be vicious criminals but not too bright. Old Barker didn't have much to do with Kate and the boys and he died early on in the story.

Ma had other boyfriends from time to time. The one who lasted longest was a rather pleasant, fairly honest man named Dunlop. When Ma got tired of him she had two of her boys kill him.

She got the name Ma, by the way, not from her own boys but from a kid from Montreal who joined their gang and called her Ma. He was a vicious gunman named Alvin Karpis. He later spent years in jail then was deported to Canada and died here only a few years back.

In the late 1920s and 30s, the mid-western United States were afflicted by more bank robberies, murders, and kidnappings than ever before in history. The new breed of criminals had all the nerve and imagination of the old bandits of the wild west plus the firepower of modern weapons and the mobility of the car. Ma Barker, the poor girl from the hills who had raised four vicious killing and robbing machines, soon put together the most successful gang of them all.

They hit banks for thousands, not putting up with any opposition. Karpis killed two bankers with his tommy-gun in one robbery. The gang also went into kidnapping and made $300,000 by kidnapping two rich men.

Ma's gang was the best because Ma was a planner. She cased banks carefully and drew up detailed blueprints for each raid. She bought off crooked cops and went over escape routes time and again until everybody knew exactly what to do.

It was her success that led to the downfall of all the big criminal gangs, including her own.

Since the local cops didn't seem to be able to do much about all this crime, the American federal government stepped in and assigned the FBI to the task. The FBI was a slow, methodical force. It didn't have much success, but gradually it closed in on Ma and other bandits by using her methods, careful planning and painstaking attention to detail.

Ma and one of her boys, Fred, set out for Florida and rented a big house at a place called Lake Weir. But the FBI was hot on their trail Agents surrounded the house on the 16th of January in 1935 and called on the Barkers to surrender. No way. There was a furious gun battle. When it was over both Ma and Fred were dead, riddled with bullets.

For years, Ma Barker was a legend. But today we live in such a violent society that she's not much news anymore so a whole generation is growing up not knowing about her. Seems a shame.

> *The new breed of criminals had all the nerve and imagination of the old bandits of the wild west plus the firepower of modern weapons and the mobility of the car.*

Originally broadcast January 16, 1992

THE INGENIOUS ECCENTRIC

Francis Galton was that most endearing of all Englishmen, the ingenious eccentric. No one knows to this day if he was smart or crazy, a hopeless dreamer or one of history's greatest practical jokers.

Galton was born in 1822 in England. His family had lots of money. His grandfather was a Quaker who had made a fortune selling guns. He got thrown out of the Quakers for that because they're a peace-loving bunch.

Galton went to school to study medicine but got sidetracked. He was incredibly curious and, in the course of his medical studies, he came across a book called the *Pharmacopea*, a list of all the drugs known to man. Galton had to try them all.

He was in the C's when he encountered croton oil, a powerful laxative. He only took two drops of it but it cured him of his curiosity about drugs and got him back to his medical studies.

Galton became a doctor but never liked medicine. He was rich enough that he didn't have to work so he travelled. He went to Africa. He brought back a strange combination of scientific observations and utter nonsense.

He wrote a travel book that became a best-seller. He told his readers that if they weren't feeling good when in the tropics they should mix a charge of gunpowder in a glass of warm soapy water and drink it down fast.

If they got blisters on their feet they should break a raw egg into each boot.

If lice were a problem, just mix up half an ounce of mercury with a handful of used tea leaves and mold it into beads and wear them on a necklace.

The best way to keep your clothes dry in a thunderstorm, wrote Galton, is to take them off and sit on them until the storm has passed.

The only way to light your pipe in a hurricane, he said, is to get off your horse and crawl under its belly and use that as a windshield.

When Galton was studying medicine, he crammed so hard he claimed he sprained his brain. And that, in turn, caused his head to over-heat. So he invented a hat with little shutters in it that he could open by pressing a bulb in his pocket. In those days, of course, a gentleman couldn't go out without a hat.

In 1899, Galton's cousin, Charles Darwin, published his famous book, *The Origin of the Species*, the theory of evolution.

That got Galton thinking about how humans develop. He figured if we breed people with the same care used to produce horses and cattle, we would soon have a master race.

He set up a booth at the International Health Exposition in London in 1884 and took detailed measurements of more than 2500 people. He weighed them and measured them and checked their reflexes and, for some reason, he took their thumb prints.

He noticed that no two were the same. So he forgot the other stuff and did a study of all those thumb prints and came up with a way to classify them. It took nine years but Galton invented fingerprinting.

In the fall of 1910, he wasn't well. So he rented a house out in the country in the south of England. The day he moved into the house he looked at the landing in the stairwell and said: "Uh oh, they'll have trouble getting my coffin around that." And they did when Galton died at the age of 88 on the 17th of January in 1911.

Galton only took two drops of croton oil, a powerful laxative, but it cured him of his curiosity about drugs and got him back to his medical studies.

Originally broadcast January 17, 1990

A Roman Ruckus

On the 18th of January in the year 52 BC on the Appian Way, the greatest highway that ran south from Rome, two parties met.

One was led by Senator Milo and it was a vast throng, strung out along the road for a quarter-mile. There were about 300 people in all, servants and cooks and dancing girls and a force of armed guards. Senator Milo himself was in the lead, in a coach with his wife.

Coming the other way, headed for Rome, was a party of 30-odd men led by a nobleman named Clodius.

Milo and Clodius were enemies. Clodius was the principal foe of the great orator Cicero, and Milo was Cicero's close friend. Cicero and Clodius had been friends at one time but for the last 10 years they had been jockeying for power in Roman politics.

Their friendship had cooled into political rivalry then into personal hatred. Cicero, in addition to being a politician, was the foremost mouthpiece of his day. He had recently defended a young man on a breach-of-promise suit brought by Clodius' sister. And, in the course of getting the young man off, Cicero had shredded Clodius' sister's reputation in very obscene and mocking terms.

Cicero was too shrewd to depend solely on his oratory and his political smarts. He also used large amounts of money to bribe jurors or politicians. Milo had started life as a muscle man, a collector, and he often used the Milo gang to have people beaten up if they stood in his way.

It was through this sort of service to Cicero that Milo became a senator.

Milo and Clodius passed each other without incident. We don't know if they smiled and waved or looked straight ahead. But as Clodius came alongside the tail end of the Milo party, about a quarter-mile from Milo himself, he made an obscene gesture. One of Milo's tough guys whipped out his sword and gave him a cut. Quite a cut. His pals took him into a nearby tavern to

have his wound looked at. It was a slash on the shoulder.

At this point, other men from Milo's party ran into the tavern with their swords drawn. Several people who worked in the tavern, including the owner, were killed. Clodius was dragged out into the road and killed with a dozen stab wounds. His body was left lying in the road.

Clodius' wife took his body to the Senate, the seat of government, and showed it to the crowd. She said Clodius had been murdered by Cicero since everybody knew that Senator Milo was just a stooge of Cicero's and had no clout of his own.

The crowd got so indignant that it broke up the place and set fire to it. Until now, Cicero probably had enough influence to have the whole case forgotten.

But it was in the middle of a very important political campaign and one of the main public buildings had just been burned down. Nobody could engineer this sort of a cover-up.

Cicero, in addition to being a politician, was the foremost mouthpiece of his day.

So Milo was charged with murder. His lawyer, of course, was his old pal Cicero, the super mouthpiece of the day. And if Milo was guilty, so was the guy who had put him up to it.

Cicero pulled out all the stops. He gave a brilliant speech, even better than the one that had cut up Clodius' sister. But it wasn't good enough.

The Jury voted to convict, 38 to 12. They had big juries in those days. The best Cicero could do was beat the death penalty. He had Milo exiled instead.

That was the best thing he ever did for him. Within a couple of years, while Milo was living in luxurious exile in Marseilles, a nice town, Cicero's enemies finally caught up with him. They probably framed him. At any rate, his head was cut off and stuck on a pike and set up in the Forum.

And who came to look at it but Clodius' widow. She stuck a needle in that tongue that had caused her family so much grief.

Originally broadcast January 18, 1988

POE-TRY IN MOTION

Edgar Allan Poe was born on the 19th of January in 1809 in Boston, the child of a not-very-successful actor and a highly-successful actress. Poe's mother got rave reviews whenever she appeared on the stage but she never managed to translate that into any large amount of money. His father disappeared the year after Poe was born. We don't know why.

Within a year of that, Poe's mother died, apparently of tuberculosis. His mother had been very popular on the stage in southern cities, and a couple from Richmond, Virginia, adopted the child because they had been such fans of his mother. Their name was Allan, hence Edgar Allan Poe's new name.

Mr. Allan was a prosperous merchant, originally from Scotland, and he raised young Edgar as his own son. The Allans moved to England for a few years and young Edgar was enrolled in a pretty good British boys' school.

He learned a lot of writing and science in a short time. They returned to the States and Mr. Allan came up with the money to enroll Edgar in the Virginia Military Academy so he could be a young southern gentleman.

But Edgar and the old man fought and Edgar walked out on him and joined the army. He spent the next few years as a common soldier, not an officer. He eventually made it up to sergeant-major while still quite young. Then he quit and set out to make his living as a writer.

All this time, it was apparent to Poe's friends that he had some sort of mental problem. Not insanity. But certainly some form of depression. He was obviously a genius. Everybody who talked to him for an hour came away with that opinion. Well, most. A few thought he was nuts.

Poe worked as a short story writer, as an editor,

With his poem **The Raven,** *Poe achieved fame in both the States and England. But he never managed to translate fame into prosperity.*

and as a reporter briefly.

He took the murder of a young prostitute in New York that was in the papers in those days and used it as the basis for a short story called *The Mystery of Marie Roget*, set in Paris. He created a detective character named August Dupin. Every detective story, from Sherlock Holmes on down, follows Poe's principles of mystery writing.

Poe was obsessed with death, especially after his young wife died. She was a beautiful girl, his cousin, and her death seems to have done him terrible mental harm.

Poe had never handled alcohol well although he was usually smart enough to stay away from it. After the death of his wife, though, he seemed determined to copy his brother who had died of alcoholism.

In 1844, with his poem *The Raven*, Poe achieved fame in both the States and England. But, like his mother, he never managed to translate fame into prosperity.

Up to that time, there were plenty of horror stories, usually ghost stories. Poe tried his hand at them. He studied science until he knew quite a bit about his subject, then he told his story with a lot of authentic scientific fact thrown in. Today we call that science fiction.

In 1849 Poe died at the age of 40. He had been drinking at the time. A New York clergyman did a biography of him soon afterwards and referred to Poe as a low-life and a drunk.

That idea was quickly picked up. A year or so later another biography of Poe was written, this time by the French poet Baudelaire. He took a much more sympathetic view, probably the more accurate of the two. But the reputation as a drunk stuck, and even today, a lot of people think of Poe as a ne'er-do-well who just happened to be also a literary genius.

Originally broadcast January 19, 1990

MADE IN HONG KONG

In the 1830s, the British Empire was on the rise and China was a crumbling giant. For thousand of years the Chinese had thought they were a superior race and culture and for much of that time they were. They had paper and gunpowder and all sorts of useful things centuries before the west.

But that situation was now reversed. The western nations, especially Britain, had developed a technology like nothing the world had ever seen, steel and steam power, chemistry and communications.

The British had owned India for a couple of hundred years and looted that land of billions to make London the capital of the world. One of the most profitable products they produced in India was opium. Naturally, they realized as well as anybody else just what a scourge it was and they tried to control it in their own territory. But they saw nothing wrong with selling huge quantities of it in China.

The emperor of China didn't want anything to do with foreigners and for years he wouldn't let the British land in his country.

But by the 1830s a few British merchants had warehouses along the lower Pearl River, around the south China city of Canton. From those warehouses they shipped tons of opium to China and made millions. Both British and Chinese officials got rich on it.

Then in 1838, the emperor of China, a thousand miles away in Peking, sent a new governor to clean things up.

He was honest and efficient and pretty soon the British weren't moving any opium into China. In fact, the new governor went even further. He made the British merchants surrender a fortune in opium that they had sitting in their ships in the mouth of the Pearl River. And I mean a fortune, hundreds of millions in today's terms. As soon as he seized it, he had it destroyed.

Hong Kong has become the most commercial place in the world, a huge financial success.

The British couldn't hold still for this insult to their flag and commerce. They sent an expedition of soldiers from India. With their modern weapons and military discipline, they easily defeated whatever forces the Chinese could muster in the area.

The British made the Chinese agree to accept opium from India, although according to British law, that wasn't strictly legal. And they made the Chinese hand over a little island near the mouth of the Pearl River, a place called the Fragrant Harbor. Or, in Chinese, Hong Kong.

The local commanders on the scene worked out the deal and drew it up formally on the 20th of January in 1841. Strangely, it was never signed. Nevertheless, the British landed on Hong Kong the following week and set about to establish a colony.

It was to be like no other colony. Hong Kong had a superb deep water harbor that would take any ship in the world. So, right from the start, they made Hong Kong a free port, one where no taxes or tariffs applied. Within a few years it was well on its way to being the commercial capital of the Orient, a position it still occupies.

A generation later, the British demanded and got more territory to add to the colony. And again in 1898. But that last acquisition had a time limit of 99 years. And today the Chinese are demanding that Britain honor that. The British have agreed and they'll get out in 1997. In the meantime, Hong Kong has become the most commercial place in the world, a huge financial success.

But the two commanders who worked out that deal were in trouble back home. Neither government liked it at the time. The Chinese commander was demoted and exiled to Turkestan. The British Commander was called home, given a lecture, and ended his days as consul in Dallas, Texas.

Originally broadcast January 20, 1992

THE RELUCTANT ROYAL

Louis the 16th was the grandson of King Louis the Fifteenth. His father had died. He was a big, awkward kid, rather slow but not actually stupid.

It was decided, since he'd be king one day, to marry him young and get him producing children so the next generation of kings would be ensured. An Austrian princess was picked out for him and given a French name, Marie-Antoinette.

Louis had some minor physical problem that prevented him from having sex with his bride and that led to a miserable life. After seven years, the royal doctors decided it was nothing major and they quickly fixed it up with a small operation. From then on, Louis and Marie-Antoinette were quite happy. Unlike most French kings, Louis was a faithful husband.

He was a generous man who was concerned about the plight of the poor people. He was about the only man in France who was. No matter how much concern Louis showed, his officials just increased taxes on the poor. The nobility paid practically nothing.

Marie-Antoinette wasn't a popular queen. She was extravagant and frivolous and got a reputation for squandering money when the people were starving. When they screamed that they had no bread, she is supposed to have said, "then tell them to eat cake."

She probably didn't say that, but a lot of people were happy to spread the story.

The day the old king died and Louis became king, he was on his knees praying to God to find somebody else for the job. He didn't want to be king.

The day the old king died and Louis became king, he was on his knees praying to God to find somebody else for the job. He didn't want to be king. The poor man wanted to be a locksmith.

The poor man wanted to be a locksmith. He had a small workbench and anvil and little forge just off his bedroom and he loved to make and change the keys to all the rooms in the palace.

He liked to work with the masons and carpenters whenever there was any work to be done around the palace. The queen was always shouting at him because his hands were dirty.

He liked to show off his strength. He would pick up a shovel and have one of the page boys sit on it while he walked around, holding the kid up. If the queen had let him out to the neighbourhood pub, he probably would have spent his time arm-wrestling. He didn't drink much although he loved food.

In 1789, the people rose in Revolution and down tumbled the old order. But the king had enough goodwill with the people that he was kept on. By now the monarchy was more like England's, not very powerful, just a servant of parliament.

But, as the various factions of revolutionaries jockeyed for power, it became a good idea, politically, to try the king for treason and execute him.

So, on the 21st of January in 1792, poor Louis had his head chopped off. Just before he died, he started a speech. He said he was innocent. We don't know what else he said, because just then the officer in charge of the execution ordered the band to produce a drum roll. Maybe he was saying he just wanted to be a locksmith.

Originally broadcast January 21, 1988

A STABBING IN THE DARK

Henry Sovereign was born in the United States, in New England, but his family moved to southwestern Ontario when he was young, in the 1790s.

Sovereign was a strange man if not outrightly crazy. When he was a teenager his mother scolded him one day for putting too much butter on his bread. He flew into a rage and vowed to never eat butter again. And he didn't to his dying day.

Sovereign married and worked a farm near London, Ontario. We don't know a lot about him except he was a troublesome neighbour, to say the least. In 1828 he went on trial for shooting a horse. As far as we know it was a neighbour's horse and the shooting resulted from some sort of dispute about a fence.

The British governor who had set out to make Ontario another little England had brought along British criminal law and imposed it on the land. And British criminal law was very severe with anyone who shot a horse. Back in England, horses were the property of the wealthy and the principal concern of British law was to keep the lower classes in their place. So the penalty for horse-shooting was death.

Sovereign was convicted and Mr. Justice James McAulay had to pass sentence. Even the judges in those days could see it was a ridiculous sentence and McAulay recommended to the lieutenant-governor that it not be carried out.

And it wasn't. We don't know what did happen to Sovereign, but if he went to jail instead it wasn't for long. Because on the night of the 22nd of January in 1832, four years later, he was at home in his farmhouse with his wife, Polly, and eight of their 11 kids. The three oldest ones were away somewhere.

In the middle of the night, Sovereign later said, two men came to the house carrying what he called sharp instruments. They woke him up, attacked him and he got away. He ran to a neighbour's and raised the alarm. When the neighbours armed themselves and went back to the Sovereign farmhouse with him, they found Polly and seven of the eight kids stabbed and beaten to death. The eighth, little two-year-old Anna, was safe in her bed, having slept through whatever happened as only a kid could.

The local cop was Constable John Massacre, appropriately enough. He arrested Sovereign for the murders and later testified that Sovereign reached into his vest pocket for a knife as he was charged. Massacre said he grabbed the knife and found blood on the blade. Sovereign said he bled from a couple of minor wounds the two strangers had inflicted on him. Then he reached into his pocket for some tobacco to have a smoke before going for help. Maybe that's how the blood got on the knife.

Some said the jury might have been buying his story about the two strangers until then. But the thought of a man stopping to have a smoke while his wife and kids were in danger, as it turned out, real danger . . . well, that was too much.

So for the second time Mr. Justice McAulay sentenced Sovereign to death. This time there was no interference from the lieutenant-governor.

Hangings were in public in those days and drew huge crowds. Tavern keepers and local merchants loved them because people came from miles around, all in a festive mood and disposed to spend. But, in that regard, the Sovereign hanging was an awful disappointment. There was a cholera epidemic at the time and not many showed up.

> *Sovereign said he bled from a couple of minor wounds the two strangers had inflicted on him. Then he reached into his pocket for some tobacco to have a smoke before going for help.*

Originally broadcast January 22, 1992

TRAGEDY AT SEA

The Valencia was a fair-sized American steamship that worked the west coast around the turn of the century.

So many people had wanted to go to the Klondike to look for gold that all sorts of old tubs had been pressed into service, in many cases by bribing inspectors in Seattle and San Francisco. Several of them sank, with terrible loss of life.

But the Valencia wasn't one of those. It was only 24 years old in 1906, young as a ship goes. Its skipper was a man named Johnston who was capable and experienced. And Captain Johnston was the sort of boss sailors liked so he had his pick of crews, no bums or drunks among them.

So, when the Valencia set out in mid-January of 1906 from San Francisco to Seattle, it should have been a short, safe trip.

But the weather turned awful. There was no radar or radio in those days. Once the ship left shore, it all depended on the skill and experience of the skipper and the crew.

A couple of days later, the Valencia was well past Seattle, creeping slowly in dense fog, away up around the south end of Vancouver Island. As the Valencia got further north, the wind got worse. It at least tore up the fog so the skipper and crew could get the odd glimpse of the coast.

The boss said the shoreline looked like the entrance to the Strait of Juan de Fuca, around Cape Flattery at the south end of the entrance. He was almost right. Except the Valencia was further north, off Cape Beale, well north of the entrance to the strait.

About 15 minutes before midnight on the 22nd of January, the Valencia was being swept toward the shore, and it hit the rocks a good half-mile or more out from the shore. The shoreline at that point was steep cliffs.

When the Valencia set out in mid-January of 1906 from San Francisco to Seattle, it should have been a short, safe trip.

The sea was like a cauldron, but Captain Johnston and the crew tried to launch the seven lifeboats over the next couple of days.

The first or second one got away and made it to the shore. The survivors had an awful time getting up those cliffs but they somehow made it. They staggered through the bush to the lighthouse at Cape Beale and sounded the alarm.

The lighthouse keeper immediately telegraphed to Victoria, and two big steamers and a powerful tug set out to save the people aboard the Valencia.

The Valencia had gone ashore at the very worst spot. It was too far out in the water for a rescue from the shore. And it was too close inshore for the ships to get close.

So, for the next 48 hours, rescuers on the shore and on the three ships stood by and watched as the waves pounded the Valencia apart.

There were three rafts aboard the Valencia and they floated ashore with people on them, many of them almost dead.

The passengers and crew climbed up into the rigging to get away from the awful waves. As they got numb from cold and fear and hunger they let go and fell into the sea.

The rescuers just stood and watched. Every now and again they would try to get close but the storm got worse over the two days after the Valencia hit.

By the time it was all over, 117 had died. It wasn't the worst Pacific coast sea tragedy by a long shot. But it was the most heart-breaking.

Skill and nerve and the best equipment available in those days were just no use.

Originally broadcast January 23, 1991

GOLD RUSH!

John Sutter was a man who dreamed of building an empire. Little did he know . . .

Sutter was Swiss, a merchant who went broke and took off in 1835, leaving his wife and four kids behind in the Alps. He travelled through Europe and eventually made his way to the United States. Along the way he made up a little background for himself. He said he'd been a captain in the Swiss Guard of the king of France.

When he reached California, Sutter figured it was paradise, with its attractive climate, rich soil, some small mineral deposits that might some day become mines, and pleasant people.

In 1839, he persuaded the Mexican government, which owned California, to let him have some land in the Sacramento Valley, south and east of San Francisco. There, he intended to build his little empire. He called it New Helvetia. Helvetia is the old name for Switzerland.

Sutter attracted a few European winemakers, and various farmers and craftsmen from the east — carpenters, tanners, blacksmiths, people like that.

He had some of the native Indians working for him and some Mexican cowboys. His colony was off to a small but steady start. He'd raised the money by selling stock in Europe.

In 1846, the Americans and Mexicans went to war and California quickly became American. A battalion of Mormons arrived from Utah to fight for the Americans, but by then the war was over. Sutter recruited a lot of them as carpenters and other skilled tradesmen.

He wanted to build two mills on the rivers, one for grain, one for timber. The timber mill was the more remote. He hired a carpenter from New Jersey to run that construction job named James Marshall. Marshall was 37 but looked and acted a lot older. He was a loner, a man reported to have proposed to two women and been turned down both times. Most of the workmen under Marshall were Mormons. There were 19 of them.

In early January of 1848, they installed the millwheel and began digging a little canal 150 yards long, to carry water from the river to the millwheel.

Toward the end of the workday on the 24th of January in 1848, Marshall was inspecting that little canal. He thought he saw flakes of gold at the bottom. He mentioned it to the others but somebody said, no such luck.

The next day Marshall ordered his men to dam the canal while he took another look. He must have been thinking about it overnight.

It was a clear, cold day and nobody else wanted to reach into the six inches or so of water left in the bottom of the canal. So Marshall did it alone. He found one piece of gold half the size of a pea and several flakes of it.

He and the others didn't know for sure if it was gold. It looked rather light in color, but it was soft like gold.

Jennie Wimmer, the only woman in the camp, the cook and laundress, threw the little piece of metal into a kettle of boiling soap and it wasn't affected by the lye in the soap. That indicated it could be gold.

On January 28th, Marshall rode downstream to report to Sutter with samples. Sutter was pretty sure it was gold.

> *The word got out — and within a year the great California gold rush of 1849 was on.*

The first thing to be done was to keep the news from getting out until Sutter could get a contract from the Indians in the area, recognizing his right to all minerals in the ground. Nobody thought that was cheating in those days, just shrewd business.

But one of the men in Marshall's construction crew who was freighting goods from San Francisco bought himself a bottle of brandy with some of the flakes of gold he'd found. The word got out — and within a year the great California gold rush of 1849 was on.

Sutter's dreams of an empire died. He couldn't get anyone to work for him. They were all busy digging for gold. He finally died in Pennsylvania and died broke in 1880.

Marshall prospected a bit but didn't get rich. In 1872 the state legislature voted him a pension of $200 a month. But he drank it all away. In 1885, just before he died, he applied for more. He was turned down.

Five years after he died, they spent $9,000 building a monument to him.

Originally broadcast January 24, 1984

THE ART OF ROMANCE

The artist history knows as Sandro Boticelli was born with the name Mariano Filipepi, in Florence in Italy, back in the time of Christopher Columbus. At that time, Italy was the artistic centre of the world and Florence was the artistic centre of Italy. The history books aren't clear why Mariano Filipepi became Sandro Boticelli.

At any rate, the artist history knows as Sandro Boticelli was apprenticed to a famous painter named Fra Filipo Lippi. That word Fra in front of his name means Brother, as in a religious title. Lippi had indeed been a monk. But he couldn't leave the girls alone so he either left or was thrown out of holy orders before Boticelli was apprenticed to him. For some reason, maybe as a profane joke, he kept his title.

Boticelli was such a devoted apprentice of Lippi's that the experts still have trouble figuring out which of them actually painted several masterpieces. To make it even more complicated, in later years, Lippi's son, also a painter, was an apprentice of Boticelli, the painter who had been his father's apprentice.

Boticelli was a strange man, a tall, thin workaholic who spent some of his time playing practical jokes on his friends and some of it in a religious passion that at times almost amounted to a trance.

He was one of the best artists of his time. He did some of the paintings in the Sistine Chapel, although the experts say they were far from his best.

But in the 1470s, when Boticelli was at the height of his genius, he did a series of religious paintings that set the tone for generations of painters.

Much of Boticelli's work was done for the fabulously rich Medici family. One of the young Medicis had a real burn for a lovely young lady named Simonetta Vespucci. This was a worship rather like what some guys get for movie stars today.

Simonetta was married, but Mr. Vespucci wasn't at all jealous. And neither he should have been. Young Medici had no hanky-panky in mind. In fact, he saw Simonetta as an almost divine creature, a gift from God to man.

Each year in Florence there was a mass tournament called the Courts of Love. Young men would fence and wrestle and carry on in a sort of decathlon. Each would carry a banner with the picture of a beautiful young lady on it. At the end of the day, the guy who won would hold up the banner of his lady and she would be a sort of Miss Florence for the rest of the year. It was sort of a mini-Olympics plus beauty contest with a vaguely religious overtone to it.

Well, on the 25th of January in 1475, young Medici went into the Courts of Love, carrying a banner with Simonetta's portrait on it, painted by Boticelli. Simonetta was all done up in a gold dress with the rising sun shining through her blonde hair. It sounds rather tacky 500 years later but it was a big hit at the time.

So much so that, after Medici won and Simonetta was the star of Florentine society, her picture by Boticelli became the standard for religious paintings of Virgins and Madonnas for a couple of centuries.

Boticelli himself painted her so many times for religious paintings and murals that he had to set up a shop full of assistants to grind them out.

Poor Simonetta didn't live to see all this fame. She died at the age of 20, before her year as the beauty queen was up.

> *Boticelli's painting of Simonetta made her the star of Florentine society, and the picture became the standard for religious paintings of Virgins and Madonnas for a couple of centuries.*

Originally broadcast January 25, 1991

DEADLY MEDICINE

The 26th of January in 1948 was a cold, blustery day in Tokyo. It was closing time at the Teikoku Bank and the staff was eager to get finished for the day. There was an epidemic of dysentery going around and everybody was feeling rotten. Two employees of that branch were off sick.

Just before they could close the door for the day, a middle-aged man in a white lab coat and an official-looking armband came in, carrying a doctor's little black bag. He explained he was from the ministry of health and presented his card to the manager. He then ordered him to line up his employees while he gave them medicine to counteract any dysentery infections they might have.

Each employee held out his teacup and the doctor put some liquid in it. He ordered everybody to drink it quickly and then hold out his cup for a second medicine. The first might burn the throat a little, he said. The second would soothe it.

All 16 employees keeled over. The doctor then walked to the cash drawers and took all the money plus a large cheque.

Nobody found the bodies for an hour. Ten were dead. Two died later. Four survived.

The survivors were able to give a good description of the man. He had a mole on his chin and a slight scar on one cheek.

The calling card he'd left belonged to Dr. Shigeru Matsui. It didn't take the cops long to find him. He wasn't the guy.

Dr. Matsui said he had bought 100 calling cards in one batch. He had four left. Painstakingly, the cops took him back over every card he'd given to someone.

Among them was an artist he met on a ferry boat during a trip to northern Japan. The methodical doctor had kept the artist's card. The artist was Sadamichi Hirasawa, a minor celebrity in Japanese art circles.

The cops in Hirasawa's home town reported he was no killer, no bank robber. The best cops in Japan beat their heads against the wall. They just couldn't get a line on the killer.

All 16 employees of the bank keeled over. The doctor then walked to the cash drawers and took all the money plus a large cheque.

It turned out that a few months earlier, and again a week before the phoney doctor hit the Teikoku Bank, he had pulled the same stunt at other banks but with harmless medicine. Apparently, those were rehearsals.

The day after the mass poisoning, the robber went into another bank and cashed that big cheque that was part of the loot.

After a couple of months, the heavy guns of the police department gave up and the case was turned over to Sergeant Tamegoro Igii. Igii was rather old to be a sergeant. He had been away in the army during the war, and when he came back most of the men his age had been promoted.

He started at square one and went over every scrap of evidence again. He checked out dozens of suspects, including Hirasawa, the artist.

He admitted later that he didn't think Hirasawa was his man when he first met him. But he slowly came to the conclusion that he was. And he built a case against him with infinite care.

Seven months after the bank employees had been poisoned, Igii charged Hirasawa with the murders. He also had a confession, both in writing and on film.

At his trial, Hirasawa repudiated his confession, saying it was tricked out of him. He said he had never been in that bank and had never stolen a dime.

Igii testified about his conversations with Hirasawa, about little lies and inconsistencies.

Medical experts testified that Hirasawa was suffering from brain damage as a result of anti-rabies shots he'd taken in 1925.

The verdict was guilty. The sentence was death.

But today, Hirasawa is still in jail, an old, old man, almost 90. The Japanese government, without any explanation, has never carried out the death penalty. And today Hirasawa is in the *Guiness Book of World Records* as the oldest man in the world on death row.

Originally broadcast January 26, 1984

A RUSSIAN REVOLUTIONARY

Alexander Pushkin was a crazy genius, a man who was born of a rich family but became the darling of the poor of Russia. He wrote passionately about freedom but he took out a mortgage on his serfs to pay his gambling debts.

Pushkin was a little guy who seldom combed his hair. His nails were so long they were like claws. He looked so lewdly at women that he was often fighting duels with their brothers and husbands.

Pushkin carried an 18-pound club in his right hand and swung it as he walked to strengthen his arm so he could hold his pistol steady. He once stood eating cherries during a duel while the other guy fired.

He was a swarthy man. His great-grandfather had been an African slave who had been given as a present by the sultan of Turkey to the czar of Russia. That slave was an excellent soldier and became a major-general.

French was the language of the Russian aristocracy, but Pushkin wrote in Russian, the first major writer to do that. The people loved whatever he wrote: plays, history, historical novels, pornography, fairy tales, poems about love and history and mythology, political essays, anything.

Pushkin poured out all sorts of writing and the public snapped it up. He was the first professional writer in Russia and made a lot of money. But he was a gambler and was always broke.

And a monumental lover. He once counted 113 great loves he'd had. One of his friends said it was the only time Pushkin underestimated anything.

Russia in those days was a police state. But Pushkin wrote about liberty and free speech until he was exiled from St. Petersburg, the capital.

When a new czar took over, he was a fan and called Pushkin back to the capital. He said: don't bother sending your stuff to the regular censor. Send it to me.

The czar didn't hack and slash it nearly as much as the censor would have.

French was the language of the Russian aristocracy, but Pushkin wrote in Russian, the first major writer to do that. Pushkin poured out all sorts of writing and the public snapped it up.

When Pushkin was 30, he married the most beautiful girl in Russia, an airhead of 16. She drove him crazy, spending a fortune on dresses, flirting with the czar and every good-looking man at the court.

Pushkin, the great lover, was consumed with jealousy. A lot of men whose wives had broken their hearts over Pushkin enjoyed the spectacle.

Pushkin's nemesis was his brother-in-law, a handsome young Dutchman who had married Pushkin's wife's sister. He made it clear he was crazy about Pushkin's wife and only married her sister to be near her.

On the 27th of January in 1837, Pushkin and the brother-in-law met on the field of honor. The brother-in-law fired first and hit Pushkin in the stomach. Pushkin fell, propped himself up on his elbow and fired. He got the brother-in-law in the chest. But the bullet hit a button and the brother-in-law got off with just a couple of cracked ribs. Pushkin died two days later.

Originally broadcast January 27, 1993

HER HIGHNESS' HERO

Francis Drake was a real hero, in the ancient, classical sense of the word, a man greater than other men.

Drake was born about 1540 in Devon in southwest England, the son of a poor farmer. We don't know his birth-date because he wasn't important enough to have it recorded. England was wracked by religious strife in those days. The Drakes were Protestants and were chased away from home by a Catholic mob. They settled near the mouth of the Thames River, a sea-faring part of the world.

Drake went to sea at 13 and for the next 10 years sailed up and down Britain's North Sea ports, learning the trade of ship's master. In the 1560s he ventured further afield to the West Indies.

Drake was a superb seaman and a tough fighter. The rivalry between Britain and Spain was partly religious. And Drake's hatred of Catholicism made him a bitter enemy of Spain. The Spanish Empire was the richest the world had ever seen and Drake delighted in looting it.

Drake returned from voyage after voyage with shiploads of loot and Queen Elizabeth quickly adopted him as her favorite seaman. A lot of titled big-shots were jealous but Elizabeth never lost her love for Drake. He returned from every voyage with riches for her.

In 1577, Drake set out with five ships to sail around the world. He battled storms and cold and the Spanish. He went around Cape Horn, the extreme southern tip of South America, then up the west coast looting Spanish ships and ports. He took so much gold and silver from the Spanish that his ship rode dangerously low in the water.

Drake sailed up to about where Vancouver is today then turned west and crossed the Pacific. He made it back home in two years, with 56 of the 200 men he had set out with, in one ship instead of the five.

He brought the queen so much treasure she met him as he dropped anchor and knighted him there on the deck of his ship.

Drake returned from voyage after voyage with shiploads of loot and Queen Elizabeth quickly adopted him as her favorite seaman. A lot of titled big-shots were jealous, but Elizabeth never lost her love for Drake.

Drake went ashore and bought a huge estate near where he was born and settled down to be a country gentleman. He became mayor of the city of Plymouth and built a fresh water system that lasted 300 years. He could do anything.

When he heard the Spanish were preparing a great armada to conquer England, he sailed into their ports and burned their supplies. When the armada sailed against England in 1588, he was vice-admiral of the fleet that defeated them, one of the greatest naval victories in history.

Drake could have stayed ashore, wealthy and showered with honors. But that wasn't his way.

When he was in his mid-50s, he led an expedition against the Spanish at Panama. It was a disaster. Disease swept through the fleet and killed dozens. Including Drake. He died on the 28th of January in 1596 and was buried at sea. Of course.

Originally broadcast January 28, 1993

THE ETERNAL PESSIMIST

William Claud Dukenfield was born in Philadelphia on the 29th of January in 1889. You never heard of him.

He was very poor. His father drove a horse and cart through the streets, selling vegetables. Young Bill went to school for four years then had to spend his time walking a block ahead of the horse and wagon, shouting "tomatoes, potatoes, cabbage," things like that.

Young Bill got tired of that and started to yell, "artichokes, pomegranates, tangerines." People came flocking to see this exotic stuff, but they walked away in disgust when they saw old man Dukenfield with his potatoes and cabbages.

The old man got so angry he hit young Bill with a shovel. Bill hit him back and ran away from home. He was 11 at the time.

At first he lived in a hole in the ground lined with oilcloth. After a while he graduated to a packing case. He stole milk from bottles on people's steps. He got bitten by watchdogs so often that he developed a lifelong hatred of animals.

Bill had a variety of jobs, none that paid very well. When he was in his late teens and working delivering ice, he set out to become a juggler. He practiced hours and hours every day. Most jugglers juggled balls. Bill figured a juggler should be able to juggle anything he can lift. So he juggled alarm clocks and knives and crystal glasses and shoes, anything at all.

By the early 1900s Bill was making big money as the world's best juggler. He had a strange sense of humor, what we'd call black humor today.

And he'd dropped the first couple of syllables off his name. By now he was just plain W.C. Fields. You've heard of him.

He had a raspy voice from bad whisky and from living in that hole in the ground when he was 11. He was a superb pool player from hanging around poolrooms. And he was one of the heaviest drinkers anywhere.

Somewhere along the way, maybe around 1915 when he made his first movie, Fields' funny lines became more important than his juggling.

He was a man of intense hatred. In the 30s he was making $6500 a week to appear on the Charley McCarthy radio show. Charley was a ventriloquist's dummy but Fields really hated him. He seemed to think he was real.

His friends never knew for sure when he was playing the comedian and when he meant it.

He had a lifelong fear of returning to poverty. He stashed his money in banks in every town he ever worked in. When he died his manager figured he had probably left three-quarters of a million scattered around somewhere.

> *Fields' friends never knew for sure when he was playing the comedian and when he meant it.*

He was never drunk. But he was never quite sober, either. Every morning, on the movie set, work stopped at 10:30 for Fields to go to his dressing room for breakfast, a thermos full of gin and orange juice. Light on the orange juice.

One day some cameramen poured it out and filled it with pure orange juice. Fields ran out of the dressing room, screaming, "Somebody put orange juice in my orange juice!"

He hated to be upstaged by child actors. Once he laced one kid's milk with gin and got him hopelessly drunk just as he was about to go on camera.

Fields was married briefly and had one child. But he said, "Women are like elephants. I like to look at them but I can't afford to keep one."

He insisted religion was for suckers and denied there could be a God. Late in 1946, as he lay dying in bed, his old pal, his doctor, saw something Fields had shoved under his pillow. He asked what it was.

Fields said, "Oh, nothing." The doctor reached in and pulled out a Bible.

"Bill," he said, "you're not reading the Bible."

"Not the way you do," said Fields, "I was just looking for loopholes."

Originally broadcast January 29, 1986

THE LONE RANGER

In 1929, a Detroit showman named George Trendle got a license to operate a radio station. He called it WXYZ. That was so he could use the motto, "the last word in radio."

At first, WXYZ was an affiliate of CBS which ground out network shows from New York and fed them to stations all over the country.

Now, radio was in a strange state in those days. It was vastly popular. The public was fascinated with people's voices and music coming out of a box in the living room. The whole family would gather around the radio and sit, silent and mesmerized, for hours.

But the advertisers hadn't yet taken to it. The traditional medium for selling breakfast cereal and perfume and cars and toothpaste was still the newspaper. If the product was upscale, like a Cadillac or a mink coat, the advertisers preferred magazines.

But radio was still a tough sell because there were no rating systems that could give an accurate picture of who was listening, if anybody.

Trendle, the new station owner, quickly got fed up with the stuff he was getting from CBS. So he ended his contract and decided to put on his own shows. He was a howling failure. By 1932 he was losing $4,000 a week.

Trendle remembered that, back when he ran a movie theatre, he couldn't go wrong with a western. Fans would line up to see even a poor western.

And there were no westerns on radio. So Trendle figured he would start a western series. Trendle was a perfectionist.

He didn't just hire any writer and say, give me a bunch of cowboys and Indians and settlers and cavalrymen and bad guys. He drew up a very definite picture of what he wanted: a tall, good-looking guy who came out of nowhere on a white horse, fought with the bad guys then, when he beat them, got on the white horse and disappeared.

A writer named Fran Striker had turned out some mystery scripts for Trendle, and Trendle liked his touch. So he phoned Striker and described what he wanted.

Striker said he would write a script and send it along. Trendle said: "Hurry. I want to be on the air by the end of January. And I already have a name for this hero on the white horse. We'll call him the Lone Ranger."

It created a revolution, although nobody knew it at the time — a story about a guy who finds injustice and corrects it. Then, before anybody can thank him, he gets on his horse and rides away to look for more injustice.

Striker sent the first script to Detroit in about two weeks. And *The Lone Ranger* went on the air on the 30th of January in 1933.

It created a revolution, although nobody knew it at the time. Here was a story that was well-written, about a guy who finds injustice and corrects it. Then, before anybody can thank him, he gets on his horse and rides away to look for more injustice.

The actor who played the Lone Ranger lost interest after a few months. He went away to Hollywood where he became a writer and director. In the 70s he created the big movie hit, *Airport.*

He was replaced by a little guy from Kitchener, Ontario named Earl Graser. Graser had a great voice and was the Lone Ranger for eight years. Then, one night on his way home from work, he fell asleep behind the wheel and plowed into a parked truck and was killed.

So the announcer on the show took over. It was just as well. Before that, when kids came around to the studio to see the Lone Ranger they had to send the announcer out to see them anyhow. He was a big guy, 6'2", who *looked* like the little guy *sounded.*

The Lone Ranger ran 2,956 radio episodes then went onto TV and the movies. You can still see it on Saturday mornings from time to time.

Originally broadcast January 30, 1990

THE UNFINISHED COMPOSER

Franz Schubert was dead for a generation before he got the fame and respect he always wanted. But that's not to say that he was ignored while he was alive.

Schubert was born in Vienna on the 31st of January in 1797. His father was a school teacher and Schubert himself became a teacher although he only taught when he was desperate for money, just for three or four years.

Schubert was a music nut. He would sooner compose than eat, sleep, or drink. He died at the age of 31 but he was a sort of Irving Berlin of his time, grinding out 650 songs, nine symphonies, five masses, a dozen operas and so many chamber pieces that no one has ever come up with an accurate count.

Mozart, the greatest musical genius of his time, died in Vienna just a few years before Schubert was born. Mozart had heard symphonies in his head. Schubert didn't have that sort of genius. He had to work at it.

Schubert was a short, tubby, awkward little man. He lived while Napoleon was fighting the Austrians, year after year. Austria was desperate for soldiers but Schubert was too short for the army. Otherwise, he would have been drafted and that might have been the end of him.

As far as we know, Schubert was only serious about one girl in his life. Her mother decided Schubert would never make much of a living as a musician so she put an end to the affair. Maybe it was just as well. Schubert probably would have been a poor husband because he was so tied up in his music.

He never made a lot of money as a song-writer until his last couple of years. He made his first royalty when he was only 19. He probably would have been pretty well off but he was a careless manager of money.

When things were tight he borrowed a lot. When times were good, he sold his songs along with their future earnings so he could have money in his pocket.

Schubert's genius brought all sorts of people together. He played his songs in the salons of the very best families in Vienna and he drew crowds in the pubs. Often, he would do both on the same night. He would play the piano at some rich man's house then top off the evening in one of the low dives in the slums.

Sometime around then, he seems to have contracted syphilis, the disease which would eventually kill him. In those days there was no cure for it.

Schubert wanted to make it as a composer of operas. But he never did. He could knock off songs by the dozen. He worked hard at them because they didn't come easily to him. He had the knack for mass production.

But he really agonized over his operas. None was performed in his lifetime. Part of that was just bad luck. Schubert was a very German composer and, in his day, the fashion in opera was very Italian.

Schubert started a lot of work that he never finished. But one symphony, his eighth, is his most famous. It was unfinished and it's known as The Unfinished Symphony.

Schubert died at 31. And it wasn't until 1865 that his brother found the manuscript. By that time Schubert was forgotten. He had never achieved much fame outside Vienna.

But that one symphony suddenly caught fire. Pretty soon it was in the repertoire of every major orchestra in the world. That, in turn, led to the popularity of a lot of Schubert's work that had been forgotten. So today, he's known as one of the half-dozen major classical composers.

> *Mozart had heard symphonies in his head. Schubert didn't have that sort of genius. He had to work at it.*

Originally broadcast January 31, 1990

THE VOICE OF REASON

Hugh Scobie did a lot to build Canada. Yet, he died so young that history books barely mention him and then, not as a great leader but as a might-have-been.

Scobie was a Scotsman, born in 1811. He became a lawyer but then, just as he was about to start practicing, his father announced he was moving the family to Canada. So they all started to pack. Then the old man was drowned in an accident. Mrs. Scobie announced the family would move, just as papa had wanted. So she, Hugh, and his four brothers and two sisters all moved to southern Ontario, near Toronto.

That was in 1833. For the next four years, Hugh worked hard and became a leader in his community and in the local Presbyterian church, although he was still a young man.

Ontario was not a well-run pace in those days. Quebec was no better. The man with most of the power was the lieutenant-governor, always a British military officer or nobleman, always more concerned with creating a little England overseas than with building a Canada.

The governor and his pals got first run at all government jobs and roads and bridges were built to increase the value of their properties, not for the benefit of the whole community.

This led to a lot of dissatisfaction and, eventually, to rebellion in December of 1837. The leader of that rebellion was another Scotsman, a fiery little man named William Lyon Mackenzie.

Mackenzie published a newspaper in Toronto called The *Colonial Advocate.* He attacked the governor and his cronies with considerable accuracy but no delicacy. Eventually Mackenzie led an armed rebellion and tried to capture Toronto. It was a fiasco. Most of the rebels were captured. Mackenzie fled to the States and lived there for years.

Scobie fought against the rebels although he sympathized with their cause. He hated the governor and his crowd but he realized that violence doesn't get results.

On the first of February in Toronto he began publishing a newspaper called the *British Colonist.* It wasn't like the other newspapers of the day. It didn't rant and rave at the governor and his greedy and incompetent pals. It pointed out, carefully and accurately and in a fairly mild tone, that things needed improving.

It said: the wealth of this new country will come from the sweat and skill of the farmers and tradesmen, not the pomp and speeches of the politicians. We don't need more confrontation and debate in this country; we need a school system that's available to all; we need roads and bridges and canals. We need political reforms, not to stamp out rebellion, but to stamp out the causes of rebellion.

The *British Colonist* made those points again and again. It was the voice of reason and common sense in an age of ranting and raving. Slowly, the politicians realized they had better start doing the things that Scobie was pointing out were needed. Of course, as they did those things, they claimed the ideas were their own. But that didn't bother Scobie.

He expanded his publishing business to books and lithography. The leading Canadian artists of the day now had someone to publish their works.

Scobie ran for election three or four times but lost every time. He kept trying and probably would have made it. He would have been one of the leading politicians of his country in the generation before Confederation. But we'll never know for sure. He died suddenly when he was only 42.

> *The* British Colonist *didn't rant and rave at the governor and his greedy and incompetent pals. It pointed out, carefully and accurately and in a fairly mild tone, that things needed improving.*

Originally broadcast February 1, 1989

TO BE, OR NOT TO BE?

Delia Bacon was born in a log cabin in the wilderness of Ohio on the 2nd of February in 1811. Her family was poor. Her father was a Bible salesman who hadn't done very well back in New England. He died when Delia was six and she was sent to be raised by her mother's relatives.

They were quite prosperous and Delia received a good education. She was brilliant and would have gone on to university if she hadn't been a woman. They didn't let them into institutes of higher learning in those days.

So Delia and her sister spent the next few years as teachers. They ran girls' schools all over the eastern United States. They had reputations as excellent teachers but poor businesswomen.

Delia went to work at other girls' schools in New England. She quickly acquired a reputation as a clever scholar. She used to add to her income by lecturing, usually to women's clubs. One of her favorite subjects was Shakespeare.

When Delia was 35 she had an affair with a young theology student who was only 23. Such things were considered outrageous in those days and it became quite a public affair. Delia had to retire from teaching.

She went back to Ohio to hide for a while. And when she emerged she was quite changed. Instead of her fascination with Shakespeare, she now had a fixation. She was convinced that William Shakespeare was just a deer poacher and a horse groom and a part-time actor.

Shakespeare wasn't bright enough to have written all those brilliant plays, she said. They were really written by a committee of the seven smartest Englishmen of his time, led by Sir Francis Bacon.

> *Bacon was convinced that William Shakespeare was just a deer poacher and a horse groom and a part-time actor. Shakespeare wasn't bright enough to have written all those brilliant plays.*

She and Sir Francis having the same surname was just a coincidence, said Delia. She never claimed any relationship.

She wrote articles, dissecting Shakespeare's plays in great detail and comparing them to the writings of Bacon and other scholars of that time. She convinced several famous Americans that they should support her research. She went to England and pored over old records.

She enlisted the great American author, Nathaniel Hawthorne, who was then the American consul in Liverpool. Hawthorne then negotiated with a British publisher to have her theory published in a huge, rambling, unreadable book of 682 pages.

At one point, Delia persuaded the clergyman of the church where Shakespeare was buried to let her dig up his grave to look for clues. For some reason, after she got him to agree, she didn't take him up on his offer.

Delia's book didn't settle the question of whether or not Shakespeare wrote his plays. Just the opposite. It got a controversy going that's still raging today. In fact there are more serious scholars now who believe that Bacon wrote Shakespeare than there were in Delia's time.

One of the few people who was able to work his way through her book was Mark Twain. He was absolutely convinced and insisted to his dying day that Will Shakespeare didn't write all that clever stuff. But Delia didn't know about Twain's conversion to her cause. She died in a mental hospital at the age of 48.

Originally broadcast February 2, 1990

THE HOUSE IS ON FIRE

In the 1850s Ontario and Quebec were united to form one big British colony. Someday they would persuade other British North American colonies to join them and make one big country. But that was far in the future.

The most urgent business of the 1850s was coming up with a suitable legislature. Sessions had been held at Kingston then Montreal then Quebec City but that didn't work very well.

The civil servants had to move all their files from place to place. In Montreal the people proved to be inhospitable, to put it mildly. In 1849, when the legislature passed a law they didn't like, a mob burned down the legislature building.

So Ottawa was selected as the site of the new parliament. That in itself caused considerable laughter. Englishmen called it Westminster in the wilderness. Goldwyn Smith, an Englishman who became the leading scholar and snob of Toronto society, described Ottawa as a sub-arctic lumber village converted by political mandate into a political cockpit.

Nevertheless, the legislature got on with the job of erecting a suitable building for its deliberations. Architects from all over the British Empire were invited to submit designs.

The winning design was by an Englishman who was now living in Toronto, a man named Thomas Fuller. He had a good reputation and he put together a pretty good design.

Contracts were let and the first sod was turned at the end of 1859. The next year the Prince of Wales laid the cornerstone.

Construction was a nightmare. The first estimate had been vague, but something in the order of a couple of million dollars was contemplated. The rock under the building was found to be cracked and excavation had to be deeper than intended. Stone quarried on the Quebec side of the river had to be brought across on barges and the cost skyrocketed.

Ottawa was such a hick town back then that it didn't have a water and sewage system so a pumping system had to be built before any work could be done.

Six years into construction, the work was so far behind and the costs were so high that construction was stopped and 1600 workmen were laid off.

The Legislature voted more money in dribs and drabs and in 1865 the first civil servants moved in. The first session of the legislature was held in 1866 with 130 seats in the chamber for the politicians.

But the next year, 1867, everything changed. It wasn't a provincial legislature any more. It was the parliament of a new country, Canada. Suddenly 181 seats had to be installed in that chamber designed for 130.

And so it went on for another 50 years, never enough space. Then, on the night of the 3rd of February in 1916, a fire started in the reading room in the centre block.

In those days, it was fashionable to have a lot of fancy woodwork inside such a building and wide, wasteful corridors.

Two guards tried to put it out instead of calling firemen. By the time they realized it was too much for them, the fire had taken hold. All that fancy woodwork burned quickly.

Seven people died. Right on the stroke of midnight, the central bell tower fell. Queen Victoria's portrait was rescued from the burning Senate. The portrait had been saved from the fire started by the mob in Montreal 60 years earlier. And the man who saved it was the nephew of the man who saved it in 1849.

> *One Englishman described Ottawa as a sub-arctic lumber village converted by political mandate into a political cockpit.*

Originally broadcast February 3, 1987

THE FUGITIVE

William Randolph Hearst was the most colorful publisher in American history and when he died in 1951 he left behind a publishing empire and a fortune of millions. Maybe even hundreds of millions.

One of his five sons, Randolph, ran the Hearst newspaper in San Francisco and was chairman of the Hearst corporation, the company that ran the whole empire. Randolph lived the quiet life of a multi-millionaire who didn't have to work very hard. He had three daughters and one of them, Patty, went to a very expensive private school.

Patty was a bit of a rebel. She took up with her math teacher, which gave the parents a bit of a shock, but they thought she would grow out of it. But two years later, Patty was 19 and still living with the math teacher who was 24. By that time she was a student at the University of California at Berkeley.

On the evening of the 4th of February in 1974, at 9:17 to be exact, there was a knock at the door of their townhouse. There was a white woman and two black men at the door. They beat the math teacher about the head with a gun then dragged Patty out of the place.

Pretty soon, the world found out why. The Hearsts got a message, including a tape recording from Patty saying she was alive and well. She had been kidnapped by a gang of crazies who called themselves the Symbionese Liberation Army. They wanted the Hearsts to distribute $2 million worth of food to the poor, and they wanted two of their comrades who were in jail awaiting trial for murder to be released on bail.

Ronald Reagan was the governor of California at the time and he ordered all the cops in the state to find Patty. The FBI put together a huge task force.

About 10 weeks after she was kidnapped, Patty Hearst had become part of a gang that held up a bank to get money for some vague revolution. She was quickly changed from victim to fugitive.

The Hearsts tried to give away food to the poor, but that triggered a riot as the poor scrambled for the free food and it did more harm than good.

The family got a couple more recordings from Patty. She was getting impatient and accused her parents of not really trying to get her back.

Then came an announcement from her that she had been convinced by her captors that they were right and society was wrong and she was joining them in their armed revolution. Sure enough, about 10 weeks after she was kidnapped, Patty Hearst was part of a Symbionese gang that held up a bank to get money for some vague revolution they had in mind. She was quickly changed from victim to fugitive.

A few months later the cops cornered most of the gang in a house in Los Angeles and burned it down. They killed six of the gang. But Patty got away. The FBI kept up the pressure and finally, a year and a half after she was snatched, Patty Hearst was captured in San Francisco, not far from where it all began.

She went on trial for bank robbery but said she'd been forced into it. She said after she was kidnapped she'd been kept locked in a closet for days at a time, beaten, raped and threatened. The jury didn't buy it and she was convicted.

She was supposed to do seven years but the president of the United States gave her a pardon after one. She never did go back to her math teacher. During her trial her father hired a cop to be her bodyguard, and she married him and has settled down to raise a family and live happily ever after.

Originally broadcast February 4, 1992

CARNAGE IN CARTHAGE

Long before Rome was a great power, Phoenicians from the Middle East had settled all along the south shore of the Mediterranean Sea on the north shore of Africa.

Their principal city was Carthage, near the modern day city of Tunisia. While the Romans were still struggling to build their small town into a city, the Carthaginians had already built a huge commercial empire, west to Spain, north to England, east to Egypt and Palestine, even a couple of thousand miles down the Atlantic coast of Africa.

It was inevitable that, as Rome became a major power, the Romans and the Carthaginians would clash. And they did, in a series of three wars that lasted more than a century.

The Carthaginians were superb sailors. Their merchant sailors went everywhere. Their naval forces could land an army anywhere they chose to defend or invade. The Carthaginians weren't very interested in war, just trade, although they were fierce fighters when the mood seized them.

The Romans called the Carthaginians Phoenicians and their word for them was Puni. So these wars were called the Punic Wars.

The Carthaginians and Romans fought over Sicily which, in those days, was incredibly rich with huge fields of grain. Today, the soil has been worked out and Sicily is the poorest part of Italy.

That first Punic War dragged on for 20 years. The Romans finally won it by putting together a fleet that surprised the Carthaginians off the west coast of Sicily.

The Carthaginians probably could have gone on fighting, but, remember, they were merchants first, and warriors second. They found it more profitable to make peace, pay an indemnity to the Romans for 10 years and keep on trading. It was a huge amount of money to Rome but it was only a drop in the bucket for the wealthy Carthaginians.

> *It was inevitable that, as Rome became a major power, the Romans and the Carthaginians would clash. And they did, in a series of three wars that lasted more than a century.*

War broke out again, the Second Punic War, a generation later. It was a strange war.

Back in Carthage, the leaders didn't care much about it. They had a military leader named Hannibal who ran the war out of his headquarters in Spain. They sent him men and supplies from time to time but they preferred to let him and his army do the fighting while they kept trading.

During that war Hannibal performed one of the most incredible military feats of all time. He marched an army, complete with elephants, over the Alps and attacked the Romans from northern Italy. They were expecting an attack from the south.

For 36 years, Hannibal fought the Romans. He won most of the battles but lost the war. That war ended as the first one had, with a treaty that required the Carthaginians to pay the Romans a bundle.

That peace lasted another generation. Then in 150 BC, the Romans and Carthaginians had their last war. It dragged on a half-dozen years and ended with another Roman victory.

This time the Romans landed an army at Carthage and besieged the city. That siege lasted three years. When the Romans finally got over the walls, the street fighting lasted six weeks.

The Romans massacred the men, sold the women and children into slavery and levelled the city. Then they spread salt on the ground and plowed it in so nothing could grow.

That third and last Punic War didn't end with a treaty because there was no Carthaginian state left to sign one.

But that situation was corrected quite recently. On the 5th of February in 1985, the mayor of Rome and the mayor of Tunis signed a treaty ending the Punic Wars after 2131 years.

Originally broadcast February 5, 1986

THE BABE

George Herman Ruth was born in the city of Baltimore on the 6th of February in 1895, in the apartment over his father's salon.

Old Man Ruth was one bad egg. Ruth's mother died when he was pretty young. He later said he was a bad kid who learned to smoke and chew tobacco and drink beer by the age of seven.

That was when young Ruth was sent to a reform school, St. Mary's, run by an order of Catholic brothers. Some say Ruth's father realized the kid was getting out of hand and took him to St. Mary's, although he wasn't a Catholic himself. A court record shows that a judge ordered it because young George was totally out of control.

No matter. It was a move that changed the youngster's life. More important, it changed the face of North American sport.

One giant brother at St. Mary's, Brother Matthias, was a baseball nut and one of the great instinctive coaches of all time. He saw young George had some talent at baseball and made him work at it.

Jack Dunn, the owner of the Baltimore Orioles, was famous throughout the baseball world for bringing on promising youngsters. He looked over young Ruth and offered him $600 a season to play for the Orioles. The day Ruth showed up to play, another player said, "Here comes the latest of Dunn's babes." Nobody ever called him George again.

Babe Ruth was so good he just tore up the game. Not only was he probably the best batter of all time, he was a superb pitcher. He was an excellent outfielder. And although few remember it today, Babe was very good at first base when he was called to fill in there.

In his first season in 1914, Babe pitched two winning games and lost one. In 1915, it was six and he struck out 112 batters.

He moved to the Boston Red Sox and really caught fire. In those days home runs were fairly rare. Even the best batters didn't get more than 10 in a season.

Even when boozing and over-eating and late nights killed Babe's conditioning, he remained a hero. Nobody could hit the baseball like he did.

Babe started hitting homers and the crowds loved it. In 1919 he was moved to the outfield so he could play every day because people were coming to the games just to see Babe hit homers. That year he set a record, 29 home runs in a season.

The next year Babe was sold to the New York Yankees for $100,000. That was huge money in those days.

In 1919, the Chicago White Sox blew the World Series. Then it turned out they didn't blow it. They gave it away. Or, to be more exact, they sold it, taking bribes from a gang of gamblers who cleaned up.

Baseball was in big trouble. Either it had to come up with something exciting or the crowds would stay away.

The Yankees built a new stadium designed for Babe to turn out home runs. They had the right field fence close in and less than four feet high. It was a little shady but it worked. Babe Ruth blasted so many home runs he single-handedly saved baseball.

He played and lived and partied like a king. His ability to eat, drink, and chase the girls was legendary. A sportswriter once asked another player who roomed with Babe on the road what it was like to live with such a hero.

"I dunno," said the player. "I just live with his suitcase." Babe was usually getting back to his room about six in the morning.

In 1927, Babe set a record when he hit 60 home runs. That record stood until Roger Maris broke it in 1961, playing a much longer season.

Even when boozing and over-eating and late nights killed Babe's conditioning, he remained a hero. Nobody could hit the baseball like he did.

When Babe was 51, he went into the hospital for an operation for cancer. Thirty thousand kids wrote him get well cards. They didn't save him. He died in 1948, only 53 years old.

Originally broadcast February 6, 1991

DISTANT EARLY WARNING

You've probably heard a lot about the Japanese attack on Pearl Harbor in early December of 1941, how the Japanese Navy struck without warning on a Sunday morning and smashed the American Pacific fleet as it lay at anchor.

It was a terrible blow to the Americans and they went into the Second World War that day, having sustained a terrible defeat before breakfast.

There were investigations and inquiries and the general in charge of army in Hawaii and the admiral in charge of the navy were both blamed and fired.

They were described as unprepared and asleep at the switch. But the warnings about the Pearl Harbor attack were numerous and went away back longer than either man had been in command in Hawaii. In fact, the first warning came, or should have, on the 7th of February in 1932, nine years and eight months before the Pearl Harbor attack.

In late 1931, the Navy Department of the United States ordered its admirals to assemble more than 200 ships and staged one of the biggest naval manoeuvres in history.

The ships were divided into two fleets, the attackers and the defenders. The defenders were to go through the motions of protecting the Hawaiian islands, specifically the big naval base at Pearl Harbor near Honolulu.

The experts figured the Americans and the Japanese would go to war one day and the Pearl Harbor base would be the key to the American position.

The defenders spread their ships out in a traditional formation, ready to intercept the attackers. The attackers made a traditional attack.

The warnings about Pearl Harbor were numerous and went away back . . . In fact, the first warning came, or should have, nine years and eight months before the Pearl Harbor attack.

But on the attackers' side was Admiral Harry Yarnell, the head of aviation of the American Navy. Yarnell believed naval battles in future wouldn't be between ships. They would be between planes flying from ships and attacking other planes and ships.

So Yarnell sneaked away to the north of Hawaii, out where there are few commercial ships to see him and radio a warning. He knew the American Navy let its men whoop it up every Saturday night in Pearl Harbor and Sunday morning was hangover time.

Yarnell sent 152 planes from two carriers over Pearl Harbor. They carried cameras instead of guns and they went through the motions of an attack. The pictures they took made it clear that if they had been real they would have blasted the harborful of ships and prevented any of the planes on the ground from getting up to fight them.

The report of the mock attack was sent to Washington and filed away. But when Japanese navy planners heard about it, they didn't file it away. They began looking at it seriously.

When the real attack came it was on a Sunday morning. The ships lying in anchor were blasted for real. The planes on the ground didn't get away in any significant numbers. The Americans lost most of their major ships and 2400 men.

But the admiral who had planned the whole affair for the Japanese knew all along that, even if the Pearl Harbor attack was a success, he couldn't win a war. Sure enough, within three and a half years, the Americans had recovered and won that war. The Japanese admiral was killed before it was over.

Originally broadcast February 7, 1992

BLOODY MARY

If you were producing a TV soap that ran every afternoon for the rest of your life, you couldn't work in the life story of Mary, Queen of Scots. She died at the age of 44 and spent almost half that time locked up. But her adventures when she was free amounted to enough to fill half a dozen lifetimes.

Mary's father was the king of Scotland and her mother was a French princess. She was born in 1542. Her father died a week later. So Mary was Queen of Scots almost from the day she was born.

Scotland was the traditional enemy of England and ally of France. England was a Protestant country; Scotland was a Catholic country with a large and growing Protestant population. And, in those days, religion and politics were hopelessly entangled.

Mary's mother sent her to France to be educated and there she married the crown prince. When the king died, her prince became king and Mary was queen of France. Then he died after only two years on the throne. Mary, the widow and ex-queen, returned to Scotland where she was still queen.

She arrived home in 1560, a widow, former queen, a bright, beautiful young woman of only 19. And she stepped into the worst hornet's nest in Europe.

England was ruled by Elizabeth, Mary's cousin. Elizabeth was firmly on her throne and her country was Protestant but not very firmly. Many of her nobles were Catholic and a significant chunk of the population. Elizabeth, more than any other monarch in Europe, tried to ignore religion. But the basis of her opposition was still religious.

Mary, in Scotland, made no attempt to tell her people how to worship. She was a devout Catholic and was content to allow her subjects to be anything they pleased. But John Knox, the founder of the Presbyterian Church in Scotland, and Mary clashed constantly.

Mary's love life complicated things as well. She married her distant cousin, Lord Darnley, a handsome young airhead. She had an affair, maybe platonic, maybe not, with an Italian who many of her subjects believed was a spy in the employ of the pope. Darnley got jealous and murdered the Italian. Then Darnley's house blew up and he was killed. Next, Mary married a rough, tough madman named Hepburn, also a lord.

By that time, what with all Mary's domestic intrigues plus the tangled religious situation plus interference by agents of the kings of France and Spain and Queen Elizabeth, the country was in a state of civil war. That war was essentially Protestant versus Catholic, although not absolutely so. It was a short war and Mary's side lost.

So after only eight years — but eight action-filled years — Mary left Scotland forever, slipped across the border into England and asked her cousin Elizabeth for shelter.

Elizabeth's first instinct was to grant it. But her very wise, very cynical, very successful advisors told her not to be too quick.

They suggested she set up a commission to inquire into just what had happened in Scotland.

After eight action-filled years on the throne, Mary left Scotland forever, slipped across the border into England and asked her cousin Elizabeth for shelter.

Historians still argue over whether the evidence before that commission was real or forged. At any rate, it accepted letters that indicated Mary was an accomplice, at least, in the murder of her husband.

Elizabeth kept Mary moving from castle to castle throughout England, always well-cared for and with plenty of servants but very much a prisoner.

Several rebellions, a couple of them quite bloody, occurred in England while Mary was there. Finally after 19 years of that, Elizabeth's advisers convinced her Mary had to go. Otherwise there would always be the threat of a civil war.

So on the 8th of February in 1586, Mary's head was chopped off. That caused her wig to pop off and it turned out her hair was pure white. It had been that way since she was 35.

Sixteen years later, Mary's side won out. Her son, James, succeeded Queen Elizabeth as monarch of England.

Originally broadcast February 8, 1991

THANKS FOR THE MEMORIAL

Abraham Lincoln was a simple man, a farm boy who managed to educate himself enough to be a lawyer and a politician.

There isn't much evidence that anyone who voted for him for president of the United States in 1860 thought he was putting a great man into office. Lincoln became the president just in time to run the Civil War.

To the people of the rebel states in the South, Lincoln became a monster, the man who was trying to take away their rights.

Eventually, before that war was over, Lincoln was the man who declared slavery was at an end. For that alone, he has been remembered as one of the great men of history. But historians are pretty well agreed that Lincoln freed those slaves as part of a political process to keep himself and his Republican Party in power.

No matter. In time Lincoln grew into the job and became one of the great men in history. When he was assassinated while still president, his reputation took on a lustre it never had in life.

Half a century after Lincoln's assassination, most Americans remembered him with great affection. So on the 9th of February in 1911, the Congress of the United States passed a law to establish the Lincoln Memorial Commission, a body to design and build a memorial to the great man.

The chairman of the Lincoln Memorial Commission was the president himself, William Howard Taft. The commission met many times. It conferred with the Commission of Fine Arts, another government body concerned with making sure that everything built in Washington was artistically perfect.

The commission decided it wanted an impressive memorial in the classic style. So after much deliberation, it narrowed down its list to the two best classical architects in the land and asked them to submit designs.

Within two years from the formation of the commission, Congress had been shown a design and approved it. It was to be an impressive building of the whitest possible marble, divided into three chambers. In the middle one would sit a statue of Lincoln, 19 feet

When Lincoln was assassinated while still president, his reputation took on a lustre it never had in life.

high, on a pedestal 11 feet high. Lincoln would be seated, looking down at visitors.

The ground was broken in a ceremony three years after the approval, on Lincoln's birthday.

Within a few months the First World War broke out, but the people involved in the project paid not the slightest attention. They moved ahead, slowly and carefully, gradually building the memorial, stopping every now and again to be sure everything was perfect.

After a while the architect thought the space above Lincoln's head looked bare. The huge statue drew the eye up high but once there, it looked at a blank marble wall.

He phoned his old pal Royal Cortissoz, the art critic of the *New York Tribune*. Cortissoz held that job for 50 years and took himself very seriously. He wrote a simple sentence: "In this temple, as in the hearts of the people for whom he saved the Union, the memory of Abraham Lincoln is enshrined forever."

The architect thought it was perfect. But by then the president of the United States was Warren Harding. He did quite like that sentence, but he wanted to change the words "the people for whom he saved the union" to "the people of the union which he saved."

Disaster! Cortissoz protested that his immortal words were being tampered with. He withdrew them. He told the architect it would be as ruinous as sticking a dormer window smack in the middle of the roof.

Poor President Harding was a hen-pecked man whose wife didn't let him decide very much. Now he couldn't even change a word or two on a public memorial. However, he bit his lip and said, "Go ahead, do it however you want." So the original words were carved into the stone and they're still there.

Pretty silly when you remember what a simple man Abe Lincoln was. One day the British ambassador arrived at his office in the White House and found Lincoln polishing his boots.

"You, the president of this country, polish your own boots?" asked the ambassador.

"Sure," said Lincoln. "Whose do you polish?"

Originally broadcast February 9, 1988

A VICTORIAN WEDDING

On the 10th of February in 1840, Queen Victoria married Prince Albert, her cousin. For her it was both love and freedom.

Victoria was headed for the throne from the day she was born. The king ahead of her was her uncle, William the Fourth. He had no children.

Victoria's father was the brother of William. He died when Victoria was still a baby. That left her to be brought up by her mother, the Duchess of Kent, maybe the nastiest woman in the kingdom.

The Duchess knew her daughter would be queen some day. That suited her fine because she was the ultimate snob in an era when snobbery was regarded as a virtue. And she spent money like a whole boatload of thirsty sailors. She figured that when she was the mother of the queen, Parliament would have to let her have as much as she wanted.

The nasty duchess hired a nasty Irishman named Sir John Conroy to run her household and to make sure Victoria stayed healthy enough to reach the throne. Conroy set up a series of spies and regulations for the little princess' upbringing. She couldn't have any conversation without a third person in the room. That person would be one of Conroy's daughters whom Victoria hated, or another of his flunkies.

She wasn't allowed to go down a flight of stairs without someone taking her by the arm. The Duchess and Conroy had a potential money making machine on their hands and they were taking no chances.

Victoria's early years were miserable.

In 1836, she met her cousin Prince Albert of Saxe-Coburg, a little speck on the map in Germany. She liked him and figured of all the young princes in Europe he was the one for her.

King William died in 1837 and Victoria became Queen. By that time her mother and Conroy were in a frenzy. Victoria wasn't behaving like the obedient little girl they thought they had raised.

Her mother demanded a bigger palace and allowance. Victoria said no. Conroy demanded he be made her private secretary and be given unlimited authority to do just about anything he wanted in her name. She said no to that, too.

She enlisted the prime minister, Lord Melbourne, to handle Conroy for her, but that power struggle went on for months and months and made her life miserable.

Victoria desperately needed a husband to help her cope. And she still remembered Albert with affection.

The Duchess knew her daughter would be queen some day. That suited her fine, because she was the ultimate snob in an era when snobbery was regarded as a virtue.

So when he came to visit her at Buckingham Palace in the fall of 1839, she was ready. She wrote in her diary that he was beautiful.

He showed up on the 10th of October. On the 12th, Albert was told through a series of intermediaries that he had made a favourable impression on the young Queen.

On the 14th, the same bunch sent the message that Albert was to prepare himself to be proposed to. That evening as they said goodnight, he squeezed her hand. The next morning he was summoned to the Queen's apartment and Victoria told him she wanted him to marry her.

There was no spy of Conroy's at that meeting. They were alone. We know what was said because the queen was a great diary keeper.

The palace made the announcement. The queen applied to Parliament for an allowance of 50,000 pounds a year for her prince. Parliament was so used to saying no to her mother that the MPs cut it to 30,000.

On the 10th of February when they were married, Victoria said it was the happiest day of her life. The only thing she feared about marriage, she said, was the prospect of having a large family. She was determined not to have many babies.

Albert must have been determined in his own way. They had nine.

Originally broadcast February 10, 1983

CAMP OUT

Everybody's heard the story of Jack the Ripper, the London killer who murdered five women in the late 1800s then disappeared.

But have you ever heard about Elizabeth Camp, who was murdered in London also, on the 11th of February in 1897, less than 10 years after the Ripper struck?

Nobody knows the name today. But back then the newspapers played it bigger, if you can imagine it, than the Ripper killings. It was front page news in New York, Chicago, Toronto, and Montreal as well.

Elizabeth Camp was a good-looking lady of 33, a little hefty by today's standards, but considered gorgeous in those days. She had started her working life as a barmaid, had become a nurse, then gone back to the bar business, this time as a manager of a pub called the Good Intent. Barmaids had pretty racy reputations but no one ever pointed the finger of scandal at Elizabeth Camp.

Miss Camp was an excellent businesswoman. She made a good profit at the Good Intent for the owner and she did quite well herself.

She was engaged to a young man named Berry, the owner of a fruit store. On the 11th of February, about a month before she was to be married, Miss Camp visited her sister for the day and went shopping with her.

She got into a train at Hounslow station and was headed for Waterloo, another London train station. The trip would take 40 minutes and make eight stops. Berry, her fiance, would be waiting at Waterloo and they would go to the theatre together.

When the train arrived at Waterloo, Miss Camp was in her compartment, dead and stuck under the seat. She had been battered about the head. There had been no sign of sexual assault and her jewellery was all on her.

There wasn't much money in her purse and her sister later told police she thought she might have been carrying most of her money in a shopping bag but that bag was never found.

This was big news all over the world for two reasons: London was the safest city in the world; there was quite a bit of sin in London but virtually no violence. And it had happened on a British train. The British rail system was not only the most efficient in the world but the safest and the best staffed. Every passenger was within sight of some railway employee every few minutes.

The strange British custom of cutting up the rail cars into small compartments that would only hold six worked for the killer. In a Canadian train all the passengers would have been sitting in one big compartment and everybody would have seen everybody else.

Scotland Yard pulled out all the stops. Dozens of detectives were assigned to the case and there were questions in the House of Commons. The police assured everyone they had a couple of hot leads and there would be an arrest soon. This was the third murder on a train in British history and the previous two had been quickly solved.

But no one was ever arrested in this case. When Elizabeth Camp was buried, she had one of the biggest funerals in the history of London. Thousands turned up. But even today the murder is still unsolved.

Elizabeth Camp's murder made headlines around the world. The British rail system was not only the most efficient in the world, but the safest and the best staffed.

Originally broadcast February 11, 1987

BORDEN SPEAKS OUT

In 1914, when the First World War broke out, Canada was at war whenever Britain was. Britain was the number one country in the Empire and its decisions were final.

The war was a horrible screw-up. The British generals had their minds away back in the 1800s. They thought they were going to win with cavalry attacks and massive regiments of infantry marching bravely into the face of the enemy guns.

But barbed wire could tie up the best cavalry and the enemy guns were now huge artillery pieces that rained death from miles away and machine guns that mowed down whole companies of men in minutes.

When the casualty lists came in, the generals just ordered more attacks and the casualty lists got longer and the same orders sent more and more men to their deaths.

When the first Canadian troops arrived in England, the British generals ordered them broken up into little units and sent to reinforce the British regiments that had been so badly hit. The Canadians refused. They insisted they would fight as a Canadian army, under British orders, but as one big unit.

The British generals didn't think the Canadians would be as reliable as English troops. In the spring of 1915, the Germans attacked at a place in Belgium called Ypres. They started their attack with poison gas and the Canadians had no gas masks.

The French troops on their flank turned and ran. The Canadians held. The casualties were terrible. And they didn't end that day. For the next generation Canadians who had stood up to that gas attack coughed their lives away at home and at work and in veterans hospitals back in Canada.

At Easter of 1916, the Canadians did it again, this time in the most spectacular attack of the war. They attacked a high cliff called Vimy Ridge, a heavily fortified German position that British and French divisions had tried to take with no success. The Canadians attacked at dawn and by lunchtime Vimy was theirs. The Germans didn't know what hit them and the French and British didn't believe it until their officers were invited over to see it with their own eyes.

All the while the Canadian politicians were demanding a voice in how the war was being run. The prime minister of Canada was Robert Borden, a Conservative, a pleasant, tolerant man who was getting less and less patient with the British.

Canadian soldiers were throwing themselves into the war with great enthusiasm. Out of a country of less than 10 million, 50,000 would die. But back home, Canadians weren't so sure. The French Canadians were reluctant to support a war that had nothing to do with them. Prairie farmers had to sell their grain at a fixed price while Ontario factory owners made millions from the war.

The British generals ordered the Canadian troops broken up into little units and sent to reinforce the British regiments. The Canadians refused, insisting they would fight as a Canadian army.

Whenever Borden said Canadians could only support a war they had a say in, the British cabinet told him he had to leave the war to them. But Borden persisted.

Finally, on the 12th of February in 1917, the British gave in and Borden was made a member of the Imperial War Cabinet, the top strategic body in London that ran the war for the empire.

At the time most British politicians saw it as just a way to keep the Canadians quiet. But Borden used that position to demand and get a Canadian seat at the peace conference that ended the war a couple of years later. Within a few years Canada was a nation, not just a dominion. When the Second World War broke out, Canada didn't join until a week after the British.

Originally broadcast February 12, 1992

FALLEN STAR

Sal Mineo was almost a big, big movie star in the Elizabeth Taylor or Clark Gable class. He was one of those unfortunate people who was successful very young and found his career going down when he was in his 30s, when most people's are going up.

Mineo was born in New York and was a bit of a problem for his teachers and his parents. His mother put him in a dancing and acting class to keep him busy. He made his debut on Broadway in *The Rose Tattoo* when he was 11. He was the prince in *The King And I*, the original on Broadway, back in the 1950s.

Mineo did well in the movies by playing the sulky, rebellious kid, which wasn't really acting as much as reconstructing his own life. His first movie was in 1955. It was called *Six Bridges to Cross* and it was about the big Brinks robbery. Tony Curtis played the main role. Mineo played him as a kid.

Then he was in *Rebel Without a Cause*, the movie that made James Dean a cult figure. Again, Mineo played a troubled teenager who finally shoots it out with the cops.

You may still see him late at night on TV in *Exodus*, where he played the teenage psycho Jewish kid fighting to establish the state of Israel.

During the 1960s, Mineo's career ran down and by 1971 he was an ape in *Planet of the Apes*. Mineo was a serious actor who preferred the stage to the movies but the big money was in the movies.

In 1956, when the movie money was pouring in, he paid $200,000 for a mansion for his folks in a rich suburb of New York. They eventually had to sell it because they couldn't afford to keep it up.

Mineo had had a mansion in Hollywood in the 50s, but by 1975 he was living in a small apartment in West Hollywood, near the Sunset Strip. At one time the Sunset Strip was the very height of glamour. Today it's pretty tacky.

Mineo was directing a playhouse show, a black humour play called *P.S., Your Cat Is Dead*. He had played the role of a crazy bisexual burglar in the play during a successful run in San Francisco and then he was rehearsing for a run in Los Angeles with him as a director instead of actor.

On the night of the 13th of February in 1976, Mineo parked his car in the garage behind his apartment house and started to walk toward the house.

Neighbours heard him call for help and when they arrived he was dying of stab wounds in the chest. The killing got a bit of publicity because Mineo was a name most people recognized. But it wasn't a big name anymore so there was no great pressure on the police to solve the killing.

Shortly afterwards, a small-time crook named Lionel Ray Williams told police he had some information about Mineo's death. He wanted to trade it for a light sentence on some bad cheque charges he was facing. He said it was part of a drug deal. There was nothing in Mineo's background to indicate he'd ever had any interest in drugs, so the police wrote Williams off as a small-time hustler trying to con them.

Then, more than a year later, in the early summer of 1977, Williams had an argument with his wife. She went to the police and told them the night Mineo was killed, Williams had come home covered with blood and told her he'd stabbed a dude in West Hollywood while he was trying to rob him.

Williams had spent most of the intervening time in jail in Michigan for bad cheques. And it turned out he had told several prisoners and guards there about killing Mineo.

They'd all written it off as jail-house talk. Williams was flown back to Los Angeles and convicted of killing Mineo and committing 10 robberies about the same time. He was sent to jail for 51 years. That rated a few paragraphs in the local papers.

> *Mineo did well in the movies by playing the sulky, rebellious kid, which wasn't really acting as much as reconstructing his own life.*

Originally broadcast February 13, 1986

A PIONEER IN CRIME

Jesse James was a farm boy from Missouri who picked the wrong side in the American Civil War.

Not that Jesse was in the army. He joined a band of guerrilla fighters on the Southern side, the one that lost. Whether these men were brave freedom fighters or a bunch of bandits masquerading as patriots . . . well, take your pick.

But the awful truth was that, away out west in Missouri, far away from the battles between the regular armies, there was an awful lot of murdering and robbing and settling of old scores.

Young Jesse was pretty good at that line of work, despite his youth. He became a squad leader. And in April of 1865, when the war ended, Jesse was in charge of half a dozen men riding in to surrender. They say they carried a white flag.

They ran into a company of 60 Northern cavalrymen and the shooting started. The Northerners either didn't see the white flag or didn't care about it.

Jesse was shot through the lung and his horse was killed. Nevertheless, he picked himself up, shot one of the Northerners dead and wounded another. He made it into some woods and lay there, badly wounded, for two days. In the shooting, his pals managed to escape.

A farmer found young Jesse and took him in then took him to the nearest town. The army commander there gave Jesse permission to go home. The trouble was that during the war the James home had been burned down. It was just a log cabin away out in the boonies but even that was now gone.

So Jesse stayed with cousins at their farm about a dozen miles from the large town of Liberty, Missouri.

There was no penicillin in those days and Jesse's wound healed slowly. His old pals from the war dropped around to see him as he lay around, caught up on his reading and fell in love with his cousin, Zerelda. He eventually married her.

Jesse was tough, a superb horseman and a crack shot. And a natural leader. He and his pals were out of work, broke and bitter. But Jesse took care of that. He found them a trade.

Jesse James was a natural leader. He and his pals were out of work, broke and bitter. But Jesse took care of that. He found them a trade — bank robbery.

A few minutes after eight in the morning on the 14th of February in 1866, Jesse and nine other men rode down the main street of Liberty. They stopped in front of the Clay County Savings and Loan Association. Four jumped off of their horses and ran inside. They came out in a few minutes with a bagful of money, about $15,000 worth.

The men who stayed outside, including Jesse, shot up the town to keep the citizens from interfering. One was killed in the process, a boy on his way to school. It was a superb piece of marksmanship. The boy had been shot four times with a revolver held by a man on a prancing horse. Any one of the shots would have been fatal.

But, more important to history, Jesse had started a whole new line of work. He had pulled off the first bank robbery.

Originally broadcast February 14, 1992

THE BLIND LEADING THE BLIND

Louis Braille was the son of a harness-maker in a little village about 25 miles from Paris. He was a bright kid and loved to play in his father's shop. One day, when he was only three, he was trying to punch a hole in a piece of leather when he stabbed himself in the eye. Doctors didn't know much about germs in those days and the wound became infected. The infection spread to the other eye and little Louis was blind.

Louis was a genius, no doubt about that. Especially at music. And blind people could play the organ and the piano.

There was a school in Paris called the National School for the Young Blind. Louis entered it on the 15th of February in the year 1819. It was the first time young Louis had been away from home. He was only 10. He knew his way around home, of course. But he had to learn all over again where the doors and the stairs and his bed and his classrooms were. It was a tough process for a little guy but Louis managed.

The school was run by a man named Hauy who had devised a way to make books that the blind could read. He had them printed in embossed letters, much bigger than in regular books. The kids could slowly dope them out by feeling the letters. The problem was that an N often felt like an H or an L like an I.

And the system was expensive and awfully

Hauy had books printed in embossed letters, much bigger than in regular books, so the blind could read them by feeling the letters. The problem was that an N often felt like an H or an L like an I.

unwieldy. A regular book would be made into maybe 20 volumes by the Hauy method, each weighing about 20 pounds. That's 400 pounds altogether.

Little Louis figured there had to be a better way. A French army officer had devised a system of raised dots and dashes that could be read at night without turning on a light, something pretty useful in the military business.

Louis asked him for some samples. Then he worked out a simpler system, taking away the dots and dashes and using no more than six embossed dots for a letter or a common word.

It took a lot of refining and fiddling but it was finally worked out.

You'd think this godsend for blind people would have been enthusiastically received at the school. Not so. The staff thought it was an act of disloyalty to Hauy, the inventor of the embossed letters. Braille had to work on his new system secretly with the help of some of the other kids.

Braille caught tuberculosis when he was a young man and died at the early age of 43. At the time of his death, he was famous as a church organist. No one paid a lot of attention to the Braille writing system at first because when Louis invented it he was only 15.

Originally broadcast February 15, 1993

A BATTLE OF WILLS

On February 16, 1926, two of the greatest tennis players of all time — Suzanne Lenglen of France and Helen Wills of the United States — met for the only match of their careers. Tennis fans had been hoping for a long time to see them play. But when they did, it didn't settle the argument about who was the better player.

The 20s were a time when all the old rules seemed to be going out the window. Women had been playing tennis for a generation or two. But at a very gentle, ladylike level. Now, the women of the 20s were slashing and serving as hard as any man.

In fact, a lot of tennis fans who were there say the hard-driving women players in those days played a tougher, faster game than the men. And Suzanne Lenglen and Helen Wills were certainly the hardest driving of them all.

Suzanne Lenglen started playing tennis when she was just a kid. Her father was a strict trainer who put a half dozen handkerchiefs on the court. Suzanne was expected to drop the ball onto a handkerchief. With training like that, she had precision no one had seen until then. Nor since. And she was fast. From the time she was in her late teens, she had never lost a tournament. She won at Wimbledon five years in a row, missed a year then came back and won it again.

Helen Wills was only 20, from California, the hardest-hitting woman in tennis without a doubt. But without Lenglen's speed, accuracy or experience.

She did very well in the eastern United States and in late 1925 announced she was going to tour the Riviera that winter to pick up some experience.

The sportswriters, not a group known for understatement, immediately decided the plucky little American lady was challenging the reigning French queen of the courts on her own turf.

Editors began sending reporters from all over the world. Workmen started building bleachers at the Carlton Club on the Riviera for the big day. Only the most influential people could get tickets and those at $50 each.

On the big day Lenglen played the queen to the hilt. She arrived in a light coat with a fur collar and a pink headband, blowing kisses to the crowd. Wills played the simple little American girl in a plain white tennis dress, looking neither left nor right, like Joan of Arc on her way to the courthouse. The American writers had already named her Little Miss Poker Face.

It was all over within an hour. But it was a very exciting hour. Lenglen took the first game without losing a point. Zap, zap, zap, like a machine. Poor little Wills was running her legs off and getting nowhere.

But Helen took the next game with her incredibly hard shots. And the next. Lenglen's precision won the next two. Helen took the seventh game, a squeaker. Suzanne easily took the last two. It was Lenglen, a pretty easy 6 to 3.

But the match had tired Lenglen. She looked ready to drop. Wills was fresher, but she had to run three times as far to get to that incredible variety of long and short shots that Lenglen gave her.

The argument still goes on. They never met again. It's probably a case of a star at the height of her career meeting one who was still in the early stages of hers.

They didn't meet at Wimbledon that year because Wills had to be in hospital to get her appendix out. Then deteriorating health gradually forced Lenglen out of sports. She died in 1937, not yet 40.

Helen Wills went on to take eight Wimbledons, setting a record.

But she won something that day on the Riviera. As the reporters swarmed around the winner, she was standing alone on the court when a young man came up to her and said, "I thought you played awfully well. My name is Moody."

Pretty soon, so was hers.

> *A lot of tennis fans say the hard-driving women players in those days played a tougher, faster game than the men. And Suzanne Lenglen and Helen Wills were certainly the hardest driving of them all.*

Originally broadcast February 16, 1983

LE GRAND PLAYWRIGHT

Molière is the greatest of the French playwrights, maybe the best French writer of them all. But he's no Shakespeare. You'd have to add up Molière, Racine and Corneille, two other great French playwrights, to equal Shakespeare. Nevertheless, he was great. And even if he was only second-rate, his story is a fascinating one.

The Catholic Church had censored the stage very severely in France for a generation or two after the time of Shakespeare. Maybe that's why France wasn't producing great plays where the English were.

At any rate, Cardinal Richelieu, the king's right hand man, liked the stage. And his successor, Cardinal Mazarin, an Italian, encouraged Italian actors to move to France. The result was that in the 1600s, after a long period of quiet, the French stage came alive.

And the principal writer and impressario of that revival was Molière. Molière was a stage name. He was born Jean-Baptiste Poquelin and his father was a prosperous upholsterer. Not just any upholsterer, but upholsterer to the king.

That was important in those days. Whatever furniture the royal upholsterer installed in the king's palace immediately became fashionable and there was a fortune to be made in selling similar stuff to the nobility. So young Poquelin would inherit a thriving business.

But he didn't like the idea of upholstery so he studied law. Another well-paying craft. In actual fact, he practiced neither. When Poquelin was a law student, just before he graduated, he fell for an actress and lived with her for a while. As a result, he met another actress, Madeleine Béjart and he fell even harder for her.

He sold his right to inherit his father's royal upholstery position and invested in a theatre company with Madeleine and her brothers. That was in 1643.

> *Molière thought there was plenty of material right around him. Especially in the king's court, where all the lords and ladies seemed to be involved in one long series of endless affairs.*

That's when he adopted the stage name of Molière.

He was usually broke. For a dozen years he played the sticks, travelling with his company from one town to another.

By 1655, Molière was also writing plays. In fact, although he loved acting, he was never going to be a star on the stage. He was pretty good but not great. But as a writer he was a hit.

Plays in those days used classical themes, like Shakespeare telling the stories of Hamlet and Julius Caesar. Molière thought there was plenty of material right around him. Especially in the king's court where all the lords and ladies seemed to be involved in one long series of endless affairs. And, as today, the common people loved to hear the stories about which duchess was making it with which earl.

Clergymen and censors were scandalized by Molière's plays, but they were very witty. Some officials saw the plays as treasonous, making fun of the king. But the king in those days was Louis XIV, the greatest French king of them all, and he felt secure. He laughed at Molière's stuff and told his officials to leave him alone.

By 1660 Molière was rolling in money and was famous. But it was easy-come, easy-go. His affair with Madeleine Béjart had ended a long time ago, but he fell in love with her daughter. And he married her. Now the great comedian was involved in tragedy. His young wife played around — on him, Molière, the man who made his name and fortune writing plays about stupid husbands who didn't realize their wives were having affairs.

Molière was only 50 when he died, worn out by a life of booze and actresses and years on the road. When he died on the 17th of February in 1673, he was a tired man. He even asked for a priest to send him on his way.

Originally broadcast February 17, 1986

MAKING A PILGRIM-AGE

John Bunyan was born in 1628 in Bedford, England . . . a fairly quiet time for England, in between two periods of upheaval. The half-century in the middle of the 1500s had seen a lot of slaughter and burning at the stake as the Catholics and Protestants fought it out for control of the country. The Protestants seemed to have won that one. But as the 1600s advanced, the Protestants had split into two main camps: the Anglicans and the evangelists.

So, into this mess of theology and politics was born John Bunyan, a simple man, a tinker, a mender of pots and pans, like his father before him. Bunyan was a strange man. Strange because he was so ordinary.

In later years, Bunyan wrote of the terrible things he did in his youth. He made it sound as if he was the sinningest poor mortal who ever walked the face of the earth.

He wrote about his conversion from Anglicanism to the Baptist faith, though, and that tells us a lot about him. It was the custom in those days for people to go to church on Sunday morning, then go home for lunch, then to the village green where the old folks would sit and gossip and the young ones would sing or play and dance.

Bunyan was in the middle of a game of tipcat, he wrote in later years. Tipcat seems to have been a game in which everybody had a stick and took a swing at the cat which sounds like it was some sort of beanbag or bundle of rags. Anyhow, it was right in the middle of a game of tipcat, said Bunyan, when he was deeply immersed in the moral degradation of hitting a beanbag with a stick, that the word came to him.

He said it was a voice that did dart from heaven and it said, "Wilt thou leave thy sins and go to heaven or have thy sins and go to hell?"

It wasn't quite that simple, Bunyan said later. He said he wrestled with his conscience for five years before he became a Baptist and an evangelist. But it doesn't take Sherlock Holmes to figure out, just from those few clues, that old John wasn't much of a sinner to start with. At any rate, no matter how good he'd been in the past, he set out to be better. He became a preacher.

John Bunyan was a strange man. Strange because he was so ordinary.

He sure picked the wrong time. There'd been quite a bit of religious tolerance up until then. The English Civil War had been fought over religion while he was still a young man; in fact, Bunyan had served in Cromwell's army. But unless an Englishman wanted to make a big thing of his religion and defy whatever law was in force at the time, he was fairly free to believe as he pleased.

But now, in the 1660s, the law said everyone had to be an Anglican and that law was enforced. It was enforced by local authorities, your neighbours. In the sticks, where Bunyan lived, he would only have had to say yeah, yeah, to the local magistrates from time to time and he could have gone on his way. But that wasn't Bunyan. He was not only a dedicated preacher by this time; he was also a dedicated martyr.

So he went to the local jail for 12 years. He could have got out any time he swore a simple oath and agreed to go to church. In fact, it wasn't a very rigorous imprisonment. He made lace in jail and sold it to feed his family. His wife and children could visit him every day. He got out at least enough to get his wife pregnant twice.

And he was allowed to write. He wrote volumes and volumes. He was finally released in 1677 and took some of his writing to a printer. And on the 18th of February in 1678, that printer turned out the first copy of *A Pilgrim's Progress*.

It's a long, dull book with a very simple theme. Christian, the hero, sets out for the Celestial City, heaven, and meets all kinds of obstacles and people along the way.

Before Bunyan died 10 years later, it had sold 100,000 copies, in a time when literacy was far from universal. As English language and culture spread over the world, so did *Pilgrim's Progress*. For almost 300 years, well into our times, *Pilgrim's Progress* was second only to the Bible as a mainstay of Protestant faith.

We curl our lips at it today and rightly so. It's an awful bore, the sort of thing that would be written by the sort of nut who defines sin as playing with a beanbag on a Sunday. But maybe that's what's great about it, too.

Originally broadcast February 18, 1983

AMERICA'S MOST UNWANTED

Benedict Arnold was born in Connecticut in the early 1700s. His grandfather had been British governor of the colony and a rich man. But Arnold's father had drunk away the family fortune.

Arnold had to drop out of school at 13. He worked for a druggist and eventually got his own business. By the time he was 26 he was a rich man, the owner of a store and three ships, trading with Quebec to the north and the West Indies.

Arnold was also a captain in the local militia. When the American Revolution broke out, Arnold took his company and marched. Other militia officers sat around and debated whether they had the authority or if the proper general had signed their orders.

The Americans had practically no artillery. Arnold knew that the British had all sorts of big guns at forts in northern New York, decrepit, poorly-guarded forts that could be captured with a quick attack.

Sure enough, Arnold pulled it off. He captured one fort and sent the guns south to Boston where they were the decisive factor in one of the early battles of the revolution. But in the process, Arnold fought and squabbled with his fellow officers.

Arnold led one pincer in the American invasion of Canada. That attack fell apart in front of Quebec City as the Americans failed to capture the city and lost heavily in the attempt. We now know that the whole venture was hopeless. The Americans assumed the Quebeckers were just itching to get rid of the British and join the new United States. In fact, the Quebeckers were bored by the whole war. They stayed neutral with a slight inclination toward the British.

The British then attacked from Canada. It was Arnold who blunted their attack, sometimes acting as the best general on the American side, sometimes going into the forest himself leading patrols like a second lieutenant.

All the time, he was fighting, squabbling, arguing, back-biting with his own people. Several of his military enemies complained that Arnold was corrupt. And he wasn't above lining his own pocket as he bought supplies for his troops.

On the other hand, if his men were hungry and the army supplies hadn't shown up, as happened so often, Arnold would reach in his pocket to feed everybody.

When Arnold was accused of embezzlement, he demanded a court martial. When the court martial convened, he was so angry he challenged each officer on the court to a duel.

On the 19th of February in 1777, the Americans dealt Arnold the blow he never forgave. Seven officers were promoted to major-general but not Arnold. Each was notably less capable than Arnold.

He sulked for a while. But then the American army was in a tight spot at the Battle of Saratoga in New York.

Arnold arrived in the nick of time, dashed onto the battlefield and turned the tide of battle single-handedly. His hip was shattered by a bullet and he walked with a limp for the rest of his life.

That battle was the turning point of the American Revolution. The French had been wavering, not sure whether they should join the Americans or not. The victory at Saratoga won them over.

From then on, the Americans were headed to victory, although it took years.

Arnold's feat was recognized and he was made a major-general and his promotion was back-dated so he outranked the seven turkeys who had been put ahead of him. But he was a bitter man and a few years later he went over to the British. And earned himself a place in American history books as the worst traitor of all time.

> *The Americans dealt Arnold the blow he never forgave. Seven officers were promoted to major-general but not Arnold. Each was notably less capable than Arnold.*

Originally broadcast February 19, 1992

THE CRUELEST COLUMNIST

Walter Winchell was a poor boy, born in a New York slum. Young Walter got his first job in 1910 in vaudeville as a singer and dancer. Then he and his brother and a pal formed a singing trio. Next he and his girlfriend did a dance act.

By 1922 he had married the dancer and had a family to support, so he started writing gossip for the vaudeville *News*, a trade paper for people in show business. That paid $25 a week, which was almost as much as he was getting as a dancer.

So Winchell concentrated on writing. Not real reporting but gossip column stuff. He was the man who invented the three little dots you still see in gossip columns. Sometimes they are used to hint at something mysterious . . . sometimes they're used instead of periods or commas . . . sometimes they just fill space.

Winchell was never a real newsman, but he was smart enough to realize that most newspapers give their readers an awful lot more on most stories than they want to read. He put together a column full of bits and pieces. And the readers gobbled it up.

By the late 20s he had a regular column in the New York *Daily News*. The Hearst newspaper chain, which owned the *News*, was syndicating his column all over North America. At one time it was in more than a thousand papers.

During the 30s, Winchell expanded into radio. The evening he was to make his first broadcast, he was nervous, of course. He had to go to the washroom. One of the radio people said it was just down the hall and he had plenty of time before they went on the air.

Winchell said, "No thanks, I want it to sound troubled and urgent." He had found the sound equivalent of those three little dots.

Winchell was a cruel, petty tyrant. As his column and newscasts became more popular his power increased. He was always a little crazy where money was concerned, no doubt a result of his poor childhood. He wouldn't invest his money. He put it in safety deposit boxes and carried the keys around with him on a huge ring.

Winchell was so powerful that dozens of press agents would line up at his favorite table in the Stork Club, the nightclub where he hung out. If they were lucky he would give their clients a plug in his column and their careers were made. If Winchell didn't like them he put them on his Drop Dead list and never used their client's names. They were ruined.

Winchell was a close pal of J. Edgar Hoover, the head of the FBI, and several big-time hoodlums. He used those contacts to get scoops in his column. But he would never run one bad word about his pal Sherman Billingsley, the owner of the Stork Club. Billingsley was a southern boy and a racist.

Once Sugar Ray Robinson, the fighter, made a $25,000 donation to Winchell's cancer fund, a promotion of his newspaper. Winchell was so pleased he promised him anything he wanted. Robinson wanted to be allowed into the Stork Club. Winchell just said: "Anything but that."

In the late 50s and early 60s Winchell's style was passé. He'd been dropped from radio and his syndicated column went to fewer than 100 papers. Hollywood even did a movie, *The Sweet Smell of Success*, in which Burt Lancaster played a nasty columnist, obviously Winchell.

His daughter hated him and wouldn't speak to him. His son had never got along with him. The son shot himself.

Winchell retired. A few years later, when he died on the 20th of February in 1972, nobody noticed.

> *Winchell was so powerful that press agents would line up at his table in the nightclub where he hung out. If they were lucky he would give their clients a plug in his column and their careers were made.*

Originally broadcast February 20, 1986

A MAN OF THE PEOPLE

It would be an exaggeration to say a governor-general ever gets to be beloved by the people of Canada. His job is too other-worldly and out of the mainstream of the real life of the rest of us for us to get to know a governor-general. But John Buchan, Lord Tweedsmuir, probably came as close as anyone.

He was a commoner by birth, the son of a Scottish clergyman, a bright boy who made it through school and university mostly on scholarships. Around the turn of the century he moved to London and worked as a journalist while studying law. He became a lawyer in 1901.

But he didn't practice. He went to South Africa to work on the staff of the high-commissioner, Lord Milner. South Africa had been badly shaken up by the Boer War which the British had just managed to win by the skin of their teeth.

Some of the toughest Boers wouldn't surrender and kept up the guerrilla warfare for a couple years. The British burned their farms and herded their women and children into tent cities where they died by the hundreds from inadequate food and medicine. They also gave the language a new phrase: concentration camps.

Young Buchan, the scholar-journalist-lawyer, was in charge of moving many of these camps from military to civilian control. It wasn't a pleasant job. But he did the job as well as anybody could have. He shut down the camps and got the people back to their homes as quickly as possible.

He returned to England after a couple of years, convinced that the British had done a superb job in South Africa and that the South Africans were now happy members of the Empire, sorry they ever went to war with the Crown.

Back in England, Buchan worked as a lawyer and writer. He preferred writing and was quite a successful novelist, not rich and famous by any means but quite acceptable.

When the First World War broke out, Buchan went to France as a war correspondent then joined military

Most of the governors-general since Confederation had been a bunch of upper class British twits, very regal and class-conscious. But Lord Tweedsmuir was different.

intelligence. By the time the war was over he was head of intelligence for the Ministry of Information — in effect, chief of propaganda for the British, a job that paid off very well. Not in money, but in experience.

From his knowledge of spying he wrote the two novels that made him rich and famous and still read quite well: *Greenmantle* and *The 39 Steps*.

So, when the King announced on the 21st of February in 1935 that he was making John Buchan Lord Tweedsmuir and appointing him governor-general of Canada, it was a popular decision.

Most of the governors-general since Confederation had been a bunch of upper class British twits, dukes and earls and marquises and such, all very regal and class-conscious.

But Lord Tweedsmuir was different. He had a reporter's curiosity and a lawyer's thirst for detail. He visited the Arctic and flew in rickety little planes into the coast of British Columbia.

He was a witty man. William Aberhart, the Social Credit premier of Alberta, who was an odd and tasteless dresser, once asked him what he should wear to the Coronation in 1937. The governor-general replied: "Anything you wear, sir, cannot help but be a social credit to Alberta."

Once, he was at a synagogue dinner in Toronto and the speeches went on and on and on. By the time he was finally able to leave, his schedule was hopelessly screwed up because he had several other places to go that night.

As he left the synagogue, he was heard to mutter, "No wonder it took those people 40 years to cross the wilderness."

Lord Tweedsmuir died in office in 1940 of a stroke. For the first time, Canadians were really sad to hear a governor-general was gone. He had made a real impression on Canadians.

His replacement Alexander Augustus Frederick William Alfred George Cambridge, son of Princess Mary, great-grandson of Queen Victoria. It was business as usual at the palace.

Originally broadcast February 21, 1983

THE INDESTRUCTIBLE MAN

Michael Malloy had been a fireman in New York since soon after he arrived from Ireland. But booze was his downfall and by the time the Depression of the early 30s rolled around, poor Malloy was a pathetic mess.

He hung around a bar owned by a thoroughly nasty character named Tony Marino. Marino was a handsome man, a flashy dresser, but absolutely unscrupulous when it came to turning a buck, something very hard to do in those Depression years.

Marino's best pal was a man named Pasqua, who owned a funeral parlor across the street from Marino's bar. The other important person in this story is Murphy, Marino's bartender.

Marino and Pasqua wracked their brains for a way to come up with some money. They finally decided on the insurance business . . . well, *their* version of the insurance business.

So they insured Betty, Marino's girlfriend and waitress and occasional hooker. They took out a policy on Betty that would pay $800 on her death. That was a lot of money in 1933.

They got Betty falling-down drunk — which was no mean feat — then took off all her clothes, doused her with ice water and left the window open at the foot of her bed one night when the temperature hit 13 below. The death certificate said pneumonia and Marino and Pasqua split the $800.

Next they looked around for another victim. And their eyes fell on Malloy the barfly. They told Murphy, the bartender, to be generous with Malloy, to give him all the whisky he could absorb on credit. On credit, Malloy could absorb an awful lot.

Next, they told Murphy that after a couple of shots of the real stuff, he was to switch Malloy to anti-freeze.

After a couple of weeks, Malloy was looking better than he had in years. The insurance policy was for $1700, double for death by accident. At this rate, Malloy would have all the profit drunk up before he expired.

They dropped the anti-freeze treatment and switched to turpentine. Not only was Malloy not dead, but he was actually seen to smack his lips and ask for more.

Next they made Malloy a sandwich of rotten sardines. They even put pieces of the sardine can in the sandwich. Malloy wolfed it down then reached for a double anti-freeze.

They tried tainted oysters. Malloy loved them.

They took him out one night when he was unconscious, took off his shirt, doused him with icewater and left him in the park. The next day Pasqua, the undertaker, had a terrible cold but Malloy was fine, although a little thirsty.

They recruited a cab driver into the scheme and laid Malloy out on the street one night when he was drunk and ran over him. Then backed up over him just to be sure.

That was the closest they had ever come to success. They actually put Malloy into the hospital for three weeks. But when he got out, after three weeks without a drink, he was so thirsty he was running through their anti-freeze like crazy.

On the night of the 22nd of February in 1933, they finally knocked off Malloy. They got him so drunk he was unconscious, then put a tube from the gas stove into his mouth. That did it.

They got their insurance pay-off. Then they started to fight among themselves about who got what. The cops heard about the dispute. And the final decision was up to a judge and jury. Marino, Pasqua and Murphy got the electric chair. The cab driver and the doctor who signed the death certificate got jail.

> *They made Malloy a sandwich of rotten sardines. They even put pieces of the sardine can in the sandwich. Malloy wolfed it down then reached for a double anti-freeze.*

Originally broadcast February 22, 1990

SHAKEN, AND STIRRED UP

About dawn of the 23rd of February in 1887 was the worst possible time for anything that required fast response and clear thinking on the French Riviera. It was the morning of Ash Wednesday, the morning after Mardi Gras. In the Catholic calendar, Ash Wednesday is the beginning of Lent, the 40 days of prayer and fasting that lead up to Easter.

The night before is Mardi Gras, the biggest party of the year, the last chance to eat, drink, dance and carry on for a month and a half. In many Catholic countries it's the biggest bash of the year. And it certainly was in the towns all along the Riviera coast, in France and eastwards into Italy.

The tourist season was in full swing. England's prince of Wales was holidaying at Cannes. The principal French nobles were at Nice. The biggest, most elegant villa at Nice was occupied by the king and queen of Wurtemberg, one of the German states.

Some of the big Mardi Gras balls were just finishing. Many of the partygoers were lurching home. Suddenly at 6:02 in the morning, the earth shook. Not just trembled a little, but shook furiously. The whole Mediterranean coast of France and northern Italy shook. The shock waves were felt hundreds of miles away in Switzerland.

Buildings were jarred and badly damaged. Many tottered, ready to fall. Then, a few minutes later came a second shock that brought hundreds of them tumbling down on the people inside and in the streets. Altogether, there were three major shocks and two lesser ones.

Most of the publicity about the calamity centred on the French resort areas because of the celebrities involved. In fact, the greatest loss of life was across the border in Italy where dozens of small poorly-built villages fell apart.

In one, the residents all ran into the church for safety. It fell with the third shock, killing at least 300. In one small Italian city the dance hall suddenly collapsed, killing 250 people.

Fortunately, no major fires broke out afterwards. Firemen in many of the towns hit by the quake were in no condition to do much good. Many were either still drunk or so hung over from the Mardi Gras celebrations that they were useless as rescuers.

That was certainly a major factor in the high death toll. More than 2000 died, many of them trapped under collapsed buildings. The rescue effort was poorly coordinated and directed.

In fact, many of the well-to-do French, English and Russian tourists just left. They took one look at their collapsed hotels and went straight to the train. A few hours later they arrived in Paris, still dressed, in many cases, in their Mardi Gras ball costumes.

One society columnist in a Paris paper looked on the bright side. "The bad news," she said, "is that there's been a terrible earthquake in the south and hundreds have been killed. The good news is that a lot of rich socialites who wouldn't normally be in Paris at this time of year have returned so we may have one of the gayest winter scenes we've seen in years."

Many of the well-to-do tourists just took one look at their collapsed hotels and went straight to the train. A few hours later they arrived in Paris, still dressed in their Mardi Gras ball costumes.

Originally broadcast February 23, 1989

REVOLUTION #2

Everybody knows about the French Revolution, the one in 1789. The mob stormed the Bastille and the king and queen had their heads chopped off and thousands died in the Reign of Terror that followed. Then Napoleon took over and French armies conquered most of Europe, spreading their ideals of liberty, equality, and fraternity.

But not many have heard of the next one, the Second French Revolution. It happened half a century or so later, in 1848. More people died in it than in the first one. But historians don't go on about it as much because, when all the noise and bloodshed had ended, not an awful lot had changed.

When the British, German, and Austrian armies finally beat Napoleon in 1815 at the battle of Waterloo, they put the French kings back on the throne. But the French kings were a pretty hopeless bunch. And in 1830, one of Napoleon's family took over France again.

But social and economic conditions were bad. France had the first of its modern depressions in 1847 and hundreds of thousands were out of work. France at the time was changing. It had ceased to be a mostly agricultural country but it wasn't yet a major industrial power.

So, a series of disturbances by the unemployed turned into the Second French Revolution. It broke out in several places all over France in the early months of 1848. But it's down in the history books as the 24th of February because that's when it hit Paris.

At first it was almost comical. Mobs of unemployed took over the houses of parliament. The revolutionaries established what they called national workshops. These were a series of public works projects to give people work. It shows how different things were in those days that it took a revolution to bring about what all governments do today as a matter of course.

Hours of work and minimum wages were brought in. The revolution didn't go much further than that because the peasants in the countryside, the ones who had been freed in the first French Revolution, were afraid the unemployed urban workers wanted to take away their land.

> *The revolutionaries established a series of public works projects to give people work. It took a revolution to bring about what all governments do today as a matter of course.*

Without the people of the countryside joining in, the new revolution pretty well lost steam. However, as a result the vote was extended to just about every Frenchman. That was a beneficial move.

Then, the inevitable counter-revolution began. In the spring, in June, the army moved in and there were long, bloody battles in Paris and several other major cities.

In Paris alone, in four days, 15,000 people were killed. That was more than had died in all the first French Revolution. In the next year, another 20,000 were exiled, sent to French colonies overseas.

For a little while, when those unemployed ran things, they had forced parliament to pass a law calling on the governments of Prussia and Russia to free Poland. That never happened. But in the process, that move encouraged a revolution in Hungary. It, too, was put down with much bloodshed.

No wonder history doesn't have much to say about that second French Revolution. It didn't change much.

Originally broadcast February 24, 1987

THE MAN OF 1000 NAMES

Henri Landru was maybe the most fascinating criminal of modern times. He's remembered in France as the modern Bluebeard, the man who killed women. Just how many he killed, nobody knows. In fact, if you want to be literal about it, nobody proved that he killed anybody although they did make a strong case that he probably wiped out a lot.

Henri Landru was a small, bald, meek-looking little guy. He'd been a choir boy. He was a bookkeeper, a furniture dealer, he owned a bicycle store, and a little toy factory. Never prosperous, but never hungry. He married and had a daughter.

Then, in the year 1900, when Landru was 31, he took to petty crime, writing bad cheques, stealing small stuff. He did several jail sentences and in 1914 he was sentenced to four years. But the cops could never quite catch up with him to send him to jail.

Maybe about then Landru began to use the first of his many aliases. Again, nobody knows exactly how many. Certainly dozens, maybe hundreds.

In 1919, two women went to the police in Paris, separately, with similar stories. Their sisters had disappeared. One had been keeping company with Mr. Fremet, another with Mr. Dupont. The descriptions of both men were remarkably similar.

The cop who was assigned to the case was just putting it together when one of the women who had called to complained called to say she had seen the man her sister had been hanging around with. When the cops questioned him, he said he wasn't Mr. Fremet or Mr. Dupont; he was Mr. Guillet.

When the cops ran him through the files they found they had finally laid hands on Landru, the bad-cheque artist who owed them four years from five years ago.

So, they were unable to throw him in a cell while they got on with their investigation. Landru just shrugged at all their questions. But in his pocket they found a little notebook with seven surnames in it. Two were names of the missing women. When they got out the old missing persons lists they found the other five names from the notebook.

Still, Landru said nothing. The cops started to painstakingly interview the relatives and friends of all the missing women.

Landru had as many names as a phone book. He had a villa in the country and four apartments in Paris, all in different names, of course. He stored furniture, clothes, ornaments, all sorts of stuff in five different public lockers.

The cops never did produce a body although they brought some ashes from Landru's villa and claimed they were bits of bone.

Landru faced 11 murder charges. Witnesses said Landru had been introduced by several

> *Landru had been introduced by several women who had since disappeared as their fiancé. Landru only shrugged and said he was too much a gentleman to ever contradict a lady.*

women who had since disappeared as their fiancé. Landru only shrugged and said he was too much a gentleman to ever contradict a lady.

When he was sentenced to death he just shrugged. On the 25th of February in 1922, as he was about to step up to the guillotine, his lawyer said: "You could clear up a lot of questions with a statement at this point."

Landru just looked at him and said, "That's an impertinence, to direct such a request to someone who is about to step into the next world."

Dozens of books have been written about the mild little man who never came right out and denied being a mass killer. Charlie Chaplin did his best movie about him: *Monsieur Verdoux.*

Originally broadcast February 25, 1992

56

THE LEGEND IS BLUE

On the 26th of February in 1829, the Strauss family in Bettelheim in southern Germany had a baby boy. They named him Lob. The Strausses were Jewish and the law in Germany in those days said Jews couldn't own land. So they couldn't be farmers.

Some were tradesmen, a few were professionals. But most were in commerce of some sort. And Lob's father seems to have been a travelling peddler. That wasn't as bad as it sounds. Many travelling Jewish peddlers in Germany in those days made good money although it was a tough life, on the road most of the time.

When Lob was 16, his father died. Two years later his mother moved to the United States with Lob and his two sisters. Two older brothers had gone ahead.

When they arrived in New York, one of the older brothers became a travelling peddler, going from farm to farm with needles and thread and pots and pans. The other stayed in town and started his own store.

When Lob arrived, he became a travelling peddler, too. At the same time his name was changed from Lob Strauss to Levi Strauss. We don't know why.

In 1853, he made the biggest move of his life. He went west to California to follow the gold rush. He arrived in San Francisco and made a killing. The miners were rich but there was very little merchandise of any sort so anybody with anything to sell did well.

Levi soon set up a store with one of his brothers. They imported goods from New York, supplied by the brother who had a store there. As the money came in, Levi invested in downtown real estate and in the gas company that was set up to supply street lighting.

But that wasn't what made him famous. The men from the mining camps who came to Levi's store for tools and supplies and clothes complained that their pants were being ripped and torn and worn out by the tough wear they got along the rocky creekbeds where they mined for gold.

Levi took some of the light canvas he was selling for tenting to a tailor and asked him to make him a few pairs of pants out of it. Pretty soon, the miners were coming back, demanding more. Levi soon set up a factory to turn out tough, wearable canvas pants.

Within a few years, cowboys and railwaymen all over the west were also wearing Levi's pants. They were known as Levis or Levis Jeans. Jeans was a slang word for pants.

In 1872, a tailor from Reno, Nevada approached Levi with a suggestion. He was making similar pants and reinforcing the pockets and seams with copper rivets. Levi liked the idea so well he adopted it and hired the man to run his factory.

Now Levi hadn't invented the idea of canvas pants. Christopher Columbus wrote that his sailmaker often made work pants for himself and his crew out of sailcloth.

Levi Strauss hadn't invented the idea of canvas pants. Christopher Columbus wrote that his sailmaker often made work pants for himself and his crew out of sailcloth.

Levi experimented with various kinds of cloth, trying to find the one that was hard enough to wear yet thin enough to be comfortable. The one he settled on was called cloth de Nîme, the name of the town in France where it was made.

de Nîme quickly became denim in English. Levi Strauss died in 1902, a rich and respected man. But today his principal memorial isn't a tombstone in a cemetery. It's worn.

Originally broadcast February 26, 1990

O, GIVE ME A HOME...

If there's one song that's known to everybody in North America, it must be *Home on the Range*, a quiet tune with gentle words. But what a fuss it caused 50 years ago.

Back in 1905, John Lomax was a professor of music and history at the University of Texas. He was given a fellowship by Harvard University to travel around and collect old cowboy songs.

Cowboy music, or country and western, wasn't as popular throughout the country as it is today and the historians at Harvard were afraid the old songs would be lost. So Lomax got a huge, heavy old Edison recording machine and he lugged it all over the west.

One day in the summer of 1908, Lomax put his machine down on the bar of the Buckhorn saloon in San Antonio while he had a glass to settle the dust. The bartender asked what that machine was.

When Lomax told him, the bartender said, "You should go down to the edge of town and look for an old black guy who runs a saloon in the bush there. He used to be a cook on the cattle drives and he rode the Chisholm trail to Kansas."

When Lomax found the place and the old cook, it was too late. He had already been into his own stock. Lomax shook him awake but he just said, "I'se drunk, come back tomorrow and I'll sing for you."

The next day the old guy sang half a dozen songs, including *Home on the Range*, which Lomax had never heard before. He later had a blind music teacher from Austin, Texas, listen to the tune and put it on paper. He'd never heard it before, either.

In 1910, Lomax published the results of his work, a collection of 112 old western songs in a book called *Cowboy Songs and other Frontier Ballads*. That book, published in the east, made western music popular all over the country.

When Franklin Roosevelt was elected president in 1932, a bunch of newspapermen covering his campaign celebrated by getting drunk and singing *Home on the Range*. Roosevelt said "I've never heard that song before but from now on it's my favorite."

Everybody played and sang *Home on the Range*. And, since it was an old traditional tune that disappeared back into history, nobody had to pay any royalties.

> *When Franklin Roosevelt was elected president, a bunch of newspapermen covering his campaign celebrated by getting drunk and singing* Home on the Range. *Roosevelt instantly declared it his favorite song.*

Then William and Mary Goodwin of Tempe, Arizona, popped up out of nowhere and demanded millions of dollars' worth of royalties from every band leader, singer and radio station who had ever used it.

Sure enough, they had copyrighted the tune, under the name *My Arizona Home*, on the 27th of February, 1905. That was before Professor Lomax had recorded it from the old trail cook.

The Music Publishers Protective Association realized it was in big trouble. The association's lawyer was Samuel Moanfeldt, an expert on copyright who knew little about the old west. But in the next few months he learned.

Moanfeldt went to Kansas, to Dodge City. There he found plenty of people who had sung Home on the Range away back in the 1890s. The Dodge City paper ran the story of Moanfeldt's search, and Moanfeldt got a letter from a woman in Osborne, Kansas.

She was able to tell him the song had been written by a strange, eccentric man named Dr. Brewster Higley. She even steered him to a man, now 86 and blind, who had first sung it in public in 1874. Moanfeldt even dug up an old newspaper from 1873 which had published all the words.

Needless to say, he won that copyright fight.

Originally broadcast February 27, 1984

LIQUID GOLD

The American history books tell us the first oil well in North America was drilled in Pennsylvania in 1859. Canadians insist they had one in Sarnia, Ontario two years earlier. They're both right, for once. The Canadian one came earlier, but it wasn't drilled; it was dug.

Indians had used oil that seeped into the creeks and rivers of southwestern Ontario long before the white man came. Early settlers in the area found the stuff was a nuisance. But they could dig oily sand out of the riverbanks, put it into burlap sacks and squeeze oil out of it. It was pretty low-quality oil and barely worth the effort but it could be used as fuel if you didn't mind a little stench and smoke.

But by the 1840s, North Americans were into some crude refining and found they could produce usable oil for lubricating machines and the axles of their carts. Generally, whale oil was still the major fuel for lamps.

A man named Tripp from Woodstock, Ontario found he could dig oily sand out of the banks of Black Creek in the Sarnia area, mix it with sand and gravel and come up with a pretty good hardtop for roads. He got into that business in a small way.

He sold out to a carriage maker, a bright, self-made young millionaire named Williams. Williams found oil nearby in a shallow water well. He figured it must have seeped up from somewhere below the bottom of the well. He realized he'd never get any major quantities of oil by digging. He'd have to drill. So in 1857 he set up the first oil-drilling rig in Canada and had a little success. In those days a few hundred barrels a week was considered enough to support a small oil operation.

A man called Shaw copied Williams a half-dozen miles away near the little village of Enniskillen. On the 28th of February in 1860, he hit a gusher that spewed out 3000 barrels a day. The oil boom was on.

Americans swarmed into southwestern Ontario and bought up oil lands. Shades of what happened in Alberta 100 years later.

Many of those early American engineers were army officers on leave from their regiments, trying to make some money. Soldiering didn't pay very well in those days. Then, in 1861, the American Civil War broke out. The American officers shot home to get back to work because the military business was booming along with the cannon. And the price of oil zoomed as American factories and railroads geared up for war.

The village of Enniskillen where Shaw had drilled changed its name to Petrolia which it is to this day.

The oil business has always been up and down. In 1862 it took another down. American factories had overbought and prices dropped. A lot of drilling had produced nothing and a lot of people had gone broke.

Then in April of 1863, an American named John Lick, a draft dodger, drilled the big one north and east of where Williams had hit his gusher in 1860.

The oil flowed so hard and fast it took four days to cap that well. It spouted out of the ground to the height of a tall man.

The oil flowed so hard and fast it took four days to cap that well. It spouted out of the ground to the height of a tall man. There weren't enough barrels to hold it so Lick and his crew dammed both ends of a small ravine and let the oil flow into it to form a little lake of oil. Prices had gone up again and the stuff was worth a dollar a barrel, payable in cash on the spot.

Lick and his crew had had to fell a huge tree to make one of their dams and they sat around the tree trunk, using it as a counter and did business there. They took in the cash from oil dealers then at the end of the day they divvied it up.

Syndicates of rich Americans came in and offered $100 thousand for the well. Lick turned them down. They raised the bid to $500 thousand. Still no deal.

One man in Pennsylvania pointed to a wheelbarrow sitting beside the tree trunk. He said, "I'll fill that with gold, all you can wheel." Still no deal. Lick knew he had a winner.

He put his money into more drilling equipment and drilled more holes. When he died 15 years later, the citizens of Bothwell passed the hat to give him a decent burial.

Originally broadcast February 28, 1983

THE PHENOMENON OF THE OPERA

They say people born on the 29th of February are unusual, if only because that date only shows up every four years. Well, Giacomo Rossini was unusual for more reasons than that.

He was born on this day in 1792, an Italian with a pair of colorful characters for parents. His father was nicknamed Lively. He was a musician and a joker. Everybody liked him. He had a few official jobs like town trumpeter and inspector of slaughterhouses that give us a clue as to the sort of man he was.

Rossini's mother was a pretty good opera singer, not good enough for the big-time but a star of sorts out in the sticks. Both were lively, cheerful people, more devoted to living a good life than making a good living.

Rossini grew up like that. He was apprenticed to a blacksmith at first but he said that involved too much work. He always pretended to be lazy.

In fact, Rossini was a very intense man, talented, painstaking, nervous. But he pretended to be exactly the opposite.

He once said to a German composer, "You people have a passion for industry. My passion is laziness."

Rossini was a genius, no question about that. His first composition performed in public won him quite a noteworthy prize and he was only 16 at the time. When he was 18 he had an opera performed. At the age of 20 another of his operas was performed at La Scala, the Yankee Stadium of opera. And when he was only 24 he wrote *The Barber of Seville*, one of the half dozen great operas of all time.

The first performance was booed and hissed. Rossini just grinned and waved to the audience. The next night he gave them an improved version. They still booed but not as loudly. A few even cheered some parts. The third night he gave them yet another rewrite and everybody cheered.

Rossini wasn't a tall man but he was big. He looked like the sort of man who would devour a chicken, wash it down with a litre of wine and look around for more.

Women threw themselves at him. And he didn't duck.

He married a woman seven years older than he was, an opera star who was the mistress of two big shots at the same time, an opera producer and the king of Naples.

When that marriage fell apart, Rossini married one of the most beautiful women in Europe, a classy prostitute who charged enormous prices. She devoted the rest of her life to looking after Rossini, almost like a mother.

In 1829, before he was 38, Rossini wrote *William Tell*, still considered by many to be one of the very best operas ever written.

Then he quit. Just like that. He'd moved to Paris several years earlier and the French government had lavished money and honors on him.

Only his friends knew, but Rossini was falling apart under that carefree exterior. His nerves couldn't take the strain of show biz in the fast lane anymore.

Rossini lived almost 40 more years. But his writing days were over. He stayed at home and everybody came to visit. He encouraged young musicians.

He wrote a little, mostly religious music, but the fire was gone. Nevertheless, in the first half of his life he produced more than most composers could in a hundred years.

> *Rossini once said to a German composer, "You people have a passion for industry. My passion is laziness."*

Originally broadcast February 29, 1988

Top Left: *Cynical comedian W.C. Fields was born William Claud Dukenfield on January 29, 1889.*

Top Right*: On June 2, 1917 Canadian pilot/gunman Billy Bishop headed out for the nearest German airfield and shot seven of the enemy's eight planes. His skill earned him the nickname "The Kid Who Couldn't Miss."*

Bottom Right: *Alexander Graham Bell, seen here with Mrs. Bell, patented the telephone on March 7, 1876.*

Bottom Left: *When Grey Owl collapsed and died on April 13, 1938, it was revealed that the environmentalist, who claimed to be part-Indian, part-Scottish was actually an Englishman named Archie Belaney.*

Top Left: *Edgar Allan Poe was born on the 19th of January in 1809, and went on to become one of the most influential writers of modern times.*

Top Right: *Sarah Bernhardt's death, on the 25th of March in 1923, was a performance as dramatic as any the great actress had given in life.*

Bottom: *The infamous outlaw Jesse James pulled off history's first bank robbery on February 14, 1866.*

KID-NAPPED

Charles Lindbergh was the greatest hero who ever came out of the United States . . . bigger than George Washington, Abe Lincoln, or John Wayne.

When the biggest names in aviation were trying to fly the Atlantic solo, young Lindbergh, an airmail pilot, did it at the age of 24. Then he went on to marry Ann Morrow, the daughter of one of the wealthiest men in the country. Then the two of them flew all over the world, Lindbergh surveying new routes for airlines, Ann writing books about it.

When Charles Lindbergh Junior was born in 1930 it was big news. When he was kidnapped on the first of March in 1932, it was front page news.

The Lindberghs lived in New Jersey, just across the river from New York, so it was assumed that New York gangsters had taken the kid. Kidnapping was a major gang racket in those days.

The kidnappers had climbed a clumsy homemade ladder to get into the baby's room on the second floor of the Lindbergh country estate. They left a note demanding $50,000. Instructions for the payoff would follow.

Literally hundreds of newsmen swarmed across from New York to make this the biggest story of the 30s. A half-dozen police forces from New York and New Jersey went to work on the case.

Most American police forces weren't very good in those days and the New York and New Jersey ones were low on the scale. The FBI was emerging as an efficient bunch of criminal investigators. But, as American law stood at the time, the FBI couldn't get involved because it was a federal organization and no federal law was broken. That law has since been changed and the FBI now investigates all kidnappings in the States.

An eccentric, retired teacher named John Condon put an ad in the local weekly paper in the Bronx where he lived, saying he would be glad to act as intermediary between the Lindberghs and the kidnappers. He was contacted and, with Lindbergh nearby in a car, he paid out the $50,000 ransom.

But the child wasn't returned. He was found dead 10 weeks later in a field not far from the Lindbergh house. He had apparently been killed as soon as he was kidnapped.

Lindbergh and the police had recorded the serial numbers of all the bills paid to the kidnapper. The first turned up even before the baby's body was found.

Two and a half years after the kidnapping, a German carpenter named Bruno Hauptmann was caught paying for a tankful of gas with one of the bills. $14,000 worth of the payoff was found in his garage.

Hauptmann at first denied any knowledge of the case. Then he said he was just holding the money for a pal called Izzy Fisch who had returned to Germany on a visit a year earlier and died there.

The cops didn't have much of a case against Hauptmann but they went to work and hyped some of their evidence and ignored some and, sure enough, they convinced a jury Hauptmann was guilty. He didn't have a very good lawyer.

Izzy Fisch, the man who died in Germany, was a conman who may very well have bought some of the ransom money at a discount to launder it and leave it with Hauptmann for a while.

We'll never know. Hauptmann was electrocuted in 1936. Several books have been written about the case in recent years, all setting out to prove it was horribly botched and an innocent man was executed. Hauptmann's widow is in her 90s now, but she's still trying to get his case reviewed and a pardon granted.

Originally broadcast March 1, 1988

WILDE LIFE

Oscar Wilde was one of the greatest writers in the English language in the 1800s, and certainly the wittiest.

Oscar Wilde was from a family of wealthy Irish screwballs. His father was an eye doctor in Dublin and a generation before Oscar became famous, the old man made it to the front pages with a court case that involved him carrying on with a patient who was young enough to be his daughter.

Oscar himself wrote poetry, prose and plays. He had a wife and two kids. Then, in his early 30s, Oscar turned homosexual.

By that time he was living in London and was famous. There was a lot of homosexuality in London in those days. In France it was called the English Vice. Many highly-placed men were involved, including a few in or on the edge of the royal family.

Oscar had affairs with many young men. The two best known were a man named Ross, the son of the attorney general of Upper Canada, and Lord Alfred Douglas. Lord Alfred was the son of the Marquess of Queensbury, the man who wrote the modern rules of boxing.

The Marquess was quite crazy, a tough-looking little red-headed man whose family lived in fear of him. His wife and other family members considered having him committed more than once but their lawyers told them they couldn't do it because of the unclear state of the law.

The Marquess and his son, Lord Alfred, hadn't been getting along at all well. They hated each other. And when Lord Alfred started carrying on with Oscar very openly, the Marquess decided to do something about it. He threatened Oscar a few times and the police were called to chase him away.

Finally, the Marquess came right out and accused Oscar of unseemly conduct with his son. He did it in writing and Oscar decided to take him to court. His friends warned him against it, since there was a strong possibility that Oscar could end up in big trouble himself. But Oscar insisted and the Marquess was arrested on the 2nd of March in 1895.

Oscar, the smartest tongue in England, figured he could match wits with any lawyer in a courtroom. When he stood up to testify he threw out the one-liners like the old pro he was.

Iced champagne was his drink, he said, although he took it against his doctor's orders.

"Never mind your doctor's orders," said the lawyer for the Marquess. "I never do," said Oscar. "That's probably why I'm in such poor health."

"Never mind your doctor's orders," said the lawyer for the Marquess.

"I never do," said Oscar. "That's probably why I'm in such poor health."

It made sensational newspaper stories and the whole world held its breath. Oscar got more and more outrageous in court. But he went too far. The Marquess had hired private detectives to get the dirt on Oscar and there was plenty of it. When into the champagne, Oscar was reckless and left a trail a mile wide.

The Marquess beat the charge. But the evidence that came out compelled the attorney-general to charge Oscar. There was a considerable wait. Oscar's friends all advised him to flee the country. But he wouldn't. He stayed and stood trial. He was convicted and sent to jail and then left the country. He died soon afterwards in France, still the master of the quip.

Lying poverty-stricken on his death bed with a glass of champagne in his hand he said: "Here I am, as always, dying beyond my means." Then he looked around at the tasteless furnishings in the room and said, "Either that wallpaper goes or I do."

And he did.

Originally broadcast March 2, 1988

THE DAWN OF TIME

On the 3rd of March in 1923, *Time* Magazine was born. It probably changed the way we see the world as much as either radio or television did. Like it or not, *Time* changed English-language journalism for all time. Until *Time* came along, reporters and editors published more words than they do today but presented fewer facts. Political speeches were covered almost word-for-word. But the reports seldom mentioned that the speaker loosened his tie or was red-faced from too much booze.

Newspapers covered the news. Magazines were more concerned with history than news, although some of the best investigative journalism in American history came from a few magazines in the late 1800s and early 1900s.

But *Time* changed all that. It boiled down the news of the week into short, very clear, stories. By covering stories over a one-week period, it could give a bit more perspective than the daily papers but still be immediate enough to be exciting. A simple idea, you say. Most great ideas are. And if they're properly packaged, they make fortunes for the people who came up with them.

The two men who thought up *Time* were Harry Luce and Briton Hadden. Luce indeed became a millionaire many, many times over. Hadden died in 1929 before he had time to become rich, six years to the day after they'd put together the first issue of *Time*.

Luce and Hadden had similar backgrounds in a way. Both were from old, moneyed families that weren't at their most prosperous when the boys came along.

Luce was born in China, where his parents were Presbyterian missionaries. He had a cold, austere childhood and he was socially awkward all his life.

Hadden was born in New York to a family of bankers and brokers. His father died when he was very young, leaving the family with little money to spare.

Both sets of parents realized the need for a good education and they scraped together the money for their boys to go to a good elementary school, Hotchkiss, and then on to Yale. They met and worked on school papers

at Hotchkiss and were close buddies ever afterwards.

They went into the army together in 1917 and were sent to a camp in South Carolina as officer cadets. There, they met men from all over the United States who had never been to college. They were amazed that there were actually young men who didn't know where Germany and France were on the map, who didn't know the history of modern Europe that had led to the war they were about to fight, and who didn't know the various powers and duties of their Congress, the Supreme Court, or the presidency.

After the war, when they graduated, Hadden and Luce both went to work as reporters, Luce in Chicago, Hadden in New York. After a year or so they both went to work for the same paper in Baltimore. There, they remembered how fascinated those soldiers had been as Luce told them of current events. They figured out how to come up with some sort of publication that would do roughly the same thing. They quit their jobs and moved to New York to start working on their idea.

> *They remembered how fascinated the soldiers had been as Luce told them of current events. They figured out how to come up with some sort of publication that would do roughly the same thing.*

They had access to people with money, partly through their families, partly through the rich kids they'd met at Yale. They figured they would need $100,000 to get going. That took about a year and they put out their first issue, dated the third of March, 1923, when they had raised only $86,000.

They didn't have any reporters. They clipped papers, backgrounded their stories with reference books and trips to the library and wrote them in a heavy, pseudo-classical style but with a light heart.

They didn't treat anyone with reverence and, in the course of putting all that was significant into 28 pages, they knew enough to put in little bits of color. Like the story of the lady who sued her landlord when a rat dropped through a hole in the ceiling and into the bathtub with her. That might not make the history books but it was certainly an indicator of the state of at least some of the housing in the country at the time.

Originally broadcast March 3, 1983

THE FIRST PHOTOGENIC DISASTER

Man first flew in a balloon. That was in France, before the time of the Revolution. The people who made the balloon didn't realize exactly what made it work. But they knew if they made a big upside-down bag of cloth and built a fire under it, it would rise and lift a load with it. It was the light air caused by the fire that did the job. Over the next century or two, other airmen perfected that technique.

The Germans realized that if they made hydrogen gas and trapped it, it could lift enormous loads. The big balloon would float and small motors at one end would push it through the air like engines push a ship through the water.

Work on the airship, as it was called, was pretty well along before the airplane was invented. Then, for a generation or so, the two types of flying machines developed side by side, the lighter-than-air airships and the heavier-than-air airplanes.

Even into the 1920s, it looked as if air travel on a big scale would never amount to anything in airplanes. Engines weren't very powerful by today's standards and airplanes couldn't be made very big. But airships could be made as big as man wanted to make them. The bigger the better.

The Germans quickly concentrated their experience in airships into one huge project. They came up with an airship more than three times as long as one of today's jumbo jets. It was launched on the fourth of March in 1936, the biggest man-made thing that ever took to the air.

It was called the Hindenberg. It could cross the Atlantic in three days from Germany to New York, about half the time of the fastest ocean liner. It was cheaper, about $240 each way. And it was luxurious.

Over the next 14 months more than 2000 people crossed the Atlantic in the Hindenberg and the Germans talked about building a whole fleet of them, some even bigger.

The Nazis had just come to power in Germany and were talking about rebuilding that ruined country and becoming a major world power. No one doubted they could do it.

These huge airships had one awful drawback, though. The Hindenberg was held up by 7,000,000 cubic feet of hydrogen gas. And hydrogen is highly flammable. Engineers had worked on dozens of safety features to make sure that no spark could get near that hydrogen.

Photographers were on hand to watch the explosion, so it was one of the best-documented disasters in the history of air travel.

Then, in May of 1937, as the Hindenberg was coming in to land at Lakehurst, New Jersey, it blew up. Photographers were on hand to watch it so it was one of the best-documented disasters in the history of air travel.

Thirty-five people were killed. The miracle was that 62 survived. People still argue over what went wrong. The skipper of the Hindenberg didn't die until 1960 and he maintained until the end that his ship was the victim of sabotage. If so, then who did it?

Germans who were anti-Nazi? Possible.

British agents afraid the Germans were establishing themselves as number one in the growing field of air travel? Not impossible.

No matter. Nobody who saw those pictures, and that was everybody, would ever set foot on another passenger airship. The age of the commercial airplane had arrived.

Originally broadcast March 4, 1988

THE IMAGINARY ATROCITY

In 1765, the British government in London began to impose import duties on lead, paper, glass, tea, and a whole bunch of other things arriving in the American colonies. The idea was to pay for the British garrison that defended the Americans. The Americans didn't see it that way. They saw it as taxes imposed by a parliament that gave them no say.

The opposition was centred in the city of Boston and it was a town that seethed with rebellion until it finally broke into open flame 10 years later. The British army kept two regiments stationed in Boston to prevent rebellion. Naturally the townspeople and the soldiers didn't get along very well.

To make matters even worse, from the soldiers' point of view, Americans lived much better than Englishmen and prices were higher than in Britain. So the soldiers found they were treated with contempt by the Americans and their pay didn't go far.

The people of Boston were probably split about 50/50. But the rebels, the Sons of Liberty as they called themselves, were a noisy, riotous lot and the loyalists were badly intimidated.

The leader of the Sons of Liberty, the chief rabble-rouser, was noisy, obnoxious, shrewd Sam Adams. Sam and his pals kept the people of Boston in a constant state of agitation. Not that the British governor did much to help things. He was a nasty, autocratic man.

On the evening of March the 5th in 1770, an officer and seven soldiers were surrounded on the steps of the Custom House by an angry mob. They claimed one of the soldiers had hit a boy. The soldiers claimed the boy was one of several who had been pelting them with snowballs. They ignored the snowballs. But the boys then started throwing lumps of ice at them and they hurt.

The mob surged forward and the soldiers fired. Five of the mob were killed and six wounded.

The lieutenant-governor just managed to forestall a riot that would have burned down the town. To do that, he had to promise the officer and soldiers would be arrested and tried for murder.

The best lawyer in Boston was Sam Adams' cousin, John Adams. John was also anti-British but he was a moderate, reasonable man who had no use for his cousin's noisy, violent tactics. He believed the Americans cause could best be advanced by having a calm, fair trial that would win over British public opinion, no matter the verdict.

Sam Adams, the rabble-rouser, had an artist draw a picture of bloodthirsty soldiers firing on an innocent mob. He had his friend Paul Revere, the silversmith, make an engraving. Pretty soon those pictures of the Boston Massacre were hanging in every pub throughout the colonies.

After about six months the trials were held. The officer was quickly acquitted when a witness said he gave no order to fire and, indeed, told the witness he didn't want his men to shoot.

The seven soldiers were then tried. Most witnesses said the soldiers were surrounded by a bloodthirsty mob and only fired to save their own lives. Five of the seven were acquitted. The other two were convicted of manslaughter. But their lawyer, John Adams, Sam's cousin, got them off by pleading benefit of clergy.

Anyone who could read or write in those days could avoid hanging. The theory was that literacy was such a rare and necessary skill that society couldn't afford to lose anyone who could read and write.

But in the end it all didn't matter. The legend of the bloody Boston Massacre persisted. Paul Revere's engraving was everywhere and by the time the American Revolution broke out five years later, Americans were convinced they'd been victims of a terrible atrocity by the British Army.

> *Pretty soon those pictures of the Boston Massacre — bloodythirsty soldiers firing on an innocent mob — were hanging in every pub throughout the colonies.*

Originally broadcast March 5, 1991

SCOTT-FREE

Dred Scott was a slave, born in Virginia in about 1795. Nobody knows for sure because nobody bothered to make a record of his birth.

Scott was a small man, rather frail and lacking in energy. When Scott was about 30, his owner moved from Virginia to St. Louis, taking Scott with him. Four years later Scott was sold to an army doctor.

The doctor was transferred by the army to Fort Snelling which was in the territory of Wisconsin. The doctor lived in the territory for about five years, then moved back to St. Louis and died. His slave, Dred Scott, was passed on to the doctor's widow.

She moved to New York to remarry, so she left the slave behind with friends, the two sons of the man who had first owned him. Their name was Blow. One of them, Henry Blow, was a lawyer and a leader of the anti-slavery movement in St. Louis.

Blow drew up the papers and had Scott, who couldn't read or write, put his mark on them. Blow intended to sue for Scott's freedom, claiming that although he'd been born in slave country, he'd lived in free country so he should be set free.

And that struck at the very heart of the slavery issue in the United States. Slavery had been abolished in the British Empire 20 years earlier but it was still the law in the southern United States. American courts had ruled for years that a slave who escaped into a non-slave state could be forcibly returned into slavery.

As the territories to the north and west became states they were permitted to join the union in pairs — one free, one slave. That didn't please either the slavery or anti-slavery people, but it was a compromise that avoided a civil war.

Now the anti-slavery people, using Dred Scott as their pawn, were hoping to get the courts to say that Scott had lived in a territory that was non-slave country, so he had become free.

The slavery people would claim that since Scott was a slave he was a non-person and couldn't be part of a lawsuit in a court any more than a horse or a cow could. Two persons could go to court over the ownership of a horse but the horse couldn't.

The Southerners believed their economy depended on slavery and that it would collapse if their slaves were freed.

The northern workmen, many immigrants from Ireland and Europe who had come to the new land to be prosperous and free, believed they could never achieve economic power as long as the wealthy could undercut their wages and working conditions with slave labour.

So everyone in the United States, and in most of the rest of the world, was watching as the case dragged through the courts for years.

The first case was filed in 1846 and the Supreme Court of the United States didn't deliver its final judgment until the 6th of March in 1857.

And it said that Dred Scott was born a slave, so he would have to remain a slave. All that high-sounding language in the Constitution about life, liberty and the pursuit of happiness was sincere, said the court. But it only applied to white people.

The decision was supposed to settle the issue. It just inflamed it. And within four years the United States split up and fought one of the bloodiest civil wars in history.

And Dred Scott? He didn't seem to comprehend just what was going on. He said from time to time that he couldn't understand what the fuss was all about. He died of tuberculosis in 1858, about a year and a half after the decision. But he died free. His owner had given him his freedom when the supreme court refused to.

> *The slavery people would claim that since Scott was a slave he was a non-person and couldn't be part of a lawsuit in a court any more than a horse or a cow could.*

Originally broadcast March 6, 1984

FOR WHOM THE BELL TOLLS

Alexander Graham Bell was a third-generation voice teacher. His grandfather and his father were both experts in speech. They were concerned primarily with teaching the deaf and so was young Bell.

The Bells were Scottish but they'd moved to London where Bell's father was a professor. In 1870 one of Bell's brothers died of tuberculosis. Another brother had died three years earlier of the same disease. Bell had a touch of it. Doctors advised the older Bell to get away from the cold, wet, damp, sooty air of London.

So the whole Bell family moved to Canada, to Brantford, Ontario. Soon Alexander Graham Bell was better.

Today it seems natural that Bell, the speech teacher and expert on deafness, would have invented the telephone, using the human ear as his model.

But that's not how it happened. Bell did experiments at Brantford on an invention he figured would make him rich, the harmonic telegraph.

Samuel Morse had invented the telegraph 30 years earlier and networks of wire had quickly crisscrossed North America and Europe. The demand for telegraph messages was straining those facilities.

Each wire could only carry one message at a time. Bell had an idea to get around that. His invention would allow one wire to carry six messages at the same time.

The idea was simple but he was having trouble working out the kinks. Bell noticed that his mouth took on a different shape when he pronounced a different sound. He was able to identify six such shapes.

If he could make something like a tuning fork vibrate only a tuning fork set to the same frequency at the end of a wire, he could send six messages at the same time, each sorted out at the receiving point because he would have six different tuning forks picking up the signal from the six sending tuning forks.

Bell had got that idea by reading a paper published by a German who had done similar experiments to his about the shape of the mouth. Bell didn't understand the German explanations under the diagrams accompanying the paper. He thought the German was sending messages by wire. The German had done no such thing. He had just used an electrical gadget to work the tuning forks. He didn't have similar tuning forks at the other end of the wire.

Bell moved to Boston to teach speech to the deaf but continued his experiments. He was working with the two wealthy young people and their fathers encouraged him with his idea of a machine to send several messages at once. They bankrolled him as he taught by day and experimented by night.

Bell came up with the idea of making a telephone by connecting by wire two iron gadgets modelled on the human ear.

The two wealthy fathers said it was very interesting, but to forget it and keep working on the gadget to send all those messages at once. Bell tried to do both. He came up with the telephone first and patented his idea on the 7th of March in 1876. One of his backers went to the telegraph company and offered them the patent for $100,000. They said no thanks, the telephone is just a toy.

So they had to go ahead with the telephone on their own. Two years later the telegraph company was offering $25 million. They were turned down.

> *Today it seems natural that Bell, the speech teacher and expert on deafness, would have invented the telephone, using the human ear as his model.*

Originally broadcast March 7, 1989

THE END OF AN EMPIRE

Riots broke out in St. Petersburg on the 8th of March in 1917. Before the end of the year they had snowballed into the greatest upheaval of the 20th century, the Russian Revolution.

The first thing you have to keep in mind when we talk about the Russian Revolution is that Russia was vastly different from the rest of the world in those days. These riots of early March are still called the February Riots because even their calendar was different from ours, about 13 days behind.

Russia was roughly the same huge country then that it is today. The head of state was the czar, a little man with a pointed beard. On paper he was the most absolute monarch in the world. In actual practice, he was a weak, not very bright man, one with no talent or inclination for government, so tied up with his own family affairs that he probably knew very little of what was going on.

And, of course, there was a vast bureaucracy, like all bureaucracies, working hard to make sure the top man knew nothing.

Since the crown held all the power on paper and the czar didn't want to exercise it, somebody had to. The queen, Alexandra, a German by birth, stepped in to fill the hole. That was a real disaster.

She was unusual, high-strung, not too with it, probably out-and-out crazy. She had come under the sway of a strange, dirty, lecherous priest named Rasputin. The poor queen, never too stable, had turned into a religious nut under Rasputin's influence. Things got really chaotic. Most of the main decisions were made in some sort of religious trance.

The First World War was nearly over. The Russians had been attacked by the Germans and their huge army had just melted. The only thing that kept it going at all was its vast numbers. Officers, equipment, ideas, discipline — none existed.

A few of the major Russian cities were quite modern with electricity and street cars but the country as a whole was pretty medieval. Under the strain of war, the primitive communications system broke down and there were awful food shortages.

In October of 1916, there had been a series of violent strikes at various factories in St. Petersburg, later renamed Leningrad, and the army had been called in. The soldiers had refused to shoot the strikers and the cossacks had been called in to put down the strike and execute the mutinous soldiers.

In December, a bunch of noblemen realized something had to be done about Rasputin, the crazy, evil priest who had so much influence over the queen. They invited him to a party, got all liquored up and slipped some poison into his drink. He loved it, drank more and sang louder. So, they got really plastered, put on the record player as high as it would go, playing *Yankee Doodle Dandy,* and shot him. Now they were rid of the man who was causing a lot, if not most, of the trouble. But they had no one to replace him. That was the terrible story of Russia at that time. Nobody had looked ahead, past the next move.

The government had been so repressive for centuries that various elements, the czar, the generals, the nobles, the factory owners, the few union leaders . . . nobody could pick up a newspaper and find out what was going on with the others.

Workers were on strike, food stores were almost empty. Most of the soldiers were kept in their barracks; in some cases, their officers had just disappeared.

Then on the 8th of March by our calendar, the 23rd of February by the old Russian calendar, the police faced a disturbance that was too big for them. They called the army. Nobody came. They called the cossacks. They came and faced the mob. A police captain gave them the order to charge. Only one did. He galloped at the captain and cut off his head with one swipe of his sword.

Then the rest of the cossacks gently walked their horses through the crowd, out the other side and back to the barracks. There they put away their horses, their sabres and an empire.

> *On paper, the czar was the most absolute monarch in the world. In actual practice, he was a weak, not very bright man with no talent or inclination for government.*

Originally broadcast March 8, 1983

CORPUS CHRISTIE

In 1949, about a month before Christmas, a young Welshman named Tim Evans walked into a police station and said he wanted to give himself up. He said, I've disposed of my wife.

Evans was not very bright and he'd been drinking heavily for the last week or two so the story he told was rather confused.

He worked in London as a deliveryman and lived in a couple of grubby rooms with his wife and baby daughter. The Welsh police called Scotland Yard and the cops in London reported they couldn't find any bodies. They looked where Evans said he'd put them and nothing was there.

Evans said he was helped by a neighbour named Reg Christie, the man who lived on the main floor of the old house. Christie said Evans seemed to be a confused young man. He said Evans had told him his wife and daughter had gone out of town to visit her father.

The police were about to give up. But Reg Christie was very helpful and kept giving them more bits of information. Acting on Christie's tips, the police kept looking. Sure enough, they found Evans' wife and daughter, both strangled, both wrapped up in blankets.

Evans was charged with both murders. He gave four statements, the police said as they presented them at his trial. In one, he said his wife died when Christie performed an abortion on her. In another, he admitted to the killings. In the third he said he was confused but he didn't kill anybody. In the fourth he said Christie did it.

Evans went on trial. His lawyer pleaded him not guilty by reason of insanity. But he didn't claim Evans didn't do it.

Christie testified against him and the jury took only 40 minutes to find Evans guilty. He was hanged

The landlord had a man in to clean up Christie's old apartment for the next tenant. He tore off some wallpaper and found a closet he didn't know was there. Out poured the bodies.

on the 9th of March in 1950. It was a pathetic case and a heartbreaker, but it didn't get the newspaper attention of many other British murders.

Almost exactly three years later, Christie's wife disappeared. He explained to her sister that she had gone away on a trip for a while and nobody seemed terribly suspicious, although the sister asked some questions. It wasn't like Mrs. Christie to do that.

In early January of 1953, Christie sold his few bits of furniture for about $75, put everything he owned into an old battered suitcase and took to the street. He lived in flop houses most of the time.

The landlord had a man in to clean up Christie's old apartment for the next tenant. He tore off some wallpaper and found a closet he didn't know was there. Out poured the bodies. Mrs. Christie and three young prostitutes, all strangled more or less the same way Evans' wife and baby had been.

The biggest manhunt in British history was started for Christie and he was found standing near the House of Commons, staring into the Thames. At his trial he pleaded not guilty by reason of insanity, just as Evans had. He also admitted that he'd killed two other women in 1943 and 1944 but no one had noticed in all the noise and confusion of the years.

There was an investigation. If Christie had killed the Evans woman and child, then an innocent man had been hanged. There were two royal commissions set up to investigate. Both reported everyone had acted quite properly.

But later, the Queen issued the dead Evans a pardon. And parliament did away with capital punishment in England.

Originally broadcast March 9, 1988

FREEDOM TRAIN

Harriet Tubman was born in about 1820 in Maryland. We don't know the day because she was a slave and nobody bothered with details about slaves in Maryland back in the early 1800s.

Harriet carried scars on her neck and back from beatings she received when she was only six or seven. When she was 13, an angry slave owner threw a lead weight at a slave who ducked. The weight hit Tubman on the head and gave her a terrible concussion. For the rest of her life she would be subject to sudden sleeping spells. She would fall asleep, sometimes standing up, for 10 or 20 minutes. She was in a sort of semi-coma for two months after that blow.

Her name had originally been Green but she became Harriet Tubman when she married a free black man named Tubman when she was about 20.

Harriet had hated the life of a slave and was determined to escape. Tubman, who was free but poor, couldn't get worried about such things. Harriet escaped and made her way north to Pennsylvania in 1840. Tubman didn't bother going with her. Her two brothers started out with her but they turned back.

Slaves couldn't usually read or write. In some southern states it was against the law to teach them. So Harriet couldn't read a map. She just knew to follow the Big Dipper in the sky at night to get north. On cloudy nights she knew to grope around the base of a tree until she could feel the moss on the north side.

She made it and started to work to save some money to get her parents out. She worked as a chambermaid in a hotel and as a laundress. But nobody made much money in those days and black people usually made only half of what white folks did.

Harriet started making trips back to the southern states to rescue slaves. Altogether she made 19 trips and brought out more than 300 slaves.

> *Black people might be free, but they weren't equal. The conductor didn't want anyone black in his passenger coaches with the white people.*

In 1851, the American federal government passed a law that allowed slave owners to take their slaves back from the free northern states. So from then on Harriet guided her fugitives across the border into Canada. She lived for a while in St. Catharines, Ontario. She guided a lot of slaves to Chatham, near Windsor, Ontario.

Harriet was one of the Americans, black and white, who plotted an armed slave rebellion in Chatham. Twenty-one men, under John Brown the abolitionist, went south to start an uprising by capturing guns at a military arsenal in Virginia. They were caught and hanged but Harriet carried on.

She made one trip south to get her husband. But he had forgotten all about her and was living with another woman.

When the Civil War started Harriet used her connections from her slave-stealing days to work as a scout for the Northern Armies. She led spies deep into southern territory. In one raid they brought back 800 black slaves.

At the end of the war, Tubman was given a military pass to ride back on a train. By then every American was free, black or white.

And that's when she learned another bitter lesson. They might be free but they weren't equal. The conductor didn't want anyone black in his passenger coaches with the white people. He threw Harriet into the baggage car so violently that she suffered a dislocated shoulder that gave her pain for months.

For years she asked the federal government for a pension for her service in the war. But she ran into another kind of prejudice. Black ex-soldiers got pensions. But not women.

Finally she was awarded a pension when her second husband died. As a widow, she was entitled.

Harriet Tubman was still fighting prejudice when she died in her 90s on the 10th of March in 1913.

Originally broadcast March 10, 1987

WHITE OUT

The Great Blizzard of 1888 wasn't the worst blizzard in history, just the most famous. That was because it hit New York, the communications capital of the English-speaking world.

It started on the 11th of March. That was a Sunday and unusually warm for March. Before noon, people were sitting on their front porches. Around mid-day it began to rain a little. That rain was caused by a storm that came up the east coast from Georgia.

After dark, another storm, this one from Canada, came across the Great Lakes and the two collided right over New York. The northern storm brought terrible winds.

The snow began before midnight and went all day Monday and most of Tuesday. The winds blew it into drifts.

The stock exchange closed down for the first time since it opened in 1790.

Nobody knows how hard the wind blew. It reached 75 miles an hour and then broke the gauge at the weather office. A man climbed the pole, 150 feet above the street, to fix it and got it working again after an hour or so. But the worst winds blew when the gauge was broken.

Hundreds of horses froze to death in the streets. One man stumbled in a huge snowdrift and was bonked on the head by something hard. It gave him quite a cut. He scraped the snow aside and discovered it was the hoof of a horse. For years he showed the scar and said he was the only man in town ever to be kicked by a dead horse.

Another man, exhausted struggling through the snow, leaned against an iron lamp-post and fell asleep for a few minutes. He finally came to and staggered on home. He slept the sleep of the dead for about 12 hours then woke up to find his false teeth gone. He went back to the lamp-post after the storm was over and found the teeth frozen to it.

Dozens of small boats were capsized in the harbor. One yacht loaded with rich people went down.

New Yorkers were then, as now, pretty cynical about their police force. It was going through yet another of its investigations for corruption. But the New York cops responded bravely this time.

Policemen struggled through snowdrifts to get people from cold houses and off the streets and took them to police stations and fire halls to keep them alive.

They pulled homemade sleighs to the station to keep the stoves going. And when that ran out they dragged in the park benches and broke them up and burned them to keep people warm.

The storm was even worse to the west in Buffalo and north in New England, but it's still known as the New York Blizzard of '88. One town in Massachusetts got more than 50 inches of snow in the storm and had a drift 60 feet high. It didn't disappear until June.

New York City itself got almost 21 inches of snow. Throughout the northeastern United States, 400 people died.

New York got more snow than that one day in December of 1947. But there was no wind with that one. So the Great Blizzard of '88 still holds the record for blizzards.

Unless you live somewhere in Canada.

> *The snow began before midnight and went all day Monday and most of Tuesday. The stock exchange closed down for the first time since it opened in 1790.*

Originally broadcast March 11, 1986

RELIEVING THE DEPRESSION

In 1929, the stock markets in both Canada and the United States crashed. Ever since the First World War had ended 10 years earlier, the economy had been booming.

The high wages of the war industries had continued as prosperity spread and everybody had a chance at owning a car, appliances, a home, and many other things that had previously been considered luxury items.

Unfortunately, in both countries, the governments were reluctant to control the banks and the stock brokers. A lot of people were paying everything they owned to get stocks that were just pieces of paper.

As long as the factories kept turning out goods that people had the money to buy, it seemed to work. But most people knew it was shaky. Nobody knew when it would fall.

That stock market crash of 1929 did the trick. If it hadn't, something else would have pretty soon.

Suddenly, banks failed. Factories closed. Farmers had lots of meat and potatoes to sell but nobody had money to buy. The result was unemployment and even starvation in the midst of plenty.

It was the worst Depression the world had ever seen and it soon spread around the world. Canada was harder hit than the States because Canada was still not a very industrialized country, just a producer of wheat and fish and lumber and materials.

Then along came Franklin Delano Roosevelt. Roosevelt was a rich boy from an aristocratic old American family. His ancestors had owned land in New York when it was still called New Amsterdam. More than a dozen members of his family tree had arrived on the Mayflower.

Roosevelt was rich, handsome, witty, hardworking and, incredibly, a socialist. His fifth cousin, Teddy Roosevelt, had been president of the United States just after the turn of the century.

Franklin got into New York state politics, became governor, was assistant secretary of the navy during the First World War and wanted that presidency that his cousin Teddy once had.

In 1932, with the country in the depths of despair, Roosevelt ran a fast, smiling, optimistic campaign. Man made this depression, and man can overcome it, he said.

The American people believed him and they voted him president in the fall of 1932. He assumed office in early March of 1933. In his inaugural speech, Roosevelt came up with a phrase that became the battle cry for Depression beating: "The only thing we have to fear is fear itself."

Franklin Delano Roosevelt was rich, handsome, witty, hardworking and, incredibly, a socialist.

Roosevelt planned to shut down the banks all across the United States, give the bankers time to straighten out their books, print more money if necessary to get things moving again, then re-open them and urge everyone to get back to normal.

His advisers warned him that he was heading down a path that the western world had always avoided, socialism with heavy government interference in the life of the individual.

"If that was such a good idea in the minds of most people, the previous president would still be in office," said Roosevelt.

"The bankers will never hold still for it," his advisers warned.

"I won't try to convince *them*," said Roosevelt, "I'll convince the people."

So a week after he became president, on the evening of the 12th of March in 1933, Roosevelt went on the radio to explain to the American people what he was doing and why. It made sense and the bankers and business moguls could do nothing but go along.

Roosevelt didn't call that radio message a speech. He didn't sound like a clergyman in a pulpit. He had a casual, warm voice and he used it effectively.

He knew that people were listening to him in ones and twos, on radios that were sitting on their kitchen tables or in bars. He made dozens more of those talks in his next dozen years as president. He called them fireside chats. And they changed the tone of political campaigning, and propaganda, for all time.

Originally broadcast March 12, 1991

A HELPLESS VICTIM

Kitty Genovese was a pleasant-looking young woman of 27. She managed a bar in New York and lived alone in an apartment about 20 minutes' drive away.

New York was a dangerous city even back in the early 1960s, although not nearly as dangerous as it's become. About a thousand people a year were murdered in New York, way more than are killed even today in all of Canada. And today about 2000 people a year are murdered in New York.

Kitty worked until three in the morning. On the morning of the 13th of March in 1964, she arrived home just about twenty after three. She parked her car and started for her apartment, about 15 seconds' walk away. She must have realized there was a man following her because she suddenly turned and walked in the other direction. It would get her to her apartment building along a well-lit street.

Also, there was a police call box at the corner, a sort of phone on a lamp post that she would pick up to talk to the police station.

She never quite made it. The man came up behind her, grabbed her, spun her around and stabbed her with a knife. Kitty screamed.

Right across the street was a 10-storey apartment building. Several lights went on and people opened their windows. A man shouted: "Let that girl alone."

The stabber hesitated then walked away and got into a white car.

All the lights went out and the windows closed. Kitty was in bad shape but she turned around and tried to make it back to her apartment. The stabber got out of the car and started after her again.

He stabbed her again, and again Kitty cried out. Again, the lights went on and the windows opened. This time the stabber went back to his car and drove away.

The police finally decided 38 people saw and/or heard the attack. Every one of them was within a step of a phone. They all said they didn't want to get involved.

By this time Kitty was probably crawling, weak from loss of blood. She got to her apartment building and was in the lobby when the killer drove back. This time he finished her off.

From the time Kitty Genovese screamed first until somebody finally picked up a phone and called the police was probably a half-hour. The police cruiser was on the scene in just under two minutes. Kitty was dead.

The police had the killer in six days. He was a crazy man who had killed another woman two weeks earlier and a teenage girl the previous summer.

The police spent most of their time and effort trying to figure out why no one called them. They questioned hundreds of people. They finally decided 38 people saw and/or heard the attack. Every one of them was within a step of a phone.

They all said they didn't want to get involved. Some had half-legitimate reasons. One woman who had come from Germany said, "The last time I called a police station, I went to a concentration camp."

The man who finally called first phoned a friend and asked him for advice. When the friend said he had to call the police, the man left his apartment, climbed over the roof to the next building and used a friend's phone. He said he didn't want the police to be able to trace the call because he didn't want to get involved.

The killer escaped and raped a woman before he was caught again. He's still in a mental hospital.

There were books and plays and a movie and a TV special about the case. To this day, social workers and police still talk about the Kitty Genovese syndrome when they can't find witnesses to a crime.

Originally broadcast March 13, 1992

DEATH INSURANCE

William Larocque and Emmanuel Lavictoire were a pair of farmers, close pals, who lived in french-speaking Ontario on the west bank of the Ottawa River.

The Great Depression was on, and prices for anything a farmer grew were low. But Larocque and Lavictoire seemed to be doing a little better than most of their neighbours.

One morning in March of 1932, the two were threshing some grain that had been stored in Larocque's barn, with the help of Leo Bergeron, a young man who worked at various farms in the area. Leo was a willing worker, but not known around the countryside as overly bright.

The three had only been working a little while when Lavictoire ran to a neighbour's hollering for help and saying something awful had happened with the horses.

The neighbours came at the run and they found young Leo lying on the floor of the barn, barely alive. The horses were standing nearby and there was blood all over. Lavictoire and Larocque said he had stumbled as the horses reared up and had been crushed under their hooves.

Now any farm boy knows that accidents can happen but, generally speaking, horses will go to an awful lot of trouble to avoid stepping on anyone.

Poor Leo had terrible head injuries and was unconscious. The neighbours sent for his father and a doctor.

The father arrived first. When he saw what had happened he accused Lavictoire and Larocque of having murdered his son for insurance. By the time the doctor arrived, Leo was dead.

The cops searched the barn and found a bloodstained handle of a pitchfork. If it had been used to beat young Leo to death, it would have left wounds rather like those from a horse's hooves.

The cops also asked Larocque if there was any truth to what old man Bergeron had said about

> *Larocque denied killing Leo but admitted he had a $5,000 insurance policy on his life. That seemed like a lot of insurance to be paying for, in a time when everybody was short of cash.*

insurance. Larocque denied killing Leo, but he admitted he had a $5,000 insurance policy on his life. He also had policies on himself and his son.

That seemed like a lot of insurance to be paying for, in a time when everybody was short of cash.

As the cops investigated they found that Larocque and Lavictoire were absolute fiends for insurance.

They had tried to take out policies on the lives of two other young men, also farm labourers, also not too bright, the previous year. For some reason, the two had balked at the idea and nothing had come of it.

But, probing even further back, the cops found that Larocque and Lavictoire had put a $10,000 insurance policy on the life of another young man in August of 1930.

The premium had been high, $62.50 a year. But somehow they had come up with the money. Just once.

They never had to pay the second year's premium because two months later the three were in a car on the Quebec side of the river, waiting for a ferry boat, when the car suddenly started to roll and went into the river. Larocque and Lavictoire escaped, but the kid didn't make it.

The trick in solving this case wasn't in figuring out what had happened. That was obvious. The tough part was getting the evidence about the death of the young man at the ferry dock in 1930 admitted into the trial of Lavictoire and Larocque when they were charged with the murder of young Bergeron. That's called similar fact evidence, and Canadian courts are very reluctant to accept it.

For weeks the cops plugged away, interviewing dozens of farmers and merchants and insurance agents.

Finally, they had enough evidence to show a similar pattern of conduct by Larocque and Lavictoire in both cases. It didn't take the jury long to find them guilty.

Late on the night of the 14th of March in 1933, just a year after the young man had died, Lavictoire and Larocque were hanged.

Originally broadcast March 14, 1984

BLOODY CAESAR

Julius Caesar was born in the year 100 BC, a descendent of a noble but poor family. Not dirt poor, like some farmer or sailor. But shabby poor, like someone from a family that had once been much richer. There was enough money for Caesar to have a good education, though.

All his life, one of Caesar's greatest strengths was his ability to get along with people from the far-flung parts of the Roman Empire.

Caesar was given a religious position while he was still very young, a sort of office rather like what a bishop would have in a modern church. Caesar wasn't a religious man, but the job paid very well.

He was married twice when he was still young. Both marriages were arranged and at least one was ordered by older men who were Caesar's bosses. Such marriages didn't bother Caesar. He ignored them. He was one of the most lecherous men of all time. He had literally thousands of affairs, with men and women alike.

While Caesar was still young, he was on a trip by ship on the Aegean when he was captured by pirates. The pirates realized they had an important young man and they held him for ransom.

While the ransom was being delivered, Caesar lived with the pirates. Caesar promised the pirates that when they released him he would put together a gang and come for them. They roared with laughter at that.

Sure enough, as soon as the ransom was paid and Caesar was freed, he hired ships and came back and captured the pirates.

He gave them a fair trial then crucified them all, killed them by nailing them to crosses. But since they'd been good to him while he was their prisoner, he ordered that their throats be cut so they didn't suffer much. What a guy.

Caesar led an army to Britain and added that distant island to the Roman Empire. He fought battles from Persia to Spain. He had affairs with Cleopatra, the queen of Nubia, and dozens of others.

Naturally, he made enemies, mostly among the old aristocratic families. Usually when he defeated an enemy — and he beat them all — he was generous and allowed the enemy to carry out his life as he had before.

Three times the crown was offered and three times Caesar turned it down. He was probably sincere. He said, "I'm no King. I'm Caesar." He really thought that was better than being king.

Caesar laid out cities and drained marshes and built roads and dredged harbors.

In 44 BC, when Caesar was about 56, he was offered the crown as king of Rome. Rome hadn't had a king for centuries. Three times the offer was made and three times Caesar turned it down.

He was probably sincere. He said, "I'm no King. I'm Caesar." He really thought that was better than being king.

But his enemies spread the rumor that he really intended to be king, that the refusal had been all part of a scheme to cover up what he was up to.

On the Ides of March in 44 BC, the 15th of March, a group of assassins stabbed Caesar to death as he sat in his seat in the Senate.

One of the conspirators was Marcus Brutus, a young man Caesar had been very good to. Centuries later, Shakespeare put the words into Caesar's mouth, "You too, Brutus?"

Brutus had been galled by rumors that he was one of Caesar's many illegitimate offspring. What Caesar really said, in Greek, was: "You too, my son?"

Nobody knows if it was a joke or confirmation of the rumors that Brutus hated.

Originally broadcast March 15, 1990

THE REAL THING

On this day, the 16th of March in 1886 in Atlanta, Georgia a druggist named John Pemberton thought of adding two new ingredients to a formula for a headache remedy: an extract of leaves of the coca plant and an extract from the kola nut.

They would eventually give his product its name, Coca-Cola, although Pemberton wouldn't live to see its incredible success.

Coca-Cola is more than just a drink. It's almost a nation. It certainly is an institution.

It employs hundreds of thousands of people all over the world, although no one has the exact count. On any minute of any day, 24 hours a day, all around the world almost 140,000 people are sipping a Coke.

If all the Coke that was ever made was put into regular size bottles and they were stacked one on top of the other, they would reach Mars.

If all the Coke ever made was poured over Niagara Falls, it would take more than 9 hours to flow past.

Coca-Cola has the second-biggest fleet of trucks in the world to deliver its product. Only the American Post Office has more.

All over the world people pay more than $3 billion every year for Coca-Cola.

All this started with a poor sickly man from Georgia named John Styth Pemberton. He had been an officer in the Confederate Army in the Civil War, although he hadn't been well enough for active service.

He appears to have been a bit of a drifter and a dreamer, not a very shrewd businessman, a druggist who was always dabbling with formulas for new patent medicines.

Pemberton produced such patent medicines and cosmetics as Indian Queen Hair Dye, Globe Flower Cough Syrup, Extract of Styllinger, Gingerine and Triplex Liver Pills.

And, most important of all, because it was the direct predecessor of Coca-Cola: Pemberton's Wine of Kola, the Ideal Nerve Tonic.

The Kola nut was said to be a source of quick energy and an aphrodisiac. When that became known in the 1890s. one New York newspaper demanded an investigation by Congress. The state legislature of Virginia actually debated a bill to ban the stuff.

We don't know an awful lot about what happened from the day in March 1886 that Pemberton jotted down his ideas until the finished product emerged a couple of months later. We do know that on that day, Pemberton lit a fire in his backyard over a 15-gallon copper kettle he used for mixing up his medicines and he stirred up the first batch of what would become Coca-Cola, using an old canoe paddle.

It isn't clear whether he was trying to come up with a medicine or a drink. The first advertisements refer to the health-giving qualities of Coca-Cola plus its refreshing taste. Maybe he was just keeping his options open to see how things went.

If all the Coke that was ever made was put into regular size bottles and they were stacked one on top of the other, they would reach Mars.

Pemberton had a book-keeper who wrote a very flowery script and he wrote out Coca-Cola in that fancy flowing trademark writing for the first time. He changed the spelling of kola so it would look nicer.

Pemberton arranged to have his Coca-Cola syrup available at the soda fountain of Jacobs' drug store in Atlanta. He and his employees passed out little tickets on the street, entitling people to one free glass, assuming the stuff tasted so good that they'd be hooked if they ever tried it.

There's quite a bit of caffeine in Coca-Cola and caffeine is bitter, so Pemberton laced the formula quite heavily with sugar. Today Coca-Cola uses 10 per cent of all the sugar refined in the United States and is the world's biggest consumer of sugar.

The summer after he started selling Coke, Pemberton was in financial trouble and he started selling off his rights in it. The following year he died. His family continued to sell off the rights and by 1891 they were gone.

Originally broadcast March 16, 1983

OLIVER TWIT

It seems impossible today to think of England without a king or queen. Three hundred years ago it was even more unlikely because the monarch in those days had an awful lot of power. He ruled, not just reigned.

Less than half a century earlier, Queen Elizabeth the First had died, leaving Britain the most powerful nation on Earth. The Queen, with her power, her prestige, and her political skill, had been the biggest single factor in that position and Englishmen knew it. Yet in 1649 they abolished the monarchy.

First, they abolished the monarch. King Charles the First, grandson of Queen Elizabeth, was beheaded in January of 1649.

Three previous kings had been executed in British history but by the time they had gone they were ex-kings. They had been removed from the throne first. But not Charles. He died a king.

There's not much doubt that he brought on most of his own trouble. He wasn't a good administrator. He was a terrible snob who believed he had been chosen by God, that all kings were, and the people were there to pay whatever taxes he told them to pay and to obey all his orders without question. Mind you, in those days, that wasn't the outrageous idea it is today.

As the king got more repressive, the people got more surly. A few leaders emerged, all good men. The foremost of these was Oliver Cromwell.

Cromwell said he supported the principle of the monarchy but he didn't agree with an unjust monarch. Cromwell later became a terrible man but everything points to his sincerity at that time.

Charles was on the throne, nominally a Protestant, almost certainly a secret Catholic, strongly influenced by his French wife, a rabid Catholic.

Cromwell and the other leaders of the people were puritanical Protestants. When the inevitable clash came in 1642, politics and religion were thoroughly enmeshed and the stage was set for a bloody civil war.

Cromwell and Co. won that one by 1646, although it had hung in the balance for a while. They still insisted they were loyal to the throne, if not to Charles. But

Charles didn't know when he was beaten and he made a secret treaty with the Scots to join with him, invade England and put an end to his enemies.

That led him to a second civil war and when Charles left that one, Parliament put him on trial and signed his death warrant.

When the axe fell on his neck in January of 1649, a tiny ripple of doubt ran through every Englishman's mind.

But doubt was quickly put aside. Cromwell had to lead his army to Ireland, where there was rebellion. That was put down with terrible cruelty and slaughter.

Then another rebellion was started in Scotland and Cromwell went north and put an end to that. That was led by Charles' son, Charles the Second. Charles the Second fled to France.

Now Cromwell was in command. Parliament voted him a hefty salary and gave him one of the king's palaces.

Cromwell was entitled Lord Protector and he became a worse tyrant than the king.

Catholics had two thirds of their land taken from them and Anglican clergymen were turned out of their churches.

All this was done by Parliament, the foundation of British liberty, at the order of Cromwell, the decent, sincere, God-fearing Puritan. In 1653, Cromwell called in his soldiers and abolished the parliament that had abolished the monarchy. Parliament wasn't going along with everything he wanted.

Cromwell was entitled Lord Protector and he became a worse tyrant than the king. Theatres were abolished. No one was allowed to eat meat on a Wednesday. Christmas was considered a Catholic holiday and no one was allowed to recognize it. People were arrested for swearing. No one was allowed to travel on a Sunday.

Cromwell, the man who put an end to royalty, named his son to succeed him.

When Cromwell died in 1658, his son couldn't handle the mess his father had left. He quit. A year and half after Cromwell died, the British people asked Charles the Second to come home from France and occupy the throne his father was dragged from 30 years before.

Originally broadcast March 17, 1983

UNDER THE VOLCANO

Vesuvius is the most famous volcano in the world for two reasons: it's on the Bay of Naples, which has been populated for longer than we can remember so every time it blows up there's somebody there to see and write about it; and its most famous explosion in the year 79 AD led to a revolution in the study of the history of Rome.

At that time the Bay of Naples was a resort area for rich Romans. Julius Caesar's favorite girlfriend, the mother of Brutus, the man who stabbed Caesar, had a villa there. So did the great Roman writer and historian Pliny. And dozens of others. It had a greater concentration of celebrities of the day than Hollywood has today.

That time, a jet of hot air and flame and gas shot straight up in the air for thousands of feet then flattened out. It formed a mushroom-shaped cloud, rather like the one that was caused by the first atomic bombs in 1945. That cloud has thus been a symbol of doom and terrible power for centuries.

That blast went on for a week. It didn't produce streams of molten rock like you see on TV when a Hawaiian volcano explodes. At Vesuvius the lava came down in blobs. We don't know for sure how many people lived in the villages on the Bay of Naples. But 16,000 were killed.

Maybe not a lot fled. As the eruption went on after several days it began to produce two new things: a cloud of deadly gas that killed people instantly, and a mixture of volcanic ash and lava, what geologists call volcanic paste. That paste landed on everything and everybody still around. And it hardened almost instantly.

The result was that three Roman villages were frozen, along with their inhabitants. Centuries later people began excavating, mostly looking for buried treasure. That excavation is still going on. On the basis of it, historians now know more about daily life in Rome than about any other ancient culture.

The volcanic paste preserved people, animals, loaves baking in ovens, wine sealed in jars, graffiti scrawled on walls...all the artifacts and activities of 16,000 people.

That was just one of 30 eruptions of Vesuvius, although by far the most famous. But not the deadliest. The one in 1631 killed 2000 more people than the one in 79.

The eruption of 1793 went on for six months. Lava flowed like a river at that one, in fact like 15 separate rivers. It ran down to the sea and was so hot that the sea was boiling 100 feet out from the shore.

The British ambassador to Naples, Sir William Hamilton, was fascinated by it and spent days watching it. Maybe that's why he was too busy to notice that his wife was having an affair with the greatest British admiral of them all, Lord Nelson.

> *For six months, lava flowed like a river, in fact like 15 separate rivers. It ran down to the sea and was so hot that the sea was boiling 100 feet out from the shore.*

The people who live under Vesuvius insist upon returning after every eruption. The eruption of 1632 followed almost exactly the same pattern as the one of 79. The village of Torre de Greco has been wiped out several times. The city of Naples hasn't been damaged, although one time the lava flowed right up to the city gates.

Naturally, the priests and religious citizens say after each eruption that it's God's vengeance on the sinful people of Naples, a notoriously bad place. The Neapolitans just wink and say, "Naples sins, Torre suffers."

The last eruption of any note occurred during the last war when Vesuvius erupted on the 18th of March in 1944. About a hundred people were killed. But hundreds more were dying at the time from bombs.

Originally broadcast March 18, 1992

THE NASTIEST NAZI

Adolph Eichmann made no splash when he was born on the 19th of March in 1906. And very little was heard of him for the next 30-odd years. Yet today we remember him as one of the most thoroughly evil men of all time.

Eichmann did nothing noteworthy with his early years. But in the late 20s and early 30s, when Germany was destitute and Hitler was plotting for power, Eichmann joined the Nazis.

From then on, he was headed for the top and fast. Eichmann was never a soldier. But he was an excellent clerk, an administrator. When Hitler and his cronies assumed power in the mid-30s, Eichmann joined their elite military corps, the SS. The SS was in charge of carrying out Hitler's plans for getting rid of the Jews and various other races that he considered sub-human.

And that's where Eichmann proved to be a genius. Extermination camps were set up, mostly in eastern Europe, especially Poland.

Hundreds of thousands of people, mostly Jews, were shipped to these camps, where they were murdered and their bodies destroyed.

Eichmann, a cold, efficient planner, was in charge of the paperwork. He was all too successful. Two-thirds of all the Jews in Europe, probably about six million were murdered, along with millions of others.

Eichmann never pulled a trigger himself. But he supervised it all. It was his idea to cut off his victims' hair and use it to stuff mattresses, to pull out gold teeth and melt them down, to render bodies to make soap.

When the world woke up from the Nazi nightmare in 1945, Eichmann was high on everybody's list of war criminals. But he disappeared.

We know now that thousands of Nazis escaped from Europe to South America, many helped by such unlikely organizations as the American Army and the Vatican. In those days, everyone was more concerned with stopping communism than with punishing the monsters who had killed millions.

Eichmann had false papers and was actually under arrest by the Americans for a while but they let him go, thinking he was just an ordinary soldier.

The Israelis had set up an organization to catch Nazis. The toughest and the smartest of their investigators was a Polish Jew named Tuvia Friedmann, a man who had just escaped a Nazi firing squad by a few minutes.

Friedmann was a very successful Nazi-catcher, a man who didn't hesitate to use Nazi methods. He was the first to admit one of his best ways of getting information was to beat it out of prisoners. The Israeli government just about disowned him because of his methods. But Friedmann ignored the orders from above. Without authorization, he announced that the Israeli government would pay $10,000 US for information about high-ranking Nazis.

It worked. A blind Jew living in Argentina wrote Friedmann to say his daughter was going out with a German boy and he had figured out that the boy's father was Adolph Eichmann.

Friedmann sent a team to check out the story. Sure enough, it was true. Eichmann was kidnapped and flown to Israel where he was tried and hanged, 17 years after the war was over.

Eichmann never pulled a trigger himself. But it was his idea to cut off his victims' hair and use it to stuff mattresses, to pull out gold teeth and melt them down, to render bodies to make soap.

Originally broadcast March 19, 1984

A LITERARY MASTER-PIECE

Harriet Beecher was born in New England in 1811, the daughter of a famous preacher. Her whole life would be based on deep religion, right up to her death at the age of 85.

Harriet's younger brother, Henry, would become an even more famous preacher than her father. Years later, he would be involved in a scandal bigger than anything in these days of sinning TV evangelists. Henry loved his fellow man. But his fellow woman more.

Harriet met a young clergyman who was a great admirer of her father's, Calvin Stowe. She married him and she has become famous all over the world by her married name: Harriet Beecher Stowe.

Calvin Stowe was a nice man, very religious and a great scholar. He taught at divinity colleges. But he never made much money.

Harriet had a talent for writing, mostly stuff for religious and young people's magazines. She had to do something to make money to supplement Calvin's meagre income. And they had seven kids.

Harriet's father had been a leader in the New England anti-slavery movement and she was brought up to believe that slavery was evil. It was legal, of course, in the southern States in those days, although the New England anti-slavery movement had been campaigning against it for years.

Harriet was living in Maine in the winter of 1850 when her brother Henry, the preacher, came by on one of his lecture tours. Calvin was away teaching at a divinity college in Ohio. Henry and Harriet sat up most of the night talking about religion and slavery. Harriet had often said she would write a book about it but had never got around to it. Henry urged her to do it.

Harriet said she'd think about it. A couple of months later she was sitting in church, her mind wandering. Harriet daydreamed about a black man, a slave in the south, who tried to escape but was chased and caught and beaten to death by his master.

A couple of days later, she wrote some of that daydream into a little story. When her husband came back from his teaching he looked at the story and told her she had to keep writing it. Actually, to go back. She had written the end of the story, but not the beginning.

> *Harriet daydreamed about a black man, a slave in the south, who tried to escape but was chased and caught and beaten to death by his master.*

While Harriet wrote the story she also sent a letter to a magazine publisher she knew. He agreed to run the story in serial installments.

That drew so much response that Calvin spoke to a Boston publisher he knew. The publisher didn't show much enthusiasm for the project.

But he said he would publish the magazine installments in book form when they were all finished. He offered to give the Stowes half the profit if they would put up some money for the printing. They didn't have money. So instead, Harriet settled for 10 per cent of sales.

The publisher told her, with any luck, she might get enough out of the effort to buy herself a silk dress.

On the 20th of March in 1852, he ran off 5000 copies. They were gone in a week. He ran off another 10,000. They were gone in less than a month. He ran off 100,000. They were snapped up.

Harriet Beecher Stowe had written *Uncle Tom's Cabin*, one of the best-sellers of all time.

Originally broadcast March 20, 1989

MAKING MONEY

John Law was either the greatest con-man or the greatest banker who ever lived. Maybe both.

John Law was a Scotsman, born in 1671, the son of a money lender who was very rich. Law's father died when he was 14 and left him two big country estates. Law was tall, handsome, charming and a genius with figures.

He was also a bit of a whiz with the ladies. He moved to London and got involved with several women at once. He married the daughter of an earl. He fought a duel over another woman and killed a man and had to get out of England.

So he travelled around Europe for another 7 years, gambling, living well and accumulating another fortune. All the time, he was trying to interest kings and prime ministers in his ideas about credit.

People would only trust coins of gold and silver, occasionally brass. Law had a theory that if a king issued paper money and backed it with gold, after a while people would get used to it. Then the king could crank up the press and issue a lot of money.

If that sounds familiar, it's how the governments of every country operate today. But back then it was too radical an idea.

Then the king of France died and his brother, an old friend of Law's, became the regent. Law returned to France and got the regent interested in his theory. The king who had just died, Louis XIV, had left the country bankrupt.

Law came up with a complicated formula for issuing bonds, some backed by gold, some backed by faith. The faith belonged to the people who accepted the bonds, thinking they were backed by gold. As long as other people would accept them for the value printed on them, everything worked fine. Law had, in effect, put paper money into circulation. Credit was created and commerce prospered.

Law was given various things by the regent, including the monopoly for the Canadian fur trade for a while.

Then Law decided to add another dimension to his scheme. He created what he called the Mississippi Company to build cities and farms along the length of the Mississippi River which belonged to France in those days. Or, at least, the French government claimed it did.

Law came up with a complicated formula for issuing bonds, some backed by gold, some backed by faith. The faith belonged to the people who accepted the bonds, thinking they were backed by gold.

People bought shares in the company and Law, in return, gave the government enough money to pay off the national debt. Of course, the national debt had been created in gold and Law paid off in paper. But nobody noticed that at the time.

Law's scheme seemed to be so foolproof that it created a panic unlike any on a modern stock exchange. One day, so many people lined up and tried to get into Law's office that three or four were killed in the rush.

Fortunes were made overnight. So many people became so rich that a new word had to be invented to describe them: it was millionaire.

Then, somebody started to ask questions. Law didn't have the answers. The next day the rush on Law's office was even bigger than before. Sixteen were killed in that rush.

Law fled the country and never went back to France. The regent set fire to all the papers involved and declared the economy was just fine. Anybody who said otherwise was a traitor. And the penalty for treason was death. Nobody complained.

Law died in exile in Venice on the 21st of March in 1729, aged only 58. Before his death, he was making a very good living offering odds of 20,000 to one against anyone ever throwing 12 with a pair of dice six times in a row.

Originally broadcast March 21, 1988

LORD STANLEY'S CUP

Considering that people are willing to die to get the Stanley Cup these days, it sure got off to a shaky start.

Lord Stanley was governor-general in the late 1880s and early 1890s. Hockey was a fairly popular game in Canada in those days but it wasn't the national obsession it's since become.

However, Lord Stanley's two oldest boys, the Honorable Algernon Stanley and the Honorable Arthur Stanley, became hockey nuts. They nagged some of the British officers on their father's staff into forming a team, the Rideau Rebels and they played on a rink they had built behind Rideau Hall.

They wore flame-red sweaters and were pretty good. Not necessarily gentlemanly, but good. They travelled to Toronto to play a team there in the early 1890s and the next day the newspapers were full of reports of what a brawl had resulted.

Toronto sportswriters expected that sort of thing from the farmboys and lumberjacks who played the game. But they were shocked to see real British officers and gentlemen so free with the fists and elbows.

When his lordship's term as governor-general was up in 1892 he returned to London. There the Stanley boys introduced the game to the royal family.

The two hockey-playing Stanleys and their three young brothers and another lord played a team of royals that included two future kings — Edward the Seventh and George the Fifth.

That bit of royal approval so delighted Lord Stanley that he wrote back to Canada, saying he thought the game should have a suitable symbol for the best team in the country. He paid about $50 to have a silver cup made and he appointed two Ottawa men as trustees.

The two looked over the records of the major teams in the spring of 1893. They ordered the Ottawa team to travel to Toronto and play the team from Osgoode Hall law school for the cup. For some reason, the Ottawa team refused. Maybe they didn't want to play with lawyers.

So the trustees looked over the records of the major teams in the country and awarded the first Stanley Cup to the Montreal Triple-As, a team that had only had one loss all season. That's not quite as impressive as it sounds today because the season only consisted of eight games back then.

So the first Stanley Cup went without a game. The next year, on the 22nd of March, 1894, that same Montreal team beat Ottawa 3-1 to take the second Stanley Cup, the first that was played for.

Lord Stanley, of course, had only amateur hockey in mind when he donated his cup. But within a dozen years it was clear that the players for most of the major teams in the country were getting paid, either officially or under the table.

So in 1909, 16 years after Lord Stanley donated his cup, Sir Montague Allen of Montreal came up with the Allen cup, strictly for amateurs.

> *Lord Stanley wrote back to Canada, saying he thought the game should have a suitable symbol for the best team in the country. He paid about $50 to have a silver cup made.*

Originally broadcast March 22, 1984

MELBA THE MUCKRAKER

Nellie Mitchell was an Australian, born in the city of Melbourne in 1861. She had one of the greatest soprano voices in history.

Nellie studied for a while with an Italian opera coach who lived in Australia. He told her she would have to go to Europe to study and make her name and nobody in the world of opera would take her seriously as long as her name was Mitchell. So she took the name of her hometown and made it into something Italian-sounding: Nellie Melba.

By the time Melba got to Europe, she was married to a rough, tough cowboy named Armstrong and had a little boy. An opera singer and a cowboy aren't the most likely ingredients of the ideal marriage. To make it even more difficult, Nellie and her husband each had terrible tempers.

So it wasn't long before they split up. Nellie didn't go lonely for long. She took up with the Duc d'Orleans, the next in line to the throne of France. Of course, France hadn't had a king for almost a hundred years at that time. But that didn't matter to the sort of people who hung around opera houses.

Melba took the European opera world by storm. Nobody had ever heard a soprano voice like hers and the experts still say she was probably the best. Queen Victoria, who was quite an opera fan, had Melba do many command performances. Then Melba's husband named the Duc d'Orleans as co-respondent when he filed for divorce. From then on, Melba was cut out of the royal programs.

Melba was always careful to not be too helpful to young sopranos who were coming along unless they were clearly never going to be good enough to be competition. She once grabbed the Irish singer John McCormack and pushed him into the wings as they headed out for a curtain call. "Nobody shares my

Melba was a curious combination of the temperamental European diva and the Australian tomboy. That made her a favorite with reporters.

curtain calls," she said.

Melba was a curious combination of the temperamental European diva and the Australian tomboy. That made her a favorite with reporters. She loved publicity but she knew she had to be careful.

No matter how an interview went, it always ended up with reporters wanting some details about the affair between her and the French duke. Melba would smoothly change the subject. That's what happened on the 23rd of March in 1901. When the reporter got the subject around to the duke, Melba started talking about food.

Thinking quickly, Melba said her favorite food was toast. She sliced the bread paper thin then baked it until it was crisp. She was such a big name at the time that several bakeries followed her recipe and called it Melba Toast, and that's what she's remembered for today. On some menus you'll also see Peach Melba. It's an unusually sweet concoction that doesn't fit in very well with today's tastes.

For someone worried about her image, Melba got into a lot of public scrapes. A drunken Australian publisher, out to hype his circulation, once started the rumor that she was a drunk. Whenever Melba couldn't make a performance or whenever she was late, her fans from then on figured she was too boozed to make the curtain on time. In actual fact, she didn't drink much.

A fellow opera star wrote in a book of her memoirs that Melba had advised her in England that when she returned to Australia she should be careful to keep her program quite unsophisticated. "Feed 'em muck," she said, "that's all they understand."

The Australians loved her for it. They called her back curtain call after curtain call, often shouting, "Great Nellie, give us more muck."

Originally broadcast March 23, 1992

GOOD-BYE QUEEN BESS

On this day, the 24th of March in 1603, the Elizabethan age came to an end. Queen Elizabeth the First, Good Queen Bess, died and an age died with her. Under Queen Elizabeth, Englishmen had laid the foundation for the greatest empire the world would see. But before there could be much built on that foundation, England had to go through a lot of turmoil.

The really remarkable thing about Queen Elizabeth's reign was that it was so stable. The years before had been bloody with the kingdom on the edge of civil war all the time. The years that followed did produce a civil war.

But between those turbulent times, Queen Elizabeth ruled over a kingdom that was sufficiently stable at home to be able to look abroad and to expand in a very few years into a world power.

The people liked Elizabeth. She was beautiful, witty, and had a sense of showmanship that attracted the average guy.

On her coronation day in January of 1559, she wore a dress of white, gold, and red, and had long red hair streaming down her back. She rode through the streets of London, packed with cheering crowds. Tears rolled down her cheeks and her subjects' cheeks too.

Queen Elizabeth said, "I care not for myself. My care is for my people." All rulers say that, of course. But she meant it. The people called her Good Queen Bess.

She could be ill-tempered and swore like a sailor. She could be fickle and banish yesterday's favorite to the corner of the kingdom. But nobody ever doubted Elizabeth put England first.

She was 25 when she became queen. She never married and became known to history as the Virgin Queen. Virginia was named after her as British sailors explored the world and started grabbing bits of it for the mother country.

But nobody who knew her took that Virgin title too seriously. She was too lusty for that. She had a few lovers but stopped short of marriage.

She flirted with several kings and princes, always with a view to putting together alliances and partnerships that would help her country.

When Elizabeth came to the throne the country was torn by fear, hatred and religious strife. She put an end to that. She was a Protestant monarch and head of the Church of England. But, aside from that formality, she didn't get too excited by how her subjects thought or prayed.

Queen Elizabeth said, "I care not for myself. My care is for my people." All rulers say that, of course. But she meant it.

Under her, British literature flowered as never before. Shakespeare, Marlowe, Milton . . . dozens of the greats wrote pretty well what they pleased in England while the rest of Europe was always under some kind of censorship.

When Elizabeth became queen, Spain was the greatest country in the world. Thirty years after her reign began the Spanish tried to invade England. They had the mightiest fleet the world had seen. But the Elizabethan spirit was part of England now and an important part of Englishmen. Britain's navy was small but good. The British ships beat the Spanish Armada and England was secure for centuries.

Old age wasn't kind to Elizabeth. The flaming red hair of her youth fell out. She wore awful red wool wigs. Her teeth were bad. Her complexion was awful so she wore chalky white make-up. When all that didn't work, she had every mirror removed from the palace.

She was well on in years when the earl of Essex made a play for her. She fell in love but wouldn't share her throne with him. He lost patience and tried an armed rebellion. It must have broken the queen's heart but she signed his death warrant.

In 1603, on the 24th of March, two years after she'd had Essex beheaded, she realized her time had come. She just took to her bed and died.

Originally broadcast March 24, 1983

QUEEN OF THE STAGE

Sarah Bernhardt is one of the most famous names in modern history. But she is just that, a name. She is remembered as the very best actress of all time.

She was almost 80 when she died in 1923. In fact, she might have been over 80. She lied so often about her age that no one knows how old she was.

The movies were well advanced in her later years and, while she was still on the stage, she made a couple. Adolph Zukor, the Hollywood director, made a biography of Queen Elizabeth in 1912 which starred Bernhardt. It was hailed as a masterpiece at the time but few people seem to have even seen so much as a scene or two from it.

Bernhardt's attempts at English were always amusing, so much so that we have to wonder if she didn't deliberately screw up our language. She would do anything for publicity. When Queen Elizabeth was first shown, Bernhardt gushed to Zukor, "For all time you have taken the best of me and, ah, ah, ah, how you say? Pickled it."

In the 1860s and 70s, when Bernhardt was the hottest thing that ever hit Paris show business, ballooning was the fad. Bernhardt, who would do anything to get a couple of inches in the papers, went ballooning. The manager of the theatre where she was working nearly fainted. Ballooning was very dangerous, like hanggliding is today, and he would have lost millions if anything had happened to her.

He fined Bernhardt a thousand francs. In those days, theatre managers were allowed by law to do things like that. Bernhardt just didn't show up at the theatre that night and the manger was soon at her place with an armful of roses, saying he was only kidding.

Any time Bernhardt ran into expenses like that, a dozen rich men appeared from nowhere, begging for the honour of whipping out their chequebooks and

Any time Bernhardt ran into expenses, a dozen rich men appeared, begging for the honour of whipping out their chequebooks and taking care of the situation. Bernhardt was so soft-hearted she often let them all do it.

taking care of the situation. Bernhardt was so soft-hearted she often let them all do it.

She made $50,000 a year and spent $100,000 a month. But she never had trouble making ends meet.

Bernhardt's love life was incredible. She had a long succession of lovers, usually one at a time, not always. If one turned out to be playing around, she would take a horsewhip to him and whoever the other girl was.

When a couple of her lovers would fight over her, Bernhardt would show up at the Bois de Boulogne, the traditional duelling ground in Paris, and watch the duel from her carriage. A bit of blood was shed by these men but no one was seriously hurt.

Some writers have suggested that her lovers knew of the thrill the duels gave her and they staged more than one to keep her happy.

Bernhardt was obsessed with blood and death. During an American tour, she was taken to see the slaughterhouses in Chicago and went back day after day. She couldn't get enough.

She was so concerned with her funeral that she bought her coffin years in advanced and liked to sleep in it.

In 1886, on her way back by ship from a tour of South Africa, she fell and injured her right knee. For 29 years the pain was terrible until the leg was finally amputated.

On the 25th of March in 1923, Bernhardt knew she was dying. She wanted to look just right. So she had her son cover her with roses, lilacs and violets, then called a priest to give her the Last Rites.

Her tombstone, she specified, should be classically simple with only one word carved on it: Bernhardt.

Originally broadcast March 25, 1986

THE MELANCHOLY MAESTRO

Maybe the greatest musical genius of all time was Ludwig van Beethoven, a sloppy, ugly, discontent man who had the soul of a great lover but, when it came to making it with the girls, seems to have struck out.

He was Ludwig *van* Beethoven, not *von* Beethoven. And that turned out to be important. If he'd been a von Beethoven back in those days, in the Germany of the late 1700s and early 1800s, that would have indicated he was a nobleman. The van just indicated he was from a family that originally came from the Lowlands.

All his life that bothered Beethoven. He had a rough life because he was born poor. Others had easy lives because their fathers had money or titles. Beethoven was a rebel on that account. But not an attractive one. He was a brooder, a melancholy man.

For a while his hero was Napoleon, the man who was going to free Europe and bring about a better world. But when Napoleon turned out to be a power-mad tyrant, Beethoven turned bitter about that too.

Beethoven was born in Bonn, Germany, the son and grandson of professional musicians. They both worked for the local duke at his court and that involved a lot of bowing and scraping. Beethoven in later life often made a big show of not taking off his hat or bowing when a nobleman came into the room. He could have carried it off with a bit of dash and good humor. Instead, he was just surly about it and irritated a lot of decent people who wanted to be his friends.

Papa Beethoven put young Ludwig to work at the piano and the violin, hoping to make him into a child prodigy who could solve all his financial problems. Mozart's father had done that and it had worked.

It didn't work in Beethoven's case. The result was an unhappy young man whose regular schooling ended when he was 10 and a father who ended up the town drunk. Beethoven never handled booze very well either, and had a reputation as a man who dipped into it too often.

However, he was such a mass of medical problems that it's hard to say just where his basic trouble lay. He had ulcers, a bad liver, and, worst of all, from the time he was 30, increasing deafness. His greatest triumph, his Ninth Symphony, was first played when Beethoven was stone deaf. When it was over a friend had to take him by the shoulder and turn him around to face the audience so he could see them cheering wildly.

Beethoven wrote music that defied the conventions of the times, just like the man himself. If he felt a melody in him he wrote it, ignoring the stylized forms and structures of what the experts said a symphony should be.

Beethoven's music defied the conventions of the times, just like the man himself. If he felt a melody in him he wrote it, ignoring the stylized forms and structures of what experts said a symphony should be.

He and his friends were packrats and they kept every letter and note they ever wrote. The result is that historians and biographers have scads of material to work with.

Someone once counted up the numbers of biographies that have been written about great men and it turned out that only Shakespeare, Napoleon, and Julius Caesar have been written about more.

Yet for all that, we don't know just what went on in the mind of this genius. He was always falling in love with rich, titled women he couldn't have. Maybe Freud would say he didn't really want them.

For all his genius, Beethoven never made much money. He had a nephew he loved like a son and he spent years in the courts fighting the boy's mother for custody. Eventually he failed at that.

The final disease that carried him off was dropsy. He had been bed-ridden and in pain for four months. Then, just about suppertime on the 26th of March in 1827, there was a strange storm in Vienna, where Beethoven lived. It rained, snowed and hailed all at once. Then, there was one terrible clap of thunder. Beethoven sat up in bed, shook his fist and fell back dead.

Originally broadcast March 26, 1985

CAPITAL CALAMITY

When Canada became a nation in 1867, the man who made it all possible, John A. Macdonald, had a dream of one country from the Atlantic to the Pacific. The only way that would work — and it was a long shot — was to run a railway from central Canada to the west coast.

That, of course, meant crossing the Prairies. In 1865 Macdonald had described the Prairies as having no value to Canada. The British government sent out an expedition to assess the west and reported back that what's now southern Saskatchewan was useless desert, unfit for human habitation.

There had been quite a bit of Metis settlement in Saskatchewan, along the Saskatchewan River, around where Saskatoon and Prince Albert and Batoche are. But nobody seemed charmed by the flat, treeless southern part, the part that runs along the American border.

Except the engineers who had to lay out the railway that Macdonald wanted to pin his pieces of country together. You don't have to spend any time in engineering school to know that it's easier, cheaper and faster to run a railway along flat, treeless country than through forests and around hills and over rivers.

In 1875, when the Canadian government created the Northwest Territories, the capital was set at Fort Livingston, a Mountie post on the Swan River, north of the flat Prairies. But Fort Livingston was too far east, near the Manitoba border, away from the centre of population. So in 1877, the capital was moved to Battleford on the Saskatchewan River.

Macdonald wished the new government well and sent it the oak table from Ottawa that had been used to sign the papers that made Confederation official. The table was six feet wide and 15 and a half feet long and had to be carried in a Red River cart from Winnipeg. So it meant a lot of sweat and huffing and puffing for somebody.

Anyway, the engineers pointed out that their railway would be closer to the border, on the flat country. That meant the capital should be there, too.

A smart British Columbia politician had made a fortune some years earlier when he somehow learned that the railway would reach the Pacific where Port Moody is today. His name was Edward Dewdney and he went on in politics. In the 1880s, Dewdney was made lieutenant governor of the Northwest Territories.

So when the capital was to be moved again, down south to the railway, Dewdney either helped decide where it would be or was very close to those who did. Historians still argue over which.

Dewdney bought up a lot of land cheap at a point on the Prairie called Pile o Bones. There was a mountain of buffalo bones left there by hunters going back generations.

Suddenly Pile o Bones became the capital of the Northwest Territories. But you can't have a capital with a name like that. Someone had to come up with a new name.

Suddenly Pile o Bones became the capital. But you can't have a capital with a name like that. Everybody in public life in those days was big on the queen, so it was decided to name the place Victoria. But there already was a Victoria in British Columbia.

The wife of the governor-general in Ottawa happened to be the daughter of Queen Victoria and she suggested the Latin word for queen: Regina.

So when Pile o Bones became the capital of the Northwest Territories on the 27th of March in 1883, it was called Regina.

Everybody was so delighted with the clever princess they decided to name the western half of the territories after her. Her name was Louise. But North America already had one Louisiana. So they used her second name: Alberta.

Originally broadcast March 27, 1990

THE TERRIBLE CZAR

The early history of Russia is an awful muddle with one czar following another, sometimes at intervals of only a few years or months, all with long, unpronounceable names. But one stands out from the crowd — Ivan the Terrible.

Everyone knows he was the ruler of Russia and a very bad man. But not many people are aware of just what a rotten person he was.

We're told that the Grand Duke Vasily the Third was tired of his wife and wanted to send her away to a nunnery so he could take up with a Lithuanian beauty named Helena. The archbishop of Moscow is supposed to have said: "If you do this wicked thing you will have a wicked son, rivers of blood will flow, and your cities will be devoured by flames."

It sounds like the stuff that legends are made of. Or, the sort of story that is made up years later to explain events that have since occurred.

Whether that story is true or not, Duke Vasily did indeed get rid of his wife and marry Helena and they had a boy named Ivan. The duke died soon afterwards, probably poisoned.

Helena was a very tough lady. She managed to gather around her enough strong men to form a council of regents to rule Russia with her boy Ivan, still a kid, as the czar, on paper at least.

This was in the 1530s, about the time that Henry the Eighth was growing up in England. But Russia was in no way like England. The czar was supposed to rule the country the way the king did in England. But, in practice, no one was sure who was in charge. The nobles, called the boyards, had more power than the czar, although they were always fighting among themselves.

While young Czar Ivan was growing up, the country was almost in a state of civil war with two factions of boyards constantly at each others' throats. Ivan was ignored most days, some days actually mistreated. The result was a young man who became quite strange, then eventually quite crazy.

He enjoyed taking dogs up to the top of walls of the Kremlin then dropping them onto the pavement below. Another of his favorite sports was to ride his horse along a crowded street to see how many people he could kill.

Ivan seems to have been a very intelligent young man at first. He studied the bible and could recite it for hours. Suddenly, when he was 17, he asserted his power and became czar in fact as well in name.

From that time on, he ran Russia. But he was getting crazier. He would howl at the moon and pull handfuls of hair out of his beard. He married a girl called Anastasia and she seemed to control him. He really loved her. But when she died while still young, there was no more control on Ivan and he won the name The Terrible.

He ordered the execution of thousands of people. He designed a huge frying pan and one of his favorite sports was to watch people being cooked on it.

He carried a short spear with an iron point and he could stab anyone who offended him. And he was easily offended.

The only person he appeared to love was his son, young Ivan, who he expected would succeed him. But one day he got into an argument with his daughter-in-law, young Ivan's wife. Young Ivan spoke up in defence of his wife and Ivan the Terrible poked him in the head with his spear. Young Ivan died after lingering for five days.

That really sent Ivan the Terrible around the bend. The whole of Russia heaved a sigh of relief when he finally died on the 28th of March in 1584, crazy, lonely, and afflicted with some terrible disease that rotted his flesh while he was still alive.

> *Ivan carried a short spear with an iron point and he could stab anyone who offended him. And he was easily offended.*

Originally broadcast March 28, 1985

NO BUSINESS LIKE SHOW BUSINESS

Annie Get Your Gun was the only show ever produced by Rodgers and Hammerstein that they didn't write.

A brother and sister writing team, Dorothy and Herbert Fields, got the idea of doing a musical on the life of Annie Oakley, the sharpshooter in the Buffalo Bill wild west show.

They intended the show to be called *Annie Oakley*. Rodgers and Hammerstein had done plenty of Broadway hits themselves, but they thought it would be an easier life to sit back and hire others to do the writing and composing.

Jerome Kern, one of the great popular composers of all time, was hired to write the music. But he died before he could get started.

Rodgers and Hammerstein went to Irving Berlin instead. Berlin wasn't very enthusiastic at first. But when Dorothy Fields said she had got her friend, Ethel Merman, to sing in the show, Berlin got interested. "I like her voice," he said, "they can hear all my lyrics in the balcony when Ethel sings."

The story is simple but a perfect vehicle for a musical love story. Annie Oakley is the star of the wild west show, the best shot in show business. She falls for Frank Butler, who is also a showbiz sharpshooter.

But Frank is enough of a male chauvinist to not be in love with Annie as long as she can outshoot him. So, to get her man, Annie lets Frank beat her in a shooting contest although she and the audience know he's not quite as good as she is.

Rodgers was afraid he would have trouble working with Berlin because the two of them were both musical geniuses and it could have been a case of too many cooks in one small kitchen.

But it didn't work out that way. Rodgers later told an interviewer he knew at the end of a week everything would turn out all right because Berlin started chain-smoking, a sure sign that he had all his problems under control.

In all, Berlin wrote 19 new songs for that show. One, a duet entitled *Anything You Can Do I Can Do Better*, was written in 10 minutes while Berlin was taking a taxi to the theatre.

When the show opened in New Haven, Connecticut, on the 29th of March in 1946, it was a hit from the start. Three songs from the show were on the hit parade simultaneously for 10 weeks in a row.

Aside from the millions the show, reruns, road shows, records and the movie brought in, *Annie* made fortunes for others too. Perry Como sold more than a million with his record of *They Say It's Wonderful*. Dinah Shore sold more than a million copies of her version of *Doin' What Comes Naturally*.

When *Annie* reached Broadway, it broke all records by running 1147 performances. That record stood until *My Fair Lady* broke it more than 10 years later.

And, of course, one hit from that show has stood by itself as the anthem for a whole industry, *There's No Business Like Show Business*.

> *When* Annie Get Your Gun *opened in New Haven, Connecticut, it was a hit from the start. Three songs from the show were on the hit parade simultaneously for 10 weeks in a row.*

Originally broadcast March 29, 1983

THE DREARY DUTCHMAN

Vincent Van Gogh was probably the most brilliant of the modern artists. Alas, he was quite unstable, a melancholy, masochistic man who was a terrible trial to his friends and family and who killed himself while he was still a young man.

Yet from this short, sad life came the beginning of what we call modern art — the Fauves, Post-Impressionists, the German Expressionists . . . all the major modern movements in art either sprang from Van Gogh's work or coincided with it.

Vincent Van Gogh was born on the 30th of March in 1853 in Holland. His father was a clergyman and his uncles were successful art dealers.

Van Gogh was a short, heavy-chested man with red hair and freckles. He considered himself ugly. His father was a handsome man but not a very talented preacher.

His mother was a plain woman who had a strong and unfortunate effect on Vincent. She had the legendary Dutch preoccupation with cleanliness. Vincent started off that way. But as his mental problems increased, he became deliberately dirty and messy and his mother nagged him about it. Vincent was already paranoid about most things so his mother's nagging made it all the worse.

Vincent went to work in his uncles' art business and seemed at first to be doing all right. The uncles were quite rich and if he'd stuck to that business he would have done all right. But Vincent didn't like getting dressed up to meet people every day. And he didn't have much in the way of personal charm.

He quit, or was fired, and started to study religion like his father. Vincent didn't want to become a conventional preacher. He wanted to be an evangelist and live and work among the poor. But when the inspectors from the theology college came around to see how he was doing, they were appalled by his dirtiness. So he was dropped from the college.

At that point, when he was about 25, Van Gogh took up art. He had little contact with his family or friends. He made friends easily but his friendships didn't last because he was so erratic.

Vincent kept in touch with his younger brother, Theo, who worked in the art business and slipped him money. The letters Vincent wrote Theo have been read and reread for years by psychiatrists who use them to trace Vincent's mental decline.

Vincent worked furiously at his art. He studied and practiced the basics until he mastered them. Then he did a series of gloomy, dull-colored paintings. He was obsessed with the dreariness of life.

The dreary Dutch climate had an awful effect on him. He moved to the south of France and became more optimistic. The vivid colors in his paintings show that he was dropping his dreariness.

He moved to the south of France and became more optimistic. The vivid colors in his paintings show that he was dropping his dreariness. But his basic mental instability was always with him.

But his basic mental instability was always with him. He had fallen in love with a girl while he was working briefly in London when he was still in the art business. She had turned him down and he had awful relations with women ever after.

He lived for a while with an unattractive, dim-witted prostitute before he moved to the south of France.

While there, Vincent developed a passion named Rachel who didn't have any feeling for him at all. In a fit of depression he sliced off part of his ear with a razor and presented it to her. We don't know if that changed her feelings for Vincent.

But it was an indication that his mental instability was becoming even more serious. Theo arranged for Vincent to be supervised by a doctor but they couldn't watch him all the time. One day he slipped away into a field and somehow got a gun. He shot himself in the chest. The wound was fatal and the doctors couldn't do anything for him. It took Vincent more than a day to die. He just lay quietly and puffed on his pipe. He smiled from time to time. Maybe he knew things could only get better.

Originally broadcast March 30, 1989

THE GRAVITY GUY

Isaac Newton was a genius as great as Shakespeare, maybe even greater. But his genius is hard for us laymen to understand.

Newton was the supreme scientist, the man who figured out what it is that holds the universe together.

Isaac Newton was born in 1642. His family had some money and Newton, all his life, didn't have to worry about making a living.

He was a little guy, just a couple of pounds at birth. Everybody expected he would die within a few hours. His mother later said he would have fit easily into a one-quart pot.

Newton, as a kid, was smaller than the other boys and didn't like to play with them. He became a bookworm, not just a kid who liked to read but one who was obsessed with books. His friends predicted when Newton was 10 that he would grow up to be an absent-minded professor. Which he did.

Newton had become so absorbed in books that he once dismounted from his horse when it was climbing a steep hill. He pulled a book out of his pocket and read it as he walked up the hill. When he got up to the top of the hill the horse was gone. Newton had let go of the bridle without realizing it and the horse had wandered off.

Newton's father died before he was born and his mother remarried when Newton was just three. He was left to be raised by his grandmother and developed a terrible hatred for his stepfather. It seems to have changed his life.

Newton was a solemn, morbid man. One biographer once said he was only seen laughing twice in his whole life.

He became a professor at Cambridge and goes down in history as the worst lecturer the place ever had. He was a genius but a terrible bore. Some days only one or two students showed up for his lectures. Occasionally, no one showed up.

Newton would be obsessed for days at a time with his mathematical calculations. He would miss meals and sleep as he pored over his books. He loved figuring things out just for acquiring knowledge. Some of his greatest works, his stuff on optics and energy, he figured out years before he published it.

On the other hand, he spent his whole professional life embroiled in arguments with other scholars over who discovered what first.

Newton discovered that what we call light was really a series of different lights, all those colors in the rainbow. With that knowledge he was able to perfect the crude telescopes of the time.

He worked out mathematically what a lot of others had realized for some time, that something holds the universe together, that something makes apples fall from trees and chairs and tables sit firmly on the floor. That's why we remember him as the man who discovered gravity.

Newton's genius brought forth immediate rewards. He wasn't one of those geniuses who dies poor then is appreciated years later. The king knighted him and he sat in parliament.

He made a lot of money and lived well in his later years. He had six servants and rode around London in a big carriage and people stopped and waved at him.

Rousseau, the great French scientist and philosopher, marvelled when Newton died on the 31st of March in 1727. "Here was a scientist," he said, "who was given a funeral as great as a king's."

Newton was obsessed for days at a time with his mathematical calculations. He missed meals and sleep as he pored over his books. He loved figuring things out just for acquiring knowledge.

Originally broadcast March 31, 1989

The Prince of Jokers

April Fool's Day is just made for someone with a sense of humour, plenty of money and time on his hands.

And that describes Horace Cole, a well-to-do Englishman who was described by the British press in 1910 as the prince of practical jokers. Cole would do anything to fool people.

One of Cole's most famous tricks was pulled on the first of April, 1919. Cole was in Venice, on his honeymoon. He took off an evening and went to a stable a few miles out of town, where he bought a pile of horse manure and rented a gondola.

In the dead of night, Cole sailed the gondola along the canals bordering the main squares of Venice and stopped here and there to shovel a little pile of manure onto the square.

The next morning, Venetians found the little piles, seemingly indicating that a squadron of horses had swum the canals and paraded around the city in the middle of the night. The citizens were scratching their heads over that one for weeks.

Another time, Cole was walking along Piccadilly in London with a friend who was a member of parliament. He challenged the man to a race then let him get ahead of him. Then Cole shouted, "Stop thief!"

A passerby grabbed the poor MP and, lo and behold, Cole had slipped his watch into the poor fellow's pocket just before he had started the race. That caused an awful furor and a committee of MPs was established to investigate. They finally decided their colleague was the victim of a hoax. The chairman of that committee, Winston Churchill, later said that Cole was a dangerous man — to his friends.

But Cole's biggest hoax, the one that got the headlines, was the Dreadnaught Affair. In 1910, Cole and a few friends, including Virginia Woolf, the author, sent a telegram to the admiral of the Home Fleet, saying the emperor of Ethiopia and his entourage would be arriving on the 4:20 train for a tour of the biggest ship in the fleet, the Dreadnaught.

Cole recruited six people who dressed up like they thought Ethiopians should be in some costumes they'd rented from a theatrical supply place.

The admiral turned out the honor guard and they got the full tour. One of the crowd acted as the interpreter, saying all kinds of gibberish. Whenever the Ethiopians were shown anything new and wonderful, like a lightbulb, they all gasped and said, "bunga bunga."

The admiral invited the Ethiopians to stay for tea but Cole and his friends were afraid they couldn't carry that off. So the interpreter explained the emperor couldn't take tea unless the waiters all wore white gloves, since he saw the waiters didn't have white gloves.

The whole tour of the battleship had only lasted 40 minutes. But the London papers got hold of the story and the controversy went on for weeks. There were questions in the House of Commons and the attorney-general sat up all night with the lawbooks to see what he could charge the pranksters with. There was nothing.

But the naval officers involved were so embarrassed by the whole affair that they sent a delegation to Cole's place and caned him.

Every music hall comic in the country did a routine that went, "What did the emperor say to the admiral?" The straight man would say he didn't know, and the comedian would say, "Well, I bet the audience knows," and the audience would roar, "Bunga bunga!"

The poor admiral had to stop going ashore from the Dreadnaught because little boys would chase him down the street shouting "bunga bunga."

Cole's brother-in-law was Neville Chamberlain, the serious little man who became prime minister of Britain in the late 30s and it's said that Chamberlain lived in constant horror that some of his brother-in-law's nonsense would ruin his political career.

Poor Cole didn't have a very happy life, aside from his jokes. He had been left so much money that he never had to work so he never really got to be anything. Then his wife ran off with one of his friends. Maybe she had a sense of humour of her own.

> *The committee finally decided their colleague was the victim of a hoax. The chairman, Winston Churchill, later said that Cole was a dangerous man — to his friends.*

Originally broadcast April 1, 1982

A TALE TOLD BY AN IDIOT

The psychiatrists would have had a field day with William Ireland. But there were none in his day. He lived in the late 1770s.

Ireland was one of three illegitimate children of a man named Samuel Ireland, an architect and rabid Shakespeare fan. The old man lived with a woman who had once been the mistress of the Earl of Sandwich. That made her a member of a not-very-exclusive club, because the Earl was notorious for having a lot of girlfriends and discarding them with great frequency. It's possible that William Ireland was a son of the Earl, but that's not clear.

Young William was starved for affection from his father, or his apparent father, anyway. Old Sam was very cold to young William, calling him stupid and showing him no love at all. Maybe William *was* rather stupid, because his mother seems to have had the same opinion about him.

In any case, one day William came home with an old book of Shakespeare's plays. In it was a hand-written note that indicated the book had been presented by Shakespeare to Queen Elizabeth.

The old man was ecstatic. Here was something written by Shakespeare himself. He wanted to know where young William had got it. William, thinking quickly, said he had been befriended by a rich gentleman who had a collection of all sorts of papers that he didn't know anything about or much care. He told William he could have anything he wanted from the collection.

Old Sam was so thrilled by the book, and William was so eager for any display of interest from him, that William came up with lots more Shakespeare things: notes and letters and receipts and contracts and all sorts of stuff. Young William was only 16 and worked as a copier in a lawyer's office. It never occurred to anyone that he could be forging this stuff.

Finally, after he'd been at it about a year, William pulled off his boldest stunt yet. He came up with a whole manuscript of a play by Shakespeare that had never been published. It was called *Voltigern and Rowena* and purported to be a tragedy about an ancient Saxon king.

Old Sam Ireland had ben showing the stuff to his friends and they were all convinced it was real. Now he took the manuscript of the play to several theatre companies and it fooled a lot of them.

The rights to perform were finally sold to the great playwright, Sheridan. He owned a theatre company and he ordered his manager and lead actor, Kemble, to perform it.

Kemble took one look at it and said, "Are you kidding? This wasn't written by Shakespeare. It's the work of a fool."

> *Kemble took one look at the manuscript and said, "Are you kidding? This wasn't written by Shakespeare. It's the work of a fool."*

Sheridan was convinced, though, and ordered Kemble to perform it. Kemble agreed, but only on April Fools Day. Sheridan flew into a rage at that, and Kemble said he would perform it the next day. So, on the second of April in 1796, the play of *Voltigern and Rowena* had its first performance. It was also its last. The audience hooted and screamed and threatened to tear down the theatre when it was announced the play would be performed again the next night. So that performance was cancelled.

Young William later confessed to his father that he'd forged the play, but the old man went to his grave insisting it was the real thing.

Originally broadcast April 2, 1992

FROG LAKE FIASCO

The Frog Lake Massacre was a part, a fairly small part, of the Northwest Rebellion of 1885. But at the time it was described as a bloody uprising by Indians in the west who were slaughtering white men and women and were intent on overrunning the whole west. Nobody back east seemed at all concerned by the fact that the west was theirs in the first place.

The great Frog Lake massacre happened on the third of April in 1885. The most wondrous aspect of the whole affair is that it didn't happen sooner.

In 1869, just after Canada became a country, the Metis of the Red River staged an armed rebellion on a pretty low scale. There was a little bloodshed and the Metis leader, Louis Riel, went into exile in Montana. And that was about all there was to that.

That had been around where Winnipeg, Manitoba, is today. By 1885, the scene of action had swung about a thousand miles to the northwest, between Edmonton, Alberta, and Prince Albert, Saskatchewan.

The Northwest Mounted Police had been formed and had moved into the area to keep peace. They did a pretty good job. The railway had moved west and almost spanned the country.

The Metis still felt they were being mistreated, that their lands and hunting grounds were being violated and their religious and political rights were being ignored. For the most part, they had a legitimate beef.

Louis Riel returned from the United States to lead them. He had been a little strange before and had spent some time in a mental hospital in Quebec. By now, he was experiencing serious mental difficulties.

His new rebellion was about to occur and it was only a matter of time. But this time, Riel had an ace in the hole: the Indians.

If he could persuade the Indian tribes of the west to join in his uprising, he would win for sure. The police could contain the Metis uprising long enough for troops to come from eastern Canada by the new railroad.

But if the Indians all across the Prairies could be persuaded to rebel also, all the forces of the federal government couldn't contain them.

Riel sent men to ask the Indians to join him. But for the most part, they didn't. The Indians trusted the mounted police who had promised they wouldn't be hurt if they kept the peace.

But around Frog Lake, between Edmonton and Prince Albert, some Crees had been gathering. They were hungry because the buffalo had disappeared. The government was supposed to send them beef but there had been a lot of promises and very little beef.

The nearest large-scale mounted police post was 40 miles away. It was under the command of Inspector Francis Dickens, the son of the author, Charles Dickens. Francis was an ineffectual turkey, one of the few mounties who didn't handle the situation very well.

The white people of Frog Lake thought the Cree would be happier if the half-dozen Mounties stationed there withdrew. Inspector Dickens let them.

Some of the younger Cree broke into a store and got some liquor. One thing led to another, and nine whites were killed, two of them Oblate fathers who ran a mission in the area.

By that time, the Metis rebellion under Riel had broken out a couple of hundred miles to the east. The whole west was aflame. Eastern newspapers headlined the Frog Lake Massacre and troops were on the way.

The whole rebellion was over in a couple of months. And today historians make little mention of the Frog Lake Massacre. Maybe both sides are ashamed of it. They should be.

> *The Metis felt they were being mistreated, that their lands and hunting grounds were being violated and their religious and political rights were being ignored.*

Originally broadcast April 3, 1984

THE PERILS OF PEARL

Pearl White was the most famous movie star of her day, and at the same time, the most unknown.

Her fame rested on a series of movie serials she starred in called *The Perils of Pauline*. She was pushed off cliffs, crashed in airplanes, drove cars off of wharfs, fell from skyscrapers — anything dangerous you can think of — and triumphed in the end.

Pearl's unknown quality was of her own making. She wasn't shy; just the opposite. She would talk for hours to any reporter who would listen. But she never told the same story about herself. Then, after a while, she started to repeat the stories she liked best, until she came to believe them.

We know Pearl White was a fascinating woman, and a very successful one. But we don't know which of her many versions of her life is the true one.

She was born in Missouri in 1889. Some sources say her real name was Madeleine White. She said her mother named all the girls after precious stones. We know she had a sister she called Opal, even if no one else did.

Pearl ran away from home to work in a circus. Her father went to a lawyer to see if he could make her come home. The lawyer pointed out that Pearl was almost 18. He could force her to live at home for a while, but when she turned 18, he couldn't keep her there. So the old man gave up and let her go.

At various times Pearl described her father as very poor, the richest banker in town, and various things in between.

We know Pearl worked in various circus acts and in travelling vaudeville shows for years. Sometime after 1910, when she would be in her early 20s, she started making movies. In those days New York was the centre of the movie industry.

Pearl's reason for going into movies was her voice. She was losing it, some say because of a throat infection. Others blame it on cigarettes and whisky. It came back eventually, but in those days the movies were silent, so a lack of voice wouldn't matter.

Pearl made all right money in the movies, a hundred or two dollars a week. But she didn't cause any great stir. She was a not-bad-looking blonde, but no great glamour girl. Then along came the serials.

The Chicago Tribune hired a movie company to run a long adventure story cut up into weekly segments to keep the customers coming. It would be shown on the screen and at the same time, the story line would be published in the paper.

Sounds corny today, but the movies were new then and having an incredible impact. The idea was so good that the Hearst papers had to copy the idea.

> *Pearl was known as Pauline and she was chained to a railroad track and pushed into a buzz-saw, held underwater — just about anything deadly.*

They hired the studio Pearl worked for and came up with all sorts of thrilling misadventures. Pearl was known as Pauline and she was chained to a railroad track and pushed into a buzz-saw, held underwater — just about anything deadly. Of course, she was in one of those life-threatening situations at the end of each episode so you'd have to go back to the theatre next week to see how she got out of it. The first of dozens of *Perils of Pauline* episodes hit the screens on April 4, 1914.

Eventually Pearl made a fortune, retired to France, ran a gambling casino, and died young, drunk, and happy.

Originally broadcast April 4, 1989

FAMILY PLANNING

By the 1660s, the little French colony of Quebec was two generations old and not very prosperous.

The king of France had given the fur-trading concessions to various merchants from time to time. They were given the exclusive right to harvest furs which were a source of great wealth. In exchange, they were supposed to send out supplies and colonists. They always managed to get their furs, but they always had excuses why they couldn't do the supplying and the colonizing.

So, King Louis the Fourteenth and his prime minister, Colbert, decided to handle things directly. They took control themselves and sent out a civil administrator named Jean Talon to make it all work.

To the south of Quebec, the New England colonies were thriving. People were pouring in from England and lots more were being born there. Immigrants from all over Europe were welcome.

Talon sent back word that what he needed most was a plentiful supply of healthy young women who could raise big families. So, shiploads of young women called "the King's girls" were sent out, off and on, for the next 20 years.

Soon the young men of Quebec had no excuse for staying single. Just to make sure they got the message, their parents were hauled into court and fined every six months a man was single after the age of 20, or a daughter after 16.

Bachelors were forbidden to go into the bush to hunt or fish, or to carry on with the Indian girls. Talon had made a survey and decided that Indian women didn't raise big enough families.

If all this seems a little heavy-handed, it was just part of the very over-governed pattern of life in a French colony. Laws dictated what people could wear, what merchants could charge, that every chimney had to be swept twice a year and the chimney sweep could charge no more than six *sous* . . . endless regulation.

To make a system like this work, the king had to make it pay. So, as soon as a couple decided to get married, they filled out the forms and were entitled to receive an ox, a cow, two pigs, two chickens, two barrels of salt meat and some money.

When the annual shiploads of girls arrived from France, the girls paraded into a room, picked out their husbands and went into the next room where a priest was waiting to marry them.

This system was going for a few years when the king decided to make it work even better. On the fifth of April in 1669, he issued a decree that conferred a pension of 300 pounds a year on any couple with 10 kids. And 12 kids produced 400 pounds. Those were considerable sums and big families became the rule in Quebec for centuries.

And in 1944, our federal government extended the idea across the country when it came up with what we still call the baby bonus, a monthly cheque to mothers.

> *Laws dictated what people could wear, what merchants could charge, that every chimney had to be swept twice a year and the chimney sweep could charge no more than six sous.*

Originally broadcast April 5, 1990

CANADA'S PET

On April 6, 1968, Canada got a new prime minister. Some may say today he's an old prime minister, but back then he looked very young and fresh.

Pierre Trudeau had been a politician for only five years when the Liberal leadership convention came along in 1968. But he took it easily. That's the Trudeau style, isn't it? Make it look easy.

Trudeau was a Montreal aristocrat, the son of a rich man, who could afford to put a knapsack on his back and wander around the world after his studies at the University of Montreal and Harvard.

Trudeau returned home to become a college professor and dabbler in politics. A brilliant dabbler. By the early 60s one of the most important voices in Canada — not just French-speaking Canada but all of Canada — was a little intellectual paper in Montreal called *The Free City*. And Trudeau was the sparkplug of it. Lots of others wrote for it and did good stuff, but it was Pierre Trudeau who did the articles with the bitter, cutting edges.

In 1963 when Prime Minister Lester B. Pearson agreed to put American missiles at Canadian bases, Trudeau wrote of Pearson's "abdication of the spirit". Trudeau said, "I have not yet agreed to tramp on democracy. So for this reason I intend to vote NDP." And he described the Liberal party as having not one man for whom principle means more than power.

Yet within two years of writing this, Trudeau was a Liberal MP; within four years he was a senior cabinet minister, minister of justice; and within five years he was prime minister, *Liberal* prime minister. And he made it all look easy.

Pearson announced in December of 1967 that he was about to retire. There was no shortage of people who wanted his job: Mitchell Sharp, the minister of finance and a career civil servant; John Turner, the most handsome man in politics in the world; Bob Winters, a millionaire who moved back and forth between the federal cabinet and the boardrooms of Bay Street, exuding power and wealth; Joe Green, who looked like Abe Lincoln and spoke like Abe Lincoln only wished he could; Allan MacEachen, the patient Maritimer who was hoping to play the victorious tortoise to everybody else's flashing hare; Paul Hellyer, the man who turned the army, navy and air force into one homogeneous green mass; Paul Martin, the oldest pro in the party; everyone.

Trudeau hadn't decided to run when Pearson said he was quitting. In fact, he was busy packing for a holiday in Tahiti. When he came back, a whole lot of people were waiting to tell him he should try for the leadership. He waited until they persuaded him. Then in February he announced he was running, but not very hard. Momentum built.

The convention vote was on a Saturday. Mitchell Sharp announced on the Wednesday just before, that he was dropping out of the race to support Trudeau. That did it.

There were about 2400 delegates to the convention, so 1200 voters would take it. On the first ballot it was Trudeau 750, Hellyer 330, Winter 290, and the others strung out behind.

On the second it was Trudeau 960, Winters 470 and Hellyer 465. That's when Judy LaMarsh, the secretary of state, leaned over to Hellyer and urged him to drop out in favor of Winters so Trudeau — that bastard, she called him — wouldn't get it. That day Judy found out Paul Hellyer wasn't a quitter and the CBC's new microphones could pick up conversation from farther away than she thought.

Finally, on the fourth ballot, Trudeau was declared victorious. And that's all there is to tell. Trudeau made it look so easy. But just like that, he was the new Liberal leader.

The Liberals had been either out of power or forming a minority government since 1957. But a couple of months later Trudeau called an election and made that look easy, too.

> *Trudeau said, "I have not yet agreed to tramp on democracy. So for this reason I intend to vote NDP." He described the Liberal party as having not one man for whom principle means more than power.*

Originally broadcast April 6, 1982

A FIRST FOR EVERYTHING

Parliament sat late on the night of the 6th of April in 1868. Canada was less than a year old and the government must have had a lot of laws it wanted passed.

The prime minister was Sir John A. Macdonald. His right-hand man, the one he depended on to do the really tough debating in the house, was D'Arcy McGee.

It was well after midnight, now April 7th, when McGee left the House of Commons and walked to his rooming house in downtown Ottawa. There had been a lot of people on the street near the House but as McGee got onto his street, he seemed to be alone.

But as he put his key in the lock, somebody sneaked up behind him and shot him once in the head at close range.

The police quickly came to the conclusion that the killer was a Fenian, an Irishman who was a member of a group much like the IRA that's causing so much trouble in Ireland and England today. McGee was an Irishman who had fought the British back home. In fact, he had escaped from Ireland disguised as a priest after a rebellion failed.

He went to the States and made his living as a writer. He returned to Ireland then left again and came to Canada, still working at the journalist's trade.

He went into politics and he and Macdonald made a great team. Macdonald was tall and lanky and retained a noticeable Scottish accent although he'd been only a kid when his family came to Canada. McGee, of course, always spoke with an Irish accent. Both men were superb speakers.

Both were heavy drinkers as well. At various times in their lives the booze got the better of them and both their careers had some pretty sad episodes in

them. McGee's best days were behind him but he had got a grip on himself and was functioning all right by the time he was killed.

In his early days, McGee had been as anti-British as any Irishman. But as time went on he liked less of the republican institutions he saw in the States and admired more the stability of the British monarchy.

The Fenians had accused him of being a traitor. Within a day the cops had grabbed a semi-literate Irishman, a tailor named Patrick James Whelan.

Whelan was suspected of being a Fenian, and he might have been. He certainly hung out with a lot of them. On the other hand, so did most Catholic Irishmen in Canada in those days.

McGee was shot with a .32 pistol and Whelan owned one. It disappeared after the trial and didn't turn up for a century. By today's standards it probably couldn't be proven to be the gun that killed McGee. Whelan denied killing

Whelan denied killing McGee but he seemed fatalistic about his chances. He said, "I guess they gotta hang me."

McGee but he seemed fatalistic about his chances. He said, "I guess they gotta hang me." He admitted he knew who did the killing but would say no more on the subject.

The evidence against Whelan probably wouldn't be admitted at a murder trial today but they were less particular about such things in those days. A lot of people still believe Whelan shouldn't have been convicted.

His lawyer was a Toronto legal hot-shot named John Hillyard Cameron who was a member of the Orange Lodge, a Catholic-hating, Fenian-hating crowd. But he believed in Whelan's innocence and handled his case for nothing.

But in the end it didn't matter. Whelan was hanged for Canada's first political murder. And practically its only one.

Originally broadcast April 7, 1992

NATIONS OF THE WORLD, UNITE

The First World War was described as the war to end war. The one international figure who really believed that was the president of the United States, Woodrow Wilson, a college professor by trade.

The First World War started in 1914 and ended in 1918. The United States didn't join until 1917. But by then the other main players were so exhausted that the Americans played a huge and decisive part.

When the peace conference began in late 1918, Wilson demanded that an international association be created to prevent future wars. It was called the League of Nations.

Its mandate was simple: to set up meetings of disputing nations so they could argue rather than fight; to intervene, if necessary; and to establish agencies to protect the health of all peoples of the world and to raise living standards everywhere. It all sounded so much like purity and motherhood that you'd think no one could object.

But the first objections came from Wilson's own countrymen. The Congress of the United States never did approve the league and the Americans never joined. By the time the war ended Americans had decided they didn't want anything to do with international affairs because the old, tired countries of Europe were always at each other's throats and to get involved with them would be to constantly be at war.

The League had some successes. In fact, some were quite impressive. It set up various public organizations that fought epidemics all over the world. First, it stopped the westward spread of cholera and typhus from Russia and Poland. They had broken out in the aftermath of the war.

It became obvious that when World War II was over, some organization more potent than the League of Nations would have to be established.

It established a series of reporting stations on the outbreak of various diseases in the Far East and started to do a lot to control them. It intervened in a couple of border disputes in South America and Scandinavia and Eastern Europe and prevented wars.

But, in the long run, the League didn't work. In 1923, Greece and Italy had a dispute over the island of Corfu in the Adriatic Sea. The League did nothing about that.

The Japanese invaded Manchuria. The League sent a commission to investigate and it recommended that the member countries intervene. But they didn't. Then in 1935 came the death blow. The Italians invaded Ethiopia and the members of the League did nothing. They set up some economic sanctions against Italy but that amounted to just an annoyance.

Throughout the 30s, as the world drifted to war, the League was less and less a player on the international scene.

The Second World War broke out in 1939, within 20 years of the First. As it progressed with the death toll running into the millions, it became obvious that when it was over some organization more potent than the League of Nations would have to be established.

The victorious powers set up the United Nations before the war was over and it took over all those international peace-keeping functions that the League had fumbled.

On the eighth of April in 1946, the League began its last session at its headquarters in Geneva, Switzerland. It was just a matter of housekeeping, and within a month it declared itself out of business.

Originally broadcast April 8, 1992

TURNING THE TIDE

Everybody has heard of the Magna Carta. It was signed by King John of England in 1215 and it's generally regarded as one of the foundations of our legal and government systems.

But the fascinating thing about the parliamentary system of government is that it didn't just happen in one day. It grew bit by bit. And the Hocktide Parliament is every bit as important to our system as the Magna Carta. But who ever heard of the Hocktide Parliament?

This all occurred back in the 1200s when the king of England and the barons were jockeying for power. The fact that it happened then is one reason why England eventually became the most powerful country in Europe. The English got this issue out of the way early in their history. Other countries were still battling it out for centuries.

In the early 13th century, in the days of King John, the king was the most powerful man in the land because he was the toughest. But from time to time, he would lose a round, as with the Magna Carta.

In the Magna Carta, the king recognized that his subjects had certain rights. Until then, the assumption was that the king was appointed by God and had all the rights.

The next major step in the development of the parliamentary system came in 1258, 43 years later, when John's son, King Henry III, was on the throne. Henry was a strange man, a gentle soul who didn't really want to be king. He would have been just as happy at home, reading books by the fire. But, since he was king, he decided to act like one. And that meant holding onto his powers.

King Henry had a brother-in-law who is one of the most intriguing characters in British history, a man called Simon de Montfort. Simon was born in France and came to England while he was young and rather poor. He married the king's sister. It was a strange marriage for those days: it was based on love, and he and his wife were deeply amorous all their days.

The way to power was to win the king's favor and Simon did this. The king put him in charge of one of his provinces in France and Simon turned out to be a pretty good administrator.

In 1250 Simon wrote a letter to the king in which he reported that, in some local hassle or other, he was upholding the rights of the king and the common people against some local barons. That was a new and radical concept, that the king and the common people had the same rights. In fact, no one had ever before mentioned the common people. They were no part of government. They were just there to be taxed and exploited, not to be considered.

> *That was a new and radical concept, that the king and the common people had the same rights. In fact, no one had ever before mentioned the common people.*

Simon supported the king in his many fights with other nobles. Then he supported the nobles in their fights with the king. He told each side that it had to define its rights and limitations and live within them.

The King had a couple of half-brothers named Lusigan, Frenchman who ignored the rights of everybody else and grabbed power and wealth however they could. That put the king on a collision course with the nobles.

The barons got together at what was called the Hocktide Parliament on the 9th of April in 1258 and demanded that the king formally recognize his power had limitations and they had some say in running the country. Later that summer, those ideas were formalized as the king recognized that he had to allow a couple of councils to advise him in his running of the country.

It was a small start, but an important one. The parliament you watch on TV sprang from it.

Originally broadcast April 9, 1986

THE FLUORIDATION CONSPIRACY

In just about every major city in North America today, fluoride is added to the drinking water, along with chlorine and other chemicals. The chlorine is to kill various harmful germs. The fluoride is to prevent tooth decay in children.

Nobody pays much attention to its presence there, if it's even known. But just a generation ago, there was an awful fuss about whether or not fluoride should be added to the water.

Scientists generally liked the idea and approved it. The opposition seemed to come from a small group of religious fundamentalists and anti-Communists.

In Toronto, when the matter was being debated, there was much noise but not a lot of public interest. Gordon Sinclair, the newsman and *Front Page Challenge* panelist, was the noisiest opponent. He described fluoride as rat poison and said it would soften the brain.

The scientists said, sure it was rat poison, if you feed rats enough of it. And it would probably do terrible things to humans, including the brain, if you ate spoonfuls of it. But just one part per million is added to water.

Fluoride was approved and put in the water without an awful lot of fuss.

But in Alberta it was different, especially in Edmonton, That's where the anti-fluoridationists decided to make their stand.

The Alberta government amended the Public Health Act on the 10th of April in 1952 to allow one part per million of sodium fluoride to be added to municipal water systems wherever the electors approved, by a majority of two-thirds.

Surveys at the time showed that 47 per cent of the voters were firmly in favor and only 17 per cent firmly opposed. That left quite an undecided vote, and the anti side went to work on them.

They imported huge amounts of literature on the subject from the western and southern States, all pointing out that fluoridation was part of a communist plot to take over the world. Huge piles of the stuff would be stored at waterworks all over the country, the pamphlets said, and when the communist leaders in Moscow gave the signal, their agents would shovel it into the water supply and everyone who drank the water would either fall over dead or become brain-numb, ready for an easy takeover.

> *They imported huge amounts of literature on the subject from the western and southern States, all pointing out that fluoridation was part of a communist plot to take over the world.*

Some people who didn't believe all that still opposed fluoridation because they saw it as an infringement of civil rights. A forcing of socialized medicine on all of us. Canada's first public medical scheme was still a dozen years in the future.

The controversy raged for years. In Edmonton, in 1957, in 1959, in 1961 and in 1964, the voters approved fluoridation by a majority but didn't get the two-thirds required. Three of those four times, the vote approved of fluoride by more than 60 per cent.

By that time, it had been added to the water in most other major North American and European cities with little or no fuss.

Finally, in 1966, the provincial government changed the law to require only a bare majority of voters to approve fluoride. With that, it was passed, and now it's in the water in Edmonton too.

There have never been any scientifically proven cases of it hurting anyone. The dentists all seem to agree that it's sharply reduced tooth decay in kids across North America.

Still, every now and again someone points out the danger of having all that fluoride stored right beside the water supply.

Originally broadcast April 10, 1992

THE MARLBOROUGH MAN

In 1689, King William came to the throne of England. He was a Dutchman and a Protestant and he replaced his father-in-law, King James II. James was Catholic. It wasn't obvious at the time, but a Protestant king on the throne of Protestant England marked the beginning of the end of religious strife in English political life.

Now, all the rage and energy that Englishmen had devoted to their religious differences could be transferred to politics. The two political parties, the Tories and the Whigs, would go at each other with terrible energy.

King William was succeeded in the early 1700s by his sister-in-law Queen Anne. Under her rule, England flowered as it hadn't since the time of Queen Elizabeth. Newton, the great scientist, changed the physical world with his calculations. Handel, the German musician, was attracted to England. Pope, Addison, Steele, Swift — some of the greatest names in English literature — all thrived in those days.

England had been fighting France, with the odd truce, since the beginning of modern history. And that war was taken up again.

This time one of England's greatest generals, John Churchill, went to Europe to lead a combined army of English, Dutch, German and Austrian armies against the French. Churchill managed victory after victory. Queen Anne called him home and made him the Duke of Marlborough.

While all this futile fighting was going on in Europe, neither Queen Anne nor King Louis XIV of France paid much attention to what was happening overseas. The French-English war had been going on in North America with as much fury, and at as great length, as it had back home.

France was a country of 20-million people while England had only 5 million. But the English colonies along the Atlantic seaboard of North America were much more populous than the French holdings. Nevertheless, the French managed to win more than their share of the battles.

Their traders were taking most of the furs out of this continent and their ships could create terrible havoc for New England's shipping. The French, with their Indian allies, could raid New England settlements almost at will. And they did.

Suddenly, in late 1712, all that changed.

The Duke of Marlborough got caught in English domestic politics. The Whigs and the Tories were fighting for control of parliament. The party that was out created a fuss over the conduct of the war. They accused Marlborough of embezzling huge funds given him to run his armies. He was called home and forced to face an investigation. He was found guilty but was so angry at the way he had been treated that he moved to Holland.

The English had no more stomach for war, not for a while anyway. King Louis had bled his country almost to death with his wars and his high living.

The English had no more stomach for war, not for a while anyway. King Louis had bled his country almost to death with his wars and his high living.

So, on the 11th of April in 1713, the two sides signed a peace treaty in the Dutch city of Utrecht, called the Treaty of Utrecht.

To hold on to some small pieces of European real estate, King Louis surrendered most of his North American possessions in the Maritimes and Newfoundland and on Hudsons Bay. He retained Quebec and a piece of Cape Breton Island but they would go too, within a generation or so.

It was the end of France as a world power and the beginning of the long climb to the pinnacle of world domination by the British. And, an indication of how Canada would go within a couple of generations.

Originally broadcast April 11, 1990

THE BISHOP'S TALE

John Strachan has been dead more than a hundred years, but in Toronto, his town, they still argue about him.

In Scotland, where Strachan was born on the 12th of April in 1778, his surname is pronounced *Strock-an*. Yet the street named after him in Toronto is given a more English pronunciation, *Strawn*. It's still a matter of argument, because so many Scotchmen have settled in Toronto.

John Strachan's mother wanted him to go to school to learn to be a clergyman. His father thought school was a waste of time and money. He wanted Strachan to learn a trade. The matter was settled when Strachan's father was killed in an accident at work. He worked in a quarry and was blown up during blasting. So Strachan set out to be a student, mostly on scholarships, then a teacher.

He was a plodder, not a natural student, but he did quite well. Strachan was a poor man who never thought of himself as poor. He spent his money as quickly as he made it and was always generous with his family and friends. As a matter of course, without giving it a thought, whenever Strachan had a few days off he would walk from the school where he taught to visit his mother. It was 80 miles away.

In 1798, after Strachan had been teaching for almost five years, he answered an ad for a teacher to found a school at Kingston in Ontario. He travelled to Canada with his last few dollars. When he got to Kingston he found that the people who had intended to start the school had dropped the idea. So Strachan founded his own at Cornwall and quickly became a success.

Right from the start, Strachan realized that he had a rare opportunity. Only the well-to-do could afford to send their boys to be educated at his school. These boys would later become the leaders of the country. The man who taught them would be in a position to wield considerable power. And he was.

As a matter of course, without giving it a thought, whenever Strachan had a few days off he would walk from the school where he taught to visit his mother — 80 miles away.

Strachan had been raised a Presbyterian back in Scotland. But in Canada he saw that membership in the Anglican Church would give him considerable advantage. So he became an Anglican, then a clergyman, and eventually a bishop.

Strachan had a good eye for a deal and he made good money, both as a teacher and clergyman. But he spent it as fast as he made it, always with generosity.

In 1807, Strachan married the wealthy widow of a man who had been a good friend, Andrew McGill.

Before McGill died, he and Strachan often talked about the need for a university in Canada. McGill left money for one and, after his death, his brother James founded McGill University in Montreal. Strachan was the first principal.

He moved to Toronto just in time to be captured, along with everyone else in the town, by American troops in the War of 1812. Strachan argued vigorously with the Americans and stood up for the rights of the townspeople when American soldiers started looting. He had it stopped.

And he was remembered with great affection by the people of Toronto for ever afterwards. He got a charter for a university in Toronto. He wanted a college to educate young men for the Anglican clergy. When the University was taken over by the government and made a non-denominational institution, Strachan started another, Trinity College, to educate those clergymen. So he was instrumental in founding McGill, the University of Toronto, and Trinity, all thriving institutions today.

As Strachan's students grew up and moved into important jobs, he became the most important non-elected politician in English-speaking Canada. Very few laws were passed or moves made without some old student dropping around to the bishop's house to get some advice. He was still at that behind-the-scenes string-pulling when he died at the age of 89 in 1867.

Originally broadcast April 12, 1988

A GREY AREA

Grey Owl was tall, slim, good looking, had a deep voice and an incredible presence. He could hold a whole theatreful of people absolutely entranced by his descriptions of life in the woods and the need for man to stop needlessly massacring animals.

Grey Owl lived in northern Ontario and Quebec with his Ojibway wife. He had been in the Canadian Army in the First World War, had been shot in the foot and gassed. He drew a wounded veteran's pension of 75 dollars a month. So, on top of all is other causes, Grey Owl was a dedicated opponent of war.

In 1929, Grey Owl sent a handwritten article from his cabin in northern Quebec to an English magazine called *Country Life*. *Country Life* bothered him with its neat, orderly view of life outside the city. And, it promoted fox hunting which Grey Owl hated.

Grey Owl explained he was no theoretical do-gooder. He believed in killing animals. He made his living as a hunter and trapper. But he opposed sport killing and reckless killing that was wiping out whole species.

The article was a sensation and the editor asked for more. Then Grey Owl started writing books that sold tens of thousands of copies. He made lecture tours of North American cities and England. He was mobbed. He spoke every day for two months on one British tour.

In 1937, he went to Buckingham Palace to tell the king and queen about life in the wild and the need for conservation. Princess Elizabeth, now the queen, clapped her little hands and asked him to go on and tell them more.

> *Grey Owl explained he was no theoretical do-gooder. He believed in killing animals, and made his living as a hunter and trapper. But he opposed reckless killing that was wiping out whole species.*

Grey Owl could be a problem from time to time. He liked to drink and was often well into the sauce by the time he stepped onto the stage.

There were plenty of women eager to get to know him better. And all those years on the trapline don't teach a man to say no. Back home, he seemed to have a somewhat bewildering series of wives, but everyone just assumed that was some quaint Indian custom.

Then in 1938, on the 13th of April, he collapsed in his cabin north of Prince Albert, Saskatchewan, where he had set up a beaver preserve in a national park. He died as soon as he got to the hospital. He was only 49.

The next day, newspapers in Toronto and London broke the biggest Grey Owl story of all. Grey Owl was actually an Englishman named Archie Belaney who had been born outside London. He had claimed to be part-Indian, part-Scottish, but there wasn't the slightest reason to believe he had a drop of Indian blood in him.

As a youngster, he'd been abandoned by a no-good drinking father and raised by a pair of aunts. He was convinced his mother was an Indian and he begged his aunts to give him the money to go to Canada and live as an Indian. He arrived here when he was only 15.

He drank away all the money he made from his books and lectures and was cruel and stingy with his wives.

It was a sensational story, no doubt about that. But today, half a century later, it doesn't seem important. Grey Owl, or whatever his name was, was a sincere and effective conservationist in a world that needed one badly. And still does.

Originally broadcast April 13, 1984

MORE THAN A MURDER

Just about everybody knows the story of the assassination of Abraham Lincoln, the great American president, by the crazy actor, John Wilkes Booth.

But there was much more to that assassination than just that one act of a madman. It was part of a plot to kill the three most powerful men in the United States, to cripple the country and to win the war the Confederate States had just lost.

John Wilkes Booth was a well-known actor of the time. His father had been a Shakespearean actor of considerable fame and his two older brothers were also. One brother was described by many critics as the best Shakespearean actor of the time, in any country. Booth himself wasn't that good, but he was no slouch.

He was a devoted Southerner, and throughout the Civil War he plotted against the Union, the North, led by President Lincoln, but Booth never actually did much about it.

When he was in Washington he stayed at the rooming house run by a Southern woman named Mary Surratt. Everybody who lived at that house supported the Southern cause. Mrs. Surratt's son was a courier for the Confederates, taking money and messages back and forth through the army lines and into Montreal.

Some of the men who hung out at Mrs. Surratt's place were simple Southern farm boys, not too swift. The brightest of the crowd was Lewis Payne. Payne was smart, brave, and handsome. He was born Lewis Powell in Florida. He joined the Confederate Army when he was only 16. He fought in two major battles, was wounded, captured and escaped. He lost two brothers in the war. At some point Powell started calling himself Payne, probably when he was an escaped prisoner.

Payne was broke, hungry, in rags and living as a beggar behind enemy lines in the city of Baltimore when Booth found him, took him in, and fed and clothed him. Payne thought Booth was great.

Booth came up with a scheme to kidnap Lincoln and hold him as a hostage until the North released all the Confederate prisoners of war. Payne was an important part of that plan. But the war ended, in early April of 1865, before they could carry out that plan.

Now Booth came up with an even crazier plan. He would kill Lincoln, Payne would kill the secretary of state, William Stewart, and George Azzerott, another boarder at the Surratt house, would kill the vice-president.

Booth came up with a crazy plan — he would kill Lincoln, Payne would kill the secretary of state, William Stewart, and George Azzerott would kill the vice-president.

All three were to strike at the same time, 10:15 on the evening of the 14th of April. Booth did. He killed Lincoln.

Azzerott went into a bar and had three drinks while thinking about his part of the plan. Then he had a fourth, said "T'hell with it," and went home.

Payne went to the home of Seward and stabbed him several times. Somehow Seward survived although he was horribly injured with wounds to the face and neck. Payne grappled with an army nurse who was on duty and with Seward's two sons. They were all injured but Payne got away.

The police picked him up a couple of hours later, back at Mrs. Surratt's rooming house. They had gone there in a general roundup of Southern sympathizers as soon as the president was killed.

Mrs. Surratt, Payne, Azzerott and another man were all hanged. Booth was hunted down and shot by soldiers.

Seward recovered although he was scarred for life. He stayed in the cabinet long enough to go down as the crazy man of the next government. He was the one who insisted the United States buy Alaska, a big pile of snow and ice for a lot of money.

Originally broadcast April 14, 1988

TO SINK THE UNSINKABLE SHIP

On the 15th of April, 1912, the greatest ocean liner ever built until then, the unsinkable Titanic, sank. Actually, it hit an iceberg off the coast of Newfoundland late on the night of the 14th. It wasn't unsinkable but it sank more slowly than it might have.

Everybody knows the story of the Titanic, the ship that was built so it couldn't sink. It sank on its first trip, killing 1513 people. But various angles to the story of the Titanic make it one of the most enduring in history.

The skipper knew he was in a sea heavily infested with icebergs in the Atlantic a few hundred miles east and south of Newfoundland. But, for some reason, he insisted on roaring ahead at almost full speed.

The designer of the Titanic put in 16 watertight compartments to seal off any part that sprang a leak. If one was flooded, it would be sealed off and the ship would stay afloat. But when the Titanic collided with an iceberg, the hole was just too big. The Titanic was designed to stay afloat with the first four compartments all flooded. But the iceberg that hit left a hole 300 feet long, and as the Titanic started to go down at the front end, the water sloshed over into the fifth compartment, and the ship filled up like an ice cube tray.

The Titanic belonged to the White Star line, a British company, and British law based the number of lifeboats on a ship on the tonnage. A 30-year old regulation said that any ship over 10,000 tons had to have 16 lifeboats. The Titanic was over 46,000 tons and the builder had installed fittings for 48 lifeboats. But, since the law only required 16 boats, that's all the White Star line installed. That meant a total of 1200 places in lifeboats for a ship that carried more than 2000 people.

Radio wasn't brand new in those days but it was novel. The Titanic had two radio operators and they were very conscious of being at the very top of their craft. They didn't condescend to reply to all messages.

The radio operator of the Californian, another passenger liner, tried several times to exchange messages with the Titanic. He couldn't get a reply although he could hear the Titanic's radio sending to other ships. He got miffed and didn't bother trying after his shift was over. He went off duty at midnight, and the Californian only had the one operator. Ten minutes later the Titanic hit an iceberg and started sending out calls for help. The Californian was the nearest ship, but with the radio operator off shift, no one heard the Titanic's call for help.

The skipper of the Californian was later described as negligent by the board of inquiry. When the Titanic's crew fired distress rockets, he saw them but figured they were just part of a fireworks display for the passengers and he kept going. He could have been on the scene in less than two hours if he had paid attention to the rockets. Not one person need have died.

The Titanic's two radio operators sent out the emergency signal CQD, come quick distress. Then they remembered that a recent international agreement had been made to drop that signal and use SOS instead. So they sent out the first SOS.

The builder had installed fittings for 48 lifeboats. But, since the law only required 16 boats, that's all the White Star line installed.

The closest ship, the Californian, was actually stopped to avoid a collision with icebergs. But the operator was asleep. The next closest, the Carpathia, was 60 miles away. The radio operator was away from his radio for a while. When he returned, about half an hour after the Titanic hit the iceberg, he sent out a "hello there" message. You can imagine his amazement at the reply: "SOS. We've struck an iceberg. Come quick."

There were three classes of passengers on the Titanic. The first- and second-class got first crack at the lifeboats. All children in those classes were saved. Two-thirds of the children in third-class died.

The sinking of the Titanic gave a brief shot in the arm to sales of a novel called *Futility*. *Futility* had been written 14 years earlier by an unknown writer named Morgan Robertson. He described the biggest passenger ship ever built. He called it the Titan. His was 800 feet long. The Titanic was 880. Robertson had the Titan hit an iceberg and go down. It had three propellers. So did the Titanic. The Titan could carry more than 3000 passengers. So could the Titanic. But it didn't have enough lifeboats.

Originally broadcast April 15, 1986

THE FLYING WOMAN

Harriet Quimby was a reporter and editor by trade, an American woman with a well-developed sense of self-promotion. Harriet was the assistant editor of *Leslie's Illustrated Weekly*, one of the most popular magazines in the States.

She was also interested in the brand new field of aviation. In those days the government didn't issue pilot's licenses, but the Aviation Club of America did. Harriet learned to fly in a lesson that lasted 10 minutes. After that, she flew solo and considered herself a pilot. Truth to tell, there wasn't an awful lot to learn about the simple flying machines of the day.

The Aviation Club debated long and hard about setting a precedent by giving a flying license to a woman. But there wasn't much they could do. Harriet was reported to have passed all her tests with flying colors, making take offs and landings as well as any male pilot. And the toughest test, the figure eight, she did better than any of the others.

So, at the age of 27, Harriet Quimby was given license number 37. That's how rare fliers were in 1911.

Harriet was soon a national figure, as she did exhibitions of flying for crowds all over the United States and even into Mexico. She always wore a mauve satin outfit while in the cockpit and big boots and a hood to the mauve satin that gave her a distinctive look.

On the 16th of April in 1912, she got ready for the stunt that would make her a world-famous figure. She had gone to France and met the great plane builder and pilot, Louis Bleriot, the first man who ever flew over the English Channel. Bleriot agreed to lend her a plane. Harriet had arranged with a London newspaper, the *Mirror*, to do an exclusive story about

> *The Aviation Club debated long and hard about setting a precedent by giving a flying license to a woman. But there wasn't much they could do. Harriet passed all her tests with flying colors.*

her flight. She had arranged back in the States for commercial endorsements and lectures and appearances. All the hype and profitable hoopla that goes with a successful stunt.

The weather was so foggy that Harriet didn't have a chance to practice with the Bleriot plane. It was much bigger and more powerful than anything she'd ever flown.

The fog was still around when she took off from a field in England not far from Dover. She did the whole flight in just over an hour and landed in a field near Calais in France. All was done in great secrecy so the *Mirror* could have a scoop on its newspaper rivals. Harriet was whisked back to London and pictures and stories were prepared and all was ready for an incredible promotion that would cover all the front pages on both sides of the Atlantic. Rights to the story were sold to a couple dozen papers in North America and Europe.

But Harriet never made the front page. That night another event pushed her way back to page 5 in the *Mirror* and right out of most papers. The biggest ship in the world, the mechanical marvel of the age, the mighty *Titanic*, on its maiden voyage, hit an iceberg and went down, taking more than 1500 sailors and passengers with it.

Harriet returned to the States and her job at Leslie's. She continued to fly and was a great crowd pleaser. She kept looking for flights that would give her the exposure and fame that would have come from the Channel flight but for a terrible accident of history. She was still looking in July of 1912, three months after the Channel flight, when she crashed and was killed at an air show in Boston.

Originally broadcast April 16, 1992

A REAL EVOLUTIONARY

Erasmus Darwin was one of those remarkable men that history throws up from time to time. He was great, but never very famous.

Erasmus Darwin was born in England in 1731 and he went to Cambridge to study to be a doctor. Records indicate that he was a great boozer and chaser of women as a young man. Dr. Darwin wasn't a handsome man by any means. He was big and heavy and talked with a stutter. But many women later told their friends they found him irresistible.

Dr. Darwin started practicing as a country doctor in the Midlands of England in 1756. He kept at it for almost 50 years, right until his death.

Dr. Darwin had an inquiring mind and loved the company of people with the same attitude. He formed an informal scientific circle called the Lunar Club. Not because its members were crazy, but because they met every month around the time of the full moon. That was important in the days before electric light because people needed the light of the moon to get home after late meetings. The Lunar Club had as members people like Josiah Wedgwood, the pottery maker and Dr. Darwin's father-in-law; James Watt, the perfecter of the steam engine; Joseph Priestley, the scientist who discovered oxygen; and a dozen others.

Dr. Darwin and his friends were very concerned with improving the quality of life around them. That's why a lot of their inventions have been forgotten. Darwin invented an improved candlestick and several gadgets that made carriage travel more comfortable on the terrible roads of the time.

Dr. Darwin spent a major piece of his life on the roads, travelling to treat his patients. He made a lot of money as a doctor, but spent much of it on his poor patients.

He not only treated the poor. He fed them too. A notorious highway robber of the time said, shortly before he was hanged, that he met Dr. Darwin several times a month on the highways because the doctor travelled so much. He never robbed him, of course, because Dr. Darwin had saved his mother when she was sick. And he had sent her food, too, when she was hungry.

Dr. Darwin was one of the first people to believe in education for girls. He set up a school for his own daughters, including two illegitimate ones. He made no distinction between them and the children of his two legal wives.

You seldom hear anyone speak of Dr. Darwin today. You often hear the name, of course, because people remember his grandson, Charles Darwin, the man who came up with the theory of evolution. Except he didn't.

It was Dr. Darwin who did that. He even wrote a treatise with the title that his grandson later made famous: *The Origin of the Species*.

One of the greatest minds of all time was lost to us on the 17th of April in 1802 when Dr. Erasmus Darwin died.

> *Dr. Darwin had an inquiring mind and loved the company of people with the same attitude. He formed an informal scientific circle called the Lunar Club.*

Originally broadcast April 17, 1986

WILD GHOST CHASE

In 1820, Lord Combermere was the governor of the island of Barbados in the Caribbean. That's how he got involved in one of the most mysterious ghost stories of all time.

It centres on a tomb in the graveyard of a church on a height of land overlooking a bay on Barbados. That height of land was a limestone ridge. In 1724, a man named James Elliott had a tomb built in the churchyard because his wife had just died. The tomb was cut into the limestone and was solidly built of limestone blocks. The floor of the tomb was two feet under ground level. The door was a huge block of blue marble and after Mrs. Elliott's coffin was put there, the blue marble was sealed by masons.

We don't know what happened to Mr. Elliott. He wasn't buried there. In 1807, the records show, the tomb was opened again and the coffin of a woman named Mrs. Goddard was put there. By that time the coffin of Mrs. Elliott had been removed. We don't know when or why.

In 1808 the tomb passed into the ownership of a family named Chase. The blue marble block was moved in February of that year to receive the coffin of a little girl, Mary Ann Chase. All was well and the tomb was resealed. A few months later it had to be opened again. Mary Ann's little sister, Dorcas, had died. Again, the records show that all was normal.

Then in August of 1812, the tomb was opened to receive the coffin of Thomas Chase, the head of the family. The coffin of Mrs. Goddard was sitting as it had been left. But the coffins of the two Chase girls were standing on their ends.

There was no sign that the blue marble door slab had been moved and it was impossible for anyone to move any of the huge limestone blocks that made up the tomb. Nobody could figure out what had happened. There had been no earthquake. Thomas Chase's coffin was set on the floor. It was encased in lead and was so heavy eight men were required to lift it.

Four years later, a nephew of the Goddards died and the tomb was opened. Again, Mrs. Goddard's coffin was in its place. But this time the three Chase coffins were scattered about.

The nephew's coffin was put in the tomb and the blue marble slab was resealed.

Just two months later the tomb was opened again for another Chase in-law who had died. The Chase coffins were scattered about. Mrs. Goddard's coffin stayed as it had been left.

Three years later, another in-law was to be buried, the tomb was opened and all the coffins of members and in-laws of the Chase family were scattered around.

> *The tomb was opened to receive the coffin of Thomas Chase. The coffin of Mrs. Goddard was sitting as it had been left. But the coffins of the two Chase girls were standing on their ends.*

The latest coffin was put there. This time the whole island was jumpy. Lord Combermere, the governor, supervised the burial himself. Just before the tomb was sealed, he ordered fine sand sprinkled over the floor. The blue marble slab was resealed and Lord Combermere and two clergymen made their marks in the mortar of the seal.

For some reason, His Lordship had the tomb opened three years later, on the 18th of April in 1820. All the Chase family coffins had been scattered again.

Lord Combermere put an end to it then and there. He ordered the coffins taken out and buried. The tomb was filled and, to this day, nobody has come up with an explanation for what happened.

Originally broadcast April 18, 1989

EVOLUTION OF A REVOLUTION

Starting about 1765, the British parliament passed a series of laws intending to help pay the cost of the army England had stationed in the American colonies.

The colonists claimed they shouldn't have to pay taxes imposed from outside; only their own legislatures could tax them.

Over the years the situation went from bad to worse. By the fall of 1774, the 13 American colonies sent representatives to what they called a Continental Congress, the first meeting of all the separate colonies. Mind you, that congress didn't have any representatives from Newfoundland, Quebec, Ontario, or Nova Scotia, the parts of British North America that later became Canada.

That congress listed the rights and duties of British subjects; they still thought of themselves as Englishmen. That was the term they used; the word American wasn't in wide usage.

All the colonies agreed to support Massachusetts, the colony where most of the opposition was centred. And they agreed to boycott British goods until Parliament dropped its taxes.

The British replied by suspending the Massachusetts legislature and imposing military rule. The commander of the British Army in North America, General Gage, was made military governor as well.

The colonists, the people we now call the Americans, had their own militia units in each community and they began to assemble and drill. They also began to assemble arms and ammunition at the town of Concord, not far from Boston.

Both sides had excellent spy networks and each knew what the other was up to. General Gage decided to send a raiding party forth to Concord to seize the rebel supplies. It would obviously be an operation that would require secrecy and a young, fast-moving commander.

Gage's first mistake was his choice of the commander, Colonel Francis Smith, a middle-aged, fat, slow-moving man. Smith was told to assemble 700 men by 10:00 one night and march them quickly and quietly to Concord by night. They would be in the town and have the supplies seized before the Americans got up for breakfast. The soldiers didn't start to assemble until 11:00, then there were several more delays. They didn't start to march until three in the morning.

The citizens of Boston knew every move they made and they sent two messengers ahead to warn the militia at Concord. And everywhere along the way.

At the village of Lexington, before the British came to Concord, they met the local militia. A force of about 70 British soldiers in the advance guard ran into 130 militiamen.

Each side claims the other fired first. Eight Americans died in a few seconds and the rest cleared out.

Colonel Smith's officers suggested they turn around and get back to Boston. Smith said no. They went on to Concord, seized some arms and burned them. But by then the Americans were behind every bush and tree and stump all the way back to Boston.

Colonel Smith sent word back that he needed help but orders got lost in Boston and that help didn't catch up with him until 2:30 in the afternoon of the 19th of April. By then 73 of his men were dead and the rest were right on the edge of panic.

The American Revolution was on. The world was changing radically. And Canada was going to come into existence as a result.

> *A force of about 70 British soldiers in the advance guard ran into 130 American militiamen. Each side claims the other fired first.*

Originally broadcast April 19, 1990

HAIL . . . SCHICKLGRUBER?

Adolf Schicklgruber was born in the little Austrian town of Branau just about suppertime on the 20th of April in 1889. His father was a customs officer and his mother was a kindly, gentle woman. His parents were second cousins.

His father was a stern, unloving man who had been married twice before. Adolf was the third child. The father was born illegitimate. Then, when he was 39, the records were changed to list him as legitimate. With that went a change of name from Schicklgruber to Hitler.

In later years, young Adolf said that was a turning point in his life although nobody realized it at the time. Can you imagine thousands of people giving the Nazi salute and shouting, "Hail Schicklgruber"?

Before he finally killed himself in April of 1945, Adolf Hitler had become one of history's most notorious dictators, a demi-god worshipped by the German people for a while, and cursed by them ever since.

Hitler was never a good student. There are still old report cards that make that clear. He was described as cantankerous, willful, arrogant, and bad-tempered. In most subjects he was called adequate. In only one did he excel: art.

Hitler tried to get into art college in Vienna but he was turned down for not having enough talent. So he wandered the streets, very much the bum, living in flop houses, eating in soup kitchens, wearing cast-off clothes, making the odd buck as a painter of houses and a hanger of wallpaper, but otherwise not doing anything noteworthy with his mediocre artistic talent.

When the First World War broke out, Hitler was 25. He turned out to be an excellent soldier, wounded twice, decorated for bravery and in a hospital recovering from temporary blindness from a British gas attack when the war ended in defeat in 1918.

Hitler was just one of millions of unemployed ex-soldiers wandering the streets in Germany. The country hadn't been physically ruined as it was in the Second World War. But its economy was shattered and unemployment was rife.

Hitler read a lot, he always had. And he developed a philosophy that was half man of action, and half anti-Semitic crazyman. His fellow unemployed veterans were looking for anybody to blame for their troubles and they ate up Hitler's speeches about the need to grasp their own future and make things work for themselves, even if it meant shedding a little blood.

In 1923, Hitler led an armed rebellion that the police easily put down. He was thrown in jail and there he wrote the story of his philosophy, *Mein Kampf*, My Struggle.

For some reason that makes no sense today, it attracted people. Hitler turned out to be a pretty good speaker. In fact, in later years, he would astonish the world as he drew tens of thousands to his rallies and they would all stand in straight lines and lift their hands in the Nazi salute and yell in unison, Heil Hitler.

The man was an organizational genius and made Germany a major power again. He was also a madman and drenched the world in blood and got Germany pounded flat, literally, before his dream of world domination ended just a dozen years after he took power.

> *His fellow unemployed veterans ate up Hitler's speeches about the need to grasp their own future and make things work for themselves, even if it meant shedding a little blood.*

Originally broadcast April 20, 1992

THE DEFOE DEBATE

In May of 1720, in London, there appeared a book that was the literary sensation of its time. It was called *Madagascar, or Robert Drury's Journal of 15 Years Captivity on That Island.* It was the story of Robert Drury, a young cabin boy of 15, who was cast up on the shore of *Madagascar*, the big island in the Indian Ocean off the east coast of Southern Africa.

Drury was on a trip back from India, said the *Journal*, when his ship sprang a leak. Some of the crew drowned. Some made it ashore. There, the natives attacked them and only Drury was kept alive, apparently because the Madagascarians wanted to keep him as a slave. According to this book, Drury spent 15 years on this island, sometimes as a slave, sometimes as a mercenary soldier for one tribe or another.

The book, purportedly a true story written by Drury himself. contained pages and pages of detail about the family trees of five clans of natives. It had a small English-Madagascarian dictionary at the back of the book.

Robinson Crusoe, one of the most successful adventure stories ever published in English, had appeared only 10 years before. The resemblances between *Madagascar* and *Robinson Crusoe* guaranteed that *Madagascar* would be a success. The first printing sold out and another came out two years later. The last came out 100 years after that, so it's safe to say *Madagascar* was one of the English language's best sellers.

But around the mid-1800s, scholars began to take a second look at it. They had devised ways to match one work of an author with another, even if he didn't always use his own name.

And it became quite clear that the similarities between *Robinson Crusoe* and *Madagascar* were more than coincidental. Daniel Defoe, the author of *Robinson Crusoe*, also must have written *Madagascar*. That was pretty clearly established by Defoe's first major modern researcher in 1869.

It had been agreed, long before that, that when Defoe wrote *Robinson Crusoe* he based it on a real incident of a man who was cast away and later returned to Britain. The question about *Madagascar* was, did Robert Drury ever exist?

At first this was just a literary curiosity and no one got very excited about it. Then, it started to become clear that the study of old records, everyday things like ships' manifests and birth and death records had been overlooked by historians. They had been so used to following official records, proclamations and debates, that they had overlooked the really valuable sources of our history.

It was assumed as late as 1910, by *Encyclopedia Britannica*, that Drury's accounts were essentially true, even if Defoe had been his ghost writer.

Then, starting in the 1940s, the truth was uncovered by two rival English professors: Arthur Secord of the University of Illinois and John Moore of the University of Indiana. They kept up a light-hearted debate on the subject in learned journals, more for their colleagues' amusement than anything else. Both men were experts on Defoe. Both agreed he wrote *Madagascar*. Moore claimed it was a work of fiction. But, in the course of looking up old records to prove his point, he found the one that didn't.

It was a diary account from a seaman dated the 21st of April in 1705. And it told of the arrival in England of a boy, not named, from a ship that had been wrecked on the coast of Madagascar. The ship had the same name as the one in Defoe's book.

Professor Moore died soon after that. But that spurred on the other professor, Secord, and he travelled to England and found the birth record of Drury. Then, to cap it all, one of his students found records from South Africa that confirmed the whole story. They had been transcribed by clerks there, shortly after the shipwreck, when they talked to survivors on their way home to England.

So, historians and students of Defoe now know that one of the bestsellers of the early 1700s was written by Defoe, and it was mostly true.

> *It became quite clear that the similarities between* Robinson Crusoe *and* Madagascar *were more than coincidental.*

Originally broadcast April 21, 1988

TRUTH ON TRIAL

On the 22nd of April in 1633, the trial of Galileo Galilei began in Rome.

Galileo was a brilliant man, one of the dozen most important scientists and thinkers in the history of man. He was famous, both for practical inventions and brilliant theories. He was the Einstein of his time.

But it's hard to understand the Galileo trial today because it occurred in an age when the major crime man could commit was one that doesn't exist in law today. That was the crime of believing something forbidden. In this case, the forbidding was done by the Roman Catholic Church.

The belief was that the earth moves around the sun. Everybody knows today that it does. And although the majority of people in those days believed the earth stood still and the sun moved, Galileo certainly wasn't unique in believing otherwise. He and other scientists had written extensively on the subject and, at least in scientific circles, no one was arguing very hard.

On top of that, Galileo was a devout Catholic and was always very concerned that anything he taught or wrote about fitted in with church policy. He had often cleared his writings with churchmen before he published them.

Galileo was born in Tuscany in Italy. He later moved to Venice, where he became quite respected and famous as a mathematician and astronomer and maker of telescopes. But he was always homesick and moved back home after 18 years in Venice.

When Galileo was still a young medical student he noticed that heavy and light pendulums swung at about the same speed. He timed them against his pulse. That ran contrary to the theories of Aristotle that had been held for a couple of thousand years. It was the length of the string the pendulum swung from, not the weight of the pendulum itself, that controlled speed. This simple observation led to the invention of the pendulum clock, man's first serious effort to accurately measure time.

Next, Galileo heard about lenses and he began to study them. By this time he had given up medical studies and moved to Venice. Galileo ground his own lenses and soon invented a telescope that would enable sentries at the harbor in Venice to see an approaching ship two hours before it was visible to the naked eye. For this he was made an important scholar and very well paid.

Galileo turned his telescopes to the stars and saw all sorts of things that disproved the theories then held. Many of them, like the sun moving around the earth, were from the Bible.

And that's what led to Galileo's troubles. That and his biting, sarcastic writing. He was a good writer, too good for his own career. He made a lot of powerful enemies as he advanced his theories and destroyed those of other scientists.

In 1633, he was summoned to Rome and tried for heresy. He was found guilty and sentenced to life imprisonment. By that time Galileo was 70 and the sentence was reduced to house arrest.

By the time he died eight years later, the theory he had been condemned for was pretty generally held by most scientists. So ever since the controversy has raged. Could the Catholic church have made a mistake? More importantly, could it *admit* it had made a mistake?

The answer came just a few years ago. The present Pope told a meeting of scientists in Rome that religion and science can get along quite well. He appointed a commission to look at Galileo's case, and it reported the church had been wrong.

> *Galileo turned his telescopes to the stars and saw all sorts of things that disproved the theories then held. Many of them, like the sun moving around the earth, were from the Bible.*

Originally broadcast April 22, 1986

PARTY FAVORS

George Brown was a Scot. He moved to New York, started up a newspaper, then left and moved to Toronto. There, he took over what is today the *Globe and Mail*, Canada's national newspaper. In those days, it was just the *Globe*.

Journalism back in the 1800s was very much entwined in politics so it was natural that Brown would soon become a politician. And a powerful one.

Brown was a Reformer. The Reform Party, not the same one that exists nowadays, later evolved into the present-day Liberal Party. Of course, in those days party politics wasn't as strong as it is today. And that made for a much more interesting political scene. Today, you know pretty well how a vote in the legislature will go. Back then, just because a member voted with Brown on one question didn't mean he'd be with him on the next.

Brown soon became one of the major figures of Canadian politics. Canada in those days consisted of Ontario and Quebec. The Maritimes and Newfoundland were separate British colonies, as was British Columbia. Everything from Ontario to British Columbia was the private property of the Hudson's Bay Company.

Another major figure in politics in those days was John A. Macdonald, a Kingston lawyer. Macdonald and Brown were both born in Scotland and that's all they had in common. They didn't like each other.

Macdonald was a slim, handsome, witty man with a light-hearted manner and a legendary thirst. Brown was a huge man, with a rather hickish appearance, and a dedicated teetotaller. And Macdonald was a Conservative, so they were also political opponents.

The Canadian parliament moved from town to town: Toronto, Montreal, Quebec. It accomplished virtually nothing. All its time was taken with debates on procedure and votes that were never conclusive because the Ontario and Quebec factions were at constant stalemate over language, religion, public works, finance, and just about any question that came up.

Governments rose and fell in months, occasionally only weeks. The record was set in 1858 by Brown. He formed a government that lasted only two days. It was the most inept piece of political blundering Canada would see for another 125 years, when the Joe Clark government fell.

> *Governments rose and fell in months, occasionally only weeks. The record was set in 1858 by Brown. He formed a government that lasted only two days.*

That mistake loosened Brown's hold on the leadership of his party. Brown's solution for the stalemate was to advocate a constitution for Canada, a written one. He would also like to see more government positions elected and fewer appointed.

Macdonald immediately accused Brown of wanting to sever the tie to Britain and become another republic like the United States. Brown denied this but was embarrassed by it.

Finally, on the 23rd of April in 1860, Brown tried to bring the matter to a head by asking it be debated in the house which was sitting in Quebec City. The Conservatives opposed the debate. But, even more troubling for Brown, so did one of the main men in his own party, a man named Michael Foley who had been feuding with Brown over the leadership.

The result, on top of Brown's fumbling performance of just a couple of years earlier, was devastating. Brown stayed in politics for a few years more. But it was the beginning of the end for him.

John A. Macdonald, his hated foe, emerged as the principal figure in Canadian politics. And when Confederation came along a few years later, George Brown, one of its earliest and most devout advocates, was little more than a footnote in Canadian politics.

Originally broadcast April 23, 1991

A MAUD-ERN CLASSIC

Lucy Maud Montgomery isn't exactly a household name. But, if you think really hard, you can probably recall that she's the lady who wrote *Anne of Green Gables*, a classic of sorts.

In fact, *Anne of Green Gables* is one of the most popular books ever written in the English language. Nobody knows exactly how many copies have been published but it's certainly in the bizillions. The reason nobody knows the exact number is rather interesting and it tells us something about our history.

Canada's copyright laws did nothing to protect authors for years. Tens of thousands, maybe hundreds of thousands of copies of *Anne of Green Gables* rolled off the presses uncounted because the publisher didn't have to pay the author any royalties. Today, we know how many are printed because the publisher is required to pay royalties.

Lucy Maud Montgomery was born in Prince Edward Island in 1874. Her mother died before she was two and her father moved to Saskatchewan and married again and started another family. Lucy stayed behind and was raised by her grandmother and grandfather. Remember that, because psychiatrists say it explains the incredible, lasting popularity of *Anne of Green Gables*.

She loved her grandparents—at least we think she did—and she loved Prince Edward Island. There's no doubt about that.

Lucy wanted to write from the time she was a child. She sent away her first story to a publisher when she was 11 and she had one accepted when she was 15.

She became a teacher when she was still a teenager but her real career was writing. She moved to Halifax, studied at Dalhousie University and worked as a reporter and editor on a newspaper called the *Echo*.

Lucy returned to Prince Edward Island and her grandparents and wrote some more. She had articles published from time to time, mostly in American magazines. She taught a bit but she was determined to make a living as a writer.

In 1904, she made $591.85 from her writing. Not much in those days, but enough to live with your grandmother on a farm on Prince Edward Island.

Her grandfather died and she promised to stay with her grandmother to the end of the old girl's days. Today, that sort of thing just wouldn't happen. But in those days it wasn't that unusual. A young Presbyterian clergyman came along, named Ewan McDonald. He wanted to marry Lucy but she said no, she would have to stay at home until Grandma was called to the great farmhouse in the sky.

Lucy put story ideas down in a book and went over them from time to time. In 1904, she read over something she'd written down sometime in the past. The idea was simple: an old couple on a farm send away to an orphanage for a boy. Somebody makes a mistake and they get a girl.

Lucy turned out that book in a few months and called it *Anne of Green Gables*. She sent it to publishers and it was rejected three times. On the fourth try a Boston publisher accepted it. The result was instant success and quite a bit of money, but no fortune. And part of the publishing contract said that the publisher owned the stage and movie rights and publishing rights to anything Lucy would write for the next five years.

Grandma died and Lucy finally married her clergyman. They moved to Ontario and she raised two boys and wrote more books, 30-odd in all. She got involved in a lawsuit, or a series of lawsuits, with her publisher and that dragged on nine years.

Every year, *Anne of Green Gables* sold more copies. The psychiatrists say it's because girls of 10 to 14 are starting to hate their mothers. Anne didn't have a mother; she was raised by grandparents, so they were safely hateable. Who knows?

All in all, Lucy had a busy life but not a happy one. She died on the 24th of April in Toronto, a place she never liked.

> *Every year,* Anne of Green Gables *sold more copies. The psychiatrists say it's because girls of 10 to 14 are starting to hate their mothers.*

Originally broadcast April 24, 1985

A MAN OF HIS WORD

Crowfoot was a chief of the Blackfoot tribe of southern Alberta. He was born in the 1820s, as nearly as he could estimate. Crowfoot's father was a chief ahead of him and so was his older brother. The brother was killed in a fight with another tribe and Crowfoot succeeded him as the Blackfoot leader.

He was about 50 when the Mounted Police arrived in his country in 1874. Crowfoot had met and had dealings with white men all his life. And he knew not to trust them.

American wolf hunters and whisky traders had ranged over his country for years, doing nothing but harm. Crowfoot was a well-travelled man. He had gone far into the southwestern United States as a young man to get horses for his tribe from Indians down there who were accomplished horse breeders. Nothing in Crowfoot's dealings with the whites made him welcome them. Nevertheless, he was an open-minded man.

So when the Mounties arrived and said they intended to enforce laws fairly to both Indians and whites and to rid the country of whisky traders, Crowfoot gave them a chance to prove they were telling the truth.

He was impressed by the Mounties and accepted them and their laws. That acceptance was crucial to the settling of the west. Crowfoot and his Blackfeet could easily have wiped out the Mounties.

Two years later, the Sioux, under their great chief Sitting Bull, destroyed a whole American regiment under General Custer, then fled north of the border. Sitting Bull was bitter toward all whites and he invited Crowfoot to join him in a war to kill all whites and take back their land. Crowfoot listened carefully then told Sitting Bull he had given his word to the Mounties and they had kept their word to him. He would join in no war. Sitting Bull and his Sioux couldn't do it alone, so they gave up and went back to the States.

Later, the federal government sent out commissioners to negotiate with all the tribes of what's now Alberta and western Saskatchewan. They wanted to open up the land for the railway and for farming.

Most of the Indians looked to Crowfoot for leadership. He listened to the promises the white people made then he made his decision. He said: "If the police had not come to this country, where would we all be now? Bad men and whisky were killing us so fast very few would be alive today. The police have protected us as the feathers of a bird protect it from the cold of winter. I will be the first to sign this treaty and the last to break it."

Crowfoot was no stooge. He realized that not all whites were as honorable as the Mounties. And not all were as sincere as the commissioners he dealt with. But he knew his people could never resist by force with any hope of succeeding.

In later years, when indifferent politicians in Ottawa and racist Indian agents on the spot broke the government's word, Crowfoot demanded justice. Sometimes he won a few small victories.

In 1885, when Louis Riel began his Metis rebellion, he sent word to Crowfoot. If the Blackfoot joined the Metis, said Riel, the whites would be driven back to the east and they could have their lands back.

"Never," said Crowfoot. "I gave my word."

Without Indian support, the rebellion collapsed after a few months and Canada's only civil war fizzled out.

Crowfoot didn't survive long after that. He caught pneumonia, a white man's disease, and died on the 25th of April in 1890. The federal government put a simple stone marker on his grave. It says, "Father of his People".

A lot of the promises made back in those times have been broken. But nobody has ever said Crowfoot didn't keep his word.

Crowfoot was no stooge. He realized that not all whites were as honorable as the Mounties. But he knew his people could never resist by force with any hope of succeeding.

Originally broadcast April 25, 1991

LIGHTNING STRIKES

The Spanish Civil War had been going for almost a year in the spring of 1937. Spain was a battleground for the two major emerging European political movements, each headed by a madman.

Adolf Hitler, the German leader, sent an army of 50,000 into Spain to support the right-wing Spanish leader, Francisco Franco. Mussolini, the right-wing dictator of Italy also sent troops.

Joseph Stalin, the Russian communist leader, sent help to the other side. He had some Russians in Spain and some communists from various countries of the world, including Canada and the United States.

The Germans were there mostly to test out their new theories of war. The Treaty of Versailles that ended the First World War in 1919 had restricted the size of the German army and had forbidden the Germans from building up an air force. The Germans got around that by forming flying and gliding clubs. The German army was being rebuilt, despite the treaty, by a bunch of young generals who had some new and radical ideas. They called their system *blitzkrieg*, lightning war.

Instead of long lines of men marching toward the enemy, they would attack with tanks, break holes in the enemy lines and keep going. The men marching behind could hold the ground. Meanwhile, the tanks would keep moving to new targets, always moving so they wouldn't be a target for the defenders.

To make this plan work, the tanks needed

> *The German army was being rebuilt, despite the Treaty of Versailles, by a bunch of young generals who had some new and radical ideas.*

something going ahead of them to disrupt the enemy they were about to attack. And that was the Luftwaffe, the German air force.

The big German air hero of the First World War had been Manfred von Richthofen, the Bloody Red Baron. His career ended when he was shot down by a Canadian. His cousin, Wolf, was in charge of the new Luftwaffe squadrons that were to pound enemy towns ahead of the advancing tanks. It was a good theory but it hadn't been tested anywhere. Richthofen went to Spain as part of the German force there. On the morning of April 26, 1937, he got a chance to try out his theories.

He sent 53 planes carrying 100,000 pounds of bombs against the town of Guernica in northern Spain. The Germans later claimed they were attacking military targets. But there were only two in Guernica — a gun factory and a bridge. Neither was hit. The bombs weren't the type used to destroy bridges and factories. They were people killers. The Germans wanted to see if they could terrorize a town into surrender by attacking the people. They killed about a thousand.

They must have thought it was a good new technique because when the Second World War started a couple of years later they used it against the British. It didn't work there. The British and the Americans then used the same tactic against Germany. This time, it worked.

Originally broadcast April 26, 1989

TAKING TORONTO

On this day, the 27th of April, in 1813, an American army captured Toronto. The army didn't stay long, but it left an impression on Canadians that lasted more than a hundred years.

In those days, Toronto was a city called York and it had a population of no more than a thousand, probably a little less.

The War of 1812 had begun about a year earlier and it hadn't gone very well for the Americans. They had been beaten at Detroit and Niagara by the fast, shrewd, brave British general, Isaac Brock. But in that last battle at Queenston, not far from Niagara Falls, Brock had been killed as he won the battle.

With Brock gone, the Americans started doing a little better. Both armies pretty well went out of business over the winter and in mid-April, 1813, an American force set out by ship from Sacket's Harbour at the southeast corner of Lake Ontario.

The American general's orders were to take Kingston, just to the north of him. But he figured it would be easier to take York so he sailed diagonally across the lake and, on the evening of the 26th of April, he appeared off the east end of York.

In the town, all was confusion. So far, most of the fighting on the Canadian side had been done by British troops and Indians. The Canadians had done very little. For one thing, their militia units weren't very good. And many of the Canadian civilians were either American-born or had relatives on the other side of the border. Some were pro-American. Even those that weren't certainly weren't very pro-British.

With Brock dead, the British commander was a general named Sheaffe. He wasn't bad but he was no Brock. When the Americans sailed past the town and landed just to the west he shifted his small British force with some Indians to attack them as they landed. But the American landing was fast and effective. The British stood in straight lines in their scarlet uniforms, just as they did in Europe, and the American riflemen cut them up.

The Americans advanced on the town and took it pretty easily. In fact, only one incident slowed them down.

General Sheaffe ordered the powder magazine blown up as the Americans advanced to capture it. Dozens of Americans were killed, including their best general, Zebulon Pike.

General Sheaffe got most of his force away and took off for Kingston. The people of York complained that he had deserted them but history says he probably did the right thing. He was outnumbered and outgunned and couldn't have held York.

The Americans did some looting but they were reasonably well-behaved. They had hoped to capture a naval ship that was under construction in the harbor but the British burned that as they retreated. The American forces burned down three major buildings, including the tiny little wooden legislature building.

Both sides believed terrible things about each other. The Canadians believed the Americans were uncouth woodsmen who would burn and rape and loot and even enter houses without removing their hats. The Americans believed the Canadians were a bunch of backwoods yokels who would snipe at them from behind trees and would turn the Indians loose on them to scalp and torture them to death. There was a grain of truth to each belief but little more.

But when the American soldiers broke into the Legislature they saw, hanging on a peg behind the speaker's chair, his wig, just like the wigs English judges still wear. The Americans assumed it was a scalp and they were so horrified they burned the place down before they left.

A lot of good it did them. Fifteen months later the British landed a force that captured Washington. Taking their lead from what the Americans had done at York, they burned the town. And when the Americans later rebuilt it, they couldn't get the smoke marks off the president's residence so they plastered it with whitewash. And to this day the president lives in the White House.

> *Both sides believed terrible things about each other. There was a grain of truth to each belief but little more.*

Originally broadcast April 27, 1982

A MATTER OF PRINCIP-LE

Gavrilo Princip was born in the summer of 1894 in a little village in Bosnia. He didn't live to see the age of 25 and he was, if at all noteworthy, a little on the dull side. But he started a war that took 9,000,000 lives.

The Turks had ruled the Balkans for centuries but in the late 1800s their empire was breaking up. The biggest of the Yugoslav countries, Serbia, won its independence. A bunch of other little ones became bloody battlegrounds with various factions trying to take over. Austria, the major power to the north, stepped in and took over two of them, Bosnia and Hercegovina. To the people involved, it was very little improvement.

This was the situation that Princip was born into. He was a sickly lad, suffering from tuberculosis. He read a lot but he wasn't bright enough to do very well in the school system that the Austrians had set up.

When he was 17 he went to Belgrade, the capital of Serbia. The school system there wasn't as demanding.

Princip studied and lived and drank with other students from Bosnia. Naturally the principal subject of discussion was the terrible state of affairs back home. Truth to tell, the Austrians were treating the Bosnians better than anyone ever had. But the Bosnians wanted their freedom.

The head of intelligence for the Serbian army at that time was a colonel named Dragutin Dimitrovich, but he went under the code name of Apis. Apis was funnelling money and officers into a secret organization called the Black Hand. It was dedicated to putting all the Slavs in the Balkans in to one country, the country that was known until quite recently as Yugoslavia. It wasn't very long before Princip was in the Black Hand and his particular cell of six freedom fighters had guns and bombs and poison supplied by Apis.

The heir to the throne of Austria, the Archduke Francis Ferdinand, was scheduled to review a military exercise at Sarajevo in Bosnia in late June of 1914. The actual day was the 28th. And if the Austrians had been sensitive to the feelings of the Bosnians they never would have made that the day for the archduke to parade through Sarajevo. That was the anniversary, 500 years earlier, of the defeat of the locals by the Turks.

Princip and other members of his cell slipped across the border into Bosnia and made their way to Sarajevo. Each carried a pistol. Three of them had grenades. And each man had a poison capsule to swallow if he was captured.

One of the gang threw a bomb that didn't kill anybody. But it caused the archduke's procession to change its route. Princip had gone into a local coffee house after the bomb was thrown, figuring the operation was now off.

As Princip stepped back into the street, the archduke, in his open car, stopped within a dozen feet of him. Princip whipped out his pistol and shot the archduke and his wife.

But as he stepped back into the street, the archduke, in his open car, stopped within a dozen feet of him. Princip whipped out his pistol and shot the archduke and his wife.

Europe was a powderkeg at the time and within six weeks the entire continent was at war. Princip was two weeks short of his 20th birthday so he was sentenced to 20 years. But he didn't make it. Tuberculosis and bad prison conditions caught up with him on the 28th of April in 1918 and he died in jail.

Originally broadcast April 28, 1986

THE NEWSPAPER TIGER

William Randolph Hearst was born on the 29th of April in 1863 in San Francisco. His father was a semi-literate miner who hit it rich and became a millionaire and eventually a senator.

The old man was once ridiculed by a political opponent for not even being able to spell the word "bird". "If b-u-r-d doesn't spell bird," he said, "what in hell does it spell?" The other guy had to admit he didn't have an answer for that one.

Young Willie was raised by his mother, a gentle, sensitive woman of considerable culture. But he was always more like his father.

By the time he reached Harvard University, he had gone through an incredible number of tutors and private schools. Even he couldn't count them all. But at Harvard, Willie underwent a radical change. He was made business manager of the school newspaper. It had been a traditional money-loser, like all college papers.

But Hearst had a talent for publishing, an ability to think up stunts that built circulation, plus an instinct for the sort of stories people liked. For the first time in his life, Hearst found himself really interested in something.

Hearst's father, the senator, owned mines and ranches and he expected his boy to come out of school and start running one of them. Hearst said no. The old man owned a small, money-losing newspaper in San Francisco called the *Examiner*. Hearst asked to be put in charge of that. The old man shrugged and told him to go ahead. Within a year, Hearst had made the *Examiner* a power in San Francisco.

When the Coast Guard said it was too dangerous to rescue a stranded fisherman in a storm, Hearst chartered a tugboat and did it.

When the city fathers cooked up a crooked deal with the water company to raise rates by 16 per cent, Hearst exposed it.

Newspapers in those days were platforms for the opinions of the rich and powerful, especially the big advertisers. Hearst ran a column in the *Examiner* called "The Workingman" and suddenly unions had a voice in the mass media.

In the next few years Hearst's power reached well beyond San Francisco. He bought a paper in New York and got involved in incredible circulation wars with the established papers there. He hired the very best writers and paid them salaries no other publisher would dare match.

The labor unions in Los Angeles asked him to start up a paper there to compete with the anti-union Los Angeles *Times*. So, Hearst started one there and called in the *Examiner*.

Wealth and success changed Hearst, just as he had changed the face of North American journalism.

All this wealth and success changed Hearst, of course, just as he had changed the face of North American journalism.

He thought he would make a great president of the United States. He started by trying to be governor of New York but he had no flare for politics and he had to give that up.

Although Hearst was married to a very classy lady, he had a long-time scandalous affair with a movie actress named Marion Davies. He got into movie-making trying to make her a star. It didn't work. Davies, although a nice person, hadn't the slightest ability as an actress.

Around the turn of the century, as a circulation-building stunt, Hearst demanded the United States declare war on Spain. The excuse was that Spain was oppressing the people in its colonies, especially Cuba. The president didn't want to but Hearst and several other publishers liked the idea so they forced the country into that war.

Theodore Roosevelt, who later became president on the basis of the fame he found in that war, called it a splendid little war.

Hearst sent an artist to Cuba to cover the war he was confident he could get started. The artists cabled back that there was no war. Hearst cabled out to him: "You furnish the pictures. I'll furnish the war."

Hearst became so powerful and ruthless that he became a caricature of his earlier self. So much so that Orson Welles used him as a model for one of the greatest movies of all time: *Citizen Kane*.

Originally broadcast April 29, 1991

MRS. DOCTOR

Emily Jennings was born in southern Ontario in 1830, the oldest of a family of six girls. Her parents were members of the Baptist church, but before that, her family on both sides had been Quakers.

In those days, women were very much second class citizens. They couldn't vote or run for public office. But more importantly, there weren't a lot of jobs for women. They could be seamstresses and store clerks. And a few were getting into teaching. But that was about all.

But the Quakers had always believed in equality of the sexes, both in terms of opportunity and responsibility. So Emily's parents saw she got a pretty good education, in terms of what was available.

Emily's mother was the teacher in the local one-room school. By the time Emily was 15, she was teaching too. Women were welcomed into teaching because the local school boards found they would work cheaper than men. A man teacher in those days got $10-$15 a week. A woman teacher got half, maybe two-thirds, of that.

Emily taught for a few years, then took a year off and went to teachers' college in Toronto for a year. When she graduated, she was offered a job in Brantford, Ontario as the first woman school principal in Canada.

After a few years, she met and married a carriage maker named John Stowe. She quit teaching and had three children. Then John took sick. Emily, always a workaholic, had to run the house and go back to teaching as well. That was quite a load.

Then, maybe because her husband needed medical attention, she decided to be a doctor. Emily worked day and night to save enough money. No medical school in Canada would accept a woman. But there were three in the States. So Emily went to New York and enrolled in one.

The Quakers believed in equality of the sexes, both in terms of opportunity and responsibility. So Emily's parents saw she got a pretty good education, in terms of what was available.

In 1867, the year of Confederation, Emily arrived back in Toronto, a medical school graduate. A law was immediately passed requiring anyone who had studied at a foreign medical school to take classes at a Canadian medical school then pass an exam set by the local medical society.

But Emily went ahead and set up a practice anyway. Women swarmed to it. They had been waiting for a woman doctor.

Emily realized the medical establishment wouldn't let her carry on indefinitely. The medical establishment realized it couldn't just shut Emily down, now that she had proven the need for women doctors. So, three years later, she was allowed to enroll at the medical school of the University of Toronto.

The professors and her fellow students, the men, harassed Emily and one other woman who had to take the same courses, Jennie Trout. They were sexist and abusive and, some days, downright obscene. Emily and Jennie put an end to the antics of the most difficult of their professors. They told him they were going to drop in to have tea with his wife and let slip some of his more outrageous comments. Things went smoother after that.

Emily's husband, John, got better and decided to drop carriage-making and become a dentist. One of her daughters became a doctor and one son, a dentist. Two of Emily's five sisters became doctors and practiced in the States where they encountered some resistance but not as much as Emily faced in Canada.

After all that, Emily moved her attention to the plight of women generally and campaigned for the rest of her life for the vote for Canadian women. But that wasn't achieved when she died on the 30th of April in 1903.

Originally broadcast April 30, 1990

NEW DIRECTION

Orson Welles was just in his early 20s when he took Broadway by storm with his Mercury Theatre productions of *Julius Caesar* and *Heartbreak House*. He was only 23 in 1939 when he produced a radio version of H. G. Wells' classic *The War of the Worlds*. It was so realistic that it produced a mass panic. People really thought Martians had landed in New Jersey and the world was about to end.

A man named George Shafer ran RKO movie studio in those days. RKO had made a lot of money grinding out mindless drivel in the 30s and Shafer wanted to take the next step and start doing great stuff, the sort of thing that would be remembered in years to come as art, not just money.

So he did something that no Hollywood mogul had ever done before. And few since.

He hired Welles, the boy genius, to turn out something that would make people talk for years to come whenever the subject of movies came up. Shafer made no demands on Welles, promised to leave him alone to turn out whatever he wanted.

Welles' favorite writer, aside from himself, was Herman Mankiewitz, a brilliant wordsmith, a nasty drunk and a night-and-day alcoholic. Mankiewitz dictated the script for Welles, at least the first draft, from his bed. He had broken his leg in a car accident while drunk. Then, when it was almost healed, he had fallen down drunk and broke it again.

The picture was called *Citizen Kane* and it was a very thinly disguised biography of the great American publisher, William Randolph Hearst. Hearst was a genius as a young man but as his power grew he became a petty tyrant. Since he spent and lived on a grand scale, everything he did made great theatre.

Welles made the picture mostly with stage actors, something that wasn't done in those days. He cast himself in the lead role as Kane, the publisher.

When RKO sent a man to the sound stage to see how things were coming along, Welles threw him out. When he returned Welles ordered work to stop and the crew stood around doing nothing at overtime rates until the man left.

Welles was a theatre director, not a movie director, so he had all sorts of ideas about camera angles and lighting and sound and sets that had never been seen before on the screen.

Hearst was furious and did everything he could to screw up Welles' career. But Welles, with his over-eating, womanizing and general tyranny, was destroying himself.

Welles wore crazy-looking contact lenses to make himself look older for the later scenes. He couldn't see properly and he fell down a flight of stairs and hurt his leg so badly that for a while, about two weeks, he had to direct from a wheelchair.

When *Citizen Kane* was first shown on the first of May in 1941, the impact was incredible. Not on the public. Not many people saw it.

But the critics either hailed it as a work of genius or toadied to Hearst by denouncing it. Louis Mayer, the owner of MGM Studios, offered to buy the film to get on the good side of Hearst. Hearst was furious and did everything he could to screw up Welles' career from then on. Not that he had to do much. Welles himself, with his over-eating and womanizing and general tyranny, was destroying himself.

Hearst didn't keep *Citizen Kane* off the screen. But he managed to keep its distribution so limited that it was a financial failure and Welles was never given total artistic control of a picture again.

He did several more clever things on the screen but nothing to compare with *Citizen Kane*. Today, on every movie expert's list of the great films of all time, *Citizen Kane* is always number one or two. Even if most people have only seen it on TV.

Originally broadcast May 1, 1992

THE GREAT EMPRESS

Princess Sophie was born in Stettin, Germany on the 2nd of May in 1729. She was a very obscure specimen of minor European nobility.

Her father had the title of prince but he was worth little more than his sword and his horse. He was a junior general in the army of Frederick the Great and not a bad officer. Princess Sophie's mother was a Romanov, from the same Russian family that ruled for centuries. But she was a pretty remote Romanov.

Nevertheless, when Sophie died in 1796, she was already one of the major figures of European history.

Princess Sophie travelled to Russia when she was 14 to be checked out by the Empress Elizabeth. Elizabeth had never married and had picked out her nephew Peter to succeed her to the throne of Russia. But she knew soon after she made the formal announcement that she'd made a terrible mistake. Peter was a jerk. He loved to dress up and play soldier and spend hours playing with his dogs and monkeys. His only adult activities were booze and women and he was a complete fool with each.

The empress liked young Sophie and decided she would be Mrs. Peter. Sophie set out to become the best Russian in the country. She studied the language, the religion and the history. She converted to the Russian Orthodox religion and took the Russian name Catherine.

So, when the empress died and Peter became czar, the German princess became the Empress Catherine.

Peter didn't last long on the throne. For years, he and Catherine had been married in name only. He had a succession of girl friends. Catherine had an impressive number of lovers.

Catherine quickly locked up Peter and proclaimed herself empress without him. He died soon afterwards, obviously murdered, probably not at Catherine's order although she did nothing to punish the guilty parties.

Much has been written about Catherine's love life and rightly so. It was impressive. The kindest biographer I've read estimates she had three lovers before Peter died and 21 afterwards. Others have come up with numbers twice that.

But this has to be said for her: Catherine doesn't seem to have allowed her numerous boyfriends to stand in the way of her being a good ruler.

Peter the Great, less than a century earlier, had set out to make Russia a western nation by importing European technology — shipbuilding, armaments, roads and canals, that sort of thing.

Catherine took the process an important step further. She imported western philosophy and art. Rousseau and Diderot, the great French thinkers, were constant letter writers to Catherine. She adopted most of their ideas about freedom and equality. Although when the French Revolution broke out, based on these ideas, she repudiated them and became quite repressive.

Rousseau and Diderot, the great French thinkers, were constant letter writers to Catherine. She adopted most of their ideas about freedom and equality.

But Catherine was a great ruler. She expanded Russia's borders southward and established seaports on the Black Sea. She also expanded westward, took Poland and made one of her former lovers the king. She introduced public schools to Russia and some of the first schools for young women in Europe.

She made a bit of a fool of herself with her lovers from time to time. But who doesn't? When she was 61, she gave command of one of her armies to her 24-year old boyfriend. But he didn't do any worse than some of the old fogeys who had been in command before.

All in all, Catherine was an empress who has been described as on par with Queen Elizabeth the First of England. Not bad for a little German girl from nowhere.

Originally broadcast May 2, 1986

GOOD AS GOLDA

Golda Meir was born in the Ukraine, where Jews had been persecuted for years. Her father was a carpenter. It was his job to nail boards across the windows of the homes and shops in the Jewish area whenever it looked as if the Czar's soldiers were about to go on the rampage, killing and smashing.

Golda was only eight when her family left for the United States but that picture of Jewish passiveness in the face of persecution stayed with her all her life. And she didn't like it.

The family settled in Milwaukee. Golda had a rough time learning English but she worked hard at it and when she finished elementary school she was near the top of her class.

Golda became a schoolteacher despite her parents' objections. They wanted her to marry as soon as possible and raise a family.

Golda met a nice young fellow-immigrant from Russia, named Morris Meyerson, and they eventually *did* get married; but it wasn't the conventional marriage that her parents or Morris had in mind. Golda didn't like fitting into other people's patterns.

Golda believed fervently in the need for Jews to have their own homeland in Israel. She insisted that they settle there. In 1921 they sailed for Palestine, as it was called then, and settled on a kibbutz. She worked first for the Israeli labour movement, then moved into politics. Golda was an enthusiast, some say a fanatic.

Morris, on the other hand, was a nice guy who wanted a quiet life. They drifted apart after they'd had a couple of children. That was the end of domestic life for Golda, although she had a few boyfriends from time to time. She never claimed to be a saint.

Now, Palestine had been promised to the Jews after the First World War by one Englishman, Arthur Balfour, the foreign secretary; and to the Arabs by another, Lawrence of Arabia.

During the 20s and 30s the British occupied the country. The Jews and Arabs squabbled with the British and each other.

All through Hitler's rise to power and the war, the Jews of Israel had to stand by while millions of their brothers and cousins were slaughtered. They wanted to open Palestine to all Jews but the British kept immigration to a trickle. Otherwise, they would have had an Arab revolt on their hands while they were fighting the war.

Some Jews wanted to go along with the British policy. Never Golda. She was always a leader of the tough liners.

In 1948, the British pulled out and the Jews established the state of Israel. Golda, the fluent English speaker, was sent to the United States to drum up support. Israeli leaders told her to tell American and Canadian Jews that all was well in Israel, that if they backed the new state they would be backing a winner. The Israelis needed money and they hoped Golda would raise a million.

Once she arrived in the United States, Golda ignored her orders. She told hushed audiences that all wasn't well in Israel, that the country was fighting for its life and its chances of survival were very slim. She said North American Jews must provide massive aid or the whole idea of a Jewish homeland would disappear in a terrible slaughter like the one that had just happened in Europe. Within 48 hours she had raised $25 million.

When Golda returned to Israel she was made ambassador to Moscow. She didn't like the idea because diplomacy impressed her as a terrible waste of time.

Golda was called home to be the foreign minister and eventually, in 1969, she became prime minister.

Her administration was just as fiery as the rest of her career. Golda never backed down from a fight from a foreigner or a fellow Israeli.

She survived the controversy over how she had handled the government during the Yom Kippur War of 1973 by facing her enemies head-on. She ended that crisis by forming a new government. Then she resigned.

And lived in busy retirement. When she died in 1978 all Israel was shocked. She seemed so healthy she would live forever. She hadn't bothered to tell anyone she'd been fighting cancer for 16 years.

> *Her administration was just as fiery as the rest of her career. Golda never backed down from a fight from a foreigner or a fellow Israeli.*

Originally broadcast May 3, 1983

DEMO-LITION

The Vietnam War was a disaster for the Americans. They went into it, they told themselves, to save all Asia from Communism. In fact, the parts of Asia that were going communist did and the parts that weren't, didn't, all without any push from the Americans.

Before the Americans finally bailed out of Vietnam in 1975, they left behind 55,000 dead, mostly young men who were being conscripted into the army because they were poor. The well-to-do could get deferments by going to university or by making all sorts of deals with the complicated conscription rules.

The campus of Kent State University in Ohio was loaded with young men staying out of the army by going to school. Or, in some cases, getting paid to go to school by the army in return for a promise to do their time later. That way, they were betting that the Vietnam War would be over by the time they had to do their service.

The kids at Kent State were the essence of Middle America, virtually all white, from families that owned their own homes, from towns or small cities or even from farms.

There was a small cell of radical student agitators at Kent State in the fall of 1969 but they seem to have fizzled out by the spring of 1970.

On the first Friday of May in 1970, the students had a mad dash through the town of Kent. The university was in the town. They shouted anti-war slogans but, to this day, nobody believes it was really a political demonstration; it was more of a student prank.

The next night, the demonstration was more political. The students burned down the army office on the campus. It wasn't as big a deal as it sounded. It was just a big wooden shack that had been there for years.

The Sunday was reasonably quiet. Classes started as usual on the Monday morning, the fourth of May, in 1970. There was another demonstration scheduled for noon but it wasn't very well attended.

By that time, the National Guard was on the scene. The National Guard is something like our militia, part of the army manned by part-timers. In the States it gets a little complicated because although it makes up the bulk of the army, which of course is federal, it's run by the state; in this case that meant it took its orders from the governor of Ohio who was campaigning at the time for re-election.

Most of the National Guardsmen were part-timers who were staying out of the war by doing five or more years of part-time soldiering rather than doing their military time all at once. Some were well trained. Others filled in their time sitting around the armories drinking beer and playing pinball machines. The ones at Kent State seem to have majored in beer and pinball.

When the demo started, the National Guardsmen threw some tear gas to break it up. Then they chased the students away from the centre of the campus. Then they turned and started to walk away. The students had been throwing rocks and a dozen or more guardsmen had been hit but none badly hurt.

Suddenly, the guardsmen turned and some of them fired. Their officers immediately ordered them to stop and most did. The whole thing lasted 13 seconds.

Four students were killed, 13 wounded. One of the dead was a girl who wasn't even in the demo. Another was a young student, also not in the demo, who was being put through college by the army in exchange for his promise to do his time when he graduated.

Nobody was ever convicted in the shootings. But within five years the Americans were out of Vietnam. And conscription ended.

The students had a mad dash through the town of Kent, shouting anti-war slogans but, to this day, nobody believes it was really a political demonstration; it was more of a student prank.

Originally broadcast May 4, 1992

THE HEAD OF THE ARMY

Napoleon Bonaparte was one of the dozen great figures in all history. He was the greatest of all Frenchmen but in his time most Frenchmen thought of him as a foreigner.

He was born on the island of Corsica, which was mostly Italian. France had only owned Corsica a year when Napoleon was born. He was raised speaking Italian and had trouble with French when he went to school in France. To the end of his days he spoke French with a thick accent.

Napoleon was a young artillery officer when the French Revolution broke out. He saw it as a chance to free Corsica. When that failed, he realized his only hope for a career now lay in throwing himself enthusiastically into service in the French Army. He did that so well that he was soon in command of the French Army. Then, he used that power to overthrow the revolutionary government that gave it to him. That was in 1800.

Never before had so much of Europe been ruled by one man. Never again would it be until Hitler came along.

Napoleon set out to rule France as a dictator and to re-establish order. The country had been torn apart by the bloody Reign of Terror and localized fighting. The French were delighted to put their affairs in the hands of this strong, decisive man who got things done.

Napoleon mobilized France's manpower and industry into the first modern war machine. He conquered Europe from the English Channel to Moscow, from the north shore of the Mediterranean to the Baltic. Never before had so much of Europe been ruled by one man. Never again would it be until Hitler came along.

At first Napoleon attacked in every direction, no matter what the odds. The French Armies were just about unbeatable. Then, by 1814 he'd done it too much. The British, German, Russian and Austrian armies all closed in on him and he was tossed off his throne.

He was made the Duke of Elba, a little island off the coast of Italy. He was told to stay on Elba the rest of his days.

A new king was put on the throne of France and Europe set out to try to restore normality. It was impossible. The new king was a turkey. The big powers that united in war squabbled in peace. The revolutionary ideas that Napoleon had taken around Europe with his armies refused to go away.

In February of 1815, Napoleon sneaked away from Elba in the middle of the night and landed in the south of France. The people who had thrown him out nine months earlier flocked to his banner and the war was on again.

It all ended with the Battle of Waterloo in June of 1815. Napoleon's comeback had lasted exactly 100 days.

This time, the allied powers weren't playing around. The German general wanted to hang Napoleon, but the British were against that. After all, Napoleon was an emperor of sorts and they didn't like the idea of killing anyone who occupied a throne. They'd done it themselves to their king in 1649 and a terrible mess had followed.

So, it was decided that this time Napoleon would be sent to the island of St. Helena, a chunk of rock away down in the south Atlantic, closer to the Falklands than to Europe. In those days of slow-moving ships, it took from August until mid-October to get there.

Several of his servants and officers went into exile with him. And Napoleon dictated his memoirs, brilliant lessons on war and politics.

On St. Helena, Napoleon fretted and chafed at the British restrictions on his movements. He was already a heavy man and he refused to go walking or riding as long as the British insisted a soldier follow him. He had a bad stomach and from early 1821 on it got worse. He took to his bed in mid-March. On the 5th of May, 1821, Napoleon murmured "At the head of the army." And died.

Originally broadcast May 5, 1986

WILDE ACCUSATIONS

Sir William Wilde was one of the pillars of the British medical establishment in the late 1800s. He was an eye and ear specialist who practiced in Dublin. He was also a specialist to the queen. In addition he was a noted scholar and had written all sorts of learned stuff about Irish history and archaeology.

Dr. Wilde was a strange man, small and uncombed and not very well dressed. Some people described him as quite dirty. Even in those days they marvelled that a medical man seemed to wash so seldom.

Lady Wilde, his wife, was a handsome big woman, bigger than Sir William. She was a writer and before they were married she had become the most famous woman writer in Ireland by writing an article encouraging young men to take up arms against the crown to drive the English out of Ireland. She was from a well-to-do family and a lady, so nothing was done to her about it.

But the magazine that published her article was put out of business and the editor was thrown in jail. That's how they did things in Victorian times.

The British regarded the bulk of the Irish people as a pack of savages, much as they do today. But they recognized the respectable Irish to be just as respectable as English leaders. The fact that Dr. Wilde had been knighted and was a specialist to the queen made him eminently respectable in their eyes.

So when a lawsuit for libel involving Sir William went to court in late 1864, reporters from all the London papers were there. The lawsuit was filed by a Miss Mary Travers, against Lady Wilde.

Travers claimed to have been libelled by a letter Lady Wilde wrote to her father, dated the 6th of May, 1864. In that letter, Lady Wilde accused Miss Travers

of having an intrigue with her husband, or claiming to. That seems to have been a polite Victorian term meaning an affair.

Lady Wilde countersued. Sir William did too, although he wasn't sued by Miss Travers.

The story Miss Travers had to tell was pretty corny. But it's the sort of tale that still sells well on afternoon TV.

Miss Travers said that when she was a teenage girl, about 10 years previously, Dr. Wilde had treated her for a sore ear and later for a cut on her neck. "In the course of all this," she said, "he . . . well, it's hard to talk about but . . ."

"As a result of Sir William's actions were you ruined?" asked her lawyer. Miss Travers gave a long pause and a sigh and a little sob and said yes.

Instant sensation on the front pages of the London papers. The queen's doctor involved in unspeakable practices with a young woman.

The jury finally found Miss Travers had been wronged by Sir William and awarded her damages of one farthing, the smallest coin in the land.

The affair seems to have gone on for years and only resulted in the lawsuit when Miss Travers started writing pamphlets about it and hiring newsboys to distribute them about Dublin.

After six days of trial, the jury finally found Miss Travers had been wronged by Sir William and awarded her damages of one farthing, the smallest coin in the land. They also ordered Sir William to pay her doctor's bill which was huge.

It all seems quite small time today. But back in 1864 it was a major story in newspapers in Britain and Canada and the United States. In fact, it was years before the newspapers had a juicier scandal.

And that involved a Wilde, too. Sir William's and Lady Wilde's son, the brilliant playwright, Oscar.

Originally broadcast May 6, 1987

WE'RE OFF TO SEE THE WIZARD

Frank Baum was a strange man. If not crazy, at least very unusual.

He was born in New York in 1856, the son of a well-to-do oilman. Baum was a dreamer from birth. He grew up to be a tall, handsome, slim man with a weak heart.

He ran his own acting company when he was a young man but couldn't make any money at it. His father put him to work for the family company as an axle-grease salesman.

The old man died and the family business fell apart. Baum moved with his wife and four boys to a little town in South Dakota where he ran a store. He went broke because he just couldn't turn down anybody who asked for credit.

Baum grew to hate the flat, treeless Prairies. He moved to Chicago and worked as a newspaper reporter but never made enough to keep his family much above the poverty line.

To make a little money on the side, he wrote a couple of books of fairy tales. One was a prose version of the Mother Goose rhymes and one a collection of stories about Father Goose.

The illustrator of those books was an artist who worked on the newspaper with Baum, a man named W. W. Denslow. Denslow was the traditional newspaperman — big, bluff, a woman-chaser and a drinker.

He and Baum didn't get along at all. Baum was a kindly, gentle man who lived in a dream world, quite literally.

His children loved to get him to tell them stories because his characters were so real but never violent. No fire-breathing dragons or evil magicians like in the traditional fairy stories.

The kids from all over the neighbourhood would come to listen to Baum tell his stories. In one story, he remembered his days on the Prairies and how he hated

Baum's children loved his stories because his characters were so real but never violent. No fire-breathing dragons or evil magicians like in the traditional fairy stories.

the country out there. So he said his story occurred in Kansas. There was a little girl in the crowd called Dorothy so he named his heroine Dorothy.

He remembered a window display he had put together years before when he ran the store in South Dakota. He had used a washtub for a body and stovepipes for arms and a saucepan for a face. So he added a Tin Woodsman to the story.

One of the kids asked the name of the place Dorothy went to after a tornado picked her up and took her away. Baum looked at the newspaper that was lying beside him, hoping to see something that would give him a clue to a place name. That was no help. But he did remember the date on the paper: the 7th of May, 1898. So we know the day he first told the story.

Baum kept looking around the room for something to give him a place name. He had a little cabinet with filing cards in it. The first drawer was labelled A to G; the second was H to N; the third was O to Z. Baum put the O and Z together and called the place Oz. That's why his modern fairy story was called *The Wizard of Oz.*

Baum didn't get along well with his mother-in-law. She was a forceful, direct, tough woman. But she insisted he get together with Denslow, the artist and put *the Wizard of Oz* on paper.

The result was one of the biggest successes in the history of publishing. *The Wizard of Oz* has sold literally millions and millions of books in dozens of languages.

It was made into a Broadway musical that made Baum a lot of money. But he never became rich. As quickly as the money came in, he blew it on one stupid invention or idea after another.

No one who could write *the Wizard of Oz* could cope with everyday life.

Originally broadcast May 7, 1990

A SLAVE TO THE CAUSE

Almost 5,000,000 black Americans were slaves. Slavery was tearing the country apart and indeed, within a few years it would result in the bloodiest war in modern history.

But not all whites believed in slavery. And a few really concerned ones were working against it actively.

For more than a generation, there had been a well-organized system for getting slaves out of the south and into Canada where they were free. That was called the Underground Railroad.

The slaves who managed to get across the border at Windsor, Ontario, the most popular escape spot, settled mostly around nearby Chatham, Ontario. In 1858, Chatham had a population of 4500, a third of it black. So it was the logical spot for a convention of anti-slavers who wanted to plot their next move.

The most active of the anti-slavers was John Brown. Brown was one of those strange men who crop up in history from time to time, absolutely dedicated to a cause, completely uncaring how they achieve it.

Brown was from an old New England family. His ancestors had been among the pilgrims who settled at Plymouth Rock.

He was an unsmiling, humourless zealot, willing to lay down lives for his cause. Other people's or his own, it didn't matter to John Brown. Eventually, it turned out to be both.

Brown had gone west to Kansas which was in the grip of terrible guerrila warfare over the slavery issue. He and his followers, mostly his sons, had murdered five pro-slavery men in Kansas, hacking them to death with old fashioned swords.

John Brown was an unsmiling, humourless zealot, willing to lay down lives for his cause. Other people's or his own, it didn't matter to Brown.

Brown himself was absolutely fearless and he had led dozens of bands of runaway slaves north to freedom.

In April of 1858, Brown sent out messages to black and white followers all over the United States and Canada that the time had come for even more aggressive action.

On the 8th of May, Brown assembled 46 anti-slavery men in a big log schoolhouse in Chatham. They knew the slavers had spies everywhere so they told anyone who asked that they were getting together to form a new Masonic Lodge. But the Masons were segregated in those days. And 34 of the 46 at the meeting were black.

So a lot of the people started dropping around the schoolhouse to see what was going on. Brown and his men moved a few miles out of town to a firehall in an all-black area.

There, they drew up what was in effect a government-in-exile. They had ministers of war and titles like that. They planned to send small, heavily armed bands of men into the mountainous areas of the South. They would set up posts in the hills and then invite the slaves to run to join them and precipitate a war that would settle the issue once and for all.

Actually, they didn't follow that Chatham plan exactly. Those mountain outposts were never set up. But Brown and his men did start shooting.

Brown himself led a raid on an army arsenal and was captured and hanged.

The rest of it went pretty well according to his plan. It did bring on a bloody war and the blacks did get their freedom.

Originally broadcast May 2, 1986

THE BYRD WHO MIGRATED NORTH

On the 9th of May in 1926, an American plane took off from the island of Spitzbergen, north of Norway, to fly to the North Pole. The time was exactly 12:37 in the morning.

Fifteen hours and exactly 30 minutes later, the plane returned. The two-man crew announced it had been to the Pole, had circled it for 13 minutes and had returned.

Crowds all over the States went crazy. Early in this century, two Americans had each claimed to be the first to reach the North Pole on foot. Peary, a naval officer, and Cook, a doctor, said they had done it.

Their claims came so close together that a controversy immediately sprang up. To this day, experts still argue over it, although most reject Cook's claim.

But this time there could be no doubt, at least in the States. Europeans weren't so sure. And now, 60 years later, it looks like the doubters may yet get to write the history books.

In 1925, the Norwegian Amundsen, one of the greatest explorers of all time, had tried to fly over the Pole. That would have been a greater feat than walking in those days, considering the primitive state of airplanes. His plane got to within 156 miles of the Pole when it conked out.

Amundsen decided the best machine for the job would be a dirigible, a powered balloon. So, in the spring of 1926, he arrived at Spitzbergen with an American explorer named Ellsworth and an Italian dirigible and its skilled pilot.

The dirigible could stay in the air indefinitely because it was lighter than air. And its motor would provide power to steer although it couldn't buck strong winds. That's why they were there in May; the winds in the area were almost non-existent.

Suddenly, a ship arrived, containing the American explorer Commander Richard Byrd and his crew. Byrd was from one of the oldest, richest, most influential families in the States, the descendent of Virginia planters who were neighbours of George Washington.

Byrd's expedition was supported by the wealthy National Geographic Society plus a few individual millionaires like John D. Rockefeller and Edsel Ford. The plane Byrd bought was named the Josephine Ford, after Edsel's daughter.

The pilot was Floyd Bennett, one of the best airmen the United States ever produced. Bennett was a mechanic by trade, a poor boy who held non-commissioned rank in the American Navy. He lived in awe of Commander Byrd, a graduate of the naval academy and an officer and gentleman by act of Congress.

Two weeks after the flight, Byrd and his ship arrived in England and the reporters were out in droves to meet him. The European reporters had a lot of pointed questions about how he could have covered all that distance in such a short time. Byrd sloughed off their questions. The British and Americans seemed to buy everything he said.

The European reporters had a lot of pointed questions about how Byrd could have covered all that distance in such a short time.

But simple arithmetic makes it hard to understand. It was more than 1,300 miles to the Pole and back. The Josephine Ford had a top speed of 75 miles an hour, according to Floyd Bennett, the pilot. It would have needed to go more than 12 miles an hour over its top speed to have made the trip. Byrd later explained they caught a strong tail wind on the way back. But nobody else reported any wind and May was the windless month around there.

In 1960, a Swedish professor wrote an article after examining weather maps for the area at the time. He said there were no winds.

In 1927, Berndt Balchen, a Norwegian pilot for some of those early flights, wrote his memoirs. He wrote in the first edition that Bennett admitted to him later that they'd never got near the Pole. Byrd had already written his own best-seller in the States about his exploits and his publishers threatened to sue Balchen. Balchen's next edition appeared without that part.

Originally broadcast May 9, 1986

STRONG AS A STONEWALL

Back in 1853, one of the big attractions in Montreal was the British garrison. Canada was still a colony so the British kept a few regiments here. There was little for them to do so their sergeants and officers drilled the men in the complicated parade-ground manoeuvres of the day.

A thousand men would line up and march and wheel and carry on as if they were all stitched together. Quite a sight, especially for a professional soldier.

And in 1853, one Major Jackson of the American Army was in Montreal watching it.

Major Jackson was an instructor at the Virginia Military Institute and he was on his honeymoon. His wife Eleanor was very close to her sister Margaret so it was a honeymoon for three. The ladies couldn't bear to be separated.

Both Jackson and his wife were religious people, Presbyterians. Both believed devoutly in doing no work but the Lord's on a Sunday. Presbyterians used to be big on that.

But the British garrison troops in Montreal did their public drilling on Sunday afternoons. And Major Jackson went to watch.

When he got back to his hotel, his bride gave him a very hard time over it. Jackson was a slow, methodical, serious man. He saw his military career as a religious experience.

He told his wife she might be right. He would think about it. When he thought about it, he had to admit his wife was right. No secular work should ever be done on a Sunday.

After he returned to Virginia, Jackson became a leader in the movement to keep the Sabbath. He wouldn't take a trip late in the week if it might involve him travelling on Sunday. He campaigned to have mail not moved on Sunday.

Eight years after Jackson's Montreal honeymoon,

the United States split in the Civil War. Major Jackson resigned his commission in the American Army and joined the Confederate Army of Virginia.

He was a brilliant soldier. His slow, methodical manner was abandoned in the field. He moved his infantry men so quickly they were known as the foot cavalry. He once had his command march 50 miles in less than two days and win an impressive victory because the enemy figured he couldn't be anywhere near where he was.

Jackson once had his command march 50 miles in less than two days and win an impressive victory because the enemy figured he couldn't be anywhere near where he was.

Major Jackson was soon made a general. And because of generals like Jackson, the Confederates won most of the battles in the early years of the Civil War.

Jackson became famous as Stonewall Jackson. One battle was won because Jackson's command stood firm while other Confederates were breaking. Lee, the head of the Confederate Army, said: "There stands Jackson like a stone wall."

Jackson wasn't popular with his fellow generals because he wouldn't obey orders until he was ready. One, a General Magruder, was in trouble one day, his command cut up by Union soldiers because Jackson hadn't arrived in time to help him. Magruder said bitterly: "Now I know why they call him Stonewall. He moves like one."

But Lee realized that Jackson was the best of all his generals and he gave him the toughest jobs. In 1863, with the fortunes of war swinging toward the Union forces, Lee decided in one bold stroke to hit the enemy where they least expected it. He gave the job to Jackson and Jackson moved his army so quickly and struck with such force that he won a great battle.

But he got so far out in front of his own army that after the battle, at twilight with darkness approaching, Jackson was mistaken for the enemy and shot by his own troops. He died in hospital on the 10th of May in 1863.

Originally broadcast May 10, 1990

HONOUR THY MOTHER

Anna Jarvis was born and brought up in West Virginia in the States. Her father was a clergyman and she had a younger sister who was blind.

Her mother was a saint-like woman who was sorely troubled by the grief of the mothers who had lost sons in the terrible American Civil War. She tried to do something for them by creating what she called Mother's Friendship days, mostly days of prayer. West Virginia was one of those border places where men from the same families had fought on different sides in the Civil War so the wounds lasted long after the casualties were buried.

Anna was heartbroken when her mother died in 1905 and she wanted a special church service to honour her and the work she'd done for all those other saddened mothers.

It took two years to organize it to her satisfaction. She suggested that everyone who went to the service wear a white carnation if they had lost a mother, a red one if mother was still alive.

It was on the second Sunday in May, 1907, which fell on the 11th that year.

The idea caught on like wildfire. In fact, it caught on so well that the next year florists raised the price of carnations from a nickel to a dollar each. That began the second half of Anna Jarvis' career, a life-long fight with commercialism.

Poor Anna was a well-meaning, decent, religious lady who was no match for the advertising agencies and marketing wizards. She ranted and raved about commercialism to every reporter who would listen. She produced pages and pages of publicity for Mother's Day and pretty soon, in 1915, the president of the United States signed a law making it an official recognition of motherhood. By then most states and Canada had already given it a semi-legal status. European countries, most of the British Empire, and Japan followed.

In case there was any danger of anybody forgetting about Mother's Day, Anna would keep making sensational speeches about commercialism. In 1923 she threatened to sue the governor of New York state for holding a Mother's Day rally without her permission.

Anna threatened to sue the governor of New York state for holding a Mothers' Day rally without her permission.

By that time Anna had copyrighted the name, she thought. Actually, she had incorporated a foundation called the Mother's Day International Association and threatened to sue anybody who called the second Sunday in May Mother's Day. Of course, no court anywhere would accept her lawsuit so the matter was never settled. But it kept the issue alive and did wonders for sales of flowers and perfume.

The florists associations offered to pay Anna a commission on every bouquet they sold for Mother's Day and that made her even angrier.

She never married. She took care of her blind sister until she died then she moved to a house in Philadelphia where she had set up a little shrine to her mother with a little bowl of china roses in front of her portrait.

As the years went on, poor Anna got stranger and stranger. Finally, in 1943, with her money all gone and her eyesight failing, Anna was moved by friends to a nursing home where she died in 1948, totally blind, almost deaf. She never knew it but the florists association had donated generously to the fund to pay for the nursing home.

Originally broadcast May 11, 1992

NEGOTIATING A NATION

When Canada became a nation in 1867, the Hudson's Bay Company of London owned just about all the land from what's now the border of Ontario to the Rocky Mountains, north to the Arctic.

The new government in Ottawa began to negotiate to take over that land and, within a couple of years, had it. It wasn't as simple as that. In fact, a lot of last-minute quibbling and haggling went on and late in the process the Canadian government didn't have the money in a London bank account to write the cheque. But it eventually happened.

At the same time the Canadian government sent survey parties into the area. They began drawing lines and driving stakes.

What's now southern Manitoba, centred on Winnipeg, had been settled a long time before by French-speaking settlers from Quebec, and about a half-century previously by Scots and English-speakers from Ontario. By this time the French-speakers were mostly Metis.

The survey crews were under orders to not offend the Metis. Those people held their land according to an old custom their grandfathers had brought from Quebec. Their farms were laid out in long narrow strips running back from the rivers. And, by custom, they were allowed to cut hay, not only on their farms but a couple of miles beyond.

In the spring of 1869, the survey crews seemed to be drawing their lines with no regard for those hay lots. The Metis got restless and complained. In October of 1869, a group of them led by a young man named Louis Riel, blocked a survey gang.

The surveyors were under orders not to argue. They just dropped that job and moved to the English-speaking area and continued their work there.

But the Metis remained nervous, afraid the survey would start up again and ignore their rights and customs. They formed a loose, not very formal government with Riel as president. They called their territory Assiniboia.

Now, the basis of the Metis economy, in the early years, had been the buffalo hunt. That was a mass, co-

> *The survey crews were under orders to not offend the Metis, who held their land according to an old custom their grandfathers had brought from Quebec.*

operative affair with the men organized along a roughly military line, into brigades, with captains in charge. The government of Assiniboia used that organization to maintain order.

At the end of October, 1869, when a new lieutenant-governor arrived from the east, they stopped him at the border.

Some of the English-speaking settlers protested and the noisiest were thrown in jail. The noisiest of the noisy was a nasty man, a big-mouth from Ontario named Tom Scott. Since the government was organized along roughly military lines, Scott was condemned at a court martial. Riel, the president, could have commuted his sentence but he didn't. In early March of 1870, Scott was shot.

After that, a military expedition was sent out from the east, and the Assiniboia government and Riel just faded away.

Representatives were appointed and sent to Ottawa to negotiate union with Canada. Those men didn't really ask for much.

They wanted to be a province, not just a territory; they wanted a governor who spoke both French and English; and, they wanted an amnesty for the people who had set up the government of Assiniboia, in case the federal government ever decided to consider that a rebellion.

Sir John A. Macdonald, the prime minister, was a foxy old devil. This was the first new land acquisition by his young country and he knew it had to come off smoothly. So he gave with one hand and took away with the other.

He agreed to the request for provincehood. But he drew the boundaries so fine that the new province just took in a small fraction of what's now Manitoba, just the area around Winnipeg and Brandon, south to the border.

It worked for the time. The Manitoba Act was passed very quickly, on the 12th of May in 1870. Canada had taken its first small step as a nation.

Originally broadcast May 12, 1983

ARABIAN FIGHTS

Lawrence of Arabia was the most famous hero to come out of the First World War. He almost single-handedly won the war for Britain in the Middle East. Then, with the war over, he became a terrible embarrassment. Or, at least, a potential embarrassment. And that leaves an air of mystery over his death.

You have to understand the story of Thomas Edward Lawrence and his times.

Thomas Edward Lawrence was born in Wales in 1888, the illegitimate son of a well-to-do Irish landowner and the Scottish nanny he had run off with. Neither was named Lawrence. The couple moved from place to place, spending no more than two years in the same spot.

A couple who lived together without being married in Victorian England was on the run just as much as if they'd been bank robbers. They finally legally changed their names, and their children's, to Lawrence.

Mama Lawrence became quite crazy over it all, racked by constant guilt. She finished her days as a missionary in China, convinced God would never forgive her. She took one of Lawrence's brothers along with her on this mission of atonement.

Lawrence himself did quite well at Oxford, not in the conventional sense. He didn't get high marks. But he learned a lot. He was interested in archeology and spent a lot of time in the Middle East, digging away at ancient cities.

He was probably also working as a spy for the British government at the time, watching German railway-building and military assistance in the Turkish Empire.

That was before the First World War. When the war came along, Lawrence organized the Arabs to rebel against the Turks in the Holy Land. In less than a year the British had pounced on the Turkish Army that was already tied up fighting Lawrence and his Arab rebels. The result was a fast, easy victory for the British.

Lawrence was also a brilliant writer and he described the whole affair in one of the best adventure books of all time, *The Seven Pillars of Wisdom*.

The British had been talking out of both sides of

When the war came along, Lawrence organized the Arabs to rebel against the Turks in the Holy Land. The result was a fast, easy victory for the British.

their mouths at once in the Middle East. One faction in the foreign office promised the Jews their own homeland in Palestine, what's now Israel. Another, led by Winston Churchill promised the area to the Arabs. Lawrence worked for Churchill after the war at the various peace conferences that cut up the area. He was terribly disappointed at the result and felt he had betrayed his Arab friends.

Lawrence announced he was retiring from public life. Lawrence was a homosexual. But, in addition to that problem, in those straight-laced times, he had severe mental strains and stresses, probably picked up from his mother's terrible guilt feelings.

Lawrence joined the Royal Air Force as an aircraftsman, the lowest rank. The newspapers found out about it and made a big thing of it, Britain's most famous colonel serving in the ranks. The air force didn't like that sort of publicity and threw him out.

He joined the army, under a false name as he had joined the air force. But he didn't like that. He went back into the air force. Then, in 1935, he left it.

He had been toying with the British Fascist movement, a pro-Hitler group that attracted a lot of titled Englishmen in those days.

Lawrence was also a motorcycle speed freak and loved to zoom over twisting country lanes. That's what he was doing on the 13th of May in 1935 when he took a spin. He died without regaining consciousness a few days later.

A mysterious black car was seen nearby but never explained. The army clamped down on all information about the accident although Lawrence was a civilian when it happened. The coroner who conducted the inquest said the evidence was suppressed. Did somebody in the British government get rid of Lawrence rather than suffer the embarrassment of having him join the fascists?

Why not? Everything else about his life was mysterious.

Originally broadcast May 13, 1986

THE WITCHING HOUR

Samuel Parris was a clergyman in the New England village of Salem. He had a Black slave woman named Tituba, a native of the West Indies. This was in the late 1600s, in the early days of the settlement of New England.

Tituba claimed to be a fortune-teller and Parris' nine-year-old daughter and his 11-year-old niece often had Tituba predict the future for them. They particularly wanted to know who they would marry when they grew up.

In January of 1692, both girls took sick. They lost their power of speech for a while, fell over and seemed to have fits. The doctor couldn't figure what was causing it so he decided they must be bewitched.

The Reverend Parris suspected his slave girl Tituba so he beat her until she confessed to being a witch. Then he beat her some more and she named other witches. The girls, plus a few others in the village who had shown similar symptoms, were questioned and they said various people in the village, mostly women, were acting like witches.

Religion in those days was a strange mixture of piety, superstition, and just plain ignorance. The doctor's diagnosis had been typical of the day. Anything he couldn't explain he had to attribute to the supernatural, good or bad. If a patient he thought would die suddenly got better, he would call it a miracle, an act of God. If it was the opposite, it must be the work of the devil. The clergymen of the time were among the worst offenders, witness the Reverend Parris.

All those named as witches were put in jail in chains so they couldn't fly away. Then local magistrates began questioning them and hearing witnesses.

From June until September of that year, 1692, 20 people were executed for witchcraft. They weren't burned at the stake as witches were in Europe. They were hanged.

Before the executions actually started, the man who would stop them arrived. He was William Phips, a native New Englander who had been to London to get his commission as governor of the colony.

Phips arrived in Boston on the 14th of May and was horrified to hear that the jails of New England were filling up with suspected witches. He established a commission to inquire and to apply some sort of rational test to the evidence that was coming forth. He was too late to stop some of the cases and the executions that followed. But his commission soon found most suspects were being improperly held and ordered them freed. More important, the commission began to question the whole concept of witchcraft.

Within two years of the executions, judges and juries were publicly admitting they had been wrong. The legislature issued pardons, too late for the people who were hanged. But it paid compensation to their families.

In Europe and England, from medieval times until the days of the Salem witchcraft trials, thousands of people had been executed as witches. The Salem trials were puny by comparison. But for some reason history remembers the Salem trials and forgets all the others.

Religion in those days was a strange mixture of piety, superstition, and just plain ignorance. Anything a doctor couldn't explain he had to attribute to the supernatural, good or bad.

Originally broadcast May 14, 1992

PRINTING PRESSURE

Jack Capstick was one of the best detectives Britain ever produced. He was born in the north of England but he couldn't join the police force there because he was too short, just 5'9". In fact, the only force in the British Isles that would take a man that short in those days was the one in London so Capstick joined there.

Within a year he was such a hot-shot cop he was posted to Scotland Yard, and began a career as a detective that took him right to the top.

In the last few months of the war, in 1945 and on into late 1946, there was a series of attacks on children in the north of England, right around where Capstick came from, near Liverpool.

In those days detectives from Scotland Yard were sent out to the boondocks to help in any major investigations and Capstick had been in the area for two months.

He got nowhere and returned to London in early May of 1947. He was back less than a day when he got a call to return right away. The worst attack yet had occurred.

Sometime just after midnight, in the first hour of the 15th of May, someone had gone into the children's ward of a hospital at a place called Blackburn.

The intruder had taken a little girl of four right out of the hospital. He'd even left the door open. The child's body was found less than a half-mile away. She'd been beaten to death.

When Capstick got back to the hospital he could see right away what had happened. The little girl had been lying in one of 12 beds in the ward. Only six were occupied.

The floor had just been highly polished and the man's footprints were quite clear in the fresh, soft floor wax. He had taken off his shoes and walked in his socks.

He had stood for a while in front of his victim's bed.

And he had lifted a medicine bottle from a bedside table and set it on the floor. Probably so he could lift the little girl out of bed without knocking it over.

And he'd left beautiful fingerprints on the bottle. Ten fingerprints and a nice big palm print.

The cops worked around the clock on all the usual stuff: known sex offenders, recently-released mental patients, comparisons with similar crimes in other parts of the country . . . nothing.

Capstick even sent a team of fingerprint men into the surrounding area to take the prints of all the men 14 to 90. Still nothing.

Capstick knew the killer had to be a local man. No stranger would have been able to just walk in and out of that hospital. So he decided to ask every male over the age of 14 in the whole city to be fingerprinted. Blackburn, remember, was a city of almost 150,000.

> *The killer had to be a local man. So every male over the age of 14 in the whole city was fingerprinted. That meant more than 45,000 sets of prints.*

That meant more than 45,000 sets of prints.

Capstick's fellow coppers told him to forget it. The British were much too much concerned with civil liberties to hold still for that sort of thing.

Sure they will, said Capstick. If we promise that once our investigation is over we'll burn all the prints. And if the mayor volunteers to be the first.

Incredibly, it worked. The mayor agreed to be first, and they did collect 46,167 sets of prints.

Thirty policemen worked 14-hour days, taking all those prints. And on the 12th of August, exactly 90 days after the little girl was snatched, they found the prints that matched those on the bottle.

After the hanging, they had the biggest bonfire in local history: 46,166 fingerprint cards.

Originally broadcast May 15, 1984

FRESH HEIR

Ivan the Terrible was the czar of Russia back in the days when Elizabeth the First was the queen of England.

Ivan had seven wives in his lifetime. But only three children. His first wife gave him two sons, Feodor and Ivan. Feodor goes down in history as a simpleton. Historians aren't sure if he really was or if he was just pretending so he wouldn't get caught up in all the violence and politics that went with being the son of the czar. No matter; Feodor was out of the picture as far as the throne went.

That left young Ivan and he seemed to be a perfect successor for the old man. In 1569 there was a rebellion in the city of Novgorod and his son arrived with an army to put it down. Then Ivan had the royal blacksmiths make a huge frying pan and had a gigantic fire built under it and sauteed the rebels. Young Ivan went along with that and thought it was a great idea. In all, 60,000 people were killed in Novgorod. So that's the sort of guy young Ivan was.

However, Ivan and his son had an argument one day and Ivan hit the prince on the head with a steel-tipped club he carried. The boy died so now there was a problem with who would succeed Ivan.

That problem became acute in 1584 when Ivan died. By that time Ivan had another son, named Dmitry, by wife number seven. But the kid was only a year old and couldn't run Russia.

He and his mother were sent to a palace in the country while a regent ran the country. Or, spent most of his time knocking off rivals and letting the country run itself.

Russia, in those days, was a violent place in the best of times. It was now drifting toward anarchy and terrible bloodshed.

Then, to make matters worse, young Prince Dmitry was playing with a knife one day and cut himself. He was reported to have bled to death. A commission was set up to investigate but its report was so garbled it didn't clarify the situation.

Then, in 1603, almost 20 years later, a young man turned up in Poland and said he was Prince Dmitry, that he hadn't died as a result of the accident with the knife.

The king of Poland liked that. He was a Roman Catholic and so was young Prince Dmitry. If the king supported Prince Dmitry in his claim to the throne of Russia then Russia would become Catholic instead of Orthodox. The two countries had split over religion about 500 years earlier.

So the king of Poland gave Prince Dmitry an army and he marched into Russia. His army was defeated and it looked as if his attempt had failed. Then, at the crucial moment, the regent died, apparently poisoned. Dmitry took over rather easily.

Although his wife was a devout Catholic and Dmitry himself followed the Catholic faith, he allowed Lutherans and Unitarians to practice their religion. That seems to have been his downfall.

And he was a good czar. He was kind to people. He ran an efficient administration. He was tolerant. Although his wife was a devout Catholic and Dmitry himself followed the Catholic faith, he allowed Lutherans and Unitarians to practice their religion.

That seems to have been his downfall. Rivals to the throne whipped up the people, saying the Jesuit priests who had come to Russia with Dmitry's wife intended to stamp out the Orthodox Church.

There were riots and Dmitry was dragged out of his palace and hacked to death on the 16th of May in 1606. His body was burned and the ashes were mixed with gunpowder and put in a cannon, pointed toward Poland and fired back to where he came from.

Originally broadcast May 16, 1988

SEPARATE, BUT NOT EQUAL

Canadians know more about American courtrooms than about Canadian ones. We watch a lot of movies and TV about the American legal system and virtually none about our own.

Canadian judges traditionally don't pay any attention to American courts. But that's changing. We now have a constitution and our judges are very concerned about how to interpret it and apply it to everyday situations. That's something the Americans are very good at.

Their most famous cases in that field concern civil rights. And the most famous civil rights case is the Brown case that was settled on the 17th of May in 1954.

Back before the turn of the century, the Supreme Court of the United States had ruled that black and white Americans had to receive equal opportunities in education. They didn't have to go to school together but they had to be on an even footing.

School boards across the country insisted they were, that black schools were just as good as white schools. This was obviously not true.

Anyone who drove past a Black school, especially in the south, could see that it was falling down, it was crowded, and the equipment was almost non-existent.

But whenever black lawyers went to court to do something about it, they lost. They presented a famous psychological study that showed all-black schools bred a sense of inferiority among the students. The courts ignored that.

They showed figures. In one county in South Carolina, the school board spent 179 dollars a year on each white student and 43 on each black student. In a school district in Maryland, the newest, lowest-paid white teacher made more than the most experienced, highest-paid black teacher.

Then, in the early 1950s, black lawyers put together five cases from various parts of the United States that showed discrimination in schools. All these cases had been lost when they took them to court.

One of the cases centred on a seven-year-old girl named Linda Brown who lived in Topeka, Kansas. She had to walk through a railway switching yard to wait for an old beat-up school bus to take her to a black school on the other side of town. But she walked past a white school to get there.

Linda Brown had to walk through a railway switching yard to wait for an old beat–up school bus to take her to a black school on the other side of town. But she walked past a white school to get there.

The Supreme Court of the United States, the highest court in the country, the one that interprets the Constitution, only takes the cases it thinks have significance for the whole country.

Some of the liberal members of that court wanted to hear the Brown case to they could end segregated schools. Others were afraid that if they did that it could lead to another civil war. The chief justice was one of those conservatives. The court heard the case but didn't make a decision. Then the chief justice suddenly died.

A new chief justice was appointed and the court decided, unanimously, that separate schools for blacks and whites cannot be equal. From now on, the judges ruled, all American kids must go to school together.

That ruling wasn't really put into effect for more than three years. And then soldiers had to march in to enforce it. But it was the beginning of integration in a society that had always been segregated.

Originally broadcast May 17, 1988

THE WRATH OF THE COMET

Edmund Halley was the astronomer royal, the head star gazer for the king, back in the late 1600s and early 1700s. When Peter the Great of Russia visited England to learn about western civilization he spent a lot of time with Halley, who was known as one of the wisest men of his time.

In fact, one night Peter spent so much time with Halley that he had to take him home in a wheelbarrow. Peter must have been in almost as bad shape himself because he kept running the wheelbarrow into hedges and the next day one of his servants had to go around and pay off the hedge owners.

However, Halley didn't spend all his time boozing with czars. He also worked a lot with Isaac Newton, maybe the greatest mathematical genius of all time.

Halley and Newton made a lot of astronomical observations and calculations. Halley checked over old records of shooting stars and comets and he came to the conclusion that several spectacular ones were really the same comet, returning to our part of the universe about every 76 years.

Halley predicted it would be back in 1758. He died in 1742, so he never knew if he was right or not.

But, sure enough, what was now called Halley's Comet was sighted by a German on Christmas day, 1758. That news didn't reach England until the next year. And, of course, England was so foggy in the wintertime that no one there could see it.

Next, people started going through history books and they came to the conclusion that whenever Halley's Comet appeared all sorts of terrible things happened — floods, earthquakes, wars, famines, that sort of thing.

Today we realize that those things are happening somewhere in the world all the time. But for the next 150 years that idea persisted.

So, when Halley's Comet was due for its regular appearance in 1910, the world was apprehensive. To add to the situation, the telegraph and radio had been invented, so news could reach more people quicker than ever before. Not just news. Nonsense, too.

Two French scientists, or pseudo-scientists, predicted terrible things. In early May, they said, all sorts of horrible disasters would happen. Then, on the 18th of May, the tail of the comet would sweep over the earth. And its tail consisted mostly of deadly cyanogen gas.

The day after the announcement, King Edward of England died. An earthquake hit Costa Rica and killed 1500 people. Bubonic plague broke out in China. One hundred and twenty five miners were killed in a coal mine in Alabama and 137 the next day in a coal mine in England.

Farm workers in the deep south of the United States put down their hoes and waited for the end when that deadly gas hit on the 18th of May. Chinese peasants were reported to be cutting off their pigtails as a symbol of their resignation to death.

The leader of a religious sect in Oklahoma had a knife poised, ready to sacrifice a 16-year old girl from his flock to avoid the death of the world when the sheriff arrived to stop him. The prophet warned that the sheriff had just saved one girl and condemned all mankind.

Winnipeg reported an epidemic of suicides. In Montreal, a breeze slammed a door shut, and a woman jumped up, shouted, "it's the comet!" and dropped dead. In Pittsburgh, another woman shot herself.

And what happened on the 18th of May in 1910? Well, we're here to talk about it, aren't we?

> *People came to the conclusion that whenever Halley's Comet appeared all sorts of terrible things happened — floods, earthquakes, wars, famines, that sort of thing.*

Originally broadcast May 18, 1984

THE GREEN-EYED MONSTER

Early one morning in November of 1971, a policeman on patrol in Portsmouth, England came across a parked car with a body in it. There was a knife sticking out of the chest and the man had been stabbed seven times. There was blood on the steering wheel. Some of it belonged to the victim, some to somebody else. There were no fingerprints on the door handles.

The police quickly established that the dead man was Peter Stanswood, the part-owner of an amusement business, a place that rented those little boats you paddle.

Before dawn they were breaking the news to the widow, a strikingly beautiful woman named Heather Stanswood. Heather said she had no idea who would want to kill Peter. But there was a good chance it would be someone somehow connected with his sex life. Peter was quite an active lover, said his widow. He had two children by other women and a third was expecting. In addition to that he had carried on affairs with a couple of dozen other women in the recent past. Cops are used to hearing this sort of thing but they were taken aback by the number of women involved with the late Mr. Stanswood.

They questioned Stanswood's women friends, his partner, Ken Thompson, Thompson's wife Elizabeth, and then the widow again.

It seems that Heather and Elizabeth were school pals who had gone to work at their first jobs together. They had met Peter and Ken, also school chums, and they had got married.

But the men had roving eyes and were out looking for girls all the time. After a while the women decided to do a little of the same. And that's where the case got really complicated.

For the couple of years previous to the murder, the Portsmouth area had been inundated with workers from the Gas Board. All England was switching from coal gas to North Sea natural gas and that involved changing the stoves in people's homes. The Gas Board had sent in a couple of hundred mechanics from various parts of the country to get the job done as quickly as possible.

Both the widow and her pal Elizabeth had had affairs with gasmen. So several gasmen were questioned. And it turned out that many, many of the housewives of Portsmouth had had affairs with gasmen.

Before the case was over, the cops had questioned 20,000 people. They took 2,640 statements. They had to take some of them several times because the witnesses weren't all too eager to give accurate accounts of who they had been hanging out with and why.

Early in the investigation the detectives had talked to a gasman named Kenneth Fromant. He had been one of the widow Stanswood's many lovers. He had given a plausible explanation for where he had been the night of the murder and had been let go.

> *Heather said she had no idea who would want to kill Peter. But there was a good chance it would be someone somehow connected with his sex life.*

Nine months later, the cops were still asking questions when a woman they were interviewing mentioned that she'd been having an affair with a gasman at the time of the murder. That gasman had driven quite a way that night to see her and he had brought along another gasman to town, Kenneth Fromant.

That's strange, said the cops, Fromant told us he was in another town at the time. They got Fromant and asked some more questions. His answers weren't too straight but they still didn't have enough to arrest him.

The investigation went on until the 19th of May in 1975, three and a half years after Stanswood's body was found. That day, the police arrested Fromant and the widow Stanswood, charged with the murder. But that wasn't the last surprise in this case. The widow was soon released, and her girlfriend, Stanswood's partner's wife, was arrested instead. She and Fromant were guilty. The motive? Jealousy.

Originally broadcast May 19, 1989

SAY IT AIN'T SO, JOE

In the spring of 1940, the German conquest of France was in its final stages. Britain stood alone.

The British navy had goofed badly trying to stop the German invasion of Norway. Winston Churchill, the British prime minister, was carrying on a secret correspondence with Franklin Roosevelt, the president of the United States.

Roosevelt was in Churchill's corner. But he couldn't do much. There was a groundswell of public opinion in the States against getting involved in another European war.

Roosevelt had another problem. His ambassador in England was quite anti-British. He was Joe Kennedy, a tough, smart, Irish-American. Kennedy had become a millionaire as a stock market swindler. When Roosevelt became president he set up an agency to police the stock market and put Kennedy in charge. Kennedy was very effective, sending people to jail for things he used to do.

Kennedy's dispatches back to England predicted that the British were finished and advised Roosevelt to abandon them. Roosevelt and Kennedy were moving apart over this. The Germans were aware of both the tension between the president and his ambassador and the secret communications between Churchill and Roosevelt.

The reason was that a code clerk in Kennedy's embassy in London was feeding them copies of everything he handled. He was a strange man named Tyler Kent, an anti-Jewish nut who had been passed over for promotion several times and had become quite bitter.

Joseph Kennedy had hoped he just might have a shot at being president of the United States someday himself. But the spy scandal finished his career.

Kent passed on copies of embassy messages to a woman who was already under surveillance by the British secret service. She was a kook, the daughter of a czarist Russian admiral who had settled in London. She went around London, putting up little stickers that said: "Don't support this Jewish war."

She seemed so crazy the British didn't pay much attention to her. But when they saw her hanging around with Kent, they decided something must be up. So they arrested Kent on the 20th of May in 1940.

In his apartment they found 500 messages, all top-secret, all passed on to the woman who, in turn, passed them on to an Italian diplomat who was feeding them to the Germans. The woman was sentenced to 10 years in jail and Kent to seven.

Kennedy had hoped he just might have a shot at being president of the United States someday himself. But the spy scandal finished his career. So he raised his son, Joe Junior, to be president.

But within a few years, the United States was at war alongside Britain against the Germans. And, among the thousands of Americans who died in that war was Joe Junior. So old Joe had to adapt his plan and groom his next son, Jack, for the presidency. Jack became president in 1960. He was assassinated in 1963.

Tyler Kent outlived him. He did five and a half years and was deported to the States at the end of the war. He died in 1988 at the age of 77.

Originally broadcast May 20, 1993

BRAVE NEW WORLD

Christopher Columbus was always a man of mystery. That seems incredible because he's certainly one of the half-dozen most famous historical figures and a lot has been written about him.

We know from reams and reams of various accounts and documents that his commission to explore the western world was signed on the 17th of April in 1492, that he spent Christmas Day of 1502 exploring near what's now the Panama Canal...plenty more. But we know very little of Columbus' early life.

He claimed to have been born in Genoa, now part of Italy. He said his name was Italian, Cristoforo Columbo. But any signatures we have by him are in Spanish, Cristobal Colon.

His son once claimed Columbus went to university in Italy and studied mathematics and astronomy. That seems logical because he was a pretty good navigator. But Columbus himself claimed to have gone to sea when he was 14.

In everything he wrote, Columbus went out of his way to point out what a good Catholic he was. He usually threw a couple of religious references in any business letter and always made the sign of the cross right beside his signature.

Yet many people believe he was really a Jew. In fact, Simon Wiesenthal, the Nazi hunter, has written a whole book about his theory that Columbus was really a Jew sailing to find a new homeland for the Jews who were being expelled from Spain, just at that time.

Columbus was a strange mixture of smart and stupid. About 1600 years before his time, the ancient Greeks had calculated that the earth was round and had come up with its exact size.

Columbus believed most of that. Yet he thought by sailing west he would reach Japan. In fact, when he reached Cuba, he was convinced he was there. That would make the world a quarter smaller than the Greeks had figured.

But he ignored that. He was a good navigator but when he took fixes with his navigating instruments in Cuba, he made a series of mistakes that put this position somewhere around Cape Cod. That's where he wanted to be so that's where he convinced himself he was.

Despite his incredible ability to delude himself, Columbus was a shrewd businessman. He tried for 13 years to convince the king and queen of Spain to sponsor his expedition. He didn't get to first base.

Then, when they said they might be interested, he laid on some very stiff terms. He wanted to be made an admiral and to get 10 per cent of whatever treasure he found. He stuck to that until he got it.

After his discovery of the New World, Columbus was sent back again to establish colonies. There were complaints that he was a harsh and crooked administrator.

He was sent back to Spain in handcuffs. The queen quickly ordered him freed but he carried the handcuffs with him to his dying day to remind himself of how easy it was to get into trouble.

Columbus became a very rich man but not a happy one. He insisted that the king and queen hadn't given him everything that was due him under his contract. He spent the rest of his life travelling from city to city, as the royal court moved, riding on a donkey and asking for yet another chance to be heard.

And that's what he was doing when he died in 1506 on the 21st of May. Or was it the 20th or the 19th? We aren't even sure of that.

> *The ancient Greeks had calculated that the earth was round. And Columbus believed that. Yet he thought by sailing west he would reach Japan.*

Originally broadcast May 21, 1984

THE LORD WHO LOVED LEARNING

The Earl of Dalhousie was appointed lieutenant-governor of Nova Scotia in 1816. Like most British governors in those days, he was a military man, a lieutenant-general in the British Army after a lifetime of service. The year before his appointment, Dalhousie had been at the battle of Waterloo, the greatest victory in British military history and one that had ended France as a world power, leaving the field entirely to the British Empire.

His Lordship was a Scotsman and had been educated at the Edinburgh High School, in those days maybe the most advanced school in all the world. The Scots had a love of learning that no other people did. In those days, no one could go to a university in England unless he had sworn he was a member of the Anglican Church. The Scots had no such rules. Their schools were open to everybody.

Dalhousie was a typical British governor, conservative, snobbish, although not as much as most, and very much a supporter of the status quo. But where education was concerned, he was just the opposite.

There was a college in Nova Scotia when Dalhousie arrived, what's today the university of King's College. In those days it was more what we'd call a snobbish boys' private school. It was run very much along the lines of the English universities in that students had to be Anglicans, or at least claim to be.

The major educator in the province was a clergyman named Thomas McCulloch, a Scotsman like Dalhousie. The two didn't get along, maybe because Dalhousie was a Presbyterian and McCulloch was a member of one of many sects that had broken away form the Presbyterian Church. McCulloch started Pictou College in the north part of Nova Scotia as a training school for clergymen.

Dalhousie wanted a real university, one free of religious restraint and teaching all sorts of subjects, not just theology and dead languages.

Money was a problem. It always is with such projects. But he had a little at his disposal.

During the war of 1812, while Dalhousie was busy fighting the French in Europe, the British and Americans fought in North America. A British force had sailed from the Maritimes and captured the town of Castine in Maine. It had occupied the town for seven months and when the war ended and the British left they took with them the money they had collected at the customs house while they were in Castine.

The Americans had been claiming it and it was sitting in a Halifax bank, more than 15,000 pounds by the time Dalhousie arrived.

In the fall of 1819, Dalhousie was promoted to be governor-in-chief of all British colonies in North America. His replacement didn't arrive until early summer of 1820 so he had to sit and wait in Halifax.

He was determined to do something about a new college before he left. So, taking the Castine Fund, and some other discretionary money he had, he founded Dalhousie College. He laid the cornerstone on the 22nd of May in 1820. It got off to a very shaky start. But it eventually became what it is today, one of Canada's major universities.

> *Dalhousie wanted a real university, one free of religious restraint and teaching all sorts of subjects, not just theology and dead languages.*

Originally broadcast May 22, 1992

HOT-TO-TROTSKY

Lev Bronstein was a Ukrainian Jew, born in 1880. He was a brilliant man and when he became a revolutionary, he was soon one of the leaders of the movement.

Russia was a worn-out, decaying empire and the czars who had ruled for centuries were about to collapse. There were several parties ready to take over.

By far, the strongest and most determined was the communists. But the czar's police were pretty efficient and Bronstein and his pals had to keep on the run.

Bronstein's first 20 years were an endless chain of arrests, escapes, exiles and stealthy retreats to Russia. He made it out to London in the late 1880s with a phony passport in the name of Leon Trotsky. That name stuck with him for the rest of his life.

In 1917, with the First World War at its height and Russia defeated by the Germans, Trotsky was editing a communist newspaper in New York.

He dropped everything and headed home, realizing the revolution he'd worked for was about to begin. He tried to go through Canada and found himself locked up in Halifax for four months. But he talked his way out and eventually made it to Russia in time for the revolution. In fact, he was one of the key people.

The communist leader was Lenin, a spell-binding speaker. His two assistants were Trotsky, the organizer, a natural leader, and Stalin, a bloodthirsty brute, not nearly as bright or as popular as Trotsky but absolutely ruthless.

The Russian Revolution became a complicated affair that turned into a civil war. Trotsky was given the job of organizing an army. And he put together the Red Army, the one that finally won.

Then, when Lenin died, Trotsky the brilliant organizer, was out-manoeuvred. Stalin grabbed power. Trotsky resisted but it was too late. Stalin just shot most of his opponents. For some reason, he allowed Trotsky to leave Russia.

A big mistake. Trotsky moved to France, then to Norway. He wrote and lectured and gathered a lot of

When Lenin died, Trotsky the brilliant organizer, was out-manoeuvred. Stalin grabbed power. Trotsky resisted but it was too late.

left-wingers around him, people convinced that he would make a better international communist leader than Stalin. Because Trotsky preached the word that communism, to succeed, must cover the world. Trotsky's propagandizing attracted a lot of converts and the communist movements in many countries were split.

Stalin, back in Russia, had made himself absolute leader with a bloodbath that still hasn't been accurately measured. The death toll was certainly in the millions, maybe dozens of millions.

Stalin protested to the Norwegian government that Trotsky was using Norway as a base to get another Russian revolution going. The Norwegians caved in and kicked him out.

The Mexicans said Trotsky could live in their country. From there, Trotsky stepped up his anti-Stalin campaign. He wrote a biography of Lenin that showed Stalin in a very bad light. Then he signed a contract with an American publisher to write a biography of Stalin. This would surely blow the lid off.

By that time the Second World War had started and all Europe was aflame although Russia wasn't involved yet.

Stalin ordered his secret police to get rid of Trotsky. On the 23rd of May in 1940, several men dressed as Mexican cops barged into his villa shooting. They fired 73 bullets into Trotsky's bed. But he had heard them coming and hid in the closet.

Trotsky said after they left, it was Stalin. And he won't give up. He'll try again.

Sure enough, within three months, Trotsky was attacked with a mountain climber's pickaxe by a young man posing as a Belgian journalist. Actually, he was a Spanish assassin who had been carefully prepared for the job.

Trotsky died and Stalin was the only major communist leader left. The assassin spent 20 years in jail in Mexico then was released and headed for Russia where a hero's welcome was waiting.

Originally broadcast May 23, 1991

CAUGHT RED-HANDED

On the 24th of May in 1936, just a few minutes before closing time, two men entered a liquor store in Sarnia, Ontario. The taller man had a gun in each hand. He jumped the counter while the other robber held a gun on the customers.

But a man about to enter the store saw what was happening and he called the cops. The police station was less than a block away and a dozen policemen arrived. The tall robber with the two guns shot the first cop. The other cops shot both robbers.

The shorter of the two robbers was quickly identified as Harry Checkley, a small-time hood. No surprise there. But it was harder to figure out who the taller robber was, the two-gun guy. His hair was dark brown, almost black. But it turned out to be dyed. He was really a redhead.

Then the story hit the headlines: Red Ryan had gone bad again.

You just can't understand today what a sensational story that was in 1936. It would be like reading that the pope had been caught shoplifting.

Red Ryan was what penal reform was all about. Red Ryan was living proof that a desperado can turn out all right. Red Ryan was the personal pet project of every prominent do-gooder in the country.

Red Ryan was as phony as a stewardess' smile.

Ryan was a tall, good-looking glib kid from Toronto who had got caught stealing a bicycle when he was 12 and a chicken when he was 13.

He was convicted once a year until he was 17. Then he went away for three years for burglary and robbery. He got out, got caught in a payroll robbery and was back in Kingston Penitentiary when the First World War started.

Ryan was released to join the army. He spent most of his military career in the army clink, then deserted, sailed around the world and came back to Toronto in 1921.

The next year he got 25 years for five bank robberies but he broke out of Kingston a year later.

He robbed several more banks and was finally caught in Minneapolis. The American newspapers referred to him as the Jesse James of Canada. Red loved that. The hometown papers had pretty well ignored him.

The priest at Kingston campaigned for parole for Red. Even the prime minister, R. B. Bennett, visited him and pronounced him completely rehabilitated.

When they caught him this time it was life. Ryan did 11 and a half years in Kingston. In that time he became the perfect inmate. He took correspondence courses, became an altar boy, worked as a nurse in the prison hospital, even gave up smoking and swearing.

The priest at Kingston, Father Kingsley, campaigned for parole for Red. Even the prime minister, R. B. Bennett, visited him and pronounced him completely rehabilitated.

In July of 1935, Red Ryan was paroled. Ten months later, he was killed in the Sarnia liquor store. In those 10 months, Ryan was a celebrity. He hung around with the rich and famous and people asked for his autograph.

A few months before Ryan died, a father and son outside Toronto were killed as they chased away burglars from their house. It turned out later that Ryan did that. Plus another half-dozen or so robberies and burglaries.

Penal reform advocates said for years that Red Ryan, with his publicized back-sliding, did more to set back parole than anything else. For years Canada had the world's highest prison population per capita and lowest number of people on parole. Thanks to Red Ryan.

Originally broadcast May 24, 1984

MASTERS OF THE MUSICAL

When they made a movie 40 years ago about the lives of Gilbert and Sullivan, the screenwriters didn't have to strain their imaginations. The real story is just like a movie script.

Arthur Sullivan was a poor boy from one of those homes the soap writers love: a talented-but-never-fully-appreciated father, a loving mother who looked and acted like an ad for apple pie, a brother who was also talented and started a brilliant career but died young. If it weren't all a matter of record you would have to laugh and scream: corny, corny, corny...

Sullivan made it to one of the very best British choir schools for talented boys, then went on to the continent to study the classics with the leading serious European musicians. He maintained those contacts to his dying day.

He rose from poor boy to the peak of British society, beloved by the Queen, knighted, hanging around with dukes and earls and the Prince of Wales himself. A fine, warm gentleman to his toes.

William Gilbert was something else. He was born into a very well-to-do family and was brilliant at school. He could do anything he wanted without much effort. Unfortunately for his career, all he really wanted to do was impress people with his keen, cold, sarcastic wit. Gilbert liked to be judged by the dozens of enemies he made.

Gilbert studied law and actually practiced for a little while, but he didn't like it, so he turned to play-writing and was an instant popular and commercial success.

It was inevitable that someone would bring Gilbert and Sullivan together. But when they first met socially in 1869, it didn't occur to either to suggest a collaboration. A couple of years later, someone did come up with the idea. In later years, the new team produced a dreary, soon-to-be-forgotten musical about life among the Greek gods on Mount Olympus. It wasn't exactly a bomb but nobody left the theatre humming the tunes.

But one man was impressed. That was a stage manager and producer named Richard D'Oyly Carte. He figured Gilbert and Sullivan could make a great team if they would just keep at it. But they didn't.

Then, in the spring of 1875, D'Oyly Carte had a problem. He had brought a very expensive actress from the Continent to London to do a series of plays by the great French composer of the 1800s, Offenbach.

They were pretty well received, making money and drawing respectable crowds. But one was too short to fill an evening. So D'Oyly Carte asked Gilbert to write something short and witty that would take up the slack.

Gilbert, the lawyer who didn't like law, came up with *Trial By Jury*, a funny, biting stab at courts, judges, lawyers, and the whole legal system.

D'Oyly Carte commissioned Sullivan to put music to it, and in the spring of 1875, it hit the stage with an incredible blast. It was the *My Fair Lady* of its day. No, even that doesn't describe its impact. *My Fair Lady* was a great musical but there had been others before it. *Trial By Jury* was probably really the first great musical in the sense that we think of the word today.

Gilbert and Sullivan quickly followed with another show, *The Sorcerer*. It wasn't one of their best but it was pretty good and it kept the ball rolling.

Then they figured they had to come up with a blockbuster. If it didn't work they would go back to their old trades. If it did, they would be assured successes.

The British liked nothing as much as their Navy. So they did a show about sailors and girls and the snobbish British social system that made admirals of nit-wits and kept bright men swabbing decks. They called their ship, and the show, *H.M.S. Pinafore*.

The audiences liked it but they didn't go crazy. Box office fell off after a couple of weeks. They announced it would close soon. Sales picked up. Then they fell off. They picked up. They fell off again. Slowly, it seemed to grow on audiences, and eventually it ran 700 nights.

Strangely, it was an instant, much greater hit in New York. That didn't help Gilbert, Sullivan, and D'Oyly Carte much. The copyright laws were so loose in those days that while New Yorkers filled the theatre, the show's creators didn't make a dime.

> *They figured they had to come up with a blockbuster. If it didn't work they would go back to their old trades. If it did, they would be assured successes.*

Originally broadcast May 25, 1983

DEAR DIARY . . .

Samuel Pepys isn't a major figure in history. But he's a very important person to historians.

Pepys was a senior civil servant in the late 1600s in England. In fact, he was probably the most important single shorebound official in the Royal Navy. The British Navy's superiority for the next couple of centuries was in great part the result of Pepys' work. But that's not why we remember him.

For a fairly short period in his life, exactly nine and a half years, Pepys kept a detailed, intimate diary that has since been deciphered and published. On the basis of that diary we judge a lot of the rest of history of the day.

One of the many things in Pepys' diary was that King Charles the Second, in the 1660s, spent millions of public money on his several girlfriends and his 11 illegitimate children.

And high-ranking men did the same. But just how prevalent was this sort of thing? How reliable are the accounts of lesser officials when they protest that they were always scrupulously honest?

Pepys was an awful lecher and was always chasing women. For years, his wife made his life miserable, often suspecting him, occasionally chasing him.

Well, one of the ladies Pepys spent an afternoon with was the wife of a master carpenter, probably a man with a small business and a dozen or so employees.

Pepys decided who got contracts to repair navy ships. And Pepys records in his diary that he and the lady got quite intimate, her payment being a few ship repair jobs for her husband. We can tell from Pepys fairly casual description of the affair that it was no big deal at the time, that that sort of thing was, if not common, at least not unheard of.

Pepys was fairly well educated but his family wasn't rich. He was cousin of a lord who used his influence to get Pepys a civil service job working for a brash, rich, clever American named George Downing in the royal treasury. Downing dabbled in real estate on the side.

That's why the British prime minister's official residence today is on Downing Street. George Downing was the developer.

Pepys was a bright man and quickly picked up the methods of government office plus the little tricks that enabled him to live well with deals on the side.

Pepys was moved to the navy office and spent more than 30 years there. Since he would be in charge of equipment and men and food for the ships of the navy, he began by studying the markets for rope and masts and sails and cannon and all that sort of thing. It was the first time in British history that a purchasing agent for the government knew anything about what he was purchasing.

He made possible a more efficient navy. He also made possible a chance to line his own pocket at the same time.

We know that Pepys was this strange combination of crook and patriot because, years after he died, someone figured out the strange code he used to keep his diaries. Altogether he used 314 characters instead of our 26 letters. He wrote in a form of shorthand he made up himself plus phrases and sentences in Latin, French, German, Greek and Dutch if he wanted to keep things secret.

We know that he had to fire a housemate because his wife caught them together. We know that one time Mrs. Pepys heated the fireplace tongs until they were red-hot then went at him with them. Her aim was just a little off. But if she had connected that time there would have been no further need to keep an eye on Sam and the maids.

We know that one night Pepys got so angry he punched Mrs. Pepys and gave her a black eye. And we know a million other details, some frivolous, some of great historic importance.

All because Sam Pepys kept a diary from the beginning of 1660 until halfway through 1669. Then he quit because he was afraid he was going blind. But he wasn't. He lived more than 30 years after that and didn't die until the 26th of May in 1703.

Pepys wrote in a form of shorthand he made up himself plus phrases and sentences in Latin, French, German, Greek and Dutch to keep things secret.

Originally broadcast May 26, 1987

CREAM OF THE CRIMINALS

On this day, the 27th of May in 1850, Thomas Neill Cream was born in Scotland. Cream attended school in Montreal, where his family moved when he was four. His father prospered as a merchant in Montreal and Quebec city, and there was enough money to send him to medical school. He graduated from McGill in 1876.

Cream married a girl from Waterloo, Ontario in his last year of medical school. When she became pregnant, he performed an abortion on her that was badly botched. She died from complications a year or two later but by that time she and Cream had split up. Cream went to London and Edinburgh for further study.

There, he spent most of his time with prostitutes; and some believe he contracted syphilis and that led to his obvious insanity. Others claim he was out of it from day one. At any rate, he moved to London, Ontario and set up practice there. He seduced a chambermaid at his hotel, then killed her during a badly-handled abortion. It was becoming a bit of a habit. Cream was charged with murder but got off for lack of evidence.

Cream then moved to Chicago and started practising there. His specialty was abortion. Two of his patients died but the police didn't seem very interested. Chances are Cream was paying someone off because the Chicago police of the day were notoriously corrupt.

A beautiful young lady who had an old husband came to him complaining that no doctor seemed to be able to cure his problems. Cream started off by curing hers, right there in the office. Then he gave her some medicine for her husband. But first he loaded him up with life insurance.

Cream would have got away with that murder, too, but the insurance company was more careful with its money than the police department was with its citizens. Cream was charged with murder and his girlfriend, the victim's beautiful young wife, saved herself by testifying against him.

Cream was convicted and sent to jail for life. That was in 1881 when Cream was 31. And that's the end of him, you say. Not so. The Dr. Cream story is barely beginning.

Cream's father died in 1887, leaving him quite well off. It's amazing how hard lawyers can work for a prisoner who has just come into some money. They went to work on the

Cream case and in 1891, after serving 10 years, Cream was released.

He went to Quebec long enough to pick up his inheritance, then sailed for London. He arrived there in the fall of 1891. Bear that date in mind. And another: 1888. That was the year that Jack the Ripper carved up a half-dozen London prostitutes.

Cream began hanging around with girls from the streets. He told them he was a doctor, that he could see they were in poor health and he had some pills for them.

Cream told the girls he was a doctor, that he could see they were in poor health and he had some pills for them. He had, too. They were loaded with strychnine.

He had, too. They were loaded with strychnine. He killed at least three girls that way. Then he wrote letters to the police and to prominent citizens, saying the girls had been murdered. That was the first the police knew about it. They had assumed the girls had died of alcoholism or natural causes.

Cream was deliberately drawing attention to himself but the police couldn't get enough on him to make a case. But they watched carefully.

In January of 1892 he sailed again for Quebec although nobody knows why. He stayed at a hotel there and showed a bottle of strychnine to a salesman from Ottawa. He said he used it to kill people.

Then he returned to London. There in April of 1892, he poisoned two young prostitutes. Both died in agony. A policeman had seen Cream with them earlier in the evening and he was charged with murder.

The salesman was brought from Ottawa and told of the bottle of poison and the strange conversation. Cream was convicted.

But during his trial a strange thing happened. The judge got a letter saying Cream hadn't killed those girls. The man who wrote the letter had. It was signed Jack the Ripper. And the Ripper never was caught.

When Cream was hanged, at the last second, he said: "I am Jack the" . . . too late. He never got out the rest.

Illinois records show that Cream was in jail for murder when the Ripper was loose in London. Some say Illinois was so crooked in those days that Cream could well have been released long before the records indicate.

Originally broadcast May 27, 1983

CLIMB EVEREST MOUNTAIN

On the 28th of May in 1953, Edmund Hillary, a New Zealand beekeper, and Tenzing Norkay, a Sherpa mountaineer, reached the top of Mount Everest, the highest point on earth. They're down in the record books as the first and they probably were. But not necessarily.

It was only 22 years since the first serious attempt to reach to top of the world. And in that time, 11 expeditions had come very close but none had quite made it. Unless a pair of Englishmen named Mallory and Irvine did. They set out in the 30s and were never seen again.

Anyhow, the British team of 1953, under a Colonel Hunt, numbered 13. Hillary and his friend Lowe were from New Zealand. They set out in early May with their food and equipment being carried by a dozen porters, hardy little men from the local tribe, the Sherpas.

The best mountaineer of them all was Tenzing Norkay, a Sherpa who was veteran of many expeditions up Everest. He was along, not as a porter, but as one of the climbers. He was teamed with Hillary.

The magic figure in Everest climbing is 29,000 feet or 8,848 metres. When the height of the highest mountain was accurately surveyed at 29,000 feet the mapmakers changed it to 29,001 in the United States and 29,002 in Britain. They were afraid people would think they couldn't measure it accurately and had made a guess.

The base camp, the one with most of the supplies, the one at the end of the fairly easy climbing, was set up at 17,900 feet. They then went forward in teams of two and three, setting up other camps and leaving supplies. At that height they needed oxygen equipment for breathing. And they had to have plenty of spare oxygen bottles because they used up a lot of breath and energy at that height. At the top of Everest, as you would expect, it's always winter.

Several climbers and porters either pulled muscles or came down sick from the thin air and exertion. But by the 26th of May they were in Camp Eight, at 26,000 feet.

The higher the camps got, the fewer men they could support because oxygen, food and fuel had to be carried up to each. So on the 26th, Hillary and Tenzing dropped back to Camp Seven at 23,000 feet. They were making room for two Englishmen named Evans and Bourdillon who would probably be the ones to actually reach the top.

The whole team made the assault but only one pair actually got to stand on the top of the mountain. Evans and Bourdillon reached 28,700 feet, higher than anyone had ever made it, unless Mallory and Irvine did it.

Then they checked their oxygen. They had enough to take them to the top. But it would be a suicide attempt if they did make it. They didn't have enough to get back. So they turned back at that point.

The body used up incredible amounts of food and energy at that height. Evans had to drink two quarts of lemon juice and hot tea before he could speak back at Camp Eight.

He told Hillary and Tenzing he was sure they could make it. So they did. They got up at 4 a.m. on the 28th of May and made it in one steady climb. They got there around noon, took pictures and shook hands.

Then they turned around and climbed back down again. Once you're at the top of Mount Everest that's about all there is to do.

> *They checked their oxygen. They had enough to take them to the top. But it would be a suicide attempt if they did make it. They didn't have enough to get back.*

Originally broadcast May 28, 1986

THE BETTER HALF

Josephine has become a fixture in history, the other half of Napoleon and Josephine. Most people don't know much about her but they do know she was Napoleon's wife. She was much more than that. And eventually a little less.

Josephine was born in the French island of Martinique in the West Indies. Her father and grandfather were French noblemen, shiftless, stupid and absolutely irresponsible. When a hurricane blew the roof off the big white house the family lived in, Papa just moved them into a storehouse and said they'd stay there until the house was fixed. It never was.

When Josephine was a little girl she played with the children of the Black Slaves around the plantation and her education was horribly neglected.

She went to France and married a wealthy nobleman who was a bit brighter and more ambitious than her father, a man named Beauharnais.

When the French Revolution broke out, both Beauharnais and Josephine were thrown in jail. He went to the guillotine and Josephine was supposed to. But Napoleon came to power and put an end to the mass executions before her name was reached on the list.

When Josephine was released from jail, she went back home and picked up her life as if nothing had happened. She was the most extravagant woman in Paris and spent a fortune, whether she had it or not, on dresses and jewelry. She usually could find some boyfriend to pick up the bills.

When she met Napoleon she was a 33-year-old widow with a boy of 14 and a daughter a couple of years younger.

Napoleon fell for her like a ton of cannonballs. Josephine was having an affair at the time with a general she met in jail and she spent a while trying to get rid of Napoleon.

They were married in 1796. She cut four or five years from her age on the wedding license and he added a couple to his so officially she was only a year or so older than he was.

They were only married a little while when Napoleon went off to conquer Egypt. Josephine stayed home and fought with his mother and sisters and found another boyfriend or two to pass the time. And shopping, of course. She bought up everything in sight and signed Napoleon's name.

Josephine was good-looking but not beautiful. She had bad teeth and spent hours in front of the mirror, practicing smiling without uncovering her teeth.

As Napoleon made it quickly up the ladder from penniless young army officer to emperor of all Europe, Josephine realized she was onto a good thing.

As Napoleon made it quickly up the ladder from penniless young army officer to emperor of all Europe, Josephine realized she was onto a good thing. She really liked him and was the only person who could soothe him at night when his troubles moved in on him.

When he was dictating his memoirs Napoleon said he had had 14 mistresses in his life after he married Josephine. People who kept score of such things estimated that she outdid him by four or five times with her lovers.

But she was always there when he came home from a campaign. Although sometimes there was a draft as the back door opened to let her latest boyfriend make a fast exit.

In 1809, after they had been married almost 14 years, Napoleon divorced Josephine. He still had a big burn for her but he was absolutely determined to have a male heir to carry on his work. So he dropped her and married the daughter of the emperor of Austria, a vacant kid whose only known accomplishment was an ability to wiggle her ears.

Josephine couldn't oppose the divorce. So she went into a prosperous exile at a country estate and continued to spend like crazy and send the bill to the national treasury. She died of diphtheria on the 29th of May in 1814.

Originally broadcast May 29, 1986

THE NAME GAME

Prince Edward Island was visited by Jacques Cartier on his first great voyage of exploration in 1534. In the years that followed, the French made several attempts to establish colonies there, none with any great success.

But in the mid-1700s, several French-speaking Acadians settled there. They had been living for a century or so in what's now Nova Scotia and New Brunswick.

In 1745 those areas were conquered by the British. The British demanded the Acadians take oaths of allegiance to Britain and those that didn't were threatened with deportation.

A couple of dozen families just moved to Prince Edward Island. In those days the French called it Ile St. Jean. The British translated that literally and it was on their maps as St. John Island.

The whole of the Maritime provinces in those days was Nova Scotia, as far as the British were concerned.

When the king of England took over, various of his officials asked for the island. They figured they would own it, sit in England and live well off the rents. The king wasn't so sure this was a good idea although he wasn't against letting his friends own land so they could collect the rents.

In 1764, the king sent a surveyor to look the place over and draw up some accurate maps. Two years later, he put the names of all the people who wanted the place into a box. The surveyor had divided the island into 67 townships. The king kept one for himself. So the first 66 names drawn were awarded a township each.

The new owners were supposed to build roads and docks, send out people to settle the land and pay the wages of the governor and officials who would be required to operate it as a colony. They were also supposed to pay an annual fee called a quit rent.

The colonists, of course, were to be Protestants. The king of England in those days didn't want his colonies settled by Catholics because there was still lots of religious struggle going on in Europe.

On the 30th of May in 1769, the king split the island off from Nova Scotia, calling it the separate colony of the Island of St. John.

The first governor was a British army officer, an Irishman named Walter Patterson. He didn't arrive until the next year and he found the place in pretty poor shape. There were two big wooden buildings and maybe a handful of log cabins about where the city of Charlottetown is today. And there were a few villages scattered around the island.

The money the owners back in England had paid as quit rents was supposed to be in a fund to pay Patterson and his various officials. But the money hadn't been paid so they went without salaries for a while.

The new chief justice arrived, expecting to find a house, lots of supplies and a courthouse for him to work in. When he saw the miserable conditions he would have to live in, he returned to Halifax for the winter so he wouldn't starve to death.

During that winter he heard the chief justice's job in South Carolina was open and he applied for that. He only returned to the island because he didn't get the South Carolina job. The poor man died five years later, obviously worn out by his ordeal. The following spring his daughter , a girl of 12, died from starvation.

In 1780, the British government decided the island needed a new name because there were eight rivers, forts and seaports along the Atlantic coast named St. John and it was getting confusing.

Patterson, the governor from Ireland, decided to call the island New Ireland. But that name was already applied to an island away off in the South Pacific.

So, in 1799, the inhabitants of the island were charmed and delighted when their island was named Prince Edward Island, after the king's son.

Lucky they didn't know what Prince Edward thought of their island. He once said it made no sense that it should be a separate colony. He wanted it to become part of Nova Scotia again.

It didn't. But the name stuck.

> *The British government decided the island needed a new name because there were eight rivers, forts and seaports along the Atlantic coast named St. John and it was getting confusing.*

Originally broadcast May 2, 1986

A MAJOR SHOCK

Major Herbert Armstrong was the clerk of the magistrates court in Hay, a large town in Wales. Armstrong was the picture of British respectability. He had studied law at Cambridge then been in the army of the First World War. He liked to be called Major Armstrong.

The magistrates courts in Britain aren't like ours. They consist, usually, of laymen, non-lawyers.

In Hay in the early 1920s, there was a retired admiral, a lady who had been in local politics, a retired farmer and a retired grocer. Usually three of them would sit as a panel of judges to hear minor cases.

If they ran into a question of law, they looked to Major Armstrong for guidance. If it doesn't sound like a very sophisticated set-up, don't knock it. It worked. Hay was a very law-abiding community and the magistrates usually had to hear only cases of speeding or petty theft or drunkenness.

The British were proud of their system and Major Armstrong of Hay would have easily stood as the symbol of British justice.

Major Armstrong didn't have the happiest home life you could imagine. He was just a little guy, 5'3". He was married to an amazon, a mouthy big lady who had all the money in the family. She wasn't slow to give the Major a blast in public if he offended her.

That didn't bother the Major too much. He spent most of his time in his garden, growing grass with fertilizer and killing weeds with arsenic.

And, one other thing. The Major made trips from time to time. He had a girlfriend in London.

In late 1921 Mrs. Armstrong was acting strangely.

The Major was arrested and the cops seized a little package of arsenic from his vest pocket. He said he used it to kill dandelions.

The Major called in the local doctor and Mrs. Armstrong was soon on her way to a mental hospital. The Major did just fine without her. But Mrs. Armstrong recovered and came home. In early 1922, she took sick and died.

She had had a history of heart trouble. The local doctor made out a death certificate although he wasn't absolutely sure her symptoms showed a bad heart. More like stomach trouble.

The Major bore up well under his sorrow. He returned to the court and continued as clerk.

Then a local lawyer went to the police with a strange story. He thought Major Armstrong was trying to poison him. He was terribly sick after dinner with the Major. He tested positive for arsenic.

The cops dug up Mrs. Armstrong and she was loaded with the stuff. The Major was arrested and the cops seized a little package of arsenic from his vest pocket. He said he used it to kill dandelions.

At his trial he stuck to that story and looked like he would get off. Then, just as he was about to step out of the witness stand, the judge asked him why he would put the arsenic in little packages and carry them around in his pocket when it would be so much easier to just dump the arsenic on the dandelions right out of the bottle. The jury got the message.

On the 31st of May in 1922, the perfect symbol of British respectability and justice, the backbone of the British legal system was hanged.

Originally broadcast May 31, 1989

MASSIVE CHANGES

Vincent Massey was the fabulously wealthy son of one of the richest families in Canadian history, the dynasty that started out making farm tools and grew into the biggest farm-machinery empire the world ever saw.

Vincent was an austere, dried-up looking little man with no talent whatsoever for business and not much more for politics. He was an intellectual and wanted to be a leader. He wasn't prime minister material because he couldn't get elected to anything. He saw himself as more of a governor-general.

In the late 1920s when Canada finally was allowed to have its own ambassador to Washington, Massey was chosen for the job. When the Second World War was on, he was Canada's high commissioner in London. The king thought he was great, the perfect English gentleman. Canadians muttered about how he was more British than the British.

At the end of the war, Massey reported the king wanted to make him a duke or some such. It was against Canadian law for a Canadian to accept such an honor but Massey hoped an exception would be made for him. He was told it wouldn't.

So Massey returned to Canada, looking for his next big-time job. He was offered the post of lieutenant-governor of Ontario and said no thanks. He was made chancellor of the University of Toronto, but that's a ceremonial job with no real power.

Next Massey hinted that he would be available to head a royal commission on science and culture. This was in 1950, at a time when Canadians were suddenly quite nationalistic. Being part of the British Empire was no longer a sufficient role for the nation that had made such a major contribution to victory in two world wars. Being just another part of the United States wasn't, either.

Canada would be defined in the next generation by its culture. And the government badly needed something to define that culture. So the Massey Commission was set up. Massey, the stiff little man who couldn't get elected, turned out to be just the perfect person for the job.

Academics and scientists and professors and artists and musicians and writers, philosophers and industrialists all appeared before Massey's Commission and told what sort of country they wanted to live in. Massey was chatty, informal, witty . . . if he'd been running an election instead of a royal commission he would have won easily.

Canada would be defined in the next generation by its culture. And the government badly needed something to define that culture.

Massey and his four fellow commissioners boiled down all that was presented to them and made their report to Parliament on the first of June in 1951. They suggested a body to foster the arts in Canada. That became the Canada Council. They suggested federal money for universities in the form of both scholarships and money to build research facilities.

Maybe most important of all, the Massey Report suggested the government double its commitment to the CBC. Remember, this was in 1951, before there was Canadian TV. There were 25,000 sets in all of Canada and 10 million in the States. It worked. Canada did develop its own distinctive TV culture.

And Vincent Massey was rewarded by being made Canada's first native-born governor-general.

Originally broadcast June 1, 1992

THE KID WHO COULDN'T MISS

On this day in 1917, a boyish-looking 23-year-old from Owen Sound, Ontario pulled off one of the most spectacular stunts in the history of warfare. It was so spectacular, so brilliant, and so brave, or foolhardy, that some people today still can't believe it happened.

It happened, all right. Billy Bishop swooped down out of the fog in one of those old wire-and-wood-and-canvas planes they flew in the First World War and shot up the German Air Force.

He did it all by himself because only one other man on the face of the earth thought it could be done and he'd been killed a few days earlier.

Billy Bishop was the son of the court registrar in Owen Sound, Ontario. That was a bit of a big deal in those days around the turn of the century. When young Billy didn't show any inclination to go into law or work very hard or do anything else useful, the old man was delighted to enroll him at the Royal Military College in Kingston with a view to him being an army officer. That, too, was a big deal in those days.

Bishop was supposed to be a cavalryman but when the war started in 1914 he soon got tired of the mud and horse manure and asked to be made a flier. The army figured if anybody was dumb enough to want to go up in one of those things he was welcome to do it.

Bishop wasn't a good flier. In fact, he was almost taken off the job. But he was an excellent gunner. He had the instinct to know to shoot not where the other plane was, but where it would be by the time the bullets reached it.

Everything about Bishop's career as an air ace was incredible and still looks made up. He shot down 21 enemy planes within a couple of months. Most pilots who lasted the war spent years without doing that.

On the day before the Canadian Corps of the British Army changed the First World War by capturing Vimy Ridge, Bishop shot down three enemy planes over Vimy. For that he was awarded the Military Cross.

> *Bishop had the instinct to know to shoot not where the other plane was, but where it would be by the time the bullets reached it.*

Bishop came to the attention of Albert Ball, the top British ace. Ball was a strange man, a bit of a religious nut. He would have nightmares after he shot down an enemy plane and burst into tears at the thought of the men he'd killed.

He would get up in the middle of the night and light a flare and walk around it in a circle for hours at a time, crying and playing the violin.

Bishop was just the opposite. He flew all day and drank all night and never gave a thought to the dangers of war, either to himself or the other guy. In May of 1917 Ball suggested to Bishop that the two of them try something no one had ever done: attack an enemy airfield while the planes were still on the ground.

If they were lucky they could get a half-dozen planes instead of waiting until they were in the air and try to shoot them down one at a time.

Bishop said he'd think about it. But before he could talk to Ball again, Ball was killed.

So in the early morning of the 2nd of June 1917, soon after 3:00, Bishop took off alone and headed for the nearest German air field. It was fogged in so he went looking for another. He wasn't even sure which one he found.

But he found one with eight planes warming up. He destroyed seven of them, either on the ground, or as they took to air.

When the war was over, a year-and-a-half later, Bishop had destroyed 72 German planes. It seemed incredible at the time. It still does.

Recently the National Film Board of Canada turned out a movie called *The Kid Who Couldn't Miss.* It questions whether or not Bishop was really as good as the record says. Have no doubts. He was.

That's what super-heroism is all about, doing things the ordinary guys don't think can be done.

Originally broadcast June 2, 1987

THE KOOKY KAISER

Kaiser Wilhelm the Second of Germany, better known to history as The Kaiser, was a strange man. He'll be remembered for generations as the man who led Germany in the First World War, a man who was at least partly responsible for the millions who died in that pointless war.

At the beginning of this century, the royal families of most European countries were somehow connected. In the cast of England and Germany, they were closely interrelated. King George the Fifth of England and Kaiser Wilhelm of Germany were cousins, both grandsons of Queen Victoria.

The Kaiser's mother was Queen Victoria's oldest daughter, also called Victoria. She had married the Kaiser's father when he was still the crown prince, a nice guy, a weakling.

When young Wilhelm was born an English doctor attended his mother. The baby was partly crippled, with a withered left arm. And for years the German press carried on about it. If a good German doctor had been on the job, they said, that wouldn't have happened.

Young Wilhelm was raised three-quarters as an Englishman. He spoke English at home and his mother took him to visit in England for weeks at a time.

But he would be the leader some day of a very nationalistic country. The Germans had a fantastic army and Wilhelm loved playing soldier. He went on manoeuvres and interfered with the generals. He designed and redesigned the uniforms of all his regiments.

He got involved in the building of a German navy that would rival England's. His grandfather, the kaiser, died. His father became kaiser. Then got throat cancer and was dead in 99 days.

Young Wilhelm became the kaiser in 1888. He set out to rule like an ancient king did, running a one-man show. Of course in modern times that was impossible and his story is the story of a man who tried ancient ways in modern times — and failed.

Historians and psycho-analysts have had a fine time looking back at the Kaiser's reign. They're agreed he was strange. Only a few say he was crazy. But he did dumb things. He once slapped the king of Bulgaria on the bottom in public and almost started a war. Kings are very sensitive about that sort of thing.

He was once on a visit in one of his warships to Italy and the king of Italy, a very short man, came aboard to greet him. The Kaiser, not realizing the Italian officers could understand German, said loudly: now we'll see how a monkey in a uniform climbs a gangplank.

By the time Europe broke up into the First World War the Kaiser's power was diminishing. There had been a homosexual scandal among several of his closest friends although no one suspected the kaiser. At least, not out loud.

The Kaiser, for all his love of things military, didn't get to run the war. When it was over, the German army was still intact. The whole war had been fought outside Germany. But the country was starving and the economy was ruined.

His generals told him the army would march home peacefully. But not with him in command anymore.

He took the hint and went into exile in Holland. He lived in a small castle there until he died on the 3rd of June in 1941.

By that time the world was involved in another war. His death rated only a couple of paragraphs in most papers. One British writer just wrote: The Kaiser died yesterday — 40 years later.

> *Kaiser Wilhelm once slapped the king of Bulgaria on the bottom in public and almost started a war. Kings are very sensitive about that sort of thing.*

Originally broadcast June 3, 1986

THE LIFE OF A LIBERTINE

On the 4th of June in 1798, in an obscure town named Duchkov in what's now Czechoslovakia, an old man lay on his deathbed.

Just before he died he made a short, painful speech of just one sentence: "Almighty God, as you witness my death, I have lived as a philosopher and die as a Christian."

It sounds like some sort of saintly old gentleman was going to his final rest. But it was really the man who has been a symbol, and rightly so, of lechery and vice for centuries: Giacomo Casanova.

Casanova was born in Venice in 1725. We don't know who his father was. His mother was a travelling actress who did more travelling than mothering. Psychiatrists who have studied Casanova's writings say the woman-chasing he did was caused by his mother deserting him to be raised by friends of the family. I doubt it. I think he was just a man who liked to enjoy whatever life had to provide and was enough of a cynic to be a taker rather than a giver.

Casanova's education only lasted until he was 12 or 13. He made his living at first as a fiddler in bars and at parties. But he had enough education in Latin and Greek and classics to pass himself off as a gentleman.

When he was about 19 he was heading home from playing a late-night gig, about four one morning, when he ran into a rich old man who took a sudden faint spell. Casanova, essentially a kindly man, took him home and called a doctor for him.

The man was very rich and very grateful. He introduced Casanova to a few of his friends and it turned out they were interested in cabalism. That's the study of foreign letters and numbers in the belief that they can reveal all sorts of ancient wisdom, like how to turn lead into gold or where to find treasure buried centuries earlier by the pharaohs or Genghis Khan, all that sort of thing.

Casanova dabbled at that kind of stuff, apparently without believing in it, rather like somebody today who reads palms or teacups for a lark.

Casanova drew up a whole lot of numbers and old Greek letters, just to humor the old guys. They eagerly jumped on them and declared their young friend was some sort of genius. The result was that Casanova was adopted as a son by one of them and became quite well off.

He could have settled down and spent the rest of his life in ease and comfort. But Casanova had a roaming spirit. He travelled all over Europe, chasing the ladies, working as a spy, conning people for the sheer love of fooling them, making a good buck at it, reading and translating, gambling . . . and chasing the ladies. That was always his major pastime.

He lived in Paris and London, always returning to his beloved Venice. In 1755, when he was 30, he was thrown in jail for his loose living. But he escaped from the escape-proof Venice jail and continued his adventures all over Europe.

His incredible success with women seems to be based on the fact that he really did love them; at first, at least.

In his late 50s, Casanova was on the run, wanted by police and angry husbands and indignant fathers all over Europe. He met Count Waldstein, who had an estate at Buchkov, and the count invited him to move there to be his librarian. So that's what Casanova did for the rest of his days. To avoid the terrible boredom of that tiny but safe haven, he wrote his memoirs.

Then he died. The memoirs were published after his death and at first they were thought to be mostly fictional. But as the years go by, historians cross-checking them find they seem to be pretty accurate. Of course, the interesting parts, the ones involving all those women, are pretty hard to check out.

> *Casanova was just a man who liked to enjoy whatever life had to provide and was enough of a cynic to be a taker rather than a giver.*

Originally broadcast June 4, 1985

STORY OF O HENRY

Nobody ever heard of William Sidney Porter, the druggist, cowboy, exile and jailbird. But everybody's heard of O Henry, the man who invented the modern short story. Well, they were the same man.

Porter was born while the Civil War was on in North Carolina. There was a drugstore in the family and Porter became a druggist. But he doesn't seem to have liked the work much.

He moved to Texas and became a cowboy. Not a hard-riding, working cowboy. Sort of a play cowboy. The Porters weren't rich but they were genteel and Will never really took to hard work.

He lived on the ranch of friends and rode a little and branded a few cows and worked on his tan and got to play the guitar well. He was a clever cartoonist and storyteller.

Everybody liked Will. He married well and got a soft, good-paying government job. Then he became a bank teller.

Will Porter liked his booze, nothing exceptional in those days. We'd think of him today as a pretty hard drinker but he was about average for Texas in those days.

His passion was writing. He ran a little literary newspaper. He spent most of his time at it. And quite a bit of his employer's money.

When the books didn't balance he was indicted for embezzlement. So he took for Honduras and hid there for a while.

When the fuss died down, Porter returned home. But he was arrested and sent to jail for five years. He served three.

In that time he amused himself by writing short stories which he sent to New York publishers. He was scared stiff that anyone would learn he was in jail so he came up with a pen name, O Henry. He never did explain how he got the name. It seems to have been from a popular poem at the time.

When he got out of jail, there was no more Will Porter. From here on he was O Henry.

He moved to New York and did very well as a writer. His stories are a little wordy today for our tastes but the plots are fascinating. O Henry almost invented the twist at the end, the sardonic little bittersweet switch that gives us a tear and a chuckle together.

He made good money. His first wife had died so he tried marriage again. But by now he was a two-bottle-a-day man and his boozing was taking him to an early grave.

He hung around with the smart Broadway gang and was always broke, although his stories brought big money. And he could grind them out. His second wife once told him they were having a dozen people for dinner that night and there wasn't enough for them all. Henry sat down and wrote a short story within a couple of hours and sold it on the phone and had the money in his hand in time to buy food and booze for all.

In early June of 1910 he took sick for the last time. He took a taxi to the hospital. As he checked in he had to leave his valuables. As he emptied his pockets he said: Here I am, going to die and I only have 23 cents to my name.

O Henry died on the 5th of June, 1910. In death, William Sidney Porter came back to life. That's the name on his tombstone.

> *O Henry almost invented the twist at the end of a story, the sardonic little bittersweet switch that gives us a tear and a chuckle together.*

Originally broadcast June 5, 1987

D-DAY

Canadian troops headed for England, for the day when the British would attack across the Channel and take Europe from the Germans. Eventually, there would be a half-million Canadian soldiers in England.

In the summer of 1942 a force of Canadians had attacked across the English Channel at Dieppe on the French coast. It was a disaster. Hundreds of Canadians were either killed or captured. The planners were shaken. They knew it would be tough but they didn't expect it would be that tough.

In late 1943, Dwight Eisenhower, an American general, was put in overall command. The first thing he had to do was to stop the squabbling and fighting among his own people. The British and Americans weren't getting along. The air force and the army couldn't agree.

Eisenhower insisted that planes that had been bombing Germany be switched to bombing French railways.

That way, when the invasion came, the Germans wouldn't be able to move men and supplies by rail. It was a shrewd move. The Germans would need 48 troop trains a day once the invasion came. The best they ever did was six in one day.

Two of the best German generals were in charge of the defence: Rommel and Runsted. Rommel believed it was necessary to defeat the invaders in the first few hours, while they were still on the beaches with their feet still wet. Runsted believed the best way was to let the British and Americans get ashore and concentrate all his forces against them.

Since they couldn't agree, Hitler himself had to make the decision. He didn't decide on either plan so neither was eventually used.

The British and American leaders promised the Russians that they'd invade France no later than May of 1944.

They didn't have a lot of choice. They would have to be ashore well before summer because they would need good weather to fight their way inland.

There were only a few days each month when they had moon for parachute troops to see at night and rising tides to float their barges onto the beaches.

The weather was bad in May so that was cancelled. It was rescheduled for the 5th of June. The weather was too bad then. Then it improved slightly but not much. Eisenhower decided it was now or never. The troops and equipment were all loaded in their boats.

So, just before dawn on the 6th of June in 1944, the biggest armada in history invaded France.

The Germans fought well but their forces were scattered. The fight was tough but not as tough as expected.

By the end of the day Americans had captured the beaches they were assigned to. British and Canadians made up just more than half the invasion force. They had not only taken their beaches but pushed about five miles inland.

The invasion was a success. Within a year the war would be over.

> *Eisenhower decided it was now or never. The troops and equipment were all loaded in their boats. So, just before dawn, the biggest armada in history invaded France.*

Originally broadcast June 6, 1989

A CANADIAN FIRST

Wilfrid Laurier was born in the little Quebec village of St. Lin in 1841. He was as Canadian as maple syrup. One of his ancestors had been at the founding of Montreal. There had been Lauriers in Canada for 200 years.

Years later, in 1896, when Laurier became prime minister, he would be the first Canadian prime minister. All the previous ones had been British subjects, who also happened to be Canadians. But Laurier would be Canadian first, British second.

Laurier was a tall, slim, serious-looking young man with a lot of charm. The ladies loved him. He reciprocated.

Laurier's father was a land surveyor, not a rich man but a clever one. Instead of raging and complaining about the English-speakers who had stolen his country, the old man wanted to understand them. When Wilfrid was 11, he was sent to an English-speaking school run by a Scotsman with a great command of English literature.

Laurier stayed there until he spoke excellent English, and even more important, until he knew Milton and Shakespeare and the English mind.

Then he went to French-speaking college for seven years. Laurier was a brilliant student but he didn't get along well with the hierarchy of the Catholic church.

Laurier was a loyal Catholic but he didn't approve of the way the Quebec bishops insisted on trying to run every aspect of life, including politics. All his life, Laurier and the church he loved would be in conflict of a sort.

For a little while Laurier was the editor of a mildly reformist little weekly newspaper. Today, we would consider it pretty tame. But opposition from the church closed it down.

Laurier moved to Montreal and studied law.

Laurier was a loyal Catholic but didn't approve of the way the Quebec bishops insisted on trying to run every aspect of life, including politics.

While he was there he met a young lady named Zoe and they got along very well.

But Zoe got engaged to a doctor and Laurier moved back to the country and began practicing law. One day he got an urgent telegram from a doctor friend of his. He dashed to Montreal to see what the trouble was.

The doctor said Zoe was supposed to marry her doctor friend within a few days. But she couldn't because she was crazy about Laurier.

Laurier and Zoe got married that night, by special arrangement with the priest.

They returned to the country and Laurier ran for parliament and lived the life of a country lawyer except for his few months a year in Ottawa.

While all this was going on, Laurier also began a long affair with his partner's wife. The wife was a wealthy, sophisticated woman and she turned Laurier from a rather awkward country boy into a beautifully tailored, impeccably mannered cosmopolitan gentleman.

Later, when Laurier became prime minister, he would make his partner a judge so he could move to Ottawa and bring his wife with him.

The wife and Laurier had two children. Laurier and Zoe had none.

Laurier would have been the obvious leader of the Liberal party soon after he went to Ottawa but he was a beach-bencher while the Liberals were in power. Then, when the Conservatives returned to government the Liberals took as their leader the premier of Ontario, Edward Blake, a brilliant, erratic man.

So Laurier had to be content to be the head of the Quebec wing of the party. Finally, in 1887, on the 7th of June, the Liberals chose Laurier as their leader. He led the opposition for nine years before he finally made it into the prime minister's office.

Originally broadcast June 7, 1990

159

A Paine in the British Behind

Thomas Paine was an Englishman who had a busy life by the time he reached his late 30s. He had been a corsetmaker, a teacher, a sailor and a customs officer.

He wrote an appeal to the government for higher wages for Customs officers and went to London to present it. As far as we know, that was his first attempt at writing.

The appeal didn't work. But in London Paine met Benjamin Franklin, the Philadelphia printer and writer who was trying to convince the British government to give the American colonies more freedom.

Franklin's mission wasn't any more successful than Paine's but he stayed on for a while, hoping he might change a few minds in London. Paine was so fascinated by what Franklin told him about life in America that he moved there.

He worked for a while as a teacher and a writer. Paine sided with the American colonists in their conflict with the British. But he never for a moment believed there would be a revolution.

No one in America or Britain, or even Paine himself, realized it at the time. But Paine was one of the major architects of that revolution.

In late 1775, he wrote a pamphlet called *Common Sense*. In it, he put in words what Americans were thinking. As were a lot of Englishmen: that government is supposed to benefit the people, not just the king; that government of any sort is, at best, a necessary evil, at worst, an intolerable one.

Everybody in America who could read, read *Common Sense*. The American Revolution was on.

During that revolution, with the British and American armies fighting and people dying and starving, Paine wrote a series of what he called his Crisis Papers. They examined the revolution that was going on and the new world that he hoped would follow it.

The first one was written in camp while Paine was hungry and cold. The war was going badly for him, so he rested his paper on a drum, and began: "These are the times that try men's souls . . . "

Later, when the revolution was won, the constitution of the United States was written by men very much influenced by Paine's writings. All that stuff about life, liberty and the pursuit of happiness was cribbed from Paine.

Paine wasn't one of those framers of that constitution. He was in France, drumming up support for the Americans from the king of France. And he was successful.

He returned to England and continued his revolutionary writings, calling for an end to the monarchy in England, just as it had been ended in America.

He went to France and wrote there and was an important founder of the French Revolution. The French were so charmed by Paine that they elected him to their new parliament.

But Paine was more than just a hot-eyed revolution-maker. He emphasized pacifism and love of mankind. When the extremists took over the French Revolution that was seen as treason and Paine was thrown in jail.

He was there almost a year before he was released.

He returned to America, broken in health from his time in jail. He was bitter toward his old friend George Washington for not getting him out of jail.

The Americans had been generous to Paine for his help in their revolution. They gave him a farm in New Jersey and a big lump of cash. But Paine, the man who loved Common Sense and the average man, turned bitter in his old age. He was a cranky drunk, twisted with pain, his body rotting from infection. He died in New York on the 8th of June in 1809.

Later his bones were dug up and taken to England, but they somehow got lost before a monument could be built.

> *Paine put in words what Americans were thinking. Everybody in America who could read, read* Common Sense. *The American Revolution was on.*

Originally broadcast June 8, 1990

TYPHOID MARY

In early 1907, Dr. George Soper, a sanitary engineer with the New York department of health, got a call from a man who owned a big summer house outside the city at Oyster Bay, Long Island.

The house had been rented the previous summer to a wealthy banker and his family. In one week six of the 11 members of the family had all come down with typhoid fever. Two of them had died. Today, with modern medicines and clean drinking water and sanitary food handling and effective sewage systems, typhoid is almost a thing of the past. But in those days it was a major killer in North America, right behind cancer.

The owner of the house called Soper because, until some explanation was found for the typhoid outbreak, no one would rent his house again.

Soper looked at all the records and decided the outbreak had started about three weeks after the banker had hired a cook, a big handsome Irish woman named Mary Mallon.

The great German scientist Robert Koch figured some people are carriers of diseases, healthy themselves but harbouring the germs in their bodies and passing them on.

Soper didn't make any connection between Mary and the typhoid at first. But as he looked through medical literature, he came across a theory by the great German scientist Robert Koch. Koch figured some people are carriers of diseases, healthy themselves but harbouring the germs in their bodies and passing them on.

Mary Mallon had left shortly after the typhoid broke out and Soper wasn't able to find her.

But as he looked through more records, he found her trail. Mary Mallon had been the cook in a home where a guest died of typhoid in 1900. She had worked there three years but left right after the typhoid broke out. There were similar cases in 1901, in 1902 and in 1904. In the case in 1902, Mary the cook had worked nursing the sick in the house after the outbreak and they all figured they owed their recovery to her. Nevertheless, she left soon afterwards.

Mary was a big, good-looking woman, somewhat shy but popular with her employers, an excellent cook and a hard-working employee. Nobody ever fired her and all were disappointed when she left.

Soper was convinced that Koch's theory about carriers was right and Mary Mallon, the cook, was a living example. But he could never find her.

Then, in the spring of 1907, not long after he began his investigation into the outbreak at Oyster Bay, Soper was in the kitchen of a home in Manhattan, where the daughter of the wealthy owner was dying of typhoid. When Soper looked in the kitchen, he saw the big, attractive Irish cook he'd been looking for.

When Soper started to question her, Mary picked up a fork and chased him out of the house.

The next day, he returned with an ambulance, a warrant and three cops. It took all of them to wrestle Mary into the ambulance and sit on her until they got her to an isolation hospital.

Mary was held there for almost two years. Then a lawyer who had been visiting another patient met her. He decided she was being held illegally so he went to court to get her released.

Nobody except Soper and a few officials knew about the case until then. But when it got to court the newspapers picked it up. That was on the 9th of June in 1909. A medical journal nicknamed Mary "Typhoid Mary" and that's how she's known in the history books.

The judge said Mary had to stay locked up. But the next year she was released on a sort of parole, supposed to report every month. She didn't. She disappeared and wasn't seen again until five years later. Soper was investigating an outbreak of typhoid in a hospital. Guess who was working in the hospital kitchen.

That was in 1915. Mary stayed locked up for the rest of her life until she died in 1938. The records showed she caused 53 cases of typhoid and three deaths but the real figure must have been higher.

Originally broadcast June 9, 1992

HOLY UNION

The United Church of Canada had 3.7 million members at the last census. That's more than a third of all the Protestants in Canada. Mind you, it's a pretty insignificant figure when you compare it with the 11.4 million Canadians who told the census-takers they were Roman Catholic.

Census figures generally don't tell the whole story when it comes to religion. Fewer than 300,000 Canadians described themselves as Jews. That figure seems awfully low.

At any rate, the United Church's 3.7 million makes it by far the biggest Protestant group. Next are the Anglicans with slightly fewer than 2.5 million. The Presbyterians were third with fewer than a million.

The Protestant church goes back to Martin Luther in Germany who was active about the time Columbus discovered America. Luther was a Catholic priest who had become disenchanted with the church of Rome. But when he formed his own church, he still followed the forms of the old one. He believed in priests and a chain of bishops and other officials linking the faithful at the bottom of the organization all the way up to God at the top.

That's called an episcopalian set-up, one with bishops. Right after Luther, in fact, right on top of him, came John Calvin, who set up *his* Protestant church in Geneva in Switzerland.

Calvin didn't believe in the episcopal set-up. He believed that each person has a direct link to God and needs no priests or bishops to intervene.

He believed some people could devote their lives to the study of religion and the leadership of the faithful. But they wouldn't be anything special in the sight of God.

One of Calvin's followers was a Scot named John Knox. He took that philosophy from Switzerland to Scotland. There it became the Presbyterian church. That name came from the presbytery, the democratically-elected body that runs each church.

All that occurred by the middle 1500s in Europe. So, you say, what does that have to do with a Canadian church that's not even 60 years old yet?

Well, it's what the controversy of the 1920s in Canadian church circles was all about.

As Canada was settled in the late 1700s and early 1800s, there was an awful shortage of clergymen. In those days, remember, a clergyman was a very important member of the community. Marriages couldn't be performed without him.

Back in the 1800s, communities tended to adopt any Protestant clergyman who was available, regardless of what church he worked for officially.

The most common Protestant sects on the Prairies in those days were the Presbyterians, the Methodists, the Congregationalists, the Anglicans, and the Lutherans.

The Anglican and the Lutheran were episcopal churches. That didn't bother many of the Anglican clergymen, who would minister to anyone who wanted their services. And, indeed, a lot of people had been talking for some time about one United Protestant Church.

> *Back in the 1800s, communities tended to adopt any Protestant clergyman who was available, regardless of what church he worked for officially.*

The Lutherans weren't too eager to lose their episcopal set-up. Then in 1888, the Church of England reaffirmed its faith in the episcopal creed at a conference in England. That effectively withdrew the Anglican Church of Canada from any potential union.

For the other sects it was one of those ideas that practically everybody agreed on but never quite got going. The Presbyterians were split. Most figured they could live with the others.

But some of the others, mostly the congregations of stubborn Scots and argumentative Irish, just couldn't go along with any plan that would include even a remote possibility of a future link with a church of bishops. On the other hand, the Methodists and Congregationalists wanted to keep the door open for a union with the Anglicans at some time in the future.

Finally the ones who could agree on union asked the government to pass an act creating the United Church of Canada. It went through on the 10th of June in 1925.

Originally broadcast June 10, 1983

OUT OF AFRICA

Marcus Garvey was Jamaican, born in the late 1880s. When he was only 16 he started working as a printer's apprentice.

He became the foreman of the printing plant. At the same time, he was a labour organizer. He led a strike that brought better money for the printers.

He lost interest in printing and became a full-time labour organizer. He organized Jamaican farm workers who went to various Central American places to work. For this, he was thrown in jail in Costa Rica.

When Garvey got out, he went to England. That was in 1911. He went to lectures at the University of London and considered a career as a labour organizer, maybe as a politician.

But, around this time, Garvey came to see his problem as something different. He was a black-skinned black man. He had known all along that whites ruled the world. And he had noticed back in Jamaica and in Central America that lighter-skinned blacks seemed to get to the top. Or near the top.

Garvey came to see the world as suffering from a very color-conscious kind of racism, one in which blackness was the sin.

Garvey moved to the United States, first to New Orleans and then to New York. Harlem was the part of New York that had become solidly black and Garvey settled there.

Most of the black leaders in the United States at the time were urging their people to think white, to copy the white man's ways in the hope that they would eventually be accepted by the whites.

Garvey preached just the opposite. He didn't come up with the phrase "Black is Beautiful," but that was his message.

He was a racist. He said black people had founded great empires centuries ago in Africa and the black man's future lay in returning to the greatness of those times. And in returning to Africa.

Pretty soon, by the mid-1920s, Marcus Garvey was the major force in Harlem and among black Americans elsewhere. Black Canadians too. His movement had a strong chapter in Toronto and another in Montreal.

Garvey preached that black Americans should get back to Africa. That had been tried several times and black American colonies in Africa hadn't prospered. In at least one, Liberia, the black Americans who settled enslaved the black natives to work on their plantations.

Garvey's message was so extreme that he found himself allied with the racist, anti-black Ku Klux Klan. He invited Klan speakers to his centre in Harlem to preach about the benefits of separating the races.

Several times a year Garvey's organization held parades and rallies. His people dressed up in garish uniforms and carried swords, strictly ceremonial, no suggestion they advocated violence.

He also founded a steamship line, the Black Star Line, to take his people back to Africa. Garvey went to jail for selling stock in his Black Star Line without warning investors that the line was on the edge of going broke. Garvey was a charismatic speaker but no businessman.

He was deported to Jamaica when he was released from jail. From there he drifted to England, where he died on the 11th of June in 1940. He was only 53.

Millions of dollars had passed through his hands but no one ever suggested Garvey kept a dime for himself.

> *Garvey said black people had founded great empires centuries ago in Africa and the black man's future lay in returning to the greatness of those times. And in returning to Africa.*

Originally broadcast June 11, 1987

BUILDING CASTLES IN THE SKY

I don't suppose there are many students of the history of Bavaria out there. But if you're one of them, you have to be careful that you don't mix up Bad King Ludwig with Mad King Ludwig. The one we're remembering today is Mad King Ludwig.

Bad King Ludwig was his grandfather. He was king of Bavaria until he had to abdicate in 1848 because of his shameless carrying-on with an Irish chorus girl.

His son, Max, became king. He had two boys, Ludwig and Otto. When Ludwig was 18, King Max died and Ludwig became king of Bavaria. This was in 1864.

Ludwig was what we would call politely these days an odd-ball.

He was a big man, 6'4". He had the strangest way of walking. He would take the biggest strides of anyone in Europe. Then, at the end of each stride, he would stamp his foot down. Someone once said he looked like a man trying to kill a room full of scorpions.

Both Ludwig and his brother Otto heard voices when there was nobody around. That had started when they were just kids. When Ludwig was 10 he tried to strangle Otto. It seems Ludwig was very conscious of being the senior prince, the one who would be king one day, and Otto hadn't shown enough respect to suit him.

For all his strange ways, Ludwig was a handsome young king. He looked a little strange at the time because he insisted that the royal barber give him a fluffed-up hairdo every day. Otherwise, he said, his food just didn't taste right.

You would have thought Ludwig would have no trouble finding a wife. And, indeed, he was engaged to a duchess for a few years but nothing ever came of it. We now know why. Ludwig's diaries are in the archives and he was a homosexual.

Bavaria in those days was an independent country, caught up in the friction between the two major German states, Prussia and Austria. Ludwig found himself in the middle of a lot of political intrigue.

In 1871, at Ludwig's suggestion, the king of Prussia assumed leadership of all the German-speaking states except those run by Austria. That new political entity became modern Germany. Remember that. It might explain what happened later.

Ludwig was a great fan of the composer Richard Wagner. Wagner was a madman in his own right, carrying on with women and constantly in debt. Ludwig gave him refuge in Bavaria and paid his bills and made possible most of Wagner's greatest work. All civilization is in debt to him for that.

The other thing Ludwig did was build castles. He had a strange idea that he was the reincarnation of a medieval German knight and he built or renovated half a dozen castles, places right out of Walt Disney with towers and drawbridges and moats and everything.

He went broke doing that and that led to his downfall. But today, the people of Bavaria bless his name. Those castles are the biggest tourist attraction in Germany and they bring in millions every year.

When government officials saw that Ludwig's castle-building was about to break the royal treasury, they had him declared insane. No trick really. Everybody had known it for years. And, on the 12th of June in 1886, they sent a committee of civil servants to lock him up in one of his castles on the shore of a lake.

The next day Ludwig and the psychiatrist who was guarding him were found drowned in the lake.

Suicide? Maybe. Ludwig had talked about it.

But there's another, more sinister explanation. Remember how modern Germany was created when the king of Prussia took over at Ludwig's suggestion? Well, a few years after Ludwig died, papers came to light in the archives that showed Ludwig had been receiving a large, secret payment each year from the Prussians. It looks like Ludwig was on the take. Crazy maybe, but not stupid.

Ludwig had a strange idea that he was the reincarnation of a medieval German knight.

Originally broadcast June 12, 1984

THE PENTAGON PAPERS

On the 13th of June in 1971, the *New York Times* began publishing the Pentagon papers. The papers were a huge mass of documents that detailed just how the United States had got involved in the Vietnam War. They were the evidence of how several governments had lied to the American people, to each other and themselves.

The French ruled what they called Indochina, what we call Vietnam, for about a century. Then, in 1954, they were turfed out by the natives. Those natives were either communist or pro-communist so the United States got very concerned.

As far back as President Eisenhower, American leaders had got involved in the war there.

That war, by the way, should have been over in 1954 but the French, then the Americans, set up a series of puppet governments to keep the communists at bay. The result was a 30-year civil war that took the lives of thousands.

In the 1960s President Kennedy escalated the American presence by sending in soldiers. They weren't to fight, he said, only to act as advisers to the Vietnamese he supported. Sending soldiers into a battlefield with orders to not fight is like telling a fox to go into the henhouse just to look around.

Kennedy knew in a general way what was happening but he didn't want to know officially. Under his successor, Lyndon Johnson, the situation got even worse. Johnson actually sent in combat troops, hundreds of thousands of them. All the time, American officials were claiming they were just there at the request of the legitimate Vietnamese government.

But the bullets that were flying didn't observe those fine points. Real American boys were shedding real blood and it was causing real trouble, both in the field and at home.

The soldiers themselves went about their task with little enthusiasm. In some cases, they actually refused orders and the American military effort was pretty feeble.

Back home, thousands of young people poured onto the streets and college campuses to protest. The United States was torn apart.

From time to time, newspapers would leak stories about lies and cover-ups. But the administration would always say those were tiny pieces of the overall picture, that the major facts were still as they were being presented officially.

That all came to a sudden end on the 13th of June in 1971. The *New York Times* began printing, word for word, a secret study that the American defence department had assembled on just how the country had got into the Vietnam mess. The study was so huge it had to be moved from place to place in sealed cartons carried in wheelbarrows.

That study was turned over to the *New York Times* by Daniel Ellsberg, a researcher who had worked on assembling the papers. He readily admitted he was the source and the American government had him arrested. At that time Ellsberg said he had given a lot of the information earlier to officials of the Congressional foreign relations committee. That information showed that the government was lying to Congress about the war.

The papers had all sorts of embarrassing information. They proved that President Johnson lied when he tried to justify his escalation of the war. They showed that President Kennedy had condoned, or at least looked the other way, as the CIA set up the assassination of the Viet leader he was supposed to be supporting.

They showed that American officials regarded Canadian diplomats as a bunch of amateurish meddlers when they tried to help end the war. Officially, of course, they had thanked the Canadians and praised them for their efforts.

Sensation was piled on sensation. Before Ellsberg could come to trial, it was revealed that the government had tapped his phone and sent burglars into his psychiatrist's files to get information to convict him. The judge said that was unfair and Ellsberg got off.

But by then, newspaper readers had something even more sensational to follow. Just a year after the Pentagon papers were published, the Watergate scandal broke.

> *The* **New York Times** *began printing, word for word, a secret study that the American defence department had assembled on how the country had got into the Vietnam mess.*

Originally broadcast June 13, 1983

BABBAGE'S BRAINSTORM

Charles Babbage was the son of an English banker who was known as Five Per Cent Babbage. Five per cent was very heavy interest in the 1800s and the old man had made a fortune.

Young Charles went to university at Cambridge where he was a lazy genius. He avoided as many classes as he could. But he threw himself with great enthusiasm into all sorts of extra-curricular studies of science and mathematics. Babbage and several of his bright young rich friends rented space and ran a science club that delved into what was much too complicated for their teachers.

It was in the science club that Babbage was going over some navigational tables one day when he saw they were full of errors. The people who had written the tables originally had made mistakes, the people who copied them made mistakes and the printers who had published them had made mistakes. Yet these were used by navigators of ships loaded with freight and people. These mistakes could cost lives and fortunes.

That encounter with those faulty tables was to change Babbage's life. And yours and mine.

Babbage, the rich kid, married a rich young woman and they eventually had eight children. Babbage had no need to work so he stayed at school and got another degree. He had a free, unstructured mind that could cut through the formalities and get at the truth. And he had a blunt, undiplomatic tongue that made him enemies as he spoke that truth.

Babbage applied for two professorships but they went to men who were much less accomplished. He had made important enemies.

Babbage then started to work on a machine that would do mathematical calculations, one that would avoid the human errors that had so shaken him when he read those navigation tables.

Babbage began with a paper he presented to the Royal Astronomical Society on the 14th of June in 1822. That paper described his incredible machine.

In 1822, there was no such thing as mass production. You couldn't run down to the hardware store and get a dozen 12-inch screws or a handful of 10-volt switches. Everything Babbage needed to build his machine had to be hand-made.

Even the Babbage fortune couldn't support years of custom work by toolmakers. So Babbage approached the government and pointed out that when his machine was made it would revolutionize navigation.

Over the years Babbage got a lot of government money. But, as fast as he developed one plan for his toolmakers, he would think of another. The result was the machine was never made and the government got angry and cut him off.

Babbage's wife and six of his eight kids died. He became a bitter old man who said before he died that he hadn't known a happy day in his life.

It took years before others could see what he was driving at. Then it took two generations of engineers to finally come up with the machine that Babbage had been carrying around in his head for years: the computer.

> *Babbage started to work on a machine that would do mathematical calculations, one that would avoid the human errors that had so shaken him when he read those navigation tables.*

Originally broadcast June 14

166

THE GREAT CHARTER

The 15th of June in 1215 was a Monday. King John of England must have thought it was an awful way to start the week. There he was, on a broad grassy field, upstream from London on the banks of the Thames. The field itself was called Runnymede. The area was called Eglinton.

King John was a clever man and a fighter. He spent about half his time fighting wars in France. The other half he spent fighting his own people. Or, at least his own noblemen. The people, the poor slobs who plowed the ground and dug the potholes, didn't rate a thought in those days.

King John's father had been King Henry the Second, another clever man. Poor Henry would be remembered by history as the king who ordered the murder of Thomas Becket, the archbishop of Canterbury.

In fact, he performed wonders of administration that made England the great country it became.

When Henry died, his oldest son Richard became king. Richard is remembered as a great king although he only lived six months in England. He spent his life battling in France and in the Holy Land in the Crusades.

When he was away his brother John acted as king and when Richard died in France John became king. He is remembered for being an unusually evil man and for that Monday in 1215 when he went to Runnymede.

John had got into squabbles with his own nobles, with the townspeople of London, with the king of France, with the Pope, with the emperor of the Holy Roman Empire...some days it seemed that John was out to take on the world.

The fact that he was still around in 1215 indicates he was a pretty smart man, if not a nice one.

At one time John got the Pope so angry at him that all England was under an interdict for six years. That meant the church went on strike. No one could be married, baptized, buried in holy ground or confess.

In those days of deep religion, or extreme superstition, whichever way you see it, that was a terrible thing. Then John made a deal that won over the pope, got his people their priests working again and left his enemies in disarray.

In the fall of 1214, John again antagonized the people of London and they joined a rebellion against him. Slowly John's support faded.

On that Monday morning in the spring of 1215, John's nobles summoned him to Runnymede to talk things over. One historian tells us that John rode up, flanked by only seven knights. The others had either joined the other side or were waiting to see how things went.

The nobles gave John a paper to sign, the Magna Carta, the Great Charter.

It had more than 60 sections. But it boiled down to this: the king was an important man but he wasn't everything. He was subject to the law, just as much as anybody else in the kingdom.

John signed then tried to have the Magna Carta declared null and void by the Pope. In those days that sort of thing happened all the time. But this time it stuck. The Magna Carta was here to stay. And today our leaders are subject to the same laws we are. Of course they show a better aptitude for getting around them.

It boiled down to this: the king was an important man but he wasn't everything. He was subject to the law, just as much as anybody else in the kingdom.

Originally broadcast June 15, 1987

ONCE A QUEEN, ALWAYS A QUEEN

In the 1600s, Sweden was a mighty power in Europe, second only to France. Religion and politics were all tied up together in those days and the mightiest king of Sweden, Gustavus Adolphus, saw himself as the champion of Protestantism. He spent most of his life abroad, leading his armies in conquests all over northern and eastern Europe.

He wanted a son but he had a daughter, Christina. He gave orders that she was to be educated as a man. In other words, she was to be educated, not just taught a little music and sewing and some scripture and housekeeping.

Little Christina turned out to be one of the best scholars in all Europe. The king died in battle when Princess Christina was only six.

Regents ruled the country until she was ready to take over. And when she was ready, she really took over. By that time she was fluent in half a dozen languages and could read and understand the classic tongues like Latin and Greek, Hebrew and Arabic. She was interested in new ideas and corresponded with the best brains of the time. She set out to have science drive superstition out of Swedish life.

When a scientist was in trouble for starting a fire with a magnifying glass, she stepped in. No, she said, it wasn't the work of the devil. It was something natural and just because no one could understand it, didn't mean that they wouldn't some day.

Christina was a good writer and was a patron of the arts. Probably as a result of her boyish upbringing, she often preferred men's clothes to women's and that caused a bit of a scandal.

As one of the foremost Protestant monarchs of the day, she was expected to take a leading part in religious life. That, she refused to do. She told her court chaplain, a gloomy Lutheran, that if she ever left the Protestant faith it would be because of his sermons.

Then, on the 16th of June in 1654, she did exactly that. She turned over the throne to her cousin who became King Charles the Tenth. They had been playmates as kids and pals later and even lovers. Then she renounced the Protestant faith and left Sweden. The Swedish parliament wished her well, gave her lots of money and voted that she be treated like a queen for the rest of her life.

Catholic Europe went mad with joy. It was assumed God himself had arranged the royal conversion and this was the end of Protestantism. Christina was greeted with such enthusiasm at every major Catholic city in Europe that it took her a year and a half to make her way to Rome.

There she was greeted by the Pope himself and formally received into the Catholic church. She turned out to be no better a Catholic than a Protestant, arguing with the Roman priests just as vehemently as she had with the Lutherans of Stockholm.

Christina still thought of herself as a queen. She got involved in a sinister intrigue to become queen of Naples. When she was betrayed by one of her staff, she ordered him executed on the spot. She was visiting France at the time and this was considered an insult to the king of France, having somebody killed in his country without his permission. But it didn't bother Christina. Once a queen, always, she figured.

Although Christina was no beauty, she got lots of offers. But never took them up. She was curious enough to try anything, she said, anything but marriage.

> *Christina was interested in new ideas and corresponded with the best brains of the time. She set out to have science drive superstition out of Swedish life.*

Originally broadcast June 16, 1992

FORM BEFORE FUNCTION

When the Lions Gate Bridge was built in Vancouver in the early 1930s, it was the longest suspension bridge in the British Empire and maybe the most beautiful, graceful one anywhere in the world.

When it was decided to build the Second Narrows Bridge 20 years later, it would be even more graceful and beautiful.

Beauty in bridges, of course, means light steelwork with graceful curves. And the Second Narrows Bridge certainly had that. Work began in 1956 beside the original Second Narrows Bridge, a rickety old steel and wood affair with a section that lifted to let boats pass under. The new one would be 150 feet over the water so boats could easily sail underneath.

In the first two years of construction, while the concrete piers and the first steelwork was being put in place, two workers were killed by falling into the water.

The British Columbia Workmens Compensation Board ordered a rescue boat be sailing around under the bridge while anyone was working on it.

On the 17th of June in 1958, the second span of the bridge was in place. Second from the north shore, that is. The bridge would join Vancouver and North Vancouver over a body of water, a big bay, called Burrard Inlet.

Suddenly, at exactly 3:40 in the afternoon, the span fell. A lot of men were working on it: iron workers, painters and other tradesmen. The wonder is that they weren't all killed.

The 2000 tons of steel in the span fell 150 feet

The tide was rising and some of the men, still alive, were trapped in the steel. As it bent and twisted, it formed cages around them.

into the water, taking dozens of men with it. Eighteen were killed. Twenty were seriously injured.

The tide was rising and some of the men, still alive, were trapped in the steel. As it bent and twisted, it formed cages around them.

That patrolling rescue boat pulled some up out of the water. Dozens of other boats and divers were on the scene in minutes. In fact, the final death toll stands at 19 because one of the divers was killed.

Naturally, there was a terrible political fuss. The opposition demanded the government resign. The Social Credit party was in power at the time. The minister of highways, Phil Gagliardi, said: "Why do they think I'm responsible? Do they really believe I was supposed to be there holding it up, and I went out for coffee or something?"

The investigation that followed showed that two engineers miscalculated and didn't design some of the steelwork heavy enough. Maybe they were trying to achieve that light, graceful look. We won't know because both were killed in the fall.

A year later, when the replacement span was ready, the high steel workers were on strike. A judge ordered them back to work to put it in place. They refused to go and their union leaders went to jail and the union was fined $19,000. The workers said they weren't sure it was safe. The judge said the engineers said it was perfectly safe. The steel workers replied: we know. We heard them say it. That was last year just before it fell.

Originally broadcast June 17, 1992

THE DOCTOR'S DICTIONARY

Samuel Johnson, Doctor Johnson, may have been the greatest man of literature who ever worked in the English language. Shakespeare was a better playwright and Milton was a better poet and Dafoe was a better novelist. But nobody, nobody anywhere in any language in any age has ever come within a country mile of Johnson at what he did: he took the English language which had been used so effectively by the hot-shots and he made it meaningful to everybody who used it.

Some languages, like German, had a separate sub-language that was for use only by the king and his circle. There was no chance of that happening in English after Sam Johnson left his fingerprints all over it.

Samuel Johnson was the son of a bookseller, but one who would sooner read books than sell them. His mother was left a small inheritance by a distant prosperous relative and she decided to blow it on sending young Sam to Oxford. This was in the early 1700s when only the sons of the rich went to university.

Sam was already a well-read man. He'd gone to school until he was 16 which made him extremely well-educated for his time.

He was a rebel at Oxford but a genius too. He came out of there with a knowledge of Latin and Greek and some Hebrew. And history. That history turned out to be very important.

He was offered jobs as a clergyman and a teacher. And he taught for a little while. But Sam Johnson wanted to make his living writing. Not literature. Journalism. Not history. But the pieces that history will eventually be made from.

He went to London in 1737 with two and a half pennies in his pocket, intending to take the town by storm. He took it but it took a while. Johnson was a ghost-writer of speeches and sermons and lectures, and a writer of essays on topics of current interest. At one time he single-handedly wrote a small newspaper that came out twice a week.

> *Johnson was against the idea of an English academy. He said the problem could be better solved, if at all, with a really good dictionary.*

People like Johnson, who took up writing for a living, were concentrated in London in a narrow lane called Grub Street. Hacking, or grinding, as we practitioners call it, was known for years in England as Grub-streeting.

Johnson sold quite a bit of his stuff to a bookseller named Robert Dodsley. One day, a bunch of literary types were talking in Dodsley's shop and the subject got around to the English language.

The French and Italians both had academies. There were bodies of scholars who would meet regularly and draw up the rules of grammar and decide which words would be allowed into the language and which old ones would be thrown out.

English was a language with an awful lot of synonyms and a frightening variety of exceptions to what few rules it had. Johnson was against the idea of an English academy. He said the problem could be better solved, if at all, with a really good dictionary.

There had been some feeble attempts at an English-language dictionary but nothing definitive had ever been done. Johnson said no, it wasn't the job for him.

But Dodsley thought it was a good idea. And he put together a syndicate of publishers and they offered Johnson 1,575 pounds to write a dictionary. On the 18th of June in 1746 they all met for breakfast at a pub called the Golden Anchor and signed a contract.

Johnson said he would do the job in three years. It took nine and the help of six assistants who he had to pay himself.

It was the most important event in the history of modern English. We have no meeting of scholars to tell us how to talk. But we can understand Englishmen, Indians, South Africans...everybody who speaks our language. And that language is spoken by millions of foreigners as a second language, the closest thing to a universal tongue man has seen since the tower of Babel.

Originally broadcast June 18, 1987

LADY LIBERTY

August Bertholdi was a Frenchman from Alsace, that part of France that borders Germany. The people thought of themselves as French although most of them spoke German.

Bertholdi was a clever sculptor. At the age of 18 he made a statue of one of Napoleon's generals that still stands in the city of Colmar. In the 1850s he travelled to Egypt to do some engineering designs. There, he got an idea for a statue at the entrance to the Suez Canal.

It would be huge, a woman with a torch in one hand, symbolizing the knowledge of Europe, pointing east with the other hand, showing sailors the way to the Orient.

It was a great idea but no one was about to come up with the money.

So Bertholdi went back to France, where he was better at raising money. In fact, he was a bit of a genius at persuading municipal politicians to commission statues of local heroes for their parks and the spaces in front of their city halls.

In 1870, when France went to war with Germany, Bertholdi was commissioned in the army. He led a force of 15 men to defend the strategic bridge at Horbourg. The Germans sent 5000 men to capture it.

Bertholdi was brave but not foolish. He let the Germans have the bridge. The war was soon over.

Bertholdi decided a trip to the United States was what he needed. As he travelled around the new world he was impressed by what he saw. The building and engineering, the incredible railways and the big canals impressed him.

But the most impressive attraction of all was the people. The Americans really thought they were different from the rest of the world, that they were really building a new society.

The Americans were going to celebrate their centenary with a world's fair at Philadelphia. Bertholdi thought a new version of that statue he had thought up for the Suez Canal would be a good idea.

He went back to France and got cracking. He received wild enthusiastic support from newspapers all over France. Government officials said it was a great idea. Fellow sculptors agreed.

Bertholdi was shooting for 1876, the centennial year. No way. Money came in way too slowly.

The centennial was long past when Bertholdi finally had the Statue of Liberty built at his workshop in Paris.

It was a steel frame covered with thin copper sheets. It was carefully taken apart and packed in 85 huge crates. They were taken from Paris in a train of 70 cars. The crates weighted half a million pounds. They were put on the deck of a French warship, the Isere, and sailed to New York harbour. It arrived on the 19th of June in 1885.

The statue couldn't be erected right away because the pedestal wasn't built. The legislature of the state of New York had vetoed the expenditure, saying it was away too much.

The *New York World*, the newspaper, ran a campaign to raise the money and the boys and girls of America paid for it with their nickels and dimes. At least, that's what the *New York World* said.

Finally, in October of 1886, 10 years late, the statue was officially opened by the president of the United States. He said it was a great project, an inspiration for all. He seemed to have forgotten that six years earlier, when he was governor of New York, he hadn't thought it was worth a $100,000 pedestal.

> *It would be huge, a woman with a torch in one hand, symbolizing the knowledge of Europe, pointing east with the other hand, showing sailors the way to the Orient.*

Originally broadcast June 19, 1987

HUN-GRY FOR POWER

Everybody's heard of Attila the Hun. We say somebody's as mean as Attila the Hun or you might as well argue with Attila the Hun. We mean Attila was the toughest guy in history. And he was.

Attila was the toughest of the Huns and the Huns were the toughest, meanest people mankind has yet produced.

The Huns came from the wilderness away up to the north of China. The Chinese built the Great Wall of China to keep out the Huns.

A lot of tough, mean people came from that part of the world. But the Huns had two things going for them: they were the toughest, meanest of all; and, they bred a superb strain of horses. Most of the horses from that part of the world were small, just big ponies. The Huns' horses were big and strong with very hard hooves. That was important in those days before horse shoes. They could gallop for days over hard, stony ground that no other horses could.

The Huns were short, ugly people and all their men were taught to fight and ride and shoot arrows with incredible accuracy as soon as they were old enough to walk.

They would have conquered the world before the time of Christ if they had ever been able to get together. But they were so mean they were always fighting among themselves.

That's why Attila gets into the history books. He was able to unite them. Attila was one of two sons of the king of the Huns. As soon as the old king died, when Attila was in early middle-age, the other son disappeared.

We can safely assume he was Attila's first victim.

The Huns had long since left the wilderness north of China and moved westward, killing and terrorizing everybody in their way.

> *The Huns would have conquered the world before the time of Christ if they had ever been able to get together. But they were so mean they were always fighting among themselves.*

By this time, in the fifth century by our calendar, the Roman Empire was falling apart. It had split into eastern and western divisions. Long before Attila, various invasions of Huns had chased people out of eastern Europe into the west. These people arriving had caused further turmoil as they fought for land with those who were already there.

Attila's capital was in Hungary, where the city of Budapest is now. It wasn't a real city. Attila had what he called a palace, really just a big log cabin. Most of his men lived in shacks and tents around him.

The Huns didn't read or write or farm or make things. They just fought and produced children. They needed huge pools of manpower and between battles they produced them in mind-boggling numbers.

By the year 440 Attila had an army of half a million men, a huge horde in those days.

He swept west into what's now France, massacring everybody as he went. Finally, on the 20th of June in 442, his army met a combined force of what was left of the Roman army and a bunch of barbarians who usually fought against the Romans.

This time they were fighting with them. That battle must have been one of the most ferocious in history.

Both armies met late in the afternoon and they went at each other with swords and spears and bows and arrows. They fought all night and until dawn.

And Attila lost, something that had never happened before. But the Romans and Barbarians distrusted each other so much that they let Attila escape, each side hoping he would keep the other busy fighting in the years to come. And he did until he died nine years later. But that battle in 442 meant Attila the Hun wouldn't conquer the world.

Originally broadcast June 20, 1988

THE SUMMER THAT WASN'T

Officially, this is the first day of summer. By this time, the weather has usually been quite summery for a month or so in most of inhabited North America. But in 1816 it wasn't. That year goes down in history as the Year Without a Summer.

Records from 1816 aren't very detailed by today's standards but they show that April was pretty close to normal. It wasn't yet very warm in North America but it got slightly warmer as the month wore on.

In western Europe it was normal, nice and bright and sunny, getting noticeably warmer every day. Then May got cooler. In North America May started off okay but it cooled a bit and stayed that way.

In June there was snow in Quebec and New England. In fact, there was snow somewhere in Quebec, in the populated part, every month of the year in 1816. That was the first time since Quebec had been settled in 1603.

In the Maritimes, the situation got worse as the summer wore on. The wheat crop just didn't exist.

The situation in New England wasn't as bad but it was much more uncertain. In the Maritimes, southern Ontario and Quebec, wheat and oats made up most of the grain crops and they just didn't mature that year.

But in New England it was a little bit warmer, and the farmers planted quite a bit of corn as well. It came up then was killed off. They planted it again. It happened again. They planted it again. Finally, in August, they realized that even if it wasn't knocked off again there wasn't enough time to raise a crop so they just quit.

Europe was already in bad shape. Farming had been upset for a generation by the Napoleonic Wars which finally ended in 1815.

1816 was to have been the first postwar year with enough men at home on the farm, instead of away fighting, to have a normal crop.

The French government put a tax on imported grain to encourage French farmers to plant big crops. The combination of the weather and the tax produced riots that almost led to civil war.

England and Ireland also had poor crops although not on as great a scale as North America and western Europe.

In June there was snow in Quebec and New England. In fact, there was snow somewhere in Quebec, in the populated part, every month of the year in 1816.

The agricultural society in Philadelphia sent out questionnaires to thousands of farmers in North America and learned that all grain was hard hit in Canada, that corn was ruined in most of the United States but wheat crops made it, for the most part. Animal fodder was in such short supply that farmers slaughtered more pigs and cattle than usual and the price of pork and beef fell that fall. But there was a shortage of meat the next year and it went up higher than ever.

What caused it all? At first, people figured it was God's vengeance on a sinful world. But people hadn't been noticeably more sinful than in years past. Or since.

A German astronomer wrote in a scientific journal in the fall of 1816 that he noticed a lot more dust in the sky, at great height, than he'd ever seen before and that could be a cause. But he didn't know where it came from.

He was right. It was from the biggest explosion the world has ever seen, on Mount Tambora in Indonesia. A hundred cubic miles of dust was thrown high into the air and it blocked enough sunlight to cancel out summer the next year on the other side of the world.

Originally broadcast June 21, 1988

HALF MOON MUTINY

Henry Hudson is down in the history books as one of the greatest explorers of all time. And rightly so.

Nevertheless, he didn't find anywhere new, at least among the places he's remembered for. His whole career as an explorer took in only four years.

Hudson was a sea captain, from a long line of sea captains. He was an excellent navigator and a good writer. We know more about his voyages than most from those days because he kept excellent logs.

Hudson lived about a hundred years after Columbus. People realized the earth was round and they could get to the east by sailing west.

And that was the way to get rich, by getting to the east. That's where all the wealth lay, in China and Japan and India. At least, that was the conventional wisdom of Europe in the early 1600s.

In 1607 Hudson was sent by a company of London merchants to reach China by sailing north through the polar regions. Europeans knew that for half the year the polar areas had long days so they thought that meant it would be nice and warm there and free of ice.

Hudson had a leaky old ship but he managed to sail further north than anyone had. He was turned back by heavy ice. But on the way he discovered Spitzbergen, north of Sweden, and reported it was rich in whales. That started a whaling industry that became Europe's principal source of fuel oil for centuries.

The next year Hudson tried again, sailing north around Russia. Again, ice blocked him.

When he wanted to make a third try his London backers said no. So he found a bunch of Dutch merchants to back him.

Hudson had another leaky little ship, the Half Moon, with a crew of 18, all tough, bad guys. Most of them went to sea to avoid jail.

Again the ice blocked him north of Russia and the crew mutinied. Hudson had to turn back.

But he was an explorer, a fanatical explorer. Instead of returning to Holland, Hudson convinced his surly crew they could get to China another way.

> *People realized the earth was round and they could get to the east by sailing west. And that was the way to get rich, by getting to the east.*

They sailed all the way to America and tried to find a way through this continent. It was then that Hudson found the Hudson River, which reaches the sea where New York is today. Hudson sailed up that river for 150 miles to about where Albany is today.

The next year Hudson found more backers and he sailed almost due west from England. Sailors had been working the Arctic waters for years but they were always turned back by either ice or land.

Hudson went into the North American land mass through the entrance that today we called Hudson Strait.

He kept going and found Hudson's Bay. He explored down the eastern shore, in what's now Quebec, and into what we call James Bay.

Always he was looking for the opening in the land that would let him through to China. That expedition set out in April of 1611. By June they were in bad shape, very low on food and fuel.

They argued among themselves over how what food they had would be distributed. Several claimed Hudson was giving plenty to his favorites and starving the men he didn't like.

Hudson was not a good leader and he let the minor irritations break into open mutiny.

On the 22nd of June the mutineers put Hudson, and his son who was only 14, along with the ship's carpenter and several sick men, into a small boat and cast them adrift. That was near land at the southeastern tip of James Bay.

Hudson said he intended to sail his little boat north along the east shore of Hudson's Bay. He and his companions in the boat were never seen again.

The mutineers went ashore to find food and they were attacked by Eskimos. Three were killed.

They headed home but along the way several more died. They made it back by September of that year and were charged with mutiny. but the survivors got off by claiming they had been forced into it by the ones who were conveniently dead.

Originally broadcast June 22, 1983

BOLD TYPE

Christopher Latham Sholes was born in Pennsylvania in a log cabin in 1819 and went to a little one-room country schoolhouse. He hated writing. In those days, kids were made to write pages and pages for hours at a time to develop good penmanship and Sholes detested those exercises.

Sholes became a printer when he was still a kid then moved west and shifted from the print shop to the newsroom. By the time he was 20 he was the editor of the Wisconsin Enquirer in Milwaukee. He eventually became the editor of the *Milwaukee Sentinel*. But he preferred tinkering with printing machinery.

Sholes came up with a method to print subscribers' names on the margin of the front page of the paper to make mailing easier. And he invented a simple numbering machine for the pages of the paper.

He thought that idea would be a winner if he perfected it, so he and a friend named Soulé were tinkering with a numbering machine in the machine shop of a friend.

A lawyer named Glidden who was also a tinkerer had his office above the machine shop. One day he showed Sholes and Soulé an article in the Scientific American about a writing machine that had been recently on display at an exhibition in Philadelphia.

It hadn't worked very well. But it had resulted in an editorial in the Scientific American that predicted it, or something like it, would soon replace handwriting which was so slow and labourious.

Glidden the lawyer knew how much Sholes hated writing and he showed him the article. He suggested Sholes might be better off spending his time perfecting a writing machine than his numbering machine.

Sholes and Soulé agreed and they started working on it right away. That was in 1867 and before the year was out they had a machine that would write, in capitals. It wouldn't write everything because it only had 11 letters. And it didn't look much like today's typewriters.

Sholes, Glidden and Soulé formed a company but Glidden and Soulé ran into financial trouble and had to drop out. Sholes formed another company with a Pennsylvania publisher named Densmore.

Densmore insisted on several improvements: keys for all 26 letters plus numbers and punctuation marks; a simple, compact way of inking, a sturdy machine that would stand up to everyday use and a design that could be mass-produced. Densmore realized if the machine was to work, it would have to be accepted by millions of people and the demand would be enormous.

Before the year was out, they had a machine that would write in capitals. It couldn't write everything because it only had 11 letters.

Sholes kept working. He argued with Densmore but he realized Densmore was right. On the 23rd of June in 1868 he came up with the machine that we now call a typewriter. Sholes himself also invented the name.

He was very proud of what he'd built but he didn't have a lot of faith in it. When the Remington Firearms Company offered to buy out his interest in the patent, Sholes sold it for $12,000. He figured the market for typewriters would quickly fade because it would be just a novelty. Densmore thought it would be better than that. He held out for a million and a half.

Originally broadcast June 23, 1988

BIERCE'S BOOK OF BITTERNESS

If Ambrose Bierce were alive today he'd be one of the top TV and screen writers, grinding out cynical one- and two-liners. He once wrote a whole book of them, called *The Devil's Dictionary*. They were especially biting in his day, around the turn of the century, when hypocrisy was more institutionalized and religion was a major factor in most people's lives.

Not Bierce's. He didn't believe in churches and most days didn't believe in God. He defined prayer as a request that the laws of the universe be annulled on behalf of someone who doesn't deserve much consideration.

Or, trichinosis: the pig's reply to pork chops.

Or, a saint: a dead sinner, revised and edited.

Or, a year: 365 consecutive disappointments.

As you can see, Ambrose Bierce was a cynic. Or at least a clever man with a sour outlook. He had reason for it, mostly of his own making.

Bierce was born on a run-down farm in the bush in Ohio, near a little hamlet called Horse Cave Creek. The date was the 24th of June, 1842. The farm was poor, the Bierce family was large, mealtime wasn't always accompanied by a meal and life was dreary.

That's why the *Devil's Dictionary* defines birth as the initial disaster.

Every time Bierce would encounter a poem or essay extolling farm life he would take up his pen and crucify the author. And, in later years, he became a very powerful writer and editor. When Bierce crucified them they stayed crucified.

Bierce's father was a dull loser. His brother, Bierce's uncle, was the family fireball. In 1837 he led a force of 180 Americans to free Canada from the British. They captured part of Windsor for an hour or two and burned down a military barracks. The British Army was so enraged at this that only 30 of the Americans escaped. Bierce later wrote that if his uncle had told him the true story of that fiasco he never would have joined the Union Army during the Civil War.

> *The Bierce family was large, mealtime wasn't always accompanied by a meal and life was dreary. That's why the* Devil's Dictionary *defines birth as the initial disaster.*

Bierce was a hero and was wounded a couple of times. Some people said a head injury turned him bitter and twisted. It certainly turned him against the army. He never had another good word to say about war or generals.

Years after the war Bierce wrote: "It was once my fortune to command a company of real soldiers. Not professional life-long fighters, the product of European militarism. Just plain, ordinary American volunteers who loved their country and fought for it with never a thought of grabbing it for themselves. Getting a piece of the pie was a trick the survivors were taught later by gentlemen who wanted their votes."

Bierce moved to California after the Civil War and became a writer and newspaperman there at the same time as Mark Twain and Bret Harte.

They moved east. He stayed in San Francisco and was one of the chroniclers of early California.

William Randolph Hearst was beginning his career then as the greatest newspaper publisher in America and he hired Bierce at big money. Bierce didn't think much of Hearst but he wrote what he was told for the money. That certainly didn't make him any less bitter.

His teenage son started out to be a reporter but killed a friend in a fight over a girl. The boy shot himself the next day.

Bierce and his patient wife split up.

He was a lonely, bitter, talented man.

He retired but was bored. By this time it was 1913. There was a bloody revolution going on in Mexico.

That's where he went, where the fighting was the fiercest and where anti-American feeling was the strongest. He's never been seen since.

In his last letter he wrote: "If you hear of me being stood against a Mexican wall and shot to rags, it's a pretty good way to depart this life. It beats old age, disease or falling down the cellar stairs."

Originally broadcast June 24, 1987

CROSS PURPOSES

For a time in the mid-1800s, France was ruled by the Emperor Napoleon the Third, the nephew of the great Napoleon Bonaparte. The only resemblance between the two besides their name was that they were both short.

Napoleon the Third had the silly idea that he had inherited his uncle's military genius and he wanted a war to prove it. He invaded Italy and got himself and his army into a horrible mess with his stupidity.

In the spring of 1859 he was a long way from home, in very bad shape and with the Austrian Army between him and France. His only chance was to fight his way out.

And he did that on the 24th of June in 1859 at a little Italian town named Solferino, not far from the Swiss border.

The Austrian commander, Franz Joseph, the young emperor, was a perfect match for Napoleon. The pair of them couldn't have commanded a troop of docile boy scouts. The two armies had 320,000 men and 900 big guns, the Austrians having a slight advantage in both.

The armies came together at four in the morning. The day grew hot and thousands of men lay wounded in the sun. Then, along toward dusk, a cold rain suddenly fell, drenching everyone. In those days armies had virtually no medical corps. The dead, the wounded, the living, all just lay there.

The French had 16,800 dead and wounded, the Austrians 21,000.

And nobody had any plan for doing anything about them.

The next day, the 25th of June, a young man in an immaculate white suit appeared on the battlefield. He was a Swiss promoter named Henri Dunant. Dunant was from a well-to-do family of bankers and he had travelled to Solferino to see the Emperor Napoleon. Dunant had a scheme to set up a colony in Algeria that he hoped would make him a millionaire.

He had tried to get the emperor's support because Algeria was a French colony. But he hadn't been able to get to see him in Paris. Dunant was hoping things would be more informal in camp and he could get an audience.

What he got was the shock of his life when he stumbled on the battlefield. There were bodies as far as the eye could see. The dead were rotting and the wounded were groaning.

Dunant got the shock of his life when he stumbled on the battlefield. The dead were rotting and the wounded were groaning. He set out to do something about it.

Dunant forgot his colonization scheme and started to do something about the terrible scene. He got the villagers to round up food and water. He got priests to open their churches as emergency hospitals. He bought and tore up all the bedsheets in town for bandages.

He rounded up doctors, then went to the French generals and had them release the Austrian army doctors they had captured. He was everywhere and did everything. That took three weeks.

Then he went back home to Geneva, so shocked at what he'd seen that he almost lost his mind. He hardly moved out of his room for three years. He thought and thought about what he'd seen. Then he wrote a little book called *A Memory of Solferino*.

He sent a copy to every ruler, politician and important person in Europe.

They got together at a conference in Geneva in 1863 and formed a committee that eventually grew into a major worldwide organization dedicated to relieving suffering in both war and peace.

The organization needed a symbol. The Swiss flag was a small white cross on a red background. So, since the organization had been thought up and convened in Switzerland, they just reversed that flag — to make a white background with a red cross. And the Red Cross was born.

Originally broadcast June 25, 1984

PERMANENT INCA-PACITATION

Francisco Pizarro was born around 1475 in a village in the middle of Spain. He had no prospects — his father was a freelance army officer, his mother was a chambermaid. Pizarro himself was illegitimate. Apparently the old man and his family played around quite a bit. There was a whole tribe of Pizarro brothers, half-brothers, cousins and uncles and nephews.

We don't know much about Pizarro's early career. He seems to have been a soldier in the never-ending wars of the time in Spain and Italy.

He emigrated to the West Indies just 10 years after Columbus found them. He explored and fought all around Central America and by 1523, when he was almost 50, Pizarro had it made. He had accumulated a small fortune and lived on an estate in Panama.

You would think he would put his feet up and settle down to the quiet life. But that was exactly the time he decided to go on his life's great adventure.

He formed an expedition team with a man named Almagro and they sailed down the west coast of South America to what's now Peru. He and Almagro had an arrangement to split whatever they made.

For three years they wandered around and explored, usually separately. Pizarro's men found a raft drifting off the coast. Aboard were some people who were obviously noblemen of a great civilization. They wore heavy, rich gold and silver jewelry, and clothes of fine cloth.

Pizarro realized he was onto something even bigger than he'd ever figured on.

He took samples of the clothes and jewelry and went back to Spain and showed them to the king. In 1529 he returned with the king's commission to find that civilization, conquer it and send 20 per cent of everything he found back to the royal treasury.

That commission was Pizarro's key to fame and fortune, and his death warrant.

Almagro joined up with Pizarro again but he figured Pizarro had gone for the royal commission to get around their contract.

You've probably heard the story of how Pizarro, with 180 men and 37 horses, found the great Inca civilization and conquered it. He captured the head Inca, Atahualpa, and held him for ransom.

The natives brought in enough gold to fill a room in Atahualpa's palace from the floor to as high as he could reach. Then they filled two other rooms with silver.

Then Pizarro killed Atahualpa.

Pizarro and Almagro were richer than the king. But they squabbled between themselves. Pizarro's brother killed Almagro. The rest of Almagro's crowd figured they were next. So they decided to strike first.

They all lived in Lima, the city that Pizarro had founded, the city that's now the capital of Peru.

On the 26th of June in 1541, Pizarro had just finished Sunday brunch and was sitting in the courtyard of his palace when a dozen of Almagro's men ran in.

Pizarro always wore his sword and armor. His men were all cut down. Then, alone, he fought on until he was run through with eight swords.

As he lay dying he dipped his finger in his own blood and made the sign of the cross on the flagstones.

> *Pizarro returned with the king's commission to find that civilization and conquer it. That commission was Pizarro's key to fame and fortune, and his death warrant.*

Originally broadcast June 26, 1984

CLASS STRUGGLE

On the 27th of June in 1858 the steamship Republic arrived in Victoria from San Francisco, carrying several hundred passengers.

Most of them were Americans who had come from the east for the California gold rush of 1849. That gold rush had petered out but a new one had replaced it.

Gold had been found in the interior of British Columbia and fortune-seekers were swarming in.

Among them was an American named Mifflin Gibbs. Gibbs was as American as anyone on the ship. But he was different. He was black.

Mifflin Gibbs was born in 1823 in Philadelphia, the son of a Methodist clergyman. He became a carpenter then moved to California at the time of the gold rush.

Americans were cruel to black people, even in the new land in the west, and Gibbs had had to work as a shoe-shiner. He saved his dimes and he and another black man named Peter Lester pooled what little money they saved and they started a store. They were both good businessmen and their store prospered.

But, over the years, it became clear to Gibbs that he and Lester would never be first-class Americans. The law said they could vote. But they couldn't.

They couldn't go to the police or the courts if they thought they needed protection. The law said they could but it didn't work out that way.

There were many successful, prosperous black people in the San Francisco area who felt the same way. When the British Columbia gold rush began, they scouted out the possibility of moving north.

Their first feelers received a favorable response from the governor in Victoria, a man named Douglas. They didn't know it but Douglas came from the West Indies originally and his mother was probably black.

Gibbs and 60 other black people from California stepped ashore from the Republic into a boom town. Victoria was the supply centre for the gold rush inland.

Gibbs brought some merchandise with him and made a good profit within a few hours of stepping ashore. He bought some property with a small house on it for $3,000 and within 20 days had it rented for $500 a month.

Gibbs sent a message back to San Francisco for his partner Lester to send on more merchandise and to come himself. The firm of Gibbs and Lester was now an important part of the commercial scene in Victoria.

Gibbs made a fast trip back to Philadelphia, married a black woman who had recently graduated from college, and returned with her. He ran for office in the first civic election in 1862. He missed election by a few votes and was elected at the next election.

Eventually, he had five children.

Governor Douglas had set up Victoria's first police force with all black constables. That idea was dropped after a few years because most of the people in the town were Americans, many from the South, and they raised an awful fuss over being arrested by black policemen, even if it was only for some minor offence.

Gibbs was a leader in the Confederation League, the movement to have British Columbia become part of Canada.

He built a small railway and wharf on the Queen Charlotte Islands and was soon shipping coal to San Francisco.

Then, when he was almost 50, he left British Columbia, returned to the States, and enrolled in college and became a lawyer. He later became the American consul on the island of Madagascar and, when he died at the age of 92 in 1915, he was president of a bank in Arkansas.

> *Over the years, it became clear to Gibbs that he and Lester would never be first-class Americans. The law said black people could vote. But they couldn't.*

Originally broadcast June 27, 1988

THE POWER OF MONEY

All too often, history remembers the people who achieved the spectacular but forgets the people who made it all happen with day-to-day jobs.

Take Jacob Fugger. Fugger was from a family in the city of Augsburg in Austria. His father and grandfather were in on the development of a type of cloth called fustian, a mixture of cotton and linen that was light and comfortable and wore well.

Fustian wasn't a classy-looking product but it made great work clothes. Young Jacob was sent away to Rome to study to be a priest but when his father died he was called home to run the family business along with his brothers.

Around that time a man named Datini invented a system of accounting that today we call double-entry bookkeeping. Jacob Fugger was one of the first to master it.

Also, around this time a new system of smelting was developed that made it easy to separate silver from copper. That, in turn, gave a major impetus to the mining and increased use of both metals.

Fugger was more interested in banking than the cloth business so the House of Fugger branched out. Kings and princes and dukes who owned land were always going to war or having coronations or throwing parties to impress each other, all activities that required money.

Fugger would loan them money, taking as security their royalties on the minerals that would be dug up in their lands. With the expanding metal industry in full swing, he couldn't lose. He would charge interest on the loan, of course, then he would collect in one currency and transfer it to another, picking up an extra point or two there. It was like the way banks trade in Canadian and American dollars and British pounds and Japanese yen these days.

Central Europe, which today makes up Austria and Germany and parts of France and Poland and Hungary and those places, was a mass of small, feuding, separate states. In theory, they were all part of a federation known as the Holy Roman Empire. But historians tell is it was neither holy, nor Roman, nor an empire.

The pope was supposed to be spiritual head but it was run along the lines of pretty grubby politics. The Roman aspect had never really existed. The ancient Romans had only ruled part of it. And it was no unified empire. On any given day, at least two or three of the states were at war with each other.

Fugger wheeled and dealed across the boundaries of the Empire. He advanced the king of Hungary huge amounts and took his mining royalties for security. Then he sent in his own engineers to make the mines more efficient.

He loaned money to one ruler and withheld it from another, making himself a power behind a dozen thrones in the process.

Fugger loaned money to one ruler and withheld it from another, making himself a power behind a dozen thrones in the process.

Fugger pulled off his biggest coup on the 28th of June in 1519 when he financed King Charles of Spain to be the Holy Roman Emperor. Charles needed millions to bribe six key voters in that election and Fugger came up with millions.

That didn't make Charles the unchallenged ruler of all central Europe, of course. It didn't end the squabbling. But it did draw lines across the map that lasted, in terms of influence and development, for centuries.

The powerful Hanseatic League of northern Europe, centred on the Baltic, fell from influence and power when it went up against Fugger and lost. That was no small factor in the decline of northern Europe.

Fugger financed many of the Portuguese voyages of discovery to South America and the Far East. If you looked at the map of today's world, you would probably find boundaries and power centres that are more the work of Jacob Fugger than of Napoleon or Alexander the Great. So why don't we know him as well? Maybe people like Jacob Fugger operate best out of the limelight.

Originally broadcast June 28, 1991

BLOOD, SWEAT AND TEARS

It seemed in the mid 30s that Germany got more powerful every day and Britain got weaker.

The German army could do no wrong. No matter what they tried, they got away with it. They had organization, skill and luck. Everything the British touched turned to mud. They were underequipped, poorly organized and in the doldrums.

Germany ruled from the north of Norway to Greece. They were on the verge of sinking the British Navy, invading England itself, and grabbing the Suez Canal.

In May of 1940, the British reorganized their government to form a coalition of all parties, headed by Winston Churchill. That was the smartest move they made although it didn't seem so at the time.

Churchill was a tough, aggressive, sometimes nasty man. He started political life as a Conservative, turned Liberal then turned Conservative again. A lot of politicians considered him a turncoat.

He had been in charge of the navy in the First World War, and masterminded the disastrous attempt by the British Navy to capture the narrow passage joining the Black Sea to the Mediterranean. If it had succeeded, it would have been remembered as a master stroke.

It didn't, and Churchill was vilified, a man who threw away thousands of lives.

But tough times demanded a tough leader and when Churchill made his first speech as prime minister to the House of Commons in May of 1940, it was hailed by all. He told the British people: "I have nothing to offer but blood, toil, tears, and sweat."

You thought he said blood, sweat and tears. He didn't. But blood, sweat and tears fitted more neatly into the headlines so that's how the papers reported it and that's how we remember it.

Churchill took over just in time to preside over the disastrous defeat in France. Then to watch the Germans take over the Balkans and Greece.

"We can expect to be invaded at any minute," Churchill said. "There must be no thought of surrender. Every man must have a weapon of some kind, be it only a mace or a pike."

The shattered remnants of the British Army that made it back from France were almost without equipment. All their big guns and tanks had been lost. In all Britain there were only 25 heavy guns.

Churchill made his famous speech about fighting on the beaches, fighting in the streets if necessary.

Some who were sitting next to him in the House of Commons said later that, as he sat down, he muttered: "and we'll fight them with beer bottles because we have little else."

The Americans eventually began to supply the British Army. Factories in Britain and Canada were cranked up to turn out the hardware required for a war. Lord Beaverbrook, the crusty Canadian publisher of Fleet Street, was put in charge of aircraft production. Churchill realized that the only war Britain had a chance at was an air war.

In June of 1941 the Germans attacked the Russians and the Russian Army collapsed within hours.

On the 29th of June in 1941 Britain's fortunes were at their lowest point ever. Churchill sent a memo to the war office: "We can expect to be invaded at any minute," he said. "There must be no thought of surrender. Every man must have a weapon of some kind, be it only a mace or a pike."

A mace, of course, was the battle club used in the days of the knights. A pike was a short spear used in Cromwell's armies 300 years earlier.

He continued his memo with further orders about how men and rations were to be distributed. Then he ended it: Let me see some blueprints for maces and pikes.

The generals and politicians had been bombarding him with stories of planes they didn't have and guns they couldn't get. Churchill told them to fight with clubs and spears.

Reading that memo today, it seems rather smart-alecky. But it worked.

Originally broadcast June 29, 1983

SCARLETT FEVER

Margaret Mitchell was born in Atlanta. Her parents were born there and her grandparents had owned plantations in the area before the Civil War.

She was called Peggy. It was assumed in 1900, when she was born, that a young lady of a good family would go to school to get a nice college education, then return home and stay there with her parents until she got married.

With Peggy Mitchell, it didn't turn out that way. She went north to Smith, one of the classy, expensive women's colleges of New England. She intended to be a doctor, although her family wasn't enthusiastic about the idea.

Then her mother died in the great flu epidemic of 1919 and she returned to Atlanta to keep house for her father and brother.

In 1922 Peggy got a job as a reporter at the Atlanta Journal and stayed there until 1927. She married another reporter. She intended to keep working, which was unusual in those days. But then she sprained an ankle, and it just wouldn't mend. The ankle was so sore she couldn't get out of bed for days at a time. She had to quit her job.

Her husband brought her library books to help her kill time, until one day, he said: "I think you've read just about everything in the library. If you want to read another book you'll have to write it."

In later years Peggy Mitchell said she had started the book in 1926, and finished all but three chapters by 1929. That would mean she started it before she sprained her ankle. But she distinguished between writing, the mental process, and typing, putting it down on paper. On another occasion, she said in took 10 years to write her novel but only a little while to type it. So I guess that means she'd had the story floating around in her head for quite a while.

When Peggy was born the Civil War had only finished 35 years ago. Plenty of people, both soldiers and civilians, remembered it.

Peggy Mitchell made it sound pretty casual, her book. But she worked hard at it. The newspapers from the time of the Civil War were all in a dusty old room in the basement of the public library. Mitchell was a tiny woman, about five feet high, and couldn't lift the big bound volumes of papers. She got all dusty lying on her tummy reading them.

She actually wrote for a couple of hours each day. She didn't start at the beginning and write her way to the end. She wrote one chapter, put it aside in a big envelope, and then started on another, not necessarily the next. As ideas for revisions occurred to her, she made notes on the envelope it was in, then corrected it later.

She had a friend about this time who worked in the Atlanta office of the Macmillan company, the publishers. One day that friend said one of the Macmillan editors was coming through town and would like to see Mitchell's book. Mitchell said: "It'll never be finished, and nobody will ever see it."

In April of 1935, that Macmillan editor was in Atlanta and Mitchell gave him her manuscript. He read it on the train to New Orleans. By the time he arrived, Mitchell had sent a telegram which was waiting at his hotel. It read: "Pls send manuscript back I've changed my mind."

But the editor was already hooked. Hooked by Scarlett O'Hara, one of the most beautiful and willful women in English literature and Rhett Butler, the dashing superman. He refused to send back the manuscript. Instead he sent a contract and predicted the book would be a best seller. Peggy's husband had always liked the book. He told her it would sell at least 5000 copies, because between them they had that many cousins scattered around Georgia.

It did better than that. From the day it was first published, the 30th of June in 1936, *Gone With the Wind* has sold more than 25 million copies. It's been translated into two dozen languages. And it still sells a quarter of a million copies a year.

It made the little ex-reporter from Atlanta a millionaire several times over. She never wrote anything again, for the rest of her life — which was ended by a drunk driver as she crossed a street in 1949.

> *Mitchell's husband brought her library books to help her kill time. One day, he said: "I think you've read just about everything in the library. If you want to read another book you'll have to write it."*

Originally broadcast June 30, 1983

Right: *Marcus Garvey, a black leader who preached that black Americans should return to their roots in Africa, died in England on June 11, 1940.*

Bottom Right: *Rodrigo Borgia was elected Pope Alexander VI on August 11, 1492. Rodrigo and his two children, Caesar and Lucretia (pictured here) have all been remembered by history as sneaks and poisoners.*

Bottom Left: *September 23 in 1926 saw the first of two showdowns between two of the brightest boxers in the history of the sport, Jack Dempsey and Gene Tunney (seen here). Tunney emerged victorious from both matches.*

Left: *In one of the great tragedies of our time, jazz legend Billie Holiday died on the 17th of July in 1959, with 17 cents in the bank, $450 hidden in her sock, and a drug charge hanging over her.*

Bottom Right: *Union activist Jimmy Hoffa had a date with some gangster friends on the 30th of June in 1975. He hasn't been seen since.*

Bottom Left: *On August 3, 1928 a producer hired a mysterious woman dressed in black to drop a single rose on the grave of Rudolf Valentino, the great lover, as a publicity stunt. It's happened several times since, without the help of the producer.*

CANADA DAY

Canada's Confederation was to have been on the 15th of July. But when the paperwork arrived from London, somebody had changed it to the first for some reason.

That change of date was awfully important to Sir John A. Macdonald. In the middle of March, the governor-general had told Macdonald he would ask him to be the country's first prime minister. That came as no surprise. But it involved a lot of politicking.

Every province and every important area of the country had to be represented in the cabinet. There was a shortage of good men from some areas, a surplus from others. And Macdonald knew the future would bring him tougher problems than he'd faced yet. He would need a cabinet he could depend on.

Or, as he once put it: I don't need men who will stand behind me when I'm right. That takes no courage. I need men who will stand behind me when I'm wrong.

Macdonald met with several men and thought by early May that he had the matter all ironed out. But he hadn't. Some who agreed to serve didn't. Some who agreed to step aside were hollering.

In fact, the membership of the cabinet wasn't finally settled until the 24th of June. The final decision was a compromise. There had to be a Catholic and a Nova Scotian to round out the cabinet.

Charles Tupper, a Nova Scotian, offered to drop out. D'Arcy McGee, the Montreal Catholic, refused. But Tupper pointed out that if he would drop out and Macdonald could find a Nova Scotian Catholic, that would simplify everything. McGee agreed and Macdonald found Edward Kenny, a politician with nothing to commend him except his religion and address.

He was the only cabinet minister not in Ottawa on the big day. There wasn't time for him to pack and get there.

When Macdonald had been in London the year before, persuading the British government to make Canada a dominion, he had entertained some pretty grand ideas about what form it should take.

When Macdonald had been in London, persuading the British government to make Canada a dominion, he had entertained some pretty grand ideas about what form it should take.

F'r instance, he figured Canada should be at least as important as India. India had a viceroy in a very fancy uniform so Canada should have one too.

The British hadn't seen it that way. The new queen's representative would be called the governor-general. He wouldn't be a member of the royal family, as Macdonald had hoped. The man chosen was the fourth viscount Monck, who had already been governor of the combined province of Ontario and Quebec. He was a big, decent, slow-moving, slow-thinking Irish nobleman who had paid his dues as a not-very-distinguised member of the British parliament. Now he was getting a not-very-distinguished payoff.

Monck went to England, picked up his commission and the great seal of the new country, then sailed back. He just made it to Quebec by the 25th of June. Macdonald was upset that he'd cut it that fine.

Viscount Monck swore in the five new justices of the supreme court, then they swore in the cabinet ministers. Then he made an announcement: Macdonald and six of the other major figures in the Confederation movement had been honored by the queen with titles. Macdonald was a knight commander of the Order of the Bath. The other six were companions of the same order.

All expected that some sort of honor would be announced that morning but they didn't know what. Monck himself had suggested making Macdonald a lord.

But advisers in the colonial office thought that might be too grand, and would make it tough for Macdonald to get along with his fellow Canadians, who were thought by the British to be less concerned with titles and much more democratic than the British. Little did they know.

Macdonald realized right away that, although he had nothing to do with it, everyone in Canada would figure he had wangled a better title for himself than for his pals.

And he was right. People said that about him until the day he died.

Originally broadcast July 1, 1983

SOMETHING ABOUT AMELIA

Amelia Earhart was an American, born out on the plains of Kansas. During the First World War she worked as a nurse's aide in a military hospital in Toronto and there she met a wounded pilot. He took her out to an airfield north of the city and let her watch him take off and land. Military regulations wouldn't allow her to get in the plane.

After the war Amelia returned to the States and took flying lessons. In 1928, she was the first woman to fly the Atlantic. She was just a passenger that time.

In 1932 she was the first woman to fly solo across the Atlantic. That was an incredible feat. Her engine caught fire at one point, her wings iced over and she had no idea how high she was above the water. Not many fliers in those days could have handled that flight.

A few months later she set a new speed record for flying from the east coast to the west. A couple of years later she broke that record. She was the first to fly from New York to Mexico City and the first to set several altitude records.

All that was quite impressive in its own right. But early in her flying career Amelia had met George Putnam, the owner of a book publishing company he'd inherited.

Putnam had to know all about promotion to sell his books and he applied that ability to Amelia. So, as well as being a real heroine in her own right, Amelia was heavily and skillfully promoted by a pro. And she had a lot of money behind her because Putnam was quite well off.

She did some dress designing and lecturing as well as flying so she was a number-one celebrity by any definition.

In 1937, Amelia was 39 and she told a reporter: I've got one more big flight in me.

Amelia set a new speed record for flying from the east coast to the west. She was the first to fly from New York to Mexico City and the first to set several altitude records.

That big flight was to go around the world the long way, around the equator.

Today it sounds like the kind of thing that happens a dozen times a day. But in those days, with the planes and equipment available it was quite a stunt.

And it was a stunt. Husband George promoted it heavily. He had all sorts of commercial tie-ins arranged and sold the serial rights to a New York newspaper.

Amelia started by flying from California to Hawaii. But as she took off from Hawaii, her plane crashed. She wasn't hurt but the plane was badly damaged.

It went back to the States for repairs. This time she took off the other way, from Florida to Puerto Rico then down to South America, across the Atlantic, across Africa, the Middle East, India, Singapore, Australia, and New Guinea.

At 1:30 in the morning of the 2nd of July in 1937, Amelia took off from Lae in New Guinea. She had a navigator aboard, a man named Fred Noonan who was maybe the best in the world despite a long time drinking problem.

They were going to go more than 2500 miles, aiming at a tiny speck of an island in the middle of the Pacific called Howland Island.

They never made it. After 20 hours in the air she was able to contact an American ship by radio but the signals weren't strong enough or long enough for the ship to get a definite location.

The navy searched a quarter-million square miles of ocean. Nothing. They're still looking. But so far, they've found nothing.

Originally broadcast July 2, 1992

OUR GANG

Ever since Hollywood made a movie about them in 1970, Butch Cassidy and the Sundance Kid have probably been the most famous bandits in western history.

Cassidy's real name was Robert Barker. He was one of seven kids of a very respectable Mormon preacher. The others took after the old man. Young Bobby wanted to become a horse thief. So he sought out the best-known horse thief in Utah, a man named Mike Cassidy. Cassidy called young Bobby Butch. When Mike took off for Mexico, Bobby took the name Butch Cassidy.

Fingerprinting hadn't been adopted yet in the late 1800s, but the good private detective agencies had started keeping detailed records. The bandits took each other's names to screw up the detectives' records. Within a couple of years the books showed that Harry Smith was a big man, a little man, red-headed, bald, fat, skinny, a teetotaller and a terrible drunk. It worked pretty well for a while.

But the detectives were getting better, especially the Pinkertons, and the bandits were mostly a bunch of hicks.

A hole was bandits' slang for a hideout. One of the best was a narrow canyon in Wyoming with steep sides like walls. So it was known as the Hole in the Wall, and it became home to the Hole in the Wall Gang.

The gang consisted of whoever was in the Hole in the Wall when someone was planning a bank or train robbery. All the big names of western banditry worked out of there — Kid Curry, Flat-nose Charley, Lonny Logan and his brother Harvey, Harry Longbaugh. . .

It was pretty hard to act tough with a name like Harry Longbaugh, so he started calling himself the Sundance Kid. There had been several Sundance Kids in the past.

Butch Cassidy was a good-natured guy who could keep the bandits from shooting each other between jobs. He was a hard worker, a good cowboy and blacksmith, and often went into town and worked for a week or two until he figured which bank or train to knock over.

Sundance was a simple kid, not too swift, more interested in girls than anything else.

The gang had various leaders at various times, starting about 1889. Then, seven years later in August of 1896, with Butch in command, they pulled a very successful job, a bank in Idaho. They didn't get a lot of money but things had been so well planned and the getaway was so smooth, Butch became the leader of the Hole in the Wall Gang from then on.

Three girls hung around with the gang. One was the wife of a gang member. When he was killed on a job, two of the survivors rolled the dice for her. Sundance won. The girl seems to have been happy enough with that arrangement.

Sundance stayed with her, faithful in his own inexact fashion, until he took up with a girl named Etta Place. Tradition has it that she was a school teacher but we're not too sure about that. Gradually, Etta switched her affection from Sundance to Butch although for most of their time together, Etta

In the days when a cowboy made $12 a month and a railway brakeman was lucky to get $25, the Hole in the Wall Gang pulled off a lot of $30- and $50-thousand jobs.

was the girl of both.

In the days when a cowboy made $12 a month and a railway brakeman was lucky to get $25, the Hole in the Wall Gang pulled off a lot of $30- and $50-thousand jobs.

But they were essentially a bunch of farm boys and the detectives were getting really professional. On the 3rd of July in 1901, just seven weeks short of their fifth anniversary with Butch in command, the Hole in the Wall Gang held up a train of the Great North Railroad near Malta, Montana and got away with $50,000.

Then they all scattered. Some were killed by the cops. Some went straight.

Butch and Sundance and Etta went to South America. The official story is that they were killed trying to holdup the payroll clerk of a mine in Bolivia. The unofficial story, the one I believe, is that they returned to the States and for years, Butch Cassidy, the robber, ran a typewriter and adding machine business around Seattle. But he got bored and killed himself in the 30s.

Originally broadcast July 3, 1987

It's a Wonder-ful Life

Charles Dodgson was an odd man. Back in the middle of the 1800s at Oxford where he taught mathematics, he didn't seem too out of place. But today we'd call him a strange duck.

Dodgson was a clergyman by training although he never preached. He made his living teaching mathematics although he had some family money, too.

His hobby was photography. And back in the 1850s and 60s that was remarkable because photography was brand-new. Dodgson paid 15 pounds for a camera back when that was more than three months' wages for a labourer.

Dodgson's other interest was little girls. That isn't as sinister as it sounds today. Dodgson never married and he seems to have found little girls to be a combination of wonder and awe and prettiness and unpredictability. He loved to photograph them. And, even more fun, he loved to tell them stories.

Dodgson's favorite little girl by far was Alice Liddell, the daughter of his boss, Dean Liddell, the head of Christ Church College at Oxford. Oxford was a very tight little academic community and Dodgson was always around the Liddell house, chatting with his boss, being very polite to the boss' wife and playing with his three little girls. Alice, the middle one, was 10, and Dodgson was 30 back in the spring of 1862.

The girls' favorite sport was to go for a long boat ride on the river with Dodgson, then have a picnic. Dodgson would row the boat and tell the girls all sorts of silly stories.

On the 17th of June in 1862 they set out on such an expedition. But it rained and they got drenched. So they rescheduled it for the 3rd of July, but it rained that day too. So they set the date for the next day, the 4th. And the 4th was hot and clear.

Dodgson teased the girls by getting started on a story about fairies and animals and all sorts of strange creatures, then pretending to fall asleep just as he was getting to the interesting part.

Both Dodgson and Alice later wrote about that afternoon but all they say to set it apart from other picnics they had is that they went for an unusually long row.

We know that they took along sweet cakes and cold chicken, and not enough dishes and cutlery because Alice and her sisters had to borrow some from other picnickers.

> *Dodgson's story on that day was an unusually fascinating one — with cabbages and kings and a mad hatter and a frantic rabbit and all sorts of other characters.*

We also know that Dodgson's story on that day was an unusually fascinating one — with cabbages and kings and a mad hatter and a frantic rabbit and all sorts of other characters.

After they got back, Alice made Dodgson promise to write it out for her. He must have realized at the time how crazy it sounded because at first he didn't want to. Finally he promised, to shut her up.

And eventually he did write it out. And it was published and immediately became famous all over the world as *Alice in Wonderland*. Dodgson used the pen name Lewis Carroll.

The story of Dodgson and Alice doesn't end. It just sort of peters out. Sometime about six months to a year later, contact between Dodgson and the Liddell family ended rather abruptly. We don't know why.

Historians have guessed that Alice's very social mother deliberately discouraged her daughter from having much to do with a mere teacher. She later tried to marry her off to a prince.

Others have hinted darkly that Dodgson became improper, as they called it in those days, with the girls. That's unlikely because he was a very proper young man.

No matter how the friendship ended, it left all us children a wonderful legacy: *Alice in Wonderland*.

Originally broadcast July 4, 1984

THE GRAND EXHIBITIONIST

Phineas Taylor Barnum was named after his grandfather. It's just a coincidence that Phineas is an old biblical name that means bold of speech.

He was born a poor farmboy in Connecticut on the 5th of July in 1810. But his big, aggressive mouth made him a millionaire and he left $5 million when he died at the age of 80 in 1891.

Barnum is remembered as the quintessential American showman. And he was. But he didn't get an awful lot of joy out of show business. He would have been just as happy if he could make the same money stacking cans on shelves in a supermarket.

Barnum's first job as a teenager was in a country store where everybody assembled to swindle everybody else. The local farmers came in to trade with the storekeeper. They knew how to comb and fluff up cotton and palm it off on the storekeeper as wool.

Barnum learned in that school and was an apt pupil. He ground up roasted peas and traded it as coffee. There was very little cash business done out in the small towns in those days.

In the 1830s Barnum bought an old woman slave. He made a good bit of money exhibiting her, billing her as the oldest human alive. In addition, he said, she had been George Washington's nursemaid and she could recite verses from the Bible and tell heart-warming tales of young George before he became the first president of the United States.

A lot of people claimed she wasn't the age Barnum claimed, 116. When she died he had an autopsy performed on her and her age was estimated by the doctors at 80.

Barnum screamed that he had been swindled. That was one of his principal contributions to the art of communication. He didn't care if he was described as good or bad, as long as his name was constantly in the newspapers.

Barnum bought an exhibition hall in New York and drew crowds to see shows and look at big paintings of exotic scenes and see animals from far parts of the world.

It all sounds pretty corny today but you have to remember that most people were from the farm and there was no such thing as a television in those days.

Barnum found a little kid in Connecticut, not far from his hometown, who had never grown. He billed him as Tom Thumb and exhibited him for years. Barnum was a good showman but an awful tightwad. He hired Tom Thumb, his mother and his father for less than 15 dollars a week.

It was a few years before Tom Thumb realized he was making a fortune for Barnum and demanded a better wage.

Barnum imported Jenny Lind, the greatest female singer in the world. She toured North America and she and Barnum made hundreds of thousands. Barnum didn't just sell tickets to her concerts. He auctioned them off.

He would send an advance man to talk to prominent businessmen a week before Jenny Lind came to town. Pay an outrageous sum for the first ticket to the concert, they'd say, and it will get you so much publicity that your business will boom.

It worked every time.

Barnum was over 60 when he went into the circus business with a man named Bailey. And the Barnum and Bailey circus is still about the biggest in the world.

Barnum was the master of clever stunts that cost him practically nothing but drew crowds. He once hired a man for a couple of dollars a week to walk around New York with an armful of bricks. The man would set down a brick at each corner as he walked along the street. Then he would double back and set each brick on end. Then he would go back again and set each brick on its side. By this time he would have attracted a crowd.

Then he'd gather up his bricks and walk into Barnum's exhibition hall. Everybody else would have to pay to get in.

> *That was one of Barnum's principal contributions to the art of communication. He didn't care if he was described as good or bad, as long as his name was constantly in the newspapers.*

Originally broadcast July 5, 1988

LOYAL TIES

In 1685, King Charles the Second of England died. This was an age when religion was all tied up with politics, so that death caused a problem.

Charles had been a Protestant and by far the vast majority of Englishmen were Protestants. They wanted a Protestant king. But the next in line to the throne was Charles' brother James. And James was a Catholic, a devout Catholic.

Charles had a son, the Duke of Monmouth, who was a Protestant. Monmouth was in Holland at the time of his father's death, passing his time carrying on with the ladies, a habit he'd picked up from his father.

The problem with Monmouth was that he was illegitimate. Charles once estimated he had 39 children, not one legitimate. An illegitimate son couldn't become king.

James was proclaimed King James the Second by his loyal but apprehensive subjects. There had been long and terrible wars over religion in the previous centuries and the thought of a Catholic king reigning over a Protestant land sounded like a recipe for trouble.

James started off, at least, as a tolerant king. He openly practiced his Catholic faith but he didn't restrict anybody else's.

Then, within a few months, came the test. Monmouth sailed from Holland and landed in the southwest of England and proclaimed himself the lawful Protestant king. He claimed that his father had married his mother. Historians have been searching for the marriage certificate ever since and it's never turned up. Catholics say it never existed. Protestants say James and his Catholic friends found it and burned it. Take your choice.

Now came the acid test of loyalty. King James sent an army out to meet Monmouth's. The cavalry was commanded by Colonel Jack Churchill, an ardent Protestant. The main force was commanded by the Duke of Faversham, a French Protestant who had settled in England years before, after fleeing Catholic persecution in his homeland.

The big battle was fought at a swampy place called Sedgmoor on the 6th of July in 1865. The royal army was camped between two streams. Monmouth marched all night and tried a surprise attack before dawn. It was a remarkable feat and deserved to win. But at the last moment, Monmouth's army was spotted by a royalist cavalryman, patrolling just in case something like that was tried. He fired his pistol and the surprise was lost.

Monmouth's army was bigger than the king's. But it was a mob of farmboys. The royals were pros. It was a terrible slaughter. Monmouth ran away but was caught a few days later and promptly executed.

The royal army that saved the Catholic king was virtually all Protestant. It could have been the beginning of an era of religious tolerance. Alas! It was not to be. James turned out to be a terrible king. Within four years, his son-in-law, King William of Orange, invaded the country and the army that had been loyal at Sedgmoor switched sides, led by Colonel Churchill. James fled and England hasn't had a Catholic monarch since.

> *There had been long and terrible wars over religion in the previous centuries and a Catholic king reigning over a Protestant land sounded like a recipe for trouble.*

Originally broadcast July 6, 1993

THE ROAD TO WAR

We in North America and Europe think of the Second World War as starting with the invasion of Poland in 1939. But that war really was a *world* war, with fighting in Europe, Africa and Asia. That fighting in Asia had been going on for a while.

The Chinese empire in the 1600s was crumbling when the Europeans first arrived. That's why they found it so easy to set up colonies there. The Russians were moving in from Siberia and the Japanese from the east.

The Japanese themselves had been isolated and rather backward for centuries. But after Europeans arrived there in the 1800s, the Japanese became westernized faster than any other race in history. They adopted western technology, warfare, dress — and the western greed for pieces of China.

Just after the turn of the century, the Japanese fought the Russians and dealt them a series of stunning defeats. In fact, the Russian weaknesses those wars revealed were important factors in the collapse of Czarist Russia in the Bolshevik revolution of 1917.

The Japanese grabbed Korea and Manchuria and little bits and pieces of north China around Beijing.

The British, French, Russians, Italians, German, Americans...just about every western power had traders and missionaries and soldiers in China. Shanghai, the country's biggest city, had a huge European settlement, with its own courts and police and municipal government. The outsiders had garrisons in Beijing and various cities and ports around there.

The Japanese had garrisons and commercial establishments along with the other major powers. But, in addition, they had that huge conquered area of Korea and Manchuria and the island of Formosa offshore.

That area was ruled by a military council called the Kwantung Army that was almost independent of the Japanese government in Tokyo. Tokyo sent out orders and the generals in the field sent back messages saying they were obeying but, very often, they ignored head office and did things their own way.

About the time the western world was all caught up in the First World War, China had a series of uprisings and

civil wars that led to a breakdown in central government. Out of those upheavals in the 20s and 30s emerged two major factions: the Nationalists, under Chiang Kai-shek, and the Communists, under Mao Tse-tung.

Neither was strong enough to defeat the other, although Chiang almost wiped out the Communists in the mid-30s. They had to retreat to the north and set up their own makeshift government. It eventually won, but that was a long way in the future.

Chiang convinced the Americans that he was the only Chinese leader strong enough to resist the Japanese. The Americans could see that they and Japan would soon be at war, so they supported Chiang, not very enthusiastically. The Americans figured that if the Japanese were having a hard time in China, they would be too busy to fight a war in the Pacific.

Some Japanese leaders wanted peace, some wanted war. In the mid-30s there was a series of intrigues and assassinations in Japan. The hawks came out on top. The leaders of the Kwantung Army then realized they could do just about what they wanted in north China. They sent troops into disputed areas.

Usually, the Chinese generals pulled back to avoid an incident because they knew their armies couldn't stand up to the Japanese. The Japanese got more aggressive, obviously trying to start a war. The Chinese avoided anything that could be construed as hostile.

Then, on the 5th of July in 1937, Japanese forces east of Beijing, near the Marco Polo bridge, a famous landmark, started very realistic manoeuvres. The Chinese did nothing. The Japanese got closer, firing live ammunition. The Chinese still did nothing, but they didn't pull back either.

Then the Japanese produced one of their men shot dead and said he had been killed by the Chinese troops guarding the bridge. They demanded that the Chinese commander be punished and that the Chinese surrender their five northern provinces since they'd shown themselves unable to keep law and order there. The Chinese refused and the fighting started.

> *The Americans figured that if the Japanese were having a hard time in China, they would be too busy to fight a war in the Pacific.*

Originally broadcast July 7, 1983

FORCES ON HORSES

Sir John A. Macdonald, the prime minister of Canada in the 1870s, knew he had to set up a presence in the west.

He'd sent the adjutant of British forces in Canada, Colonel Robertson-Ross, out there to investigate. And the colonel had come back with an alarming report: American whisky traders were supplying booze and guns to the Indians. Since the buffalo were disappearing, the Indians of the west were often hungry and a bad situation was developing.

In the previous year alone, 88 of the Blackfoot Tribe had been killed in drunken brawls. A Metis named Gaudin had killed his wife and crippled his mother-in-law but there was no one to arrest him.

A Cree named Ta-ha-kooch had killed several people near Edmonton. No one knew just how many. He was strutting around, terrorizing Indians and the few whites in the area. There was no one to arrest him, either.

In his report, Colonel Robertson-Ross recommended that a small cavalry force be set up to establish posts and string telegraph wires all across what we now call the Prairie provinces. In those days the whole land mass from about Kenora in northern Ontario to British Columbia was called the North West Territory.

Sir John authorized the establishment of a force of 300 men, preferably veterans of military service. The colonel had recommended that the force be split up into detachments of about 50 men at a post, more at the bigger posts. He recommended old soldiers who knew the cavalry drill. He suggested about 500 men in all. But Sir John, although he'd never been to the west, realized that wasn't the sort of force he needed. These men wouldn't work in squadrons of 50 with flags flying and brass sparkling.

These men would operate alone for weeks at a time, occasionally in patrols of a half-dozen if some emergency occurred. He wanted them to wear the traditional British scarlet tunic because the Indians had bad experiences with the American army in its blue coats.

Just before the bill was to go to parliament to authorize the North West Mounted Rifles, Sir John drew a line through the last word. Parliament approved the formation of the North West Mounted Police instead. That sounded

less war-like and wouldn't offend the Yanks.

Three divisions of 50 men each were sent out from Toronto that fall and spent the winter in the old Stone Fort at Winnipeg, rented from the Hudson's Bay Company.

In the spring, the new commissioner of the force, Colonel George French, sent out from Toronto with 150 more men. They had to travel through American territory much of the way because there was no railway on the Canadian side of the border.

When they arrived at Fargo in North Dakota in June of 1874, the men and their equipment landed in a heap at the railway station. The local plainsmen scoffed at them and said they wouldn't be ready to set out for Manitoba for a month. But Colonel French kept the men working all night, packing and sorting, and they set off in the morning. They made it to their headquarters at Camp Dufferin in Manitoba in less than two weeks.

The night after they arrived, an eight-hour thunderstorm hit the area, the worst in history. It scattered their horses. Some ran for 35 miles. But the new Mounties rode across the prairie for several days, rounding up their herd. They eventually recovered all but one and it was presumed to have drowned in a creek.

By the eighth of July Colonel French had his force ready to move out. Some patrols started then, some didn't go until the ninth and tenth. That's why the history books give all three dates.

No matter. The force moved west, roughly along the border. At Roche Perce, south of where Regina is today, it split. Colonel French continued on to the foothills of southern Alberta. A detachment rambled north and eventually got to Edmonton.

Along the way they established small outposts and dropped off a few men at each. In the fall when French returned to Winnipeg, he had covered almost 2000 miles.

It had been a tough march and the men had had their share of hardship. Some days they blundered along like kids on a hike. But they got better as time went on. And, most importantly, they stayed.

> *Parliament approved the formation of the North West Mounted Police instead of the North West Mounted Rifles. That sounded less war-like and wouldn't offend the Yanks.*

Originally broadcast July 8, 1983

A RIDE TO REMEMBER

Fewer than a dozen people have tried to go over Niagara Falls in a barrel. At least three have died in the attempt. Some were pulled out before they reached the Falls itself.

But on the 9th of July in 1960, a 7-year-old boy made it without a barrel. Not intentionally, but he made it.

Roger Woodward and his sister, Deanne, who was 17, went for a boat ride with a neighbour. Their father was a construction worker and his boss and pal James Honeycutt dropped by the house and offered to take the kids for a boat ride.

They got into Honeycutt's outboard on the Niagara River. Honeycutt made the kids put on life preservers. He had one for himself and decided he would put it on later after they were going.

They were about a mile above the Falls when a shear pin broke in the outboard motor. Honeycutt started to row but, even that far from the Falls, the current was too strong for him.

By now, Honeycutt was afraid if he quit rowing, even long enough to put on his lifejacket, the boat would be lost.

Young Roger realized what was happening and he started to scream: We're going to die.

Honeycutt told him to be quiet, everything would be all right.

A minute or two later the boat overturned. Roger and Deanne were both swept down toward the falls. Honeycutt was drowned.

Deanne's screams attracted a New Jersey policeman who was there on his holidays. He and another man climbed through a fence and snatched Deanne just before she went over the falls. She was shooting past so fast they'd only have one grab at her.

That would have been a big-enough miracle story for one day.

Maid Two was calling Maid Three: "I've got a lifejacket here, up in The Shoe." Then Maid Two called again: "There's a boy in it. And he's alive."

As Deanne was pulled out she was crying that Roger had gone over the Falls. Police on the American side, where Deanne was rescued, called police in Canada, across the river. They warned them to watch for a body in the whirlpool below the Falls.

Just as that message was being received at the police station, the skipper of a cruise boat named the Maid of the Mist received a frantic call, also from a cruise ship called the Maid of the Mist. There are two Maids of the Mist to carry passengers in to the swirling water at the base of the Falls.

Maid Two was calling Maid Three: "I've got a lifejacket here, up in The Shoe." The Shoe is that part of the Niagara River right at the base of the Falls.

Then Maid Two called again: "There's a boy in it. And he's alive."

Sure enough, young Roger had somehow survived.

He was only seven at the time and weighed 55 pounds. The lifejacket he was wearing was designed for an adult.

But obviously, luck played a major part in it. Scientists still puzzle over it but they say he must have just bobbed like a cork and floated down on a mixture of water and air. Then, by sheer chance and against all the odds, missed the hundreds of rocks at the bottom.

Soon afterwards, the Woodward family moved to Florida to get away from all the publicity that resulted. In a few years Roger was old enough to buy a motorcycle.

He crashed it but walked away with only a broken finger. His sister Deanne was hit by a falling power line. Doctors said she should have been killed but she escaped unhurt.

Roger is now sales manager of a business machine company in Florida. He got his promotion a few years ago. On Friday the 13th.

Originally broadcast July 9, 1986

THE ACCIDENTAL ASSASSIN

It rains a lot in England but it doesn't storm much. So the two-hour thunderstorm of the night of the 9th and 10th of July in 1923 was really something. Hospitals and police stations were deluged with calls from people frightened by the lightning and thunder.

Several hospitals reported attacks of nerves by men who had been in the war and were reminded of the artillery fire.

Shortly after 2:00 in the morning of the 10th of July, a porter at the Savoy Hotel heard three bangs. At first he thought it was noise from the storm. Then he was sure they were three pistol shots. He'd heard enough of them when he was in the army to know.

He went up and down the hall, trying to figure out what room the shots came from. Suddenly, the door of one of the biggest suites flew open and a beautiful young woman came out, screaming: "What have I done? I pulled the trigger three times."

What had she done indeed. She'd just set in motion a murder trial that would sell newspapers by the millions all over the world.

The man on the floor with three holes in him was Prince Fahmy Bey, an Egyptian nobleman with bags of money that couldn't do him any good where he had gone; a gorgeous young French wife, who had just made the what-have-I-done speech; and some unorthodox habits that included young men.

Under British law, when you're in a scrape like this you don't holler "Get my lawyer." You holler, "Get my criminal solicitor." He assesses the situation and calls in the lawyer who will eventually defend you in court, the barrister.

The gorgeous widow sent out a call for a man named Freke Palmer, the best criminal solicitor in London. He, in turn, rang in Marshall Hall, the best barrister. Hall was very much in demand and very hard to get.

He asked the Prince and his wife if there was any particular tune they'd like to hear. The wife replied: "Thank you, but my husband is going to kill me and I'm not much in the mood for music."

But he knew to come running when Freke Palmer called. Freke Palmer was also in charge of the investigation and his private investigators soon came up with the band leader of the orchestra of the Savoy and a pair of handsome young men from Paris.

The band leader was able to testify about a strange conversation the night before the shooting. Or, as the prosecution insisted on calling it, the murder.

He said he stopped at the table of the Prince and his wife and asked if there was any particular tune they'd like to hear. He said the wife replied: "Thank you, but my husband is going to kill me and I'm not much in the mood for music."

Marshall Hall, the hot-shot lawyer, was also able to produce a letter that Mrs. Prince had written a few days earlier. It was a statement sworn before a lawyer which said that the Prince had sworn on the Koran that he would kill his wife and she was scared stiff that he would.

Somehow Marshall Hall also got a page of a letter thatthe prince had written to his sister saying he was forcing his wife to do exactly what he wanted. The two young men from Paris testified that the Prince was a sexual weirdo.

On the witness stand the widow said she had a pistol to protect her jewelry which was worth a fortune. She and the Prince had an argument, he made a dive for her and she pointed the pistol at him and — lo and behold — the silly thing just went off.

The betting was that the poor princess was headed for an English jail, that a British jury wouldn't buy all that hysterical foreign carry-on. The betting was wrong. The jury said not guilty. The princess walked and newspaper circulation soared. It was a great deal all around. If you weren't an Egyptian prince.

Originally broadcast July 10, 1987

DUEL PURPOSE

As the 1800s began, the two brightest men in American politics were Aaron Burr and Alexander Hamilton.

They were the same age, just under 50. Each had been an officer on Washington's staff during the American Revolution. Each had founded a bank. Each had published a newspaper. In 1804, each was practicing law in New York.

Most people agreed that one or the other of them would some day run the country. But not both. They hated each other so much that that would be impossible.

Hamilton was the illegitimate son of a handsome, dissipated rich man and a West Indian beauty, a man known for fire and dash and flamboyance. Burr was from a well-to-do New England family, a cool customer, some said stuck-up.

In those days, the president of the United States wasn't elected by the people. He was put into the job by representatives of the state legislatures.

In the election of 1800, it was a three-way race. John Adams, the president, was running for re-election. Thomas Jefferson of Virginia and Aaron Burr were also running. Adams lost out and Jefferson and Burr tied. That meant the house of representatives had to break the deadlock.

That only happened after much politicking and many votes. Jefferson won. Alexander Hamilton had worked hard to defeat Burr. And Burr knew it. He had to settle for being vice-president.

Next, Burr tried for the governorship of New York. He did all the back-room politicking necessary and seemed to have it in the bag. But something went wrong at the last minute and he was beaten out by a nobody.

Burr set out to find out what had gone wrong. He soon learned that Hamilton had been doing back-room work just as hard as he had, maybe harder. Not that Hamilton wanted the job himself; he was just trying to keep it from Burr.

Burr seethed and waited for a chance at revenge. In the spring of 1804 he got the excuse he was looking for. An Albany newspaper quoted Hamilton as calling Burr despicable.

Burr didn't even bother to check it out; he sent a message to Hamilton challenging him to a duel. Hamilton couldn't say no, although he hated the idea of duelling. He had always opposed it in general, and when his son was killed in a duel three years earlier, that really set his mind against it.

On the 11th of July in 1804 Burr and a friend arrived by boat at a landing on the New Jersey side of the Hudson River, across from New York.

They climbed a cliff to a little ledge about six feet deep and 30-odd feet long. It was screened by trees so no one could see. Duelling was illegal at the time.

Burr learned that Hamilton had been doing back-room work just as hard as he had, maybe harder. Not that Hamilton wanted the job himself; he was just trying to keep it from Burr.

The men cleared away some brush to make an open area. Shortly after 7:00, Hamilton and his second arrived. So did a doctor.

The men stood 12 paces apart, each with a pistol. Hamilton, the man who hated duelling, left a letter saying that no matter what happened he didn't intend to fire.

He didn't. It was a one-shot affair. Burr hit Hamilton in the right side of the belly. The bullet went through the liver and lodged in the spine. Hamilton died 30 hours later.

As for Aaron Burr, the shot that killed Hamilton also killed Burr's political career. He became the most notorious man in America. People would walk blocks out of their way just to catch a glimpse of him. But nobody would vote for him again.

Originally broadcast July 11, 1984

SUCCESS STORIES

Mazo de la Roche was born in southern Ontario, near Toronto, in the late 1800s. Her ancestors had settled in New England long before the American Revolution. When that Revolution came, they moved to Canada to stay British.

Mazo later wrote that her mother's side of the family were handsome, intelligent-looking people who never amounted to much. They were what she called distinguished-looking nobodies.

Mazo had a cousin named Caroline Clement and they were raised together. They always referred to themselves as sisters.

Mazo and Caroline set up housekeeping together when they were young women. They didn't have much money, although they were both very genteel. Caroline was an organized person and a worker.

Mazo was artistic, a writer, but not the most practical person in the world.

The only place they could afford was a little wooden house in the country west of Toronto. Caroline would take the train to Toronto where she was an office worker for the provincial government. Mazo would stay home and write. She seldom did any housework.

Mazo was trying to make a living at a style of writing that we today would describe as part Gothic novel, part soap opera script.

The area where they lived, near the town of Oakville, was home to a lot of retired Englishmen, people who had been in the army and the colonial service. They usually named their homes after places they'd worked at in years gone by.

Mazo took the homes and mannerisms of her neighbours plus the distinguished looks and bearing of her nobody family. Caroline asked a man at work, another former British civil servant, for a list of names of places he'd been. That list included the name of a town in India called Jalna.

So Mazo created a distinguished Canadian family of achievers, called the Whiteoaks, and gave them an estate named Jalna.

She added cranky old grandmothers and seductive, man-stealing aunts and a story line that will never win any award for gripping plot structure. But it was an instant success.

It was in 1927 and Mazo, who wasn't exactly the hottest author in the English language, submitted the manuscript to two American publishers at once. They both wanted it. She was in her first legal hassle, but it was a pleasant one.

Mazo made a lot of money out of that book, called simply *Jalna*. Then she set out to write another novel about something else.

"No, no," said the publisher, "we need a sequel to *Jalna*." And that was the story of her life from then on. Publishers kept demanding more Jalna stories. The public kept paying fortunes for them.

By the time Mazo died, on the 12th of July in 1961, she had written 16 of them. The critics saw some merit in some of them but sneered at most.

The readers couldn't have cared less. They had the same grip on the customers that *Melrose Place* does on TV watchers today.

Mazo's stories were mostly sketched out years before, when she and Caroline had made up stories as girls. They discussed everything Mazo wrote and worked on it together.

Once they had money, they moved to England, bought a big estate and settled down. Neither ever married.

They returned to Canada when the war started in 1939 and bought a big place, like an English country estate, outside Toronto.

The Jalna books still sell well. And in the '70s, the CBC turned out a series based on them.

> *Mazo submitted the manuscript to two American publishers at once. They both wanted it. She was in her first legal hassle, but it was a pleasant one.*

Originally broadcast July 12, 1984

A ROBBER AND A GENTLEMAN

One nice day in the summer of 1875, a stagecoach was travelling in the mountains of central California, taking passengers and gold dust from one town to another.

The horses were barely moving then they reached the top of a long hill. Suddenly, a man appeared in front of them, wearing a long linen coat, what was called a duster in those days, one that cowboys wore in dusty country. It was like a long white lab coat.

The man's face was hidden in a flour sack with a couple of eyeholes in it. And he pointed a shotgun at the driver.

The driver threw down the strongbox. The five passengers, without even being told, knew to throw out their wallets. One was a lady's purse. The bandit bowed down to her and handed back the purse and the wallets to the men. He said he intended to make his living only by robbing Wells Fargo, the stagecoach company.

When the sheriff galloped up a couple of hours later the strongbox had been pried open and the bandit was gone. In the empty box was a folded paper.

And on it was a little poem, not very good but kind of touching:

I've laboured long and hard for bread
For honor and for riches
But on my corns too long you've tred
You fine-haired sons of bitches.

And it was signed Black Bart the PO8. PO8 apparently meant poet.

Over the next eight years, Black Bart struck 27 more times, always hitting stagecoaches, never hurting anybody, always bowing to any ladies in the coaches.

Sometimes Bart left one of his poems, usually not.

Bart was the darling of the newspapers. Most citizens saw him as a good guy, one who stood up to the banks and other big shots. Within a short time, there were rewards totalling $800 for his capture. Eight hundred dollars in those days was a lot of money.

The head of security for Wells Fargo, the stagecoach company, was an ex-copper named James Hume, one of the best man-hunters North America ever produced.

On the 13th of July in 1882, seven years after Bart's first robbery, a stagecoach driver got a shot at him. He missed but Bart dropped his mask and the driver saw enough of him to get a not-bad description.

In November of 1883, while pulling off robbery number 27, Bart was nicked by another bullet. He dropped his handkerchief and Hume traced him by checking out the laundry mark. He caught up with him as he arrived to pick up his shirts at a laundry in San Francisco.

Black Bart turned out to be a small, dapper, retired mining engineer named C. E. Bolton, a fastidious little guy with a starched collar and cane and diamond stickpin.

He pleaded guilty and got a very light six years. He only did four and a half. The newspapers smelled a deal and raised a fuss. But nothing came of it. Bolton did his time and disappeared. And left Hollywood with enough material to turnout more than a half-dozen Black Bart movies over the years.

Originally broadcast July 13, 1992

> *Over the next eight years, Black Bart struck 27 more times, always hitting stagecoaches, never hurting anybody, always bowing to any ladies in the coaches.*

GLOOM AND DOOMED

The word everybody used to describe Gary Barrett was gloomy. From his childhood in Detroit to his death in Edmonton more than 55 years later, everybody who met Gary Barrett was impressed by his melancholy manner.

Barrett was married when he was 20 and the father of eight by the time he was 30. He never had much of a job and the prospect of life with a wife and eight kids and never enough money was more than he could stand.

So sometime around 1900 he just walked away. He next turned up in Utah, working as a laborer on the railway.

There, he met a widow named Johnson, a lady with three children, and a few dollars. Barrett must have been missing the domestic life by this time. He told the widow Johnson how much he liked her, how good cheap land was available up in Canada, what a pleasant life they could have together . . . he seems to have told her about everything except the wife and eight kids back in Detroit.

So the widow Johnson became Mrs. Barrett, she thought. She sold some property she had in Utah and she, Barrett, and her three kids moved to Egg Lake, Saskatchewan, near Prince Albert. There, they homesteaded.

We now know that throughout all this time Barrett had terrible dreams and urges. He was obsessed with the idea of shooting people, especially his wife. Obviously, he was quite crazy by today's standards. But there were few psychiatrists in Canada at the time, none of them at Egg Lake.

In October of 1907, Barrett finally snapped. He had thrown his shotgun into the lake a few weeks before because he was afraid he would give in to one of his urges to shoot his wife.

But he still had a revolver. His wife began to argue with him about his gloomy moods. Barrett grabbed the revolver, put it to her head and pulled the trigger. Click.

For some reason, it didn't fire. Two of the three children then tried to pull Barrett away. He pointed the revolver at Burnett, the 12-year-old boy, and pulled the trigger. This time it fired. The boy was wounded in the arm.

Mrs. Barrett ran to a neighbour's two miles away. Pretty soon young Burnett was in hospital in Prince Albert and Barrett was in jail.

But the wound became infected and, in the days before penicillin, that could be fatal. It was.

Barrett went on trial for murder. He was convicted with a recommendation by the jury that he not be hanged.

So Barrett went to the penitentiary near Edmonton for the rest of his life.

The deputy warden there was a man named Richard Stedman, one of those rare prison officers who was popular with the prisoners. For some reason, Barrett got the idea that Stedman hated him and was giving him a hard time.

The opposite was true. When Barrett seemed to become listless, Stedman arranged for him to get a lighter job in a prison workshop and be examined by a doctor. Sure enough, Barrett had developed a heart condition.

The possibility of early parole under those circumstances became a definite likelihood. But before that could happen, Barrett took an ax as Stedman walked through the shop and hit him once on the back of the neck. Stedman was dead within minutes.

This time, the jury that convicted Barrett of murder didn't recommend mercy. So he was hanged on the 14th of July in 1907, a gloomy man who obviously had mental problems. But in those days, the law was reluctant to look at mental problems.

> *Barrett had terrible dreams and urges. He was obsessed with the idea of shooting people, especially his wife. Obviously, he was quite crazy by today's standards. But in those days, no one could help him.*

Originally broadcast July 14, 1988

ONWARD, CHRISTIAN SOLDIERS

To a medieval European Christian, the single most pious act possible was a trip to Jerusalem to worship at the site of the Crucifixion. Jerusalem had been occupied for centuries by Moslems but that was no problem. The Moslems were broad-minded people who allowed Christian pilgrims to worship in Jerusalem. In fact, they encouraged them. They provided a profitable tourist business.

Then, there was a series of wars within the Moslem world and the new rulers of Jerusalem, the Turks, wouldn't allow Christian pilgrimages.

In the year 1095, the pope ordered all Christians to stop fighting amongst themselves, which they were always doing, and to unite and march on Jerusalem and make it secure for Christians.

At first, peasants swarmed to form an army and started off without any organization or supplies. They burned and looted and massacred Jews they encountered along the way. They died in their own quarrels or drowned in leaky ships or starved to death in mountain passes. Their sorry, silly venture fizzled out before they left Christian territory.

Next, four big-time European leaders, from France and Germany, formed an army with proper organization and supplies and they made it to the Holy Land. That one is called the First Crusade.

It was a success of sorts. On the 15th of July in 1099, these crusaders captured the city of Jerusalem.

They massacred every Moslem man, woman and child they could find. Then they set fire to the Great Synagogue where the Jews of the city had gone for refuge and killed the few who escaped the flames.

Then they gave thanks to God for allowing them to plant the cross once more in the holiest of cities.

Next they settled down to fighting amongst themselves. They did that with great gusto, slaughtering friend and foe. After 90 years of that, the Moslems counter-attacked and took Jerusalem back and held it until the British Army captured it in the First World War, 800 years later.

In all, there were eight or nine great crusades, depending on which historian is doing the counting, plus a couple of dozen other half-baked ventures like the peasants' march. They always started with religious fervor and ended with greed, jealousy and in-fighting. They lasted 250 years and when they ended, the situation in the Holy Land was remarkably like it was when they started.

Nevertheless, the crusades were a turning point in the history of the world. Peasants who had been tied to the land in Europe took off. Some never came back. Sugar and glass and spices and ideas began to flow to Europe along the trade routes that followed the crusading armies.

The world was changing and, once started, that change never stopped.

> *In all, there were eight or nine great crusades. They always started with religious fervor and ended with greed, jealousy and in-fighting.*

Originally broadcast July 15, 1993

THE END OF AN ERA

For 300 years Russia was ruled by the Romanoffs, a royal family that intermarried with various other European monarchies.

By the time the First World War broke out in 1914, Czar Nicholas was a cousin of both the kaiser of Germany and the king of England. He looked exactly like the English cousin, King George the Fifth, grandfather of the present queen.

The czar's wife, the czarina, had started life as a German princess. They had four daughters, all titled arch-duchesses, and one son, the czarevich.

In theory, the czar was the most absolute monarch on earth, responsible to no one, answerable to no parliament. In fact, the Russian government was hopelessly inefficient, the empire was so huge it was ungovernable, and Nicholas was disinterested in ruling.

The German Army beat up the Russian army with incredible bloodshed soon after the war started. The Russian Army collapsed, the communists who had been in exile returned and the country dissolved into an orgy of civil war, famine and massacre.

The Reds, the communists, fought the Whites, the monarchists. And for a while it was impossible to say who was going to win.

The czar threw up his hands and abdicated. The communists took custody of him but they didn't come right out and say he was under arrest. They said he and his family were being moved a thousand miles to the east, to Siberia, away from the fighting. The vast mass of the Russian people had a strange reverence for the czar and the communist leaders were afraid they might be in trouble if anything happened to the czar

while he was under their care.

So the whole family was put under guard in the small city of Ekaterinburg. They had a few servants and the czarina filled her days supervising the kids' school work. The czar got a woodpile and kept himself in shape by sawing and chopping.

But the civil war spread and pretty soon there was an army of monarchists threatening Ekaterinburg.

The communist leaders back in Moscow were afraid that if the czar and his family were rescued the people would think the civil war was over and the communists had lost.

So they ordered that the royal family all be shot. On the night of the 16th of July in 1918, they were lined up in the cellar on the house where they were living.

The firing squad was half-drunk. The czar and czarina and the servants were killed quickly. But the arch-duchesses were wearing corsets packed with jewels. Apparently they hoped to be rescued and figured they might have to move in a hurry.

> *The communist leaders back in Moscow were afraid that if the czar and his family were rescued the people would think the civil war was over and the communists had lost.*

The jewels acted as armor and the bullets bounced off them although they were badly wounded. They were eventually clubbed to death.

Since the collapse of the communists, there has been a lot of digging in that area. Some bones were sent to England where experts have extracted DNA to compare with royal blood samples, including Prince Philip's.

Sure enough, the bones of Ekaterinburg are what's left of the Romanoffs. Or at least some of the family. The remains of arch-duchess Anastasia and the czarevich are still missing.

Originally broadcast July 16, 1993

LADY SINGS THE BLUES

Billie Holiday is the most tragic story in the history of show business.

Other artists have had bad luck and been the victims of injustice. Others have been talented. But you can't find a case anywhere of anyone as talented as Billie Holiday who was hounded to an early death. Mind you, she was her own worst enemy and caused most of her own trouble...

Billie Holiday was the greatest jazz singer this world has ever heard. Ella Fitzgerald, Sarah Vaughan, Cleo Laine, Lena Horne, Frank Sinatra . . . they all acknowledge that on their best night they're trying to be as good as Billie Holiday was.

So what went wrong? Well, everything. And right from the start.

Billie was born Eleanor Fagan in Baltimore in 1915. Her mother was 13 and her father was 15. He was a bright man, half-Irish, half-black, the son of a slave.

There was no worse time to be born in the United States and be black. It wasn't a society based on discrimination: it was outright oppression.

Eleanor was a jazz nut and her favorite movie actress was Billie Dove so she changed her name to Billie Holiday.

When she was 12, a man tried to rape her. She called the cops and they let the man go and put Billie in a reform school. She got out at 13, very bitter. She moved to New York, where her mother was working as a maid. Her father was a very good musician and was away all the time on the road with some very big-name bands.

Billie worked as a prostitute in New York and spent time in jail for it.

She loved to sing. And she started singing in the Harlem jazz clubs. Despite that stint as a prostitute she wouldn't snuggle up to either the club owners or the customers; and the other singers and dancers started calling her "Lady." Sarcastically. The name stuck. Later, Lester Young, the sax player, called her "Lady Day" because she lit up his life. That's the name that stuck and that's what her fans called her.

In the mid-30s, Billie cut a few records, pieces that are collectors' items today, the best jazz vocals ever done until then, maybe the best jazz vocals ever — period.

And she got 20 and 30, occasionally 50 dollars per record. That's all. No royalties, nothing more.

She went on the road with Count Basie. But Billie liked to drink and puff marijuana. And she rebelled noisily when she was told that, as a black, she had to go in and out of the back door of hotels and clubs she played.

Basie dropped her and Artie Shaw picked her up. He dropped her too after a while. Everybody agreed about Lady Day: a brilliant singer but a bad attitude.

> *Lester Young, the sax player, called Billie "Lady Day" because she lit up his life. That's the name that stuck and that's what her fans called her.*

She played in England and Europe and was a huge hit. She tried marriage, a couple of times. When that failed she tried something stronger than booze and marijuana. She became a hopeless heroin addict.

She went into clinics and tried to straighten out. She did time for heroin possession. At least once the cops tried to frame her with planted dope.

A lot of sentimental nonsense has been written and put on the screen about Billie Holiday, Lady Day. But she was her own worst enemy. No question about that. Most of the injustice she complained about has been eliminated today by black people who swallowed their anger and used their brains instead.

Billie Holiday wasn't one of them. When she died in a hospital room in New York, on the 17th of July in 1959, she had 17 cents in the bank, 450 dollars strapped to her leg, another dope charge hanging over her head — and a talent we can only weep for.

Originally broadcast July 17, 1984

THE OTHER BROTHER

Late on the night of the 18th of July in 1969, Senator Edward Kennedy left a party at a rented cottage on Chappaquiddick Island in Massachusetts, in summer holiday country.

The senator and five of his pals had thrown a party that night for six young women who had been workers in the political campaign of his brother Bobby, the previous year. That campaign had come to an abrupt and tragic halt.

Teddy was the youngest of the Kennedy brothers of that generation. Many have said he's the least bright. Old Joe Kennedy, their father, was a man of incredible ambition and rare genius. Joe became a millionaire in various businesses, mostly construction and liquor. He was a Boston Irishman, a man who thoroughly disliked the English. Yet, in the late 1930s he had been appointed the American ambassador to England.

When the war began, Ambassador Kennedy openly predicted the Germans would win. The British, he said, were finished.

The British complained to Washington that Ambassador Kennedy was undermining their war effort. Eventually he was recalled.

Kennedy wanted more than anything for his son, Joe Jr., to be president of the United States one day. But Joe was killed in the war, fighting to defend England, the country his father hated.

So Kennedy transferred his plans to his next son, John. And John became president in 1960, masterminded by his father's plans and fueled by his wealth.

But John was killed by an assassin in Dallas in 1963. The next brother, Bobby, was John's attorney general and in 1968 he was running for the Democratic Party nomination so he could be president. But an assassin got him in Los Angeles in the fall of 1968.

That left Teddy. It was assumed he would run in 1972. He probably would have made it. Everybody who knew the Kennedys said Teddy wasn't nearly as bright as the other brothers, but he was a relaxed charmer, the sort of person who could shake your hand once and have your vote for life.

Like his brothers, Teddy directed a lot of his charm towards women. He liked them and they liked him.

Kennedy left the party with Mary Jo Kopechne, a young woman who had worked on Bobby's campaign the previous year before he was killed.

Chappaquiddick Island was joined to the nearest major piece of land by a big old wooden bridge, 85 feet long with a high hump in the middle. A car that tries to cross it in a hurry will bounce in the air.

Several hours later, some time after dawn on Monday morning, Kennedy called the local police. He said he had made the wrong turn as he approached the bridge and had driven into the water. He got out of the car but Mary Jo Kopechne had been drowned.

Kennedy said he dived several times to get her but he couldn't. The tide at that point was too strong. He then swam 500 feet across a channel to the motel where he was staying, fell asleep and called the police when he woke up in the morning.

His story came out slowly and in small pieces. He didn't make any public statement until after his lawyers and advisers talked to him for a long time. Then Kennedy went on TV and asked the people of Massachusetts to be understanding.

They were. And they have been ever since. He's still their senator. But he's never again been a serious contender for the presidency.

> *Everybody who knew the Kennedys said Teddy wasn't nearly as bright as the other brothers, but he was the sort of person who could shake your hand once and have your vote for life.*

Originally broadcast July 18, 1988

FAMILY PLOT

Lizzie Borden was born on the 19th of July in 1860 in Fall River, Massachusetts, the daughter of a well-to-do property-owner named Andrew Borden.

Her father loved Lizzie even more than most fathers love their daughters. In fact, Lizzie's middle name was the same as her father's — Andrew.

Lizzie's mother died and her father remarried. The new Mrs. Borden was a nice, kindly woman named Abby. Everyone spoke well of Abby but Lizzie and her sister Emma hated her.

Lizzie's father was a decent man but a bit of a character. He put in his time collecting rents from properties he owned in and around Fall River and investing in various small business schemes.

He could be very much the tightwad. His taxes were once raised by the local assessor who was a member of the same church he was. In a rage, he quit that church.

But where Lizzie and Emma were concerned, Andrew was the soul of generosity. On Lizzie's birthday in 1892, Andrew gave Lizzie and Emma a house. When they said they didn't like the house he took it back and gave them $5000 instead, more than the house was worth.

Apparently the reason Emma and Lizzie didn't like Abby was because they were afraid their father was going to leave everything to her and cut them out of his will. There was nothing to suggest that was a valid fear.

One hot day, three weeks after Lizzie's birthday, the one that resulted in the big present, Andrew left the house after breakfast to do some business. It was a scorching hot day.

Emma was out of town. So was most of the Fall River police department. This was the day of the police annual picnic. Only one cop was left behind.

Lizzie and Bridget the maid and Abby were working around the house. The maid was working outside most of the morning. Lizzie was in and out.

On Lizzie's birthday in 1892, Andrew gave Lizzie and Emma a house. When they said they didn't like the house he took it back and gave them $5000 instead, more than the house was worth.

Abby, the stepmother, was doing housework in a second-floor bedroom.

Andrew, the father, returned late in the morning and Lizzie reported Abby had gone out to visit a sick friend. Andrew said he was exhausted from the heat and he lay down. After a while Lizzie shrieked and called Bridget the maid. She had found her father dead. He had been attacked with an axe and badly cut up. Lizzie said it must have been a tramp she'd seen hanging around the house. Nobody else ever saw him.

The one town cop on duty arrived, looked at the body and went back to the station to file a report.

A doctor was called. While he was looking at the body of Lizzie's father, somebody found the stepmother, also done in with an axe. But she had been dead an hour and a half.

Enough neighbours had seen Bridget the maid going in and out of the house to establish that it wasn't her who had killed the Bordens.

Lizzie said she'd been in the loft of the barn most of the morning, looking for fishing equipment. But a messenger boy who heard her explain that to the one cop on duty went to the loft and checked. It was covered with dust and cobwebs and hadn't been disturbed in weeks, maybe months.

Lizzie was charged with the murder but got off. It's obvious she did it. Newspapers all over the world ran the story on the front page. Not that the murder was that unusual. But Lizzie was a wealthy young woman of refined family. And, in those days, that was really something.

Oh, there was one other factor in making the story big. Little boys all over the English-speaking world loved to recite a little poem. It went: Lizzie Borden took an axe and gave her father 40 whacks. And when she'd seen what she had done, she gave her mother 41. It is kind of catchy, isn't it?

Originally broadcast July 19, 1988

THE HEN WHO FLEW THE COOP

Marie Manning was a misfit. She was the daughter of a Virginia gentleman and was sent to an expensive finishing school. But she didn't want to pour tea or embroider or play the harpsichord. She wanted to be a reporter.

This was 1890 and the sort of girls who went to finishing schools weren't expected to work. And the sort of girls who worked didn't go in for racy jobs like reporting.

Marie was at dinner one night and sat beside Arthur Brisbane, a famous New York editor. She said she wanted to be a reporter. He said, c'mon around to the office.

So, at the age of about 20, Marie went to work for the *New York World*. She covered murder trials and city hall and fires and speeches and all sorts of things. After a while, Brisbane, her boss, was hired away by the *New York Journal* and took several of his top reporters with him, including Marie.

Newspapermen were radical enough in those days to allow women into their business. But they weren't so radical that they'd actually let them work in the newsroom. At the *Journal*, Marie worked in a room down the hall with a few other women reporters. It was called the Hen Coop.

Marie stood almost six feet tall and she liked to wear her hair combed up high. So they called her the Phone Pole.

One day, Brisbane came into the Hen Coop with three letters. In those unsophisticated days, readers thought editors knew everything and they often wrote for advice. Three readers had written, all within a few days, asking what to do about boyfriends and girlfriends and broken hearts.

Brisbane figured the ladies in the Hen Coop could handle the job. He suspected there were lots more readers out there with similar problems.

Male reporters' names appeared on their stories in those days but it was considered quite improper for a woman to use her own name.

Since Marie got stuck with answering the letters, she was allowed to pick the name. She was reading a book at the time about a woman named Beatrice. She had been born in Fairfax County, Virginia. So she called her column Advice from Beatrice Fairfax. It appeared on the 20th of July in 1898. And it started something.

Pretty soon the post office told the *Journal* it couldn't handle the flow of mail. Two men had to be hired to carry it all. It reached 1400 letters a day in no time.

> *Newspapermen were radical enough in those days to allow women into their business. But they weren't so radical that they'd actually let them work in the newsroom.*

Marie kept it up until 1905. Then she quit, married a Washington real estate man and settled down to raise a family.

In 1929, she and her husband lost everything in the stock market crash. So she went back to writing the Beatrice Fairfax column until she died in 1945.

By then, every major newspaper in the English-speaking world had a column like it. The most successful columns carry the names of two Chicago sisters, Ann Landers and Abby van Buren. They appear in 2400 different papers a day.

Originally broadcast July 20, 1993

MONKEY BUSINESS

The most revolutionary act of the 1800s, a very revolutionary century, was the publication of a scientific paper. Charles Darwin, the English biologist, came up with his Theory of Evolution. Or, as he called his book, *The Origin of the Species.*

In his book, Darwin claimed that man and various other animals, like monkeys, are descendants of a common ancestor, probably more like today's ape than man.

Science, until Darwin's time, had been very much a descendent of religion. Now, a reputable scientist was saying that the story of creation in the Bible couldn't be true. That argument is still going.

By the 1920s, it was clear to most people that Charles Darwin was right, in a general way at least. His theory, by the way, has never been absolutely proven and scientists, even those who believe it, say there are still some significant holes in it. But they say, as human knowledge advances, the theory of evolution will be proven, more or less as Darwin wrote it.

Nowhere was opposition to Darwin's theory so spirited than in the southern United States. That's the world stronghold of fundamental Christianity. And fundamental Christianity is based on total belief in the literal meaning of every word in the Bible.

Evolution had been taught legally and with little fuss, in the schools of Tennessee for almost a generation. Then, in 1925, the Tennessee legislature passed a law called the Butler Act.

The Butler Act said it was a violation of the law to teach the theory of evolution or to deny the truth of the Bible in a public school.

Liberals were appalled. Conservatives liked the new law. Many of them didn't deny evolution. But they saw it as a part of a general loosening of morals.

The lines were drawn. The most distinguished lawyers in the United States stood in line to test the Butler Act.

A young high school teacher named John Scopes volunteered to be the guinea pig. He admitted he taught evolution in the high school in Dayton, Tennessee.

The leading lawyer for the prosecution was William Jennings Bryan. Bryan had been a candidate for the presidency three times and was known as a populist leader from the midwest. He was the voice of fundamentalism.

Defending Scopes, and evolution, was Clarence Darrow, a Chicago lawyer who is still remembered as the most brilliant courtroom lawyer in American history.

The trial began in July, 1925 and more than a hundred newsmen came from all over the world. This wasn't an American story. This was a major international event that just happened to be in the States.

They argued and hassled. The audience broke into applause at the end of each speech. Hot-dog stands were set up outside the courthouse and did a raging business.

A small carnival arrived and the monkeys were the most popular act.

The Monkey Trial, as it was called, is remembered as the end of the anti-evolution movement. Most people will tell you it ended in victory for Darrow and the evolutionists on the 21st of July in 1925.

But actually it didn't. Scopes was convicted and fined $100. Darrow, in his speech to the jury, said it was clear he had broken the law and he should be found guilty.

But that provided a springboard for appeal that eventually had the law declared invalid. But, legislatures being legislatures, it stayed on the books another 30 years before it was repealed.

> *Science, until Darwin's time, had been very much a descendent of religion. Now a reputable scientist was saying that the story of creation in the Bible couldn't be true. That argument is still going.*

Originally broadcast July 21, 1987

WORKING A MIRACLE

On the 22nd of July in 1604, King James I of Scotland drew up a set of instructions to the 54 wisest men in the kingdom. They were ordered to come up with a new English translation of the Bible, a Protestant Bible and that, as nearly as possible, would use original names.

Anyone who lived in the time of King James would surely have thought, of all the things the king did, this had to be the least important. The truth is that, of all the things King James did, this is the only one that has survived.

How could anyone expect 54 scholars of varying skills and backgrounds to agree on anything? It would require a miracle. Some say the result is, indeed, a miracle.

The chairman of the committee, the man the king conferred with in drawing up instructions, was Bishop Bancroft, the Anglican primate of London. When the king had suggested the idea six months earlier, Bancroft had objected. He said there were plenty of translations of the Bible in existence and another one would just confuse things.

The Catholic church in those days opposed the idea of having a bible that the average person could read, if indeed the average person could read. The Anglicans were split on that subject but obviously Bishop Bancroft favored the Catholic position.

But the king insisted. So the committee was put together.

Queen Elizabeth's Greek tutor was among them. So was a professor of languages who could read 15 different languages. There was another one who had been a child prodigy, who read the Bible in Hebrew when he was six.

Also among them was a scholar who was a refugee from religious persecution in Belgium. As well as a couple of brilliant but erratic alcoholics. And one widower who died before he was finished his part of the translation, leaving 11 destitute orphans.

Maybe at least part of the success of the project was based on the democratic nature of British society. Noblemen were still all-important and snobbery was rife. But smart poor boys could get to the top.

How could anyone expect 54 scholars of varying skills and backgrounds to agree on anything? It would require a miracle. Some say the result is, indeed, a miracle.

The final revisions were written into one book by the foremost Bible scholar in the land, a professor at Oxford whose father had been a butcher.

Seven years after King James issued those orders, the King James Version of the Holy Bible rolled off the presses.

The book contained 1500 pages and sold for 30 shillings a copy, a very stiff price in those days.

Universal literacy was still a long way off but this new Bible, in those religious times, gave a lot of people the motive to learn to read.

The writing itself was wonderful. You don't have to be at all religious to appreciate it. The Lord is my shepherd . . . For God so loved the world . . . blessed are the meek . . . words and phrases that shaped our language and our civilization.

The great English historian Macaulay said it all: "This book, which if everything else in our language should perish, would alone suffice to show the whole extent of its beauty and power."

Originally broadcast July 22, 1985

BRING US YOUR WOUNDED . . .

In 1929, a group of Saskatchewan farm women put together an organization called the Anti-Tuberculosis League, an early socialist experiment in medical care. In the years that followed, even the Saskatchewan Medical Association had good things to say about a government-run prepaid medical plan. Of course, in those days many doctors were on welfare along with their patients. The depression hit Saskatchewan hardest of all the provinces.

In 1944, the CCF party was elected in Saskatchewan and it set up North America's first socialist government. Gradually, it introduced free medical, hospital and dental care for the elderly and anyone on welfare; then, free mental hospitals; then, air ambulances...

The premier of Saskatchewan was Tommy Douglas, a Scottish clergyman and a dyed-in-the-wool socialist. He said in speech after speech that he wouldn't be happy until every Canadian had free access to medical care, paid for by the state, financed by taxes.

In the late 1950s, Douglas stepped up his campaign. The doctors by this time had switched their stand and were vigorously opposed.

In 1960, there was a provincial election and medicare became the central issue. The CCF and Douglas both won big, their fifth straight victory. Douglas announced he would sit down with the doctors to work out the details. The doctors said they weren't really being consulted, that it was already in the bag.

A sick baby died the first day of the strike as his parents drove from hospital to hospital, trying to find a doctor. An inquest never did establish whether or not the lack of medical care killed him.

Douglas figured his overwhelming victory in the election settled the issue. The government passed the necessary law in the fall of 1961. Douglas quit and turned Saskatchewan over to his successor, Woodrow Lloyd. Douglas went to Ottawa to head the re-organized CCF, the NDP.

Twice, the plan was delayed. The minister of health wasn't moving quickly enough so Lloyd fired him. Then, at the beginning of July in 1962, free medical care for all became the law in Saskatchewan.

Saskatchewan's 900 doctors went on strike. The Canadian Medical Association and the American Medical Association both backed them.

A sick baby died the first day of the strike as his parents drove from hospital to hospital, trying to find a doctor. An inquest never did establish whether or not the lack of medical care killed him.

The Saskatchewan government started recruiting abroad and began to fly in British doctors. It also brought in Lord Stephen Taylor, a British nobleman and doctor, to sort out the mess.

Taylor persuaded the doctors to go back to work on the 23rd of July in 1962, three weeks after they walked out.

The other provinces followed Saskatchewan's lead. Now every Canadian has free medical care.

But it didn't help the CCF. They lost the next election. So did Tommy Douglas.

Originally broadcast July 23, 1993

AND THERE WAS LIGHT

For centuries, light at night was provided by torches and candles, both not very good, the candles quite expensive. Then came whale oil, also not very good. Then came coal oil and naptha gas, much better, but the lamps they powered were dangerous and caused many fires.

In 1802, the great English inventor, Humphrey Davy produced a bright glow by running an electrical current through platinum strips. That demonstrated that electricity could produce light but Davy's experiment didn't come up with a practical way.

But that experiment did show it could be done and the race was on. Inventors all over the world got to work on the project.

Another Englishman, a man named Swan, realized that if the electricity ran through something that glowed, contact with the air would soon make that something burn up. So he enclosed it in a bulb and pumped out the air. That way the something, called the filament, would glow and provide light without burning up because there was no oxygen in the air around it to support the burning.

But Swan couldn't find the right stuff to make an efficient filament. He used paper.

By this time, hundreds of inventors were working on the project, maybe thousands. Two were in Toronto: a medical student named Henry Woodward and a hotel owner named Matthew Evans.

Woodward owned a battery and an induction coil and the two used to experiment with it. Electricity then was still quite new. One winter evening in 1872 they were making sparks from the coil when they noticed how bright it was. Evans pulled out his watch and they could read the dial in the dark room. If only they could catch that light in some sort of bottle.

> *Evans pulled out his watch and they could read the dial in the dark room. If only they could catch that light in some sort of bottle.*

We don't know if they were aware of Swan's problem with the filament burning up or if they just figured it out by trial and error. But they went to a brass foundry with drawing of what today we would call a light bulb.

It was a tube of glass from a water gage with wires running in each end. The wires were attached to a carbon filament and the ends were sealed with copper. And the air was exhausted to form a vacuum, as in Swan's bulb.

Then they added something Swan didn't. Instead of just leaving a vacuum in the glass, they pumped in nitrogen. Now there was not only no oxygen to allow the filament to burn but there was a gas surrounding it that acted like a fire extinguisher, something that prevented burning.

It worked. Evans and Woodward were granted a patent on their light bulb on the 24th of July in 1874. They put together a company of businessmen to perfect it and get rich. But the costs of development were too high.

Five years later, one of those Toronto businessmen was in New Jersey and he met the great American inventor, Thomas Edison. Edison said he was working on a light bulb. The Canadian said, you're too late. I'm part owner of a patent that did that five years ago. Edison said he knew all about that patent and the principle behind it was all wrong.

The next day a friend of Edison's approached the Canadian and bought up the patent. A few months later Edison got a patent on his light bulb, the father of the one we use today. It incorporated that vital element from the Canadian patent, the gas that won't burn.

Originally broadcast July 24, 1992

TAKING A CHANCE-LLOR

Engelbert Dollfuss was a smart little guy. He'd been born of poor farmers out in the country but was so bright that he made it through two universities on scholarships. During the war he fought well and was wounded.

He was a charming little man, not much taller than five feet. Before anyone could make fun of his size, he would make a joke about it and pretty soon everybody would be on his side.

In 1932, when he was only 40, Dollfuss made it to the top as chancellor, the head of the Austrian government.

He married a tall, beautiful woman, and he would clown for the photographers by sitting on her knee. Shortly before he got the top job he was coming out of the parliament house one day and a crazy man who disagreed with his politics fired a pistol at him. He missed. The reporters all swarmed around Dollfuss and asked what he thought it meant, who he thought had put the man up to it. Nobody, he said, the poor man was just trying to split the atom.

But anyone who took Dollfuss for a clown was in trouble. He was one tough politician. He was a right-winger and a devout Catholic. He saw Communists, socialists, anyone to the left of him as an enemy of himself, his country, and the church.

The socialists and the right wingers each had their own private armies. The socialists were concentrated in a vast housing project in Vienna. Dollfuss ordered them to disband their army. They refused.

Dollfuss ordered in his army plus the national army. The socialists refused to budge. Dollfuss ordered in the artillery. About a thousand were killed, mostly women and children.

You would have thought that would have made Dollfuss a strong enough man to please any right-winger. But there was a party even further to the right, the Austrian Nazis. They were so impressed by Hitler's miraculous revitalization of Germany that they wanted to dissolve the Austrian government and become a province of Germany.

Anyone who took Dollfuss for a clown was in trouble. He was one tough politician. He saw Communists, socialists, anyone to the left of him as an enemy of himself, his country, and the church.

Dollfuss' politics were very much like Hitler's but with one main difference: he was an Austrian patriot. He wouldn't consider union for a moment.

Hitler, on the other hand, dreamed of ruling the world. But he was too cunning to say that out loud. He said the German-speaking people of Europe had been badly treated, needed protection, and he was the man to protect them. He wanted to expand Germany's borders simply so that all the German speakers lived in one country. And since he'd been born in Austria, it was first on his list.

The Austrian Nazis held rallies. Dollfuss threw them in jail. Hitler demanded they be released. Dollfuss told him to mind his own business.

So on the morning of the 25th of July in 1934, less than a year after Hitler came to power in Germany, a troop of Austrian Nazis broke in to the chancellor's office. Obviously, his guards were paid to look the other way.

Dollfuss' office was part of the suite of rooms that had been the location of the Congress of Vienna, the international conference that ended the Napoleonic wars.

So many foreign ministers had shown up for that conference that a problem in precedence had sprung up. If the Russian minister entered the room ahead of the British minister, a terrible diplomatic furor could result.

If the Prussian came in ahead of the Austrian, the war could break out again. So the Austrians cut a door in the walls of the main salon for each minister. After the conference, they bricked up the new ones but left the ornate door frames in place.

A few months before he was assassinated, Dollfuss was showing off his office to a British diplomat. "They did such a good job," he said, "that I can't remember which is the real door, and which are the phoneys."

On the 25th of July he still didn't have it figured out. When he saw the men coming he ran for the door. The wrong door. He was shot and left all day on his office floor to bleed to death.

Originally broadcast July 25, 1983

OUT, OUT DAMNED SPOT

The Bennett family lived in a farmhouse in the township of Pickering, just east of Toronto.

Ellen Bennett was the mother of five children. Her husband was a hired hand who was away from home five nights a week. He worked at a farm an hour or two away to the north.

On the 26th of July in 1877, while her husband was away, Mrs. Bennett was raped and savagely beaten. There were two men armed with some sort of stuff that knocked her unconscious, maybe ether or chloroform. They got in through a broken window.

We know almost exactly what happened because Mrs. Bennett lived for a couple of weeks after the attack. And the detective who handled the case was a very careful man who piled detail on detail on detail.

That detective was John Wilson Murray, the Scotsman who had been appointed a detective to cover the whole province of Ontario. Criminal science was pretty primitive in those days — no fingerprints, no comparison microscopes to match bullets, none of that fancy stuff.

But Murray took careful notes, piled up lots of evidence and pushed scientists to their limit to tell him everything they could about clues he gave them.

Murray didn't have any trouble figuring out who had done it. The bad guys were a wealthy young man named McPherson, the son of a rich farmer, and a not-too-bright farmboy named Burke, who sometimes worked for the McPherson family.

Mrs. Bennett, the victim, knew McPherson slightly. Although she couldn't see the men clearly in the dark she was able to identify McPherson's laugh, which was quite distinctive.

Murray interviewed everybody for miles around until he knew exactly where McPherson and Burke had been during the couple of days before and after the attack.

He carefully examined wheel tracks and was pretty sure McPherson's buggy had been near the Bennett house.

He interviewed McPherson and Burke several times, never accusing them, always acting more curious than hostile, sometimes being sympathetic. Pretty soon he had them contradicting themselves and each other over a whole bunch of petty details. No <u>one</u> was important; but together, they amounted to a pack of lies.

Then he seized McPherson's trousers, which had been washed recently but appeared to have had bloodstains on them. Murray took them to Professor Croft at the University of Toronto. Croft did some tests and was able to prove the stains had been blood although he couldn't swear it was human blood.

Detective Murray seized McPherson's trousers, which had been washed recently but appeared to have had bloodstains on them.

Murray pushed him for more detail, more detail, about the number of stains, the size of them, the pattern of stains on the trousers, and anything else that might provide a lead.

Murray also lined up plenty of other witnesses who could testify about a lot of details. McPherson and Burke were convicted although they had the best lawyers in the country.

McPherson's family had enough clout to save them from hanging and they did long jail terms instead.

It was the first time in the English-speaking world that scientific blood evidence had been presented in court in such detail.

But the irony of the Bennett case is that by today's standards it would have been open-and-shut. There was a blood smear on a window blind. Murray knew it came from a hand because he could see the loops and lines that are distinctively indicators of the human hand. But there was no way of knowing which human hand. The science of fingerprinting hadn't been invented yet. That came 20 years later.

Originally broadcast July 26, 1984

LINES OF COMMUNICATION

The invention of the telegraph in the 1840s was a huge step in the history of man's progress. For the first time man could send a message further than he could see or hear. Until then the only way to extend the range of communication was to relay signals from hilltop to hilltop or beat a drum.

In 20 years, with incredible speed, telegraph lines were strung beside roads and railway tracks all over North America, Europe and England. It was only a matter of time until someone built a long wire, covered it with rubber insulation, and dropped it off the back of a ship sailing from Britain to North America. There already was a message service and telegraph line in Newfoundland.

The distance from the west coast of Ireland to the east tip of Newfoundland was a little less than 2000 miles. A generation earlier a hundred miles was a long distance. But now, it was just a step. A long, uncertain step some days, but still just a step.

A bright young American named Cyrus Field was the man for the job. Field had started working for a paper manufacturer when he was only 15 at a dollar a week. By the time he was 33 he was a millionaire. He retired and devoted the rest of his life to the Atlantic cable.

Looking back on it, the amazing thing is the incredible optimism of Field and his partners. They raised huge amounts of money for ships to lay the cable and for the cable itself.

British manufacturers knew very little about making wire or covering it with rubber insulation and spent hundreds of thousands on raw material, new machinery and new techniques.

All sorts of basic knowledge about electricity, things that are in high school physics books today, were unknown then.

In the summer of 1858, a British warship and an American one met in the mid-Atlantic, each carrying a huge cargo of cable. They spliced the ends of the cable together, then the American sailed to Ireland and the British ship to Newfoundland.

The Americans landed their end in Ireland and connected it to a telegraph station. In August, the British ship brought its end of the cable ashore in Newfoundland. It was connected and fuzzy messages were actually sent back and forth.

The British ship brought its end of the cable ashore in Newfoundland. It was connected and fuzzy messages were actually sent back and forth.

The Newfoundlanders, who had prepared bonfires to celebrate the great occasion, started a forest fire that caused some small panic for a while.

The fireworks at the city hall in Saint John's also got out of hand. For a few minutes there, it looked as if the great new technical success might cost the town its city hall.

Then the messages fizzled out. The line went dead. The insulation was no good.

Field and his friends wanted to start again right away. But it took a few years to raise the money and to design and make a better cable.

Then the American Civil War came along and stopped things for a while.

So, in the summer of 1866, 2000 miles of cable were put aboard the Great Eastern, the biggest ship in the world at that time. The ship sailed from Ireland, staying in contact all the way over the cable as it was being laid.

And on the 27th of July, 1866, the western end of the cable was brought ashore at Heart's Content in Newfoundland and the old world and the new were linked.

Originally broadcast July 27, 1984

Posthumous Popularity

Even if you don't agree that Bach was the best composer in history, you have to admit he was right up there with Beethoven, Mozart, and Cole Porter.

The amazing thing about him is that he wasn't regarded as a top-notch composer in his lifetime. He was famous as an organist who could write music pretty well too. He was dead more than 50 years before music scholars began to realize what a genius he'd been. Today, he is more popular than ever. Especially among jazz musicians who find he wrote a lot of stuff that they can use as the basis for some very modern-sounding work.

Bach was the greatest of a huge tribe of German musicians. The Bach family of notable musicians went way back for three generations. It gets really confusing because these musical Bachs had a habit of naming their boys Johann. So we have Johann George and Johann Emil and Johann just-about-everything-else. But the best of the bunch was Johann Sebastian who was born in Germany.

After he died several of his sons and nephews made names for themselves. They were known by the places they worked so we have the Milan Bach and the Leipzig Bach and the Berlin Bach. To make it even more confusing, the Milan Bach worked in London for a while so at one point in his career he was the Milan Bach and at another the London Bach.

But Johann Sebastian was the greatest of them all. He was a heavy man, described by some who knew him as a bit of a bear in appearance, but with arched eyebrows that made him look as if he was always asking questions or trying to pick a fight.

He was a devout Lutheran and most of his music was written for church services. He worked in several cities, usually as an organist and choirmaster.

He never made much money. He had such a big family, 10 kids altogether, that he could have kept busy just teaching them music.

At various times in his life he squabbled with his employers over wages and working conditions. They certainly didn't behave as if they had one of history's all-time geniuses on their hands. At one point he got into a

scrap with the committee that ran a church because they wanted him to teach his pupils Latin and mathematics as well as music.

Bach spent a lot of his time worrying about money. In 1729 he wrote a friend that he was short of cash because they were having such a mild winter in Leipzig, where he was living, that not many old people were dying. That cut down on the number of funerals he was playing.

At one point he was reprimanded by the board of the choir school for not maintaining discipline among the choirboys, who were getting out of hand. Another time he got into a feud that dragged on for three years over whether Bach or the principal of the local school had authority over the choir.

Twice Bach grabbed the principal's assistant by the neck and gave him the bum's rush out of the organ gallery.

But throughout all his life, Bach was essentially a quiet man, deeply religious without being a pain to his fellow man.

> *The critics of his time usually praised Bach for his organ playing and suggested he stick to it. His compositions didn't impress many of them.*

Frederick the Great of Prussia was quite a capable musician himself and a great friend of Bach. He sent for Bach one day and when Bach arrived Frederick dismissed his court musicians for the day saying, "Take five boys (or whatever you said to musicians in those days to get rid of them). Old Bach is here." Then they sat and played together for hours. Frederick's instrument was the flute so Bach wrote flute music for him.

The critics of his time usually praised Bach for his organ playing and suggested he stick to it. His compositions didn't impress many of them.

In the last year of his life, when he was 64 Bach's eyesight failed rapidly and he became blind. An operation didn't work. He was very low and he dictated a composition to his son-in-law. The words went: "Come kindly death, come for life is dreary."

Then suddenly and without explanation on the 18th of July in 1750, Bach's sight returned. His family gathered around him to celebrate. But the excitement was too much for the old man and 10 days later he died.

Originally broadcast July 28, 1983

THE ITALIAN STALLION

Benito Mussolini was born on the 29th of July in 1883 in northern Italy, the son of a blacksmith who was a lifelong socialist. He named his boy after Benito Juarez, the great Mexican revolutionary.

The Mussolinis were grindly poor. Young Benito left home when he was a teenager, to work in Switzerland. Life there wasn't much better.

He was thrown in jail and deported by the Swiss police a few times. Each time he sneaked back into Switzerland and either worked as a bricklayer or spent his time organizing Italian immigrant workers.

And it was there that Mussolini discovered women liked him. All his life he would be a big-time skirt chaser. He and women couldn't leave each other alone. Neither tried very hard.

Mussolini returned to Italy and became editor of a socialist newspaper. In 1914, as war threatened all Europe, the socialists in Italy, Germany and France all vowed they wouldn't go to war.

Mussolini did an about-turn and published an editorial in his paper, saying that all Italians, socialist or otherwise, must fight if the country went to war. He was thrown out of the socialist paper and branded a traitor.

The war came and Mussolini joined the army. The Italian Army wasn't very good, to put it charitably. But many of its soldiers were brave and Mussolini was one. He was horribly wounded when a shell exploded right beside him and doctors had to perform 27 operations on him, some without anesthetics.

When Mussolini returned to civilian life, he joined the fascists, a right-wing group, dedicated to the destruction of his old pals, the socialists.

Mussolini became editor of the fascist newspaper — and love of the paper's art critic. He was married and had kids by then but his wife and family knew he'd be away for days, sometimes weeks at a time, as he chased and conquered scores of women.

In 1922, with Italy paralyzed in one of its many political crises, the Fascists marched on Rome and seized power.

Mussolini, who had spent his time knifing other fascist leaders, was now the top man in Italy. Within the next few years, he became Il Duce, the leader, He closed down parliament and crushed all other parties.

Nobody realized that the Italian army wasn't much good and a couple of battalions of the British Army probably could have nipped Mussolini's grand plan in the bud if they'd stood up to him.

There were no unions and no employers' associations, only 22 corporations that mobilized all Italy into Mussolini's private empire.

Mussolini built up the Italian army and invaded Ethiopia in Africa as the start of an Italian overseas empire. The other nations of the world protested but did nothing. Nobody realized that the Italian army wasn't much good and a couple of battalions of the British Army probably could have nipped Mussolini's grand plan in the bud if they'd stood up to him.

But they didn't. And Mussolini and the fascists grew more powerful. They joined up with the Germans under their power-made leader, Hitler.

When the Second World War started the Italians joined on the German side. Eventually, the British and Americans invaded Italy and the whole country was devastated by war.

As the country collapsed in hunger and blood and anarchy, Mussolini was deposed. The Germans rescued him and set him up in power again.

Next, Mussolini was captured by Italian communists and shot, along with his latest girlfriend. The fact that she stayed with him, knowing she'd be killed just for being his girlfriend, is an indication of the attraction he held for women.

Originally broadcast July 29, 1992

STATE OF THE UNION

Jimmy Hoffa was the most fascinating union leader in history, either the best or the worst thing that ever happened to the labour movement, depending on who you listen to.

To hundreds of thousands of North American workers, Hoffa was the man who got them decent wages and working conditions, who put an end to the old sweat shops and won them the right to refuse to drive unsafe trucks.

Hoffa was a poor boy from Indiana who left school when he was 13. He never read a book in his life until he went to jail at the age of 54. But he had a photographic memory. He could remember every line of a 40-page labour contract he'd negotiated years before. Or the face of a truck driver he'd met only once. Or the slightest insult he'd received when he was only a kid.

Hoffa was working for 32 cents an hour, unloading groceries in Detroit when he was 17. But the unloaders only got paid for the hours they actually worked. They might have to sit around for hours waiting for work.

Hoffa waited until a load of strawberries arrived one hot day. Then he led the unloaders out on strike, leaving the strawberries sitting in the sun. The boss quickly settled.

That started Jimmy Hoffa's career as a labour organizer. He led the unloaders into a bigger union, the Teamsters. And, over the years, Hoffa rose until he became number-one man in the Teamsters, the biggest union in the world.

Hoffa waited until a load of strawberries arrived one hot day. Then he led the unloaders out on strike, leaving the strawberries sitting in the sun. The boss quickly settled.

There was a lot of violence involved in the early days of organizing unions. The bosses hired gangsters to beat up the organizers. So Hoffa hired other gangsters to beat up the bosses and their gangsters.

It worked. But it led to Hoffa's undoing. Pretty soon, he was in bed with the gangsters. Millions from the Teamsters pension funds were loaned to the Mafia to allow it to take over Las Vegas.

Many Teamsters locals were the best unions in the world, taking care of their members. Others were run by gangsters, who used them to extort and intimidate and leave the workers with nothing.

In the mid-50s, a rich young lawyer named Bobby Kennedy went to work for a congressional hearing committee in Washington that was looking into labour racketeering. Kennedy used the publicity he got investigating Hoffa to enhance his own career and that of his brother Jack, a senator. Soon Jack became president of the United States and he made Bobby attorney-general.

Bobby had Hoffa prosecuted four times. Each time Hoffa got off. In 1967, Bobby finally got him. Hoffa was sentenced to 10 years for fixing the jury at one of his trials. But after he'd done four years he was pardoned.

Hoffa played at being retired but he worked hard to take over the Teamsters again. That's what he was doing when he left home of the 30th of July in 1975 to meet some of his old gangster friends. And he hasn't been seen since.

Originally broadcast July 30, 1993

MEDICINE MAN

Nobody ever includes Thomas Kelley in the list of the greats of show business. But he probably brought more entertainment to more people in North America before the invention of the radio than anyone else.

Because Kelley was king of the medicine show. It sounds corny today to the point of impossibility. But Kelley lived and worked in a world quite unlike ours.

Kelley was born in southern Ontario in 1865. His parents were farmers and Kelley went to work when he was 12. He became a cook on a tugboat on the Rideau Canal. He learned the art of highwire walking by walking along the tow rope from the tug to the barges it was pulling. From there, it was a short hop to a travelling circus.

Kelley wasn't in that business very long before he realized that the only way to make money was to own his own travelling show.

In those days there were two kinds of travelling shows: the circuses, which charged admission, and the medicine shows, which were free.

The operators made their money by selling medicine to the crowd that was attracted to the show. The word medicine was strictly an honorary term. There is no known case of anyone ever being healed of anything by a bottle of the homemade slop that was sold by the medicine show people. And if it ever killed anyone...well, that's one of the great things about a travelling show, isn't it? By the time the customer keels over, you're long gone.

Kelley and a partner started their own medicine show when Kelley was only 22. It ran for a couple of years, then went broke. Kelley started up again on his own.

In those days North America was mostly inhabited by hicks. The show people called them rubes. Most people lived far away from cities. They worked on farms. They didn't get daily papers. There was no radio. Life was tough and not very glamorous.

Kelley realized people went to the travelling shows for excitement and glamour. So he gave them dancing girls and acrobats and exotic animals. He widened their horizons.

Then, after the acts had gathered a crowd of about a thousand, Kelley would go into his pitch for one of his wonderful medicines: East Indian Tiger Fat or Shamrock Healing Oil or the New Oriental Discovery.

While the rest of the crew was pitching the tents and setting up the stage, Kelley would be behind the scenes, brewing up the latest medical marvel in an old tub and bottling it. He liked to have something for five dollars a bottle to cater to the well-to-do; something for the average man at two dollars; and something at a dollar a bottle for those poor rubes who only had a buck in their pockets and some imaginary ache in their bones.

Kelley wowed them with his Lady Minstrels, an all-girl singing act; with Freda the Powerful Fraulein, a big, muscular girl who lifted weights and bent iron bars; and a dozen others...

Every spring, beginning in 1897, Kelley went on the road with his show and kept it going until September.

Then, in the spring of 1930, he could see it all coming to an end. He told his son: Progress has doomed us. Paved roads, fast cars and radios have crucified the med game. There's no such thing anymore as a simon-pure, dyed-in-the-wool rube. They've smartened up.

Nevertheless, the Kelley show got through that season. And it was well into the next when Tom Kelley took a weak spell in Uxbridge, Ontario near Toronto.

He died on the 31st of July in 1931. And the old medicine show died with him.

> *Kelley realized people went to the travelling shows for excitement and glamour. So he gave them dancing girls and acrobats and exotic animals. He widened their horizons.*

Originally broadcast July 31, 1984

HIGH AND LOW

In 1919, Prohibition hit North America. On paper, that meant nobody could get a drink of beer, whisky or wine and the age-old curse of alcohol was banished from society.

In practice, it meant booze was just as available as ever but much more expensive.

The law that forbade alcohol in the States was federal. It applied equally all over. In Canada, the Prohibition laws were provincial and varied a bit from province to province. Quebec didn't have one, at least it didn't have one that changed anything.

Within months, Windsor, Ontario, became the busiest place in Canada. Millions of gallons of beer and whisky were shipped to the States.

Canadian law said Canadians couldn't buy or drink the stuff but it was all right to make it. In fact, the federal government continued to tax it.

So, breweries and distilleries worked as busily as ever and shipped their stuff to the States, across the river that separates Windsor from Detroit. Detroit became the major booze-importing centre of the States.

The Americans had a vast army of federal agents waiting on the other side of the border to grab the stuff. But it didn't take long for that army to desert the cause and go on the take.

After a while, the American government brought pressure on the Canadian government to do something. So the Canadian Customs department came up with a form that had to be filled in by every Canadian exporting booze. It had to state the country it was going to. And if that country was the States, the booze wouldn't be allowed to go. So nobody wrote on the form that he was taking booze to the States.

A Windsor man would buy a few cases from the distillery at $2.50 a bottle, fill out a form that said he was shipping the stuff to Peru, row it across the river, sell it for $10 a bottle and be back in a couple of hours, ready to buy a few cases to take to Bermuda.

That was too good to last. Big businessmen soon took over and shipped shiploads, not cases.

The biggest operator in Windsor was a machinist named Harry Low. Harry and his brother Sam ran a poolroom. They raked in millions but nobody knows how much they had to pay in bribes on both sides of the border to operate.

> *The smuggling became so open, and the Canadian Customs department became so corrupt, that a royal commission was set up to investigate.*

It became so open, and the Canadian Customs department became so corrupt, that a royal commission was set up to investigate.

By that time, Harry and his brother owned Carling's Brewery. They had waterfront warehouses along three blocks of Windsor. They also had two ships.

Their books were so tangled the government auditors couldn't figure them out. But they said it appeared that a few of the Lows' many companies seemed to have made half-a-million dollars in one six-month period.

The yardmaster of an American railway in Windsor testified that he was offered $100 for each boxcar he would allow to be loaded with booze and shipped to the States.

Harry lived like a king. The problem was that the business was full of crooks. He was kidnapped and held for ransom. He seems to have promised to pay but then he went back on the deal. For years afterwards, Harry was afraid the mob was trying to get him.

Prohibition ended and the Lows were poor again. Sam always loved flowers so he set up a greenhouse business and raised roses for the rest of his life. Harry died broke and unhappy on the first of August in 1955.

Originally broadcast August 1, 1989

HARD-ING TIMES

Warren Harding was a small-town publisher from Ohio. He was everybody's idea of what a newspaperman was like. He drank like a fish. He had a long series of affairs with various women. In fact, when he was a senator he used to duck out of debates late at night and meet his girlfriend for a quickie in the Senate cloakroom.

And poker! Harding played poker like other people breathed. After he became president he thought it looked a little more dignified to play bridge but he did that from breakfast until midnight.

As president, Harding put all his old poker-playing, girl-chasing, whisky-swilling pals into the highest offices in the land.

Prohibition was in force at the time. One close old pal from Ohio made millions selling permits to make and distribute medicinal alcohol. If every man, woman and child and dog in the country had a sore throat they couldn't have accounted for all the medicinal alcohol turned loose on the land by the Harding administration.

A couple of other old pals convinced Harding he should transfer control of a lot of western oil land from the navy to the department of the interior. The navy had jurisdiction to make sure ships would have enough fuel in case of war. The secretary of the interior promptly sold the rights to the oil to a bunch of crooked western oilmen. In exchange for millions under the table, of course.

Another old buddy milked the Veterans Administration for millions. Harding couldn't very well fire him because the old man was looking the other way while Harding carried on with his wife.

Harding played golf twice a week at least. He stepped out onto the White House lawn at noon every day to shake hands with tourists. And he dropped into the Gayety Burlesque Theatre an afternoon or two a week to look at the girls.

Harding had spent six years in the Senate, and was known in Washington for his poor attendance and his windy speeches. One fellow senator called those speeches a series of pompous phrases moving over the landscape in search of an idea.

At the Republican convention of 1920, two strong candidates canceled out each other and the convention went for Harding as a compromise. He easily won the election. Harding was a big, handsome man. Someone once said he was the only senator who could wear a toga and not look ridiculous.

By the spring of 1923, things were coming unstuck in Washington. The attorney-general's assistant blew his brains out. A few of the medium-rank fixers got caught and it looked as if the high-ranking ones would be next. Including the president himself.

Harding decided to take a trip to the west and Alaska. The trip was a disaster. Two newspapermen covering the trip were killed in a car crash. Then the train carrying the president dropped him off at one stop and ran into a landslide just before the next. In Alaska, Harding and several of his aides got ptomaine poisoning from a meal of bad crabs.

> *Harding was a big, handsome man. Someone once said he was the only senator who could wear a toga and not look ridiculous.*

On the 26th of July, on the way back from Alaska, Harding's ship stopped at Vancouver and he became the first American president to visit Canada. He made a couple of big speeches and was a huge hit. More people showed up in Stanley Park to listen to him than had turned out to see the Prince of Wales there three years earlier.

After Harding left Vancouver, aboard an American navy cruiser, the ship rammed a destroyer in the fog. Harding was jolted awake. When his valet assured him that all was well, he said: I wish the ship would sink.

Assistants were bringing him news every couple of hours of scandals coming to light back in Washington. His battle-ax wife was nagging him something awful about his personal life.

Soon after they reached San Francisco, the president died in his hotel room. Only his wife was with him. Within a year his doctor died too. Only Mrs. Harding was with *him* when *he* went.

Even in death, Warren Harding kept the rumour mill churning at double-time.

Originally broadcast August 2, 1983

THE GREAT LOVER

Rodolfo d'Antonguolla was just one of thousands of young Italians who emigrated to the States in 1913. Rodolfo arrived with a few bucks. He managed to live the good life in New York for a while. He went to the best restaurants and shows.

He was a dark, handsome man who danced well. One day, while Rodolfo and a friend were visiting the zoo, the subject got around to dancing. The friend told him about an Argentinean dance he had learned while he was in South America. He showed Rodolfo how to do it. In fact, he taught him, there in front of the monkey cage with the monkeys for an audience.

The dance was called the tango. And Rodolfo cut quite a swath at nights as he showed the ladies of the expensive nightclubs how to tango.

When Rodolfo's money ran out, he kept himself alive as a gigolo, dancing with rich women.

That led to a career as a professional dancer. Nobody could be expected to pronounce his name so he used his middle name as his last name and became Rudolph Valentino.

Valentino did all right as a dancer but he certainly didn't hit the big time. He was dancing with Al Jolson's show in Los Angeles when he left and took a chance on the movies.

He went a long time before he got a part. But he was an almost instant success. These were silent pictures so it didn't matter that Valentino spoke broken English.

Then he really hit it big. He starred in a terrible, corny picture called *The Sheik*. It was about an Arab chief who fell for a woman and grabbed her and dashed off with her aboard his horse to his tent in the desert.

Suddenly, every adult female who could find her way to a movie theatre was in love with Rudolph Valentino.

The Hollywood publicity mill wasn't as sophisticated as it later became. But it fanned the sparks that were already there. Pretty soon, Valentino was so popular his life was in danger. Women mobbed him.

One broke her leg falling from a ladder as she tried to get into his dressing room.

Valentino loved the fame and money. He carried his own silk sheets with him when he traveled in case he had to check into a hotel with the plain, ordinary, cotton ones.

But the Great Lover, as he was known, wasn't such a howling success in his personal life.

He married an actress named Jean Acker and that lasted six hours. Then he married a brilliant, cold, heartless woman named Natasha Rambova. Valentino was mad about her but she treated him like a doormat.

Pola Negri, a gorgeous blonde actress he worked with, fell for him. They were pretty happy together. But Valentino was still in love with his wife, the nasty, icy Natasha.

Then suddenly in the summer of 1926, Valentino died of a perforated ulcer. Tens of thousand of women lined up for his funeral. Dozens were injured in the rush.

Two years later, in 1928, a Hollywood producer was trying to drum up some publicity for a rather poor movie he was about to release. It had a story line vaguely like Valentino's romantic stuff.

So he had a mysterious lady in black appear at Valentino's grave in Hollywood, drop a single rose, kneel for a minute then walk away. Photographers were on hand, of course.

The legend of the woman in black was started. The next year, to the producer's surprise, a lady in black appeared at Valentino's grave and went through the rigamarole. It's been happening on and off ever since.

It usually happens every 23rd of August, the date of Valentino's death. Except the first time. That appearance, the one the producer paid for, happened on the 3rd of August. The producer knew he was jumping the gun but his picture was due for release the next week.

> *Valentino loved the fame and money. He carried his own silk sheets with him when he traveled in case he had to check into a hotel with the plain, ordinary, cotton ones.*

Originally broadcast August 3, 1989

MARK OF BRILLIANCE

An Englishman once said everything there is to say about *Huck Finn*: I would give a thousand pounds to have never read that book. So that I could read it again for the first time. That Englishman, whoever he was, spoke for millions. If *The Adventures of Huckleberry Finn* isn't the best book ever written in the English language, it's gotta be very close behind whatever is.

Mark Twain was born Samuel Clemens in Hannibal, Missouri, a rough, tough, bawdy, brawling town. Young Sam went to work before he was 13, first as a printer's assistant, later as a riverboat pilot.

He left that and drifted west to Nevada and California. He became a newspaperman again and discovered he preferred writing to printing. It was an affectation among writers in those days that they had to have a separate name to sign to their stuff. So Clemens took Mark Twain from the shout that riverboatmen gave as they took soundings in the shallow Mississippi. Usually "mark twain" meant they were out of danger.

Twain married a rich girl from Elmira, New York, whose family owned a coal business and a newspaper plus a few odds and ends. They lived in a mansion that took up a whole block. Twain said their greenhouse was so big that one of their major problems was not having enough friends dying to use all the flowers. Somedays, he drawled, there just wasn't a confounded corpse to be seen.

He continued his old hard-drinking ways, and that didn't please wife or in-laws. His mother-in-law wrote out west for references when her daughter said she was going to marry Twain. The ones from the decent people, the clergymen and pillars of the community, weren't very flattering. Twain said he couldn't very well have her write to his friends because they were either illiterate or jealous.

Twain made good money but he threw it away as fast as it came in. He was an awful sucker for inventions. He put money in a typesetting machine, in a fire extinguisher that worked like a hand grenade, in just about anything that came along. As a judge of inventions, he was a fine writer.

For a few years he'd had rattling around in his head the story of the boy who runs away from home and drifts

down the Mississippi on a raft. Finally, he wrote a friend: Today, the 4th of August 1876, I got started on it. I'm tearing along. He might actually have got started sooner because he wrote to another friend five days later that he was already half done, about 400 pages.

That doesn't add up but Twain was always a writer, never a mathematician. As other books occurred to him, he set *Huck Finn* aside. He pigeonholed it for two years, worked on it again in 1879 and 80, then let it lie for another two years. When it was finally finished in 1884, Twain had written seven other books since he began it.

Just as Twain finished *Huckleberry Finn*, he got in a fight with his publisher. He set up his own publishing house to handle it, but he was no businessman, and he just couldn't get the project off the ground. Months and months were spent in pointless arguments, legal and personal. His inventions were draining his money away.

He had trouble with the illustrations. The first pictures of Huck made him look too Irish. The Irish were unpopular and Twain didn't want to risk hurting sales. He was shooting for the Christmas rush of 1884.

Then the unthinkable happened. The printing was all done and the engravings were bound into the books. Then someone discovered that a dirty-minded saboteur in the engraving department had added a sex organ to one of the men in one of the pictures. You had to look for it but it was clearly there. This was 19th century America. The pictures had to be cut out of thousands of books by hand. *Huckleberry Finn* missed the Christmas trade and didn't come out until February of 1885.

Twain should have saved himself all the grief and trouble of taking out those pictures. The critics noted the book contained references to nakedness, blasphemy, bad smells, sweat and dead cats. They pronounced it unfit for the perusal of decent folk.

The library committee of Concord, Massachusetts, banned it. It would eventually be a success but that was a long time in the future.

> *Twain made good money but he threw it away as fast as it came in. He was an awful sucker for inventions.*

Originally broadcast August 4, 1983

GENTLEMEN PREFER BLONDES

Marilyn Monroe was the ultimate Hollywood glamour girl: gorgeous, sexy, a combination of little girl and super-sophisticate . . . and made up, created, absolutely unreal.

She was born Norma Jean Baker in 1926, the daughter of a woman who ended her days in a mental hospital. So did Norma Jean's grandparents, and a brother. Norma Jean was sent to a foster home when she was 12 days old and she lived in an endless series of them until she was an adult. She and her mother lived together briefly for just a matter of months. Nobody knows who her father was.

In the 1940s, Norma Jean was working as a model and she and her agent came up with a new name: Marilyn Monroe. She did some modeling and a lot of small movie parts. Some of that modeling was nude which was pretty risqué in those days. The most famous was a calendar picture that made millions for the publisher. Marilyn was paid $50.

In the 1950s, Marilyn had had small roles in more than 20 films. Then she hit it big: *Gentlemen Prefer Blondes* in 1953, then *The Seven Year Itch*, then *Bus Stop* and *Some Like it Hot*.

Marilyn Monroe, on film, was the sexiest movie star on earth. In reality, she was pathetically insecure. She married Joe Dimaggio, the baseball star. That lasted nine months. She married Arthur Miller, the playwright. That lasted a bit longer.

Marilyn had dozens of affairs, some very brief, some quite lengthy. Today, there's a Marilyn Monroe industry, based mostly on supermarket tabloids that grind out story after story, most obviously untrue, some maybe a bit true.

Marilyn was a pill-popper and had big psychological problems. In her later days she saw her psychiatrist at least daily. For a while she lived at his place. Friends say she got a kick out of overdosing on downers then making last-minute phone calls for help.

Marilyn was making a comedy called *Something Has to Give* in the spring of 1962 and missed 12 out of 33 camera days. The studio fired her.

Marilyn Monroe, on film, was the sexiest movie star on earth. In reality, she was pathetically insecure.

A month later, Marilyn appeared on stage at Madison Square Garden in New York at a fund-raising birthday party for John Kennedy, the president of the United States. She sang a sexy *Happy Birthday* that made clear what insiders already knew: she was having an affair with the president.

That became such a public scandal that the president's brother, Bobby Kennedy, was assigned to tell Marilyn to get lost. Some stories say she also had an affair with him.

About 3:00 in the morning of the 5th of August in 1962, Marilyn's housekeeper phoned her psychiatrist to say something was wrong. Marilyn was dead in bed.

The cops weren't called for an hour. The sergeant who arrived first called it murder, a clumsy cover-up. His bosses insisted it was suicide, an overdose.

We'll never know. There's plenty of investigation still going on into the subject but it's by the people who write supermarket tabloids. The real investigators, the cops and coroners, they say the case is closed. Not solved, just closed.

Originally broadcast August 5, 1993

THE DAY THE EARTH STOOD STILL

One of the first things Hitler did when he came to power in Germany in the mid-1930s was to persecute the Jews. Pretty soon, a lot of European Jews decided to head for Canada and the United States, just in case that madman took over all of Europe.

Among those was Albert Einstein, already acknowledged as the greatest scientist of his age. Einstein settled in the States but kept up his contacts with scientists in Europe.

When World War II got started, Einstein came to realize that German scientists were working on a bomb based on splitting the atom. He was worried about the chances of German scientists being successful. It was hard to explain to a layman, but any scientist knew that the country that invented the atom bomb would win any war it was in.

Einstein got a message to Roosevelt, the American president, and he got Roosevelt appropriately alarmed. Roosevelt ordered a maximum effort project started under absolute secrecy.

The scientific part of the project, the splitting of the atom, was done at the University of Chicago, right in the middle of the second-biggest city in the States.

Then the practical part, the bomb-building, was started out in the desert in New Mexico, miles from anybody.

Roosevelt made the decision that the bomb, no matter how terrible, would be used as soon as it was ready. He figured it would be so awesome that the enemy would surrender right away and, in the long run, lives would be saved.

Roosevelt died before the war in Europe ended, before the first bomb was built. He was succeeded by Harry Truman who ordered the work to go ahead.

The work in the desert was so hurried that the first bomb had as some of its components, Kleenex and Scotch tape. But it worked. In July of 1945 the first bomb was detonated in the desert in New Mexico and it turned night to day. Even the scientists who designed the bomb were stunned by the explosion.

When they reported their success to Truman he ordered them to get the next one built as quickly as possible and drop it on Japan.

The American army had already assembled a squadron of flying hot-shots, the very best airmen it had. They had been practicing a long flight over water followed by a fast bomb run with a single bomb that would explode 1980 feet above the ground. The pilot was practicing a fast turn away as soon as the bomb was released so the plane wouldn't be hit by the blast.

The scientists had the next bomb ready in two weeks. It was moved by truck to the coast and a cruiser was waiting to dash with it to the little island of Tinian, a few hours flight from Japan.

The plane it was put on was called the Enola Gay, named after the pilot's mother.

The bombardier was the best in the American air forces. The plane made it to its target, the port city of Hiroshima, right on schedule. The bombardier had been shown aerial photographs of the city and told to use a peculiar t-shaped bridge as a reference point. He spotted it easily.

There was no indication they were even noticed . . . no enemy planes, no gunfire. He pressed the button, and the world hasn't been the same since.

We know the exact second the bomb went off: 8:15:31 in the morning of the 6th of August, 1945. We know because hundreds of corpses were wearing watches stopped at that time.

> *Any scientist knew that the country that invented the atom bomb would win any war it was in.*

Originally broadcast August 6, 1987

CAROLINE THE CRASS

When Queen Caroline, wife of George the Fourth of England died, everyone heaved a huge sigh of relief. Not very good manners, maybe, but perfectly understandable when you hear her long and tangled story.

Old King George the Third, the one who is remembered for losing the American colonies, died mad. But even before he was locked away, for years he hadn't been too alert.

His son, who eventually became George the Fourth, was the worst and most dissipated man who ever sat on the British throne.

He was brilliant and handsome and all the women in the kingdom were mad for him. So he set out to have them all. By the time he was in his early 20s he looked like he just might make it. His father, the king, seemed blissfully unaware of his son's scandalous conduct although he was the only man in the realm who was.

The king ordered the young prince to get married and produce an heir to the throne. The prince was so angry at this that he deliberately chose a German princess who was eminently unsuited to be queen of England. She was his cousin, Caroline of Brunswick.

Now, if the young prince led a fast life, you should have seen them in Brunswick. It was a little one-horse dukedom in Germany where the whole ruling family was into boozing, gambling, wife-swapping and sitting around talking about all the above in loud voices.

And Princess Caroline was never known to have missed a beat in that racy company. In addition, she was loud-mouthed and crude.

Now, ten years earlier, the Prince of Wales, young George, had secretly married a woman named Maria Fitzherbert. He couldn't have that made public because she was both a commoner and a Catholic. But everybody in the kingdom except the king knew about it.

There's an old Irish saying: "As the Lord made 'em, he matched 'em." And if the prince thought he was going to beat Princess Caroline in the lechery game, he was sadly mistaken.

Then, on the king's orders, the prince married Caroline, and she quickly became pregnant and had a daughter. The prince then told Caroline that he couldn't stand her and he'd done his duty, so she was to get out of his hair. He then took up with a duchess. Mrs. Fitzherbert, his real wife, had since gone to live in Europe.

There's an old Irish saying: "As the Lord made 'em, he matched 'em."

And if the prince thought he was going to beat Princess Caroline in the lechery game he was sadly mistaken.

Caroline had so many boyfriends nobody could keep count. And she made no secret of it. A commission was appointed to investigate a rumour that she'd had an illegitimate son. She told the commissioners: Go ahead and prove it. That'll make the little bastard your king, won't it?

Next Caroline took off for Europe where she really scandalized everyone. At one fancy ball in Vienna she showed up topless. Her antics went on for years.

Then the old king died, and she and the prince became king and queen. The king told the prime minister to take care of Caroline's behavior; it wasn't his problem.

The poor prime minister charged Queen Caroline with treason and put her on trial before the House of Lords. The trial went two months then fizzled out when the lords wouldn't show up for the trial. They figured no matter which way they voted they'd be in trouble.

The king's coronation was held up for a year until that trial was over. And on his coronation day guards were stationed around Westminster Abbey in case the queen tried to crash her own coronation.

She didn't. She stayed home, too worn out to make it. And within a year she died. To everyone's relief.

Originally broadcast August 7, 1984

THE QUINTESSENTIAL CANADIAN

Allan McNab certainly isn't my favorite Canadian hero and I doubt if he's very high on anybody's list of great men. But he is a symbol of the difference between Canada and the United States. And, whether we like to admit it or not, there's a bit of him in all of us.

McNab's family was quite well-to-do in Scotland. But there wasn't enough land and money for the whole family so McNab's father moved to Canada. He did all right but you couldn't say he made his fortune.

Young Allan McNab was just 13 when the American army captured his hometown of York that's now Toronto and burned it down. Before that war of 1812 was over, young McNab had served as a midshipman in the primitive navy the British built and sailed on Lake Ontario. He was mentioned in dispatches and was under fire before he was 16.

When he got out of the navy he went to work in a lawyer's office in Toronto. He was one of those no-nonsense lads with his eye on the future: hard-working, respectful to the boss, a devoted subject of the crown.

Allan McNab was one of those no-nonsense lads with his eye on the future: hard-working, respectful to the boss, a devoted subject of the crown.

He must have had a small streak of irresponsibility in him because he served a brief stint in debtor's prison. But the debt wasn't much, and he was from one of the town's better families, even if it was a family with no money. So the other good folk passed the hat.

It took McNab 10 years to become a lawyer. Then he moved to Hamilton, just west of Toronto. He arrived in the 1820s, in time to be in on the ground floor there. Eventually Hamilton became one of the major industrial cities of North America, and McNab and the town prospered together. He bought a thousand acres of choice land and built a castle, just like grandpa's castle back in the old country. He even named it the same, Dundurn.

You may wonder how he could go from a debtor's cell to a castle in so short a time.

Well, the answer provides a lesson that still applies to anyone who wants to be a success in Canada: stay on the right side of the government.

Alan was a loyal follower of the crown. And he got his share of legal work from the government.

The British who settled what's now Ontario had set out to create a little England here. They had plastered the map with British names and had set up a little aristocracy. If people did as they were told and prospered they might even get knighthoods.

That sort of thing suited Allan McNab to a T. There was a rebellion in 1837. The tame legislature was so arrogant that the farmers finally blew their corks and armed themselves and marched on Toronto to capture it.

The rebellion vanished in the first puff of gunpowder. On the government side, the winning side, was Allan McNab, colonel of the loyal militia. In fact, he was soon Sir Allan McNab.

The rebels fled to Navy Island in the river just above Niagara Falls. McNab led a force to set fire to their one-ship navy, cut it loose and let it drift over the Falls.

For that, he was mentioned in the House of Commons in London as the saviour of Canada. The man who lavished all this praise on him was the Duke of Wellington himself.

McNab was a member of the pre-confederation legislative assembly years. He was a speaker of the house when a mob in Montreal burned it down, in anger at the governor-general for signing a bill to compensate people for property damage in the rebellion of 1837. McNab always said that wouldn't have happened if they'd listened to him. He wouldn't have paid one dime.

He prospered. He started the bank that today is the Canadian Imperial Bank of Commerce. He was one of the founders of the Great Western Railway. In 1859, 60 passengers were killed in a rail crash. It was pretty apparent that it was the railway's fault. But nothing much came of the investigation. Nobody looked too closely into the affairs of a man with a sir in front of his name.

McNab was actually premier for a few years before Confederation. When he died on this day, the eighth of August in 1862, he was loaded with honours and could look back on a very successful life. Riches, honours and no surprises.

Originally broadcast August 8, 1983

THE LEANING TOWER

The city of Pisa developed before the year 1000 as a prosperous port. It's in northwestern Italy, not on the sea but several miles inland, up the River Arno. The name of the city, Pisa, is derived from an old Greek word that means swampy. That word describes the ground the city of Pisa sits on and it explains what made Pisa famous.

Pisa had colonies on Corsica and Sardinia and on the islands off the coast of Spain. A Pisan fleet raided the city of Palermo in Sicily and returned with a fortune in loot.

The Pisans were pious people and decided to give thanks to God for providing them with this great score by building the greatest cathedral in the world. The cathedral they had in mind was a complex rather than one building. There would be the main cathedral building plus a separate baptistery plus a separate bell tower and cemetery.

They started the cathedral in the year 1063, using marble from old Roman ruins. It wasn't finished for 300 years.

Ninety years after they started the cathedral itself they started to build the baptistery. The great renaissance scientist Galileo was baptized there in the 1500s.

Twenty years after they started the baptistery, the Pisans started on the bell tower, on the 9th of August in 1173. And that's what's made Pisa famous.

The tower is one of the most beautiful pieces of medieval architecture anywhere: 180 feet tall, 50 feet in diameter, made of limestone faced with white marble. It had seven storeys plus the penthouse on top

By the time the first storey was finished it was clear that there was a southward tilt. So the architect just made the second story an inch higher on the south side than on the north and went ahead.

to hold the bells.

The tower, plus the cathedral, plus the baptistery, plus the cemetery made of 53 shiploads of earth from Jerusalem . . . all make up what the Italians call the Square of Miracles in Pisa. But it's the tower that makes it all famous, the Leaning Tower of Pisa.

The first architect was named Bonnano. He could only put foundations down 10 feet because of that marshy ground that gave that city its name. But he figured that would be good enough.

But by the time the first storey was finished he could see there was a southward tilt. So he just made the second story an inch higher on the south side than on the north and went ahead.

Work stopped and started on the tower over the years and the architects that followed Bonnano used the same technique, lengthening the low side. The result is that the tower isn't exactly straight. It's a modified curve, sorta like a banana standing on end.

The tower was finally finished, 199 years after it was started. By that time, it was leaning almost 16 feet off centre. But it was firm enough and became a much greater attraction than if it had been straight. Pisa has had a flourishing tourist business on the basis of the leaning tower ever since.

Not only does the leaning tower lean, but it leans a little more every year, about a millimeter. It will fall in a hundred years unless something's done.

Now, the tower is closed to tourists. But they still flock to Pisa in thousands to marvel at it.

Originally broadcast August 9, 1993

A GLOBAL THINKER

History hasn't been good to Fernando Magellan. He was the greatest navigator of his time. Columbus is more famous because he made a short, simple voyage west from Europe and found a land that was quickly and easily colonized.

Magellan, just a little later, did something even more impressive. He sailed all around the world — well, *he* didn't but that's getting ahead of our story. And he made pretty accurate maps and took careful sightings as he went.

Magellan is what we call him in English. He was born sometime in 1480 in Portugal. His family was sort of small-time nobility but that didn't mean much because all Portugal was very poor. That was about to change.

Because of his noble birth, Magellan went to the court of the queen as a page boy. He learned there that he wasn't cut out to be a yes man. He was a doer, an adventurer, not a courtier. That would cause him a lot of trouble later.

When Magellan was 18, Vasco da Gama, the great Portuguese explorer, sailed around Africa, reached India and came home with a cargo of spices that made him rich.

Right away, the king of Portugal realized he was onto something. In 1505 he sent an expedition around Africa into the Indian Ocean, to shatter the Arab fleets there and to make the route to India safe for Portuguese ships.

Magellan was on that expedition and fought well. In fact, he made a name for himself as a superb sailor and a loyal subject. After seven years he returned and fought in another expedition the king sent to North Africa.

He received a wound in the right knee that caused him to limp for the rest of his life.

Magellan asked the king for a raise. He didn't really want the money. But it would be confirmation of a slight promotion in rank. The actual amount of that raise he asked for would be about a nickel a month in our money.

The king was now one of the richest men in the world with the wealth of the Orient pouring into the royal treasury. But he didn't like Magellan. In fact, he not only refused the raise but he said he didn't care if he never saw

him again. He sneeringly referred to him as Clubfoot because of his limp and told him he could leave the court and work for anyone he pleased.

Maybe the dumbest stunt pulled in history.

Magellan went to the king of Spain and was put in charge of an expedition to get to the Orient by sailing west, specifically to get to the Philippines and Indonesia where the gold and spices were.

Magellan's expedition had five ships. He had two major problems before he even sailed. The Spanish ship captains under him were jealous because he was Portuguese. And Portuguese agents did everything they could to sabotage him.

In 1493, after Columbus came back from his great expedition, the Pope had divided the new world between the Spanish and the Portuguese. The Portuguese claimed virtually all of what they knew of it then. But if Magellan could prove the world was round, as a lot of them suspected, at least half, maybe more, of that newfound territory would belong to Spain.

> *The Spanish ship captains under Magellan were jealous because he was Portuguese. And Portuguese agents did everything they could to sabotage him.*

And, of course, that's exactly what happened.

Officially, the expedition sailed on the 10th of August in 1519. Actually, contrary winds and a shortage of supplies delayed it almost a month.

For Magellan, it was a constant hassle. His captains mutinied a few times and on the east coast of South America, near Argentina, he barely managed to maintain control. His captains were scared and wanted to turn back.

He found the way through South America. Today it's called Magellan Strait. And he went into the Pacific and made it to the Philippines. There, he was killed in a battle with some natives.

And in 1522, three years and one month after his five ships set out, one limped home. The captain in charge was allowed to have a coat of arms that said he was the first to circle the globe.

He was one of the five treacherous captains who had mutinied in South America because he wanted to turn back. He had told Magellan it couldn't be done.

Originally broadcast August 10, 1984

CARDINAL SIN

Rodrigo Borgia was a Spaniard, a clever man, the nephew of a cardinal in the Catholic church. Between his own ability as an administrator and his uncle's influence, he became an important figure in the church himself. He was made a cardinal when he was only 25 although he didn't become a priest for another dozen years.

He was made the vice-chancellor of the Vatican when his uncle the cardinal became the pope. The vice-chancellor was the man who ran things.

Borgia had a girlfriend back in Spain and had a son and a daughter by her. He seems to have been a faithful mate, albeit not married.

If all this sounds terribly scandalous, you have to remember in those days it was considered only mildly scandalous. Priests weren't supposed to have girlfriends but many, maybe most of them, did.

When it became obvious to Rodrigo that he might be pope one day, he found a husband for the mother of his children and was on friendly terms with her for years.

As the principal administrator of the church, Borgia knew how to run things. He did it efficiently and well. When the pope died in 1492, Borgia was elected by the other cardinals as Pope Alexander the Sixth. That was on the 11th of August in 1492. In the three weeks between the death of the previous pope and the coronation of Alexander, there was a terrible crime wave in Rome. The people were terrified. There were 220 murders.

Pope Alexander's first act was to have one of the killers hanged, along with his brother who seems to have been there when the killer was arrested. Then he had their home torn down. That established a law-and-order administration.

The Vatican treasury was in bankruptcy. The new pope had the budget balanced in two years.

In those days the pope was an important political as well as a religious figure.

And Pope Alexander was one of the best in the field of statecraft. He raised an army and had it conquer all central Italy under the generalship of his son, Caesar, one of the brightest men of the age.

He married his daughter, Lucretia, off a couple of times to important dukes, thus creating political alliances that strengthened the church.

Pope Alexander wasn't above some pretty shifty dealing in the field of external affairs. He even made a deal with the Sultan of Turkey to fight with him against some Christian princes who were challenging the power of the church.

All the while, he was living a happy home life. He had taken up with a girl named Julia, the most beautiful woman in Rome. He was 57. She was 16.

Politics was so tangled and underhanded in those days that Pope Alexander could only trust his own kids, Caesar and Lucretia.

> *All three Borgias have been remembered by history as sneaks and poisoners. And poison was a popular way to get rid of enemies in those days.*

The people who wrote the history books in the hundred years or so after Alexander died have given him and Caesar and Lucretia awful reputations. And they were certainly capable of some pretty bad things.

All three Borgias have been remembered by history as sneaks and poisoners. And poison was a popular way to get rid of enemies in those days. But there's never been any proof presented that they were guilty of it. In fact, medical knowledge was so slight in those days that many sudden deaths were explained as poisonings. When Alexander died suddenly in 1503 when he was 72, poisoning by other cardinals was suspected. But researchers say it's obvious he died of malaria and a lot of the deaths called poisonings were likely from the same cause.

Originally broadcast August 11, 1989

THE JEWEL OF THE NILE

We'll never know the true story of Cleopatra. She's sure a romantic figure that writers keep straying from the truth to turn out soap operas about her. And for centuries, everything that was written about her was written by her enemies and their descendants.

Cleopatra was the queen of Egypt in the time of Caesar, just a generation before the birth of Christ. But she wasn't Egyptian. She was Greek. She is described as slim and beautiful. Though today we envision her as dark-skinned and raven-haired, she might even have been fair-skinned and blond or red-headed. Three hundred years before she was born, her ancestor had been Ptolemy, one of the generals who conquered Egypt along with Alexander the Great.

The Romans ruled the world, or were in the process of conquering it, when Cleopatra became queen of Egypt. Her capital, Alexandria, was a grander, richer city than Rome.

The Egyptian royal family still thought Greek. Cleopatra was the only one, in all those years, who ever learned the language of her people. She went out of the palace and mingled with them, and was fairly popular as a queen.

Cleopatra was bright. She spoke several languages and handled a lot of her diplomacy herself, rather than trust it to the civil servants. She was a bit of a scholar and wrote essays about coinage, the measurement of weight and distance and cosmetics.

Throughout the 300 years of the rule of the Greeks, there had been many revolts by the Egyptians. Under Cleopatra there were none.

But none of that would have won Cleopatra a place in history.

The reason we know her is that she became part of the most dramatic struggle for power in the history of Rome. And the history of Rome is the foundation of the history of the western world.

Julius Caesar, the most brilliant of the Romans, set out to conquer the world in league with two others. They were doing pretty well when they began to fight among themselves.

Caesar went to Egypt to see if he could nail down that corner of the world. North Africa in those days was quite fertile, not the big sandpile it is today. And the wealth of Egypt was incredible.

No sooner had Caesar got to Alexandria in Egypt than his enemies besieged him there. So we had three armies in and around the city — Caesar's, the smallest; his Roman enemies'; and the Egyptian army nominally loyal to Cleopatra.

Cleopatra arranged to have herself delivered to Caesar who had apparently refused to see her. She came rolled up in a mattress.

She and Caesar soon put the mattress to use and a child was born. Caesar won the struggle with his enemies in Egypt then went back to Rome and was assassinated.

Cleopatra moved to Rome and took up with Caesar's old pal, Mark Anthony, one of those who had turned against him and assassinated him. She had an affair, or a series of affairs, with him.

Again the Roman leaders fought amongst themselves. This time Cleopatra chose the wrong side. She and Anthony lost.

Their enemies were closing in. Anthony heard Cleopatra had killed herself so he slashed himself with his sword. The report was wrong. Cleopatra was alive. Anthony was taken to her and died in her arms.

It was an ancient Egyptian tradition that a king or queen who died from the bite of an asp, a deadly snake, went right to heaven. So on the 12th of August in the year 30 BC, as nearly as historians have been able to pin it down, Cleopatra grabbed an asp and held it to her arm. She had asked to be buried beside Mark Anthony and she was.

She wasn't yet 35 when she died. She'd been 30 years younger than Caesar when they had their affair.

> *Cleopatra was the only one, in all those years, who ever learned the language of her people. She went out of the palace and mingled with them, and was fairly popular as a queen.*

Originally broadcast August 12, 1987

NURSING MOTHER

Florence Nightingale was born in 1820 and that meant she should have led a useless life. Her parents were rich and English and such people in those days didn't believe that their girls should be either educated or trained to work.

The Nightingales were so rich they spent most of their time abroad. Florence was named for the city in Italy where she was born. Her sister, poor thing, was born in Naples. Naples didn't have a nice ring to it so her parents named her after the ancient Greek name for the city: Parthenopey.

Florence was a bright, active person and she fought with her parents over things that were a big deal in those days but seem ridiculous now. F'r instance, she was fascinated by mathematics and wanted a tutor to teach her more of it. She won that one for a while but it was an awful struggle.

Florence was a lovely young woman, slim and intense and a superb dancer. Several rich young men came around and her mother spent most of her time figuring out which ones would make good husband material for her daughters. She did a superb job for sister Parthenopey. She got her a lord. But Florence decided not to get married.

She was fascinated by nursing. This was not only remarkable; it verged on crazy. English hospitals were terrible places, cold and dirty and unhealthy. The women who worked in them were at the very bottom of the social scale, often regarded as mere prostitutes, often with good reason.

Florence had the biggest fight of her life until then, persuading her parents to let her go to a hospital in Germany where nurses were trained. Her mother and sister were so angry they barely spoke to her when she returned. In fact, in later days, they and Florence didn't speak for nine years.

On her return Florence ran a small hospital, really a sort of nursing home, for elderly ladies of good family.

English hospitals were terrible places, cold, dirty and unhealthy. The women who worked in them were often regarded as mere prostitutes, often with good reason.

Her ability to organize and get things done was remarkable and she made the place a real wonder of the medical world.

By that time the British Army was fighting in the Crimean War. Wounded soldiers were dying from lack of proper attention and supplies. Healthy ones were dropping off like flies as diseases thrived on the unhealthy living conditions of camps with no pure water or proper sewers.

The situation was so bad that some influential politicians asked Florence to go the war zone to do what she could.

Well, the whole world knows now that she succeeded. She had to fight army bureaucracy and pig-headedness. The chief surgeon of the British Army didn't believe in anesthetics because he felt they were only for cowards. Wounded soldiers should have their arms and legs amputated while biting a bullet.

By the time Florence came back from the war, she had accomplished two things: she had brought about a revolution in medical treatment and living conditions for British soldiers; and, she was a legend, the woman who ignored diseases and fatigue and poor food and bureaucracy and devoted herself 100 per cent to her patients.

Queen Victoria thought Florence was the greatest thing since bottled beer. Royal commissions hung on her every word and changed the set-up of hospitals throughout England. Since the Empire covered the globe in those days, that meant the same standards became world-wide within a few years.

Florence lived on and on. She brought about all sorts of improvements in health and sanitation with her painstaking research and crystal-clear reports. Her health failed and she was blind and forgetful when she finally died on the 13th of August in 1910, 90 years old and a legend.

Originally broadcast August 13, 1992

PUBLIC SPEAKING

Admiral William Penn was a wealthy man and an important one in the England of the late 1600s. He led the expedition that captured Jamaica for Britain.

His son, also named William, was a terrible disappointment to the old man. He was studying at Oxford, as befits the son of a well-to-do Englishman, when he was expelled for refusing to go to church.

Religion was all tangled up in politics in those days. The Puritans had won the English Civil War. They were sour, unhappy Protestants. They had put the country under such a joyless dictatorship that the English people asked the exiled king Charles the Second to return to rule them.

Charles, who was raised a Catholic, was on the throne and nominal head of the Church of England. Everybody was supposed to be a member of that church. Those who weren't were called dissenters. Among the dissenters were several sects that were outstanding in their opposition to the Church of England.

Among them were the Quakers. The Quakers believed in non-violence so they didn't actively oppose the Church of England. They just went about their business ignoring its rules.

That's the group that Penn joined. On Sunday, the 14th of August in 1670, Penn and his fellow Quakers went to their church, which they called a meeting-house, in downtown London. It was locked and they couldn't get into it. Soldiers had locked it to prevent them holding a service there.

So Penn and another Quaker leader, a former army captain named William Mead, said they would hold their service in the street.

That's what they were doing, before a crowd of about 500, when they were arrested. They went on trial for unlawful assembly.

The trial was in the most famous court in the English-speaking world, the Old Bailey. It was before a panel of 10 judges, all members of the Church of England. The 12 jurymen were dissenters but not Quakers. Penn and Mead were the only two Quakers.

The judges made it clear to the jury from the outset that they expected a conviction. Penn and Mead were refused pens and paper and weren't allowed a copy of the indictment against them. When they protested the way the trial was going, they were taken out of the court and heard the proceeding from the courtyard. From time to time they shouted into the courtroom. As he cross-examined several witnesses, Penn showed that there wasn't much case against him.

The whole proceeding lasted four days. The jurors retired and returned in an hour-and-a-half. They said they couldn't agree.

They were sent back to reconsider. They returned and said Mead was not guilty of anything and Penn was only guilty of speaking in the street.

The judges said that was no crime. They ordered the jurors to reconsider and return with a proper verdict. When they didn't the judges ordered them locked up all night with nothing to eat or drink and no candles to see by.

When they persisted in their stubbornness, they were locked up the next night, too. When they still refused to bring in the verdict expected, they were thrown in jail for two months. By this time Penn and Mead were free.

The jurors appealed and the appeal court said they were right. That decision established for all time the right of an English-law jury to make up its own mind without interference from the judges.

When Penn's father died, the king owed him 16,000 pounds and didn't have it. Penn said he would settle for a huge land grant in the new world. It was heavily forested country so he gave it the Latin name for forest, Sylvania. The king suggested he add the name Penn before it, in memory of his dead father.

When soldiers locked their church to prevent them holding a service there, Penn and another Quaker leader said they would hold their service in the street.

Originally broadcast August 14, 1992

Mister Rogers

When Will Rogers died, Americans were stricken, just as if a member of their own family had been killed. The only other death in American history that hit the average person as hard until then was Lincoln's assassination.

Rogers was famous for saying, "I never met a man I didn't like." It sounds like a line you'd get from someone trying to sell you aluminum siding. But when Will Rogers said it people believed it.

Rogers was part-Indian, born in Oklahoma, the son of a wealthy rancher. His father sent him to six private schools before he realized Will wasn't much for books.

By the time the old man got that message, Will had run away to Texas to work as a cowboy. Then he wandered all over the world. He was in South Africa, breaking horses for the British Army during the Boer War, when he was offered a job doing rope tricks with a traveling wild west show.

Every cowboy had to be pretty good with a rope. After work they amused each other doing tricks, spinning incredibly long loops or making a loop then jumping through it, that sort of thing.

That job in South Africa got Will into show business and he traveled all over the United States and most of the world. He became the greatest rope trick artist in history. But that's not what made him famous.

One night Will felt the audience wasn't paying much attention. So as he spun his rope, he said: "Not bad work, spinning a rope. If your neck's not in it."

That got a laugh and Will decided not to do it again. He saw rope-spinning as unusually serious work. But other actors urged him to keep throwing in the funny lines. Pretty soon he was rich and famous. Flo Zigfield hired him at big money to appear in the Zigfield Follies as a comedian, along with W. C. Fields and Eddie Cantor and the other big names of the time.

One night, as he was spinning his rope and making wisecracks, Rogers said: "I'm just here to fill in the time while the girls change. Although that shouldn't take long. They wore practically nothing in the last number and they'll wear practically nothing in the next one."

That led him into commentary on dress and manners and morals and politics. Pretty soon, Will Rogers was also writing a newspaper column, then doing a radio show. He'd already been in the movies, first as a cowboy doing rope tricks then as a comedian. In 1934 he was the number one movie star in Hollywood.

He invented the roast. When he was invited to a banquet he would always poke gentle humour at the guest of honour. In fact, this technique was credited with the re-election of a politician named Ogden Mills to the American Congress. Although Mills was reputed to be so humourless he just sat through the speech, wooden-faced, unable to understand what people were laughing at.

Rogers was a great enthusiast of aviation. In his few serious speeches, he kept warning that Americans weren't building enough airfields or training enough pilots.

He was on a flight around the world with a famous pilot of the time named Wiley Post, also an Oklahoma boy, when their plane crashed in Alaska on the 15th of August in 1935. Headlines all around the world were the same, just two words: "Will Killed." Everybody knew who.

The day of his funeral movie theatres closed. The two major radio networks went silent for half an hour. Thirteen planes flew over New York, each trailing a long black banner.

And people repeated his lines, not cruel jokes but gentle ones with just a kernel of truth in them: "Everybody is ignorant, only on different subjects." Or, "I'm no fisherman and I hope I never get lazy enough to take it up." Or, "Income tax has made more liars out of people than golf." Or, "You can't accuse America of secret diplomacy; our dealings are an open book; usually a cheque book." Or, "Liberty doesn't work as well in practice as it does in speeches."

> *Rogers was famous for saying, "I never met a man I didn't like." It sounds like a line you'd get from someone trying to sell aluminum siding. But when he said it, people believed it.*

Originally broadcast August 15, 1986

CORTES' CONQUEST

Hernando Cortes was a Spanish nobleman from an old but poor family. In the dozen years after Columbus discovered the new world, hundreds of such men arrived to make their fortunes. Because they were nobles back home, the crown made huge grants of land to them and put them in charge of expeditions.

The Spanish had colonized most of the islands of the Caribbean and some of northern South America. But it wasn't until 1517 that they went ashore in Mexico and started to look around.

The country, at first, seemed rather poor. But the natives wore trinkets made of pure gold. And that was exactly what the Spanish were looking for — gold. They were gold-happy.

You would think that the Spanish of the new world, thousands of miles from home and surrounded by hostile natives, would stick together. Not so. They argued and fought constantly. They sent back to Spain for orders to settle their fights and when those orders came they interpreted them as they saw fit.

Cortes had fought in the expedition that took Cuba for Spain. The governor of Cuba was authorized to send an expedition to explore Mexico and he put Cortes in charge.

Cortes was 32 at the time, an experienced soldier. We know he had studied law for a couple of years back in Spain and he'd suffered a serious head injury in a fall from a lady's bedroom window. He'd been laid up a couple of years with that.

Cortes set out in late 1518 with a small group: 600 men altogether, 11 ships, 10 cannons and 17 horses. Those horses would later prove to be worth their weight in gold, many times over.

Cortes was just ashore in Mexico when mutiny broke out and he spent his first few months fighting his fellow Spaniards.

The Mayans owned the country he landed in and they were a tribe in decline. They had once been a mighty power. To the west of them the Aztecs ruled. Their power was also on the wane and Cortes was able to take advantage of the various tribal conflicts to make some progress. He said the Spanish had a disease that only gold could cure so he persuaded the Mexicans to part with a lot of their gold that way.

Then, on the 16th of August in 1519, he headed inland for the Aztec capital of what's now Mexico City.

He knew quite a bit about where he was going because he'd been given an Aztec slave girl soon after he landed. She spoke Aztec and Mayan and he taught her Spanish.

Before the expedition set out, Cortes destroyed his ships. The history books say that was so his party couldn't turn back; glory or death.

Before the expedition set out, Cortes destroyed his ships. The history books say that was so his party couldn't turn back; glory or death.

The real reason was that he was afraid some of his men would desert and go back to his boss in Cuba and tell stories on him.

Cortes and his men won many battles against Indians who outnumbered them a thousand to one. At first the Indians ran from the horses. They thought the horse and the man on it were one animal.

And they were frightened by the cannons. Cortes made it into Mexico City, partly by the sword, partly by diplomacy.

Then he had to leave and head back to the coast to fight a second expedition of Spaniards, led by another Spanish nobleman who was coming to take over Mexico and Cortes. Cortes arrived in the middle of the night at the other Spaniards' camp, surprised them and quickly won. Most of the men from that second expedition joined him.

Then Cortes went back to Mexico City. But by now the Aztecs realized he was just out for their gold and they organized a fierce resistance.

Cortes conquered the city after a siege of 55 days. In one day he slaughtered 40,000 people. The conquest of Mexico was pretty well over. Cortes was appointed governor and, strangely enough, he was a good one. After all the bloodshed and brutality, he turned out to really like the people and he governed them well. At least, by the low standard of the time.

Originally broadcast August 16, 1988

A CREDIT TO THE CAUSE

Nobody knows to this day if the social credit theory would work because it's never been tried.

In its simplest form, as I understand it, it goes something like this: since we all deal in paper money anyhow, when there are plenty of apples on the trees and loaves and steaks on the shelves in the stores, and times are tough and buyer and seller can't get together because no one has any money...why can't we go ahead and take the apples and the loaves and the steaks and give the merchants pieces of paper for them because isn't that what money is anyway? I have the vague idea in the back of my mind that nothing that simple could work, but why not?

The theory of social credit was thought up by a Scotsman, an engineer named Major Douglas, back in the 1920s.

In the early 30s, it came to the attention of Bible Bill Aberhart. Now Aberhart was one of the most fascinating characters Canada ever produced. Good or bad, take your choice.

Aberhart was a big man. He was born in Ontario and became a schoolteacher and a very good one. He moved to Alberta and was soon principal of one of the biggest schools in Calgary.

He was also a lay preacher. He studied the Bible and preached in Presbyterian and Baptist churches then he started his own Bible institute.

That was supported by a Baptist church. In an incredibly long and complicated deal, Aberhart ended up holding the deed to that church. Some people thought he was a saint, sort of like some look at Billy Graham today. Some thought he was the evilest man that ever set foot in Alberta. There are still people out there who refer to him as the man who stole a church.

Aberhart became the best-known man in Alberta because in the early days of radio, he put his church services on the air and they blanketed the Prairies.

He got his church by selling bonds to raise the money. Then when the interest was due on the bonds, he persuaded most of the bond holders to put their interest cheques on the collection plate. It sounds like chasing money around in a circle but it got Aberhart his church.

Naturally, when a man with a mind like that read of Major Douglas and his social credit theories, sparks were struck. Aberhart decided social credit was the answer to the problems of the poor people of Alberta.

And evangelism was the way to sell social credit.

So he grafted social credit onto his network of church workers and his broadcast audience and in 1935 he swept the provincial election. The previous government, the United Farmers, didn't get a single seat.

Not one of the newly-elected Social Credit Party members had ever sat in a legislature before.

Aberhart cabled to Major Douglas, who lived in England: "Victorious. When can you come?" Douglas apparently considered Aberhart a nut who didn't understand social credit and couldn't make it work. He never did come.

Aberhart said he would issue certificates worth $25 every month to every adult Albertan. They would have to be spent. Merchants would

> *Aberhart decided social credit was the answer to the problems of the poor people of Alberta. And evangelism was the way to sell social credit.*

have to accept them for goods. That way the economy would get rolling again. Remember, this was right at the depth of the depression and Alberta was in terrible shape.

Aberhart promised to do that within 18 months. Meanwhile the province was broke and had to borrow from the federal government. Aberhart's legislature passed two laws to make all that possible. Plus a third one that gave him the power to decide what newspapers could print. That was because the reporters and editorial writers were giving him a hard time, calling him a nut and social credit a harebrained scheme.

Nothing ever came of any of those laws because on the 17th of August in 1937, the federal cabinet disallowed them. It claimed his press law restricted one of Canada's basic freedoms and his $25 certificates would amount to printing money and only the feds can do that.

Aberhart and his followers let out an awful howl and said they'd leave Canada. But they didn't.

Nothing much happened at all. The social credit government stayed in power until 1971, long after Aberhart died. But nobody has ever tried social credit.

Originally broadcast August 17, 1983

THE WRATH OF KHAN

When Genghis Khan died, on the 18th of August in the year 1227, away off in the middle of China, the world lost one of the most remarkable conquerors of all time. Genghis conquered an empire, by himself, bigger than the one the Romans took centuries to build. Yet he knew nothing about administration and it soon all fell apart.

He held it all together with a series of horsemen who could take messages a thousand miles in a few days. But he didn't do anything to advance art or science within his huge empire.

Genghis Khan was his name by the time he died. He was born with the name Temujin, way out in the wastes of what's now Mongolia. The trickiest part of reconstructing the story of Genghis Khan is to get all the people straight.

Today we think of him as a Chinese warlord who spread out. Not so. The Mongols were racially very different from the Chinese. They conquered the Chinese, not the other way around.

Later, when they spread westward and came into contact with Europeans, the historians of Europe referred to them as Tartars. Again, not so. The Tartars were a fairly small tribe the Mongols conquered and absorbed.

The Mongols were cowboys. They lived on their horses and when they moved their herds of cattle and sheep they took everything they owned with them and lived in felt tents.

When there was food they gorged themselves. It was nothing for a Mongol cowboy to eat 10 or 12 pounds of meat at a sitting. The rest of the time they starved. And they could live on less than anybody else.

Water and pasture and game were all in short supply away out on the edge of the Gobi desert where Genghis Khan and his Mongols lived. So they were used to being on the move, always searching.

Until he was about 30 Genghis spent his life in a hundred petty wars and battles with neighbouring tribes. He won all those skirmishes and became a major local leader.

Then he sent out to conquer the world. And he eventually ruled about half of what was then known as the world.

His horsemen just took those skills they'd honed out in the wilderness and applied them to conquest. No army could stand up to them. If they met resistance, they just rode past it and attacked in the rear. They burned and looted and left opposing armies out in the field without supplies.

Genghis' conquests seemed to be almost effortless. His soldiers could be killed but his army couldn't be beaten.

Genghis' conquests seemed to be almost effortless. His soldiers could be killed but his army couldn't be beaten.

He moved south into China and his sons moved southwest to India and west to about where the Ukraine is today.

The Mongols didn't read or write so they had to use the scribes and administrators of the countries they conquered. Genghis did this as little as possible. He knew that once you hire the bureaucrats, they soon take over.

But it had to be done. The result was that Genghis was a conqueror, not an administrator, and rebellious states had to be conquered all over again.

In 1226 Genghis fell from his horse and hurt himself. He was never the same. Eventually, after about a year, he died, aged about 60, on the 18th of August in 1227.

The Mongols loaded his body on a cart and took it a thousand miles away to a sacred grove of trees on a hill in Mongolia. The guards accompanying the body killed everybody they met on the way.

No real reason for that. That was just the way the Mongols were. With Genghis gone, his empire melted like the snow. His grandson, Kubla Khan, was still running China when Marco Polo arrived there a few years later. But within a hundred years of Genghis' death, just about all trace of him and his armies and his empire had faded.

Originally broadcast August 18, 1987

ON THE ROPES

Jean-Francois Gravelet was the son of a tightrope walker. He started practicing his father's craft when he was only five. And by the time he was 27 in 1851, he was the most sensational high-wire man in Europe. He had light hair and blue eyes and performed under the name of Blondin.

Blondin came to North America in 1851 as part of a circus troupe. He played near Niagara Falls and went to take a look.

He decided he'd like to stretch a rope 200 feet above the Niagara Gorge a little upstream from the falls and walk it. It actually took eight years before he made the attempt, in 1859.

First a small rope was carried across the river from the Canadian to the American side on an excursion boat. Then it was used to pull the three-inch rope that would eventually be Blondin's sidewalk. Teams of horses had to be used. The process of anchoring it securely took days.

Then it had to be steadied with guy ropes. No matter how calm a day it is, the air above the falls is always turbulent because of the rushing water under it.

Each guy rope was attached to the main rope then balanced with a six-pound sack of sand. Blondin had to install them all himself because no one else could go out on that rope. Or was crazy enough to try.

On the night of the 29th of June it rained like crazy and the rope was wet and slippery. But Blondin made his try anyhow on the 30th and did it easily.

The crowds went crazy. Blondin was the wonder of the age and steamers and trains brought tens of thousands from all over North America to see him.

Blondin did it again and again. He did it tied in a sack and dressed as an ape. He stopped halfway and stood on his head. He took along a little chafing dish and a sidetable and stopped halfway and cooked himself an omelette.

Niagara Falls was the Las Vegas of its time. It was the hottest tourist property in the western world. It had hotels, bars, strip joints, plenty of gambling although it wasn't legal, pickpockets, conmen, easy ladies . . .

Blondin had to do something sensational for the Prince of Wales' visit. So he offered to carry a man on his back. Strangely enough, there were no volunteers.

everything people look for in a holiday.

Blondin kept trying for more and more exciting ways to cross Niagara on his rope.

Then it was announced that the Prince of Wales would be visiting the Falls on the 19th of August. Blondin had to do something sensational for that. So he offered to carry a man on his back. Strangely enough, there were no volunteers.

Finally, Blondin talked a wiry little ex-sailor into it. He was Harry Colcord, a Boston Irishman. The French newspapers assumed Blondin would only take a fellow Frenchman for a partner so they named him Colcourt.

The bookies had cleaned up at first when thousands bet that Blondin wouldn't make it. But as he did it several times people started betting that he would. The only way the bookies could clean up would be if he fell.

Well, Blondin carried Colcord fairly easily on his shoulders. He had a half-dozen hooks hanging from his belt and Colcord could use them as footholds. The two men were tied together with a short rope. If one felt the other falling he was to throw himself in the opposite direction and hope the rope would hold as it hit the tightrope.

As it turned out, that wasn't necessary. Blondin had to put Colcord down a half-dozen times to rest but they made it.

About 50 feet from the American side, the arriving side, the bookies had loosened a guy rope and that almost tumbled them into the water. But not quite.

The poor prince of Wales looked more exhausted than Blondin when it was all over. Blondin went on and on and did his last tightrope act when he was 72.

Colcord rode Blondin's back twice more across Niagara then gave up. He was terrified each time. In fact, he would wake up at night in Chicago where he lived 40 years later all broken out in a sweat because he'd dreamed of that cold, fast, green-grey water 200 feet below.

Originally broadcast August 19, 1983

REAVIS, WILLING AND ABLE

If you're a fan of people who think big and take painstaking care to set up a huge score, you'll want to draw a circle around today in the calendar, because on the 20th of August in 1841, James Addison Reavis was born. And nobody thought bigger than Reavis.

Reavis was born in Missouri. He fought on the losing side in the Civil War, then drove a streetcar in St. Louis, did a little business in South America, then returned to St. Louis and went into real estate.

And that's where it gets interesting. Sometime about 1871, Reavis met a doctor and small-time swindler named George Willing.

Willing had traveled all over the American west and he'd uncovered something interesting. It seems that at various times the American government had taken bits of the west from Mexico. It took huge chunks — like California, Texas, New Mexico and Arizona — as well as little bits from time to time, to straighten out borders and things like that.

At first the Mexicans complained but they eventually gave up and signed away the land in a treaty. According to that same treaty, the American government promised to recognize the old land grants that had been made by the king of Spain when he ruled that part of the world more than a hundred years earlier.

Dr. Willing had found that record-keeping in Mexico and Spain had been very haphazard. He had a piece of paper that claimed to be from a Spanish nobleman named Peralta in which Peralta signed away his land claims to Dr. Willing.

We don't know exactly what sort of deal Reavis and Dr. Willing made between themselves. But we can figure it out.

There was another piece of old, brown paper all written in Spanish and covered with seals and emblems. It gave Peralta's grandfather a big chunk of what is now Arizona, a piece of land 10 leagues wide and 30 leagues long.

Reavis went on a trip to Mexico and visited a lot of places where records were kept, courthouses and churches and the like. Then he returned to the United States and his partner, Dr. Willing, dropped dead.

The coroner said it was a clear case of poisoning but no one was ever arrested. Those old pieces of paper became Reavis' property.

And he used them to lay claim to a huge chunk of the richest land in Arizona, an area of farms, ranches and homes and businesses as big as the states of New Jersey and New Hampshire together.

The Southern Pacific Railway forked over $50 thousand rather than run the risk of a lawsuit. The Silver King mine came across with $25 thousand. Dozens, then hundreds of ranchers, farmers and businessmen made settlements with Reavis rather than risk going to court and being turfed off their land. We don't know how much he took in but it must have been a huge amount because he lived like a king.

> *Hundreds of ranchers, farmers and businessmen made settlements with Reavis rather than risk going to court and being turfed off their land.*

He even married a Spanish-speaking lady who he said was the last survivor of the original land grant holder, so that now his claim was twice as good. In fact, it was too good.

The American government had to do something because this one man owned too much. When they started to investigate, they found the original land grant was printed on paper with a watermark indicating it was made in a mill in Minnesota 130 years after the grant was dated. It was printed in type that had only been designed a few years earlier.

When they sent experts to look at the original documents in Spain and Mexico, they found they, too, had been forged and planted.

At the Reavis trial it was proven that his wife the baroness was really a chambermaid from a flophouse near San Bernardino, California. The poor woman had been sucked in and really believed she was a long-lost Spanish noble.

She divorced Reavis and when he got out of jail she was long gone out of his life. Reavis was sent away for six years but he was paroled after two.

Originally broadcast August 20, 1984

MISSING MONA

In 1963, when the French loaned the Mona Lisa for display in the United States, it was valued for insurance at $100 million. The premiums would have been so high that it was cheaper to spend several hundred thousand dollars on a special carrying case and extra guards.

The Mona Lisa was painted about 1503 by the great Leonardo da Vinci. It's a rather usual-looking portrait of a youngish woman — except for one feature. The lady has a strange smile: half-smirk, half-grin, certainly not a full-blown laugh. Could she be making fun of somebody? Or thinking of a boyfriend? Or a joke she'd heard? Or making fun of the painter?

Nobody knows. But that smile has made the Mona Lisa the most famous picture in the world.

It hangs in the Louvre, the great art museum in Paris. It's been there forever, it seems. But it was missing for a while.

On the morning of the 21st of August in 1911, a carpenter who used to work at the Louvre stole it right off the wall. His name was Vincenzo Perugia. He was an Italian who had worked for a few years in Paris. Perugia lived better in Paris than he could in Italy. Still, he was an Italian patriot and a hater of everything French.

We don't know exactly how Perugia got the Mona Lisa. At one point he told the police he was helped by two brothers, also Italians, who went into the Louvre with him and helped to watch for guards and to carry the Mona Lisa. Perugia later said that was a lie, that he'd done it all himself.

However he did it, Perugia got the Mona Lisa out of the Louvre and was long gone before somebody finally noticed it was missing.

There was a terrible outcry. The director of the Louvre and the French deputy-minister of culture lost their jobs. Rewards of thousands were offered and tips came pouring in. Police ran all over the place.

However he did it, Perugia got the Mona Lisa out of the Louvre and was long gone before somebody finally noticed it was missing.

Nothing. After it was gone for two years, an art dealer in Florence, Italy, got a letter from a man who said he could produce the Mona Lisa. At first the art dealer thought it was a letter from a crazy man and paid no attention.

Then he decided to call the cops. They quickly found Perugia living in a grubby little hotel in Florence with the Mona Lisa hidden in the bottom of his trunk.

Perugia explained that, as a red-blooded Italian, he was enraged that the greatest picture ever painted should have been stolen from Italy by Napoleon and was hanging for all the world to see in a French museum.

When he gave that speech in the courtroom in Florence, the audience was on its feet cheering. The problem with that was it wasn't true.

Leonardo da Vinci had taken the picture, several years after he painted it, with him when he left Italy to go to live and work in France. He sold it to the king of France for what was in those days a very handsome price, almost $1500.

But it was a good enough story to get Perugia off. He was sentenced to seven months in jail for possession of stolen goods. But since he'd been in jail awaiting trial for seven months he was turned loose.

The Mona Lisa was sent home to Paris.

The art dealer got a small reward. He sued for 10 per cent of the value of the Mona Lisa. His case was thrown out of court because no one could say what the value of the Mona Lisa was worth — what he should get 10 per cent of.

And Perugia, the ardent Italian, the great hater of everything French? He spent the First World War in the army then set up a paint and wallpaper store in France, of all places, and did quite well. He died in 1947.

Originally broadcast August 21, 1989

HELLO DOLLY

When the Los Angeles cops were called to the home of Fred and Dolly Osterreich, shortly before midnight, Fred was lying dead on the floor with three bullets in him and Dolly was locked in a bedroom closet. Dolly said a burglar had invaded the house, fought with Fred, then shot him and locked her in the closet.

The whole thing looked awfully phoney and the cops didn't believe a word of it. But they couldn't prove anything. They kept checking the case, off and on, for years but they came up with nothing.

There was a lot of money in Fred's pocket but his expensive watch was missing. That seemed strange, too. Eleven months later the cops found the watch. It was on the wrist of Dolly's lawyer. She explained that she had found the watch around the house so maybe Fred hadn't been wearing it the night he was killed. She had reported it missing at the time because she thought it was missing. No law against making a simple mistake, is there? That made the case even more peculiar but the cops still couldn't prove a thing.

They were still wondering what had really happened eight years later in 1930, when Dolly's lawyer walked into the station and said he'd been instructed to explain the case to them. And then it came out, the weirdest tale they'd ever heard.

Dolly and her husband Fred were from Milwaukee, where Fred owned a factory that made women's aprons and lingerie.

One day in 1903 one of the sewing machines broke down and a repairman came to fix it. He was a little guy named Otto Sanhuber, 17 years old and less than five feet tall. Dolly was then 36. And Otto fixed more than the sewing machine. He turned Dolly on. They had an affair and eventually, when Fred found out about it, they ran off together to California.

But after a while they ran out of money and Dolly

Each morning, Fred would go off to the lingerie factory. And Otto would come out of the attic where Dolly had stashed him.

returned to Fred. She said she'd been foolish and asked if he would take her back. He did.

No further mention was made of Otto. In fact, Fred had never seen him.

Then the case got strange. Each morning, Fred would go off to the lingerie factory. And Otto would come out of the attic where Dolly had stashed him. Each evening, just before Fred was due back home, Otto would return to the attic.

To pass the time in the evenings in the attic, Otto took to writing short stories and actually had a few published. When Fred remarked that he and Dolly seemed to use an awful lot of groceries for a family of two, Dolly explained to him that when he came home drunk from time to time he ate like a horse.

Once, Fred was sure he saw somebody in the attic but Dolly convinced him he was working too hard and he went to a doctor who told him to get more rest.

One day, the inevitable happened, of course. Fred walked in early and found a strange man sitting at his kitchen table, polishing off a plate of food. Fred thought he was just a passing tramp and threw him out.

Dolly told Otto to move to California and she would soon follow. She then convinced Fred he should sell the business and retire to California. And that's what happened. They bought a house in Los Angeles. With an attic, of course.

When the cops heard this story, they went to Dolly's place, grabbed Otto and Dolly, and charged them with murder.

The jury let Dolly off and convicted Otto of manslaughter. But he beat it on appeal. It seems in those days there was a statute of limitation of seven years on manslaughter and he hadn't come out of the attic until eight years after Fred was dead. Altogether, Otto had spent 19 years in Dolly's attic.

Originally broadcast August 22, 1984

NO MORE MR. NICE GUYS

The Mounties had a reputation as a police force of nice guys by the time the Yukon gold rush began in 1898. They had helped settlers on the Prairies by fixing their harness and carting in their seed for them. They had delivered babies and fought prairie fires.

In the Yukon, they had to keep the peace among tens of thousand of men who swarmed in from all over the world. They spent most of their time taking care of frost-bitten miners and delivering the mail.

The worst crime they had to contend with was usually thefts from caches of supplies. In that cold, snowy country, if a man reached his cache of food and equipment and found it had been stolen, the result could be death.

Constable Alex Pennycuick, a former officer in the British Army in India, was investigating some thefts along the trail that led from Dawson southward to Skagway in the United States. Nothing serious, just petty stuff.

As Pennycuick worked his way south along the trail he met a fellow Mountie, Corporal Paddy Ryan. This was in the last week of 1900. Ryan was looking for a telegraph lineman, a Norwegian named Olsen who was supposed to have been at Ryan's post for Christmas dinner a few days earlier. He hadn't shown up.

A half-dozen miles north of his post at Hutchiku, Ryan had run into something strange. Someone had cut a trail through the bush, to the edge of the river a half-mile away. Then he'd built an observation post near where that new trail joined the old one.

The Mounties couldn't understand why anyone would do such a thing. They soon found out. They learned that Olsen the lineman had set out for Ryan's post about 8:00 Christmas morning with two Americans who were headed for Skagway. Both the Americans were carrying a lot of money and gold.

Ryan and Pennycuick questioned people up and down the trail. They soon realized that the three travelers had got as far down the trail as the observation post — but not past it. The other travelers didn't seem to be accounted for either, a pair of Englishmen named Miller and Ross.

The Mounties telegraphed messages up and down the trail for all cops to watch for the missing five.

On the sixth of January in 1901, 13 days after Olsen

The three travelers had got as far down the trail as the observation post — but not past it.

missed his Christmas dinner with Corporal Ryan, a man arrived at Tagish, the last police post in Canada before the trail crossed the border into the United States.

He answered the description of the missing Englishman, Miller. He admitted his name was really O'Brien when the Mounties questioned him closely. He had a sled and a big St. Bernard dog and the usual camping equipment. Plus a pair of binoculars. Nobody on the trail in the Yukon in those days carried binoculars. The Mounties threw O'Brien into a cell while they looked for more evidence.

When Ryan and Pennycuick took O'Brien's binoculars to the observation post they discovered they could see an hour up the trail. When they told his St. Bernard to go home, the dog trotted down the trail for a while, then lay down. They deduced that O'Brien had lay down there to wait for people coming along the trail.

The new trail had been cut with a dull axe with three nicks on the blade. They found people who had seen such an axe in the kit of Ross, O'Brien's missing partner.

O'Brien was carrying a distinctive-looking double gold nugget, two small nuggets fused together. One of the missing Americans had a nugget like that.

It seems incredible but Constable Pennycuick swept and sifted the top three feet of snow for a half-acre around that observation post. He identified and labeled everything they found — a garter, a comb, two buttons, three cigar butts, a medicine label, a whisky bottle, a spent bullet, six shells, a dull axe with three nicks in the blade, a piece of a tooth, a piece of bone from a human skull, frozen bloodstains . . . and on and on.

In May the ice broke up on the river and four bodies came up — Olsen the lineman, the two Americans, and O'Brien's partner Ross.

O'Brien went on trial for murder. The Mounties had 400 exhibits. They brought in 80 witnesses from all over North America. Including one guy they'd found in jail in Oregon, who testified that O'Brien had told him he and his partner had done the killings, then O'Brien had knocked off his partner.

When the trial was over, the Mounties' reputation was made — as highly-skilled investigators, not just nice guys.

Originally broadcast August 23, 1983

THE BEAR WHO MADE IT BIG

The First World War began in early August of 1914. Within weeks, young men in western Canada were rushing to join the army and troop trains were pouring eastward to Halifax to get the men overseas.

One of those trains filled with Prairie soldiers stopped for water and fuel at White River in northern Ontario on the 24th of August in 1914.

While the train was being serviced, the soldiers were allowed out on the platform to stretch their legs.

Among them was a veterinary lieutenant from Winnipeg named Harry Colborn. Vets were important in armies in those days because everything on the battlefield was moved by horses.

There was a trapper on the platform, a man who had come to watch the train come in. This was a big deal.

The trapper had killed a bear a few days earlier but didn't have the heart to kill the little cub she had with her. He'd kept the cub which was small and fluffy and cute.

Lieutenant Colborn paid the trapper $20 for the cub and took it back aboard the train as a mascot.

All through camp in Quebec, on the train trip to Halifax, on the boat ride overseas, Lieutenant Colborn and his men kept the cub.

Colborn named the little bear after his home town, Winnipeg. The soldiers shortened that to Winnie.

When it came time in early 1915 for the soldiers to go to France where the fighting was, Colborn realized he couldn't take along a bear.

He asked the keeper of the London Zoo if he would give Winnie a home for the war. Pretty soon, Winnie was the most popular animal in the zoo. She would play with the kids and do all kinds of clever tricks that Colborn had taught her.

Colborn asked the keeper of the London Zoo if he would give Winnie a home for the war. Pretty soon, Winnie was the most popular animal in the zoo.

In 1919, when the war was over and Colborn was headed home, he went to the zoo to get Winnie. But he didn't have the heart to take her away from the kids of London. So he returned to Canada and Winnie lived out her days at the London zoo. She didn't die until she was about 20. That was in the 1930s.

Among the swarms of little British kids who loved Winnie was a little boy named Christopher Robin Milne.

His father, A.A. Milne, was a strange, introverted man who made his living as a writer. He had written funny magazine articles and a few plays that had some success in both London and New York.

A.A. Milne told little bedtime stories, as most parents do. They were kids' tales, populated with Christopher Robin's toy donkey and other toys, and, of course, Winnie the little bear at the zoo who was Christopher Robin's very favorite.

In 1924, old man Milne published a collection of Winnie stories in a book. It took off like a shot.

Over the next few years, he wrote three more. They have turned out to be the most successful kids' stories in the English language. And several other languages, too.

Christopher Robin never called Winnie a Pooh. That was a name he had for a swan that swam on a pond near his home.

Winnie the Pooh made A.A. Milne rich but not happy. He was always bugged by the fact that for the rest of his life he was known as a writer of kids' stories.

And in White River in northern Ontario, about 300 miles north of Sault Ste. Marie, there's now a statue of the little bear who caught the train out of town and hit the big time.

Originally broadcast August 24, 1992

CAPTAIN MORGAN'S RUM TALE

Henry Morgan was a thoroughly unpleasant man, a pirate, a thief, a killer, a torturer, a kidnapper, and a cheater of his own comrades.

But he was one of history's most successful men at all these things so we know him as Sir Henry Morgan.

Henry Morgan was a Welshman who moved to Jamaica when he was just a kid, apprenticed to a plantation owner.

When Morgan was 19 he went pirating. It beat plantation-operating as a trade and it paid a lot better.

Jamaica, in the West Indies, was just a few days away from Spain's American empire, the richest the world had ever seen. The Spanish were looting so much gold and silver and jewels from their colonies that they didn't bother to protect them. It was easier and cheaper to replace a stolen shipload than to maintain a huge army and navy to defend it.

Also, the people on the scene in the Spanish outposts who were expected to fight and die to protect the treasure, ended up with very little of it. That all went back to Spain, to the king and his pals.

Morgan shrewdly assessed this situation. He put together small bands of poor, desperate men. He told them the fewer they were, the more loot there would be for each.

The result was that on most of Morgan's raids his men were outnumbered at least a dozen to one. But they seldom failed because they were hungry.

Morgan's men were excellent sailors and marksmen. They raided Spanish settlements all up and down the mainland of North and South America, from Mexico down to Venezuela. They would capture a town and grab all valuables in sight. Then they would torture any inhabitants they could find, making them tell where they had hidden any valuables.

Or, they would have them send messages to relatives in other towns, demanding ransom. Those who couldn't raise the ransom were taken back with Morgan's gang to Port Royal in Jamaica, the pirate stronghold.

Port Royal was called the most sinful port on earth.

There, the pirates drank and chased girls and got rid of their loot then signed on with Morgan for the next raid.

Morgan took terrible advantage of his own men. Most were illiterate and he cheated at divvying-up time. But he was shrewd enough to always set aside a substantial share for the king back in England and the king's brother, the Duke of York.

The result was that in 1674, instead of being hanged for piracy, as he should have been, Morgan was knighted and made deputy-governor of Jamaica.

He had led a raid on the city of Panama, the richest in the western world, and had looted it of millions. He had treated the people even more roughly than usual.

The king of Spain demanded Morgan be punished. The king of England had him arrested and brought to London for trial. There, of course, he was acquitted. He probably bribed the judge and jury.

But the king announced that evidence at Morgan's trial indicated he knew a lot about piracy. So he made him Sir Henry Morgan, the deputy-governor of Jamaica, with a special commission to get rid of pirates.

Morgan returned to his old haunts and started hanging his old comrades. The result was that pretty soon there was nobody left who could testify against him if he should ever get into trouble again.

A book, detailing his crimes, was published in England but he sued the publishers and won a small award and an apology.

He spent his last years in Jamaica in an alcoholic fog and in the constant company of bad women, a pirate's idea of paradise.

He finally died on the 25th of August in 1688. Five years later an earthquake and tidal wave wiped out his haunt at Port Royal. Since then, history has been kind to the old scoundrel and he's remembered as a lovable old rascal. Canadians have even named a brand of rum after him.

> *The king announced that evidence at Morgan's trial indicated he knew a lot about piracy. So he made him the deputy-governor of Jamaica, with a special commission to get rid of pirates.*

Originally broadcast August 25, 1986

A BATTLE OF CONSEQUENCE

There were only a dozen or two battles that changed the course of the history of the whole world. Yet, strangely enough, one of them has been almost ignored by our historians. That was the battle of Manzikert in 1071 in Asia Minor, in what today is eastern Turkey.

A historian could take a couple of pages just to list the important results of the battle of Manzikert. It was the beginning of the end of the Roman Empire which had endured for more than a thousand years. It meant the end of Christian domination of the eastern Mediterranean, the beginning of the map of the Middle East that keeps the world on the edge of war today.

It was a stunning defeat for the Christian west. For the first time in the history of the Roman Empire, an emperor was not only defeated in battle but captured on the battlefield.

And in the long-term, maybe the most important of all, it led to the Crusades, that incredible series of exoduses and battles that covered a couple of centuries and brought the eastern and western cultures into close contact, for better or worse.

The world in 1071 was a pretty brutal place. The Romans had built the greatest empire the world had ever seen then it had split.

The world in 1071 was a pretty brutal place. The Romans had built the greatest empire the world had ever seen then it had split. The western part, the part dominated by the Roman Catholic Church, had gone into decline, what we call the Dark Ages.

The eastern part, more Greek than Roman, dominated by the Greek Orthodox Church, got both better and worse than the original Roman Empire had ever been. Its art and technology and military and administrative sciences surpassed anything the old Romans had achieved. But, at the same time, its morality, public and private, was absolutely rotten.

Bribery and corruption were deeply ingrained in the government and vice and double-dealing and dishonesty were integral parts of daily life.

The capital was Constantinople, Istanbul today, right where Europe meets Asia. The area just to the east of that, Asia Minor, is the country of Turkey today. Now it's pretty poor and the soil has been leached out and eroded by centuries of over-farming. But in those days it was the richest part of the world, loaded with prosperity and civilization and Greek culture.

But the hordes from the steppes of Asia had invaded it and the whole area was a battlefield. Those Asian hordes, from somewhere in southeastern Siberia and northern China, fought amongst themselves as much as they did against the Roman Empire. Otherwise they would have conquered the whole area in a matter of months. Then, a century or two before the time we're talking about, the Moslem religion came along and unified them to a degree.

So, in that pivotal year of 1071, we had the not-quite-united Asiatic horsemen, fierce warriors, pushing in from the east. Their leader was a brilliant man named Arp Arslap. But no matter how good he was, he could only devote a small fraction of his time, his attention and his army to fighting the Romans in the west. Most of his time was spent in endless civil wars.

The leader in the west, the emperor, was a capable soldier named Romanus the Fourth Diogenes. Emperors were lasting an average of three or four years in the Roman Empire at that point. A few did better. Many were on the throne and deposed in months.

Romanus was a good general but nobody could breathe any fire or efficiency into the army by that time. It was huge but ineffective because of corruption and inefficiency. Some historians say the Romans had as many as 100,000 men in the field at Manzikert the day of the battle, the 26th of August, 1071. Arp had as few as 15,000, no more than 25,000.

There isn't much to say about the battle itself. Nothing sensational happened. The Romans attacked and the Turks retreated slowly, depending on their mobility to keep out of the grasp of the Romans and their superb archery to pick off the Roman soldiers one at a time.

Romanus was captured but Arp let him go. He returned to Constantinople and was killed by his rivals for the title. Arp went back to his civil wars and was stabbed to death within a year.

Originally broadcast August 26, 1986

The Slick Yankee

Thomas Chandler Haliburton liked to say he and his father were born in the same house, miles apart. The old man was from a family of New England Yankees who fled to Nova Scotia at the time of the American Revolution. They settled out in the country. The house he was born in was later put on rollers then floated down river to the town of Windsor. And that's where it was when Thomas Haliburton was born in it.

Old Man Haliburton was very much part of the establishment and was a judge. Young Tom went to Kings College in Halifax, in those days a bastion of the establishment. He grew up a staunch right-winger.

But soon after he started practicing law he ran for the legislature, claiming to be the friend of the working man.

He always claimed that and always made great speeches on behalf of the poor and disenfranchised. But there's no indication that he ever voted for their welfare if it would run contrary to his own.

When Haliburton rose to make a speech in the legislature, all other work stopped dead. He was the speaker of the age. Joe Howe, the editor of the *Nova Scotian* and a real, true friend of the poor, would sit and the pen would drop from his fingers in the press gallery. He often confessed he didn't give accurate reports of Haliburton's speeches because he was so enthralled he couldn't take notes.

When Haliburton's father died, young Tom got his job as judge. Then as now, judges didn't work too hard so he was able to spend his time at his favorite pastime, writing. He created a character called Sam Slick.

Sam was a Yankee, a traveling salesman who went about the countryside, peddling clocks to farmers' wives. The clocks were cheaply made and didn't run

well but Sam did just fine by appealing to his customers with outrageous flattery.

Haliburton meant to reform Nova Scotia farmers who he figured were foolish and idle. At one point he had Sam note that the Nova Scotians had their fields all sown in oats to feed their race-horses while they bought wheat for flour from the Americans. They feed horses, said Sam, we feed asses.

You can understand why Haliburton's work found only modest success in Nova Scotia although it was pretty funny. But British publishers and their public loved the doings of Sam Slick and Haliburton was very popular there.

> *Sam noted that the Nova Scotians had their fields all sown in oats to feed their race-horses while they bought wheat for flour from the Americans. "They feed horses," said Sam, "we feed asses."*

He and Howe traveled around Europe together but Haliburton was such a cruel man that he would never resist a chance to write some funny story about the well-meaning rube in Europe. Everybody knew he was writing about Howe but Howe seemed to forgive him, even if others didn't.

Haliburton had married young to a woman he loved greatly. She died in the early 1840s and the light went out of Haliburton's life. He applied for early retirement then got involved in a lengthy dispute over his pension.

He moved to England, where he was still a popular writer. He married a wealthy widow and ran for parliament.

But he couldn't duplicate the brilliant speeches of his time in the Nova Scotian legislature. But was a bit of a pathetic figure when he died on the 27th of August in 1865. Although his writing was never very popular in Canada, you can still find the odd volume in your local library. And bits of it are well worth the effort.

Originally broadcast August 27, 1992

HYDE AND SEEK

In 1885 Robert Louis Stevenson, the great Scottish novelist, wrote his story of Dr. Jekyll and Mr. Hyde and the phrase Jekyll-and-Hyde entered our language to describe someone with both a good and a bad side. But the story of the man who provided Stevenson with the idea for his story is even more fascinating than the story itself.

William Brodie was one of the most prosperous and most respectable men in Edinburgh. He was born in 1741, the son of a well-to-do cabinet maker who lived in a big house on the best street in the city.

Young William inherited his father's business and expanded it. He not only built fine furniture but he also did house and shop renovations, installing the wood panelling that was fashionable at the time. He was a deacon of the church and went into politics and sat as an alderman on the city council.

But Deacon Brodie also had a racy side to his personality. In addition to his wife and family, he had two girlfriends, and several children by each.

He had to maintain apartments for these other two families. He loved to gamble. Or rather, he loved to play cards. The way Brodie played, there wasn't much gambling involved.

He used loaded dice and marked cards and made a fair bundle on the side that way. But, what with his two other households to maintain and a taste for general high living, Brodie was always on the lookout for extra money.

In those days in Scotland, it was the custom for storeowners to hang their keys on a hook just inside the door. Brodie took to carrying a wad of putty in his palm. As a shopkeeper was busy looking for a shirt or tie-pin or pound of nails or whatever else Brodie said he was looking for, sharp Deacon Brodie would press the putty against the shop key.

Using that imprint as a pattern, he would make a key and he'd be in the burglary business.

Another time, he made a major score at the biggest jewelry store in town. He'd made a copy of the

> *Brodie's raids amounted to the worst crime wave Edinburgh had ever seen. The police sent out extra patrols but they couldn't catch the burglars.*

shop key when he was hired to install new paneling.

In all, Brodie's raids in the mid-1780s amounted to the worst crime wave Edinburgh had ever seen. The police sent out extra patrols but they couldn't catch the burglars.

Brodie started off working alone but soon added three or four men to his gang. Then he would win their share of the loot with his marked cards and loaded dice. And that brought about his downfall.

In March of 1788, Brodie and his gang pulled off their biggest score yet. They hit the Excise House and got a bundle. But the government offered a reward plus a pardon to anyone who would point the finger. One of the gang ratted on Brodie.

He fled but he was soon traced to Amsterdam and brought back for trial.

In those days in Scotland, they didn't fool around. The penalty for burglary was death. And a death trial had to keep going once it got started. For 21 hours, Deacon Brodie stood at the bar of justice until, on the 28th of August, 1788, the jury said guilty. Brodie was hanged a few days later.

He had shoved a silver tube down his throat and bribed the hangman to not break his neck. His friends put the body into a buggy and rushed to a doctor who tried to revive him.

Some say they saw Brodie years later, living well in Paris. There's a tombstone with his name on it in Edinburgh.

Young Robert Louis Stevenson was brought up on the story of Brodie. In fact, in his bedroom was a cabinet that Brodie had made.

He was fascinated by the story. His first effort at writing, at the age of 15, was the story of Deacon Brodie. And he later wrote a play about him.

But Brodie lives today because in 1815 Stevenson had a terrible nightmare about him. He woke up in a sweat. Then he locked himself in his room for three days and emerged with the dream about Deacon Brodie, *The Story of Dr. Jekyll and Mr. Hyde.*

Originally broadcast August 28, 1986

THE PRODIGIOUS PEACEMAKER

Hugh de Groot was what the newspapers call a child prodigy. He was born in Holland in 1583. At seven he was writing compositions in Latin, the learned language of the time. In fact, historians still refer to him as Grotius, the Latin version of his name.

Grotius went to university when he was only 11 and graduated with several doctorates when he was 14.

He was made a doctor of laws, the highest university honour of them all, at the university of Orleans in France when he was only 16. He was pleading cases before the highest court in Holland when he was 17.

When he was 18, he was made official historian of Holland. When he was 19 he began writing the treatise which has been the basis for all international law ever since. He was the man who first thought up the idea of freedom of the seas.

At 24 he was the attorney-general of Holland.

And at 30 he was sentenced to death.

Holland had been ruled by the Catholic Spanish although most of the people were Protestants. Two hundred years before the American Revolution, the Dutch won a long, bloody war of independence and set up their own free republic.

Gradually, those Protestants, who believed in John Calvin's theory of predestination, won power in the new country. Predestination preaches that some of us are intended to go to heaven and some to hell, that God makes the decision before we're born.

Grotius didn't believe that and wrote learned papers disputing it. He and two other leaders of the anti-predestination faith were arrested in 1618. Catholic tyranny had been replaced by Calvinist tyranny.

The other two stuck to their guns and were beheaded. Grotius wrote a long apology, saying he was wrong. He got off with life imprisonment.

Grotius and his wife and children were shut up in a castle. They stayed there three years, Grotius studying all the time and eating very little.

One day, when he had reduced himself to less than a hundred pounds, his wife packed him into a trunk with some books he was supposed to be sending to a fellow scholar and he escaped.

Twenty years earlier when he had been a brilliant teenager, the king of France had offered him a job as an ambassador. Grotius had preferred to go home to Holland. Now he couldn't. He moved to Sweden.

He wrote about war and international law. He wrote that women and children and unarmed civilians shouldn't be harmed by armies. That countries should hold conferences and go to third parties to settle their problems, and should try anything before they went to war.

Grotius was made a doctor of laws, the highest university honor of them all, when he was only 16. He was pleading cases before the highest court in Holland when he was 17.

He wrote that prisoners of war should be held only long enough to keep them from fighting, then sent home to their families.

The Thirty Years War, one of the bloodiest in European history, was ending and its terrible toll made sense of everything Grotius had written.

Once more he was regarded as a genius. He was made Sweden's ambassador to France. Then the queen of Sweden called him back and asked him to stay at her court as her most trusted adviser.

But Grotius said he preferred to retire to Germany and spend the rest of his life reading and writing. The queen put him aboard a ship and wished him godspeed. But a storm came up and the greatest peacemaker Europe ever knew was drowned on the 29th of August in 1645.

Originally broadcast August 29, 1985

242

AN ATTACHÉ CASE

Alfred Dreyfus was a Jew and an officer in the French Army in the late 1800s. That was unusual. The French Army was a very reactionary organization and its officers were mostly quite anti-Jewish.

In the fall of 1894, Major Henry, who was in charge of security for French army headquarters was given some pieces of a torn-up note. The French bribed a cleaning lady at the German embassy to bring them the contents of the German military attaché's wastepaper basket. When Major Henry put the pieces together he found that someone, apparently a French Army officer, had offered to sell the Germans plans for a French gun and a secret army manual.

Major Henry said the guilty party appeared to be Captain Dreyfus. When Dreyfus was accused, he denied it. So he was court-martialed.

The Dreyfus family had lots of money and they hired him a very good lawyer. But the court-martial wouldn't even let the lawyer look at the torn-up list.

Dreyfus was convicted and sent to Devil's Island, off the coast of South America.

A few years later, that cleaning lady at the German embassy brought in some more scraps from the military attaché's wastepaper basket, part of a note from a spy to the attaché. Apparently, the attache had started to write a reply then tore it up, along with the spy's note. The attaché's note pointed to a French officer named Major Esterhazy. And Major Esterhazy's hand-writing was the same as on the list that had sent Dreyfus to Devil's Island.

> *The Dreyfus family had lots of money and they hired a very good lawyer. But the court-martial wouldn't even let the lawyer look at the torn-up list.*

The boss of Major Henry, the security officer who had fingered Dreyfus, went to the head of the army with this startling new evidence. He was told to shut up and was transferred to a remote post in Algeria.

Major Henry went to work to create a phony file on the Dreyfus case to make it look stronger than it really was. He created other notes that were supposed to have been found in the German embassy.

And he dummied up reports from imaginary agents who reported seeing Dreyfus going into the German embassy.

But all this activity came to the attention of the newspapers. The novelist, Emile Zola, wrote a sensational account of what was going on. He was convicted of insulting the army and had to flee to England to avoid jail.

On the 30th of August in 1898, Major Henry was questioned by a committee consisting of the minister of war, the chief of the French army and his assistant.

At first, he stuck to his story. But after a while he got all tied up in his lies and finally had to admit he'd framed Dreyfus.

He was arrested and the chief and the assistant submitted their resignations all on the spot. The next day, Major Henry killed himself.

The army's attempts to cover up got clumsier and clumsier. Eventually, Dreyfus was reinstated in the army.

Major Esterhazy, the real traitor, was allowed to slip away. He took a phony name and lived out his life in a little town in England.

Originally broadcast August 30, 1993

CALIGULA THE CALLOUS

I don't think even a professor of ancient history could get all those Roman emperors straight. We all know which one was Julius Caesar. But aside from that, only one sticks in the mind, the crazy guy who tried to make his horse a consul. That was Caligula. And the stunt with the horse wasn't his craziest by any means.

Caligula became the emperor of Rome in the year 37 AD when the Roman empire was at its most decadent. Tiberius had been the emperor. He didn't like Rome much so he spent most of his time at the Isle of Capri, which is still a great summer resort.

He intended to have his grandson and his grandnephew rule Rome together when he died. The grandnephew was Caligula.

When Tiberius had all that down on paper, Caligula got impatient. He either smothered Tiberius with a pillow then had a witness bumped off, or had someone else do the smothering then had him put out of the way. Either way, he was off to a nasty start.

His cousin, Tiberius' grandson, realized he would get the same treatment if he hung around so he cleared out and left Caligula in sole command of the empire.

Caligula, the name we know him by, was just a nickname. His real name was Gaius. But his father had been an army officer in Germany and young Gaius was brought up in army camps on the frontier of the empire. The soldiers wore a kind of sandal or boot called a caliga. When Gaius was just a little kid he had a pair made for him so he could march with his father's soldiers. They called him Caligula, which meant little boot. And the name stuck.

When Caligula became emperor he was able to consolidate power because the army still liked him. The whole empire was held together in those days by the army and the free handouts of food and the elaborate shows in the forum that the emperor put on.

Caligula doubled the handout. That made people love him. And he put on even bigger and better shows. Better in show business in those days meant gorier.

The Romans really loved blood.

Caligula had teams of gladiators slaughter each other. Then bigger and better teams. Finally he had his soldiers drag the spectators from the first half-dozen rows into the arena.

He bet fortunes on the chariot races. In fact, it was the greatest horse of Roman times, Incitatus, that he considered making a consul. He never actually did that.

About the time Caligula became emperor he also went crazy although he was only 25 at the time. But his mind wandered. However, he kept it on the horse long enough to set it up with its own marble stable, ivory manger, and retinue of slaves.

When Caligula liked a girl he just snapped his fingers and she was his. One time he was invited to a wedding. He liked the bride so much he took her home and married her himself. When he was finished with a girl she was finished — period. He liked to run his hands through a girl's hair and say: "Lovely. And just imagine, when I'm finished with it, the head comes off."

> *Caligula had teams of gladiators slaughter each other. Then bigger and better teams. Finally he had his soldiers drag the spectators from the first half-dozen rows into the arena.*

When he found his sister and brother-in-law plotting against him he had the brother-in-law killed. Then he made his sister carry her husband's ashes around all the time, even sleep with them.

Caligula was convinced he was a god and he ordered people to worship him. As long as he was good to the soldiers they kept him in power.

But eventually he got arrogant with the praetorian guard, the soldiers who guarded him. Each day he would have to give the commander of the guard a password for the day.

Caligula amused himself by thinking up a more obscene one every day. The commander of the guard seethed.

The one he thought of on the 31st of August in the year 41 must have been really vile. Because the guard commander pulled out his sword and killed him.

Originally broadcast August 31, 1984

TREMOR TROUBLE

We know the exact instant of the Tokyo earthquake. It was at 11:58 and 44 seconds on the first of September in 1923.

Japan had always been earthquake country. And when the Japanese began their enthusiastic copying of western technology in the last half of the 1800s, one of the first things they did was set up earthquake study centres in their universities. Pretty soon European and American experts were going to Japan to study.

By tradition, the second of September in the Tokyo-Yokahama area is Storm Day. The summer heat seems to build up and every year on the second of September there's a gigantic rain- and thunder- and wind-storm.

It usually did a lot of damage. The result was that people in that area, even the poor, were used to buying insurance.

The Great Tokyo Earthquake was actually a long series of tremors. The first struck just a minute and a half before noon. But over the next six hours there were 171 more, one every two minutes.

That first quake forced some of the ground to rise nine feet. Just a mile or so offshore, the seabed in one spot dropped 1200 feet. That caused a terrible tidal wave in the port of Yokahama.

The well-to-do had stone and brick homes built along western lines. In some cases, this was a disadvantage. The falling bricks killed the people inside. The poor lived in flimsy wooden houses with paper interior walls.

Since the quake struck just as everyone was stoking his kitchen stove for lunch, there was an instant mass fire. In Yokahama, every firehall was wrecked and there wasn't one fire truck or one foot of hose to fight the fires. Most of the firemen were killed in their halls.

All those small house fires worked their way into one huge firestorm. The normal temperature in Tokyo late in the afternoon on the first of September is 25 degrees. That day it reached 46.

The Great Tokyo Earthquake was actually a long series of tremors — 172 of them over the course of six hours.

In addition, terrible winds blew. At six in the evening and again at 11, wind speeds of 150 miles an hour were recorded. Then the weather office burned down.

The very efficient Japanese police immediately set up refugee centres in the city. One was at a high school. But the firestorm swept toward it faster than anyone could run. Thirty-two thousand, five hundred and sixty-four bodies were later identified at the school and the park around it. Another 25,000 couldn't be recognized.

By a superhuman effort, railway officials got a train moving shortly before midnight to take refugees out of the city. So many people tried to get aboard they were lying on the roofs of the cars. A hundred were killed when they were swept off at a tunnel.

In Yokahama, the chief of police managed to find one phone line open and called Tokyo for help. He couldn't understand why he was getting no answer.

The tidal wave had done most of the damage there. So he ordered all the ships in the harbor and nearby to anchor a mile or two offshore and ferried thousands of refugees to them. There, the ship's kitchens fed them and the people slept everywhere. Two Canadian Pacific liners, the Empress of Japan and the Empress of Australia, were pressed into service.

It was the worst disaster in the history of modern Japan. One hundred twenty-four thousand people died. Twenty years later, 100,000 more than that died in the explosion of one bomb at Hiroshima.

Aid poured in from all over the world, especially from the United States. The man in charge of American aid was General Douglas MacArthur. He impressed the Japanese with his efficiency. Twenty years later he impressed them again as he commanded the American forces that beat their armies in the Second World War.

All those policy holders got something for their wrecked homes. Many insurance companies went broke doing it, but most paid off at eight cents on the dollar.

Originally broadcast September 1, 1986

LET THE GAMES BEGIN

On the second of September in 1937, a dapper little man with a white moustache was taking his daily stroll in the park in Lausanne, Switzerland. He suddenly had a stroke and fell dead.

Within hours, telegrams of tribute and condolence arrived from all the major heads of state of the world: Hitler, Mussolini, the king of Greece, the emperor of Japan . . . the message from the president of France didn't come for more than 24 hours.

And that was a fitting postscript to the life of Baron Pierre de Coubertin, the founder of the modern Olympic Games. He was a Frenchman, from one of the oldest families in France. He was showered with honours from every corner of the world. But somehow, his fellow Frenchmen always looked on him as some sort of freak.

Coubertin's family got its title from King Louis the Eleventh, away back before Columbus discovered America.

Coubertin was a little man, 5'3". But, as one charitable writer once noted, he had the nose of a much bigger man.

He never really did anything for a living. The family had been rich for centuries and none of the Coubertin's had to do anything except clip coupons.

After the French lost the Franco-Prussian War in 1870, Coubertin began writing angry letters to editors, claiming that Frenchmen had become soft, that they didn't have the love for sport that the British and the Germans had.

In 1890, Coubertin was invited to spend a few days at the country home of an eccentric Englishman, Dr. W. P. Brooks. Dr. Brooks was a scholar of ancient Greek. Every year he held a sports meet and booze-up for the people of a nearby village. He hung banners with old Greek proverbs from the trees and called the whole thing his Olympic get-together, because he had named his estate the Olympian Fields.

Maybe that's where Coubertin got the idea. He never said. Anyhow, in November of 1892, Coubertin was making a speech to the Union of French Sports Associations when he suggested an Olympic Games, modeled on the games of ancient Greece, as a substitute for war.

Unfortunately, the baron left his speech until late in the evening when everyone had drunk lots of wine. The meeting saw fit to regard it as a big joke and the poor man left with tears in his eyes.

A beautiful young girl who had been in the audience ran after him and stopped him and said she thought he was a great man with a great idea and the others were all wrong. They fell in love on the spot and were married within a couple of years.

Coubertin now had a strong-willed woman behind him and he really went to work on his Olympic Games idea. He got the crown prince of Greece interested and got a rich Greek cotton merchant from Alexandria in Egypt to put up the money. The first modern Olympic Games were held in Athens in 1896.

When Coubertin got back to his hotel room on opening day, his wife chewed him out. Not once, not one time at all, in all the opening ceremonies, she said, was the Coubertin name even mentioned.

That pretty well told the story of the rest of their lives. Coubertin devoted his life and his fortune to the games.

Eventually, the Baron and his wife and daughter moved to Lausanne in Switzerland. The city council of Lausanne recognized his contribution to world peace through the games and voted him a free hotel suite. By that time he needed it. He was almost broke. His wife was an awful shrew, doling out his spending money a penny at a time. He had hoped to win the Nobel Prize in 1936. His name was mentioned. But it didn't happen.

> *Coubertin suggested an Olympic Games, modeled on the games of ancient Greece, as a substitute for war.*

Originally broadcast September 2, 1985

COUNTING THE DAYS

As far as we can figure, the ancient Egyptians were probably the ones who came up with what we call a calendar. Egypt was, and still is, a dry, sterile country with a band of very rich soil along the Nile River. Each spring, the Nile flooded and left inches of rich earth that supported the farming that fed the Egyptians. So it was important for them to know when the flood was coming.

Over the years, they noticed that the Dog Star flashed on the eastern horizon just before sunrise a few days before the floods began. And the Dog Star did that every 365 days.

Well, not exactly 365 days, but the Egyptians didn't have watches so they didn't know that a year is really 365 days, 5 hours, 48 minutes and 46 seconds.

Considering that, the Egyptians did a remarkable job. But that extra quarter day left over every year meant that the Egyptian calendar was out of whack by about a month every century. In the year 238 BC, the king got upset about having to celebrate his June holidays in January and tried to take away some time to make things fit. But the priests who ran the calendars and such things were very jealous of their power and they prevented him.

So, when Julius Caesar, the boss of the Roman Empire, arrived in Egypt a couple of hundred years later, he found a badly screwed-up system. But better than the Roman one. The Romans had been using a calendar based on the moon. They had to add a month every now and then to make things work out.

Again, that was the responsibility of the priests. But the priests could be got to, especially by the politicians. Some years they wouldn't add any extra time. Some years, they would really pile on the extras. That made a longer year, usually a year when one of their friends was in office.

Caesar saw right away that the Egyptian system was better. So he consulted with a Greek astronomer named Sosigenes and they came up with a new calendar. To make it work, Caesar had to stretch out

In the year 238 BC, the king got upset about having to celebrate his June holidays in January and tried to take away some time to make things fit.

the year before his new system began. It was the year 46 BC by the way we now measure things. It was known back then as the Year of Confusion. Caesar had to make it last 445 days instead of the usual 365.

But it worked. At least better than any other system anybody had seen up until then.

At the same time, we got the names we now apply to our months. The Romans had numbered some months. September, October, November and December mean seven, eight, nine and ten. They had named some after gods, like March after Mars, the god of war, and June after Juno, the goddess of marriage. That's why we're still big on June weddings.

The Romans had left a few lumps of time with no names. So Caesar took a month's worth and named it after himself, Julius Caesar, therefore, July. The next head was Augustus and he didn't want to be outdone so he named the following month after himself.

That system worked for centuries. In fact, it was only out about eight days per thousand years.

By the year 1582, that meant the calendar had shifted 10 days. At that rate, Christmas was going to be in the middle of summer after a while. So, Pope Gregory the Thirteenth ordered the system that slips in an extra day every four years, leap year. All the Catholic countries obeyed his order and that was that.

But England, Holland and the northern European countries were Protestant by that time. And they hated the Catholics so much they refused to go along with the new system.

They held out for almost 200 years. Then, in 1752 the king of England decreed that there would be no 3rd of September that year. Or 4th or 5th or 6th either. His subjects would go to bed on the night of the second and wake up on the 13th.

Today, we're all appropriately thankful that His Majesty had the wit to do that. But at the time, his subjects weren't. They figured he'd shortened their lives by 11 days and they rioted.

Originally broadcast September 3, 1991

PICTURE PERFECT

Away back in the 14- and 1500s, artists used a thing called a camera obscura. They punched a little hole in one side of a light-tight box and let the light fall on the opposite side. That side was either glass or paper oiled to make it transparent. Then they were able to trace the image they saw on a piece of paper laid over that transparent surface.

Most good artists didn't need a camera obscura and the ones who did weren't going to amount to much anyhow, so it remained a toy for several centuries.

Then, in the late 1700s and early 1800s, it occurred to several people, all around the same time, that if they could find some way to hold that light image that came through the tiny hole they would have something valuable, a system that recorded what they could see.

A Frenchman named Niepce was the one who did it first in 1826. He had a camera he designed made by an instrument-maker and he used a film he had invented himself. He set the camera on his windowsill in Paris and left it there for hours.

The picture he got was a roofscape, looking out over the eaves and chimneys of Paris. It wasn't very clear. In fact, you have to be told what's in it before you can recognize a pigeon coop and a tree and a patch of sky.

But it was, sure enough, a photograph. Except Niepce didn't call it that. He called it a heliograph, a sun picture.

Another Frenchman, a painter of theatre scenery named Louis Daguerre, heard about Niepce's experiments and wrote him suggesting they work together. And they got quite good at heliography rather quickly.

The head of science for the French government, an astronomer, heard about what they were doing and he had a brilliant idea. He arranged for the government to get the rights to all their work in exchange for giving them pensions.

That way, all their findings were published. Right away, everybody had access to them and could make improvements.

And it turned out that others in France, Germany and England had been tinkering around with the same ideas. Within a couple of years they had advanced the new science remarkably.

One of the Englishmen didn't like the word heliography. He preferred photography, light picture. That was the name that stuck.

A German put a lens in the little hole where the light came in and the time required to take a picture dropped from hours to seconds.

By the time the Crimean War got going in the 1850s, photographers could go just about anywhere and some of their war pictures from Crimea are still impressive. Mind you, their equipment was so bulky and the developing process so cumbersome that they had to have a horse and wagon to lug it around.

> *One Scottish photographer did brilliant work but his glass plates for capturing the image were so big they weighed 44 pounds. That's more than a case of beer.*

One Scottish photographer did brilliant work but his glass plates for capturing the image were so big they weighed 44 pounds. That's more than a case of beer.

But each year, got smaller and handier. Then, in the United States, a moody young bank clerk named George Eastman started making film to capture the picture by smearing the chemicals on rolls of celluloid.

On the 4th of September in 1888, Eastman patented his film, plus a name he had invented for it. He wanted a word that had a sharp, precise, businesslike sound but didn't mean anything in any language. He called it Kodak. The customer took 100 pictures then sent the camera to the factory and got his snapshots back. Kodak's motto was: "You press the button, we do the rest."

And within a dozen years, one American in 10 owned a camera.

Originally broadcast September 4, 1991

FIGHTING GENDER ROLES

Emma Edmonds is also known to history as Sarah Seely. And that's appropriate because Emma, or Sarah, made her mark in the history books because of a double life.

She served in the American Civil War as a soldier, one of 40- or 50,000 Canadians who fought in that war. But she served as Private Frank Thompson in a regiment of Michigan infantry.

Sarah Emma Edmonds was born in New Brunswick on a farm near the town of Magundy. Except back in those days there was no Magundy and the Edmonds farm was away out in the bush. That was in 1841.

Father Edmonds seems to have been a bit of a psycho. He had five girls and a boy. What he really wanted was six boys. The one boy was sickly and epileptic. Maybe that's why he let Sarah Emma grow up a tomboy, a girl who could ride a horse and shoot a rifle and do all the boyish things.

Old man Edmonds was very much the 19th century biblical father, demanding the girls wait on him like servants and treating his wife like something God had given him so he wouldn't have to do any of life's menial tasks.

When Emma was a teenager, she ran away, probably to be free of the old man. The family wrote a lot of letters back and forth and we have many of them. But like most Victorian families, they carefully avoided any open mention of family scandal.

Today, we would have to consider that Emma might have been a homosexual. But there appears to be no evidence of that. Remember, back in those days, women didn't hold down jobs away from home, they didn't travel alone, they didn't go out in public unless accompanied by another woman or a husband or brother . . . life was vastly different.

Emma went to Michigan and made her living, dressed as a young man, as a traveling salesman of bibles. When the Civil War broke out, she was shocked that all the young men didn't rush to join the army, to fight for the cause of anti-slavery. She

considered it un-Christian.

So Emma joined the army in 1861 at the outset of the Civil War. A lot of women did, several hundred at least. In most cases, they wanted to be with their husbands or boyfriends. Many were found out, many weren't. I can't help but wonder if a lot of people didn't turn a blind eye.

In later years, some of Emma's old comrades said they knew all along that she was a girl but figured she had reasons of her own for wanting to do what she did.

> *Some of Emma's old comrades said they knew all along that she was a girl but figured she had reasons for wanting to do what she did.*

Emma served in the first half of the civil war in some of the worst battles. She also worked as a nurse and a mail clerk.

She got quite friendly with a couple of senior officers, one of them a brigadier named Poe.

She began spying for the army, slipping through the enemy lines and bringing back reports. In fact, in 1863, she posed as a woman — if a woman posing as a man posing as a woman can be called posing. She brought back valuable information that resulted in the Union army capturing the city of Yorktown, although it was later lost.

Emma left the army, just walked away from it halfway through the war and wrote about her experiences. Her book was a bestseller but she gave all the money to military hospitals.

In later years, she married a man from, of all places, Saint John, New Brunswick. His name was Linus Seely and she then began using her other name, Sarah, maybe because she liked alliterative names, Emma Edmonds and Sarah Seely.

In 1882, she applied for an army pension and had to put all this on the record. At that time, several of her old comrades in arms invited her to one of their reunions. But Sarah later said it was quite embarrassing, that many of their wives, especially the wife of Brigadier Poe, treated her as if she'd been carrying on with their husband all through the war.

When Sarah died on the fifth of September in 1898, she was the only woman member of the Civil War Veterans' Association.

Originally broadcast September 5, 1985

SUB MISSION

In the late summer of 1776, things looked grim for the Americans who had rebelled against the king of England. They had managed to chase the British army out of Boston, but the British had arrived at New York with one huge fleet and an army that was twice the size of the Americans'.

And that British army was a good, professional one. The American army was a pretty sorry organization.

But what worried the Americans most was that British fleet. They figured if they could drag a war out long enough, they would have to win because they were on their home ground. The British had to supply their army over a 3,000 mile ocean.

But they would have to do something about that British navy. In the New York area alone, the British had 350 ships manned by 10,000 sailors. And they were very good.

In late August that fleet landed troops and badly beat the Americans in a hilly countryside that's now downtown Brooklyn. The Americans managed to escape under cover of night.

As the American generals were standing around, wondering what to do, up stepped a man named David Bushnell. He said he thought he could get rid of the British fleet with a machine he'd invented. He called it the submarine.

Bushnell was a strange man and we know very little about him. He was a Connecticut farmer who sold his share of the family farm to his brother and used the money to go to college. He enrolled at Yale when he was 31.

In the spring of 1775, when college stopped for the holidays, Bushnell and his brother went to work on his idea for a sub. They didn't have the time or money for plans or a model so they just started hammering.

The machine they came up with looked rather like two turtle shells clamped together. So they called it the Turtle. It would hold just one man and he made it go by turning a crank that operated a driveshaft with a propeller on it.

It sank and rose when the operator pumped leather bags that pulled in and forced out water. It had a long screw auger that looked vaguely like a wood drill. That would be used to screw the Turtle tight against the bottom of a British ship. Then the one-man crew would set a time bomb and get out as best he could. The time bomb would go off in about a half-hour or so and blow up anything around.

Bushnell himself wasn't a strong enough man to operate the sub. It took a lot of muscle power. His brother could operate it well. But he fell ill with a fever that had afflicted the whole American army about that time. So they quickly trained a young sergeant named Ezra Lee.

Just after midnight on the 6th of September in 1776 in New York harbour, Lee and the Turtle were towed as close as they could get to the British flagship, a huge battleship called the Eagle. Lee then drifted with the current and cranked his propeller furiously until he was under the Eagle.

He couldn't get the Turtle attached to the Eagle because the bottom of the British ship was copper-covered to protect the wooden hull against sea worms.

Actually, if he'd had enough time, his screw attachment would have bored through the soft copper. But daylight was coming and Lee was running out of air in the Turtle. So he drifted away.

At the same time he cut loose his time bomb, which had 150 pounds of gunpowder in it. That bomb went off with such a crash that the whole British fleet scattered. Nobody was hurt, but the British were badly scared.

The Turtle had come very close to being a success.

We don't know what happened to the Turtle. Some say Bushnell sank it so the British wouldn't capture it. And for years we didn't know what happened to Bushnell. Then, some old papers discovered in Georgia in 1884 cleared up that mystery. He went back to Yale, graduated in medicine, and changed his name to Bush. Then he moved to Georgia and spent the rest of his life practicing medicine in a little, out-of-the-way town. But we don't know what he was running from.

The machine they came up with looked rather like two turtle shells clamped together. So they called it the Turtle.

Originally broadcast September 6, 1984

CANADIAN MARTYRS

Today should be an annual school holiday. And it should be called Pickersgill Day, after the bravest Canadian who died in the Second World War.

Frank Pickersgill was a big, awkward, very clever man from Winnipeg who was doing postgraduate work in Paris when the war broke out.

That was in the fall of 1939. At first, the war didn't cause any change in his life. He wrote to his brother Jack, then the secretary of Mackenzie King, the prime minister of Canada, saying he couldn't see any point in joining the army. He said he couldn't see an awful lot to choose between the British and the Germans. He figured both were corrupt.

Then, in the spring of 1940, the Germans suddenly invaded France and grabbed Paris in a couple of weeks. Pickersgill got on a bike, with two dollars in his pocket, and tried to get away. A Frenchman hid him out in the country, but the Germans caught up with him late that summer.

He was locked up in an internment camp for civilians from various Commonwealth countries. But on the way there, while he was being held in a little country French jail, he saw two German guards beat a Frenchman to death with their rifle butts.

That made up his mind. The British might not be perfect, but the Nazis were animals.

Pickersgill stayed in that internment camp for 15 months. Then, in March of 1942, with help from the French underground and a hacksaw blade smuggled to him in a loaf of bread, Pickersgill got away.

He hid in France for six months, helped by French patriots and an American woman he knew who was living in France. He got to England in October of 1942.

He immediately enlisted in the Canadian army and was assigned to the British. The first time he appeared on the street in his lieutenant's uniform a couple of military policemen arrested him. He'd put on the right tunic and pants but he was wearing a dark blue shirt and a civilian tie with them. Pickersgill just never did take to soldiering in the official sense.

All that winter, Pickersgill was trained by British intelligence in codes, espionage and sabotage. Then, in June of 1943, he was parachuted into France.

Within a week he was betrayed by somebody in the French resistance and the Gestapo got him.

He was thrown into jail and tortured. Pickersgill wasn't alone. He had another Canadian with him, John Macalister from Guelph, Ontario. Neither man told the Germans anything.

After the war, investigators found a message scratched there by Pickersgill and he wrote that he'd been told he'd been condemned to death less than two weeks after he'd been captured. But he wasn't to be executed right away. He couldn't understand that.

Pickersgill and Macalister were sent to Auschwitz concentration camp that winter. In the spring of 1944, just skin and bones, they were taken to Paris to be questioned by the Gestapo again. Again, they didn't say anything.

Pickersgill knocked out a guard with a bottle and made a break for it. He jumped 30 feet out of a window and broke his ankle when he landed. The Germans shot him twice, but he kept running. They finally stopped him with another shot.

He and Macalister were then sent to Buchenwald, the worst of the concentration camps. There, Pickersgill became a soldier. He insisted on marching in step like a soldier. He wouldn't give in.

On the night of the sixth of September in 1944 the camp loudspeaker named 16 prisoners and ordered them to report to the guards. Pickersgill lined them up and marched them away singing *Alouette* and *Tipperary*.

On the morning of the seventh they were all executed.

> *At first Pickersgill couldn't see any point in joining the army — there wasn't an awful lot to choose between the British and the Germans.*

Originally broadcast September 7, 1984

UNDER THE INFLUENZA

In early 1918, there were outbreaks of a serious cold-like disease in army camps in the western United States and in Britain.

Half a dozen times in the 1800s, versions of this same disease had swept the world. When epidemics cover more than one country, the doctors call them pandemics. And these were serious pandemics.

Because the First World War was on at the time, the outbreaks in Britain and the States were kept secret by military censors. Spain wasn't involved in the war so the outbreak there became the first to be widely reported. So, the disease became known by what the Spanish called it, influenza, or as we say today, the flu.

The war was winding down and ships bringing soldiers home docked in Montreal, Quebec and Halifax. The army doctors put sick soldiers in military hospitals and kept them there and that seemed to limit the spread at first.

But it spread to some places. Four hundred of the 410 live-in students at Victoriaville College in Quebec came down with it.

The school couldn't cope so it shut down and sent the students home. That did it. The flu spread throughout Quebec and half-a-million people caught it. More than 13,000 died.

By the time Quebec authorities realized what a crisis they had on their hands, it had spread to Ontario. From there, to the Prairies. Returning soldiers didn't like being cooped up in military hospitals after being overseas for years and lots of them just slipped away and spread it when they got home.

The flu itself wasn't what killed people. But it left them so weak they were sitting ducks for pneumonia. And in those days before penicillin, pneumonia was a big killer.

Nobody knew what to do, but everybody had a theory. Heavy drinkers seemed to catch it less than most, so some said booze was the answer. But Prohibition had just been passed and there wasn't much good booze available, though there was lots of the bootleg stuff.

All sorts of crazy home remedies were tried. On the Prairies, they hung garlic around their necks. Some people sprinkled sulphur in their shoes on the theory that it killed germs.

All sorts of crazy home remedies were tried. On the Prairies, they hung garlic around their necks.

Some people sprinkled sulphur in their shoes on the theory that it killed germs.

There was already a shortage of doctors and nurses because of the war. Volunteers tried to fill in and many of them worked themselves so hard they had no resistance when the flu hit.

By Christmas of 1918, the government of Alberta passed a law requiring everyone who went outdoors to wear a gauze surgical mask. Nobody knows to this day if it worked. Some say it stopped the spread of germs. Some say the masks themselves became germ catchers.

One Canadian in four caught the flu and 50,000 died. That was when the population was less than a third of what it is today.

Around the world, the flu killed millions, more than the First World War.

Originally broadcast September 8, 1993

COLOR BLINDNESS

John Howard Griffin packed more fantastic adventure into 60 years than would fill a shelf-full of novels.

He was born in Texas in 1920 and for no reason he could ever explain, he wanted to be educated in France. He wrote to a high school there, saying he would do anything, even scrub floors, to get a French education. The principal of the school wrote back: If you can get here, we'll educate you.

When the Second World War broke out in 1939, Griffin was still in France, studying medicine. He was put in charge of a ward in a mental hospital when all the doctors were hustled into the army. German and Austrian Jews fled to France ahead of the German army and the death camps. Griffin put them in straight-jackets and had them evacuated to England, disguised as mental patients. When France fell, he escaped.

When Griffin got back to the States he was put in the American Army and sent to the South Pacific. He was hit in the head by shrapnel and seemed to be dead. Just as they were about to bury him, somebody noticed he was breathing.

Griffin appeared to recover with just a sensitivity to light that made his eyes sore. That meant he couldn't study for long so he dropped his plan to be a doctor and returned to France to study medieval music. But his sight kept failing and, by 1947, Griffin was blind.

He returned to Texas and for 10 years made a good living as a livestock breeder, impressing everybody by his skill despite his blindness. Then, suddenly, in a flash, one day after 10 years of blindness, his sight returned.

Griffin couldn't go into a decent restaurant, he had to use the "Blacks Only" washrooms in bus stations, and he often couldn't find anywhere to get a drink of water.

Griffin became a writer and went to work for a black magazine called *Sepia*. As a white Texan he had always taken segregation for granted. But now, working on a black magazine, he started to wonder how blacks really felt about being second-class citizens.

Griffin took a drug that darkens the skin and shaved his head to change his appearance, then wandered around the South. He was a shoe-shine boy in New Orleans and a manual labourer in several places. Whenever he applied for an office job he wasn't even given an interview.

He couldn't go into a decent restaurant, he had to use the "Blacks Only" washrooms in bus stations, and he often couldn't find anywhere to get a drink of water.

Griffin only did that for a month or so. But he had enough material for a series of articles in *Sepia*. He later wrote a book he called *Black Like Me*.

It was a sensational bestseller. John Kennedy had just been elected president and *Black Like Me* was a major factor in his commitment to ending segregation. Kennedy and his brother Bobby, the attorney-general, sent the FBI into the south to gather evidence and make cases against racists, enforcing the federal laws that outlawed segregation that local cops wouldn't enforce.

Griffin was a convert to Catholicism and a religious mystic, and he spent the rest of his life working on a biography of the 20th century Catholic philosopher, Thomas Merton. But he never got it finished. He died at the age of 60 on the 9th of September in 1980.

Originally broadcast September 9, 1993

GAMBLING ON GUADALCANAL

In December of 1941, the Second World War had been going in Europe for two years and the Japanese invasion of China had been going on for four years. The Japanese won every battle, but they couldn't finish off the Chinese. They just couldn't cope with all that geography and all that population.

So, they decided to gamble everything on one last chance. They would suddenly attack the Americans, the French, the British and the Dutch in Asia.

On the first Sunday morning in December of 1941, while most western soldiers and sailors in Asia were sleeping off their hangovers, the Japanese struck. They sank much of the American fleet in Hawaii. They launched the attacks that, in just a few months, would take French Indochina, the Philippines, the British colonies of Hong Kong, Malaya, Singapore and the South Sea Islands, and the Dutch East Indies, what today we call Indonesia.

The Japanese were invincible. Nothing could stop them. They captured the biggest naval base in the world, at Singapore, although the defenders outnumbered them.

In the next couple of months, the Americans managed to squeak out a couple of important victories at sea. But on land, nobody could stop the Japanese.

They landed an army in New Guinea, the big island just north of Australia, and their planes bombed the northern Australian city of Darwin. They landed forces in the Solomon Islands, a bunch of jungly British colonies that controlled the route from the American base at Hawaii to Australia. If they took all the Solomons, the Americans would have trouble coming to help the Australians when they were invaded.

The main island in the Solomons was called Guadalcanal. The Japanese took a couple of small islands nearby and landed a thousand men with orders to build an airfield. If they got that airfield operating, they would be able to bomb American and Australian targets.

So the Americans decided they would start their counteroffensive, the one intended to win the Pacific back, on Guadalcanal. Although neither side knew it, both planned to invade Guadalcanal on the same day in early August.

The American admirals assigned the task to a Marine division and a few squadrons of planes. On paper, there would be 19,000 men in the force. In fact, they had fewer than that. And many had been civilians only six months earlier.

The Marine general in command of the operation was so short of everything he called it Operation Shoestring. The admiral in charge of putting the force ashore thought it had such a slim chance that he sailed his ships away as soon as the Marines were landed. He wanted to be out of the way when the trouble started.

The Japanese airfield builders had done a great job. The Marines were able to capture the field, fully equipped with supplies, radio links, a dock to land supplies, and a road to move them.

The Americans managed to squeak out a couple of important victories at sea. But on land, nobody could stop the Japanese.

Then the main Japanese force arrived. On land, the Marines could hold them off, although just barely. There was seven months of fierce jungle fighting.

At sea, the Japanese swarmed all over the American navy. They sank so many American ships off Guadalcanal that the Americans said they lined the ocean floor and even today that stretch of sea is called Iron Bottom Sound.

In the air, the battle swung one way, then another until the Americans finally won.

The absolute low point for the Americans came on the 10th of September in 1942. Of the hundreds of planes they had thrown into the battle, only 11 were left. But they were reinforced and slowly they took command of the air. The superb Japanese navy controlled the sea but never completely.

In February of 1943, the battle of Guadalcanal was finally over. The Japanese victories had ended and ahead was a long string of defeats.

Originally broadcast September 10, 1991

SEW WHAT

Elias Howe was a desperately poor man. By the time he was 20, Howe had a wife and three kids and a dead-end job in a machine shop in Boston.

One day he heard a customer saying to his boss that anyone who could invent a workable sewing machine would make a fortune.

From that day on, Howe ate, drank, slept and thought about nothing else. Until then he had seemed a morose, beaten man. Now, his wife and kids and neighbours found out he was also a desperate man.

One night Howe fell asleep after working for hours on a sewing machine that wouldn't work. He had a nightmare. He dreamed he was captured by a bunch of fierce cannibals who gave him 24 hours to come up with a sewing machine. He couldn't do it. They came for him to put him in the pot, all armed with spears. Not ordinary spears, but spears with little holes near the points.

Howe jumped out of bed and started sketching. He moved the hole in the needle from the blunt end to near the point. When he tried it, it worked. Not perfectly by any means, but it worked.

Howe's machine would make 250 stitches a minute, many times more than the best seamstress. But it couldn't sew in a straight line for very long, the thread kept breaking and the cloth kept bunching up.

Nobody was interested. But he got a patent on it on the 11th of September in 1846.

Then Howe packed up his family and sailed to England. There, he interested a corsetmaker in his invention. The corsetmaker bought the rights to the machine and hired Howe to work in his factory, perfecting it. Once he did that, the corsetmaker fired him.

He borrowed money to send his wife and kids back to the States. He had to stay several more months in England to make enough to get back himself.

When he returned to Boston almost a year later, he found his wife had died and the ship carrying their clothes and furniture had been wrecked. They had no insurance.

He also discovered that another American, Isaac Singer, had taken his invention and improved on it.

If Howe was a character, Singer was even more so because of his lifestyle.

Singer was, like Howe, a genius with his hands. But he didn't care for machine shop work. He preferred to be an actor. He'd only been to school a few months in his life, but he could spout hours and hours of Shakespeare.

He had an actor's flair for the good life. And an actor's attraction for women. Singer would eventually have 24 children by five women. He was actually married to two of them for a while.

Howe and Singer got into a strange sort of partnership. Singer said he didn't need Howe, and he probably didn't. But that 1846 patent of Howe's presented all sorts of legal problems. It was easier to join him than fight him.

Howe was paid a few thousand dollars and a royalty on every sewing machine built. There were years of legal battles. Others had invented sewing machines of one sort and another, a couple even earlier than Howe, although he held the first patent in the States.

Howe just drifted through life and didn't do anything very spectacular with his money. Singer built mansions in New York, moved in and out with his various women, moved to Paris, then to England then back to the States. Sixteen of his children survived him, and among them, they had 35 marriages — nobody knows how many kids. The lawsuits over the will went on for a dozen or more years after Singer died. There was plenty of money to fight over.

> *Howe dreamed he was captured by a bunch of fierce cannibals who gave him 24 hours to come up with a sewing machine. He couldn't do it.*

Originally broadcast September 11, 1989

THE COLD-HEARTED COLONEL

The most famous duel in modern British history occurred on Wimbledon Common in London on the 12th of September in 1840, at exactly 5 p.m. The two men involved were Lord Cardigan, the most hated man in England, and Captain Harvey Tuckett, a retired army officer who became a wealthy merchant.

Lord Cardigan was one of the richest men in England and the boss of the 11th Hussars, by far the classiest regiment in the British army.

Cardigan had always wanted to be a cavalry officer, but his father had forbidden him to join the army until the Napoleonic Wars were over. That made him a bitter man.

In those days, a rich man could buy himself command of a regiment. When Cardigan finally got permission to join the army, he bought the 15th Hussars and installed himself as colonel.

He spent a fortune on horses and uniforms. But he was an impossible officer, a short-tempered man who despised anyone who wasn't rich.

In 1834, he began persecuting one of his officers, a man named Captain Withen. Withen was an excellent officer and it was soon clear to everybody in the regiment that Cardigan had some sort of personal vendetta against him. When Cardigan wouldn't let up, Withen demanded Cardigan be court-martialled.

The court martial quickly made it clear that Captain Withen was a good officer and Colonel Cardigan was a nut. Withen was acquitted and Cardigan, although he wasn't even charged, was removed from command of the 15th Hussars.

But he was determined to run his own regiment and he used his considerable influence with the queen to get another regiment. This time, in spite of an awful howl in the press, he bought command of the 11th Hussars. Here he was, only two years after being found unfit to command a regiment, in command of one.

The papers described Cardigan as everything that was wrong with the British army and they watched him closely.

In the spring of 1840, the 11th Hussars were stationed at Canterbury in the south of England. One day, some of the junior officers were fooling around and they galloped their horses through a field of standing grain near the camp. The owner of the field wrote Cardigan. Cardigan, of course, felt it beneath his dignity to enter into correspondence with a farmer. So he ignored the letter. The farmer gave his letter to the newspapers and soon Lord Cardigan was on all the front pages again.

Then a retired officer named Captain Tuckett wrote another letter, this one to the editor of the *Chronicle*. It accused Lord Cardigan of having insulted one of his officers then having refused to fight a duel with him when it was demanded. The officer involved obviously couldn't take such a gentlemanly affair to the papers, so Captain Tuckett, as a retired army man, was doing it for him.

Well, Cardigan might have been a fool, but he was no coward. He immediately challenged Tuckett to a duel and that's the one that was fought on the 12th of September in 1840.

Tuckett was shot in the lower right rib but recovered without any great trouble. Lord Cardigan was charged with dueling.

Now the charge of dueling was a serious one. In fact, if even one drop of blood was shed in a duel, the sentence was death. And there certainly had been blood shed.

The powers that be didn't charge Cardigan with shedding blood, just with intending to duel. As a lord, he was entitled to be tried by the house of lords, not by an ordinary jury. All the lords looked at their fellow nobleman and figured, that could be me standing there, so they acquitted him.

The papers let out a terrible howl.

Did that end Lord Cardigan's career as commander of the 11th Hussars? Well, yes it did. He moved from there to another fashionable cavalry regiment, the Light Brigade. And 13 years later he led them in the most famous charge in military history. He got most of them killed, 525 out of 700, in less than 20 minutes. But Lord Cardigan rode away without a scratch.

> *The papers described Cardigan as everything that was wrong with the British army and they watched him closely.*

Originally broadcast September 12, 1985

DANCES WITH WOLFE

In 1758, the British captured the great French fortress of Louisburg on Cape Breton Island. The French had spent more than 20 years building it and it should have been able to defend itself for years. It fell in a few weeks.

One of the deputy-commanders of the expedition was James Wolfe, a 31-year-old general in the British army.

The king of England decided that, with Louisburg out of the way, he could now send an army to capture Quebec. And he chose Wolfe as commander.

Right away, there was an awful fuss. Many generals were senior to Wolfe and they protested. One even accused Wolfe of being mad. "If so," said the king, "I hope he bites some of the other generals. They could do with whatever he suffers from."

No question about it, James Wolfe was a bit of an oddball. He was tall and skinny, with practically no chin at all. His skin was paper-white and his hair was bright red.

He was a hypochondriac, a man who would be popping pills today. In those days, he was a sucker for every phony medicine on the market. In fact, some modern doctors have suggested most of his medical problems came from his addiction to quack remedies.

Wolfe was given an army of 8500 soldiers. It was carried by a big fleet under an excellent admiral named Charles Saunders. Saunders sailed up the St. Lawrence River and put Wolfe's army ashore just outside Quebec, most on the opposite shore, some a few miles downstream from the city.

It was a superb feat of navigation. The French had been sailing in and out of Quebec for 150 years and they still couldn't do it that smartly.

Wolfe set up guns and the siege began. But the French were alert and their commander, the Marquis Montcalm, moved his army to counter every move of Wolfe's.

It was the sort of plan that could fall apart over any tiny detail. Somebody sneezing in the middle of the night could ruin everything.

Wolfe sent out scouts and they reported that the French outposts were thinnest just upstream from the city. The reason was obvious: the riverbanks there were high cliffs. Any man who attacked up there would be slaughtered as soon as the defenders saw them coming.

And that was the key to Wolfe's plan. He would send a small party up the cliffs at night when the French couldn't see them coming. Once they were at the top, they would suddenly attack the French posts and hold the heights until the rest of the army could follow.

It was the sort of plan that could fall apart over any tiny detail. Somebody sneezing in the middle of the night could ruin everything. Nevertheless, that's the plan Wolfe went with, and it worked.

The attack began quietly at 9:00 on the night of the 13th of September in 1759. Twelve hundred men were moved in boats to the south shore of the St. Lawrence, right opposite the point of the attack.

The boats that left them there went back and got the one company of soldiers under three officers who would make that first attack.

French sentries challenged them in the dark, but the officers all spoke French and convinced them they were French reinforcements arriving to take over.

They managed to pull their way to the top of the cliffs and jump the surprised French guards. Then the boats went back for those 1200 men who had been stashed just across the water.

When the French realized what had happened, their army poured out of Quebec City. But it was too late. The British army had gone ashore, up the cliffs and all formed up on the Plains of Abraham outside the city walls.

By noon, it was over. Quebec was no longer a French colony.

Originally broadcast September 13, 1990

ELBE ROOM

About the year zero, when the calendar we now use stops measuring in BC and begins AD, the Romans had the greatest empire the world had ever seen. The ruler was Augustus Caesar, a superb administrator and a man of vision. Augustus expanded the Roman Empire in just about every direction.

Then he fortified the borders and began what he saw as his real work: the task of building roads and harbours and cities and imposing Roman law on the whole huge mass, an area as big as all Canada is today.

In the northeast, Augustus figured he would use the Elbe River as his border. The province of Gaul, which has since become France, ran east to the Rhine River. The Elbe was the next main north-south river to the east, a couple of hundred miles further on.

This was wild country, mostly forest, inhabited by a dozen fierce tribes. The Romans sent armies into the area and the Roman administrators tried to make friends with some of those fierce Germans. They had a lot of success with a tribe called the Cherusci who lived in what's now northern Germany.

The Cherusci had two princes who were their leaders. The Romans called them Arminius and Flavius. Arminius' German name was Herman. We don't even know what Flavius' original name was. He became such an enthusiastic Roman that he moved to northern Italy and settled down and became the Roman Flavius.

Arminius was a handsome, blond giant who acted as a scout and middleman for the Romans in their dealings with the tribes of the wild east.

He was an important part of Augustus' plan to extend the Roman Empire, and Roman civilization, east to the Elbe.

Another important man in this plan was a Roman officer named Varus. Varus had distinguished himself, both as a soldier and an administrator, in putting down a Jewish revolt in Palestine. Augustus was so impressed that he transferred him to Germany to handle things there.

Varus soon was using Arminius as his right hand man. In the summer of 9 AD, Arminius went on a scouting mission into the forests in what's now north-central Germany. He returned slightly wounded himself and reported two of his men had also been wounded and one of their horses had been stolen by hostile tribesmen.

He suggested that Varus return with him into the area with his whole army and teach the people there a lesson.

It impressed Varus as a great idea. He set out in September of 9 AD with 20,000 men in three legions.

The legions were the most powerful formations in the Roman army, what we would today call divisions. They were self-sufficient and had their own engineering and baggage units. No military formation in the world could stand up to a Roman legion. A few disorganized tribesmen wouldn't stand a chance against three of them.

A couple of days out, in a dense wilderness called the Teutoberger Forest, the Germans attacked. Their attack was superbly planned and executed.

No wonder. It had been all worked out, a year or more in advance, by Arminius, the German the Romans thought they owned.

Every last man of those 20,000 Romans was killed. It was the most stunning defeat in the history of the Roman Empire.

It's hard to pin down the exact date. But historians agree that either Varus set out on the 14th of September in 9 AD, or that was the day his army was attacked and massacred.

When word reached Rome, Augustus gave up his plans to extend the empire to the Elbe. He pulled back to the Rhine. And for the next 1800 years, the German tribes were left alone to put together their own society, quite different from the rest of Europe.

> *No military formation in the world could stand up to a Roman legion. A few disorganized tribesmen wouldn't stand a chance against three of them.*

Originally broadcast September 14, 1990

WHEN STOCKS WENT SKY-HIGH

At just one minute past noon on the 15th of September in 1920, a bomb went off on Wall Street, the main drag of American finance. Thirty-eight people were killed or later died of wounds. Several hundred were severely injured. To this day, nobody knows who planted the bomb or why.

In 1920 there were lots of cars and trucks on the road, but a lot of freight was still moved by horses and wagons. A small wagon with stake sides, pulled by one horse, pulled to a stop in front of the offices of J.P. Morgan, the king of American finance. Across the street was the Treasury Building with $900 million worth of gold in the vaults. And that's where the bomb went off.

A Morgan employee who was standing at the window was killed instantly. But it couldn't have been a bunch of anarchists out to kill Morgan. He was away in Europe at the time and his movements were well known. There were items about him in the newspapers almost daily.

It couldn't have been a gang of robbers intending to make off with all that gold in the Treasury vault. In the confusion that followed this explosion, they would have taken the whole Treasury Building. But no attempt was made on the gold.

The local police and the secret service from Washington put hundreds of detectives on the job. Police investigations weren't very thorough in those days. But this one was.

All that was left of the horse who had pulled the wagon that blew up was two horseshoes and a pile of horsemeat. One of the horseshoes was traced to a blacksmith. He had shod the horse only a few days earlier. But he was a funny old guy who could describe the horse in great detail but not the owner. It turned out that was a peculiarity of his. Everybody who knew him told the police he could describe horses he'd shod 30 years ago. But he couldn't tell you about the owner of the horse he was working on right now.

There was a big Communist scare on at the time. There always is on Wall Street. Several well-known communists were rounded up but they all proved they were nowhere near the scene.

Witnesses were useless. Several described seeing wild-eyed foreign-looking people just after the explosion. But everybody was wild-eyed after being through that blast.

The Pittsburgh police came up with a great suspect. He spoke Russian and was reading a Russian newspaper when they kicked in the hotel room. Or so they thought. The newspaper turned out to be Polish, not Russian, and it was a Catholic, not a communist, paper. The man was a devout Catholic and very anti-communist. But the Pittsburgh cops still liked him as a suspect and held him for weeks.

Experts even looked at the grass in the stomach of the horse that pulled the wagon. They agreed it wasn't from a New York stable. Some said it was from a pasture in New Jersey, others claimed New England. It would have been a tired horse that had pulled that wagon all the way to Wall Street from either. For a couple of years, the police announced from time to time that they had new clues. But today they don't know any more about who planted that bomb than they did the day it happened.

> *Several described seeing wild-eyed foreign-looking people just after the explosion. But everybody was wild-eyed after being through that blast.*

Originally broadcast September 15, 1988

LAW OF AVERAGES

Andrew Bonar Law was born in New Brunswick on the 16th of September in 1858. His father was a Presbyterian clergyman, an Irishman, a strange man who would probably be diagnosed by a modern doctor as depressed.

Bonar Law's mother was a gay, laughing woman, just the opposite of his gloomy father. She intended to name her child Robert, after a famous Scottish clergyman. But she was already mother of one Robert, so she couldn't do that. As a compromise, she named him after the writer who had done a biography of the clergyman she admired so much, and his name was Andrew Bonar.

Bonar Law's mother died when he was just a baby. His aunt raised him. When Bonar Law was 12, his father remarried and the aunt took him aboard a ship and sailed for Scotland. He never returned to Canada. In Scotland, Bonar Law went to school, where he was rather dull, then into business as a banker and later as a hardware wholesaler.

His aunt, her cousins and his own sister all lived with Bonar Law in three houses all together in a little dead-end.

There was a lot of money in the family but no wit or cheer. All were devout teetotalers, devoted to work, suspicious of anything that smacked of frivolity or laughter.

When he was 33, Bonar Law met a rich young woman who was just his opposite — gay, laughing, a big fan of dances and parties.

Bonar Law changed completely. Or, so it seemed for a while. He took to the gay life to please her. Once he even got dressed up as a sailor to take her to a masquerade. She went as a Swiss milkmaid.

Bonar Law's friends heaved a sigh of relief. They were afraid he was going to spend his whole life as a chain-smoking workaholic, only taking time out for a game of chess or bridge now and again.

As soon as the gay young lady agreed to marry, Bonar Law reverted to his real dull self and never changed for the rest of his life.

As the various relatives from his dull youth died,

> *Bonar Law had the same dull, bleak, unimaginative approach to the House of Commons as he did to the rest of his life.*

Bonar Law became quite wealthy from the money they left him.

In the 1890s Bonar Law gave up business and went into politics as a Conservative. He had the same dull, bleak, unimaginative approach to the House of Commons as he did to the rest of his life.

Bonar Law's closest friend was Max Aitken, another New Brunswicker who had gone to Britain and was doing well. Aitken was the opposite, a brisk, cheerful, outgoing man. He was always after Bonar Law to smile and try to get along with people. He once told Bonar Law he was a great man.

Bonar Law just looked bored and said, "If I'm great, then an awful lot of great men have been frauds." That's as close to a smart crack as he ever made.

Bonar Law made it to the leadership of the British Conservative Party by sheer hard work. When he was chosen, the whole world was amazed. Some very bright men had been after the job.

During the First World War, two of Bonar Law's boys were killed within six months. His wife took sick and died when she was only 45. His sister, just as glum and strange as he was, took over and raised the children.

In the 1920s, Britain was going through strange times, still a major world power, but no longer in complete control of the Empire.

Somehow, in those upside down times, Andrew Bonar Law became prime minister of England. He only served seven months then had to resign. He was dying of cancer of the throat from a lifetime of cigarettes.

When he died, in 1923, he was buried at Westminster Abbey, the first prime minister buried there in 25 years. One of his pall-bearers said: "Appropriate. The Unknown Prime Minister now lies beside the Unknown Soldier."

In British history books, Andrew Bonar Law is rarely mentioned. In Canadian history books, he rates a footnote. He's the only person born in Canada who ever became prime minister of Britain.

Originally broadcast September 16, 1991

THE AMERICAN EMPEROR

Joshua Norton was born in London, England in 1819. His father was a merchant who moved to South Africa and did very well. Young Joshua worked for the old man as a merchant and land developer in South Africa. Later, he sailed on his father's ship as it traded between South Africa and South America.

In 1849, he was running a branch of the family business in Brazil when he heard that gold had been found in California. He took his considerable fortune, $40,000, and moved to San Francisco.

In those boom days, a shrewd businessman could do well, and Joshua Norton did. He made money in bricks, tea, flour, coal and beer.

Then he took everything he had, a quarter-million dollars, and set out corner the market in rice. He bought at four cents a pound and held on, even after the price rose to 32 cents. Then, just as he had all the rice in San Francisco and was about to make the killing, several ships arrived with rice from South America.

Norton couldn't even get four cents a pound for it. He lost his fortune and in 1856 he went bankrupt.

Norton had always been a decent, gentle man, and people liked him. His friends stayed with him, even after he lost his luxurious mansion and had to move into a seedy room.

They would discuss business and politics by the hour. Norton was sincerely concerned with the state of the world. His friends took to calling him Emperor. Whether that was originally his idea or theirs, we don't know.

On the 17th of September in 1859, Norton walked into the newsroom of the *San Francisco Bulletin* and asked for the editor.

He handed him a proclamation in which he declared himself Norton the First, emperor of the United States.

The editor ran it in his paper without comment.

He ate in the best restaurants and wasn't given a bill. When he went to the theatre, again without paying, the audience all rose and saluted him.

The people of San Francisco loved the idea. Norton walked around town in a crazy outfit, an old army officer's uniform with a top hat that had a green plume. Often he carried a sword that had been presented to him by a blacksmith.

Ladies curtseyed and gentlemen bowed when they met Emperor Norton in the street. The emperor was in the streets daily, inspecting sidewalks and sewers, checking to make sure the horse-drawn buses were on schedule, discussing crime prevention with the cops.

When the American Civil War broke out, Norton sent telegrams to the leaders of both sides, ordering them to come to him immediately to have the matter settled.

He once walked into the state legislature, which was deadlocked over two men who wanted the same job. Norton spoke favorably about each then added he only knew one. So the legislature gave the job to the man Norton knew. It wasn't a bad appointment.

Norton would walk into a store and tell the storekeeper he was behind in his taxes. If the store was a small one, the storekeeper would pay a quarter. If he had a big store, he might pay as much as three dollars. If business was poor, the emperor would come back another day.

He ate in the best restaurants and wasn't given a bill. When he went to the theatre, again without paying, the audience all rose and saluted him.

Once, a rookie cop ran him in for vagrancy. The chief of police got out of bed and rushed down to the station to turn him loose with profuse apologies.

For almost 21 years, Emperor Norton was accepted and loved by the people of San Francisco. And when he dropped dead on the sidewalk one day in 1880, the whole town stopped. Norton the First was buried in a rosewood coffin with 10,000 mourners walking behind. Just like an emperor.

Originally broadcast September 17, 1990

CHANGING WITH THE TIMES

Henry Jarvis Raymond was a bright young man who went to college in New England then found his way to New York to make his fortune. He arrived about 1840. We don't know the exact date.

New York was emerging as the major city of North America. The brainy Americans from Boston and Philadelphia were all heading for New York.

Raymond wanted to be a newspaper publisher. So he sought out Horace Greeley, the best editor in town, and offered to work for him for nothing to learn the business.

That appealed to Greeley. No publisher in those days liked to pay reporters much. They still don't. But Greeley was unusually tight-fisted and took Raymond on.

In 1841, Greeley launched a new paper called the *Tribune*. It would become one of the major forces in American politics. Some say that Greeley's anti-slavery stand was so firm, and his Tribune editorials so effective, that they were a major factor in starting the American Civil War.

Raymond was a small man, with a neat black beard. Someone once wrote that the part of his face that showed was no bigger than a snuff box.

Raymond came up with his own type of shorthand and was soon a valuable fixture at the *Tribune* and its number one reporter.

Greeley had to break down and start paying him. Raymond was a tough bargainer and he held out for eight dollars a week, a wage that brought tears to Greeley's eyes.

The *Tribune* was a good, accurate but very opinionated newspaper. Mind you, that was common in those days. Readers expected to know where an editor stood and they would allow a few little white lies to advance the editor's point of view.

There were plenty of newspapers in New York. And, as the city became the centre of communications for all North America, they would be more and more important. Most of the news we get today was patterned on how those New York papers behaved in the mid-1800s.

Another major successful paper was the *Herald*, quite brightly written, the first one to give good, clear, accurate, detailed crime news.

And there was the *Sun*, bright, chatty, easy to read, not too concerned with accuracy. And there was a bunch of lesser ones.

Henry Raymond left Greeley's *Tribune* after a few years. He went into politics and became a big-time Republican, eventually the speaker of the New York state legislature before he was 30.

But, always, he remembered his initial ambition to start his own paper. With his brisk, business-like manner and his political connections, Raymond had no trouble attracting investors. He raised more than $100,000, a huge sum in those days.

On the 18th of September in 1851, the first edition of his new paper hit the streets of New York. He called it the *Times*. He started off selling it for two cents. The others were selling for one cent so he had to drop his price.

Pretty soon, Raymond's accurate reporting and careful writing found readership and his *Times* was as big as the other leading New York papers within a short time.

In 1861, when the American Civil War broke out, Raymond himself went south to cover the fighting. It began with a successful attack by the army of the North.

Raymond ran back to the telegraph office and soon had a story on the front page under the heading "Rebellion Crushed."

After Raymond left the field, the Southern army counter-attacked and won the battle, a crushing defeat for the North. But the *Times* got better and today is maybe the best newspaper in the world. But Raymond didn't see its success. He died at the age of 49.

> *Raymond's accurate reporting and careful writing found readership and his* Times *was as big as the other leading New York papers within a short time.*

Originally broadcast September 18, 1990

PRINCE CHARMING

The most colourful, exciting character in British history is Bonnie Prince Charlie. He was handsome, fearless, brave, a charmer, a man willing to endure any discomfort for the cause he believed in — for 14 months of his life.

The rest of the time he was arrogant, thoughtless, totally self-centred and so ill-tempered that he drove his supporters away.

In 1689, King James the Second, a Stuart and a Catholic, was driven out of England by his subjects. His son-in-law, William of Orange, became the next king. James' daughter, Ann, took the throne when William died. Ann had no children, so there was a dispute over who should be the king next.

James' son, also named James, landed and raised an army in 1715, but he was soon defeated and escaped again to exile in France.

There, he married a Polish princess and they had a son named Charles. Charles was tall, handsome, an excellent swordsman and rider. He was also sulky, vain, and hard to get along with.

In the summer of 1745, 30 years after his father had tried it, Prince Charles landed from a French ship on the coast of Scotland. The Highland Scots were eagerly waiting for him. They called him Bonnie Prince Charlie and they worshipped him.

The spoiled, nasty Prince Charles blossomed over the adulation of his people into Bonnie Prince Charlie, a good-natured young man who slept on the ground with his soldiers and shared what little food they had. He was a brave leader and, under him, the Scots won several battles against the British Army.

In fact, in the spring of 1746, Bonnie Prince Charlie led his army almost to London, sweeping the British aside.

If his luck had held, he would have been King

> *The spoiled, nasty Prince Charles blossomed over the adulation of his people into Bonnie Prince Charlie, a good-natured young man.*

Charles of England that summer. But the Scottish army was poorly disciplined and the British finally stopped them and drove them back. It all ended on the bloody battlefield of Culloden with Bonnie Prince Charlie standing to the end as his army melted around him.

At the last minute, he escaped into the heather with a couple of friends. The British were not graceful victors. They hunted down every Scotsman who had supported Charlie and hundreds who might have. Some were hanged, hundreds were thrown in jail, and thousands were exiled.

For months, Charlie slipped from one hiding place to another. Several times he was almost caught. But no one would betray him.

For three days he was disguised as a woman, the maid to Lady Flora Macdonald, the daughter of one of his supporters.

For weeks, he worked as a porter, dressed like a bum and making a few pennies a day lugging parcels.

The French navy kept ships off the coast all this time, ready to pick up Charlie if he could get to a beach and signal them. The British navy was patrolling the coast, chasing the French away.

Finally, after enough adventures to fill five books, Charlie got to the beach at a deserted place called Moidart on the 19th of September in 1746. It was the same place he'd landed 14 months earlier.

That night a boat picked him up and took him out to a French ship and he got away to rejoin his family on the Continent. He reverted to his old ways, lazy, nasty, arrogant, a thoroughly unpleasant person who alienated all his friends and eventually ruined his cause. No other Stuart was ever a serious threat again to the British throne. But for 14 months, he'd been the stuff legends are made of.

Originally broadcast September 19, 1986

GREECE IS THE WORD

Of the thousands of battles that man has fought since the beginning of time, only a few really settled anything. And the battle of Salamis is one. Some say it is *the* one.

It happened in Greece in 480 BC, on the 20th of September. At that time, the mightiest empire the world had ever seen was the Persian Empire. It stretched from India to Turkey. It took in several dozen countries and peoples, some of them very civilized.

The next major people to the west were the Greeks. They weren't one nation by any means. In fact, they had almost as many little cities and states in what's now Greece as the Persians had in their mighty empire. The Greeks were great squabblers, always debating every minor point and going to war among themselves over the most trivial things.

When Xerxes, king of the Persians, decided to invade Greece, everybody figured it was over for the Greeks. They were outnumbered by an incredible margin. Also, the Persians were a very military people and they'd built their empire by beating every army they met.

If the Persians had conquered the Greeks, our civilization would be vastly different from what it is today. The Greeks were curious, they were inquisitive, and they questioned authority. Just as we do.

The Persians were primarily an oriental people, with a society and religions that functioned to help millions of people live close together — usually by accepting whatever fate sent them and not rebelling against whoever was in power.

Some historian once said it was the difference between European hunters and Asian rice-growers.

Previous Persian kings had tried to invade Greece and hadn't done very well. So Xerxes spent four years making careful preparations. The Persians were mighty engineers. They built a floating bridge across the Hellespont, the narrow strip of water that separated Greece and Turkey.

They cut a canal a mile-and-a-quarter long across a peninsula in northern Greece to give their ships safe passage.

Xerxes captured and devastated Athens, the principal Greek city. Then he blundered into the naval battle of Salamis and blew the whole operation.

When Xerxes' army finally started to march, in the spring of 480 BC, it was huge. Greek historians have claimed he had more than two million men and the Greeks had fewer than a quarter-million. Both figures are probably inaccurate, but it's a fact that the Greeks were horrendously outnumbered.

Most of the Greeks surrendered as the Persians approached. The army marched along the coast, protected and supplied by a huge navy, more than 2,000 ships.

The first resistance came at Thermopolae, a narrow pass. There, 300 Greeks from the city of Sparta held up Xerxes' army for four days.

That one goes down in history books as one of the great battles of all time but, truth to tell, it didn't prove anything except that Spartans were very brave men. Not too smart, but brave.

Xerxes captured and devastated Athens, the principal Greek city. Then he blundered into the naval battle of Salamis and blew the whole operation.

The Persian fleet had been hit by two bad storms and had lost one medium-sized battle to the Greeks. Salamis is a peninsula near Athens, and Xerxes hoped to bottle up the Greek fleet in the narrow Channel just off it. He sent his best ships and men to cut off the Greeks so they couldn't retreat. That meant that force was out of the battle.

Then he sent he rest of his fleet into a narrow channel after the Greeks. One part of the Greek fleet retreated in front of him. That made him think he had them on the run.

But the other part of the Greek fleet was hiding inshore. And as the Persian ships passed in single file, the Greeks shot out from shore and hit them on the side.

It was all over in a morning. The campaign lasted another season but Xerxes knew he was beaten and he went home.

And the Greeks settled down to the philosophy and science and mathematics that made them great. Which they passed on to us.

Originally broadcast September 20, 1984

FREE TRADE, TAKE ONE

In 1910, Wilfrid Laurier was the prime minister of Canada, leading a Liberal party that had won the last four elections. But the Liberals were getting tired and nobody knew it better than Laurier.

He took a trip to the Prairies to look around and get the mood of westerners. He found western farmers were bitter because of Canada's high tariffs on manufactured goods. The factory owners of Ontario and Quebec loved the high tariffs. But for the westerners, they meant high cost farm machinery.

Laurier didn't say anything but he returned to Ottawa with a plan. The Americans had already approached him quietly with a suggestion that maybe a reciprocity treaty might make sense. Reciprocity was the buzz word in those days for what today we call free trade. Usually it was the Canadians who went to Washington trying to sell the idea.

Now, Laurier saw his chance for a coup. He would please the Americans, win the western votes and maybe even bring down prices enough to raise the Canadian standard of living to something like the American level. In those days there was quite a difference.

Laurier's minister of finance held secret talks with the Americans in a hotel room in Albany and the matter was settled in no time. And on terms very good for Canada. There would be no tariffs at all on the things that Canada sold the States: grain and vegetables and fruit and salt and fish and lumber. And there would be none on farm machinery shipped into Canada. And there would be very low tariffs on a lot of other manufactured things like clocks and engines.

> *Laurier saw his chance for a coup. He would please the Americans, win the western votes and maybe even bring down prices enough to raise the Canadian standard of living.*

When Laurier made his deal public the Conservatives were thunderstruck. They were pretty discouraged after losing the last four elections but they thought they might have a chance this time. But with Laurier's deal, they figured they'd be out of power for another hundred years.

Laurier was so confident he adjourned parliament and took a trip to London.

But he had reckoned without the rage of the Ontario and Quebec manufacturers. They'd been living very well since the Conservatives brought in high tariffs back in 1879.

They knew they couldn't win an election arguing against lower prices. So they took the patriotic approach. "What would this do to the Empire?" they shrieked. "Laurier is trying to break ourtie to the throne and make us part of the States."

American politicians were already making speeches about how reciprocity was the beginning of political union, how the stars and stripes would soon be flying over Canada. Newspapers in Ontario and Quebec front-paged this stuff every day.

The Conservatives, who hated the Quebec nationalists, suddenly saw merit in them because they were Laurier's foes. A lot of money was spent on a very expensive campaign. And by the time Laurier realized what was up, it was too late.

The election was held on the 21st of September in 1911 and the Liberals were smashed. They were out of power for less than ten years, though. And when they returned, they never again uttered the R-word.

Originally broadcast September 21, 1993

SETTLING IN

In the 1890s, just as the Canadian government was looking for settlers, a strange sect from Russia was looking for a home. The Doukhoubours were a religious group who believed in communal living and having not much to do with governments. They refused to recognize the authority of the czar and their young men refused to join the army.

This kept them in constant trouble with the Russian government and they would have been happy to move anywhere else. But the government wouldn't allow that.

Just about then, Count Leo Tolstoy, the novelist, became interested in their plight and he used his influence with the czar's wife. She persuaded the czar to allow the Doukhoubours to leave Russia.

The czar had that sort of power. He also had the power to lift that permission without a moment's notice. Poor Nicholas, the czar, wasn't a man cut out for high office and spent very little time on affairs of state.

Strangely, although the Doukhoubours were peasants themselves, they attracted the sympathy of a lot of well-to-do people, even noblemen. One of these was a Russian Duke named Kropotkin.

Kropotkin had been an army officer and landowner in Russia. But his modern thinking had brought him into conflict with the government. He'd been sent to Siberia, had escaped and moved to France. There, he got into trouble with the French government for plotting a revolution.

He went to England, where he became interested in the plight of the Doukhoubours. Kropotkin was a mapmaker and zoologist as well as those other things.

So he volunteered to look over western Canada on behalf of the Doukhoubours.

He arrived in Winnipeg on the 22nd of September in 1897. He travelled all over the Prairies and reported back that the country that's now Saskatchewan would be ideal for the Doukhoubours. The Prairie was exactly like the steppes of southern Russia, where they came from.

That set the project in motion. The Doukhoubours piled aboard ships in the Black Sea and headed for Canada.

> *The Doukhoubours had become a fashionable cause, just like the starving Ethiopians of our generation.*

By this time, they had become a fashionable cause, just like the starving Ethiopians of our generation. Other exiled Russian noblemen, British politicians, a professor from the University of Toronto, an Englishman who had been a factory manager in Russia . . . all got to work to get the Doukhoubours to Canada.

Within a year, 7500 Doukhoubours were settled in Saskatchewan, or what would become Saskatchewan. The whole thing had happened so quickly that there were misunderstandings about their status. In later years, they would claim their young men had been promised they wouldn't have to join the army. They would claim they were guaranteed they wouldn't owe allegiance to the crown, like other Canadians do. All sorts of trouble would result.

But, at the time, it was a remarkable feat, the biggest mass movement until then in the history of Canada. And an important addition to the tiny population of that huge area. What one writer had called 50 years earlier the vast lone land.

Originally broadcast September 22, 1986

BOXING DAY

There's a strong movement underway, especially in England, to outlaw the sport of boxing. It might not be a bad idea. A lot of boxers have been killed in the last few years and the brutality of the sport offends most people today.

But, like it or not, no sport is like boxing. It appeals to something primitive in all of us.

And two of the best fights in history of boxing were between two brilliant men. And that's unusual in a sport not noted for attracting brainy people.

These two fights were held 364 days apart: on the 22nd of September in 1927 and the 23rd of September the year earlier. The boxers were heavyweights, Jack Dempsey and Gene Tunney.

Jack Dempsey was a tough boy from the west who was known as the Mauler. He went to work on his opponent and systematically punched him up one side and down the other, until the fight was over. He would invest a couple of rounds pounding away at the other man until he found the opening then land the hardest uppercut anyone had ever seen. That made him the champion.

Gene Tunney was the very opposite. He was a bookworm. He was born in New York and his family expected him to be a priest. His favorite hangout was the local library.

In the First World War, Tunney joined the Marines and boxing was part of Marine training in those days. Before the war was over, Tunney was lightweight champ of the American army in Europe.

He liked boxing but he wasn't a natural boxer. He had to sweat and practice for hours to learn every move. The sports writers didn't take him seriously because he was usually reading a book when they came around to interview him.

The other boxers took him seriously, though. When Tunney went into the ring he was ready. And he beat them all.

Finally, on the 23rd of September, 1926, Jack Dempsey, the heavyweight champion, met Tunney in Philadelphia. This was before the age of TV and if you wanted to see the fight, you had to go to the park.

Dempsey was the 2-to-1 favorite. But the oddsmakers were wrong that night. Dempsey won his fights by brute strength, although he was a scientific puncher if he had to be. Tunney was known as a skillful boxer.

> *Dempsey won his fights by brute strength, although he was a scientific puncher if he had to be. Tunney was known as a skillful boxer.*

That night Tunney was both and Dempsey was neither. For 10 rounds, all in pouring rain, Tunney did his careful, methodical thumping on Dempsey. Finally, with no knockout, the decision went to Tunney.

Nobody argued the decision. But a lot of people pointed out that Dempsey had been rusty. He had defended his title five times in five sensational fights. Then he couldn't get anyone to fight him for three years.

Then Tunney and another fighter named Jack Sharkey challenged at the same time. Dempsey took on Tunney.

Dempsey defeated Tunney, then took on Sharkey and managed to beat him in a terrible slugfest. Most boxers agreed that Tunney wouldn't have beaten Sharkey that night. Dempsey almost didn't.

Three hundred and sixty-four nights after he lost the championship to Tunney, Dempsey was back in the ring with him in Chicago. Fans paid more than two and a half million to see that fight.

In the seventh round, Dempsey floored Tunney with four incredible punches that all landed in less than a second. Then, instead of going to a neutral corner, Dempsey stood over Tunney. The referee didn't start counting until Dempsey went to the corner. And Tunney got up at the count of nine and won that one, too.

Originally broadcast September 23, 1986

GREAT SCOTT!

We've all been fascinated by F. Scott Fitzgerald ever since he started writing, more than 60 years ago. He wrote some very good books — *Tender is the Night, This Side of Paradise, The Great Gatsby* — but never any great ones. Practically everyone knows who F. Scott Fitzgerald was and most of use can name at least a few of his books. But more of us talk about those books than ever read them.

A few years ago, Hollywood did a lavish production of *The Great Gatsby* and sent it around to the theatres of the world with an incredible promotion budget. Everybody talked about it, which should have made it a huge success. It wasn't.

And that's the story of F. Scott Fitzgerald. It's easier to say he wasn't a success than to explain why not. He certainly had everything going for him.

Fitzgerald was born in St. Paul, Minnesota on the 24th of September in 1896. He was named Francis Scott after Francis Scott Key, the author of the *Star-Spangled Banner,* an ancestor on his father's side. On his mother's side there was plenty of money.

But not quite enough for him to play the rich boy, a role he coveted all his life. Scott went to Princeton, where he wanted to be a football star but he wasn't quite big enough. That's strange, because he weighed over 10 pounds at birth.

When the First World War came along, he joined the army and longed to be a hero. He was stationed in the South for a while and he became engaged to Zelda Sayre, an 18-year-old southern beauty who had scads of boyfriends.

Then his regiment was ordered overseas and Fitzgerald was about to be a hero. He was in Quebec, waiting for a ship to sail him to glory, when the war ended.

Fitzgerald decided to be a writer and he moved to New York. But no newspaper would hire him, so he went to work writing copy in an ad agency.

The only thing he ever wrote that drew praise from his boss was a streetcar poster for a steam laundry that operated in Muscatine, Iowa. It said: "We keep you clean in Muscatine."

All the time, Fitzgerald was writing short stories and working on a novel. At one time, in his garret in Greenwich Village, he had 122 rejection slips pinned to his walls.

Not one editor thought his stuff was good enough to rate a letter of rejection. He just got the printed rejection slip back with each submission.

All this sounds like the stuff that a lifetime of failure is made of. Not so. Fitzgerald was very fast. He wrote 19 short stories in less than three months. One was done in an hour-and-a-half. The longest took three days.

He got out of the army in February of 1919. He had his first novel accepted by July of 1920.

> *Fitzgerald was drinking like a fish. He couldn't write unless he was half-drunk and he couldn't write when he was all-drunk.*

All this time, Fitzgerald was drinking like a fish. He couldn't write unless he was half-drunk and he couldn't write when he was all-drunk.

Scott and Zelda lived for the next few years in big rented houses in France, or the New York area. Fitzgerald got good money for his short stories and published half-a-dozen books. Zelda was from a family with a wide streak of insanity in it. Their drinking and her mental condition worked together to bring about a series of breakdowns. Finally, she went into a mental hospital in 1937 and was never out again for any significant length of time.

Fitzgerald could barely take care of himself, let alone their daughter. So the kid lived apart from them. Fitzgerald's letters to her were some of the best stuff he ever wrote.

Fitzgerald moved to Hollywood and lived with Sheila Graham, the gossip columnist. He wrote good stuff, when he was sober enough to write.

But Hollywood in those days was ruled by a bunch of puritanical censors and not much of his good writing ever got to the screen. His drinking brought on a heart condition and that's what killed him in 1940, when he was only 44.

Originally broadcast September 24, 1986

FREEDOM FIGHTER

Simon Bolivar was born in Caracas in Venezuela in the late 1700s. His family was incredibly rich. They were Spaniards who had lived in South America for more than 200 years. Bolivar's father owned 12 mansions in Caracas alone.

Young Simon was just another rich boy. If he had any characteristic that made him outstanding, it was his fixation with women. He fell in love with them all.

He was sent to Europe to complete his education and got there as Napoleon was conquering everywhere in sight and bringing about great reforms.

For some reason that Bolivar himself couldn't understand, he was suddenly seized with a mad desire to free his native country. All Latin America, except Brazil, was owned by Spain. Brazil was owned by Portugal.

The wars in Europe were keeping the Spanish army busy. So Bolivar went back home, joined a revolutionary movement and was incredibly successful.

Bolivar was one of those great leaders of history who could convince people to do anything. He started with a starving, tattered little army of 2500. He won battle after battle.

He freed all northern South America, five nations. One of them, Peru, split and the new part was named after him, Bolivia.

Bolivar was also a great administrator. He redistributed land to the poor, set up schools, encouraged mining and agriculture, and built roads.

But the South Americans split up into little factions and began fighting among themselves. Although Bolivar is remembered as the Great Liberator, he spent most of his time fighting those endless internal wars.

His position was made more difficult by his personal life. His wife died of a fever when they were both very young. Bolivar had vowed never to marry again.

But he didn't vow to never have anything to do with women again. Everywhere he went, the slim, brilliant, intense Bolivar had women throwing themselves at him. Nobody ever heard him say no.

As Bolivar was riding his horse, leading his triumphant army through the streets of Quito in Ecuador, he was bopped on the head by a bunch of flowers.

Women often threw flowers at Bolivar. But this bouquet was intended to get his attention, not just call him hero.

It was thrown by a beautiful young woman named Manuela Saenz, a wild lady who wanted Bolivar more than anything else.

It was lust at first sight. From then until Bolivar died, they seldom had their hot little hands off of each other.

Back in Bogota, Colombia, where Bolivar ruled from, there was a plot to kill him, on the night of 25th of September in 1828.

Some historians say the plot was political. Some say it was revenge by several dozen of the husbands Bolivar had made angry. No matter. As the plotters seized the palace and hunted for Bolivar, Manuela pushed him out a window then stalled the plotters until he was safely gone. Later that night, Bolivar rallied his troops and captured the plotters.

But he was worn out. A couple years later, Bolivar was dead. Manuela became a bag lady and lived another 26 years.

> *For some reason that Bolivar himself couldn't understand, he was suddenly seized with a mad desire to free his native country.*

Originally broadcast September 25, 1989

DODGING THE DRAFT

When the First World War began in August of 1914, Canadians trampled each other to get into the army. The biggest fear of young Canadian men was that the war would be over before they could get into it. By April of 1915, Canada had 32,000 men overseas.

Nobody noticed at the time, but there was something significant about the make-up of those 32,000. Two-thirds were from the British Isles, Englishmen, Scots and Irishmen who had moved to Canada.

Many of them were homesick. Many had tried the tough life on Canadian farms and frontiers and decided it wasn't for them.

The Orangemen of Ontario, solidly for king and country, joined up in pretty impressive numbers. The second year of the war, 1915, 180,000 more Canadians enlisted. A pretty impressive performance for a country of 10 million.

But by the next year, 1916, it was apparent that not enough men were coming forward. The principal reason was that the British and French generals who were running the war were a bunch of incompetents who didn't know their jobs.

They sent tens of thousands of men marching right into machine guns to win a few yards of mud so they could move their pins along the map.

The Canadians stopped a major German attack at Ypres in Belgium in 1915 by ignoring the latest German weapon, poison gas. The British generals thought that sounded like a promising weapon, so they tried it. But they picked a nice, clear day with no wind to carry the gas towards the Germans. It fell on their own lines and killed their own men.

Oh well, back to the drawing board. The Australians and New Zealanders sent thousands of young men to the war, but they voted against conscription. Only volunteers would go.

The Americans imposed conscription on their young men, but they stayed out of the war. Halfway through the war, the British brought in conscription. It didn't really matter. All the eager young men joined the army, and the only ones who were forced to go didn't make the best soldiers.

Sir Robert Borden, the Canadian prime minister, had said he didn't want conscription, but he would impose it on young Canadian men rather than lose the war.

Quebeckers were dead-set against conscription, although their young men had joined the army in about the same proportions as the rest of the country. Western farmers wanted to keep their sons at home.

At first, most Quebec politicians favored the war. But when Borden proposed conscription that would take everybody, including student priests, the bishops of Quebec turned against it.

Sir Wilfrid Laurier, the leader of the opposition, was in a terrible bind. He was a staunch supporter of the British Empire, more so than any Ontario Orangeman. When he was prime minister before the war, he had once said, "When Britain's at war, Canada's at war. It's as simple as that."

Overseas, the Canadians were such superb soldiers that the generals kept clamoring for more of them as they threw away their lives by the thousands.

Borden figured he had no choice. On the 26th of September, 1917 he imposed conscription on Canada. It was a move that split the country as it's never been split before or since.

In Quebec, 62 seats went to the anti-conscription Liberals, only three to the conscriptionists. In Ontario it was the other way around, 74 to 8.

The whole operation only produced about 20,000 more soldiers, less than 10 per cent of the Canadian army. And of Canada's population of 10 million, 50,000 died.

> *Overseas, the Canadians were such superb soldiers that the generals kept clamoring for more of them as they threw away their lives by the thousands.*

Originally broadcast September 26, 1985

COMMISSION OF ERROR

The assassination of President Kennedy in November of 1963 hit the people of the United States right in the pit of the stomach.

There had been assassinations and attempts on other presidents. Virtually all had been by nuts or fanatics. But one, the assassination of President Lincoln a century earlier, had left disturbing questions. Many people wanted to see Lincoln dead. The investigation that followed didn't settle many questions, although it resulted in the shooting of the assassin and the hanging of several associates.

Now, the Kennedy assassination seemed to be a repeat of the Lincoln one in that respect. Kennedy had stood up to the Soviet Union in the Cuban missile crisis. They might have wanted him dead. He had vigorously opposed Castro in the Caribbean, even approved the disastrous invasion at the Bay of Pigs. So Castro had no reason to love him.

Under President Kennedy, and his brother the attorney-general, the American government was effectively fighting organized crime for the first time. A lot of mobsters who usually murdered people who bothered them also wanted the president out of the way.

Most disturbing of all was the assassin himself, Lee Harvey Oswald. Oswald was a 24-year-old former Marine who hated the United States and had gone to live in the Soviet Union. He had returned after a couple of years. But the FBI knew he remained in contact with the Russians because the tapped the phone of the Soviet embassy in Mexico City and heard Oswald on that line not long before the assassination.

Put it all together and you get a terrible mess. There had to be an investigation that would settle the affair and put people at ease.

The new president, Lyndon Johnson, set up a commission to investigate, headed by the chief justice of the U.S., Earl Warren. Warren was known as a defender of civil liberties, and his court had angered right-wingers by vigorously standing up for poor people accused of crimes.

There were six other members of the commission, including Gerald Ford, who later became president, and Allan Dulles, who had been head of the CIA until a couple of years earlier. He'd been fired by President Kennedy, the man whose death he was to investigate.

No one has ever suggested that chief justice Warren was either stupid or dishonest. Far from it. But the awful truth is that the Warren Commission was one of the worst screw-ups in modern history. Consequently, it achieved exactly the opposite result of what was intended: it settled nothing and reassured no one.

There were indications that the FBI and CIA might have known of connections between Oswald and the Russian secret service. They weren't followed up.

There were glaring discrepancies between the evidence of the doctors in Dallas, where the president was killed, and in Washington, where his body was taken. The commission's report ignored them.

Warren had more power to investigate than anyone in the country. But he decided to do very little investigation of his own. He relied on reports from government agencies, like the FBI and CIA.

Oswald, the assassin, had been gunned down himself two days after the president was killed, so he wasn't available to tell his story.

The assassination of President Kennedy, on the 22nd of November in 1963, was a tragedy. The publication of the Warren Report, on the 27th of September in 1964, compounded it.

> *The Warren Commission was one of the worst screw-ups in modern history. It settled nothing and reassured no one.*

Originally broadcast September 27, 1984

WHO KILLED THE POPE?

In early August of 1978, Pope Paul the Sixth died at the age of 80. As soon as his funeral was over, the cardinals, the princes of the Roman Catholic Church, assembled in Rome to pick a successor from among them. The man they would choose would be one of the most powerful in the world.

Love him or hate him, you can't ignore the pope. He's the spiritual leader of all Roman Catholics, and there are two-thirds, maybe even three-quarters of a billion of them in the world.

Traditionally, the job goes to one of the cardinals who has worked his way up through the Vatican bureaucracy.

Pope Paul the Sixth had been a brooding, serious man, not hard to understand when you realize what a pile of problems lay on his shoulders. With each passing year, the problems of the Vatican, like those of any major world power, get more complex, so it was assumed that the new pope would be any one of a half-dozen brilliant scholars or diplomats.

When the decision came, it was a surprise. In the shortest deliberation in centuries, the cardinals chose Cardinal Albino Luciani, the bishop of Venice. Luciani was a quiet, unassuming man, a parish priest more than a church administrator.

He walked the sidewalks in Venice, talking to people. He took his lunch at a sidewalk cafe and played the old game of bocce, that Italian lawn bowling game.

The new pope was 65 years old, reasonably young to be a pope. It was assumed by all that when he took the job he would adopt the elaborate ceremonials that are part of the papacy.

Not so. On his first speech from the balcony in St. Peters Square he joked. The Latin he spoke was informal. When he had an audience with journalists, one of the pope's first audiences, he joined them more as a colleague than their pope. As Father Luciani, he had been a writer for Italian newspapers on religious subjects, and a good one.

In the shortest deliberation in centuries, the cardinals chose Cardinal Albino Luciani, a quiet, unassuming man, a parish priest more than a church administrator.

The official word from the Vatican press office was that the new pope was a young, healthy one.

At his coronation, he carried the informality further and refused a lot of the ponderous part of the ceremony. It was obvious to Catholics, and everybody, that the papacy was in the hands of a simple, unassuming man, a man of the people.

Then, on the early morning of the 29th of September in 1978, only 33 days into his papacy, John Paul the First, as Luciani was known, suddenly died.

The cardinals assembled again and chose the present pope.

But even before the new pope was elected, the rumor mill got churning. How could a healthy man suddenly die, just like that? The new pope had uncovered scandals in the secretive Vatican and heads were about to roll, so he'd been poisoned, or so people said.

Well, there were scandals in the secretive Vatican financial office. The head of the bank that handled Vatican investments was found hanged under a bridge in London. His death supposed to look like a suicide, but nobody to this day believes it was.

The bishop in charge of Vatican finances was a prisoner in the Vatican, afraid to step into Rome because the police had a warrant for him. An Italian bank swindler, who was in jail for his high-level chiseling connected to the dead banker, was mysteriously poisoned in his jail cell.

So, what happened to Pope John Paul the First? Nine years after his death, Vatican officials invited a British writer and former Catholic named John Cornwell to go into the Vatican, rummage through the records and interview whomever he pleased.

His conclusion, and it seems to be accurate, is that the pope was a sick man, that those early descriptions of his good health were little white lies. And his immediate staff were more concerned with his privacy than getting him proper medical care.

Originally broadcast September 28, 1990

CREATING A BY-PASS

On the 29th of September in 1783, two British army engineers were ordered to leave Montreal and make a survey.

Lieutenant Jones was to travel up the east shore of the Ottawa River to where Ottawa is today. He was to cross the river there and return on the south shore. Along the way he was to survey and report back on the soil, the rock and the forest.

At the same time, Lieutenant French was to take seven soldiers and three local guides in canoes and go up the Ottawa River, turn into the Rideau River and make a similar survey along the way.

Both reported they found rich soil and plenty of timber. Lieutenant Jones reported lots of stone suitable for building all along the Ottawa River.

Lieutenant French went south from the Ottawa River, through the Rideau River and Rideau Lakes, as ordered. Then he made his way over a few small portages, south to Lake Ontario and back to Montreal.

Although that wasn't why he was sent out, Lieutenant French had made the first survey for the Rideau Canal.

It was obvious that Britain and the United States would go to war sometime in the future and southern Canada would be the battleground. With that in mind, the British had to find some way to supply Kingston and other forts to the west along a supply route the Americans couldn't capture.

So, it was decided to build a canal, or a series of canals, to link up the Ottawa River to Lake Ontario at Kingston. That would be best done by following the route Lieutenant French had taken along the Rideau River and Lakes. In some places channels would have to be dredged and canals dug and locks built.

The government of Upper Canada, what's now Ontario, wanted the British government to do the building because it would be expensive. The British government wanted the government of Upper Canada to do it for the same reason.

The British and Americans did go to war and the British managed to keep their western forts supplied. The Americans didn't make the obvious move of capturing the north shore of Lake Ontario.

Nevertheless, when the war was over, the British government still wanted the canal built in case there was another war with the Americans and they were smarter this time.

So, Colonel John By was sent from England to supervise the building. He set up his headquarters on the south bank of the Ottawa River, where the Houses of Parliament sit today. He called it Bytown.

Colonel By arrived in 1826 and was finished and back home in England by 1832. He put a canal more than 123 miles through uncharted wilderness. No detailed preliminary survey was done.

No record was kept about how many men worked on the canal or how many died. The total work force was in the thousands, maybe two to four thousand. Hundreds died, many from blasting accidents as they cut the canal through solid rock, most from malaria in the unhealthy swamps.

The Rideau Canal has been called the biggest engineering project the British Army has ever undertaken in eastern North America. Colonel By should have been knighted for his work. Instead, he was called home to explain why the canal cost more than budgeted for.

It was never used to fight the Americans. Today, every summer, it's crowned with American pleasure boats.

Colonel By should have been knighted for his work. Instead, he was called home to explain why the canal cost more than budgeted for.

Originally broadcast September 29, 1989

NOT ALL'S FAIR IN LOVE AND WAR

In the spring of 1945, the Second World War finally ended. In just a decade, Europe had gone through the bloodiest period in its history. And Europe had a very bloody history.

The most vexing questions facing the winners was what to do with the Nazi leaders who had brought on all this bloodshed and destruction.

Stalin, the Russian leader, had a simple solution: take all the Nazis and their principal followers and hang them, all 50,000 of them. While we're doing that, we'll think of what to do with the others.

But the British and Americans insisted that the final chapter of this most brutal of all wars had to be written legally. They demanded a trial of the Nazi leaders.

The Russians and French pointed out that most of the Nazi leaders had broken no laws that existed at the time. There was no law against starting a war.

So, in the fall of 1945, the four major powers met in London and drew up the London Charter. It said that starting war and waging it cruelly and bringing on the conditions that cause war were all crimes against humanity.

The Russians wanted to hold the trial in Berlin, the German capital. But it was shattered and didn't have a big building standing that would accommodate the trial.

The Americans suggested Nuremberg. It was the city where the Nazis had held their party rallies and where the Germans had first enacted their anti-Jewish laws. Besides, it was in the American zone of occupation and the Americans were the only ones left with the money and equipment and energy and will to stage a major media event.

So they quickly rebuilt the old Nuremberg Palace of Justice which had been damaged by bombs.

> *The methodical Germans had carefully filed and saved the evidence that would be used against their leaders.*

There were four judges, one each from Britain, Russia, France and the United States. The chief was the British one.

Each of the major powers also put together a prosecution team. The first was the American team, which prosecuted the prisoners for taking part in a huge conspiracy to start the war. The British handled the next charge, secretly preparing for that war. The French and Russians jointly handled the other two charges, crimes against humanity and war crimes generally.

The evidence was nearly all written. Boxcarsful of minutes of meetings and copies of memos sent from one Nazi leader to another were presented. The methodical Germans had carefully filed and saved the evidence that would be used against their leaders.

Hitler had been killed in the last days of the war. Martin Borman, his principal aide, had disappeared about the same time. Rudolph Hess, who had been Number Three in the Nazi party at the beginning of the war, was in Britain. He had flown there early in the war to try to negotiate a peace.

In all, 24 Nazi leaders were indicted. Borman was charged in absentia. One committed suicide in his cell just before the trial.

The trial ran almost a year. On the 30th of September, 1946 the four judges started delivering their judgment. Three of the accused men were acquitted. Seven were sent to jail, terms ranging from 10 years to life. Hess is still in jail, an old man.

The others were sentenced to be hanged. And they were, two weeks later. All but Hermann Goering, the number-two Nazi, that is. He killed himself just before he was to be executed.

Originally broadcast September 30, 1986

Right: *Sharpshooter Annie Oakley died on November 3, 1926. Her life inspired the musical* Annie Get Your Gun, *which opened in New Haven, Connecticut on March 29, 1946.*
Bottom Right: *Norman Bethune, a Canadian surgeon and social activist, died on the 13th of November in 1939 when he cut his finger during an operation and caught blood poisoning.*
Bottom Left: *On the 5th of October in 1813, Tecumseh, the Shawnee chief who had joined the British forces, was killed in battle with invading Americans near London, Ontario.*

Top Left: *Orville and Wilbur Wright invented the first airplane, which took flight December 17 in 1903 — and stayed airborne for 12 seconds.*
Top Right: The Mousetrap, *a play by Agatha Christie, opened on November 26, 1952. It's now the longest-running play in history.*
Left: *Canada's most famous humourist, Stephen Leacock, was born in England on December 30, 1869.*

A SWEET STORY

Laura Ingersoll was born in Massachusetts in 1775, the year the American Revolution broke out. Her father fought against the British in that war.

But, strangely, after the war was over, he moved to Canada and became a staunch monarchist. The family lived near Niagara Falls for a while then they moved further west and founded a settlement. It was named after him and today it's the city of Ingersoll.

Laura met a fellow American at Niagara and married him. But his history was quite different. He had been born James DeSecors, the son of a large family of prosperous New Jersey lumber merchants. The family split during the Revolution and the ones who remained loyal to the crown changed their name from DeSecors to Secord.

So Laura Ingersoll became Laura Secord and settled down with her husband to raise children. By the time the War of 1812 broke out, they had five kids and were living in the village of Queenston, near Niagara Falls.

James was a fairly prosperous merchant and an officer in the local militia regiment. When the war began the Americans invaded Canada and occupied the village of Queenston.

Laura, although born an American, was now a loyal subject of the crown. Legend has it that she warned one of the Americans in the invading army that all of Canada he'd ever conquer would be the six feet needed to bury him. And later that day the poor man was killed.

The American invasion was turned back at the bloody battle of Queenston Heights, not far from the Secord home. James was badly wounded in that battle, shot in both the shoulder and the leg.

Laura set out to warn Fitzgibbon. She travelled the whole dozen miles on foot, through rough bush and through a really terrible swamp.

Laura went to the battlefield after it was over and found her husband lying, almost dead. She took him home and nursed him.

In the spring of 1813 the Americans invaded again. This time the officers of one of the regiments used the Secord home. And one night in June Laura heard them planning an attack.

The British and Canadians in that area were hopelessly outnumbered and they had retreated but kept up guerrilla warfare against the Americans. The Americans had figured out that the British headquarters for that war was a dozen miles away in a farmhouse. They decided to attack with 500 men, a force almost 10 times what the British commander had.

He was a young Irishman, a lieutenant named James Fitzgibbon. Laura set out to warn Fitzgibbon. She travelled the whole dozen miles on foot, through rough bush and through a really terrible swamp.

Fitzgibbon was warned and sent an ambush for the Americans. They were either killed or captured and it was one of their most ignominious defeats.

James Secord never did recover fully from his wounds and life for the Secords wasn't the same from then one. They had two more children, making seven in all.

Laura didn't talk much about her exploit. But in 1860, when she was well on in years she told about it, hoping to get a pension. It got her a hundred pounds, which was quite a bit in those days. But it made her story known and made her one of this country's foremost heroes, which was her status when she died on the first of October in 1868 at the age of 93.

Originally broadcast October 1, 1992

THE FIRST TV PRODUCER

John Baird was the inventingest son-of-a-gun who ever came along. Nobody knows his name today because most of the things he invented never got off the ground. And he wasn't as well organized as, say, Edison who patented everything he thought of.

Baird was an inventing genius from the time he was a kid. His father was a clergyman and young Baird was born and raised in Glasgow in Scotland.

When he was just a teenager he built a generator powered by water that created enough electricity to run all the lights in the house. His father was impressed. But, he pointed out, they didn't live beside a stream that could turn the waterwheel to run the generator. No problem, said young Baird, we'll just set up the wheel beside the sink and let the water from the kitchen tap do it.

Unfortunately, in those days in Glasgow, the rates for water were higher than for electricity. The machine worked fine. It was just cheaper not to use it.

Baird invented a gadget that he hitched to a camera so he could take his own picture while he was asleep. He didn't know just where to take it from there. If he'd given that one more thought it might have made his fortune. Today millions of camera owners have remote-controlled shutters.

He worked on a process to make artificial diamonds by exploding a rod of carbon embedded in concrete. That one used more power than the diamonds were worth.

He moved to the West Indies and built a factory to make jams and jellies. That went broke. He moved to England and invented an inflatable insole to put inside a pair of boots so the wearer would be walking on air. One of the insoles had a blowout and he limped from a badly bruised foot for a couple of weeks.

He imported honey from Australia. He invented a new kind of fertilizer. He became a dealer in soap. But everything he touched lost money.

All this time Baird kept going back to one invention he just couldn't get off his mind. He was convinced that pictures could be transmitted by radio. He knew roughly how it would be done. It would take high voltages of electricity and it would somehow involve selenium, a rare metal with a peculiar property: selenium is a good conductor of electricity when it is exposed to light, but a poor one in the dark.

A selenium plate that had an image flashed onto it would transmit the same pattern of lights and darks to a similar plate miles away if some way could be found to carry a signal on a radio wave.

Baird came up with that idea when he was in his early 30s, after years of failure at everything else. That's still the basic idea of TV. But it took a lot of tinkering and money to get a lab and equipment.

Baird kept going back to one invention he just couldn't get off his mind. He was convinced that pictures could be transmitted by radio.

Baird tried to finance his TV by perfecting another of his superb ideas, a glass razor. If you break a piece of glass you get an edge so sharp you have to be careful with it. That's the sort of edge you need to shave with. So, why not a razor made of glass? Baird just about hacked his face to shreds before he realized that was an idea whose idea wasn't likely to come.

So he bugged his family to come up with a few pounds to back him in his TV experiments. He raised a couple of hundred with an ad in the papers.

He had a spectacular series of failures. In the fall of 1923, he was almost killed when he carelessly touched a bare wire as he was working on the high-voltage part of his machine.

On the 2nd of October in 1925, Baird was ready. He set up his machine in one room and a receiver in another. He played in front of the machine with a puppet. The puppet could be seen on the receiver in the next room.

He ran downstairs to an office on the floor below his and got somebody's office boy to come upstairs and sit in front of the machine. The kid was so scared when he saw all those wires and sparks that Baird had to pay him to sit in front of it. So, the first person to ever appear on TV was paid for his performance.

Alas! Baird's story doesn't have a happy ending. American researchers took his experiments and perfected them and became rich. Poor Baird died broke in 1946, just at the beginning of the age of TV.

Originally broadcast October 2, 1984

A CRY IN THE DARK

When you look back at those years between the First and Second World Wars, you have to wonder if anyone, anyone at all among the politicians was really trying to avoid war.

They all said they were. One or two, like Woodrow Wilson, the president of the United States, tried hard. But most of them just let matters drift.

Take the Italian invasion of Ethiopia, a shameful event that could have been stopped at any one of a dozen stages.

The Italians came out of the First World War, like every other European country, thoroughly shattered. Things got so bad that in 1923 there was a huge uprising, led by a socialist schoolteacher named Benito Mussolini. Once he got into power, Mussolini quickly switched from socialism to fascism. In fact, he and his pals invented the word when they created the fascist party and made it a synonym for tough, one-man rule, the very opposite of democracy.

Italy hadn't even become a country until the 1860s, about the same time Canada did. By then, all the choice land for colonies was gone except in a couple of not-very-fertile places of Africa, in Libya in the north and in the east, just south of the Red Sea.

In 1896, the Italians tried to expand their couple of tiny colonies in east Africa by invading Ethiopia. That should have been a push-over.

The Ethiopian army, such as it was, carried spears and threw stones. That was a one-battle invasion. It's known to history as the Battle of Adowa and ranks as one of the great military exploits of modern times. Somehow, the Italians managed to lose.

Not only that, they lost 6,000 men and two generals. And everybody knows that no matter how badly a battle goes, generals just never get hurt.

By the time Mussolini had been in power a dozen years, he could do remarkable things with his military forces. British and German and American spies were reporting back regularly that the Italians didn't really have an army, just a bunch of people who wore military uniforms and marched in step.

Once, when Mussolini complained to his generals that the army wasn't big enough, the general staff sat up all night reorganizing. In the morning, by transferring regiments from one division to another and changing a few names and commands, the staff officers had expanded the army from 29 to 73 divisions. But they hadn't added a single soldier.

Mussolini had ordered the army to start getting ready for another invasion of Ethiopia in late 1932.

The generals kept putting him off but announced they would be ready by late 1935.

The British and French complained to the League of Nations, an international organization that operated much like the United Nations does today. They demanded that other countries join them in stopping the Italian invasion before it started.

None of the others did anything. The British suggested an embargo. To lead the way, they stopped shipping several things to Italy, including fish. That didn't stop the invasion but it ruined the Newfoundland fishing industry.

The Germans weren't quite sure where they stood. So they sent the Ethiopians 600 machine guns and 16,000 rifles, then cheered for Mussolini, figuring they were covered no matter what happened.

The British could have stopped the invasion by forbidding Italian troops to use the Suez Canal but they chickened out at the last moment.

At five in the morning of the 3rd of October in 1935, 400,000 Italian troops poured across the border into Ethiopia.

They took the whole country in a few months. The Ethiopian emperor, Haille Selassie, fled and turned up at the League of Nations in Geneva. There, he gave a speech.

"If you don't help us, if you don't stop this invasion, you'll be next. The whole world will be at war," he pleaded.

But nobody listened. Nobody cared.

> *The British could have stopped the invasion by forbidding Italian troops to use the Suez Canal but they chickened out at the last moment.*

Originally broadcast October 3, 1984

THE KISS OF DEATH

The Black Death wasn't an event. It was a long series of them, spread out over a century or two. Nevertheless, we can tell almost to the day when it started. A fleet of naval ships from Genoa sailed into the harbour of Messina in Sicily in 1347. Their crews were dead or dying from a terrible disease. It hit its victims with eruptions under the skin that produced black marks like bruises. Hence the name, the Black Death.

The first record of this event mentions the fourth of October. Those ships had just sailed from Caffa, a city on the Crimean Peninsula in the Black Sea. Caffa was a Christian city that had been under siege by Mongols from away to the east around China.

Caffa had withstood that siege for two reasons: first, that Genoese fleet arrived with help; and, second, the Mongol army had been almost wiped out by an epidemic of that awful Black Death.

The harbour authorities wouldn't let any of the men ashore after they tied up. But the Death spread anyway. Within days people started dying in Messina. Within six months, half the population of the whole region was dead.

Within two years, the plague moved like a marching army, taking in northern Ireland, southern Scotland and Denmark and Norway. Within another year it had spread east and north into Russia.

We know of specific projects that were interrupted by the Black Death. Construction on Winchester Cathedral in England, for instance, was halted for a few years because of a shortage of skilled stoneworkers.

Historians still argue about just where the Black Death fits into history. European and American scholars seem to think it caused terrible disruption; that it led to the end of the Middle Ages, the collapse of the monopoly of the Catholic Church and the beginning of the Protestant Reformation. Marxist historians admit it was serious but they say European society was corrupt and about to collapse anyhow.

At any rate, at least a third of the population of Europe died, maybe a half. Whole towns were wiped out.

Today we know the Black Death was an attack of bubonic plague, a disease that isn't at all a problem these days. It's easily controlled by the antibiotics that were developed in the 1940s.

We also know that it didn't matter that those harbourmasters in Messina made the sailors from the Genoese ships stay aboard. Rats and the fleas they carried ran down the mooring ropes as the ships tied up. And it's the rats and fleas that carry it.

This wasn't known until the late 1800s. In 1855, there was a rebellion in Mongolia and Chinese troops went in to put it down. When they returned they brought bubonic plague with them and it wiped out hundreds of thousands.

European scientists had just begun to understand about germs and that sort of thing so they dashed into the area and started researching. They quickly found out about the rats and fleas and, from that, they figured out how the Black Death had spread.

It was one of the great examples in history of Monday morning quarterbacking. You can almost hear the ghosts of those millions who died 500 or more years earlier saying, "Now you tell us. But where were you in 1347 when we really needed you?"

> *The plague moved like a marching army, taking in northern Ireland, southern Scotland and Denmark and Norway. Within another year it had spread east and north into Russia.*

Originally broadcast October 4, 1984

UNITED WE STAND . . .

Once the American Revolution ended and the United States became an independent nation, the Americans started their westward expansion. As long as they were part of the British empire, the government in London prevented them from stealing all the Indians' land to the west.

Not that the British were great friends of the Indians. It was just that, as long as the Americans were expanding, there would be Indian wars and the British would have to send their army to fight them, at terrible cost in money and manpower.

The most expansion-minded Americans were the ones who assumed leadership in the westward move. The most beautiful and fertile of the lands to the west of the original Atlantic colonies were in the Ohio valley, in what's now the states of Ohio and Indiana, south of the Great Lakes. Several Indian tribes lived and hunted there.

One such tribe was the Shawnee. A chief of the Shawnee was Tecumseh, a brilliant man and a bold warrior.

Tecumseh had a hatred of white people ever since his father was killed by frontiersmen in their western march. Tecumseh was only seven at the time.

Tecumseh gradually became a leader in the endless skirmishes with the white settlers. He preached to the Indians that, as long as they remained in their separate tribes, they could do nothing. Unite and they could resist the white invasion and form a nation of their own. He had plans for such a nation in the rich forestland south of where Chicago is today.

Tecumseh had a younger brother who was a no-goodnik and a drunk. Then, apparently without explanation, the brother cleaned up his act and became a spiritual leader among his people. He was known as the Prophet. He travelled from tribe to tribe preaching clean living and resistance to the whites. Tecumseh, between battles, travelled as far south as the Gulf of Mexico, trying to persuade all tribes to join his plan. He got a lot of agreement as they listened to his speeches. But not much concrete came of it.

The British, to the north of the Great Lakes in Canada, were sympathetic to the Indians' plight. At least, they said they were.

The Americans were quite conscious of Tecumseh's power and every time they were defeated in their conquests, they blamed him.

In 1812, when the British and Americans went to war, Tecumseh joined the British with about a thousand of his warriors. Tecumseh and the British leader, General Isaac Brock, were a natural team — both men of action, both ready to attack in the face of any odds. Between them, they gave the Americans a terrible series of defeats in the first months of the war.

Then Brock was killed in the fall of 1812. His successor was a no-talent bum. Tecumseh saw him for what he was an bluntly said so.

In 1813, the Americans invaded again, from the Detroit area. They drove the British eastward with Tecumseh protesting that they should stand and fight. He finally persuaded the chicken-hearted British general to do battle just west of where London, Ontario, is today. That was on the 5th of October in 1813. It was a mistake. The Americans won and Tecumseh was killed. And the last chance of an independent Indian nation died with him.

> *Tecumseh had a hatred of white people ever since his father was killed by frontiersmen in their western march when Tecumseh was only seven.*

Originally broadcast October 5, 1992

CEREAL STORY

John Harvey Kellogg was a genius, everybody agreed. He taught at the high school in Battle Creek, Michigan before he graduated from it. He was editor of the town paper before he was 20.

John's father was owner of a small broom factory and a Seventh Day Adventist. He was one of the founders of a health clinic called the Battle Creek Sanitarium.

Now, there was another Kellogg boy, young Will, eight years younger than John. Will was just another boy, pretty dull beside his brilliant brother. John gave the orders and Will obeyed. In fact, while they were both still young, the elder Kelloggs turned Will over to John. John told him what to do, even spanked him when he was bad. All this was in the 1860s and 70s.

John graduated from medical school when he was only 24 and returned to Battle Creek to run the sanitarium. The Battle Creek sanitarium was a sort of convalescent home for people in poor health. It was run partly on the basis of modern medicine, partly on the basis of the Seventh Day Adventist religion. This meant the diet had little or no meat and a lot of cereals.

When Dr. John took charge of the sanitarium, he put Will, the young brother, to work as an errand boy, shipper, gardener, cook, bottlewasher, floor sweeper, bookkeeper, just about everything. Some of the patients were a trifle disturbed and when they ran away Will was sent to round them up. Years later he said he never came back without one, because if he did he knew what would happen to him. He never explained what he meant by that. Maybe Dr. John was still in charge of spanking him.

But Will wasn't just a menial. He was also in charge of the administration. Will worked at the sanitarium 16 hours a day, seven days a week. Still, Dr. John referred to him as "the Loafer".

For all this, Dr. John paid him nine dollars a week. After Will had a wife and two children, Dr. John raised that to 10. In addition to that, Will took care of some horses that belonged to a farmer nearby and for that he got another three dollars a week. When he was 42, Will

had been working at the sanitarium for 25 years and had been raised to 87 dollars a month.

Not that Dr. John was any layabout. He performed more than 20,000 operations over his career and wrote 45 books on health and diet.

Some of the patients at the sanitarium complained of the monotony of the diet, which was mostly grains. So one night, Dr. John boiled some wheat to soften it, then had Will press it in a pastry roller. Then he baked the flakes. The patients seemed to find them more palatable.

Some of the patients at the sanitarium complained of the monotony of the diet, which was mostly grains.

They tried the same thing with corn and found it tasted even better. So it became part of the sanitarium diet.

One of the patients was a salesman. He urged the Kellogg brothers to go commercial with their corn flakes.

Dr. John didn't think much of the idea, but Will liked it. Finally they formed a company with Dr. John holding 75 per cent of the stock. He threw his stock certificates in the bottom of a drawer and used them from time to time as tips or bonuses for employees at the sanitarium.

Will believed in the product and he bought up the certificates as fast as Dr. John gave them away. One day he figured out he now owned 51 per cent of the company. That was the day he told Dr. John to go to hell.

The company did very well and made millions. The two brothers fought bitterly over ownership of it.

In the 1920s they had a battle in the supreme court of Ontario over the Canadian rights to Kelloggs. That went on for eight years. Will was allied with the Seventh Day Adventist Church on that one.

Dr. John had argued with the church and had been thrown out.

Finally, Will and the church won.

When Dr. John died in 1943, Will had pictures taken of his grave and sent copies to everyone who had worked with them at the sanitarium years before.

When Will died at the age of 91 on the sixth of October in 1951, he left his millions and the Kellogg company to a medical foundation.

Originally broadcast October 6, 1983

BALLOON RALLY

When the Americans invented modern warfare during their Civil War in the early 1860s, the German Army had officers on hand to watch.

They went home, wide-eyed with wonder. Here was a war fought by hundreds of thousands of men who had been civilians only months earlier. They were transported to battle by train and they fought with machinery that had been turned out in factories conscripted to a war machine. The factory had become more important than the barracks.

In the next few years, these German officers rebuilt their army and their whole philosophy of war. Then, in 1870, the Franco-Prussian War began between France and Germany. The Germans won it, easily at first, eventually reducing their demands as victors to be rid of a war they couldn't lose but they couldn't finish.

France was run in those days by an emperor who called himself Napoleon the Third, a pathetic little man who insisted he was a military genius, although every time he tried to prove it he inflicted terrible disasters on his fellow Frenchmen.

The war began with an awful French defeat in the northeast, near the German border. The Germans surrounded almost the whole French Army and captured it.

That was the professional army and the harebrained emperor who led it.

But a popular opposition movement sprang up. The leader was a Parisian lawyer named Leon Gambetta and Gambetta mobilized the patriotism of the people against the German invaders.

The German army drove right to the outskirts of Paris. And there a popular French army stopped them. The siege of Paris was on. Eventually the people would be reduced to eating dogs, cats and rats.

They would stretch their meagre coffee ration with roast chicory. And to this day, Parisians have a taste for bitter coffee heavily laced with chicory.

As the German hold on Paris tightened, it was almost impossible to get supplies into the city. Or for leaders to get out. It was essential that Gambetta escape to the hinterland and rally the rest of France to the fight.

So, on the seventh of October in 1870, a giant balloon was fired up in Montmartre in the middle of Paris and Gambetta stepped into the basket slung beneath it. He was accompanied by his secretary and the pilot.

Balloons had been used for almost a century. In fact, during the American Civil War, the Union armies had used them to give artillery officers a view of what was going on.

The French army had tested them a few years earlier but abandoned them.

Now, a few of the old army balloons were brought out of their warehouses and were filled with hot air from bonfires. The first few attempts had mixed success. A couple got away. A couple came down behind German lines.

But Gambetta was desperate to get away to continue the fight.

So the balloon took off. It soared over the countryside for more than three hours. Gambetta and his friends didn't know where they were.

There were no such things as aerial charts in those days. And the weather was foggy, so they didn't have a very good view.

Finally, they came down in a forest, hung up in an oak tree. Peasants found them and whisked them to freedom.

Months later, the war ended with a German victory. Paris was captured. But the war had dragged on long enough that the French were able to negotiate a not-bad peace treaty.

As the German hold on Paris tightened, it was almost impossible to get supplies into the city. Or for leaders to get out.

Originally broadcast October 7, 1985

THE SOCIAL REFORMER

Clement Atlee was a bald, mousy-looking little man who looked like a movie director's idea of a bookkeeper. Atlee was an Englishman, born into a prosperous lawyer's family. He studied to be a lawyer but, instead, became a social worker.

He ran a boys' club in a slum area east of London and slowly became a socialist. England, in those days before the First World War, was populated by millions of poor people, all of whom were badly housed, horribly underpaid, poorly fed, and absolutely without health care.

Atlee lectured at the London School of Economics, not because he was a brilliant scholar, but because he had a very practical grasp of social work. Despite his mousy appearance, he was an excellent speaker. He never had Winston Churchill's talent for the grand phrase. But he knew how to paint pictures that made his point simply and graphically.

For instance, he once told this story: "I met a young girl, barefoot, on the street outside the community centre the other day, and she asked me where I was going. I said I was going home for tea. 'Oh,' she said, 'I'm going home to see if there is any tea.'"

Atlee was an officer in the First World War, was wounded, recovered and went back into the trenches. His experience in the war made him quite contemptuous of Europeans and in later years he fought to keep Britain out of the Common Market.

Between the wars, Atlee was elected to parliament and became a big shot in the British Labor Party. Just before the war, he was made leader.

When the war came along and Winston Churchill took over as prime minister, his Conservatives formed a wartime coalition government with Labour.

Atlee became the deputy prime minister and did the detail work while Churchill ran the war. In the middle of the war, the British Labour Party announced its plans for a socialist society for the post-war years — old age pensions, unemployment insurance, health care, education available to all. . .

In 1945, as soon as the war in Europe was over and before the war in the Pacific had ended, Britain had an election.

Nobody was more surprised than Atlee when Labour won and he was prime minister.

Atlee brought in his socialist state despite the fact that Britain was broke from the war. He set a schedule for granting independence to India and other parts of the empire. He joined with the Americans and western Europeans to form NATO.

In his quiet way, Atlee performed miracles. You might not agree all his miracles were for the better, but he brought them about.

Churchill was now the leader of the opposition and he had a field day, making fun of Atlee.

"His friends say the prime minister is a modest man," said Churchill, "and they're right. He has a lot to be modest about."

Or, "An empty car pulled up and the prime minister got out."

Or, "This island is a lump of coal sitting in a sea of fish, yet Mr. Atlee has managed to create shortages of coal and fish."

Churchill once described Atlee as a sheep in sheep's clothing.

Atlee's friends said that if he'd wanted to, he could have replied and cut up Churchill just as effectively. But he never did. That wasn't his way. In 1951, the Conservatives won the next election and Churchill was prime minister again and Atlee was back in opposition.

He eventually retired, and died on the 8th of October in 1967, the quiet, capable man who led Britain into socialism.

> *In his quiet way, Atlee performed miracles. You might not agree all his miracles were for the better, but he brought them about.*

Originally broadcast October 8, 1990

GUERRILLAS IN THE MIST

Ernesto Guevara was born in Argentina, the son of an architect and the grandson of an American woman. Two factors were big in his early days: his left-wing American grandmother and his asthma.

His grandmother died of cancer when Guevara was in high school; that made him want to be a doctor.

Because of his asthma, his family moved to a little mountain town where the air was clear. There, Guevara learned to ride and shoot, to run with a street gang and to grow up with a strange combination of a rich kid's formal, private-school education and a poor kid's street smarts.

He also picked up the nickname Che, which was slang for "hey you".

Part way through medical school he quit to motorcycle and hitchhike the length of South America. He tried to get into the United States for a visit but he was turned back at Miami. The American government already had him on their list of communists.

He worked for a while as a male nurse in a leper colony then went back to Argentina and finished medical school.

Then he went back on the road, travelling to most of the countries of South America and Central America.

He was in Guatemala in 1954, as a low-level government clerk, when the CIA financed and masterminded a revolution.

Che had come to the conclusion by this time that the Americans were the major enemies of the struggling peoples of the world. The CIA overthrow in Guatemala confirmed that belief and he became a pretty hot communist from then on.

About the same time, Che met a young Cuban exile named Fidel Castro who was determined to start a revolution and free his country from American influence. Che went with Fidel to Cuba, landed at night, went into the hills and started a guerrilla army.

Che was the head military man in Fidel's revolution and when they finally won in 1959, he became number-two man in Cuba.

He was also the head economic man in Cuba. Alas! The revolution had its problems and the basics were in short supply. A lot of Cubans blamed Che.

In 1966, Che announced he was tired of fighting the revolution from a desk. He was going into the field again. He led a band of 44 men into Bolivia and tried what he had worked in Cuba. They went into the hills and started a long, slow guerrilla war to topple the American-backed government.

But Bolivia wasn't Cuba. The peasants didn't flock to join. The Bolivian army was American-trained and very good.

On Sunday, the 8th of October in 1967, after months of patient tracking, a counter-guerrilla company of the Bolivian Army cornered Che in a ravine out in the boondocks. The 44 men had shrunk to 17. Most had malaria. Che was in bad shape from his asthma.

The first bullet went through Che's black beret, his trademark. The next two got him in the leg.

The soldiers took Che and two other prisoners to a schoolhouse a few miles away and radioed for orders.

The word came back from the capital: kill him and write a report saying he died of wounds.

So, on the morning of the 9th of October, 1967, a sergeant went into the schoolhouse and killed Che Guevara and his two friends.

Then the Bolivian army tore down the schoolhouse so it wouldn't become a communist shrine.

> *Che was the head military man in Fidel's revolution and when they finally won in 1959, he became number-two man in Cuba.*

Originally broadcast October 9, 1985

MARCHING BAND

It's hard to believe the Long March really happened. It sounds like one of those tales that has been embellished over the generations until no truth remains. But it did happen. And so recently that there are still a few hundred survivors alive today.

The people of China had a revolution in 1912 and overthrew the Manchus who had ruled the country for a few centuries.

The revolutionaries looked to Russia for help and the Russians gave it. That divided the revolutionaries into two groups: the communists and the nationalists.

They began fighting amongst themselves. At the same time the Japanese invaded the country from the northeast and the southeast.

China was a terrible mess. It had millions more people than it could feed and the Japanese Army was gobbling up great chunks of land.

The British, Americans and Europeans who could have helped with their superior technology were, for the most part, just there to exploit the country and the people.

And the two groups who intended to build a new nation out of that chaos were fighting between themselves.

The communists were mostly concentrated in the southeast. The nationalists held the rest of the country, except what was under the control of the Japanese or local warlords.

The Nationalist leader, Chiang Kai-shek, had the support of the western countries. That didn't mean a lot. They would send him some money and arms but they certainly weren't going to send any armies to help him.

The Russians would have sent help to the communists if they had had any. But Russia, the centre of communism, was on the verge of starvation, weak as a kitten after its revolution and civil war.

So the communists were on their own. Chiang Kai-shek was much more interested in fighting than in resisting the Japanese invasion.

For a couple of years he kept the communists surrounded and kept pushing them into a smaller area.

Finally, the communist leaders passed the word to their people: get ready to move. One hundred thousand people were involved directly and another 200,000 joined along the way.

So we can't say the Long March began at one place at one time. But the official version is that the first units took off from a little village schoolyard at a place called Ruijin on the 10th of October, 1934, in the middle of the night.

Chiang Kai-shek's forces attacked them as they marched. They had to cross rivers and mountains. They marched 6,000 miles, in all sorts of weather, across all sorts of country.

Of the 100,000 who set out, 80,000 died on the way. It would be like starting in Labrador, walking west to the Rockies, then turning north and walking through the mountains to the Beaufort Sea — fighting 200 battles along the way. That doesn't include the minor skirmishes. They had an average of two of those a day.

They crossed 18 mountain ranges and 24 major rivers. They occupied more than 100 cities, sometimes having to fight their way into them, sometimes being greeted with open arms.

They paid for everything they used along the way. They often got the money for that by knocking off banks as they marched.

When they finally arrived at the opposite corner of China, the northwest, they set up their own government and began to build an army that would eventually drive out the Japanese, then Chiang Kai-shek and his American friends.

Maybe the most important product of the whole march was a leader: a tough, chain-smoking round-faced man named Mao Tse-tung.

The communist leaders passed the word to their people: get ready to move. 100,000 people were involved directly and another 200,000 joined along the way.

Originally broadcast October 10, 1985

HERE COMES SUN YAT SEN

Sun Yat Sen was the first president of modern China and the leader of the revolution that freed the country from the rule of the Manchus who had taken it over centuries earlier. But he almost didn't live to lead that revolution. Only a British servant and a swarm of London reporters saved his life.

Sun Yat Sen was born of a well-to-do Chinese family and he studied medicine under Scottish professors at university in Hong Kong. He went back to China and became an agitator for reform.

For drawing up a petition, Sun Yat Sen was sentenced to death and he had to flee. He went to Hawaii, San Francisco, and eventually London; there he looked up two men who had been both old friends and teachers, Dr. Cantlee and Dr. Manson.

The two doctors helped him find a place to stay and he wandered around London, visiting the doctors quite often. He had been raised a Christian and often joined them on Sunday morning to go to church.

The 11th of October, 1896 was a Sunday and Sun Yat Sen was walking along Portland Place in London, going to Dr. Cantlee's house to go to church with him.

The door of number 49 opened and a Chinese man came out and began chatting with Sun Yat Sen. Another man, then a third arrived. They invited Sun Yat Sen in for tea, but he said he didn't have time.

Suddenly they grabbed him and dragged him inside. Sun Yat Sen hadn't realized that 49 Portland Place was the Chinese embassy. He was on Chinese soil and under arrest.

Dr. Cantlee wasn't too worried when Sun Yat Sen didn't show up for church. He figured he was busy.

Inside the embassy, Sun Yat Sen was locked in a room. He was interviewed by a tall, white-haired, very distinguished-looking Englishman. That was Sir Halliday McCartney, a lawyer for the embassy. McCartney questioned him. Then an embassy official named Tang questioned him.

Tang came right to the point: Sun Yat Sen was wanted in China, where he would be executed. He would be loaded aboard a ship within a week.

Sun Yat Sen now realized he was in trouble. He tried writing notes and throwing them out the window, weighted with coins. But the embassy guards found them and sealed his window.

A young Englishman named Cole worked as a servant in the embassy and Sun Yat Sen tried to interest him in his case. Cole was reluctant at first but eventually he took a note from Sun Yat Sen to Dr. Cantlee.

It arrived exactly a week after Sun Yat Sen had been kidnapped, a Sunday. Dr. Cantlee went to the Foreign Office, Scotland Yard, everybody he could think of. Nothing could be done because everybody with any authority was off on Sunday and couldn't be disturbed.

Dr. Cantlee tried to hire private detectives to keep watch on the embassy. They were all shut down on Sundays, too.

He went to the *Times*, the most influential paper in the world. No editor with the authority to order a story written would be in until late Sunday night.

Dr. Cantlee finally hired an ex-policeman to watch the embassy. The next morning he went to the *Times* and told the story. The *Times* called the embassy. The embassy denied the whole story. As the official British newspaper, the *Times* naturally believed an embassy official.

Sun Yat Sen would have been spirited away within a couple of days but another paper, the *Globe*, got onto the story. The *Globe* didn't believe the embassy's denials. So it cornered Sir Halliday McCartney, the embassy lawyer, and caught him in a series of contradictions.

The *Globe* reporter then went back to the embassy and told the ambassador if he didn't turn Sun Yat Sen loose he would write a story that would have a thousand angry Englishmen in the street in front of the embassy, blocking the way. Sun Yat Sen would never be allowed to get to a ship.

So the ambassador caved in, and Sun Yat Sen was freed to lead his revolution 25 years later.

> *Sun Yat Sen went back to China and became an agitator for reform. For drawing up a petition, he was sentenced to death and had to flee.*

Originally broadcast October 11, 1985

Bound by Duty

On this day, the 12th of October in 1915, a British nurse, Edith Cavell, was shot by a German firing squad for helping British soldiers escape after the Germans had conquered Belgium. The British cranked up their propaganda machine, and pretty soon Edith Cavell was a symbol of all that was pure and righteous in the fight against the Germans.

Edith Cavell was the very picture of a brave, efficient, no-nonsense nurse. She was brisk, competent, commanding, very skillful at her trade, equal to any occasion — a sort of Mary Poppins with no sense of humour.

Edith was born in 1865, the daughter of a Church of England clergyman. She was brought up in a nice big house with plenty of culture and sense of responsibility and a maid or two — and not a dime left to spare at the end of the month.

Edith began to work as a governess, and was hired after a year or two by a Belgian family. She lived with them in Brussels, raising their two daughters.

Edith was a nice-looking girl, no beauty but very pleasant-looking. She was religious, devoted to her work and her employer, and not at all interested in frivolous things like young men.

After a while, she got the urge to go into nursing. It was probably a combination of homesickness and a sense of duty. She returned to England, took up nursing and went through the whole apprenticeship system of long hours, virtually no pay, hard work, and intense study. It sounds more like drudgery than an attractive life but Edith prospered on it. She had found her life's work and was happy. Not happy in the giggly sense. Happy in the stern, dedicated sense. Edith didn't laugh a lot.

In 1907, she took the job that shaped the rest of her life and made her a legend. In Belgian hospitals all the nursing was done by nuns. They were patient and dedicated, but not very professional. The Belgian doctors envied the British doctors with their efficient, professional nurses. So they set up a nursing school in Brussels and hired Edith Cavell to run it. She was the perfect choice.

Religious people were opposed to the idea because it displaced the nuns. But they couldn't argue with Edith's dedication, at least equal to any lady of holy orders.

Nationalists opposed the idea of a foreigner running the school. But Edith spoke perfect French and was completely at home in Belgium, which she loved.

The school was a spectacular success. Within a few years, it was the symbol of modern, efficient nursing in Europe. If nothing else had happened in her life, Edith would have been remembered in the nursing business as a pioneer educator.

But the First World War came in 1914 and the German Army drove through Belgium in a couple of weeks. The British and Belgian Armies just about collapsed.

Thousands of soldiers were wandering around, vaguely aware they should avoid the Germans and get back behind the British lines. Belgian patriots set up an escape network. They included Edith Cavell and her nursing school in it without asking her. She never argued, just assumed it was her duty because she was British.

The Germans finally caught up with her and she and a few dozen Belgians were court-martialed.

Several were convicted. Edith and a Belgian leader were shot. The sentences of the others were commuted.

The Germans have argued since, and quite rightly so, that Edith Cavell knew what she was doing, that she knew that the penalty was death, and she was treated with proper military justice.

But when the Germans stood her in front of a firing squad at 7 o'clock on the morning of the 12th of October in 1915, they pulled the dumbest trick of the war. The world was horrified at the thought of a gallant nurse being killed, just because she was faithful to her profession and comforted the wounded.

That wasn't what she was shot for at all. But the British knew a good thing when it fell into their laps and they pushed that line for all it was worth.

The German army had started the war as a collection of brisk, efficient military gentlemen. With the death of Edith Cavell they became a mob of bloodthirsty Huns.

When the Germans stood Edith in front of a firing squad, they pulled the dumbest trick of the war.

Originally broadcast October 12, 1983

DEADLOCKED

The War of 1812 began in June of 1812 with the Americans invading Canada. They poured across the river and captured Sandwich, a village where the city of Windsor, Ontario is today, across from Detroit.

The British commander was General Isaac Brock, one of the great British military heroes. Brock was tall, handsome, athletic, a boxer and a swimmer. He liked soldiers and they liked him.

That was unusual in those days. There was often more hatred between the officers and men of the British Army than there was for the enemy.

Brock had served briefly in Europe, fighting Napoleon, then had been sent to Canada. It's not clear why. In those days the best officers were sent to fight Napoleon, and Brock was certainly one of the best.

But he wasn't always as respectful as he should have been to those above him, especially when those above him were stupid. And many were.

Brock sent one small force to capture the American fort at Michlimackinaw, near where Sault Ste. Marie, Ontario is today, a very strategic narrow point in the Great Lakes.

Once he had that important place, Brock led a force himself to recapture Sandwich and chase the Americans off Canadian soil. Once that was done, instead of waiting around for reinforcements he knew would never come, Brock did what the Americans least expected.

He took his small, very small, army across the river and captured Detroit. That was the only time in American history that one of their cities fell to an enemy.

Then he dashed back to the Niagara Peninsula because he knew that was where the Americans must attack next.

They had amassed thousands of troops just across the river from Fort George at the mouth of the Niagara River where it pours into Lake Ontario. To defend Canada Brock had about a third, maybe only a quarter, as many men.

In the dark, before dawn on the 13th of October, the Americans attacked. Not at Fort George, where Brock expected them, but up river at Queenston.

When Brock got word the Americans were landing troops at Queenston he didn't believe it. He figured it was just a feint to draw him away from Fort George.

If the Americans captured Queenston and left the British with Fort George, the American army would have bottled itself up on a high hill and the British force, smaller but better, would still be intact.

It was hours before Brock realized the Americans weren't kidding. They really did intend to hold the heights above Queenston.

It was hours before Brock realized the Americans weren't kidding. They really did intend to hold the heights above Queenston.

He realized he had to get them out of there. If the Americans planted big guns up on that high ground they would prevent British troop movements in the area.

So Brock galloped off to Queenston and led his men in a charge up the hill.

The first charge broke. The Americans had a lot of men up that hill and the British soldiers dropped like flies.

Brock rallied his men at the bottom of the hill and jollied them into trying again. He was that kind of leader. He was in the lead, taller than anybody else, all done up in his red scarlet coat and waving his sword. A Tennessee militiamen drilled him right through the heart with his squirrel rifle at 30 yards. Brock was dead before he hit the ground.

The British waited for some Indian scouts to catch up with them. The Indians didn't kill many Americans but they scared them. The Americans had heard terrible tales about Indians.

When they heard those war whoops their knees turned to water. With the Indians whooping and the British soldiers now re-organized, they chased the Americans off the hill and killed or captured most of their army.

But they had lost Isaac Brock, the best general the British had in North America. If he had lived, he could have won the war in a year. Without him, neither side was weak enough to lose but neither had a general who could win.

Originally broadcast October 13, 1987

Spectre of Doom

John Schrank was a quiet young man, short and chubby. He never caused anybody any trouble in his life until the 14th of October in 1912. That was the day he shot the president of the United States.

Schrank was born in Germany and raised in New York City where he worked in his uncle's saloon. He never married, got drunk six times a year and then not noisily, and never discussed politics. He voted sometimes for the Democrats, sometimes for the Republicans.

In 1895, when Schrank was 19 and working for his uncle, Theodore Roosevelt became the police commissioner of New York. He immediately closed down a bunch of saloons that had been ignoring the licensing laws, including Schrank's uncle's. It was out of business for two months then reopened. Schrank later said he didn't hold that against Roosevelt.

The careers of both men prospered. Roosevelt went on to be vice-president of the United States. In the fall of 1901, the president, William McKinley, was assassinated by a madman and Roosevelt became president. He served that term then another, then was defeated.

Schrank inherited his uncle's saloon in 1904 and ran it for seven years. Then, he suddenly lost interest. He sold the place and spent his time reading and brooding.

On the night that Roosevelt inherited the presidency back when McKinley was killed, Schrank had a dream. McKinley's ghost told him that Roosevelt had murdered him.

In 1912, Roosevelt decided to make a come-back. He ran, not as a Republican as he had in the past, but as the candidate for a newly-created outfit called the Bull Moose Party. By now, Schrank was quite crazy, although nobody realized it because he was as quiet and well-mannered as ever. Besides, he was quite well-to-do and nobody questions the prosperous.

As Roosevelt set out on his campaign, Schrank followed. He bought a new revolver in a gun shop in Charleston then followed Roosevelt from city to city. He had chances to shoot him in Chattanooga and Chicago but he seems to have lost his nerve.

The next stop was Milwaukee. And that's where Schrank struck.

Roosevelt left his hotel and stepped into a car which would take him to make a speech. Schrank was waiting on the sidewalk. He reached between the heads of two men in the crowd around the car and fired once.

The bullet went through Roosevelt's coat, the metal case he kept his glasses in, and through the text of his speech. That speech was 50 pages thick and was folded once, so it took most of the force out of the bullet. The bullet went into Roosevelt's chest. The doctors left it there.

Roosevelt didn't bleed much. He insisted on giving the speech before he went to the hospital. That lasted 50 minutes.

Before Schrank could fire a second shot, he was grabbed by Roosevelt's secretary, a former football player.

Roosevelt lost that election and retired. Schrank was declared insane and spent the rest of his life in a mental hospital. He died on the 42nd anniversary of the night he dreamed he saw McKinley's ghost.

> *On the night that Roosevelt inherited the presidency, Schrank had a dream. McKinley's ghost told him that Roosevelt had murdered him.*

Originally broadcast October 14, 1993

THE PRINCESS OF ESPIONAGE

Just before dawn on the 15th of October in 1917, a French officer went to the cell of Margaret Gertrude Zelle McLeod. She had been living in that cell for seven months.

There were three beds — one for her, the others for a pair of nuns who lived with her to make sure she didn't try to commit suicide.

The officer told her that her appeal had been turned down. If she was pregnant, she should say so now. Otherwise, the firing squad was waiting.

The woman looked at the two nuns' beds and said: "You must be fooling."

Then she got dressed in her best grey dress, straw hat and black shoes and went to meet the firing squad.

Margaret McLeod was a small-time spy, if she was one at all. She had once been a high-priced prostitute and dancer but that was in the past.

Her real fame, strangely enough, lay in the future. Under her old stage name of Mata Hari, she has become the most famous spy in history.

After the war, the French claimed she had been a master spy who had stolen secrets that cost the lives of maybe 200,000 men.

But of course the French shot her, so they were eager to tell stories justifying their action. The British had caught her a year or so earlier and they had merely told her to go home. And the British weren't famous in the First World War for being easy on spies.

Margaret Zelle was born in Holland and raised in an expensive convent school. She married an army officer 17 years older than she was, a Dutchman named McLeod, the great-grandson of a Scotsman who had settled in Holland.

Mrs. McLeod went out to the Dutch East Indies with her husband. He was a bad guy, a drunk and a bully. Later, in divorce court, they each accused the other of awful things. Probably the worst Mrs. McLeod did was hustle a few rich Dutchmen out east then later blackmail them. She said her husband put her up to it.

They returned to Holland and split up. Mrs. McLeod, the ex-Mrs. McLeod now, went to Paris and tried to make a living as a dancer, a prostitute and an artist's model. She was a spectacular failure at all three.

Then she had a stroke of genius. She put together a dance act based on what she recalled of the native dances she had seen in the east. She was tall and dark, and claimed she was a Malaysian princess, Mata Hari, the daughter of the dawn.

In the course of what she called her authentic Malaysian dances she took off all her clothes. That was really something in those days, although figure-wise she didn't have . . . well, if she was in business today she'd be no threat to Dolly Parton.

She was tall and dark, and claimed she was a Malaysian princess, Mata Hari, the daughter of the dawn.

She became a big show-biz sensation and hung around with a lot of rich men who showered her with money and diamonds. Easy come, easy go.

When the First World War broke out, she was certainly involved in a little low-level spying for the Germans, the British and the French. But they all knew about her.

She was reported to have kept a lot of letters from various rich and powerful men, including the foreign minister of France. That turned out to be true years later when researchers went through her papers.

So, it just might have made a lot of sense for the French to get rid of her. The politicians who had known her in the past wanted her out of the way, and the French intelligence officers who hadn't been able to protect their country's secrets needed a scapegoat.

And it gave history a great legend.

Originally broadcast October 15, 1984

COMFORTABLY NUMB

Since the dawn of history, doctors of one sort or another had been looking for ways to kill pain as they worked on their patients. Various narcotics were used in the Orient before biblical times. In the 1800s, a Scottish doctor who worked in India had quite a bit of success with hypnotism. So did a Viennese doctor named Mesmer. In fact, mesmerize is still a synonym in our language for hypnotize.

The Congress of the United States offered a reward of $100,000 for anyone who could make surgery painless.

In late 1844, a young dentist named Horace Wells was watching a vaudeville show in Hartford, Connecticut. The showman was giving various members of the audience whiffs of nitrous oxide, known as laughing gas. The inhalers were laughing loudly and hopping around the stage, apparently quite happy.

Dr. Wells noticed that one of them had hit his leg quite hard on a table but didn't seem to be in any pain.

Intrigued, Dr. Wells went to another young dentist, a former partner of his named William Morton. Wells knocked himself out with laughing gas, then had Morton pull one of his teeth. He didn't feel a thing.

About that time, people were experimenting with ether. Nobody saw it as having any medical use. People would hold parties and sniff it and get happy. It was a drug like marijuana is today.

So Wells tried ether, too. He became convinced that it was an even better pain killer and he arranged to demonstrate it before a class at Massachusetts General Hospital in Boston.

Wells knocked out a medical student with ether and then pulled a tooth. As the student woke up he began to groan. The class burst into laughter and Wells fled in embarrassment.

If he had stayed around long enough to question the student he would have found out he hadn't felt a thing. The groan was caused by a stomach cramp from the ether. That cramp passed in a few minutes.

Wells' partner, Morton, kept looking into anesthetics, mostly under the supervision of a doctor and chemist named Charles Jackson.

Morton was suspicious of Jackson and rightly so. Jackson had tried to steal Samuel Morse's invention, the telegraph, just a couple of years earlier and had been caught at it.

On the 16th of October, at Massachusetts General Hospital, where Wells had failed two years ago, Morton put a patient to sleep with ether. Then a doctor removed a tumor from his neck and sewed up the wound. The patient didn't feel a thing.

Morton, who was only 27, figured he was on the verge of fame and fortune. But Dr. Jackson, the invention stealer, claimed a part of the discovery. Morton offered him 10 per cent. Jackson agreed, took it, then sued for more.

Morton put a patient to sleep with ether. Then a doctor removed a tumor from his neck and sewed up the wound. The patient didn't feel a thing.

Dr. Wells, the laughing gas man, now appeared and said he was the inventor of anaesthetic. Within two years Wells went crazy and killed himself.

By now, the lawyers were making money as everybody involved sued everybody else. Wells' family kept his lawsuit going after his death.

In 1865, Morton died penniless. He had gone crazy as well. He was buried in Boston and Jackson went to visit his grave.

When he saw the tombstone of his old enemy, Jackson snapped and began prancing around, laughing like a madman, which he was. They carted him off and he died seven years later in an asylum.

So who did discover anaesthesia? Well, it turned out that while Morton, Wells and Jackson were fighting over it, a doctor named Long in Georgia had first used ether, then chloroform, for operations a good two years before any of them. But he had never got around to patenting it, until years later.

Originally broadcast October 16, 1985

THE PALLID POLE

Frederic Chopin was a strange mixture of French and Polish. His father was a Frenchman who moved to Poland about the time of the French Revolution, apparently more for economic than political reasons.

The older Chopin was a musician, although not a particularly good one. He was a schoolteacher who did rather well, rising quickly and becoming a well-to-do citizen of Poland. He married a Polish girl and they had several children.

Two of them, Frederic and a sister, had tuberculosis almost from birth.

Young Frederic was a genius but a difficult one. He could play the piano soon after he could talk. And he was a clever cartoonist and actor. He could have made his mark at either career.

But he wasn't a very good student; if he wasn't interested in a subject, he didn't pay much attention to it. His parents hollered and whined as parents always do when he came home with bad report cards.

But they were very proud of his musical talent and they hired a good pianist to work as a tutor with him. This pianist was the perfect teacher, a happy, irresponsible man who loved playing the piano, chasing the girls and sipping vodka.

The result was that young Frederic Chopin was a big name in Polish music while he was still in his early teens.

He went to Vienna a couple of times and did very well there. But he couldn't stay away from Poland long because he had a strange sort of patriotism. He was a typical artist, very self-centred and an awful strain on his friends. But at the same time he had a deep feeling for his country that was quite mystical.

All the books and plays about pale young men who fall in love but die tragically are Chopin's life story told and retold.

In 1839 he set out for Paris, the musical capital of the world at the time. His friends ambushed his coach and sang a song they had written for him, a sort of schmaltzy, pseudo-patriotic song. Then they gave him a package of Polish soil.

Chopin made a teary, patriotic speech then continued on his way and never saw Poland again.

He took Paris by storm. He was a superb pianist, maybe one of the dozen best the world has ever seen. And he loved to write for the piano.

He was just what the ladies loved — pale, always on the verge of death, a very snappy dresser, with a habit of sitting down at the piano and playing just for every woman in the room, they all thought.

All the books and plays about pale young men who fall in love but die tragically are Chopin's life story told and retold.

Chopin's most famous love affair was with the French novelist, George Sand. Despite the name, George Sand was a woman. She used a man's name to overcome the prejudice that was common in those days against women writers.

Sand was just the opposite of Chopin, a tough woman who wore men's clothes and smoked a cigar. They lived together for seven or eight years but drifted apart because the other ladies wouldn't leave Chopin alone. And, poor fellow, he was too weak to fight them off.

On the 17th of October in 1849, only 39 years old, pale, frail and handsome in a sickly way, poor Chopin coughed his last. And when they buried him in Paris they spilled his little package of Polish soil over his coffin.

Originally broadcast October 17, 1985

WOMEN ARE PEOPLE, TOO

Emily Murphy was one tough lady. Nice, but tough.

She was born in Ontario and married a clergyman when she was only 19. She later admitted to friends that she had first met him when she was 12 or 13 and decided then she'd marry him. And what Emily wanted, Emily got.

There was plenty of money in both families. Emily had lots of time to write and paint and travel because she had a couple of servants to take care of the house and kids.

Her husband was able to take on whatever church work interested him so they travelled a lot. For two years they wandered around England.

Emily was an excellent writer and she wrote articles and books using the pen-name Janey Canuck.

Although she was rich herself and didn't lack for anything, Emily had a strong social conscience and worried about others, especially women who were poorer than she was.

In 1911, when she was living in Alberta, she met a farm woman who had worked all her life to help her husband make a farm out of the bare prairie. Then he ran off with another woman, sold the farm and left her penniless.

The law allowed that because it assumed women couldn't handle money so everything they owned was really their husbands'. They didn't even own what they owned. Because, under Canadian law, they weren't people.

Emily set out to correct that. She started by button-holing the attorney-general of Alberta. He smiled and wished her well but said he wasn't interested in helping her.

Emily stood on the steps of the Legislature and grabbed each member as he went in and out. In 1911, she got the law changed.

In 1916, a group of Edmonton ladies tried to go to court to see how young prostitutes were being treated. They ran into trouble. The prosecutor said the evidence in the cases of such women was unfit for the ears of ladies in mixed company and asked them to leave.

So the ladies left and went to Emily to ask what they should do. Emily was so angry she stormed into the office of the attorney-general, the same man who hadn't helped her the last time.

Emily had an ingenious idea. If the trials of prostitutes weren't fit for mixed company, then they should be heard in courts run by women. Of course, the idea was preposterous. There wasn't a woman judge in the whole British empire.

> *Emily had an ingenious idea. If the trials of prostitutes weren't fit for mixed company, then they should be heard in courts run by women.*

The attorney-general, a man named Cross, smiled his bland smile again. "How soon can you be ready to be sworn in?" he asked. That's how she became Judge Emily Murphy.

Naturally, Judge Murphy was a heroine among the women who were agitating to get the vote. Women, of course, couldn't vote in those days.

And she became a leader in the women's vote movement. But that got nowhere. So she decided to take another tack.

She began agitating to have a woman made a senator. If a woman could sit in the Senate then it would be a short step to give all women the vote.

In 1921, the Montreal Women's Club asked the prime minister, Robert Borden, to appoint Emily to the Senate. Mr. Borden replied he couldn't because the law said a senate seat could only go to a qualified person and women, under Canadian law, weren't persons.

There it sat until 1927. Then Emily and four others got the case to the Supreme Court of Canada. The court ruled Mr. Borden had been right, women weren't persons under Canadian law.

In those days, there was one court above the Supreme Court of Canada, the privy council in London. So they appealed there.

And, on the 18th of October in 1929, the privy council announced what Canadian men had known all along: Canadian women are persons.

Originally broadcast October 18, 1985

A MAN OF MANNERS

Historians have got into the habit of being concerned with dates and battles and politicians and soldiers, and ignoring the people who really count: the ones who decide how we dress and eat and act toward each other.

That's why you seldom hear Beau Nash's name mentioned these days. But he was a man who had a real and lasting effect on the whole English-speaking world.

Nash was the son of a young woman of good family and an unknown father. His mother book up with a man who was in the business of making bottles. He wasn't rich, but he had a few bucks to spare and his wife's son, young Richard, seemed to be very bright. So the family saved up its pennies and sent him to Oxford.

There young Nash studied hard at the two subjects that he was eventually to make his life's work: women and gambling. He was booted out after only a few terms because of his involvement with a woman.

Next he tried the army, but that wasn't for him. He stayed in London and studied law. Nash would have made a great courtroom lawyer if he could ever have left the girls and cards alone. But that wasn't possible.

However, he did make quite a name for himself. He was put in charge of the social life of the law school, the Inns of Court, an ancient institution that involved a lot of pomp and ceremony. In 1694 he threw a celebration to mark the coronation of King William.

That was such a success that the king offered him a knighthood. Nash modestly turned it down. He couldn't afford the high cost of carrying on at the high court.

Instead, he dropped out of law school and made a very good living as a gambler and boyfriend of rich women.

In 1703, the queen was very sick and she went to the hot springs at the town of Bath for a cure. Actually, they didn't help her; she died soon afterwards of a whole medical catalogue of ailments.

But going to Bath became fashionable. And Nash decided to look the place over and see if there was a buck to be made there.

A moneyed class was emerging in England and a lot of people with time and money were looking for ways to rid themselves of both.

Nash made Bath the fashionable place to do it.

The town council ran the hot springs and what little entertainment was in the town. That consisted mostly of a dance hall.

Nash gradually talked the councilors into improving the baths and the dances. He convinced them they should set up a casino. But they didn't know how to run one. No problem. Beau Nash, as he was then known, would lease if from them and pay them a handsome rent.

The nickname Beau was applied to Nash because it meant a man of fashion in those days.

Pretty soon, all the wealthy people in England and France were flocking to Bath. It was the place to be and be seen.

Nash was a kindly dictator. He demanded that men wear light shoes instead of heavy boots on the dance floor. He demanded they stop wearing their swords there. That cut down on the fights and it also made dancing more comfortable because the sword hilts had been jabbing the ladies in the ribs.

Nash demanded good manners. He set new rigorous standards for proper behavior in public places.

He was also a kindly man and talked the wealthy into building the most advanced hospital in the world at Bath.

He made a fortune at his casinos. But he wouldn't let foolish young men throw away their inheritances there.

He never married and he was a great hit with the women. But he wouldn't take advantage of a young lady out for her first big adventure in society.

Beau Nash was born into a crude, uncultured England. He left it more polished and a more pleasant place to live.

And, when you think about it, as England was embarking on its great era of empire-building, that was very important. Because now that British Empire is pretty well gone, what has Britain left all over the globe?

Parliamentary government, trial by jury, the language of Shakespeare and Milton — and good manners.

> *Beau Nash was born into a crude, uncultured England. He left it more polished and a more pleasant place to live.*

Originally broadcast October 19, 1983

CAPITAL GAINING

Quebec was the capital of the British colony of Canada after the conquest of 1759, just as it had been the capital under French rule.

A generation later, the colony was split in two and a new province was created, Ontario. Its first capital was on the Niagara River at what's now the town of Niagara-on-the-Lake. In those days, it was called Newark.

The first governor intended to establish a capital in southwestern Ontario at London. But he had to spend most of his time at York, what's now Toronto, so that became his capital.

In the 1840s, Ontario and Quebec were amalgamated into a double colony called the province of Canada.

The first governor of the new set-up didn't like the idea of running his business out of Quebec City, probably because he subscribed to the official belief of the time that the French-Canadian people would eventually lose their language and culture and disappear into a bigger, English-speaking Canada.

He liked Kingston at the eastern end of Lake Ontario, so he declared that his capital.

But Montreal was emerging as clearly the biggest and most important commercial city in British North America, so there was a lot of pressure to make it the capital.

In fact, it was for a while. Then, in 1849, a Montreal mob got so angry at a law the assembly had passed that they burned down the building that was being used as the Legislature. And they chased the governor-general across town, and would have killed him if a troop of cavalry hadn't protected him.

That put an end to Montreal's ambitions as a capital.

It was decided next to alternate between Quebec City and Toronto. That was a set-up that pleased no

Any time the opposition wanted to bring down the government it would introduce a motion about establishing a new capital.

one and was incredibly awkward. All the files and papers of government had to be packed up and moved every year.

The double colony idea wasn't working. The balance of members between Ontario and Quebec was almost exact and they couldn't agree on anything.

Any time the opposition wanted to bring down the government it would introduce a motion about establishing a new capital and the government would fall in the hassle that followed.

In the early 1850s, one such government fell over the capital issue and a new one was established. It set a record for short Canadian governments: two days.

From time to time, someone would suggest that Ottawa might be a nice compromise, not big or old enough to have violent supporters; in Ontario but right on the border of Quebec, with a nice balance of English- and French-speaking citizens.

The names of six cities were put forward. The Queen was asked to choose. She never came to Canada so she hadn't seen any of them. She went by the advice of her ministers and it was announced in 1857 that Ottawa would be the new capital. Not the capital of Canada, the country we live in today. But the capital of the United Province of Canada, one of several British North American colonies.

For the next 16 or 18 years, the argument went on despite Her Majesty's declaration.

The parliament buildings of the new province were started before the new country was formed. They became our national parliament buildings, which officially opened in July of 1867. But it wasn't until that first session of parliament was over, on the 20th of October in 1867, that a royal proclamation made it official: Ottawa is the capital of Canada.

Originally broadcast October 20, 1992

SHOWING HIS STRIPES

Horatio Nelson was the greatest fighting sailor in history, not just in British history.

On sailors' uniforms of many countries, not just Britain's, there are three white bands on the back of the wide collar. They are there to recognize Nelson's three great victories.

Nelson was born the year before General James Wolfe died while capturing Canada for Britain. He was a big Wolfe fan. He was the same sort of leader: young, aggressive, not at all tied to old methods or traditions, and not at all very interested in anything but his career.

Nelson went to sea when he was 12 and was a young officer of note in less than 10 years. He devoted his whole life to the British navy — with maybe one exception.

Nelson was married and seems to have loved his wife, at least at first. But in the 1790s, he met Lady Hamilton, Emma, a beautiful creature with a long and fascinating history of her own. Emma was married, but that didn't bother her or Nelson — nor, strangely enough, her husband. Before Nelson's death, all three lived together and Nelson and Emma had a daughter.

That was Nelson's sole attempt at humanity. Otherwise, he was a fighting machine. He lost an eye and an arm in battle and it didn't bother him a bit. In fact, he seems to have been very proud of his injuries and did everything he could to draw attention to them.

In 1798, Napoleon was emerging as the bright star of the French Revolution. He had led French armies to victory in Italy and now convinced the French government to allow him to conquer Egypt, cutting England off from India.

Napoleon conquered Egypt. Then Nelson came along with a small fleet and sank the French fleet at the mouth of the Nile River, in the battle of Aboukir Bay. That put an end to Napoleon's plans for conquest in the east. And that's the first of those white stripes on a sailor's collar.

In 1801, Nelson sailed to the Danish capital of Copenhagen, a port city. The Danes had decided to fight against the British, with the French. Nelson wasn't in command of that battle and the man who was was a very timid admiral.

Nelson said the only way to win this one was to sail right into Copenhagen Bay and out-gun them. So he did. At the last minute, his boss signalled him to pull back; it was too risky.

Nelson put his telescope up to his blind eye and said: "Can't see any signal from the admiral. I guess it must be all right to go ahead."

He did. And he won. And that's the second white stripe on a sailor's collar.

Then in 1805 came the big one, the third white stripe: the Battle of Trafalgar. Napoleon intended to invade England. If he succeeded, he would be the ruler of all Europe. He already had the rest.

Nelson was a fighting machine. He lost an eye and an arm in battle and it didn't bother him a bit. In fact, he seems to have been very proud of his injuries.

The only trouble with that plan was that the British Navy ruled the seas. Napoleon figured the way to beat it was to put together a huge fleet of French and Spanish ships and batter the British navy. Then, with it out of the way, he would send his army across the English Channel.

It happened just the other way. Nelson, who had been trying for years to get the French fleet to fight, couldn't wait.

On the 21st of October in 1805, the two fleets met. It was Nelson's masterpiece. He sank 17 or 18 of the enemy ships and didn't lose one of his own, although a couple were so badly damaged they were useless. Napoleon never again had a navy that threatened the British.

Nelson triumphed. But in the process, he was killed.

Originally broadcast October 21, 1987

LISZTOMANIA!

Franz Liszt was born in Hungary on the 22nd of October in 1811. His father was an amateur musician of some talent and he got young Franz interested in music.

The old man had also spent a couple of years in a monastery as a young man and he also gave him an interest in religion.

Franz started writing music when he was only eight. When he was nine he gave a concert and was so impressive a group of rich Hungarians put up the money for him to get a musical education.

Old man Liszt took the boy to Vienna then to Paris. Fifty years earlier, Mozart's father had paraded his boy around Europe, showing off his genius, and became wealthy in the process. Old Man Liszt tried the same. With no success.

The old man was a bit of a fumbler. Everything he touched turned to mud.

Young Franz' genius overcame his father's failing and he was a showbiz sensation. He gave concerts in Paris, London, Berlin — all the big-time musical towns. Then the old man died. So at the age of 16, Liszt sent for his mother and supported her with his music. Mama had stayed home in Hungary when Papa and young Franz went on the road.

Unlike her husband and son, Mama Liszt had no use for religion.

As you would expect, the strain of constant concerts and being the breadwinner soon proved too much for a youngster and Liszt collapsed, had what we'd call a nervous breakdown. That brought on a desire to turn his back on the world and become a priest.

That was too much for Mama. She threw up her hands and went home.

Liszt snapped out of whatever was ailing him and stayed in Paris and a life of music. Not just playing music for a living but a life of music. For the rest of his life, Liszt would be very much a keystone of European culture.

He wrote hundreds of musical works. He also tried to write a history of music and criticism. Unfortunately, his wandering life and erratic education left Liszt unskilled in any tongue. He spoke practically no Hungarian. His German had a French accent, his French had a German accent, and his English was just awful.

But that doesn't mean Liszt couldn't communicate; he just didn't do it very well with language.

As a musician, Liszt might have been one of the great communicators of all time.

His audiences, mostly all women, went crazy over him. They literally fainted. Liszt himself was also a fainter. The writers came up with a name for his fans' adoration: Lisztomania.

Liszt's audiences, mostly all women, went crazy over him. They literally fainted. The writers came up with a name for his fans' adoration: Lisztomania.

Liszt would step up to the piano, usually dressed in green velvet. He would remove his green gloves slowly and throw them away.

By the time he sat down and touched the first key, the ladies were squealing and fainting all around the hall.

Liszt had so many affairs with women nobody has tried to count them. He lived for a while with a French countess who left her husband and children for him. They had three children. Liszt, the soft, doe-eyed charmer, was quite cold to them.

Later, he left the French countess and took up with a Polish princess, while all the time having affairs on the side with some of the female big names of the time: Lola Montez, the dancer, Marie Duplessis, the woman whose life was the basis of the novel *Camille* . . . and others and others and others.

Liszt moved with George Sand, Paganini, Baudelaire — all the big literary and musical names of the time. His pal Wagner eventually married Liszt's daughter.

Then, when he was 44, Liszt turned religious again. He moved to Rome and took holy orders. He didn't become a priest. That would have involved a vow of chastity.

And so, Franz Liszt lived out the rest of his life studying religion and music. When he died 20 years later, his friends were busy organizing a music festival. No priest was handy so they had Franz Liszt, the musical genius and devout Catholic, buried by a Lutheran minister who happened to be nearby.

Originally broadcast October 22, 1990

WRITER OF THE PURPLE SAGE

Zane Grey was the man who invented the modern conception of the wild west.

He wrote more than 80 books, mostly about cowboys and Indians and miners and saloonkeepers. Others had written westerns before him and plenty of others after. But it was Zane Grey who came up with the strong, silent hero, the absolutely evil villain and the sweet, virtuous rancher's daughter who rides off into the sunset with one after being rescued from the other.

Zane Grey was a strange man with a life history at least as interesting as anything he wrote.

The Zanes came to the New World from Germany before the American Revolution. One of them was involved in a terrible battle and siege at a fort that later became the town of Wheeling, West Virginia.

The family later moved west and the town of Zanesville, Ohio was founded by them. That's where Grey was born and raised.

His full name was Pearl Zane Grey. Grey always said there was nothing peculiar about a boy being named Pearl. He used that first name for years. But once he was away from his mother, he started calling himself Zane.

Old man Grey was a dentist and he insisted that Zane and his brother Red follow the same trade. Red wasn't very enthusiastic about the life of a dentist. Zane detested it.

Both were ardent fishermen, despite their parents' prejudice against fishing. They thought people who fished were time wasters and, as often as not, drunks.

The Grey boys travelled all over the world fishing. But they didn't drink. Zane once bought a ship in Nova Scotia, one of his favorite fishing spots. He had it converted into a luxurious floating fishing lodge. But he wouldn't sign the papers to buy it until he'd been assured it had never been used as a rum runner.

Grey was a superb baseball player. If he didn't invent the curve ball, he was certainly one of the first

to use it. Then the ball diamond was changed. The pitcher's mound was moved back 10 feet from the plate, 60 feet instead of 50. That threw off Grey's curve, although he was still good enough to go through dental college on a baseball scholarship. That was his father's idea.

Brother Red was even better at baseball. He played in the National League for some years.

Grey was practicing dentistry in New York and hating every minute of it when he met a beautiful young rich woman. They fell in love and were married.

She realized how much Grey hated what he was doing. He wanted to be a writer. So she told him to quit and write full-time.

It took several years. His first four books were turned down by publishers. Then, in 1912, Grey hit it big with a book called *Riders of the Purple Sage*.

> *Grey was no businessman but his wife handled all sales and even came up with a new idea: selling movie rights.*

From then on, the books just poured out. Grey was no businessman but his wife handled all sales and even came up with a new idea: selling movie rights. Actually, leasing movie rights.

In exchange for a lot of money, a movie producer would have the rights to a Zane Grey western for seven years. After that, they were up for sale again.

More than a dozen of Grey's books were made into movies several times. Many of them three and four times.

Grey travelled all over the road fishing. He was away from his wife and kids for months at a time, fishing and researching. On these trips he usually had along a young woman or two, always described as his niece or his secretary. Nevertheless, he and his wife had a life-long love affair.

Grey died of a heart attack on the 23rd of October in 1939, a rich and famous man. He had written so much, and his wife had played the market so carefully, that more of his books have been published since his death than before it.

Originally broadcast October 23, 1990

BLACK THURSDAY

Until the First World War, mankind consisted pretty well of the rich and the poor. In North America and, to a lesser extent, in western Europe, there was a prosperous middle class. But generally speaking, you were near starvation or you ordered champagne by the bucketful.

Or, at least it looked that way.

When governments discovered the war was costing more than any other in history, they went to their people for loans. In a wave of patriotism, people reached into the mattresses and came up with some incredible amounts.

In Canada, in 1917 alone, more than half a billion dollars was invested in wartime government bonds.

Stock market sharpies on both sides of the border became aware that North Americans could be induced to part with an awful lot of money if the pitch was right.

So, once the war was out of the way, the stock market swung into a new phase. Stock salesmen didn't make their pitches to businessmen anymore. They went after Mr. and Mrs. Average. They extended credit and they sold stock like there was no bill being presented someday.

Toward the end of the 20s it was quite common for people to buy stock with only 20 per cent down. As long as the price of the stock kept climbing, all was well.

And it kept climbing. During the summer of 1929 alone, the *New York Times* stock index jumped from 340 to 440.

The brokers who were extending the credit had to get it from somewhere, so the banks were lending to them. Money was in such demand that the brokers were paying 15 per cent for it. But not complaining.

They were passing it on to the customers.

> *Toward the end of the 20s it was quite common for people to buy stock with only 20 per cent down. As long as the price of the stock kept climbing, all was well.*

During the 20s, everybody wanted the latest entertainment machine, a radio. The stock of the Radio Corporation of America was selling for 94 dollars in 1928. In the fall of 1929, it was at $505. General Electric jumped from $129 to $396. Everybody wanted a phone. AT&T, the phone company, jumped from $180 to $336.

The suckers thought it would go on forever. The smart guys closed their eyes and pretended it would.

Stock exchanges in Toronto and Montreal did even better than New York. In addition to all those industrial stocks, northern Ontario and Quebec seemed to be sprouting gold mines.

Even nature was co-operating. The Prairie harvest in the fall of 1928 was more than half-a-billion bushels of wheat, the greatest in history.

Then, on the afternoon of Wednesday, the 23rd of October, in 1929, the stock players figured it was time to take their money out.

Nobody knows who started it or why. Millions of dollars have been spent on research and hundreds of books have been written about it.

But nobody knows exactly what happened.

By the close of trading that day, there were a lot of sell orders unfilled.

The brokers got on the phones to their customers overnight and told them there was nothing to worry about. The buyers would take over the market the next day.

But they didn't. Thursday, the 24th of October is down in the history books as Black Thursday.

The market rallied a bit but then it started down again. The boom was over. The Great Depression was on.

Originally broadcast October 24, 1985

FROM PISTOL TO PENCIL

On the 25th of October in 1921, Bat Masterson, the great western gunfighter and lawman, died. Not out west, as you'd expect, but in New York City, at his desk as he wrote his column. Bat Masterson had become a sportswriter.

Anyone who owns a TV set knows that Bat Masterson was one of the greats of the wild west. He was a pal of Wyatt Earp and Doc Holiday and all those other good guys.

If you missed the series about Bat Masterson, you probably saw him in the series about Wyatt Earp. Or in the dozens of movies that were either about Bat or had him as a secondary character.

Well, they were pretty close to the truth. Sheriffs and marshalls in the west in those days south of the border spent most of their careers somewhere between the edge of the underworld and outright corruption. By those standards, Bat Masterson was a good guy. But his brand of honesty isn't to be confused with the rigid, Boy Scout attitude of the Mounties to the north.

And his pals, the Earp brothers, weren't always as scrupulous. In fact, at one stage in their careers in Tombstone, while Bat was their pal, Wyatt and Virgil Earp were known as The Fighting Pimps.

Like many famous Americans, Bat Masterson was born in Canada, at Henryville in Iberville County in Quebec in 1853. That's south of Montreal, eight miles from the American border.

Before Bat was 10, his family moved to Illinois and that's where he was brought up. He went west and worked as a hunter, guide, scout for the army, cowboy, lawman, and gambler. That was his principal occupation all his life, gambling. And he was good at it.

In the 1880s, Bat's career as a lawman was pretty well over and he became a saloon keeper and gambler. He ran places in Denver and that area. He also promoted prizefights and was a referee in some of the big ones of the time.

Despite all his playing around well into his later years, Bat was a devoted family man. And that was a lot of playing around. Bat probably had more success with the ladies than any of the western heroes.

In May of 1902, Bat and his wife moved to New York. He took with him a mighty reputation. He was reported to have killed 38 men in his career. Bat was modest about it. He said it was only about 27 because he didn't count Indians.

That sort of racist remark was commonplace in those times. But Bat said several things in his last few years that indicate he became genuinely ashamed of the way he and many other white men had treated Indians out west in those days.

Bat was reported to have killed 38 men in his career, but he was modest about it. He said it was only about 27 because he didn't count Indians.

We'll never know how many men he actually killed. Bat told several stories at various times because he was a great kidder.

On his arrival in New York, Bat was arrested for swindling an elder of the Mormon Church in a card game on the train east. He indignantly denied the charge, and indeed, the alleged victim didn't show up in court.

Teddy Roosevelt, the president, appointed him a federal marshall for New York. That was a job that paid well and involved no work.

Bat had done a bit of writing out west for the sports pages and he took up that trade with the old *New York Morning Telegraph*. Mostly he covered boxing.

Sports writers in those days, just like today, seldom wrote anything critical of the sports they covered. But Bat was a boxing fan first and a writer second.

He never hesitated to expose crooked fights and he was knowledgeable enough at the fight game to know one when he saw it. Bat became a very popular columnist and eventually was a shareholder in the *Morning Telegraph* and treasurer of the company that owned it.

He had a bright and droll style of writing. He once wrote about ice: "I notice things work out fairly evenly in the end. The poor and the rich get about the same amount of ice, for instance. Only the poor get it in the winter and the rich in the summer."

He was at his desk, pounding the typewriter when his heart stopped on the 25th of October in 1921. He would have been 68 in another month.

Originally broadcast October 25, 1983

CODE NAME: CICERO

Until almost the end of the Second World War, Turkey was neutral. That made it a very important place for the German, the British, and the Russian secret services. Here was a country, right in the middle of things, where each of the fighting countries maintained embassies and ran elaborate intelligence operations out of them.

Each group tried to spy on the others and each was conscious of what was happening and spent a lot of time and effort on security. The result was something like a fight between two perfectly matched boxers. Every blow was perfect. Every counterblow was perfect. So nothing happened.

Neither side got anything of any value out of the other. Until the night of the 26th of October in 1943, that is.

Then a man who spoke bad French knocked on the door of the first secretary of the German embassy, a man named Jenke.

Jenke vaguely recognized the man as a former servant, a man who had been his valet about a half-dozen years earlier. He couldn't recall his name but he remembered he was an Albanian.

The man said he had some very valuable British secrets and he wanted to sell them to the Germans. Jenke asked the man to wait and he put in a call for a man named Moyzich who was in charge of spying at the embassy.

When Moyzich arrived, the man got right to the point: he had some very valuable British documents. Actually, not the documents themselves, but photographs of them. He had two rolls of film that would cost 20,000 British pounds. That was $100,000 Canadian in those days.

The man said he wasn't there to dicker. It was take it or leave it. He would expect an answer in three days. If they did business this time, he would continue to supply the Germans at a price of 15,000 pounds per roll of film.

> *The British ambassador was one of the Foreign Office old boys and he kept a lot more stuff in his safe than he really should have.*

He said two other things: first, he hated the British; and, second, he was the valet to the British ambassador.

Moyzich had to call Berlin because he didn't have that sort of money on hand. In fact, the amount was so huge that only the foreign minister himself could decide whether or not to do business with the man. He mulled it over for a couple of days then decided he couldn't afford not to. That doesn't mean he was convinced.

In fact, he was pretty sure it was a trap the British were setting for him. Things like that just don't happen.

When Moyzich gave the man his 20,000 pounds a day later, he found he'd really got a bargain. The British ambassador was one of the Foreign Office old boys and he kept a lot more stuff in his safe than he really should have, top-secret policy papers and that sort of thing.

The valet opened his safe with a key that the ambassador left lying around and took pictures of everything in it with an ordinary camera.

The Germans code-named the man Cicero and continued to do business with him. They paid him several hundred thousand pounds.

So, you say, how come the Germans lost the war if they had this pipeline to the most important British secrets? Well, nothing's as simple as it first seems.

The British had their own spy in the office of the German foreign minister, so they soon found out he was getting their secret stuff. And, some of the Germans agreed with what the secret papers were saying and some didn't. They spent the rest of the war arguing over whether they were accurate or not.

Cicero? He got away to South America with his money. But when he tried to spent it he found out the Germans had paid him in counterfeit. After the war he sued the German government, but he lost.

Originally broadcast October 26, 1984

THE KING WHO WASN'T

Bessie Wallis Warfield was born in Pennsylvania in 1896. There had been money on both sides of her family, but by the time she came along it was mostly gone. But relatives took pity on her and paid for her education at a finishing school for young ladies in Baltimore. When she was young her family and friends called her Bessiwallis, as if her two names were one.

Bessiwallis married an American naval officer in 1916, but that only lasted five years. Then she married an American named Ernest Simpson. Simpson lived in London and was more British than most Englishmen. He had been an officer in the Coldstream Guards during the First World War and the Simpsons moved in the very top levels of British society. So much so that in 1930 they met the Prince of Wales.

The Prince of Wales, the king's oldest son and heir to the throne, was known to the family as David, although he would be King Edward the Eighth. The prince was maybe the most popular British royal in history. He was a handsome little guy and had a smile that melted any hostility. As he travelled around the country during the hungry 30s he was clearly disturbed by the suffering and unemployment he saw. He wasn't above mentioning it, although members of the royal family aren't supposed to say things like that.

Alas, underneath the charm, the prince was a bit of a lightweight. He was a great chaser of the ladies and by the time he was 40 he'd had long, intense affairs with three women, all of them married. The first was the wife of a Liberal politician he met during an air raid in London in the war.

The second was Lady Thelma Furness, an incredibly rich woman whose husband had inherited a bizillion. Lady Furness introduced him to Mrs. Simpson. And the Prince really fell for her, although he was still carrying on with the other two at the same time. He finally dropped Lady Furness when she took

up with the Aly Khan, the guy who eventually married Rita Hayworth, the movie star.

The prince would soon be king. His father, King George the Fifth, wasn't well. And as king, the prince would be the head of the Church of England. The Church of England was against divorce.

The prince wanted to marry Mrs. Simpson. But if he did, she would have to get a divorce, her second.

None of this was known to the public. In fact, it was carefully concealed. Lord Beaverbrook, the Canadian who had settled in London to publish newspapers and become a lord, was put in charge of keeping the secret. He got a hold of all his fellow publishers and got them to agree to not let the public in on what was happening.

American papers published various stories of royal romance, but the British didn't pay any attention to foreign papers in those days.

The prince had it all figured out. If Mrs. Simpson got her divorce in October of 1936, they could be married in May of 1937. In those days there was a six-month waiting period in England between divorce and remarriage.

The old king died in January of 1936. The prince became king right away, but his coronation wouldn't be until mid-May of 1937. So Mrs. Simpson would be Mrs. King by then and, the new king figured, would be crowned queen along with him.

So a quiet divorce was held on the 27th of October, 1936. Two photographers tried to take pictures as Mrs. Simpson left the divorce court, but policemen were waiting and smashed their cameras.

All was now ready. Except that the Archbishop of Canterbury raised a fuss over the religious issue. The new king said, take us both as king and queen or find a new king. And that's what happened. It was his brother Albert who became king — George the Sixth.

> *By the time of Edward's coronation, Mrs. Simpson would be Mrs. King and, the new king figured, would be crowned queen along with him.*

Originally broadcast October 27, 1987

CRISIS AVERTED

On the 16th of October in 1962, the president of the United States was John Kennedy. Kennedy's military advisors told him that day that they had been examining aerial photos taken of Cuba and they could say definitely that Russian missiles were being installed there.

Much of the hardware had already been delivered. Most of the concrete launching pads had already been built. The rest of the missile hardware was probably at sea, aboard Russian freighters, on its way to Cuba.

Within a very short time, maybe just a couple of weeks, Russian missiles would be able to hit the United States from Cuba.

That news wasn't, in itself, that alarming. The Russians and Americans had each had long-range missiles aimed at each other's cities for a couple of years. The missiles being installed in Cuba were only medium-range, not the most sophisticated in anybody's arsenal.

But President Kennedy was in no mood to take any nonsense from anybody about Cuba.

When Kennedy took over as president, the CIA had been plotting its invasion of the Bay of Pigs for months. Kennedy was told that president Eisenhower, his predecessor, had authorized it. He told the CIA to go ahead, although he had misgivings about it.

It had turned out to be a clumsy, embarrassing failure.

The Russian head man at the time was Khruschev. At their first meeting in Vienna, Khruschev was clearly the winner, brow-beating Kennedy, who was then a brand-new president.

Kennedy was determined that this time he wouldn't back down.

He ordered his military people to prepare for two possible orders he might give: one, an air strike that would take out the missile sites; and two, a naval blockade of Cuba.

The military advisors got cracking on those alternatives, plus another of their own devising, a plan to drop the atom bomb on Cuba. The president's brother, Robert Kennedy, the attorney-general, looked over that plan and said to one of the generals: "You guys just can't be found wrong, can you? If this turns out to be a bad idea, there'll be nobody around to say you made a mistake."

For the next six days Kennedy and his people worked in secret. On the second day they discarded the idea of the air strike. It would have killed 25,000 Cubans and might still not have smashed all the missile sites.

On the seventh day, Kennedy went public. He said he was starting a naval blockade of all missile equipment headed for Cuba. He didn't call it a blockade; that sounded too warlike. He called it a quarantine.

It was the closest to war that Russian and the United States have come. Americans figured they were on the edge of World War Three. Supermarkets were crowded as people hoarded food.

There was an anti-American outburst from peace groups in Canada, Britain and Europe.

In Moscow, Khruschev said the Americans had just about declared war. But at the same time he sent a secret message to Kennedy: we'll dismantle our missiles if you'll promise not to invade Cuba.

On the 28th of October, two days later Kennedy sent the message to Khruschev: you've got a deal.

In the calendar of the Roman Catholic church, it was the Feast day of St. Jude, the patron saint of the impossible.

> *At their first meeting in Vienna, Khruschev was clearly the winner. Kennedy was determined that this time he wouldn't back down.*

Originally broadcast October 28, 1985

CHEF'S SPECIAL

On the 29th of October in 1828, an Irish sailing ship, the Granicus, left Quebec, bound for Britain with a load of lumber. It carried passengers, a small crew and the captain, for a total of 25.

Among the crew was a man named Harrington, apparently a cook or cook's assistant. We know little about him, except he appears to have been a mulatto and his mother lived in Liverpool.

The Granicus was at sea less than a week, making very little headway against strong winds. It was off the east end of Anticosti Island, in the St. Lawrence River, not very far from Quebec. It was foggy and the Granicus grounded on a reef.

The weather was bad and the water was choppy, but all hands managed to get ashore without much trouble. They must have been able to make several trips in the ship's boats because they were able to bring along all their clothes, plenty of food and tools, and even the ship's log.

When they got ashore they found a cabin that had been built and stocked with food, just in case of shipwreck. So they settled down to wait for someone to rescue them.

They realized it might be quite a while. It certainly was. They were still all alive and well more than three months later. Then the entries in the logbook suddenly stop.

In May, 1929, more than six months after the Granicus was wrecked, a sailing ship ventured into the same area, looking for fresh water. The captain and three sailors went ashore.

Right away they found a slashed, blood-stained dress that had belonged to one of the passengers. They went back to their ship for guns, then returned.

They made their way to the cabin and found everybody dead. Bodies were lying all over the place, hacked and slashed. Some were hanging by ropes from the roof beams.

Lying in a hammock in the corner was Harrington, a big man. He couldn't have been dead long, according to the men who found him. At first, they thought he was just sleeping.

He had left a note, asking that a letter he had written be sent on to his mother in Liverpool. The men opened that letter and found out what had happened.

Apparently the ordeal had unbalanced Harrington's brain. He decided the only way to survive was to kill all the others, who were going to die anyway, or so he thought. He would survive by eating them.

The big mystery of the whole affair is just how he managed to kill every single one of them without the others being warned in time to defend themselves.

A mystery that's perhaps better left unsolved.

> *The survivors of the shipwreck were still all alive and well more than three months later. Then the entries in the logbook suddenly stop.*

Originally broadcast October 29, 1984

DIVINE INSTIGATION

The southern United States had had slavery since before the American Revolution. It was, in every sense, an institution, an integral part of southern society and economy.,

In many ways, the system was an easy, relaxed one. Both blacks and whites knew where they stood. Many blacks lived free, although not a majority by any means. Many slave owners were decent men who provided churches and schools for their slaves. But they were still slaves.

Most were reconciled to it. But a few weren't. Among those was Nat Turner. Nat was born in 1800 in a remote rural county in southern Virginia. It was a poor area with a very high number of free blacks, almost 2,000 in the county.

Nat was an unusually bright man. His first owner allowed him to learn to read and write and Nat became a Christian preacher among the slaves. His primary job, of course, was to work his owner's plantation.

Nat was a mystic, a man who could recite whole chapters of the old testament and who often fasted for days at a time. Once, he escaped and was gone for a month. Everybody assumed he'd made it to Canada and they'd never see him again.

But Nat came back. He said God wanted him to work among the slaves. He married a slave named Cherry. Their owner died and they were sold to separate owners so they seldom saw each other again.

In the spring and summer of 1831, Nat started hearing voices from God and saw signs — bloodstains on leaves in the fields, and symbols in the sky. God wanted him to lead a slave rebellion.

In February of 1831 there was an eclipse of the sun. In early August there was some sort of atmospheric disturbance, sunspots or some such. Nat now knew the time had come.

He led a rebellion of six other slaves that lasted less than 48 hours. They murdered about 60 whites, mostly women and children.

At first they didn't want to use guns. They were afraid the noise would arouse the countryside. So they hacked their victims to death with axes and swords and farm tools. The whites organized the militia and the reaction was swift and bloody.

In many cases, the rebels were captured by other blacks, both slaves and free men. At the height of the rebellion, there were probably fewer than 50 rebels. A dozen were put on trial and hanged within a couple of weeks.

But Nat escaped for a while. As long as he was on the run, he became a symbol of freedom for a lot of blacks and a symbol of injustice for northern Americans who opposed slavery.

Then, on the 30th of October, 1831, a couple of months after the rebellion started, Nat Turner was captured. It was all over. Two weeks later he was hanged.

But in that two weeks, a Virginia lawyer interviewed Nat at great length. He wrote down his confession in considerable detail. And it became clear that Nat Turner was a much brighter man than average. He was a fanatic, maybe even a bit crazy, but he certainly wasn't stupid.

And that confession, when it was published, made a lot of people think. It made northerners question the whole idea of slavery. And it made southerners more defensive than ever about it.

Nat Turner died a generation before the Civil War. But some people say he started it.

> *As long as Nat was on the run, he became a symbol of freedom for a lot of blacks and a symbol of injustice for northern Americans who opposed slavery.*

Originally broadcast October 30, 1984

BABY BOOM

Charles Miller was a strange man by anybody's definition. He was one of the best lawyers in Toronto in his time and made a respectable sized fortune.

He was a farmboy who put himself through college, never married, only took an occasional drink, and loved owning racehorses.

One night in 1914 he was sitting around with some of his racetrack friends arguing the fine points of horse training. Miller said: It's not as hard as you guys make out. I'll bet you a thousand dollars I can win next year's King's Plate. And he did. He hired a trainer, told him to buy the best horses available, and took first and second in the Plate in the spring of 1915.

On the 31st of October in 1926, a Sunday, Miller dropped dead in his office. He'd been having lunch at a hotel with a couple of lawyer pals and they'd started to argue about law. Miller went back to his office to look up in a lawbook to prove his point. Apparently the dash up three flights of stairs was too much for his heart.

In the preamble to his will, Miller noted he had no family and was under no obligation to provide for anyone, so he was going to indulge himself a little.

He left stock in the Jockey Club to a former attorney-general of Ontario and two clergymen who had been lifelong opponents of horse-racing. He left stock in a Windsor racetrack to every Protestant clergyman in Windsor. He left stock in a brewery owned by Catholics to every Protestant clergyman in Toronto.

The newspapers had great fun watching the various beneficiaries explain how they weren't compromising their principles without actually saying no thanks.

Miller also left stock in the Catholic brewery to each Orange Lodge in Toronto. And he left money for masses to be said for the soul of a lawyer who had died ahead of him, an Orangeman.

He left his winter home in Jamaica to three Toronto lawyers who didn't like one another at all and could be depended on to fight and squabble all the time they were there.

Then he ordered that the rest of his estate, with

Miller noted he had no family and was under no obligation to provide for anyone, so he was going to indulge himself a little.

accumulated interest, be given to the mother who, since his death, gave birth to the greatest number of children as shown under the Vital Statistics Act. The contest was to be decided 10 years after Miller's death.

Now that seems like pretty straightforward language. But right away the lawyers went to work on it.

"Surely that wouldn't include illegitimate children," said one. "That would be encouraging immorality."

"What's legitimate?" asked another. "Everyone knows a child born to an unmarried woman isn't legitimate. But what about a child born to a married woman but whose father isn't her husband?"

And what about babies who are born dead or have since died? Do you include those?

It wasn't long before the courts in Toronto had a constant flow of Miller will cases as people joined what the newspapers called the Great Stork Derby.

One woman forgot to register the births of three of her 10 kids, so she was knocked off the list of potential beneficiaries.

Another had five children by her husband then another five by her boyfriend. She too was out of the running.

What finally happened was that the four major contenders, with 10 children each, and their lawyers got together. They took $165,000 each, and gave $12,500 each to two other contenders with slightly clouded titles.

Those two, in exchange, had to sign away any future rights to the estate.

The estate came to about a million dollars. The lawyers got the rest, of course.

The people who won the money were all decent, hard-working types, all suffering badly from the Depression that was on at the time.

One of the winning families promptly paid back $1800 to the city of Toronto that they'd collected in welfare. One bought a farm, another a small country hotel.

And Charley Miller's name was in the papers long after he'd died.

Originally broadcast October 31, 1983

THE BLUNDERING GUNMEN

Today, nobody's surprised to hear someone has taken a shot at the president of the United States. But back in 1950, that sort of thing just didn't happen. True, three presidents had been assassinated in American history and a gunman almost got President Roosevelt in the 1930s. He missed, and instead killed the mayor of Chicago who was standing behind him.

In 1950 things were different. Harry Truman was the president, the war was over, and except for the fighting in Korea, it was a time of peace.

Puerto Rico was part of the United States, in a way. The Americans had grabbed it from Spain at the turn of the century. It wasn't a state. And it wasn't a territory like Alaska or Hawaii. But it was American.

Most Puerto Ricans seemed happy enough with the set-up, but there was a strong, small nationalist contingent. There's been fighting among various factions in Puerto Rico, but, as wars and revolutions go, it didn't amount to much.

Then, on the first of November in 1950, two Puerto Ricans tried to kill President Truman. If two people hadn't been killed in the attempt, it would have made a funny story.

The two would-be assassins were Oscar Collazo and Griselio Torresola, and they were a scriptwriter's dream. They were an odd couple.

Collazo was 36, a serious man who had a wife and a couple of daughters. He worked as a metal polisher and was active in his union and in the Puerto Rican independence movement. He was such a serious man that when he decided to kill the president he went out and bought a new suit, three shirts, underwear, socks and a snap-brim hat. This was almost like going to church.

Torresola was just the opposite. He was 25 and a bit of a swinger. When the FBI set out afterwards to investigate his background, they gave up when the list of his wives and girlfriends hit about a dozen.

He lived in New York, like Collazo, but he was collecting welfare. In fact, at one time he was a welfare

fraud, drawing cheques in three different names.

There had been some shooting between two rival factions in Puerto Rico and both men took it very seriously. They discussed going back to Puerto Rico to join the fight. Collazo gave Torresola $50 to get a gun. The next day Torresola came back with the gun and $15 change.

Then Collazo said they would probably do more good for their cause if they killed President Truman. That would plunge the United States into civil war and Puerto Ricans could get their independence while the Americans were fighting amongst themselves. Of course, no civil war had ever followed the shooting of a president, but Collazo was a patriot, not a historian.

So they took the train to Washington, walked around for a day and got the lay of the land.

The White House was being repaired at the time, so President Truman was living across the street at Blair House, a residence usually used for visiting dignitaries.

Just after two o'clock on the afternoon of the first of November, Collazo walked up to the guards in front of Blair House. One was standing with his back to Collazo. Collazo pulled his gun and aimed at the guard's back.

The gun misfired and went click. That started the fight. Torresola had walked around to the side of the Blair House and he started shooting from there.

The whole thing lasted three minutes. The Puerto Ricans fired 17 times and the guards 10. Torresola and one guard were killed. Collazo and two guards were wounded.

Collazo was convicted of murder. He said he wouldn't ask the president for mercy. But he got it anyhow.

Just eight days before he was to die, President Truman commuted Collazo's sentence to life. Truman had been in Blair House at the time of the shooting, but he didn't even know about it until it was over.

Two Puerto Ricans tried to kill President Truman. If two people hadn't been killed in the attempt, it would have made a funny story.

Originally broadcast November 1, 1984

THE UNSOCIABLE SOCIALIST

George Bernard Shaw was a genius and a weirdo, both at the same time.

Shaw was born in Ireland, the son of a drunk. His early life seems to have been very disturbing. Dozens of books have been written about him and how his early years twisted his mind. They certainly did strange things to his love life.

Shaw moved to London and started working as a critic and playwright. He was a prolific writer. In his day he turned out 52 plays, writing 1500 words a day in shorthand. He also kept detailed diaries in code that researchers have since deciphered.

As far as we know, Shaw had no sex life until he was 29. Then he took up with his mother's best friend, a woman 15 years older than he was. The woman, Jenny, seems to have been a kind soul but terribly jealous. Shaw suddenly took an interest in a lot of women. Jenny would burst in on him at the most awkward moments.

In 1893, after Shaw and Jenny had been lovers for eight years, she burst in one night when he was with an actress. That was the last straw and ended their affair.

Shaw was an active socialist and that was reflected in most of his plays. He was also a great believer in the power of language.

He spent a lot of time studying how various accents in English determine where a person came from and where he would go — or couldn't. He observed that every Englishman despises most other Englishmen as soon as they open their mouths. He was also concerned with the crazy, illogical spelling of English.

Shaw made a lot of money from his plays. His best, *Pygmalion*, made a fortune. Long after he was dead it was turned into the best musical of all time, *My Fair Lady*.

Shaw wrote *Pygmalion* after he met a language professor from Oxford named Henry Sweet to discuss language. He turned him into Henry Higgins and had him help the flower girl, Liza, climb the social ladder just by teaching her a more cultured accent.

Shaw had affairs — a few real, a few others innocent flings — with practically all the glamour girls of the London theatre.

He married a rich woman and seems to have ignored her most of the time. That probably wasn't as hard for her as it sounds. He was an ill-tempered old devil.

He had all sorts of nutty theories about germs and epidemics and was convinced that doctors were all charlatans. He didn't believe in operations for appendicitis or a lot of other ailments.

In 1950 he was playing croquet at the age of 94. He missed the ball and was so angry he kicked at it. He missed that, too, and fell over. He broke his hip but wouldn't call a doctor until things got really bad. He died of complications, as nasty as ever, on the 2nd of November in 1950. But he left some great plays.

> *Shaw observed that every Englishman despises most other Englishmen as soon as they open their mouths.*

Originally broadcast November 2, 1989

HOT SHOTS

Phoebe Annie Oakley Mozee was born in 1860 away out in the country in Ohio. In those days, little boys played with guns and little girls learned to cook and sew.

But not in the Mozee family. Little Phoebe was a natural marksperson. She could bag a rabbit at 75 yards with her little .22 rifle or knock the head off a quail from the other side of a cornfield.

When a child is as talented as Phoebe and a family is as poor as the Mozees, tradition is quickly ignored and little Phoebe was sent out with her rifle whenever the subject of mealtime came up. And, since Phoebe was one of eight kids, it came up quite often.

It wasn't long before Phoebe discovered that hotels and restaurants in Cincinnati were paying real money for rabbits and quail, and she was soon the family breadwinner.

She was still in her teens and very small. But cute.

Pretty soon Phoebe was dropping into country fairs and turkey shoots and making big money by listening to the local hot shots boast about what good shots they were. Phoebe would wait until they'd talked themselves into a corner then she'd suggest they put up their money. Even after her fame spread, none of them could be seen to back down from a little girl.

When Phoebe was about 18, a sharpshooter named Frank Butler came to town with a wild west show. Butler was the best shot in show business. He had a standing offer of $100 to anyone who could outshoot him. The offer had been up for years and nobody had collected yet.

Until the day he went up against Phoebe. Phoebe outshot Frank. Then she smiled at him and the poor sap was in love. He married her and they went on the road together, as a husband-and-wife sharpshooting act.

She dropped her first and last names and became Annie Oakley. They were a sensation. Annie could shoot a playing card in half by putting a bullet through the thin edge. If Frank threw a handful of bullets in the air, Annie could hit three out of five before they hit the ground. Frank put a ball on his head and Annie shot it off, standing with her back to him, sighting in a mirror. When the crowd was amazed by that, she threw away the mirror and polished her hunting knife and she used the shiny blade as the mirror.

In 1885, Frank and Annie joined the Buffalo Bill Wild West Show, the very best of the circus acts.

Annie shot the ash off the end of the Kaiser's cigarette in Germany. He had such faith in her that he insisted she do it.

They travelled all over the world together. Annie amazed the Prince of Wales and Queen Victoria. She shot the ash off the end of the Kaiser's cigarette in Germany. He had such faith in her that he insisted she do it.

She went up against the grand duke of Russia, the best shot in Europe. She took him 15-to-3. She said later she shot so poorly because she was impressed by anybody with a title that grand.

All along, Annie and Frank were having one of the great love affairs of all time. No matter where they went or who they met they just had eyes for each other.

They had no children of their own. Annie dropped into orphanages wherever she went and adopted little girls. In all, she raised 18 of them.

In 1901, the wild west show train was heading south for winter quarters when it was in an awful head-on collision with another train. Four were killed, more than 100 injured. Frank tore at the wreckage with his bare hands and pulled Annie out, unconscious and near death.

She was paralyzed and her hair had turned white. It took five operations and a couple of years. But Annie came back, as good a shot as ever. She was still at it when she died on the 3rd of November in 1926. Frank seemed fine. But he just shut his eyes and died within a month.

Originally broadcast November 3, 1988

FALSE TESTIMONY

Around the beginning of this century, *Collier's Magazine* in New York ran a series of exposés about quack medicines and the blatantly false advertising that was used to sell them. Remember, back then most North Americans lived on farms and weren't very sophisticated. The very fact that some ridiculous claim was published gave it a lot of credibility.

Those articles in *Collier's* were quite effective. Several readers wrote to the magazine, pointing out that while *Collier's* was running those articles, it also ran the type of ads the articles described.

So, on the fourth of November in 1905, *Collier's Magazine* ran an announcement that from now on it would refuse such ads. *Collier's* would no longer publish ads making claims to medicinal effect.

That announcement ran right next to an ad for Postum, the caffeine-free coffee substitute.

That caused an even bigger furor than the original announcement. Hundreds of readers wrote to Robert Collier, the publisher of the magazine. They accused him of doing what he said he wouldn't do. That Postum ad had been a testimonial-type spiel in which a Postum drinker was supposed to have sworn Postum had cured his nervousness and heart trouble.

Collier's wrote to the C.W. Post Company, the makers of Postum, saying they wouldn't take those ads anymore. But they would continue to take regular display ads with pictures of people happily drinking Postum and smacking their lips. They just wouldn't take any more ads saying Postum cured ailments.

The same, of course, applied to C.W. Post's other major product, Grape Nuts, the breakfast cereal. Post had been making similar claims about Grape Nuts.

> *Collier's would continue to take display ads with pictures of people happily drinking Postum. They just wouldn't take any more ads saying Postum cured ailments.*

C.W. Post was just as fiery a man as Robert Collier and he didn't take that lying down. He ran an ad in 44 newspapers throughout the state of New York. He accused Collier of blackmail.

He claimed that Collier wasn't at all concerned about false advertising. He just wanted Post to buy display ads, which were more expensive than the simple columns of words he'd been using to sell Grape Nuts and Postum.

That caused such a fuss that within a year, the first modern pure food act had been passed in Washington.

But that was just a by-product of the feud that had begun between Post and Collier. Each sued the other. Collier claimed he had been libeled by Post's ads. That case didn't come to trial until November of 1910, five years and a couple of weeks after Collier's original announcement about refusing false advertising.

By the time the trial was finally over, very little had been said about libel. Post had been cross-examined at length about the claims he made for his foods. He was asked to describe in detail what was in them. He refused on the grounds that if he answered fully, it would give away his formulas and competitors would copy his products.

The jury awarded $50,000 damages to Collier, the biggest libel award in American history until then. Post appealed and won. The case finally just fizzled out.

There was nothing wrong with Postum and Grape Nuts. They were both good products and still are. But Post had to change the way he advertised. And so did hundreds of other manufacturers.

Originally broadcast November 4, 1987

A LEADER BY DEFAULT

When Sandy McKenzie became Canada's second prime minister, the governor-general said: "He's honest, industrious and sensible and has very little talent."

A Toronto writer said, "McKenzie's strength is that he was a stone-mason. His weakness is that he still is."

Sandy was born in Scotland, but settled at Sarnia in southwestern Ontario when he was 20. He made his living as a stone-mason, a contractor, the editor of a local newspaper and an investor in insurance companies. He worked hard but never made much money.

Sandy was a great fan of George Brown, the publisher of the Toronto *Globe*. Brown was a strong, forceful man, a champion of the temperance crowd and a Liberal.

Sandy followed Brown, did what he was told and became a member of parliament in 1861.

The Liberals were a badly organized lot, not really a party by today's standards. They spent much of their time fighting among themselves. They always made a poor showing against the Conservatives, who were led by John Macdonald, the first prime minister.

Macdonald was a superb politician and Canadian politics has never seen a smoother machine than Macdonald's. The days it was working, that is.

The Liberals had several people better qualified for the leadership of their party than Sandy. But none of them relished the idea of spending years in opposition, pounding their heads against Macdonald the unbeatable. So, in the spring of 1873, they chose Sandy as their leader. He was the only one dumb enough to take the job.

Then, along came one of those flukes that makes politics interesting. Macdonald got caught taking money from the people who were supposed to build the new railway to the Pacific.

The Macdonald government fell. In the election of the 5th of November in 1873, only eight months after Sandy took over as Liberal leader, he found himself Canada's second prime minister. Nobody was more amazed than Sandy.

> *Only eight months after Sandy took over as Liberal leader, he found himself Canada's second prime minister. Nobody was more amazed than Sandy.*

As a prime minister and leader of the country, Sandy was everything you would expect: a disaster. His cabinet ministers came and went at intervals of months, sometimes weeks.

A depression came along. The railway to the west ran out of money. British Columbia had only joined Canada on the promise of that railway being built.

Sandy made a free trade deal with the States but the American Senate backed out. And, through all this, Sandy was Sandy: dull, colourless, humourless, and ineffective.

At the next election, the voters decided they preferred the crooked, drunken, humourous Macdonald. Sandy returned to his seat on the back benches of the opposition and was still there when he died.

Originally broadcast November 5, 1992

HOLY TERROR

In the First World War, Britain had fought the decaying Turkish Empire in the Middle East with considerable success. While Britain's armies were bogged down and barely hanging on against the Germans in Europe, the British in the Middle East did spectacularly. They captured Palestine, what's now Israel, Syria, Iraq, Jordan and chunks of Arabia.

Much of their success was based on the help they got from various factions within the Turkish Empire, people who expected they would be rewarded by being given their independence when the war was over.

The British promised anything they had to. In Palestine they promised both major groups of inhabitants, the Jews and the Arabs, that they'd have the country for their own. Obviously, they couldn't be telling the truth to both.

In the 1920s and 30s, Britain ran Palestine as part of its empire. The Jews and Arabs fought each other and, when the British stepped in to separate them, they fought the British.

The British could handle the Arabs. But the Jews were tougher and more determined and, as time went by, Palestine degenerated into a state of terrorism.

When Hitler came to power in Germany and began persecuting the Jews there, the situation became more urgent. The Jews already in Palestine demanded that the British allow the fleeing European Jews to settle there.

The British were afraid that would cause the Arabs to rise in open revolt so they refused.

Now the situation verged on civil war. When the Second World War started, and the Germans drove across north Africa for the Suez Canal, the Jews in Palestine and everywhere else threw in with the British.

But not all of them. There were still hard-line terrorists in Palestine who wouldn't stop fighting the British. They were a minority, but they were tough.

They started a campaign of terror, attacking any British soldier or civil official they could catch unawares.

> *The British could handle the Arabs. But the Jews were tougher and more determined and, as time went by, Palestine degenerated into a state of terrorism.*

Their campaign was an annoyance but it wasn't about to drive out the British. Then, in late 1944, those Jewish terrorists decided they would pull off a stunt so spectacular the world would have to sit up and take notice.

They would assassinate the British resident minister in Cairo, the man who ran all British civil operations in the Middle East.

That man was Lord Moyne, a hard-working, capable but not very understanding man. At one time a Jewish leader, desperate to get the Jews out of Europe, offered to give the British Army 10,000 trucks if Moyne would let a million Jews into Palestine.

"I wouldn't know what to do with a million Jews," said Moyne.

Two young assassins were chosen, one just a teenager. They were Eli Bet Zouri and Eli Hakim. They made their way from Palestine to Egypt in the uniforms of Jewish soldiers in the British army.

Their leader, the director of the operation, was a sergeant in the Royal Air Force.

They watched the home and office of Lord Moyne and decided to kill him as he arrived home for lunch. He always took a long siesta in the middle of the day.

On the 6th of November in 1944, as Lord Moyne arrived home they jumped out of the shrubbery around his house and shot him and his chauffeur.

They jumped on bicycles to get away but they were caught by an Egyptian policeman on a motorcycle. They were put on trial for murder but refused to defend themselves. They were fighting for a just cause, they said, and history would prove them right.

They were hanged, of course. Today, Israelis still argue about whether or not the two Elis were patriots or terrorists. But within four years, the British withdrew from Palestine and let the Jews there set up the state of Israel.

Originally broadcast November 6, 1990

THE LAST SPIKE

On this day in 1885, a grumpy little hunchbacked photographer from Winnipeg named Ross took the most famous picture in Canadian history.

It was cold and wet, not quite raining. It had been raining and would rain again in a little while.

Ross was just one of a big mob standing on the railway tracks in the Eagle Pass in British Columbia, in a range of mountains called the Monashee.

This little spot in Eagle Pass is called Craigallachie, a Scottish name. And that's because most of the key players who set up this moment were Scots.

In the centre of Ross' picture is an old man in a long white beard and a tall hat. He crouches to bang a spike with a big hammer. He doesn't hit it straight on the first time. The spike bends and somebody pulls it away and hands him another. This time he drives it into the tie.

It's the last spike of the Canadian Pacific Railway. A huge construction job is finished. But, more important, a huge country is beginning. In 1867, the political union was put together in Ottawa and named the Dominion of Canada. But it wasn't really a country. There were four provinces in the east, a couple of thousand miles of water and rock and prairie, a few mountain ranges, then British Columbia, the colony that was supposed to be the other end of the country. The British Columbians, with great doubt, had joined Canada only on the promise that they'd be connected to the rest of the country by a railway.

Actually they had only asked for a pack trail big enough to get a horse across the mountains. But the eastern politicians got carried away with their speeches and promised a railway.

The best scientist in Canada, maybe in the world, was there that morning. He was Sir Sanford Fleming, the man who invented standard time and gave Canada

The British Columbians had only asked for a pack trail big enough to get a horse across the mountains. But the eastern politicians got carried away with their speeches and promised a railway.

its first postage stamp. He had said it would take 25 years to build the railway. He was right. But he was also wrong.

He had meant 25 years to lay the tracks. Actually, it had taken 20 years to raise the money and get the politicians to quit fighting and stealing long enough to get on with the project. The actual, physical building was done in a little less than five years.

The old man who drove the spike, in the centre of the picture, was Donald Smith, a canny, cranky old Scotsman who had arrived in Canada years before as a clerk with the Hudson's Bay Company and had amassed millions. Then he gambled them, and his friends' money too, on this railway. He would soon be named Lord Strathcona.

Beside him in the picture is William Van Horne, the American who had supervised the building of the railway. For that, he was allowed to make the speech when Smith drove the last spike.

It was a short speech: "All I can say is, the work has been done and done well in every way."

If anybody didn't think that was a very good speech, they didn't mention it to Van Horne. They knew better. His favorite speech was one he'd delivered several times to people who disagreed with him: "I eat what I want, I smoke what I want, I drink what I want and I don't give a damn for anybody."

Also in the crowd was a little man with those huge Victorian sidewhiskers some men wore at the time. He was A.N. Rogers, the surveyor who found the notch through the mountains that made it all possible. He got a $5,000 bonus for that but he refused to cash it. He framed it and hung it on his wall. He said he wasn't after money; he was after glory and he wanted his name on the map of Canada. And it is. The Rogers Pass is named after him.

Originally broadcast November 7, 1988

THE MAN OF STEEL

On the 8th of November in the year 1519, Montezuma, the emperor of the Aztecs, stepped through the gates of his capital of Mexico City to greet a creature like he'd never seen before.

His spies had told him this creature was a man but he had trouble believing it. His skin was very fair and he had a beard and seemed to be encased in steel. But he was more than a man. He was very tall because the bottom half of him was almost another creature, a four-legged thing with a big head.

When the top of the man moved, so did the bottom part, the creature. Then the man-creature split and the man part stepped forward. He was indeed a man. But poor Montezuma couldn't figure what that part was that was left behind, swishing its tail.

Like most Indians, Montezuma had never seen a horse before.

The man in steel was Cortes, an officer of the king of Spain. In the 27 years since Columbus had discovered this new world, the Spanish had been colonizing the islands of the Caribbean.

Cortes was the first of the Spanish to land on the mainland of the Americas who intended to stay.

He had with him a Spanish sailor who had been shipwrecked some years before and had learned the language of the peoples of the east coast of Mexico. He was half of the interpreting team.

The other half was a beautiful young woman named Malinche. She could speak the language the Spanish sailor knew plus the language of the inland people.

Montezuma, the emperor back at Mexico City, sent word when he heard of these strange creatures, that they were to be dazzled with precious gifts to show them how rich and powerful he was. Then they were to be told to go away or they would be killed.

But the gifts given to Cortes and his men contained a lot of gold. That made the Spanish more determined than ever and they began marching inland.

With their horses and steel swords and guns they defeated army after army that Montezuma sent against them.

Now they had reached the capital and Montezuma came out to greet them.

The Spanish moved into the city. When it looked like the Aztecs intended to surround them and kill them, Cortes grabbed Montezuma as a hostage.

Malinche, the interpreter, who was also Cortes' girlfriend, uncovered a plot to murder the Spanish and cook them up in cannibal pots.

The Spanish locked themselves in Montezuma's castle. The Aztecs attacked but were afraid of killing their emperor. Finally, during one half-hearted attack Montezuma was hit on the head by a stone thrown by his own people. He died.

There was plenty more bloodshed but eventually the Spanish took the city and destroyed it. Then they built modern-day Mexico City on top of it.

Cortes ruled Mexico for the king of Spain and he sent for his Spanish wife. He gave Malinche to one of his officers and she had a baby daughter. She'd already had a son with Cortes.

Malinche died within a few years. She was probably about 25 when she died. Her husband immediately disowned their daughter.

> *Cortes was the first of the Spanish to land on the mainland of the Americas who intended to stay.*

Originally broadcast November 8, 1989

DO NOT GO GENTLY . . .

Every now and then, along comes a genius, somebody with the capacity to amuse us as nobody else can. And then, just as we're all excited and waiting for more, he kills himself.

Edgar Allan Poe, Elvis Presley, Janis Joplin, Brendan Behan . . . and the brightest of them all, the Welsh poet Dylan Thomas.

If you just look back on Thomas the man, you don't see much to admire. But if you think of Thomas the wordsmith, the man who knew how to put words together for their sounds . . . wow, nobody was better than Thomas at his best, probably not even Shakespeare.

Thomas was born in Wales in 1914. His father was a schoolteacher who had wanted to be a poet, and he seems to have hit the bottle from time to time to blunt his disappointment.

He read Shakespeare to young Dylan when he was just a little kid. His mother spoiled him too, and that seems to have set his character.

His mother said later that Dylan was never happier than when he was sick, tucked into bed and with everybody waiting on him, running around with medicine and hot milk and sympathy.

Thomas was a poor student at school. But when he was 13 he began filling notebooks with poetry. When he was 16 he flunked out and went to work as a proof-reader and junior reporter on a little newspaper in Wales.

About the only thing he got out of that brief fling at journalism was a habit of spending his evenings in pubs. He was a bad drinker but a very enthusiastic one.

He did a little amateur acting about this time but he gave that up when he was dropped one night for showing up too drunk to go on.

Strangely, it was just about this time, 1933 and 1934, when he was barely 20, that Thomas wrote some of his best stuff. Mind you, it was poetry, and even if it was very good nobody makes much money at poetry.

Thomas was on the edge of marriage to a well-known poet but he dropped the idea, in favour of what he called Comrade Bottle. He'd sooner be a drunk than a husband.

By the late 1930s Thomas was acknowledged by the critics as a poetic genius and by his friends as a monumental bore, a guy who got drunk and bit the caps off beer bottles or got down on his hands and knees and barked and bit people on the ankle.

He got married and had a daughter and barely made a living. A rich old woman provided a house in Wales for him but he didn't write much. His whole life's output only fills two or three very slim books.

During the war he stayed out of the army. They didn't want to put up with his drinking.

He did a bit of film writing but nothing noteworthy. In 1950 he made a tour of the States, reading his poems and making plenty of money. But he drank it as fast as he made it.

He returned to England and started working on a couple of plays. Then in 1953 he made another tour of the United States.

At least, he started one. His drinking was so bad that he went into convulsions in New York and he died in a coma in Greenwich Village on the 9th of November, 1953. He was only 39.

He must have had his own death in mind when he wrote some of his best lines:

Dressed to die, the sensual strut begun,
With my red veins full of money,
In the final direction of the elementary town
I advance for as long as forever is.

> *Thomas was on the edge of marriage but he dropped the idea, in favour of what he called Comrade Bottle. He'd sooner be a drunk than a husband.*

Originally broadcast November 9, 1984

REVOLUTION REJECTED

When the American Revolution broke out in 1775, the governor of Nova Scotia issued an order for the militia to mobilize.

The town of Halifax was loyal to the crown and there was no problem there. But when news of the revolution arrived inland, things were different.

Around the Chignecto Isthmus, where New Brunswick and Nova Scotia join, there were a lot of people who weren't cheering for the British. The British army had expelled the Acadians, the French-speaking settlers, barely a generation earlier. They had missed some. Others had drifted back. So there wasn't much sympathy for the crown from them.

The Indians of the area were split. Most had found British rule quite pleasant. But the French missionaries who had worked in the area before the British came, about 40 years later, had made a profound impression on some of them.

Most important of all, many of the settlers at Chignecto were New Englanders. They had settled only a few years earlier and if there was war they would be expected to fight their brothers and cousins who would invade from Massachusetts. This didn't appeal to them at all.

Their leaders were Colonel Jonathan Eddy and Sheriff John Allen. Allen was also the local member of the legislature. They collected a petition, asking the governor to rescind his mobilization order so they wouldn't have to fight their kinfolk.

The governor sent the petition on to London, with a note saying this was evidence of rebellion in his territory and asking for more troops.

He then sent a note to Allen and Eddy, telling them to assemble their men and report at once. When they didn't do that, he declared Allen's seat in the legislature was vacant and he posted rewards for both men.

Colonel Eddy took out for New England to get help. Sheriff Allen tried to raise a force to attack the British army posts in his area. He had no success so he took out for New England and disappeared forever from Canadian history.

But Eddy managed to recruit 20 New Englanders to sail back with. He figured hundreds of Nova Scotians would join him. He started off by capturing a supply ship sent from Halifax to help the garrison at Fort Cumberland.

On the 10th of November, 1776 he and his small force sneaked up on the Fort itself and he sent a message to the commander, Colonel Gorham, to surrender.

Colonel Gorham sent back a message that Eddy had just one hour to surrender himself and disband his small army or they would all be in deep trouble.

> *Colonel Gorham sent back a message that Eddy had just one hour to surrender himself and disband his small army or they would all be in deep trouble.*

Eddy made a fake attack at the back of the fort while one of his Indians jumped the wall and tried to open the main gate. A British officer saw him at the last minute and cut his head off with one swipe of his sword.

Eddy retreated and later tried to set fire to the wooden fort. But Colonel Gorham was on the alert. Soon a ship arrived with reinforcements. Eddy managed to ambush one detachment of the British troops and killed a dozen or two. That was as close to success as he got.

Eventually Eddy's force melted away on him and he managed to get into a boat and take off after a couple of close shaves with British troops. And that was the end of the American Revolution in the Maritimes.

Originally broadcast November 10, 1987

REQUIRED READING

Of all the kings of England, only one is known to history as The Great. That's Alfred, who was king in the last half of the 800s.

The Romans had built quite a civilization in Britain. Then, as barbarians attacked Rome, they pulled their armies out of the far parts of the empire and brought them home to protect Rome itself.

Into the vacuum in Britain moved two groups of people. The Angles, and Saxons and Jutes moved from about where northern Germany and Holland are today. They settled and were, for the most part, Christians, carrying on a primitive version of the civilization the Romans had left behind.

After they were settled, but before they were firmly established, came the second group, the Vikings or Danes. These were pagans, tough warriors and skilled sailors. Their principal pastimes were rape and pillage, and they were quite good at them.

In the days of Alfred, Britain was a whole bunch of little kingdoms. The ones in the north and east were mostly Danish. The ones in the south and west, mostly Anglo-Saxon. There was constant warfare and the boundaries changed all the time.

Alfred was the fifth son of the king of Wessex, an Anglo-Saxon kingdom on the English Channel that ran inland almost as far as London.

Alfred's father, the king, was quite a devout Christian and he sent Alfred to Rome to be blessed by the Pope when he was only four years old. Just why isn't clear. As the fifth son, he was unlikely ever to be king.

A couple of years later, the king went to Rome himself, taking Alfred along. So by the time he was six or seven Alfred had been to Rome, the centre of religion and learning, twice.

When they got home, the wars with the Danes, which were always going on, got even hotter. Young Prince Alfred spent a lot of his time fighting.

The king died and the eldest son became king. Then he died and the next one took over. And so on. Until, in the year 871, Alfred became king at the age of about 22.

He won some battles and lost others. A couple of times it looked like the Danes would prevail. But Alfred was a tough man and would retreat into the swamps when he was beaten and come out to fight another day.

After a half-dozen years of this, Alfred won a big battle and converted the defeated Danish king to Christianity. From then on, he was acknowledged as king of England, or at least most of it. He conquered London and that meant he pretty well ran the whole country.

In the course of all this, Alfred had organized an efficient army, built a chain of forts to protect his kingdom, and started a navy. The navy would never be strong enough to keep away the Vikings. But it kept the English Channel pirates under control.

With war no longer threatening, Alfred settled down to establish a kingdom with wise laws, honest judges and a tradition of literacy.

Now, with war no longer threatening, Alfred settled down to establish a kingdom with wise laws, honest judges and a tradition of literacy. That was what was important about Alfred, why the historians call him great, that literacy part.

On the 11th of November in the year 887, the feast of St. Martin, Alfred told his assistant, a Welsh priest named Asser, that he wanted to learn Latin himself and he wanted all the important books translated into the Anglo-Saxon language, the language we call English. And all the sons of important people were to learn to read.

He even required judges to learn to read. Not an awful lot did, so he later altered that rule to say they either had to read themselves or hire assistants who could.

It took Alfred himself five years to master Latin. Then he did a lot of the translating himself.

By today's standards, his kingdom wasn't very literate. Maybe only one in a hundred could read and write, maybe not even that. But every community had someone who could. And England was well on its way to being what it is today: the most literate nation on Earth.

Originally broadcast November 11, 1991

SCARLET LETTERS

Emma Magdalene Rosalia Maria Josefa Barbara Orczy was born in Hungary in 1865, a real, live baroness.

The Baroness' daddy was a well-known composer and conductor of a symphony orchestra. So she grew up in a house where Wagner and Massenet and Gounod and Liszt and a whole bunch of musical heavy hitters were always around.

Young Baroness Emma was sent to private schools in Paris and Brussels and London. She had a talent for drawing.

After she was finished studying, Baroness Emma became a bit of a star as an illustrator in the London magazine business of the late 1800s.

And she acquired a husband, a bright young Englishman named Montagu Barstow.

The Baroness began to dabble in fiction writing for magazines, pretty syrupy stuff about young ladies in love with earls and dukes and stuff like that. Not terribly good but acceptable.

Then, in 1905, the baroness burst on the literary scene with her book *The Scarlet Pimpernel*. A pimpernel, by the way, is a little English flower.

The Scarlet Pimpernel was such a success that it soon became a play and it drew crowds for 10 years. There's no doubt that Mr. Baroness, good old Monty Barstow, had an important hand in the writing of the play. It isn't clear just how vital a part he played in the novel.

> *The Scarlet Pimpernel is a British nobleman who travels to France in disguise and rescues French aristocrats from the guillotine. Sort of paying his dues in the aristocrats' club.*

The story of the pimpernel is rather simple, although the baroness added all sorts of complications to give the tale some suspense. It's set in Paris and London at the time of the French Revolution and French aristocrats are having their heads chopped off. The Scarlet Pimpernel is a British nobleman who travels to France in disguise and rescues French aristocrats from the guillotine. Sort of paying his dues in the aristocrats' club.

The story was made into a movie in 1917 and again in 1929. Then again, in 1935, starring Leslie Howard. That's the one you see on TV late at night, an excellent movie, way better than the book.

The Baroness became wealthy and famous from the *Pimpernel*. She lived on an estate in England in the summer and in a villa in the south of France in the winter.

When the Germans captured France in 1940, she was caught there and had to stay for the war. The local German headquarters was in the next villa and the British bombed it. At least, they tried and missed and smashed up the Baroness' villa.

No hard feelings, though. She returned to Britain after the war and that's where she was living when she died on the 12th of November in 1947, very old, very rich and very famous.

Originally broadcast November 12, 1992

A MEDICAL MARTYR

Norman Bethune was born in Gravenhurst, Ontario, the son of Presbyterian clergyman.

He studied medicine at the University of Toronto then joined the army as an ambulance driver when the First World War started. He was the tenth man in Canada to join up. He was wounded, left the army and went back to school. He graduated as a doctor then joined the navy as a surgeon. After the war, he stayed in London, studying and practicing.

Bethune did everything in a hurry, like having a wound and a degree and a new medical career, all in one four-year war. He was a hard man to understand. He had dozens of affairs with women, all quite open, never caring what anyone thought. Bethune made a very good living buying art and sculpture in France and Spain and selling them back in London. Most people got the impression, with his parties and cars and expensive clothes, that he was quite wealthy. He wasn't. He just lived with a lot of style.

Bethune married a rich Scottish girl then moved to Detroit and made a lot of money specializing in treating rich women with imaginary ailments.

He caught tuberculosis and almost died. He spent a couple of years recuperating and thinking. It seems, looking back now at Bethune's career, that he felt a lot of guilt about all that money he made for doing nothing useful.

When Bethune recovered he moved to Montreal and he'd changed. Now he was a medical martyr, working far into the night, joining communist groups concerned with the health of poor people, agitating for government-paid health care.

This was the 30s and his medical colleagues started calling him Comrade Beth. He took it as a compliment.

When the Spanish Civil War started, Bethune went to Spain. He had been one of the best-paid chest surgeons in Canada. He walked away from it all.

In Spain he threw himself into medical work with an incredible energy. A lot of the people who saw him then thought he was crazy. A saint but a mad one.

Bethune just about invented modern blood transfusion techniques. He saved thousands of lives. He wasn't able to save tens of thousands more.

He was only in Spain for seven months, but he came back completely changed. He travelled all over Canada, preaching that fascism had to be stopped. The Germans and Italians had turned Spain into a testing ground for their armies.

Stop them there now, he warned, or watch them start another world war.

People shouted him down and called him a communist. Bethune shouted back: "And if Christ were on Earth today, wouldn't you call him the same thing?"

Next Bethune went to China. The next world war was already here, he said. It started with the Japanese invasion of China in the early 30s.

Bethune went into the hills with the Chinese communists and set up hospitals and first aid teams. He designed simple operating rooms that could be made from common materials and carried on the backs of two mules. He told his doctors and orderlies: don't wait until the wounded are brought back from a battle. Go to them. Get up close. Save lives fast. Ignore the shooting. Get to where the wounded are.

And that's just what Bethune was doing in the late fall of 1939, just two months after the rest of the world went to war.

Bethune operated with kitchen knives sharpened on whetstones. He used old torn shirts for bandages. Infection was everywhere. He ignored that, too.

He cut his finger during an operation and caught blood poisoning. He died on the 13th of November in 1939. He's been described as the only Canadian the Chinese ever heard of.

> *People shouted him down and called him a communist. Bethune shouted back: "And if Christ were on Earth today, wouldn't you call him the same thing?"*

Originally broadcast November 13, 1986

A DREAM COME TRUE

The trouble with dreams that come true is that the dreamer usually tells us about them after the event has come true. Very seldom does someone describe an event in great detail before it comes true. And, even more seldom, an unusual and sensational event.

That's why the case of John Lee is so fascinating.

John Lee was a good-looking, agreeable young man who lived in the southwest of England in Devon. Now, the folklore of Devon is full of all sorts of superstitious stuff. And when Lee was a teenager, around 1880, there were still a lot of people in that part of the country who believed in all sorts of supernatural nonsense.

But a couple of things stand out. Lee worked as a stableboy for Miss Emma Keyse, a wealthy old maid who had once been a lady-in-waiting to Queen Victoria. Miss Keyse' carriage horse refused to go past a certain piece of road. Local legend had it that it was haunted.

No matter the reason, the horse just stopped dead when it got to that stretch of the road. But when John Lee drove the horse it trotted past without any trouble. Also, Lee once predicted that a maid of Miss Keyse would be drowned in a nearby river. The girl disappeared soon afterwards and hasn't been seen to this day.

Lee left Miss Keyse' service and joined the navy. He was a bright lad and was marked for promotion. But one day he was ordered to lower a boat from the ship and row an officer to another ship. Lee started to shake all over and fainted. Another sailor was told to do the job and Lee was taken to the hospital.

The boat overturned and the other sailor and officer were drowned. Lee was in a coma for five days and when he was revived he was discharged.

He returned to Miss Keyse' place and continued to work for her. The household consisted of Miss Keyse, two old woman servants and a younger maid who was Lee's half sister.

On the day of the 14th of November in 1884, Lee's half sister, Elizabeth Harris, had had the day off but she returned to the house just before suppertime. She seems to have been either sick or very distraught because she lay down for a while in her room and old Miss Keyse went to see her.

Miss Keyse and the three woman servants slept on the top floor of her big house and Lee slept in a little room off the kitchen.

Lee was an incredibly sound sleeper and everyone in the area made jokes about it. A burglar could have come in the night and made himself a meal in the kitchen, they used to say, and John Lee wouldn't hear a sound.

Well, somebody came in the night on the 14th of November in 1884. Just about dawn, Lee was awakened by screams from the women. He dashed upstairs and found Miss Keyse' bed was on fire. Somebody had stabbed and slashed her and set fire to her mattress.

It looked like the work of a man and Lee was the only man in the house, so he was charged with murder. He denied it but didn't appear very interested in the trial. He sat quietly through it. When he was convicted, he just shrugged. He was to be hanged the following February at 8 o'clock one morning. The night before he slept like a log.

The warden and a clergyman and three guards went into his cell to get him. Lee was sleeping and after a while he woke up. When he saw the five men he said, "Hi there, this is the day, eh? Well, I just dreamed that I was marched out of here and along the corridor and into a yard . . ." And he went on to describe the part of the prison he'd never seen. He said he dreamt that the trapdoor on the gallows didn't work. They tried again and again. But it never worked.

Then they marched him along the corridor to the gallows, past the places he'd described. He climbed the gallows and . . . Well, you know by now the end of the story. Three times the gallows trap wouldn't spring. Each time Lee was removed and it worked just fine.

The next day the newspapers were full of nothing else and Queen Victoria commuted Lee's sentence and told her prime minister to never again mention his name.

Lee served 23 years' time then was released.

> *Lee once predicted that a maid of Miss Keyse would be drowned in a nearby river. The girl disappeared soon afterwards and hasn't been seen to this day.*

Originally broadcast November 14, 1984

THE LAST EMPRESS

Zu-si might have been the most powerful woman who ever lived. She was empress of China, absolute ruler of a third of the world's population, when she died in 1907.

She had intrigued and murdered and plotted her way to the top and stayed there for half a century. She had very little to do with westerners and the Europeans who were invading China in her later years. They knew her name, but little about her.

She was born in 1835, two years before Victoria became queen of England. Her given name was Yehonala and she had a cousin named Sakota. Both girls were from the Chinese nobility of the time, the Manchu dynasty. The whole dynasty was old and weak and corrupt and would soon collapse.

As nobles, they were eligible to be concubines to the emperor and were moved into the Imperial Palace in Beijing. What was called the Palace was really a series of palaces, all walled within the city and forming a city of their own. The emperor was worshipped as a kind of god.

All this had made some sort of sense centuries earlier when the emperor had to keep order over millions of subjects from Siberia to the tropical China Sea. But by the 1800s, not only was the dynasty tottering but the emperor himself was a sorry wreck.

He was a weak young man who ruled in name only. Although the emperor's word was law, his mother had most of the power and the head eunuch ran a close second.

The term head eunuch was just a term, too. Actually, he became Yehonala's lover. One of the officers of the palace guard was Yenohala's cousin's lover although that, too, was strictly against the rules.

Yehonala and her cousin were just two of many dozens of beautiful young concubines in the emperor's stable. But they quickly beat out the others. The cousin bore the emperor a son which moved her right up to the head of the class.

Yehonala herself made a big play for the emperor's mother and became her favorite. She saw right off that the emperor was a mama's boy and that was her way to power.

Books have been written about how Yehonala made her way to the top, first as the emperor's favorite, then as the favorite aunt of his son and so on. But the incredible fact is that, in this most rigid of all hierarchies, she became empress in fact if not always in title and ruled China for more than 50 years.

The name we know her by, Zu-si, was a title she took about 1850 when she first seized power. In 1860 she ordered her army to attack the Europeans who were establishing trading posts around the edges of China.

The old, outdated Chinese army was no match for the newcomers and she had to flee Beijing as the European armies invaded and attacked the city.

That made her hatred of foreigners, which was always strong, even worse.

In 1899, when a sect of religious fanatics called the Boxers started attacking foreigners, she approved and encouraged them. The result was the Boxer Rebellion and another humiliating defeat for the Chinese on their own soil.

China was falling apart and the foreigners were grabbing the pieces. Only one cruel, treacherous, but brilliant old woman was holding things together. And when she died on the 15th of November in 1907, the end of the old China was at hand.

Originally broadcast November 15, 1985

> *Yehonala made a big play for the emperor's mother and became her favorite. She saw right off that the emperor was a mama's boy and that was her way to power.*

THE BIRTH OF THE BLUES

William Christopher Handy was born in Florence, Alabama on the 16th of November in 1873, the son of a clergyman.

Handy is famous all over the world today as the man who invented the blues, that form of ragtime music that gets right to the soul. But Handy had an awful time getting started in music.

His father once told him, I'd rather see you in a hearse than in a band.

The old man associated professional music-making with sinfulness, and he wasn't far off. The black musicians of the Old South were a pretty hard-living, high-living crowd.

Young Handy bought his first trumpet for 25 cents down. He had to practice away from home. His father insisted that Handy go to school to get an education, so he studied to be a teacher. But he liked music so much that he travelled all over, just looking for a chance to play with good musicians.

This was back in the late 1800s when black people were really oppressed throughout the States, especially in the south. After Handy graduated, he found he could make a better living as a labourer than as a teacher.

He bummed his way around the country, playing in bands, doing odd jobs, pan-handling.

For a while he went back to his old teachers' college and taught music. In 1909, Handy was living in Memphis, playing and writing music. A politician named Crump was running for mayor and he hired Handy to write a campaign song that would bring out the black vote.

Handy wrote a blues number called *Mr. Crump*. Crump was elected and went on to become one of the really noteworthy crooked politicians of American history.

The song remained so popular that Handy renamed it the *Memphis Blues* and gave it new words. A New York publisher bought it for $50 and it became a big hit all across the country.

Handy saw the blues would be a great money-maker, now that it was introduced to prosperous white audiences.

> *Handy saw the blues would be a great money-maker, now that it was introduced to prosperous white audiences.*

So he sat down and dredged his mind for old blues tunes he'd encountered in the past. He remembered when he was doing odd jobs in St. Louis, so poor he had to sleep on the hard cobblestones along the Mississippi River docks. He dreaded every night because of that. So he started his song: "I hate to see the evening sun go down . . ." And that was the *St. Louis Blues*. It's one of the dozen most famous songs in the world. The Queen Mother has said she loves it. During the Ethiopian War, Emperor Haile Selassie had it arranged as a march. It was the biggest selling song in the English language until *White Christmas* came along.

Handy lived until he was 85, but he was a bitter man. He did all right from music but white musicians and song publishers made a lot more from his songs than he ever did. He claimed to have invented the blues but music historians have always insisted he just wrote them down. Maybe both are right.

Originally broadcast November 16, 1989

FREEDOM OF THE PRESS

John Peter Zenger was a German. He arrived in New York in 1710, when he was 13, and he never did speak English without a thick accent. His grammar was pretty bad and reflected the writing of a man who spoke German at home.

Zenger was apprenticed to a printer and set up his own show when he was 29.

New York in those days was a grubby little place, not as big as either Boston or Philadelphia. It had a population of 10,000. Barely half used English as their first tongue. The town had been founded by the Dutch and just taken over by the British less than a generation earlier.

In 1732, just a few years after Zenger set up his press, a new governor arrived from England. He was an arrogant ex-British army officer, an Irishman named Cosby, infamous for his terrible temper tantrums.

Cosby had been fired from his last job as governor of a tiny British island colony because there were discrepancies in his books. In other words, he was a crook.

The legislature voted the new governor a rather generous wage. But instead of being grateful, Cosby pointed out that he had been appointed to the job a year before he bothered to show up. So, by his figuring, they owed him a year's pay when he arrived.

The legislature refused to pay. Cosby then took the case to the local court and juggled the membership of the court so he himself would sit in judgment on his own case.

A bunch of New Yorkers got angry at this and they prevailed on Zenger to start a newspaper to stir up public opinion against the governor and his high-handed ways. Zenger was no dummy. He knew he was asking for trouble. But he did it anyway.

In November of 1733, Zenger began publishing

> *A bunch of New Yorkers prevailed on Zenger to start a newspaper to stir up public opinion against the governor's high-handed ways. Zenger knew he was asking for trouble. But he did it anyway.*

the *New York Journal*. And it began attacking the governor. We know Zenger did at least some of the writing himself because the grammar was so bad. We also know the better-written pieces were done by two or three lawyers who were leaders in the fight against the governor.

Zenger was warned to stop. He didn't. Within a year he was arrested, on the 17th of November in 1734, charged with seditious libel. That's legal talk for bad-mouthing the government.

Two judges presided at Zenger's trial and they were both dead-set against him. The attorney-general prosecuted and he was out for blood. Zenger was defended by Andrew Hamilton of Philadelphia, the best courtroom lawyer in the American colonies.

They started by admitting that Zenger had printed the paper and the articles that offended the governor. The attorney-general said: In that case, the jury just has to say guilty, because anybody can see the articles are offensive. The judges said the same thing.

Hamilton said: But we claim they're true.

The attorney-general said: all the more reason why they shouldn't have been published. And Zenger persisted even after he was arrested. That was true. Each day Zenger's wife had come to visit him in jail and he had told her what to put in the *Journal*, which was still being published in his absence.

The judges told the jury they had to say guilty. The judges had decided the articles were guilty, as a matter of law. Judges decide the law; juries decide the facts. So the jury had to say guilty.

But the jury said: not guilty. Zenger was released and the principle was established that the truth can be published, even if the big shots don't like it.

Originally broadcast November 17, 1988

PLANNING A REVOLUTION

No one knew it at the time. But on the 18th of November in 1789, the industrial revolution landed in North America. The man who brought it was a 21-year-old Englishman named Sam Slater. And he carried it in his head.

Mechanization had come to the textile trade in England in the 1730s with the invention of a few small, simple machines. They didn't do much more than the hand looms and spinning wheels that had been around for centuries.

But they did make one important step: they were powered by something other than the hand or foot of the operator. Usually, they were connected to a water wheel that turned the shaft and made the wheels roll.

The next step was to put several things together, like spools or spindles so that the machine could do several times as much work as the old hand-powered ones.

For the next generation, that was about the extent of modernization. But, just about the time Sam Slater was born in the midlands of England, mechanics were beginning to think bigger.

They were thinking in terms of machines that would take dozens of spindles and turn out miles and miles of thread an hour.

Very few of the basic tools like lathes and drills existed in those days. So the early inventors had to be their own toolmakers and engineers and designers and maintenance men.

Young Sam Slater was apprenticed for seven years to one of the early inventors and factory owners. He was fascinated with machines. He worked only an hour's walk from home. But he lived at the factory and for the first six months he didn't go home to see his mother once. He was so interested he stayed at the factory on Sundays to see what improvements he could make.

The problem in those days was almost constant breakdowns. Young Sam was always climbing under or over or into the machines to keep them going or get them started again.

By the time Sam was 21 and finished his apprenticeship, he carried the plans to all of the spinning machinery in England in his head.

The result was that by the time Sam was 21 and finished his apprenticeship, he carried the plans to all of the spinning machinery in England in his head. His boss was friendly with all the other manufacturers and they had been to his factory and Sam had picked their brains.

He had also got used to the constant lawsuits and bickering that went with the inventing and improving business. The British government was so afraid of losing its leadership in the textile industry that it passed laws forbidding the export of skilled machine makers or plans or models of machines.

But Slater had decided to leave England and try his hand in the new United States. Perhaps he had heard of rewards and subsidies being granted by governments and merchants associations in New York, New England and Pennsylvania. Perhaps he just got tired of the British economy, dominated by titled landowners who were very stingy with wages.

At any rate, Slater described himself as a farm labourer so had no trouble leaving the country. He didn't have to take any plans with him. They were all in his head.

He landed in New York on the 18th of November in 1789. Within a few days, he moved to New England, a part of the world with abundant water power.

He went into partnership with a Quaker who had been trying to build a mill with some bits of old broken-down machinery. Slater used some of the old parts. He designed and made others. He had to train his own machinists. He had to do some things by hand because the tools required didn't exist on this side of the Atlantic.

But in December of 1790, in Pawtuckett, Rhode Island, Slater opened America's first factory, a water-powered spinning mill employing seven boys and two girls. He lived another 25 years and died rich and respected.

Originally broadcast November 18, 1987

The World-Famous Address

Edward Everett, in the year 1863, was considered the brainiest man in the United States. He had graduated first in his class from Harvard University at the age of 17. He had been an ordained minister at 19. He had been president of Harvard, governor of Massachusetts, and secretary of state.

Now, he was an old man but still considered the finest orator in the United States, maybe the whole English-speaking world.

Abraham Lincoln, on the other hand, was considered a bit of a klutz. He was the president of the United States and today he's considered some sort of legend. But in his time, Lincoln wasn't very highly regarded. He was a tall, skinny, ugly man, a farm boy who had studied law and been a petty politician away out west. He got the nomination for the presidency by the Republican Party in 1860 more through default than any wide following.

When he travelled to Washington to be sworn in, secret service agents had to create a diversion and hustle him through Baltimore because a pro-slavery mob wanted to lynch him.

They thought Lincoln would be such an inept president that the country would split and a disastrous Civil War would follow. And that's exactly what happened, although it's hard to blame Lincoln. That war was inevitable.

That war was a bloody one and one of its worst battles was fought in the summer of 1813 at the town of Gettysburg in Pennsylvania. The Southern forces drove deep into Northern territory and for three days the fate of the whole divided nation hung in the balance. The Northern forces, Lincoln's army, held firm and the Southerners had to turn back. It was their high tide and from then on they were on the losing side, although it would be another two years before the war ended.

The slaughter at Gettysburg had been terrible, more than 50,000 killed and wounded. In those days of primitive medical care, many of the wounded died.

Lincoln was asked to say a few words, but just out of respect for his office, not because anybody considered him at all great enough for such a noble occasion.

It was decided to create a national cemetery on the battlefield and Everett, the great orator, was chosen to deliver the speech of dedication. The date was set for the 19th of November, 1863. Lincoln, the not-too-popular president, was asked to say a few words but just out of respect for his office, not because anybody considered him at all great enough for such a noble occasion.

Everett performed as expected. He gave a speech that ran an hour and 57 minutes, full of references to ancient Greeks and riddled with classical references, just the sort of thing that audiences of the 1800s expected.

Many of the people in the audience left when Everett was finished. Lincoln was next on the program. Everett had once described him as a man totally inadequate to his task, and that was a view widely shared.

Lincoln pulled out a few notes and began to speak. "Four score and seven years ago," he said, "our fathers brought forth on this continent a new nation, conceived in liberty and dedicated to the proposition that all men are created equal."

Lincoln uttered only 271 words. It was all over in two minutes and 13 seconds. We have no photograph of him delivering his Gettysburg address, because the photographers didn't have time to set up the clumsy cameras of the day.

When Lincoln was finished he stood looking around awkwardly for a few seconds, then sat down. He said to somebody beside him: "It was a failure. They didn't like it."

Everett later sent Lincoln a note saying all his words were pointless beside Lincoln's few well-chosen ones. He seems to have been the only one who saw any greatness in it. Today, of course, everybody can quote the last phrase about government of the people, for the people and by the people. Who can tell you who Edward Everett was?

Originally broadcast November 19, 1991

TANKS A LOT

The First World War was a terrible blood bath. The manufacturers came up with machine guns and poison gas and the airplane. But the generals still directed their armies as they had for centuries, marching their infantry straight at the enemy.

At least the British generals operated like that. The Germans adapted better to modern methods. They organized their whole war machine to move men and supplies by railway. Since Europe was a web of efficient railways, they had the fastest-moving army in history.

And they had been quick to realize that the machine gun would revolutionize war. No longer would victory go to the side that massed its soldiers into the tightest formations. In fact, when a machine gun started to shoot, smart officers scattered their men.

General Haig, the British commander, once said the machine gun was an amusing military toy but it would never replace the horse.

For three years, from 1914 to 1917, Haig sent his men marching in masses into the muzzles of the German machine guns.

Not all the British leaders were as stubborn as Haig. There were some new ideas. One of these was to mount a steel box on the caterpillar treads that worked so well on construction machines. And put a gun on top.

When this gadget was under development, it was important to fool any German spies who might be watching. So, the British minister of munitions, Winston Churchill, spread the story that it was just a carrier for moving water in the desert, just a sort of tank. So the new war machine was called the tank.

Machine gun bullets bounced off them. But the caterpillar treads didn't work too well on ground that had already been chewed up by three years of war.

The generals didn't consider tanks when they were planning their battles. They coordinated infantry and artillery. But no military textbook mentioned tanks.

Churchill spread the story that it was just a carrier for moving water in the desert, a sort of tank. So the new war machine was called the tank.

That changed on the 20th of November in 1917 when the British attacked the German line at Cambrai in northeastern France. Almost 400 tanks led the charge.

The ground they attacked over hadn't been chewed up so they made good time. Two miles an hour on dirt, four miles an hour on the road.

One of the attacking divisions was commanded by a general who would have nothing to do with tanks. The rest of the attack was a success. That division was soon bogged down.

Did the generals learn the lesson? The German ones did. They lost that war a year later.

But when the Second World War started 20 years after that, their army got off to a great start, attacking behind masses of tanks.

Originally broadcast November 20, 1992

DECLINE OF THE AUSTRIAN EMPIRE

Franz Josef became emperor of Austria in 1848 when he was only 18. He took over from an uncle who was too crazy to carry on in the time of crisis. Both the royal family and the Austrian empire were much the worse for wear at that point.

The royal family was the Hapsburg clan, a tribe of monarchs that went away back centuries in history. The empire took in great chunks of northern Italy and southern Germany and went into what's now the Balkans and southwestern Russia and Hungary. It had been called the Holy Roman Empire for centuries and it was a citadel of Roman Catholicism.

There were dozens of racial groups within the empire, most of them hating each other.

The court of the new emperor was encrusted with a lot of stodgy tradition. Various nobles had privileges and responsibilities and everything was stuffy and artificial.

The new emperor's first problem was a rebellion in Hungary. A Polish general put it down quickly and the young emperor ordered the leaders hanged.

And that pretty well set the pattern for the next 68 years. Various officials did things for Franz Josef and he sat in his palace in Vienna, signing papers. He was known as the emperor of the empire, the king of bureaucrats.

Thousands and thousands of tiny details required his personal attention. The result was that the head man knew very little of what was happening, day to day.

For his first few years, young Emperor Franz Josef only had to sign papers. His mother, the terrible-tempered Archduchess Sophia, ran things. When Franz Joseph was in his early twenties, he and his mother had an awful set-to.

She wanted him to marry a Bavarian princess. He wanted to marry her sister. He won that argument.

He lived to wish he'd lost it.

The princess he won, Elizabeth, was sweet but

The Austrian army had the snappiest uniforms in the military world. But it couldn't fight a modern war.

crazy. He was madly in love with her. But the generations of inbreeding that were part of the noble families of all Central Europe finally got to her. For years, she left Franz Josef and wandered around Europe, having affairs with young men, going on fad diets, falling under the spells of fortune tellers.

All the while, Emperor Franz Josef was at his desk, reading and signing papers. He would get up at 3:30 every morning and work through until suppertime. He would be in bed by 8:30 most nights.

His son, Crown Prince Rudolf, was quite nutty. He finally killed his girlfriend then himself. The emperor worked day and night for a month to cover up that scandal. And it still got out.

He had a war with the Italians in the 1850s and lost. He had one with the Germans in the 1860s and lost. Each time he lost great chunks of his empire.

He had an affair with an actress that lasted more than a dozen years. He didn't find her himself. His wife picked her out for him then went back to her young lovers and fortune tellers.

The empress was assassinated in Switzerland by a crazy man. The actress left Franz Josef within a year.

And all through that, he got up at 3:30 every morning to attack that pile of paperwork.

His army had the snappiest uniforms in the military world. But it couldn't fight a modern war.

And it had to. In 1914, when Franz Josef had been on the throne more than 65 years, his nephew, the new Crown Prince, was assassinated in Yugoslavia. That started the First World War. The Austrian army collapsed. The country was in ruins.

And on the 21st of November in 1916, Emperor Franz Josef sipped a cup of tea and died. So did the Austrian empire.

Originally broadcast November 21, 1988

Mae Queen

Mae West was born in New York in 1892. Her mother was a vaudeville addict and took little Mae to shows every day of the week.

Cute little Mae was imitating the stars when she was five, taking singing and dancing lessons when she was seven and on the stage at 15. She started off as a straight lady to a comedian.

When she was 19 she got a brief mention in the *New York Times* for what it called her snappy, grotesque delivery in a show called *À La Broadway*. For the next 15 years she worked around New York theatres, always making a pretty good living, never giving any indication that she was star quality.

She wore blonde wigs and had a full, busty figure that she exaggerated with the way she dressed and the way she moved. Mae managed to be sexy but still a little less raunchy than a stripper.

Mae would come up with a lot of her own funny, sexy lines but nobody thought of her as a writer.

Then, in 1926, when she was 34 but still looking 10 years younger, she wrote a show called *Sex*. If you think the title wasn't very subtle, you should have heard the dialogue.

It was outrageous. The show ran on Broadway, not in one of the major theatres. It was real gutter stuff, about a bunch of prostitutes in Montreal.

Variety, the show business paper — which was pretty hard to shock — called it nasty, infantile, amateurish and vicious. The *New York Times* — which was easily shocked — called it crude, inept and poorly acted.

The police and various church leaders expressed great concern. Looking back, 60 years later, we can only conclude that something crooked was involved. Either the reviewers were paid off to make it sound worse than it was or the cops were paid to let it run. Either was rather common at the time, and it's quite possible that both may have occurred.

At any rate, in 1927, after *Sex* had been running 14 months and making a fortune, the police raided the theatre and closed it down. Mae was convicted of corrupting the morals of minors and sent to jail for 10 days.

Mae showed up for her trip to jail in a dress that fit like a sunburn and had all sorts of sexy quips for the reporters. She sold so many papers they were there when she got out. She gave them more snappy lines and they gave her more ink.

Mae West never looked back. She did a show about homosexuals called *The Drag*. Homosexuals saw her as their champion and she had a big following among them until she died.

> *Mae showed up for her trip to jail in a dress that fit like a sunburn and had all sorts of sexy quips for the reporters.*

In 1932 Mae went to Hollywood. She got off the train and told reporters: I'm not a little girl from a little town trying to make it in the big city. I'm a big girl from the big town coming to a little city.

She ground out movies that sold like crazy: *Night After Night, She Done Him Wrong, I Ain't No Angel, It Ain't No Sin* . . . Mae West was a money machine.

She did one of the most famous movies of all time with W. C. Fields, *My Little Chickadee*. She hated Fields. They each had huge egos and one screen wasn't big enough for them both.

In 1937, she did a radio show with Edgar Bergen and his dummy, Charley McCarthy. It sounds pretty tame today but church groups protested and Mae was booted off the air. This time she stayed off. She'd made so much money she didn't need to work again. She wrote an outrageous autobiography that wasn't likely very true. She was a ham who made news long after she'd quit working. And she was still a celebrity, if not a star, when she died on the 22nd of November in 1980.

Originally broadcast November 22, 1988

DEAD SEA DISCOVERY

On the 23rd of November in 1947, Professor Sukenik of the Hebrew University in Jerusalem had a meeting, of sorts, with an Armenian dealer in old documents. I say a meeting of sorts because Jerusalem in those days was in Palestine, a country run by the British. The British had run a barricade of barbed wire right through Jerusalem, trying to keep the Jews and Arabs apart. Professor Sukenik had to reach through that wire to get what the dealer had for him.

He took it home and examined it and figured he had one of the most important finds in history. It was a sheepskin scroll that contained writings of the old Jewish Bible.

The oldest known such bible was a thousand years old. If some of the writings on this one were an accurate indication, this scroll was a thousand years older than that. It had been written about the time of Christ.

Professor Sukenik met the dealer again a few days later and bought three scrolls from him. There were others, but they disappeared for a while. Then, a few years later, Professor Sukenik's son went to New York in response to an ad in the *Wall Street Journal.*

He paid a quarter-million for four more scrolls. They seem to have been in the possession of the head of a Syrian monastery, although they were obviously part of the same batch as the first three.

We now know they came from a cave overlooking the Dead Sea. They had been found, probably not long before Professor Sukenik encountered them, by a shepherd boy looking for a lost sheep. Hundreds more scrolls, some complete, mostly just powdery fragments, have been found since in other caves in the area.

Plus an awful lot of forgeries. The going price is one British pound for a square centimeter of scroll, which makes them very valuable. And well worth forging.

> *Professor Sukenik had one of the most important finds in history: a sheepskin scroll that contained writings of the old Jewish Bible.*

Scholars have been examining the scrolls ever since. Some say they're making great progress. Others say they're poking along or that they're deliberately keeping the scrolls out of reach of rival scholars.

In 1991, a biblical research centre in California published photographs of the scrolls so scholars everywhere could examine them. The Israeli government, which controls the scrolls, threatened to sue, but it didn't.

Meanwhile, the scholars keep examining the scrolls. So far, they've found several things of interest to professionals but nothing that you or I would be likely to understand.

Originally broadcast November 23, 1992

EVERYBODY GOES TO RICK'S

Everybody Goes To Rick's was a play that died on the road before it could make it to Broadway. This was about 1940 when the standards on Broadway were very high.

Warner Brothers, the movie studio, bought the movie rights to the play, then lost interest.

In 1942, the studio was looking for a script with a strong male lead role. Humphrey Bogart was emerging as a big draw at the box office and Warners owned him. They wanted a picture that would show off Bogart to his advantage.

At that same time, a producer named David Selznick, owned the contract of a new Swedish actress, at least new to Hollywood, named Ingrid Bergman. Selznick didn't have any script for her right then and he would be willing to rent her out to another studio if he could be convinced that other studio had a script that would advance Bergman's career.

Warner Brothers liked Bergman. In fact, they were more enthusiastic about her than the man who owned her, Selznick.

They sent two screenwriters to Selznick's with orders to convince Selznick he should rent out Bergman to Warner's. The Epstein brothers, Julius and Philip, were so-so scriptwriters, but great salesmen. They convinced Selznick.

They came back with a contract for Bergman's services for a picture. Warner Brothers told them to outline the story they'd told Selznick would be used for Bergman's picture.

They had taken *Everybody Goes To Rick's*, the story with the strong male lead, and strengthened the female lead to make it attractive for Bergman.

But the Epsteins couldn't write like they could sell. So Warner Brothers assigned another writer, Edward Koch. Koch was a young lawyer who much preferred writing plays to practicing law. He had written most of Orson Welles' *The War of the Worlds,* the radio play that everybody thought was real and started panic in the streets across the United States in 1938.

Koch had done some screenwriting and was quite good. So he was told to get cracking with the story of Rick and make sure the girl had a strong part.

The original play was about an American named Rick who owns a little bar overseas and everybody goes there to drink and flirt and do various bits of illegal business.

Koch looked at the situation that then existed in Europe and set Rick's bar in Casablanca, in French North Africa. He put in Nazis and Jewish refugees and crooked black marketeers.

He threw in a black American pianist who played the boss' favorite song, *As Time Goes By.* When Rick, Humphrey Bogart, gets lonely and sentimental, he sits at the bar after the place is closed and says, "Play it Sam." Not "Play it again, Sam," like most people think.

Today, no matter how often we see it on TV, *Casablanca* comes across as a superbly written screenplay, maybe the best ever done. Koch says he had only a couple of dozen pages written when the cameras started to roll and two-thirds of the way through it, the camera caught up with him and he was writing each day's shooting the night before.

But when *Casablanca* opened in New York on the 24th of November in 1942, it sure looked good. And it's become the number one film classic of all time.

> *Koch looked at the situation that then existed in Europe and set Rick's bar in Casablanca. He put in Nazis and Jewish refugees and crooked black marketeers.*

Originally broadcast November 24, 1986

CARRY ON

Carry Nation is remembered as a nut, a religious fanatic, a do-gooder, an object of laughter.

And she was all that. She was also a very serious, dedicated campaigner against one of the greatest evils North American society has had to cope with: alcohol.

Carry Moore was born in Tennessee on the 25th of November in 1846. Her family was prosperous. On her mother's side, there was a long history of insanity. Her mother thought she was Queen Victoria and caused much hilarity by carrying on like how she thought Queen Victoria would.

Carry's brother and sister and mother all died in asylums. And that was Carry's terrible tragedy. She knew there was a streak of craziness in her family. She realized it would probably eventually claim her. But she wasn't stupid; she lived with this prospect every day of her life.

Carry's first husband drank himself to death. Her second, Mr. Nation, eventually wished he had.

Mr. Nation was no hot-shot at it but, for some reason, he chose to be a preacher. He had already failed as a farmer and lawyer. Carry would sit in the front row of the church on Sunday morning and criticize her husband's sermons in a loud voice, often correcting his grammar.

One Sunday, Carry found the sermon so bad she walked out, taking the whole congregation with her. As she left, she turned back to the pulpit and said: "That will be enough for today, David."

In 1891, the Nations lived in Kansas, a state that was legally dry. Legally was the key word. Despite the law, Kansas had more saloons than milk stores. They operated openly and by paying off the local politicians and making no secret of it.

Carry lived in a large town called Medicine Lodge. She became interested in the work of the Women's Christian Temperance Union there. She led prayer meetings on the sidewalk out in front of the saloons. It didn't bother either the saloonkeepers or the customers.

Carry then followed the saloonkeepers down the street, screaming at them: "Fiend, maker of drunkards,

Carry's first husband drank himself to death. Her second, Mr. Nation, eventually wished he had.

friend of the devil!" That didn't change anything either.

Then one day Carry decided on more direct action. She took an ax and walked into the local drug store, right into the back room where the druggist kept a barrel of whisky that he sold by the shot.

She smashed the barrel and told the druggist she'd be back when he got a new barrel. If he wanted to call a cop to arrest her, that would be just fine. Each would explain in court just what was going on in that drug store.

The druggist closed his store and left town.

Carry then went to the next big town, a place called Kiowa. She walked into the biggest saloon in town with her ax in her hand and broke up the place, screaming all the while for someone to come to arrest her, for the owner to sue her.

It worked. She started closing down places.

In 1900, she walked into the bar of the Carey Hotel in Wichita, one of the plushest and more famous bars in the west. She broke all the bottles and glasses and, horror of horrors, slashed the nude painting behind the bar. Then she threw her ax through the $1500 plate glass mirror and waited for the cops to come.

Over the next few years, Carry spent almost as much time in jail as on the road. But the day she got out, the newspapermen gathered. They knew she would march from jail to saloon and break up another place.

Everybody laughed at her. But Carry Nation was doing good work. Alcoholism was a much bigger problem then than now because it was combined with low wages and unemployment and poor housing and sweat shops and a lot of things we've either eliminated or softened.

Her movement spread north to Canada and east to the older parts of the United States. Eventually, it led to Prohibition in both countries. But Carry didn't live to see it. She was struck dumb one night while delivering a temperance lecture. She died five months later in a padded cell in a Kansas hospital, the victim of the family insanity that she had always feared.

Originally broadcast November 25, 1987

THE PLAY'S THE THING

Agatha Christie was a young English woman, married to a flier in the First World War, working in the pharmacy of a hospital, partly to fill in time, partly as her contribution to the war effort.

She mentioned one day to her sister that writing a mystery story seemed like an easy task. Her sister laughed and dared her to try.

Since Christie was working around all sorts of chemicals, she did a story about a poisoning. Her husband was serving in a squadron with a man who worked for a London publisher in peacetime and he arranged for an editor to look over the story. He didn't think it was worth publishing.

Christie rewrote and edited and fiddled with it for a few more years and it was finally published four years later, in 1920, under the title *The Mysterious Affair at Styles*.

That was the beginning of an incredible career of dozens of books and short stories and a few plays. Twenty-two of Christie's works were made into movies. The best by far was *Witness For The Prosecution*.

The queen, her mother and her grandmother were all big Christie fans. In 1947, the queen's grandmother, Queen Mary, was 80 and the BBC asked her what sort of radio program she would like to celebrate the event. She said: A radio play by Agatha Christie.

Queen Mary was turning 80 and the BBC asked her what sort of radio program she would like to celebrate the event. She said: A radio play by Agatha Christie.

So Christie was commissioned to do a half-hour mystery. It was called *Three Blind Mice* and it began with a murder being committed by someone whistling that old nursery rhyme.

It was a success but nothing sensational. But Christie liked the basic story and, over the next few years, worked with it.

In late 1951, Christie was having lunch with a producer who had staged a couple of her works. She handed him a script and suggested he give it some thought. She had obviously been working on it for quite a while. Several pages had coffee cup rings on them.

It was a tricky little mystery with 10 characters and two sets. The producer dropped two characters and condensed the action into one set to save money.

The Mousetrap, as it was called, opened in London on the 26th of November in 1952. The actors weren't very impressed. The critics liked it. Christie figured it could run for a couple of years, maybe even three. It's still on the stage, the longest-running play in the history of the world.

Christie's been dead over 20 years now. She never made a dime from *The Mousetrap*. She gave her grandson the rights to it for a birthday present. He's a millionaire several times over.

Originally broadcast November 26, 1992

A CALCULATING LADY

Lord Byron was the major celebrity of Britain in the early 1800s. He was brilliant, a poet who achieved worldwide fame at the age of 24 with his masterpiece *Childe Harold*. He was an athlete who could fence and swim like nobody else, despite a club foot.

And most important of all, he was a real hell-raiser. Byron's affairs with women made him a household name in a shocking kind of way. If there had been supermarket tabloids in those days he would have been on their front pages most weeks. There were a few affairs with men too, but they were more hinted at in polite society than actually talked about. One woman who had an affair with Byron, one of many, described him as mad, bad, and dangerous to know.

Although Byron had affairs with dozens of women, rich and poor, he had never shown any inclination for marriage. Then he met Annabella Milbanke, a brilliant young woman of good family. Their romance went on for two or three years, in an on-again, off-again way. Naturally, it didn't interfere with Byron's other affairs. No one had any influence on the others.

Finally, after a rather stormy courtship, Byron and Annabella were married.

It was, as you would expect, a disaster. For one thing, by the time Byron got around to marrying Annabella he was already having a long-term affair with another, his half-sister.

The marriage produced one child then ended after 11 months. The child was a pretty, brilliant daughter named Ada.

Needless to say, the split between Ada's parents was a messy one and most of her mother's time was spent with lawyers, fighting tooth and nail to blacken Byron's name and hound him through the courts. Byron never saw Ada after he left Annabella, but he tried to contact her. Annabella saw that never happened.

Instead, she set out to educate Ada according to her own ideas, which were quite advanced for the time. She got her good tutors and, when she saw Ada had an interest in mathematics, she encouraged it, though it was considered rather improper for a female to have an interest in anything but painting and embroidery and a little literature.

Annabella had a real fixation about Byron and even forbade Ada to see a picture of him until she was 20.

She was always trying to get Ada interested in good works. This back-fired twice in ways that were to change Ada's life, but not how Annabella intended.

First, she took Ada to a horse race to show her the evils of gambling. Ada got hooked and spent the rest of her life trying to beat the horses. Needless to say, she had as much success as thousand of others before and since and died broke.

Annabella had a real fixation about Byron and even forbade Ada to see a picture of him until she was 20.

Annabella also showed Ada a factory to demonstrate the evils of the industrial revolution and how it was enslaving workers. Ada couldn't get interested in that. But she got fascinated by machinery.

That led her to meet and become a disciple of a brilliant mathematician named Charles Babbage. Babbage invented the first computer but couldn't figure how to make it work. Ada, with her mathematical mind, added the necessary steps and was the world's first programmer. She rewrote Babbage's papers on the subject and translated them so continental students could get an introduction to Babbage's work. It's only in recent years, as the computer has become a major force, that her work has been appreciated.

Ada married a nobleman, Lord Lovelace, and he encouraged her in her work and financed a lot of it. He tried to discourage her addiction to gambling but without any success. Poor Ada, brilliant long before her time, caught tuberculosis and died at the age of 36 on the 27th of November in 1852.

Originally broadcast November 27, 1991

THE SPORTING LIFE

Jim Naismith was an Ottawa Valley farm boy, born in the mid-1800s. He was an outdoors type, not much interested in school. He worked on his uncle's farm, ploughing and logging. He was also a big hunter and hiker.

After a few years of this, Naismith felt he should be doing something else, something more useful to society. He had left school at 14 so he had to go back to finish high school then to university at McGill in Montreal. There, he intended to be a clergyman.

Naismith was an athlete and while he was getting his B.A. he played every game going. By the time he graduated he was the McGill director of athletics. He supported himself at that job while he went on to get a degree in theology as a Presbyterian clergyman.

Naismith was one tough cookie, although he had trouble convincing people at first. They thought his constant Bible study indicated he was some sort of sissy. He had to lay out the toughest star of the McGill football team before he made his point. He did that with one punch.

In the three years it took to get a degree in divinity, Naismith did a lot of thinking. He couldn't see himself spending life in a pulpit, although he was an excellent preacher. One of his best sermons was preached while he had two black eyes from a football game. That scandalized the congregation.

Naismith decided he could further his religion better as an athlete than a preacher, so he went to the YMCA's Christian school at Springfield in Massachusetts. There he played football under one of the most famous American coaches, Amos Alonzo Stagg. Naismith was only 160 pounds, but Stagg played him at centre. Naismith said he would be killed by the bigger guys. "You play centre," said Stagg, "and you do the meanest things in the most gentlemanly way."

Naismith got a soccer ball. Then he had to find some sort of target. The janitor came up with some bushel baskets that peaches had come in.

There was a class of 18 young men at the Springfield school, studying to be YMCA secretaries. They were supposed to spend part of their time at athletics and they did that eagerly during the summer and fall because they all loved baseball and football. But in the winter they refused to do their gym exercises because they found them dull.

Naismith tried to devise an indoor form of football but it just didn't work.

Back on the farm in the Ottawa Valley, when Naismith was a boy, he had played a game called Duck on the Rock. A small rock was set on a bigger flat rock and the point of the game was to knock it off by throwing another rock at it. But the rock had to be thrown high in the air to land on the small rock from above.

It seemed to Naismith that something like that might make an interesting indoor game. Of course, not with rocks.

He got a soccer ball. Then he had to find some sort of target. He asked the janitor to look around for something. There was a pair of bushel baskets that peaches had come in and the janitor came up with them.

So Naismith had the game and the name for it: basketball.

He played it first with nine players on a team because he had 18 men to keep busy. That was in 1891. Four years later somebody tried it with 100 players. That created such a mob scene that the rules were changed to provide for five on each team.

A few years later Naismith went to medical school, but after he graduated he still preferred sports so he went to the University of Kansas as athletic director. In all, he held 11 university degrees by the time he died. That was on the 28th of November in 1939.

Originally broadcast November 28, 1991

THE MAN WHO LOST HIS MARBLE

Lord Elgin, the seventh Lord Elgin, was the British ambassador to Turkey from 1799 to 1803.

He was a fabulously wealthy man and had promised his new bride that he would build her one of the most elaborate homes in his native Scotland. And he would decorate it with the Greek statues that were fashionable at the time.

With that in mind, he hired an architect and an artist and dozens of workmen and they measured and sketched the architecture and statues at the Parthenon in Athens. The Turks ruled Greece at the time.

When the local Turkish governor interfered with his employees' work, Lord Elgin used his influence as the ambassador to get a paper from the sultan of Turkey allowing his people to sketch and examine and move various pieces of the Parthenon, the great ancient Greek temple, and any other artifacts that interested them.

That paper was originally written in Turkish, translated to Greek, then to Italian. Somewhere along the way, the Greeks now say, the word "move" was translated to "remove".

From 1802 until 1812, for 10 years, various statues and pieces of sculpture were crated and shipped, usually aboard British warships, from Greece to England.

By then, his new bride had run off with somebody else and His Lordship's career as a diplomat was on the rocks because of various political problems.

He almost forgot about the 80 crates of marble that had cost him a fortune. One warship had sunk in a storm and it cost him 5,000 pounds to send down divers and recover the cargo. That was a fortune in those days.

Then there was a storm of protest over Lord Elgin desecrating and looting the sites of ancient art treasures. That was all bewildering to his lordship because he'd only visited the work site once. It now seems likely that the idea to ship and crate the stuff and send the bill to Lord Elgin came from that architect he hired.

Lord Elgin got permission for his people to move various pieces of the Parthenon. Somewhere along the way the word "move" was translated to "remove".

The French demanded that the artifacts, by now known around the world as the Elgin Marbles, be given to them for safekeeping. King Ludwig of Bavaria wanted to buy them.

A committee of the British parliament was established to decide what to do. It paid Lord Elgin half of what they had cost him and the pieces of marble are now in the British museum. The Greek government keeps demanding them back but the British refuse to part with them.

The controversy got so hot that Lord Byron wrote a poem about what a philistine Lord Elgin was.

That stirred interest in ancient Greek sculpture and led to more trips to unearth ancient treasures. A young, wealthy British student of architecture named Charles Cockerell led an expedition to the Aegean island of Aegina. There, he found 16 statues and 13 pieces of others. They were buried in soft earth that had preserved them beautifully. He called up a British warship to cart them away.

But by then the Greeks were protesting about the theft and the Turks were trying to hold them for ransom.

So Cockerell had them shipped to a safe place and announced they would be sent to the highest bidder, but the bidder had to be a recognized collector, not just somebody rich.

The warship that was sent from Britain to take the statues back there arrived on the 29th of November in 1811 in the middle of a huge controversy and all sorts of threats by all the major powers to go to war with each other to stop this desecration.

They eventually were sold to King Ludwig of Bavaria. Much underhanded dealing was involved. Poor Lord Elgin wasn't involved in any way in this transaction. But somehow, history has become confused over the two separate incidents and, in most accounts of the affair, Lord Elgin is blamed for breaking his word, stealing the statues and almost causing a war.

Originally broadcast November 29, 1990

THE PERFECT GENTLEMAN

You say you've never heard of Sir Philip Sidney, the perfect English gentleman? No wonder. Philip might have been perfection itself, but he was no winner. He was living proof, if you need any, that good guys finish last.

Sidney's father was Sir Henry Sidney, one of the few hard-working and honest servants of the crown. England, in those days, was involved in a lot of fighting in Wales and Ireland, and Sir Henry was away, running armies and administering conquered territories. He was one of the few who wasn't lining his own pockets on the job.

In fact, the Sidneys were known as an honest but poor family. All his life, Philip would live under the shadow of poverty.

We don't know for sure, but it appears that young Philip couldn't read or write until he was 10. Then his father sent him to a free school because he couldn't afford tuition at a private one.

Young Philip took to learning like a horse to oats. And not just book-learning. He became an excellent horseman and swordsman, an athlete and a man quite accomplished in all the social graces that were so important in those days.

The original idea of chivalry, the basis of gentlemanly conduct, had been founded on the customs and traditions of the Catholic courts of the kings of Europe. Sidney became known as the first Protestant courtier, a man who could be learned and witty and humble and dedicated to a life of service within a new Protestant tradition.

In four years, Sidney became a remarkable scholar, able to write fluently in both French and Latin. When he was 14 he went to Oxford, where he excelled.

Then he went abroad for two years to perfect his languages and to learn something of diplomacy. He worked in English embassies in Paris, in Italy and Vienna. He took some time out to study in Italy.

He returned to London and worked at the court of Queen Elizabeth. He was the ideal young man. The queen was rather cynical. She used young Sidney, holding out many promises to make him rich but paying off on none.

The Duke of Anjou, a French nobleman, wanted to marry Queen Elizabeth. She intended to have nothing to do with him. But she couldn't just put it that flatly. So she arranged for Sidney to write a brilliant attack on the proposed marriage. Then she was able to show it to the king of France as evidence that the English people would rebel if the marriage came off.

You'd think Sidney would be knighted for that. Not at all. The queen then forced him to retire from the court, as a phony sort of punishment.

Sidney, still only in his 20s, then revolutionized English prose by throwing himself into writing. Today only scholars read his stuff. But they're pretty well agreed that he invented the English novel, or at least its forerunner. Then he threw himself into poetry and did

> *The queen needed someone to command one of her armies in Holland, where she was fighting the Spanish. Young Sidney was called out of retirement and sent.*

the same there.

Then the queen needed someone to command one of her armies in Holland, where she was fighting the Spanish. Young Sidney was called out of retirement and sent.

The army was tired and hungry, unpaid for months, not adequately fed or equipped. Sidney borrowed money from his rich father-in-law and led the army into battle.

He was wounded and died in agony 25 days later, a month before he would have been 32. As he lay on a stretcher, half-mad with thirst, he was handed a canteen of water. But a wounded soldier lay nearby. Sidney handed it to him, saying: "Thy necessity is yet greater than mine."

Three months later, all the important people in England crowded into St. Paul's for his funeral, led by the queen who had treated him so heartlessly — the perfect subject buried by the perfect cynic.

Originally broadcast November 30, 1984

EVIL GENIUS

Aleister Crowley was a genius. He was born in 1875, the heir to a fortune. His family was Scottish and he not only inherited hundreds of thousands of dollars, but also a gloomy old Scottish castle.

Hundreds of thousands back then, of course, meant that by today's standards he was a millionaire several times over.

Right from the time he was a little kid, it was clear that Crowley had a superior intellect. He went south to England and taught ancient mythology and anthropology at Cambridge.

In his lifetime, Crowley wrote 45 books of poetry, most of it not easily understood. He also wrote several volumes on black magic and all sorts of ancient superstitions and beliefs. He was probably the world's foremost authority on the subject.

Crowley moved in an intellectual circle, so it was expected he'd be a little on the weird side. It was some years before it became obvious that he was out-and-out nuts.

Crowley wrote articles for various learned publications, expounding his philosophy. Anything you want to do is all right, he wrote. The only sin is restriction.

Each generation comes up with something like that, so nobody took it as a sign that Crowley was unusual.

About this time he was also emerging as an athlete of some note, a mountain climber back in the days when mountain-climbing was big-time.

Crowley was the first man to make a serious attempt to climb K2, the second-highest mountain in the world, considered by the experts to be tougher than Everest.

He organized an expedition on one of the other Himalayas. Five men from his party died in that attempt. Next Crowley went to Mexico and climbed one of the big mountains there.

He wrote several hymns for the Anglican church. Two of them became minor classics. But by then Crowley had crossed the line from slightly strange to really weird.

The honours bestowed on Crowley for his hymn-writing seemed to mark a turning point in his life. He turned his back on conventional society and started his own religion, a sort of black magic, devil worship.

He moved into his Scottish castle and assembled a pack of weirdos and started to practice a nutty religion he invented. It consisted mostly of sex.

He was told to leave Scotland and he wandered around the world, first to New York. He was an artist for a year and some thought he had considerable talent.

By now he was an out-and-out pervert and drug addict. He had no trouble assembling women, mostly rich ones, who became his disciples. He moved his harem for a while to Sicily until word of his orgies and dope reached the ears of Mussolini, the dictator of Italy at the time. Crowley was exiled.

He lived in Paris in the 20s. Ernest Hemingway knew him and thought he was the most evil man he had ever met. He lived for a while with Somerset Maugham, the author. Maugham wrote a novel about him called *The Magician*.

Crowley's drug habit used up all his money eventually. He ended his days in Bristol, England, still surrounded by a few old women admirers. They panhandled on the streets to get enough money to keep Crowley in drugs. He died on the first of December in 1947. The day before, he wrote in his diary: "What an ass I am. Will heroin help me forget it?"

> *Crowley moved into his Scottish castle and assembled a pack of weirdos and started to practice a nutty religion he invented. It consisted mostly of sex.*

Originally broadcast December 1, 1988

THOSE DARN QUAKERS

Lydia and William Darragh were Irish Quakers who emigrated to America and settled in Philadelphia about 1760. William was a prosperous merchant and they lived in a big house in the centre of the city. In those days, Philadelphia was the second-biggest English-speaking city in the world, next only to London. It was the centre of the Quaker movement, a religion that was based on Christianity and love of peace.

When the American Revolution broke out, the Darraghs found their patriotism was at odds with their religion. In the early years of the Revolution, the sympathies of the Quakers were split. Some favoured the American cause. Some preferred the crown. But none took up arms.

Well, practically none. A few joined each of the opposing armies. That meant, of course, that they had to leave their church.

Charles Darragh, the oldest child, joined the American Army as a lieutenant. Lydia, his mother, believed in what he did, although she remained in the church.

The first American government made its capital in Philadelphia. But in 1777, the war was going badly for the Americans, and the British Army occupied the city.

So Lydia was in enemy territory while her son was serving in the opposing army just a few miles away. Lydia collected bits of information about the British army and sent them to her son. She usually stitched them into some sewing she was doing and had her youngest son take them to his brother Charles, the lieutenant. It looked as if she was just doing his sewing and darning his socks.

Lydia knew quite a bit about what was going on

Lydia collected bits of information about the British army and sent them to her son. She usually stitched them into some sewing and had her youngest son take them to his brother the lieutenant.

because the British general used her living room as a conference room.

On the night of the second of December in 1777, an unusually large number of British officers arrived to hold a meeting. Lydia was supposed to be upstairs in bed. She sneaked down the stairs and listened at the door.

And she learned that the British were marching out their army in 48 hours, in the middle of the night, in two columns, to surround and smash the American army that was out in the suburbs.

Lydia decided this was much too important news to be entrusted to the kid and the sewing basket. So Lydia set out the next day on foot, carrying a flour bag. She told British sentries she was heading for a mill out in the suburbs to get flour.

They let her through their lines and pretty soon she met an American officer who was a friend of her son's. She told him exactly what the British had in mind.

When the British force tried its midnight ambush, the Americans were waiting and they were sent back into Philadelphia, badly battered.

By that time Lydia was back at home. The British immediately suspected a spy had learned what they were up to. A few old letters and military dispatches show that Lydia was on a list of suspects, but she was just one of many and she came to no harm.

The American army she saved went on to eventually win that war. Her son returned home safe when the war was over. But peace didn't bring happiness to Lydia and her family.

For participating in the war, they were turfed out of the Quakers.

Originally broadcast December 2, 1988

A TOUCH OF CLASS

George Gershwin was a New York boy who took piano lessons as a kid. He was good enough to play from time to time at his high school assembly. He went to the High School of Commerce to be an accountant.

But music was more fun. So, at the age of 15, he quit school to be a song plugger.

Gershwin was paid to play his boss' songs, to show them off to prospective users like theatre owners or entertainers.

Song pluggers were the work horses of the music industry and they put in long hours for low pay. The smart ones took their jobs as opportunities to learn the gritty end of the business. No one learned it better than George Gershwin. He developed a cocky self-confidence that saw him through the bumps and slumps of show business.

At the same time, Gershwin realized he needed training in the techniques of sophisticated music, and for the rest of his life he took lessons in composition from the best symphonic composers he could find.

In 1919, when Gershwin was 1919 and had been making a living pounding the piano for six years, he wrote a song called *Swanee*. It was a mild success. Then Al Jolson, the night club and musical comedy singer, adopted it as his signature song. That was it. Gershwin was in the top rank of American song writers with Jerome Kern and Cole Porter. The experts still argue who was Number One.

Gershwin was in the top rank of American song writers with Jerome Kern and Cole Porter. The experts still argue who was Number One.

But, despite his light-hearted music, Gershwin had a compulsion to unite classical music, the symphony hall stuff, with jazz. In those days, jazz was considered very low-brow.

In 1927, he did his *Rhapsody in Blue* at the Aeolian Hall in New York, backed by Paul Whiteman's very classy band. That broke the ice. But there was still considerable reserve in the classy end of the business.

That was ended on the afternoon of the third of December in 1925. Gershwin played his *Concerto in F*, a piece he had written especially for the occasion and for the New York symphony. And he did it in Carnegie Hall, the very temple of respectable music.

After Gershwin signed the contract to write the concerto and perform it at the piano, he went out and bought a book on composing concertos.

The critics liked the *Concerto in F*, but didn't go crazy over it. But it slowly but surely caught on. Two years later, it was played by a symphony in Paris.

Gershwin lived to see popular and classy music blend into the popular and classy music we have today, a much more sophisticated product than the moon-croon-June stuff of his early song-plugging days. But he didn't live much longer. He died of a brain tumour when he was only 38.

Originally broadcast December 3, 1992

THE KING'S RIGHT HAND MAN

Armand Jean du Plessis de Richelieu was the son of a high official in the court of the king of France in the 1500s. But by the time he was born, most of the family money had been frittered away.

Young Armand was supposed to be an army officer. But he was sidetracked into the priesthood. The Richelieu family had the right to nominate the bishop of one of the cities of the French provinces. And they usually kept it for one of their own.

The older son who was supposed to get it had no interest in the church. So it went to Armand. Armand was a brilliant, cold young man and it didn't matter to him if he became a soldier or a bishop. So he studied briefly, just enough to be sworn in as a priest, then took the bishop's office.

He was too young, by church law, so he travelled to Rome to get permission from the pope. The pope's officials said: Don't bother. He'll say no.

Young Father Armand made a clever pitch for the job in a speech he delivered himself to the pope in Latin. In it he listed all his qualifications, including being old enough. The pope was quite charmed and confirmed him as a bishop. Richelieu then asked the pope if forgiveness was important for a man of the church. "Yes, indeed," said the pope, "all important."

"Then you'll have to forgive me," said Richelieu, "because I just lied about my age."

The pope laughed and called him a rogue, but he didn't take away his bishopric.

Richelieu went home to France and threw himself into his work. Pretty soon, he had done a lot of work for his people. Taxes in those days were crushing and he negotiated a series of tax breaks in his area that made life easier for the people and created some prosperity.

From there, he moved to Paris and got involved in the king's affairs. The king was Louis the 13th, a royal loser. Louis suffered from tuberculosis, a chronically nervous stomach, and a stutter. He was skinny to the point of emaciation and had an oversized head. He was weak and if he caught a cold it took him to the verge of death.

Worst of all, he couldn't seem to be able to produce a son. If he couldn't France would be plunged into endless civil war over the succession to the throne. But not only was Louis not very interested in women, he *was* interested in men.

Eventually, under Richelieu's guidance, Louis became the father of Louis XIV, the greatest of all French kings. Some historians say that was Richelieu's greatest accomplishment; some say it was the most spectacular of his many examples of getting something done by means no one could prove.

Richelieu was the prime conspirator, the fixer, the sneaky behind-the-scenes manipulator. In effect, he was the king of France.

He subdued the Protestant rebels who threatened to tear the country apart. Then he treated them with great leniency, allowing them to prosper.

He crushed the nobles who questioned the king's authority. Then he treated them with great cruelty, wiping out virtually all noble houses that didn't bow to the throne.

In the midst of all his reforms and controls, Richelieu put the government of New France, Quebec, on a firmer basis. Champlain had established the first colony at Quebec City but it wasn't prospering. Richelieu provided government support and arranged for a new colonization company to take over, one that would really strengthen the colony, not like the previous frail attempts.

When all is said and done, that was probably his greatest accomplishment.

When Richelieu died, still in his 50s, on the fourth of December in 1642, the king was at his side. All Europe paid homage to this strange, efficient, cruel super-bureaucrat who had made France such a great nation. But within a century and a half, France was torn apart by revolution. But Quebec by then was quite prosperous, even if it wasn't French anymore.

> *Richelieu was the prime conspirator, the fixer, the sneaky behind-the-scenes manipulator. In effect, he was the king of France.*

Originally broadcast December 4, 1987

The Best Burglar

Dr. Michael Halberstam was a heart specialist who was also interested in both writing novels and politics. A brilliant future seemed in store for him.

On the evening of the 5th of December in 1980, Dr. Halberstam had been at a cocktail party with his wife. They arrived home, and Mrs. Halberstam waited in the car while Dr. Halberstam went into the house to get the dogs. They were going to take them for a walk before bedtime.

Inside the house, Halberstam surprised a burglar. The burglar pulled a gun and fired five shots. He hit Halberstam twice in the chest.

Halberstam ran out of the house and jumped into his car. He told his wife what had happened and started driving to the hospital.

He didn't seem to be too badly hurt. A few blocks away they saw the burglar running along the sidewalk. Dr. Halberstam drove the car right over the curb and hit the man, knocking him over a hedge.

Halberstam lost consciousness. An ambulance was called and took him the rest of the way to the hospital. But he died within a few minutes. He'd been more seriously wounded than he thought.

The first police on the scene grabbed the burglar. He was groggy and had been knocked out but he wasn't badly hurt. At the station he wouldn't give his name or say anything. Detectives questioned him for hours but all he ever said was, "you're going to be surprised."

It took a few days for the FBI to check out his fingerprints. And the cops were certainly surprised. It turned out the man they had was Bernard Charles Welch, a 40-year old who had been on the wanted list for six years, since escaping from a jail in Connecticut. Before that, Welch had been the burglary genius of upstate New York.

In his own way, he was just as clever as Dr. Halberstam. He had had an alcoholic father and a crazy mother and had been on his own from about the age of 12. He'd made his living by skipping school and running a trap line, selling muskrat and mink skins.

He had become a plumber, a workaholic who went at it seven days a week, plumbing all day, stealing all night. He was quite well-to-do when he was caught back in the

> *In his own way, Welch was just as clever as Dr. Halberstam.*

60s. His wife had divorced him while he was in jail.

The cops got ready to try him for murdering Halberstam. Then they got a call from an FBI agent who lived out in a suburb of Washington. He said the pictures of Welch in the newspaper looked an awful lot like a neighbor of his, a man named Hamilton. He had been suspicious when Hamilton moved into the neighborhood a few years ago, he said, because he seemed to have an awful lot of money.

When the cops went to Hamilton's house, they were stunned. They found three cars in the garage, each worth more than $50,000. They found a house and elaborate security system that was worth more than $1,000,000. In the huge basement they found piles of gold bricks, each worth $10,000.

They found jewellery, fur coats, coins, guns and antique furniture and vases worth millions. They figured it had all come from more than 3500 burglaries. There were more than 13,000 separate items. The catalogue of loot took 20,000 pages.

The police put two and two together and realized that Mr. Hamilton was really Mr. Welch. Whatever name you want to call him, he was clearly the most successful burglar of all time, a rich man who could have retired years ago.

He had an equally palatial house in Duluth, Minnesota. Each summer he drove there with a moving van full of loot and sold it through furniture and coin collectors all over the midwest. He kept a seamstress working all summer, replacing the linings in his endless supply of fur coats.

The people Welch dealt with, his wife and three kids all figured he was just an unusually successful businessman.

The gun that killed Dr. Halberstam had been stolen from the apartment of an FBI agent.

Welch knew what every cop knows. If you live in one area, steal in another and fence your loot in a third; that way, it's almost impossible to get caught.

Welch was convicted of killing Dr. Halberstam and sentenced to 15 years to life. In other words, he could be out before he's 50.

Originally broadcast December 5, 1983

AN EAR-IE TALE

Thomas Walker was a stubborn, cranky man. He was an Englishman who made his living as a merchant in Boston. In 1763, when Quebec became British at the end of the Seven Years War, he moved to Montreal and was soon one of the leading citizens of the town.

At that time, Montreal was still under martial law and the army ran everything. Walker, a civilian to the core, didn't enjoy that situation at all.

He had a dispute over wages with one of his clerks. Since the army ran the courts, he figured he was victim of a military plot when the clerk won.

Soon afterwards, in early 1764, martial law was ended and civil rule was established. As one of the leading citizens of Montreal, Walker was appointed a magistrate.

The law still said that the army could billet officers and soldiers in civilian homes around the town. But Walker, now a bit of a legal expert, started to read the law. It said a householder had to supply a room for a soldier if the army demanded it. But it didn't say he had to supply anything else.

So, at Walker's direction, householders who found soldiers billeted in their homes refused to give them firewood, a candle, a wash basin or use of the kitchen.

Life in the British army in those days was tough enough. With Walker adding to their misery, the soldiers were soon pretty agitated.

On the evening of the 6th of December in 1764, after this situation had been going on for a few months, Walker was having dinner with his wife, his clerk and a couple of servants.

Suddenly, the door flew open and in dashed several men — at least four, maybe as many as seven. They were disguised with blackened faces and scarves over their mouths and noses.

Mrs. Walker ran out the back door to the barn. Walker stayed to fight and put up quite a struggle. But he was knocked down and stabbed a couple of times with a sword. Then one of the attackers grabbed his hair and slashed off half his ear. He grabbed the severed half-ear then they all ran out.

Walker and his friends and neighbors raised the alarm and the army went looking for the attackers.

Now, everybody knew they were soldiers. Nobody really expected the army would arrest whoever was responsible.

But the governor in Quebec City, a military man, was already in hot water over the high-handed treatment the military had been handing out to civilians. So he and the attorney general went to Montreal to investigate.

> *They offered a huge reward for any information that would solve the case of Walker's ear.*

They offered a huge reward for any information that would solve the case of Walker's ear. They even offered any soldier who came forward a discharge from the army plus free passage to any colony he named.

Nothing. Four soldiers were arrested but nothing came of it.

Two years later, with a new governor in Quebec City, Walker came forward with a witness who named six other men, three army officers and three leading citizens.

But the witness was a drunkard and an army deserter and the trial, when it finally came off, ended with the jury saying not guilty after only five minutes deliberation.

Walker remained in Montreal and remained a hater of the army. When the American Revolution broke out in 1775 and the Americans sent an army to capture Montreal, Walker joined them and took up arms against the British. When that American expedition ended in failure and the Americans retreated, Walker had to go with them.

Benjamin Franklin had come up to be civilian governor when Quebec became a state of the new United States. Instead, he found himself retreating in the middle of the winter, sharing a sleigh with Walker and Mrs. Walker. A more miserable, complaining man he never met, Franklin said. He noticed that somebody, sometime in the past had cut off half his ear. "They must have been aiming for his throat," said Franklin.

Originally broadcast December 6, 1990

BONES OF CONTENTION

Davidson Black was a Toronto man who was a doctor by trade and a scientist by inclination.

Black didn't make much money at medicine. He worked in Cleveland and in north Canada as a specialist in anatomy for four years.

Then he studied geology and anthropology. Then he went to England to study more anatomy. Black was regarded by his fellow doctors as a superb anatomist.

In 1919, Black was hired by the Rockefeller Foundation to go to the medical school it had established in Beijing, China. There, he was to teach anatomy.

Black soon got a reputation as a brilliant teacher, as much for his good nature as his medical knowledge. He was one of those bright, friendly, optimistic people who made work seem easy.

While he was teaching, Black was also spending some time in the hills outside Beijing where ancient bones and fossils had been discovered for years. The local farmers thought the strange bones they found were from dragons. Black knew they were from animals that had become extinct.

He also knew that there was an excellent chance that if the digging was thorough and careful, he would someday come up with ancient human bones that could help man understand how our ancestors looked.

The Rockefeller Foundation complained that Black was spending too much time with old bones and not enough with current ones.

So Black established a crew of workmen who would dig all week and he would inspect what they had found on weekends. That went on for quite a while. Black had a young Chinese assistant named Pie who was just as good with the old bones as Black was.

> *There was an excellent chance that if the digging was thorough and careful, he would someday come up with ancient human bones that could help man understand how our ancestors looked.*

Sure enough, in 1929, Pie found an almost complete skull, somewhere between a quarter-million and a half-million years old.

It's known today as Peking Man and it provided an important piece of vital information. It was the skull of a creature more human than ape, although to us it would look a little ape-like.

Casts were made of it and sent to the States for further study. Black was showered with honours from scientific organizations around the world.

He died in China in 1934, age 60, worn out by his two jobs, anatomy and anthropology.

The political situation in China got grimmer and grimmer. Finally, over the protests of the Chinese government, the Americans decided to move the Peking skull and other valuable bones to the States, where they would be safe from Japanese invasion.

A detachment of American marines who had been guarding the embassy at Beijing were to be transferred home and it was arranged for the bones to be carefully wrapped in cloth and taken along as part of their baggage.

The Marines got on the train headed for the nearest port where a ship would pick them up. But they had waited too long.

They were arrested by the Japanese along the way. It was the 7th of December in 1941, the day the war between Japan and the United States began. In all the confusion, the bones of Peking Man disappeared and have never been seen again.

Originally broadcast December 7, 1987

A FAN'S 15 MINUTES OF FAME

The Beatles were the most sensational act in the history of show business, four nice-looking young men from Liverpool.

After a few years of drawing huge crowds all over the world with their frantic act, they settled down to turning out great melodies.

After a dozen or so years of that, they split up and retired. Separately, they dabbled at exotic religions and music, sometimes they sat back and enjoyed their millions.

John Lennon, probably the deepest thinker of the four, got divorced from his wife Cynthia. He married Yoko Ono, a wealthy Japanese woman.

The other Beatles lived in England. But Lennon and his new wife moved into the Dakota, a gloomy-looking old apartment building in New York. They took over the seventh floor and made the five apartments there into a 28-room suite.

Fans hung around the Dakota day and night and the Lennons' comings and goings were well-chronicled and photographed.

Those comings and going were closely followed by Mark David Chapman, a 25-year old psycho who had spent most of his life playing with drugs and religion and toy soldiers and making his living as a security guard.

Chapman had worshipped Lennon in his younger days. Then he read that Lennon had told an interviewer that the Beatles were actually more popular than Jesus.

Actually, what Lennon had said was, that because of modern communication, TV and records and movies, more people knew of the Beatles than had ever known of Jesus in Jesus' day.

No matter. About then, Chapman, a born again Christian, started to consider killing Lennon.

Chapman figured he would become the most famous person in the world if he killed Lennon. So he flew from Hawaii, where he was living, to New York. He had a gun but no ammunition. So he flew to Atlanta and borrowed five bullets from an old friend who was now a deputy sheriff.

He returned to New York and started hanging around the Dakota. On the 8th of December in 1980, shortly after 11 p.m., Lennon and his wife pulled up in a limo. Lennon got out, his arms loaded with cassettes and a tape recorder.

As Lennon walked past, Chapman fired two shots into his back. The impact spun Lennon around and Chapman fired two more into his chest.

Lennon died almost instantly. And Chapman was right. He was the most famous man in the world. For a while. But few people even remember his name today. He's stuck away in a cell in upstate New York, doing 20 to life.

> *Chapman figured he would become the most famous person in the world if he killed Lennon.*

Originally broadcast December 8, 1992

THE INVENTIVE VENDOR

Timothy Eaton arrived in Canada from Ireland in 1854, a year that saw a lot of Irishman arriving.

The potato famines had hit Ireland in the 1840s and thousands had died of starvation. Eaton was from the north of Ireland, the part where the fighting is going on today, and there wasn't much starvation there. But the potato famines had so upset the economy of all Ireland that it was a good time to get out.

The Eatons were fairly prosperous by the standards of Ireland, but pretty poor by ours. Young Timothy was only 20 when he arrived. He'd been apprenticed to a merchant when he was just a teenager and he had put in his time working from before dawn until almost midnight.

His boss would have him up early to sell whisky to the farmers bringing their goods to market. And the store stayed open late at night to catch any late customers. Young Eaton often slept on a cot under the counter in the store.

The apprenticeship left him with a liking for the retail business but a dislike of several things about it.

He saw no need to stay open two-thirds of the day. There was no reason why business couldn't be done in a normal working day. He saw no need for the boss to make all the money and the employees to exist on the edge of poverty.

And, most important of all, he saw no reason why one price couldn't be set for each item. The custom in those days was to dicker at great length with each customer over each sale. The result was that it took a long time to sell anything and no two people ever paid the same price for the same thing.

Eaton saw no reason why one price couldn't be set for each item. The custom in those days was to dicker at great length with each customer over each sale.

Like most northern Irishmen, Timothy Eaton had been raised a Presbyterian. The Irish Presbyterianism of the 19th century was a pretty austere religion, one that claimed we're all marked out as saved or sinners from birth.

Eaton was a religious man but he'd always been bothered by that definition of what God had in mind for man. At Kirkton, near London, Ontario, he opened a store with his brother. He also encountered the Methodists there and embraced their religion with great enthusiasm. It disapproved of smoking or drinking or dancing or cards, but it was based on a belief that man could improve himself.

That faith was to shape Eaton for the rest of his life. And he became so important and powerful in Canada that it shaped us all to some degree.

A third Eaton brother joined the first two and they opened a store in St. Mary's, also near London. They did pretty well but Timothy felt things could be better. He was eager to try his theory of one set price with no haggling.

But that wouldn't work in a small town in the mid-1800s in Canada because there wasn't enough money in circulation in rural areas. People paid with eggs and chickens and apples and turnips.

So, in late 1869, Timothy packed up his wife and first kid and moved to Toronto.

And he opened his store on the 9th of December, 1869 — a store that would become one of the world's biggest retailers and would be an important part of Canada from that day to this.

Originally broadcast December 9, 1985

A Nobel Effort

Alfred Nobel was a genius. And he was a man devoted to peace, although most of his fortune was based on war.

Nobel was a Swede, the son of another genius. The old man was an inventor who was always going broke. The Nobel family saw more suppertimes than suppers.

Nobel Senior went to Russia and made explosives for the Russian government. He became quite wealthy and young Alfred was educated by private tutors and quickly learned six languages and more chemistry than anybody else in the world. Until then, he'd only gone to school for six months back in Sweden. Mind you, at the end of that six months he stood first in his class of 82 students.

The Nobels returned to Sweden and in the 1860s, they set out to come up with an explosive that would be more efficient than the gunpowder then being used in mining and excavating. It never occurred to the Nobels that the principle use for such a thing would be war, although it was obvious to everybody else.

Just before they succeeded, an explosion wrecked the Nobel family lab, killing five of their workers, including Nobel's younger brother.

The shock to Nobel Senior was so severe that he suffered a stroke and took to his bed. He lay, staring at the ceiling and thinking. He got the idea for plywood, dictated the details to a secretary, then died.

Alfred was left in charge at the age of 31. He put a few finishing touches on the formula for the new explosive and presented it to the world.

It was an instant hit. It was in liquid form and was called blasting oil. Right away, mining became more efficient, tunnels were built that could never have been built before. Rivers were diverted and canals were dug.

The problem with blasting oil, what we call nitroglycerine, was that in its liquid state it wasn't easy to handle. People were blowing themselves up with it. So Alfred went to work and came up with a formula that blended the nitro with clay to make solid, safe, easy-to-handle sticks. He named it dynamite, after the Greek word for power.

But Nobel wasn't just a brilliant chemist. He was also

It never occurred to the Nobels that the principle use for the explosive they were developing would be war, although it was obvious to everybody else.

an organizer, a shrewd businessman and a supersalesman. He had homes, mansions, in all the major cities in Europe. He was known as Europe's wealthiest vagabond, travelling from Stockholm to Paris to Berlin to Vienna constantly, building factories, making deals . . . and looking for women.

Poor Alfred the genius was probably the unluckiest lover ever. He fell madly in love with a woman who seemed to feel the same way about him. But she died.

He fell just as hard for another woman. But she looked right through him like he wasn't there and married somebody else.

Nobel was a flower nut. He had a steam-heated greenhouse where he raised orchids beside his Paris mansion.

One day, when he was in Vienna on a deal, he stepped into a flower store and fell for the clerk. She was a beautiful girl named Sophie, probably 16 or 18 at the time. Alfred was 46.

Sophie certainly didn't love Alfred as he loved her. But, left alone, she would have made him happy. He certainly made her happy. Sophie loved the good life and with Alfred money was no object. Even Sophie probably couldn't have spent what Alfred had pouring in.

But Sophie had a family, a big, hungry family and they reached deep, deep, deep into Alfred's pockets. That made his affair with Sophie an on-again, off-again thing.

But he still loved her. When she became pregnant by a Hungarian officer, Alfred gave her a fortune so she could marry him and support him in the grand style Hungarian officers were supposed to live in.

Alfred's love for Sophie was so great that he poured out his heart to her in love letters, 216 of them. When Alfred died, on the 10th of December in 1896, his will set up the Nobel Prizes that go to give huge annual awards to people who have made significant contributions to mankind.

Those prizes would be bigger if Sophie hadn't taken a fair chunk of Nobel's estate, making the executors buy those 216 love letters rather than have her publish them.

Originally broadcast December 10, 1990

HOLY WAR

Around the year 1000, the Turks, an Asiatic people who followed the Muslim religion, conquered what we call the Holy Land, that eastern shore of the Mediterranean that takes in Israel, Lebanon, Syria, Jordan, part of Egypt, parts of Turkey, parts of Iraq . . . the lands mentioned in the Bible.

The thought of the cradle of the Christian religion being in the hands of the unbelievers galvanized the European Christians into a couple of centuries of action called the Crusades. Army after army went east to the Holy Land.

But in the end, they all failed. So, from then on, the Holy Land was part of the Turkish Empire.

As years went by, the vigorous, progressive Turkish Empire got fat an lazy and corrupt and feeble.

By the 1800s, it was on the ropes. The British and French set up colonies with it, usually not even bothering to fight battles.

They just sent consuls and regional managers and went through the motions of calling them advisers and adopting the polite fiction that the Turks still ran things. It was easier and cheaper than a real conquest.

The French built the Suez Canal but the British quickly snatched it from them because it was the lifeline to the huge British Empire in India that's the basis of Britain's wealth.

And, that's how things stood when the First World War broke out with the British and French on one side and the Germans on another.

The Germans persuaded the weak, crumbling Turkish Empire to join them. The war in France bogged down into years of immobile trench warfare.

The British showed no initiative there. But in the Holy Land, things were different. The British realized they had to move smartly to keep that line to India open.

In early 1915, the Turks attacked and tried to capture the Suez Canal. The British beat off that attack easily. But it frightened them.

First, they tried a daring plan to end the war against Turkey in one brilliant stroke. They put a big British and French army ashore at Gallipoli, right where Europe and Asia come together, in Turkey.

It should have worked. But the British generals on the spot didn't have enough youth and spark to move quickly.

Although the Turkish empire was crumbling, the individual Turkish soldier was one tough cookie. The Turks hung on and eventually the British got the message and gave up.

So now it was decided to do things the tried and true way: start a conventional military campaign, marching slowly and carefully from Egypt, north through what's now Israel, Lebanon and Syria, until all the Holy Land was in British hands.

And that's how it was done. The British sent out a general named Edmund Allenby, a slow plodder who hadn't distinguished himself in the war so far. He had on his side some Arabs who wanted to revolt against the Turks. He kept them in line with a man called Lawrence of Arabia.

A lot of Jews lived in what's now Israel and they wanted to be free of the Turks. They provided a superb intelligence network behind the Turkish lines that kept Allenby better informed about the Turkish army than the Turkish staff was.

Allenby had under his command some Australian cavalry, tough happy drunks who hated to take orders. As Allenby once said, they were terrible soldiers but great fighters.

It worked. On the 11th of December in 1917, Allenby entered the holy city of Jerusalem. He walked because he thought it would be sacrilegious to ride where Christ had walked.

The campaign dragged on a few more months. But when it was over, so was the Turkish empire. What was just starting was the endless series of struggles in that part of the world that still go on.

> *Although the Turkish empire was crumbling, the individual Turkish soldier was one tough cookie.*

Originally broadcast December 11, 1990

RADIO ACTIVITY

Guglielmo Marconi was one of those men who look, act, and are rich and lucky. His father was a rich Italian landowner and his mother was an Irish heiress who had been brought up in a castle.

Young Marconi was handsome, well-to-do and very natty, a real fashion plate. He never claimed to be a great scientist, although he's remembered as the man who invented radio.

He didn't, really. He perfected it, made work what others had discovered.

In 1894, Marconi was on a holiday in the Alps. He was 20 at the time and fascinated by science. He read about the experiments of a German researcher who was working with electromagnetic waves. Marconi suddenly thought: if those waves could be controlled and sent from one place to another, they could carry messages.

So he dashed home and started experimenting with aerials and transmitters. He was soon able to send a message from one end of his father's estate to another, about three-quarters of a mile.

Of course, there was plenty of papa's money to finance this sort of thing. In addition, Marconi had everything done for him by his mother so he had plenty of time. When he was in his late 20s, his mother would still remind him to wear a scarf on cold days.

Marconi ignored a lot of the scientific wisdom of the day and his experiments seemed to work. He patented several of his discoveries then moved to England. He wanted to install radios on ships so they could sent messages to each other and to shore; Britain was the major shipping nation of the world back then.

By early 1899, Marconi was sending messages across the English Channel and to and from ships not too far from shore.

Queen Victoria sent for him and had him install a radio on her yacht so she could get regular medical reports on the Prince of Wales, who wasn't well. In the course of doing the installation, Marconi walked across a piece of the royal garden that was reserved for the queen. She flew into a rage and had him banned from the palace grounds.

But nobody else could install the radio, so the queen had to finally break down and send for Marconi again.

Marconi wanted to send a message across the Atlantic. The experts said it couldn't be done because the radio waves would travel in a straight line and shoot off into space. They could prove it.

Marconi admitted he couldn't dispute theory with them, but insisted it could be done. He built huge aerials at Cape Cod and in England and was ready in November of 1901.

Then a storm blew over the Cape Cod aerial. Marconi jumped into the next ship and crossed the Atlantic, looking for another spot for an aerial. The ship landed in St. John's, Newfoundland, so he started looking there.

And on the 12th of December in 1901, Marconi and an assistant picked up a signal, the letter S in Morse code. It had come from England despite an awful sleet storm at the time. They got the first signal at 30 minutes past noon and two others that afternoon.

Marconi couldn't explain why, but the signal had crossed the ocean, just like he'd predicted, instead of shooting off into space.

All St. John's went crazy and the governor of Newfoundland arrived with congratulations.

The governor urged Marconi to establish a station in Newfoundland for his new invention. Cable in those days cost 30 cents a word. Obviously, Marconi could beat that price because he had no expensive cable to install and maintain.

Just as Marconi was considering that offer, lawyers from the Anglo-American Telegraph Company served him with legal papers pointing out they had a monopoly on all telegraph communication in Newfoundland.

So Marconi installed his radio the next year on Cape Breton Island with a $75,000 subsidy from the federal government. And Newfoundland never saw him again.

> *Marconi suddenly thought: if those electromagnetic waves could be controlled and sent from one place to another, they could carry messages.*

Originally broadcast December 12, 1984

HOWE TO SUCCEED IN POLITICS

Joseph Howe was born in Nova Scotia, at Halifax, on the 13th of December in 1804. When he was only 24, and the editor of a newspaper, he won a famous trial that is one of the foundations of Canadian freedom of the press.

Howe started as a printer and a reporter at the age of 14 and within half a dozen years owned a small newspaper.

In 1835, he ran a series of articles that exposed the committee of magistrates that ran Halifax as a pack of crooks.

He wrote that they stole $4,000 a year from the taxpayers. That was a huge amount of money in those days.

Howe was hauled into court. Everybody knew what he had written was true. But he had attacked the most powerful men in Nova Scotia. No lawyer would take his case.

So Howe borrowed law books and studied for a week then defended himself. His defence consisted of a long speech about what was legal and what was right. He got off.

From that day on, Joe Howe was a politician. He was the spark plug that moved the Reform Party of Nova Scotia. Rather quickly, the old British colonial administration was replaced by a democratic government. Not very democratic by today's standards, maybe, but pretty good for the time.

There were bloody rebellions in Ontario and Quebec at the time but none in the Maritimes. Howe was an important factor in that.

Howe was absolutely honest. In fact, at a time when government jobs paid poorly and everybody else grabbed a little for himself, Howe was too honest for his family's good.

What money he made he either gave in handouts to the poor or he spent on trips to England and Europe to advance his own career or further the interests of his country.

That country, at first, was Nova Scotia. But, as time and history moved on, Howe became a supporter of the idea of one big country.

He was too much his own man to get along smoothly with Sir John A. Macdonald, the first prime minister of Canada, but he did help him make this one country.

Then, a couple of years later, he was one of the leaders in the move to have Nova Scotia drop out of Canada.

When he saw that wouldn't work, Howe accepted a post in the federal cabinet. His political enemies howled that he was a turncoat. Most people wouldn't have survived that sort of attack.

But Howe could. He was so honest that when he changed parties or changed his mind the voters saw it as his honest response to changing conditions.

Nobody could stay mad at Joe Howe for long. His wife once wrote when he was in England that she'd heard he was seeing other ladies. "Five hundred," he replied, "and not one has come up to your standards."

In 1872, Sir John A. Macdonald wanted Howe out of the cabinet because he was embarrassing him. So he made him lieutenant-governor of Nova Scotia. Howe accepted the honour but it was no job for a fighter. Six weeks later he died.

> *In a time when government jobs paid poorly and everybody else grabbed a little for himself, Howe was too honest for his family's good.*

Originally broadcast December 13, 1988

FOUNDING FATHER

George Washington was one of the great men of history. He was a rich, aristocratic Virginian who fought for his king in his early years and who led the fight for his country's independence against that king later.

When the 13 colonies of New England, the South, set themselves in defiance against the mighty British Empire in 1775, only George Washington could have led them to victory. It was a long, hard fight, but he won.

When the 13 former colonies, now separate states, didn't know what to do next, only George Washington could lead them in peace to form the first modern republic, the United States of America.

In his last years as a president, Washington sent an ambassador to England to write a treaty that would put the final touches of American independence. It surrendered American rights to trade in the West Indies and got the New Englanders thoroughly aroused against him. It forced the new national government to pay a lot of the debts of Washington's native Virginia, getting the rest of the country angry at him.

Then Washington, the warrior for democracy, silenced opposition with a series of laws, the Alien and Sedition Acts, that read like something Hitler would come up with. People could be thrown in jail for uttering criticism of government officials or not reporting those who did.

When Washington left public life in 1797, a newspaper published by the grandson of the great Benjamin Franklin described it as a day for rejoicing to be rid of him.

So, when George Washington died on the 14th of December in 1799, the chances were that he would go down in the history of his fellow Americans, at least for a generation or two, as just another grubby politician.

Then, suddenly, along came Mason Locke Weems, better known as Parson Weems.

Weems had been ordained as an Anglican clergyman but didn't have much aptitude for the pulpit, although he was a great preacher. But his medium was the printed page and the stage.

Weems could grind out books like a machine. And he could promote them like nobody else.

He travelled all over the United States in a garishly painted wagon, running something like a medicine show. Except he didn't sell medicine. He sold books. He was an agent for several publishers. But he never liked what they produced as much as the ones he wrote himself.

Americans were hungry for heroes and Weems figured Washington would be the ideal one. He was a great man. But most importantly, he was a man of the people.

Weems could see that Americans were hungry for heroes and he figured Washington would be the ideal one. He was a great man. But most important of all, he was a man of the people.

Weems urged one of his publishers to print a little 80-page book about Washington that he wrote.

The publisher refused. Instead, he brought out a long, dull, five volume *Life of Washington*, printed to sell at three dollars a volume. He printed 5000 and we don't know how many he sold. But not many.

So Weems' 80-page life of Washington, the hero, was printed. It sold thousands. And more and more, as fast as the presses could turn it out.

Nobody knows how many dozens of thousands of copies were sold. The presses ran so fast there was no time to keep count. At 25 cents a copy, the money piled up.

Eventually Weems expanded it into a 200-page version that sold even better. To fill out those 200 pages, Weems had to come up with a lot more material. Some he found in his research.

Some he made up. Including the most famous story of all Washington's life — the one about him admitting to his father that he cut down his favorite cherry tree because, even as a child, he couldn't bear to tell a lie. A great story that was. But a lie.

Originally broadcast December 14, 1990

DIZZY IN LOVE

Benjamin Disraeli was England's most brilliant prime minister. Maybe not the greatest, but certainly the brightest.

He was the son of a well-to-do Jewish merchant who had joined the Anglican church. But in those racist times he was still The Jew and he had to work hard to overcome that sort of prejudice.

Disraeli really had only one love in his life until he was well on in years: his sister.

He was a novelist and his books reveal a man who didn't really think of women with much affection. He once wrote to his sister that everyone he knew who had married for love either beat his wife or was split from her. He didn't intend to make that mistake.

Disraeli had some money, enough to live the social life he liked; but in his late 20s he decided on a career in politics. He had to look around for a wife with plenty of money to allow him to follow his ambitions.

Disraeli ran for parliament for the Conservatives twice and was beaten. Then he ran in a riding that had two MPs. That was common in those days.

The other MP was a man much older than he was, an old political pro named Lewis. Disraeli, no matter what he thought of women, never missed a chance to flirt.

Within a pretty short time, Mrs. Lewis' heart was going bumpety-bump.

The ingredients for romantic disaster, you say. But wait. Mr. Lewis did the decent thing. He died in March of 1838, leaving his widow very well off.

Disraeli's family had been pushing him to get married to someone with bucks. So he waited four months and popped the question.

Mrs. Lewis, of course, couldn't say yes with the sod over Mr. Lewis barely yet taking root. But she didn't say no. In fact, there's reason to believe from their piles and piles of letters back and forth that she liked the game. Well, she certainly found the perfect partner.

Disraeli pulled out all the stops. He wrote her love letters and poems and all sorts of nonsense. Needless to say, it worked.

Disraeli once wrote to his sister that everyone he knew who had married for love either beat his wife or was split from her. He didn't intend to make that mistake.

The 47-year old widow Lewis married the 34-year old Disraeli and he never had another worry in his life about money. He was able to devote himself to his career in politics and eventually became prime minister.

Disraeli was a bit of a fashion plate, albeit more notable for his colours than his taste. He always wore a primrose in his lapel and his favorite color in vests was canary yellow.

The new Mrs. Disraeli threw herself into her new career — Disraeli. Looking back on it, she just might have been working to deliberately make him look better than he really was by always acting dumber than she really was.

Disraeli could go on and on for an hour about history. Mrs. Disraeli would giggle and say she could never remember which were the Greeks and which were the Romans.

Disraeli could talk knowingly about foreign affairs. Mrs. Disraeli would look helpless and say she knew the French weren't the same as the Russians. One had wine and the other had snow. But which was which?

When parliament sat late Mrs. Disraeli would show up with some supper and she and the prime minister would sit in her carriage and eat it together in the parking lot. She cut Disraeli's hair and laughed at his jokes. And they weren't all that funny.

Once she wrote out a list of their characteristics and found they shared practically no interests or abilities or ambitions; just each other.

Disraeli's health wasn't the best and she acted as his nurse. She hated formal receptions, but she went to them all to be with him. She was a superb political campaigner and pulled in the votes.

She was over 80 when she died on the 15th of December in 1872, and Disraeli was in his late 60s. History hardly remembers her first name, Mary Ann.

But the historians do remember one thing she said shortly before she died: "Dizzy married me for my money. But if he had to do it again, he'd marry me because he loved me."

Originally broadcast December 15, 1983

ON THE ROCKS

In the spring of 1943, Lord Louis Mountbatten went to visit Winston Churchill. It was halfway through the war and things were grim. The Germans were almost starving Britain to death with their U-boats.

The most effective weapon against U-boats was the long-range patrol plane, but the planes in those days weren't very long-range and they couldn't fly far enough long enough to cover the whole Atlantic.

Churchill was in the bathtub when Mountbatten arrived and that suited Mountbatten just fine. He barged into the prime minister's bathroom and reached into a bag he was carrying. He pulled out a big lump of ice and threw it into the tub.

Churchill said, "get that out of the tub before it melts and makes my bath cold."

"That's why I put it there," said Mountbatten, "to show you it won't melt."

Churchill turned on the hot water and let it run until he had to get out of the tub. But the ice didn't melt.

"There you are," said Mountbatten, "that will win the war for us. We'll make huge floating aircraft carriers out of this unmeltable ice and float them in the middle of the Atlantic. Planes will use them as bases to wipe out the U-boats."

"Brilliant," said Churchill. "Let's get cracking."

It was assumed that since everybody knew Canada was a land of snow and ice, Canada would be the ideal place to build huge ice airfields.

Scientists were moved from other jobs to work on this one. A pilot project was started at Lake Louise in Alberta. Hundreds of carpenters were put on the job, building a framework.

There were three different teams of scientists working on developing the unmeltable ice. They were in London, Montreal and Brooklyn.

The stuff was called pykrete. It had been thought up by a British genius or madman, or both, a man named Geoffrey Pyke. Pyke figured if water was mixed with wood pulp, then frozen, preferably in layers, the stuff would be hard and almost unmeltable. He was right. The Canadians worked first with pine pulp and then with spruce pulp and came up with that virtually unmeltable stuff that went into Churchill's bathtub.

Churchill and Mountbatten were mad with enthusiasm for the scheme. But back in Canada scientists from the National Research Council were warning that it wasn't such a good idea. The cost in time and money and materials that were in short supply would be too great.

The British wouldn't hear anything that knocked their pet project. In fact, their plans got even more elaborate. Within a short time they had a plan for an iceberg of pykrete 2000 feet long, housing 2000 men, costing $70 million and moved around by 26 engines.

Canadian officials were aghast. The rest of the country's war effort would grind to a halt. Then somebody got a great idea. Geoffrey Pyke had thought up the iceberg airfield idea while in a mental hospital. He'd been sent by the British government to Washington on some other war work. He was brilliant but such a nasty, abrasive man that the Americans demanded he be withdrawn.

The British had told him that he was obviously overworked and needed a rest. That's how he got to the mental hospital.

The Canadians suggested that, since the idea would cost a fortune, maybe the Americans could be persuaded to take it over. Then they pointed it out to the Americans that it was Pyke's idea. That was the end of it. The Americans dropped the idea on the 16th of December, 1943, the day after they heard Pyke was involved, eight months after Mountbatten had put the ice in Churchill's bathtub.

> *Pyke figured if water was mixed with wood pulp, then frozen, preferably in layers, the stuff would be hard and almost unmeltable.*

Originally broadcast December 16, 1985

THE WRIGHT WAY TO FLY

Man always wanted to fly. Leonardo da Vinci designed an airplane, a helicopter and a parachute, although he never built them.

In 1709 a Portuguese priest managed to hitch a small boat to 14 hot-air balloons and got it off the ground. But he was hauled up before the Inquisition on charges of sorcery and that put an end to his flying career.

In the 1780s, a pair of French brothers named Montgolfier built the first practical balloons and they had people flying within a year or two.

But balloons flew because they were lighter than air. That made them slaves to the winds. They went where the winds blew, not where the pilot wanted them to go.

In 1809, an Englishman named Cayley wrote, after much scientific research and experiment, that the only practical way for man to fly would be in a heavier-than-air machine with a fixed wing. There was no point in trying to come up with a machine that flapped the wings like a bird.

People and goods would be transported easier by air than by water, said Cayley, and at speeds of at least 20 miles an hour. Everybody scoffed. Then he added something even more ridiculous: maybe as fast as a hundred miles an hour.

So much for Crazy Cayley. He disappears from history about that point.

But he left behind one important discovery: the glider. He made a kite-like thing that would fly, after a fashion. Several people thought of putting an engine in a glider. But the only engines in those days were steam engines and they were much, much too heavy.

A Scotsman named Percy Pilcher first came up with the idea of putting one of the new gasoline engines in a glider. But before he could do it, he was killed when his glider crashed.

A German named Lilienthal spent a lot of time with gliders. He worked on them and refined them and was the first to work out mathematical tables to show the various effects of different air pressures on glider wings.

And those tables make him the grandfather of aviation. In 1895, an article about his work appeared in an American magazine. It was read by a pair of brothers who ran a bicycle shop in Dayton, Ohio. The brothers were Orville and Wilbur Wright.

The Wrights started to study what was written about flight, which was very little.

Then they were discouraged when they read that Lilienthal had been killed in a glider crash. They almost gave up.

It was clear that the problem was shifting weight. When a bird dipped to one side, he flapped that wing and righted himself. But the rigid wings of gliders wouldn't allow that.

Then, one day, Orville said to Wilbur: "What law says the whole wing has to stay rigid? Why can't we put a panel on each wing that's hinged? We can have the pilot push a lever that moves the panel as the plane starts to tip."

Later, they took that a step further and had the panel on the opposite wing move the opposite way as the lever moved.

There were a lot of problems to be overcome. But that was in 1899 and the Wrights flew four years later.

In 1900 they managed to get their glider off the ground, controlled by ropes they held as they stood on the ground. It worked all right but it didn't carry a pilot.

Back to the drawing board. In December of 1903, they tried again. On the 14th of December, Wilbur took off and was in the air three and a half seconds then the plane stalled.

They made a few adjustments. Three days later, on December 17th, it was Orville's turn in the pilot's seat.

He flew in a wind of 27 miles an hour, stayed up for 12 seconds and went about 40 feet. That was the first real flight.

> *When a bird dipped to one side, he flapped that wing and righted himself. But the rigid wings of gliders wouldn't allow that.*

Originally broadcast December 17, 1986

SITTING FIRM

Everybody knows the story of Sitting Bull and General Custer. Custer went up against Sitting Bull and his whole tribe of Sioux at the Little Bighorn in June of 1876. Custer's force was wiped out. Custer himself, every soldier and all their horses except one.

But nobody seems to have heard of the battle six months later between Sitting Bull and Lieutenant Frank Baldwin. Baldwin won that one and Sitting Bull's career was over.

Sitting Bull, by the way, wasn't a general. As a young man, he had done his share of fighting and had been famous among the Indians of the plains as a brave warrior. But just another brave warrior, nothing outstanding.

During the days of his real fame, from about 1865 on, he was sort of a spiritual leader, a medicine man. In fact, he sat out his last dozen battles, off to one side, usually in a religious trance.

As the Americans moved west after their Civil War in the 1860s, they broke just about every treaty they made with the Indians. As quickly as ranchers or miners or farmers found some Indian land they wanted, the army arrived to roust the Indians off it.

Sitting Bull's people, the Sioux, had been promised they would be allowed to live and hunt forever in the Black Hills of Dakota. Then gold was discovered there and they were told to move on.

They were to surrender all their guns and turn themselves in at army posts by the 31st of January in 1876. Sitting Bull refused. In fact, the army posts were hundreds of miles away and the prairies were covered with deep snow so he couldn't have obeyed that order if he wanted to.

The army set out to teach him a lesson as soon as the snow was off the ground. Sitting Bull went into a trance and advised his warriors to stand up to the soldiers in the valley of the Rosebud River in early June.

The result was a great victory for the Indians. The army then attacked the Indians as they retreated and camped along the Little Bighorn River. The Indians won that battle, too, the one that wiped out General Custer.

But not all the American army officers were boneheads. Captain Nelson Miles quickly figured out how to put an end to Sitting Bull's rebellion.

Troops of cavalry galloping across the prairie looked nice but they could never beat the Indians. The Indians were the best light cavalry history has ever produced.

Captain Miles asked his bosses to give him half their infantry, 500 men, for about six weeks.

Then he marched them across the prairie, slowly but steadily, well-disciplined and not likely to panic under fire.

A company under Lieutenant Baldwin was moving slowly but carefully along Redwater Creek in northern Montana on the 18th of December when they found Sitting Bull's camp of 122 teepees.

For two days they skirmished with the Indians. They didn't actually charge them. They just moved slowly and steadily. Baldwin insisted that his men make every shot count.

If they weren't sure of a hit, they were to hold their fire. They were to shoot only at warriors, not at the women and children and old folks.

It was probably the least spectacular operation in the history of the American army. It was also the most successful.

Sitting Bull and his people melted into the snowstorms that were raging at the time and headed for Canada.

> *Sitting Bull was sort of a spiritual leader, a medicine man. He sat out his last dozen battles, off to one side, usually in a religious trance.*

Originally broadcast December 18, 1984

FRANKLY SPEAKING

Benjamin Franklin was one of those geniuses that shows up in history from time to time. He was the founder of the United States, much more than George Washington, the man who gets the credit.

Washington was a clever man, a great general and the first president. And a wealthy man.

Franklin was a tradesman, a printer who became wealthy by hard work and frugal management.

In his later years, he was the American ambassador to France and handled most of the delicate diplomatic manœuvering that kept the United States alive in its early years. To the British, Franklin was known as the most dangerous man in America.

But before all that happened, Franklin had already made a name for himself. He was probably the best-known man in all the American colonies.

That was because of his writing. There were no newspapers as we know them in those days. There were news-sheets but they contained only brief news reports. The features, the columns, the astrology columns, the puzzles, all the things we look at first in a newspaper today . . . they were in things called almanacs. They were based on the same idea as the Farmer's Almanac is today.

The almanac was a sort of little magazine that contained predictions about the weather, which was very important in a country where most people were farmers. It had little stories we would call features.

And, maybe most important of all, it had a sort of column, the writings of a smart guy. And of them all, Ben Franklin was the best. He was Peter Mansbridge, Pierre Berton and Farley Mowat all rolled into one.

In his early days in Boston, Franklin had written a column named Silence Dogood. Ms. Dogood had a wry way of admitting that men were vastly superior to women but did it in such a way that the reader was left with the idea that women were really brighter. That was pretty radical stuff back in the 1700s and many have called Franklin the first feminist writer in America.

Franklin had a fight with the publisher of that paper, his brother, and he left his native Boston and settled in Philadelphia.

And that's where, on the 19th of December in 1732, he published what he called *Poor Richard's Almanac*. Franklin the printer was now a publisher and a writer.

Poor Richard was a homespun character with all sorts of opinions. Franklin didn't make up many of Poor Richard's sayings, but he phrased them well and he was soon a rich and famous man. Most of what he wrote still sounds good.

> *Franklin didn't make up many of Poor Richard's sayings, but he phrased them well and he was soon a rich and famous man.*

Eat to live, not live to eat. A lie stands on one leg, the truth on two. An old young man will be a young old man. Now that I own a sheep and a cow, everybody talks to me. He who has patience will have whatever he wants. The absent are never without fault, the present without excuse. Poverty, poetry and titles make a man ridiculous. Eat to please yourself; dress to please others.

The incredible success of *Poor Richard's Almanac* gave Franklin the money and time to go into politics.

Just about everything Franklin did was successful with one notable exception. In 1775 he came to Canada with an army to either persuade or conquer. He did neither.

Originally broadcast December 19, 1988

BARGAIN SALE

On the 20th of December in 1803 in the centre of the city of New Orleans there was a brief military ceremony that marked the end of the greatest real estate deal in history.

The United States, a country just 20 years old, doubled its size by buying the whole centre of the continent of North America. And the price was about four cents an acre.

But what a complicated deal it was!

Until the French were chased out of Canada in 1759 they had controlled the Maritimes and Quebec and a chain of fur-trading forts that reached west onto the Prairies and south all the way to the mouth of the Mississippi River. There, they had the great port of New Orleans.

On paper, it looked as if the French controlled enough territory in the middle of the continent to ensure that the New England colonies would never be able to expand very much. In fact, the French held that land so thinly that, in case of a dispute, they wouldn't have been able to enforce their claim.

Then, within a generation of the British winning Quebec, they lost New England. The British colonists there formed their own country.

Then France had its revolution. With the major countries of Europe busy at each other's throats, it didn't really matter who held the title. The people in North America could run their affairs pretty much as they pleased.

Then, revolutionary France had a series of revolutions within the big revolution. But out of those emerged a strong leader, the strongest France ever had: Napoleon.

All that takes us to the year 1799. And if it seems muddled up to now, it really gets complicated.

Napoleon was trying to make himself the emperor of Europe by replacing the various kings he found there with members of his own family. The black slaves of Haiti had revolted and declared their independence. Napoleon sent a huge army commanded by his brother-in-law to reconquer Haiti.

That expedition was a miserable failure.

Now he really had troubles. Without a strong French garrison in Haiti, the British navy could control the West Indies and the Gulf of Mexico. It could probably attack and capture New Orleans and the territory surrounding it, Louisiana.

So, in 1800, Napoleon signed a secret treaty with Spain. Spain would take control of Louisiana because Spain wasn't at war with England. That way, the British would have no excuse for attacking the territory. At the same time, Napoleon didn't want the Spanish ownership generally known because it might look like a sign of weakness.

Just then Thomas Jefferson, the president of the new United States, was worried about Louisiana.

If Napoleon strengthened the colony there, it would be a threat to the new country. It would force Jefferson to make an alliance with the British. And, since Americans had been fighting with the British less than 20 years earlier, it would be a very unpopular move, the kind that loses an election.

Jefferson sent an emissary to France to see what could be worked out. He told him to raise the question of the United States buying some of the territory.

The reply was so fast, it took his breath away: how about the whole works for $15 million?

When the Americans said yes, Napoleon sent a governor to formally take the country back from Spain, to hold it for three weeks then to surrender it to the United States on the 20th of December in 1803.

> *Thomas Jefferson was worried about Louisiana. If Napoleon strengthened the colony there, it would be a threat to the new country.*

Originally broadcast December 20, 1984

SNOW MAN

The Disney family left Ireland in the early 1800s and headed for southwestern Ontario. One generation prospered in the milling business near the town of Goderich on Lake Huron.

Then things turned sour, so the Disneys moved to the American west where they went into farming. They were living in Chicago in 1901 when a son was born. He was named Walter after the clergyman who baptized him and Elias after his father. But you and I know him as Walt Disney, the man who invented Mickey Mouse and Disneyland.

Disney's father owned a jelly factory, a place that puts jam into jars. Disney preferred art. He had been a truck driver in the American army in France at the end of the First World War and he'd made a few hundred dollars drawing cartoons for his fellow soldiers.

Disney started off in Kansas City because he wanted to become a cartoonist for the *Kansas City Star*, a big-city paper. That was his goal.

But Disney couldn't get hired at the *Star*, not as an artist, not even as an office boy. So he turned his hand to whatever was available.

What turned out to be available was cartooning advertisements, one minute long, black-and-white and silent, to be shown between movies at the local theatres.

It wasn't awfully successful. North American moviegoers have never liked commercials on their silver screens.

But it convinced Disney that the movie camera was the cartoonist's best tool.

So Disney hung around the Hollywood studios for a while, learning whatever he could about moviemaking. Then he bought an old second-hand movie camera and built a frame for it out of scrap wood in his uncle's garage in Hollywood. At that point he was being bankrolled by his older brother Roy. Since Roy was living in a veterans hospital and drawing an $85 a month disability pension from the army, Disney wasn't living very high.

Disney's cartoons got a bit of play in theatres. Then he got more ambitious.

In 1929, in a cartoon called *Steamboat Willie*, he introduced a talking mouse named Mickey. He was so popular Disney used him again and again. He also created other characters like Donald Duck, and Goofy and Pluto, the dumb dog.

Audiences were amused. Disney was making a good living. But he wasn't going to get rich.

All this time he was dreaming of making a feature-length cartoon, one with a strong story line. Disney was famous for cartooning, but he knew what sold: the story. He was always spending more time looking for good writers than good artists. He could train artists. Writers, the people who made the stories, were hard to find.

Disney hit on the Grimm Brothers' story of *Snow White*. He had his writers rework it. Then he had more than 750 artists work on it for three years, making two million separate drawings.

Then he unleashed it on the world, at the Carthay Circle Theatre in Los Angeles on the 21st of December in 1937.

One big-time Hollywood producer sneered: Nobody's going to pay to see a bunch of little cartoon animals when they can see Joan Crawford for the same price.

Snow White and the Seven Dwarfs brought in $8 million.

That was back when movie admission was cheap. The average ticket price paid to see *Snow White* was 23 cents.

And that year Walt Disney won the Oscar. Or, to be exact, eight of them. They gave him a big Oscar and seven little ones.

> *Disney was dreaming of making a feature-length cartoon, one with a strong story line. He was famous for cartooning, but he knew what sold: the story.*

Originally broadcast December 21, 1987

A DICKENS OF A TALE

Charles Dickens was not a religious man but he was a great fan of Christmas.

Early in his career as a writer, Dickens put a Christmas scene in one of his stories. Again, in the *Pickwick Papers*, another of his early successes, he goes deeply into Christmas festivities.

But Dickens, in both those accounts of Christmas, stayed away from the religious aspect of the season.

1843 was not a good year for Dickens, especially late 1843. He brought out a novel called *Martin Chuzzlewitt* and it wasn't nearly as well received by readers as his previous stuff.

He had written *American Notes* the previous year, and it had sold well. It was an account of his travels in Canada and the States. But now, in 1843, he was feeling a backlash. Americans were enraged at his making fun of them.

Martin Chuzzlewitt, like Dickens' other writing, was in installments. He had a few chapters with Chuzzlewitt travelling to the States. English readers lost interest and the Americans were further infuriated.

Then Mrs. Dickens told him she was expecting another baby, their fifth.

All in all, late 1843 was shaping up as a bad year for Dickens.

Dickens had been a poor boy himself and was interested in doing what he could to change the terrible working conditions of English people, especially children.

A report on children working in mines had recently been published and Dickens was writing articles on that subject. They were popular and seemed to be convincing a few members of parliament that something should be done. But they took a lot of time and they didn't pay very well.

In October of 1843, Dickens travelled from London to Manchester to speak at a series of meetings about the poor and child labour.

The sight of all those healthy, well-fed people in the lecture halls contrasted with the poor, semi-starved kids he saw working in the mines touched him. The contrast impressed him especially at that time of year, as people were making plans for Christmas.

Plus, of course, the need to write something that would breathe life into his stumbling career and produce some money was ever-present.

Dickens returned to London and locked himself up and started writing. Scrooge the miser was a reworking of a character he had created years before, a nasty old grave-digger.

Tiny Tim was based on his own little brother who had died. Dickens turned out *A Christmas Carol* in less than six weeks.

Then he got into a terrible argument with his publishers. He wanted the edition to be top quality but to sell for a low price.

The publisher said it couldn't be done. Dickens insisted. He even made a deal to pay all the expenses and take the profits. The publishers would just get a printer's fee.

The first copies were made available to the public on the 22nd of December in 1843, *A Christmas Carol* was an immediate hit. It sold by the thousands.

But the publishers were right. The edition was too lavish and the price was too low. Dickens made very little profit from it.

Then he got into a lawsuit with another publisher over the copyright. The publisher went bankrupt and Dickens was stuck with a lawyer's bill of 700 pounds. As Scrooge would say, "Bah, humbug!"

> *The sight of all those healthy, well-fed people in the lecture halls contrasted with the poor, semi-starved kids Dickens saw working in the mines touched him.*

Originally broadcast December 22, 1989

RISING STAR

Joseph Atkinson is a name few Canadians have ever heard, but Atkinson changed the lives of all of them. He turned Canadian journalism on its ear and, even today, more than 40 years after his death, what we read and listen to and watch is very much a product of what Joe Atkinson, Holy Joe, created.

Atkinson was born in a little town east of Toronto on the 23rd of December in 1865. His parents were poor and when his father was killed while walking along the train tracks, their situation got even worse.

Atkinson's mother ran a boarding house. Atkinson himself went to work in a flour mill when he was just a kid.

The drunkenness he saw there made him a confirmed teetotaler. The misery he saw from layoffs made him a firm believer in social legislation to provide a cushion for workers. Unemployment insurance and things like that.

Atkinson was a shy kid with a bit of a stammer. He had no special interest in journalism but he had to take any job that was going. So he went to work while still in his early teens for a newspaper in Port Hope, near Toronto. He worked in the office, collected accounts and sold advertising. After a while he began writing stories. And at that trade he took off.

He got so good he was hired by a big paper, the Toronto *Globe*. The *Globe* sent him to Ottawa in the early 1890s. There, Atkinson met Sir Wilfrid Laurier and became a firm Liberal. He was convinced that only the Liberal Party would ever bring in the unemployment insurance and old age pensions he figured Canada needed.

In 1897, Atkinson was hired away by the *Montreal Herald* to be a managing editor. Soon, he was being considered a managing editor of the *Montreal Star*, the biggest and richest paper in the country.

But before Atkinson could take that job he got another offer. From the *Toronto Star*.

It was a small struggling paper, number six in a field of six in Toronto. It had been started in 1892 by a bunch of striking printers and was about to fold.

Ten rich Toronto businessmen bought it then looked around for an editor. Joe Atkinson went to them as editor at an incredible sum, $5,000 a year.

Atkinson realized what everybody knows today but very few people saw then: people love to read about people. Instead of columns of long, dry speeches by politicians, the *Star* under Atkinson ran stories about people having babies, being evicted in the winter and robbing banks and having operations and getting killed in car crashes. That was new then.

Good writers went to the *Star* because it was run by a good writer.

Atkinson realized what everybody knows today but very few people saw then: people love to read about people.

While all this was building circulation, the *Star* was becoming rabidly Liberal, none of that objective stuff that's important in journalism today.

When other publishers saw how successful the *Star* was, they copied the new tactics.

As the original investors took their money and got out, Atkinson bought their stock. Pretty soon the *Star* was his.

Atkinson saw when radio came along that it would be big. He used radio to get stories ahead of anybody else. And he started up a radio station.

Before long, the Star had the biggest circulation in the country, and it still has.

Atkinson never smoked or drank or approved of anyone who did. But his reporters were the best, the best-paid and the most boozing in the land. They were the sort of people other writers wrote plays about.

Atkinson spent a fortune to get a story and the reporters didn't let a few facts stand in the way. The *Star* was great entertainment.

But it was more than that. Atkinson pushed government into social legislation and regulation of industry. He made Canadian Press, the news co-operative, work better.

And that's how he affected us all. By far the majority of news we get originates with newspapers, whether we get it on radio or TV or read it in magazines.

And when Joe Atkinson made the *Star* a great paper, he guaranteed that all Canadians would be well-informed.

Originally broadcast December 23, 1988

CHRISTMAS PAST

Considering that the Christian religion has been going for a couple of thousand years, Christmas as we know it arrived quite recently.

The sixth of December was the feast of St. Nicholas, one of the early bishops of the Christian church. He lived in the 300s in what's now Turkey.

He got a reputation as a generous man because of a good deed he did for three poor girls. He was going past their house one day when he heard them crying. He stopped to listen and he could tell by what they were saying that they were afraid they were never going to get married.

Their parents couldn't afford to provide dowries for them. Nicholas returned later and threw some gold coins down the chimney for them. They used the gold to get husbands and, presumably, settle down to lives of domestic bliss. This was early in Nicholas' career. He became a bishop and is supposed to have performed miracles, like reviving a drowning man and bringing back to life a man who had been murdered by robbers.

In the centuries that followed, Nicholas became the patron saint of travellers, beggars, virgins, sailors and pawnbrokers.

At one time, he was one of the stalwarts of the Christian church, right behind Jesus and the Virgin Mary. As the years went by, he was almost forgotten, associated only with generosity and chimneys.

Even before Christianity arrived in northern Europe, the pagan tribes saw something sacred about evergreens. Even when leaves fell from other trees and the ground was covered with snow, they remained as symbols of life and fertility. So, when Christianity arrived, the Germanic people transferred their awe of evergreens to the new religion.

German troops who were hired as mercenaries to fight for the British in the American Revolution brought the custom of the Christmas tree to North America.

In 1781, the Baroness Riedesel found herself in Sotel, Quebec, at Christmas. Her husband, the baron, was a commander of some of those troops. When they were defeated in the Revolution, they retreated to Canada.

And that Christmas Baroness Riedesel decorated a fir tree with white candles for her little girls, just as her mother had done for her back in Germany. So the Christmas tree custom was well established in Canada a generation or more before Prince Albert introduced it to Queen Victoria and to England.

Old Saint Nicholas had evolved over the years into a bit of a Christmas symbol, but not a terribly important one. He was usually shown as a long, lean, unhappy-looking man with a bishop's staff in one hand and a bag of gifts for kids in the other. He was accompanied by an assistant with a stick who used it on the kids who hadn't been good.

Then, in 1822, the Reverend Doctor Clement Moore told his nine kids if they were good and went to bed early on Christmas Eve and let him go out and visit his friends for a Yuletide glass, he would write them a poem he would read to them on Christmas morning.

Moore's coachman was a Dutchman named Peter, a big bluff old guy with a red face and a cheery manner. Doctor Moore later wrote that he was thinking of the poem he had to write and watching Peter drive the horses as he headed home. Just before he went to sleep, he sat down and dashed off *The Night Before Christmas*. He used Peter, not tall, lean, unhappy Saint Nicholas, as his model. He turned the horses into reindeer and he gave them the names of some of his horses plus some Dutch words that Peter the coachman used.

The Moore kids were delighted with the poem and learned it and often recited it. A few years later, a friend who had heard them wrote it down and sent it to a newspaper and it was published.

In the 1920s, a commercial artist named Haddon Sundblom, doing a job for the Coca-Cola Company, drew a red, jolly fat guy in a red suit for a Christmas ad. And that's the Santa Claus we have in mind today: an early Christian saint, the figment of the imagination of a clergyman who liked a late night glass and a picture used to sell a soft drink. But who cares? It works.

> *Saint Nicholas was usually shown as a long, lean, unhappy-looking man with a bishop's staff in one hand and a bag of gifts for kids in the other.*

Originally broadcast December 24, 1990

HUMAN SACRIFICE

In 1939, the Second World War started in Europe. The Germans won from the outset, leaving only Britain still fighting; and doing that with a shattered, under-equipped army. Britain's first priority was just staying alive. If necessary, various bits of the Empire would have to be written off because the British army just wasn't big enough to defend them.

If that situation sounds gloomy, there was much worse to come. All the fighting for the first year or so was in Europe or North Africa. But it was clear that the Japanese would soon start to pick off the British, French and Dutch colonies in the Pacific.

The British colony of Hong Kong, on the southeast coast of China, was an obvious target. It was equally obvious it couldn't be defended. In January of 1941, Winston Churchill, the British prime minister, wrote to his military chiefs: "If Japan goes to war with us, there is not the slightest chance of holding Hong Kong or relieving it."

Yet, eight months later, two battalions of Canadians arrived in Hong Kong: the Royal Regiment of Canada, from Quebec, and the Winnipeg Grenadiers.

Just why Canadian boys from Quebec and the Prairies had travelled halfway around the world to defend a British colony isn't clear. Just why these two battalions were sent is even less so. At that time, the Canadian Army classified all its units as A, ready for battle; B, not yet ready; and C, a long way from ready. Both battalions that landed in Hong Kong were in the C class. Some of the men had been in the army less than 16 weeks, including the time spent sailing from Vancouver to Hong Kong. Virtually all were untrained.

Through some goof at headquarters, they arrived without any trucks or scout cars or gun carriers; as one officer said, without even a wheelbarrow.

The British in command had a low opinion of the Canadians. The Canadians weren't at all impressed by the Brits.

Three weeks after the Canadians arrived, the Japanese attacked with a strong, well-equipped, battle-hardened force. It should have been a turkey shoot for the Japanese. The first British units they encountered pretty well collapsed.

But once they got onto the main island of Hong Kong they ran into the untrained, unequipped Canadians. Again and again, the Canadians counter-attacked. Maybe if they'd been trained, experienced soldiers they would have known their situation was hopeless. But they just kept fighting for 17 days until they finally were ordered to give up. It was on Christmas Day, 1941.

> *Two hundred and ninety Canadians died in defence of the colony that everybody but them knew had been written off.*

Two hundred and ninety Canadians died in defence of the colony that everybody but them knew had been written off. Two hundred and sixty-seven more died over the next 44 months in the terrible, brutal captivity of Japanese prison camps. Of the 1418 who made it back to Canada, virtually all were suffering from malnutrition and tropical diseases. They found the army's medical establishment wasn't equipped to treat them.

There was a royal commission into what had happened. It was held in secret and found no high authority was to blame. Three senior officers who had failed to send the vehicles with the troops were fired.

The Hong Kong vets suffered poor health, mental breakdown and, worst of all, official indifference.

They asked for proper pensions for themselves and for the widows and orphans of those who died.

The government always had some reason for doing little or nothing for them without actually saying no. The Hong Kong vets finally got their pensions topped up in 1976. Those who were left.

This entry was written expressly for this collection.

THE KING'S ENGLISH

Henry Watson was a teacher of English for 17 years at a school in Yorkshire in northern England. Then he was promoted and that was the end of his career. In his new job, with higher pay, he would have to prepare young men to take exams to be clergymen in the Church of England. Fowler wasn't a religious man and he was afraid it would be hypocritical for him to take the job.

So he quit. His father had left him a little bit of money, about $500 a years. That was back in the last years of the 1800s, and Fowler thought it would be outrageous that anyone would need more than that to live on.

He moved to London, did a little bit of freelance journalism and lived modestly. He went for his run and swim every morning. The swim was in the pond in Hyde Park. One morning he returned home with cuts on his chest from ice in the pond. Another time he got lost in a thick fog on the pond and was just rescued in the nick of time by a man who was boating on the pond, another odd character out in the pre-dawn hours.

Fowler wanted to be an author, so he moved to the island of Guernsey in the England Channel and lived in a little granite cottage and wrote. His brother Fred had a similar place nearby. Fred was a writer, too.

The Fowler brothers had one thing in common as writers: they collected huge numbers of rejection slips. No publisher was interested in their stuff.

They collaborated on a translation of the works of the Latin author Lucian and had that published by the Oxford University Press. But it was no best seller.

Then Henry Fowler wrote to the publisher suggesting a new kind of book. He called it a sort of English composition manual from the negative point of view for journalists and amateur writers. Oxford Press liked the idea and in 1906 it published it under the title *The King's English*.

It was a success. Fowler realized there was an awful lot of people out there who could read and write just well enough to know they couldn't do it very well.

Brother Fred took sick and Henry went to visit him in the hospital. He met and fell in love with Fred's nurse and they were married when he was 50.

The First World War came soon afterward and both Fowler brothers lied about their ages and joined up. They were in such good shape that they easily fooled the medical officers, although Henry was 56 and Fred was 44.

Henry survived the war but brother Fred didn't.

Back at work, Fowler suggested a new kind of dictionary, one that would tell people how to use words. It would be useful, he said, for the half-educated Englishman who has idioms floating in his head in a jumbled state. And knows it.

He produced another brother, Arthur, to help him. The result was published in 1926 as *Fowler's Modern English Usage*, maybe the most practical book on the English language ever written. It's sold millions of copies and run through dozens of editions. Author after author has described it in flattering terms.

All these years, as he was becoming one of the most read authors in history, Fowler lived the life of a recluse. Only two people at the Oxford Press had ever seen him. In late 1933, they got a 12-word telegram from brother Arthur to say Henry had died, quietly and modestly as ever, on the day after Christmas, 1933.

> *Fowler realized there was an awful lot of people out there who could read and write just well enough to know they couldn't do it very well.*

Originally broadcast December 26, 1991

MISERABLE WIFE

On the 27th of December in 1610, thousands of miles from Canada, in Paris, there occurred one of the most fascinating events in Canadian history.

Samuel Champlain, the great explorer and founder of Quebec, signed a marriage contract with Helen Boullé, the daughter of a very important official at the court of the king of France.

Champlain was 40 at the time. Helen was 12.

Champlain had made several trips to and from Canada over the years and he was deeply involved in a lot of problems, religious, political and financial.

France was, generally speaking, a Catholic country. But many of the businessmen and some of the noblemen involved in the organization of Quebec were Protestants. Champlain always went out of his way to point out to everyone that he was a good Catholic. But there are hints in his background that indicate perhaps he and his family hadn't always been.

Champlain seems to have been a well-to-do man but the finances of the colony were always shaky.

Champlain kept detailed diaries and journals but there is absolutely no mention in anything he wrote about marriage to Helen Boullé, right up to the day he signed the contract. The marriage itself took place two days later, a formality.

Helen's father paid a huge dowry. He paid three-quarters of it down and the marriage contract specified that the wedding was to take place as soon as possible.

In the spring, Champlain left his wife in Paris and returned to Canada. He was there without her for 10 years, then she sailed for Quebec in the spring of 1620. She had seen Champlain from time to time as he often went back to France for the winter.

Quebec was a terrible place, cold and dirty. Helen seems to have done her best to fit in. She nursed the sick and tried to teach the Catholic religion to the Indians. She was now a very devout Catholic. But after four years she gave up and went back to France and never returned.

Some old records hint that Helen was living for a while in France with Champlain when he was back from Canada. She was 15 at the time and she seems to have run away. Whether it was after an argument with Champlain or whether it was with another man, we don't know.

Anyhow, after her return from Canada, Helen lived in Paris and seems to have spent quite a bit of time taking care of Champlain's business and political affairs.

Her younger brother Eustache had gone to Canada ahead of her and worked for Champlain. He returned to France after a few years and he and Helen were very close. Helen was probably a major factor in Eustache's conversion to Catholicism. He moved to Italy and became a monk and Helen sent him money for years.

When Champlain was old and returned to France one winter, Helen suggested to him that she go to live in a convent. Champlain didn't like that idea.

He died a few years later, in 1635. He left everything he had to Helen and she was quite wealthy.

Ten years later she went into a convent. But she was a tough lady, very hard to get along with. She had some sort of disagreement with the people who ran the convent so she moved out and started her own. She died in 1654, 44 years after what must have been one of history's most unhappy marriages.

> *Quebec was a terrible place, cold and dirty. Helen seems to have done her best to fit in. But after four years she gave up and went back to France and never returned.*

Originally broadcast December 27, 1988

GOING DUTCH

King Charles the second of England had a nasty brother, the Duke of York. The king and his brother the duke had spent years in exile on the continent. Then, in 1660, their fortunes changed and they returned to England.

Charles was a high-living man who had felt deprived of the things he wanted to do during his penniless exile. Now, as king, he could really cut loose. And he did.

Historians argue over how many illegitimate children he had. Some say as many as 19.

His brother, the duke, had similar tastes. But at least the king enjoyed himself with a laugh and everybody admired him for it. The Duke was a sour, moody man.

One other complication: the duke was Catholic. England had been torn by religious wars for years and parliament was now determined that religion would split the country no more. There would be no Catholic king again. The duke had two daughters, Mary and Ann. They weren't very well educated. In fact, they were little better than illiterate by today's standards.

But, despite their father's opposition, they were thoroughly drilled in the Protestant religion by chaplains and bishops. That was an order from Parliament.

Despite all his procreating, the king didn't have any legitimate children, so his brother, the duke, was next in line for the throne.

Parliament was determined he wouldn't get it.

When Mary, the older of the duke's daughters, was 15, she was married off to Prince William of Orange, the king of Holland. William was a gloomy,

reserved man of 27. Mary had nothing to say in the matter, and she cried for two days when she was told about it. Then she sailed off to Holland with her morose husband and there she lived for 11 years.

Strangely, she grew to like Holland and she even fell in love with Prince William. He gave no indication of returning the feeling.

King Charles died and the Duke, Mary's father, became king. The Catholic king and the Protestant parliament were soon at each other's throats and civil war loomed.

Then, a bunch of landowners sent word to Holland that they wanted Mary to return and be their queen.

Prince William came on ahead and had a confrontation with the king, his father-in-law. The king backed down and fled to Ireland.

There was a short but bloody war there and William and Mary were firmly on the throne of England.

William was a gloomy, reserved man. Mary had nothing to say in the matter, and she cried for two days when she was told about the marriage.

Then, still only 27, Mary turned out to be a pretty good queen. William was away a lot in Europe, fighting one pointless war after another. The girl who hadn't received a very good education was suddenly forced to make all sorts of hard decisions.

She certainly wasn't brilliant, but she did better than anyone expected.

Then, suddenly, she caught smallpox and died on the 28th of December in 1694, only 33 years old.

Then, the strangest thing happened. King William, the austere Dutchman who never showed emotion, broke down and cried for days. It seems that, just as Mary fell in love slowly with William, he had been falling in love with her. But he never told her.

Originally broadcast December 28, 1989

THE RHODES NOT TAKEN

Cecil Rhodes was an Englishman in the late 1800s who wanted to be rich and to have an Oxford education. So he went to South Africa and looked for diamonds. He found them. He looked for gold and found that, too. He was soon one of the richest men in the world.

While all this was going on, Rhodes was travelling back to England each year to take classes at Oxford. It took him about 10 years to get his degree.

Rhodes believed that the English-speaking people were meant to save civilization. He intended to bring the Americans back into the British Empire. Then the white adult males of Britain, the States, Canada, Australia, New Zealand, and South Africa would rule the world.

With this in mind, Rhodes went into politics and became the premier of the Cape Colony, part of what's now South Africa. Then he got a royal charter to rule a huge chunk of south-central Africa he named after himself, Rhodesia.

Rhodes' first step was to get all the British colonies in Africa rolled up into one. The English-speaking whites of South Africa thought Rhodes made sense. But not the Dutch-speaking ones.

And they had their own republic, Transvaal. So Rhodes cooked up a plot with the British colonial secretary. He would have his man in Rhodesia, Leander Jameson, lead an expedition into Transvaal. The English-speakers there would greet him as a liberator. The British army would then move to rescue them and, once there, it would never leave.

Jameson led his force into Transvaal on the 29th of December in 1895. Disaster right from the start. Within five days, Jameson had been defeated and captured.

A committee was established to investigate, naturally. The colonial secretary denied he knew anything about the crazy plan, naturally.

Rhodes blackmailed him by threatening to show the committee the telegrams they had exchanged during the planning of the expedition. Jameson, the leader of it, was sentenced to 15 months in jail, but went back to South Africa without doing any time.

Rhodes was exposed for the schemer he was and his plan to save the world collapsed. He died within a few years.

He left his fortune to carry out his crazy racist plan. But the administrators of his estate have since changed things. Now Cecil Rhodes' money goes to supporting the most prestigious educational awards in the world, the Rhodes Scholarships, open to everybody, including women and all races.

And Leander Jameson, the guy who goofed? He did better than Rhodes. He went into politics and was successful, and is remembered with some affection as one of the founders of the modern union of South Africa.

> *Rhodes believed that the English-speaking people were meant to save civilization. The white adult males of the British Empire would rule the world.*

Originally broadcast December 29, 1992

THE FUNNY PROFESSOR

On the 30th of December in 1869, Canada's best known funnyman, Stephen Leacock, was born. Leacock kept readers laughing all over the world and made himself a fortune at it.

Plenty of bright, witty people have knocked their brains out trying to write humour. But the Canadian who did the best job of all was an economist. When was the last time you ever heard an economist predicting anything but doom and bankruptcy?

Leacock was born in England of a well-to-do family. He used to say that his ancestors had made so much in the wine business that no one had to work for three generations — and he was the fourth.

But his father moved to southern Ontario on the west shore of Lake Simcoe and took up farming. There seems to have been plenty of money in the family, though Leacock often told stories of his poor farm days.

His folks had enough to send him to Upper Canada College, the classiest boys' school in the country, then on to the University of Toronto. After he graduated, Leacock went back to teach at Upper Canada for several years. He said it was the only trade he could find that required neither intellect nor experience.

He went to the University of Chicago and got a doctorate in economics, then was appointed a professor at McGill University.

He was vastly amused at being entitled to call himself "doctor". He got married and took his bride to Europe. He put himself down on the ship's passenger list as Doctor Leacock. The second day at sea, a steward knocked at his door and said, "Dr. Leacock, come quickly. The chief stewardess has fallen and we think she's broken her hip."

"I dashed off," said Leacock, "but a doctor of divinity beat me to the lady."

After a while Leacock was made head of the department of economics.

He would get up very early every morning, make a pot of tea and start writing. He would be at it by 4:30 or 5:00, put in a few hours, then show up at McGill at 10.

At first his works were serious. He wrote his first book, *The Elements of Political Science*, in 1906.

But a lot of that early-morning writing was for his own pleasure, funny little sketches of life: the difficulty of opening a bank account, or the story of the local barber. Leacock enjoyed that sort of writing more than the serious stuff. He noticed that people were much more intrigued by his story-telling than they were by his lectures on economics.

In 1910 it was suggested that his publisher put together some of his light stuff. His friends tried to talk him out of it. They said if it got around that he wrote for laughs, no one would take his economic writing seriously. His career would be over.

But Leacock insisted and he was right. His first book of humour, *Literary Lapses*, came out in 1910, the year Mark Twain died. The publisher billed Leacock as the Mark Twain of the British Empire. That caused Americans to be curious and pretty soon Leacock's books were big sellers.

No one knows how many copies of his books sold, but it was certainly in the millions. They were translated into every popular language plus dozens you've never heard of. Leacock made about $60,000 a year in the 20s, and when he died in 1944 he was worth $150,000, a fortune in those days.

While all this was going on, he was becoming an economist with an international reputation. He was offered big money to leave McGill. He always refused. "I have more leisure here at college," he said to one offer, "in just one year than the average businessman has in a lifetime. I have the freedom to think. Even better, I have the freedom to stop thinking for months at a time."

McGill made Leacock retire at 65, although he said there was nothing wrong with his brain at 65 that hadn't been wrong with it at 64.

He went lecturing and made big money. Finally, he said he'd lectured all over the United States, all over Britain, all over Canada. If he was to get a new audience he would have to lecture in China, and he was too old to learn the language.

> *Leacock noticed that people were much more intrigued by his story-telling than they were by his lectures on economics.*

Originally broadcast December 30, 1983

PLAY HOUSES

On the last day of 1935, a man named Charles Darrow filed a copyright application with the American Patent Office for a board game he called Monopoly. I don't know why he chose that day, but I assume it had to do with getting the application filed before the end of the year.

Monopoly is one of those games that comes in a box with a cardboard layout you fold out on the kitchen table. Then you roll the dice and advance your markers and, depending on which squares you land on, you win or lose.

But when I say Monopoly is one of those board games, I do it a terrible disservice. It is *the* board game of all time. Until a bunch of Canadians came up with Trivial Pursuit a few years ago, there was nothing to rival it.

A lot was written about Darrow — how he realized in the depth of the Great Depression that people needed a game they could play at home because they couldn't afford to go out; how they loved the play money in the Monopoly set because they didn't have any of the real stuff.

Darrow sold his game to Parker Brothers, a New England game firm and it made them both millions.

In 1973, a professor of economics invented a board game he called Anti-Monopoly. Parker Brothers sued. The professor hired a lawyer and the lawyer filed the usual papers. In any such lawsuit, the lawyers always claim the other side doesn't have a valid patent. It doesn't matter if that's true or not. These are lawyers.

In the course of trying to shoot down the Parker Brothers copyright, the professor found people who recalled playing a board game called The Landlord's Game long before Darrow filed his copyright. He even found somebody who recalled Darrow playing it.

The Landlord's Game had a whole bunch of similarities to Monopoly: squares, dice, various names on the squares that were alike or identical to the Monopoly names . . . and the Landlord's Game had been patented in 1904. It wasn't just for amusement. It had been invented to create interest in the teachings of a man called Henry George, an economist who wanted to reform the tax system.

The professor won that lawsuit and Parker Brothers had to pay him a bundle. But they still own Monopoly and it still sells like crazy.

Darrow didn't care. He'd been a poor man when he got his copyright. After he sold it he moved to a big estate outside Philadelphia, raised prize cattle and bred orchids in his greenhouses. He died, rich and happy, half a dozen years before the professor came along.

> *In the depth of the Great Depression, people loved the play money in the Monopoly set because they didn't have any of the real stuff.*

Originally broadcast December 31, 1992